A Political Companion to
Henry David Thoreau

# POLITICAL COMPANIONS TO GREAT AMERICAN AUTHORS

*Series Editor:* Patrick J. Deneen, Georgetown University

The Political Companions to Great American Authors series illuminates the complex political thought of the nation's most celebrated writers from the founding era to the present. The goals of the series are to demonstrate how American political thought is understood and represented by great American writers and to describe how our polity's understanding of fundamental principles such as democracy, equality, freedom, toleration, and fraternity has been influenced by these canonical authors.

The series features a broad spectrum of political theorists, philosophers, and literary critics and scholars whose work examines classic authors and seeks to explain their continuing influence on American political, social, intellectual, and cultural life. This series reappraises esteemed American authors and evaluates their writings as lasting works of art that continue to inform and guide the American democratic experiment.

# A POLITICAL COMPANION TO
# Henry David Thoreau

Edited by Jack Turner

THE UNIVERSITY PRESS OF KENTUCKY

Scholarly publisher for the Commonwealth,
serving Bellarmine University, Berea College, Centre
College of Kentucky, Eastern Kentucky University,
The Filson Historical Society, Georgetown College,
Kentucky Historical Society, Kentucky State University,
Morehead State University, Murray State University,
Northern Kentucky University, Transylvania University,
University of Kentucky, University of Louisville,
and Western Kentucky University.
All rights reserved.

*Editorial and Sales Offices:* The University Press of Kentucky
663 South Limestone Street, Lexington, Kentucky 40508-4008
www.kentuckypress.com

13  12  11  10  09      5  4  3  2  1

Library of Congress Cataloging-in-Publication Data

A political companion to Henry David Thoreau / edited by Jack Turner.
    p.    cm. — (Political companions to great American authors)
    Includes bibliographical references and index.
    ISBN 978-0-8131-2478-0 (acid-free paper)
    1. Thoreau, Henry David, 1817–1862—Political and social views.
2. Politics and literature—United States—History—19th century.
I. Turner, Jack, 1975–
    PS3054.P65    2009
    818'.309—dc22
                        2009007427

This book is printed on acid-free recycled paper meeting
the requirements of the American National Standard
for Permanence in Paper for Printed Library Materials.

Manufactured in the United States of America.

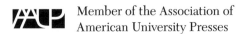
Member of the Association of
American University Presses

# Contents

# Series Foreword

THOSE WHO UNDERTAKE A study of American political thought must attend to the great theorists, philosophers, and essayists. But such a study is incomplete, however, if it neglects American literature, one of the greatest repositories of the nation's political thought and teachings.

America's literature is distinctive because it is, above all, intended for a democratic citizenry. In contrast to eras when an author would aim to inform or influence a select aristocratic audience, in democratic times, public influence and education must resonate with a more expansive, less leisured, and diverse audience to be effective. The great works of America's literary tradition are the natural locus of democratic political teaching. Invoking the interest and attention of citizens through the pleasures afforded by the literary form, many of America's great thinkers sought to forge a democratic public philosophy with subtle and often challenging teachings that unfolded in narrative, plot, and character development. Perhaps more than any other nation's literary tradition, American literature is ineluctably political—shaped by democracy as much as it has in turn shaped democracy.

The Political Companions to Great American Authors series highlights the teachings of the great authors in America's literary and belletristic tradition. An astute political interpretation of America's literary tradition requires careful, patient, and attentive readers who approach the text with a view to understanding its underlying messages about citizenship and democracy. Essayists in this series approach the classic texts not with a "hermeneutics of suspicion" but with the curiosity of fellow citizens who believe that the great authors have something of value to teach their readers. The series brings together essays from varied approaches and viewpoints for the common purpose of elucidating the political teachings of the nation's greatest authors for those seeking a better understanding of American democracy.

Patrick J. Deneen
Series Editor

# Acknowledgments

I AM GRATEFUL TO Patrick J. Deneen and Stephen M. Wrinn for inviting me to edit this volume for the University Press of Kentucky's Political Companions to Great American Authors series. Their counsel and encouragement have been indispensable. Thanks to the authors of the previously published essays for letting me reprint their work and for modifying it to fit this volume. The authors of the newly commissioned essays completed their pieces on time, revised with good cheer, and were great fun to work with. Several anonymous reviewers pored over the original book proposal and first draft of the manuscript; their feedback significantly improved the volume. Candace Chaney, Linda Lotz, Ila McEntire, and Anne Dean Watkins provided excellent editorial assistance. Benjamin Gonzalez provided expert research assistance. Rachel Sanders helped with the index. The Department of Political Science at the University of Washington is a wonderful atmosphere for scholarly work. My mother, Chris Turner, and life partner, Jillian Cutler, positively inspirit everything I do.

Works like this one are intensely collaborative, and the editor can take credit for only a portion. Nevertheless, I dedicate my portion to the memory of Joyce Johnson (1911–2005). My great aunt—in both senses of the term—she was also my first teacher.

Acknowledgments for the reprinted works appear in the chapter endnotes.

# Introduction: Thoreau as a Political Thinker

*Jack Turner*

WRITER, NATURALIST, THEORIST of civil disobedience, and anti-slavery activist, Henry David Thoreau (1817–1862) both inspired and irritated audiences in his time, and the words he left behind both inspire and irritate readers today. Thoreau's inspiring quality derives from the eloquence of his call to live more intensely, to "suck out all the marrow of life . . . to put to rout all that [is] not life . . . to drive life into a corner, and reduce it to its lowest terms, and, if it prove[s] to be mean, why then to get the whole and genuine meanness of it . . . or if it [is] sublime, to know it by experience, and . . . give a true account of it."[1] Thoreau's irritating quality proceeds from his tendency to insult "the mass of men" and to appear hypocritical. In "Civil Disobedience" (1849), for example, Thoreau protests slavery vehemently and characterizes those who do not share his moral vehemence as "men of straw" and "lump[s] of dirt."[2] Yet just a few pages later he writes, "As for adopting the ways which the State has provided for remedying the evil, I know not of such ways. They take too much time, and a man's life will be gone. I have other affairs to attend to."[3] Such statements provoked Vincent Buranelli—in a famous 1957 *Ethics* article—to dismiss Thoreau's political thought as "false and bizarre."[4] Buranelli had trouble deciding which was worse—that Thoreau was so illogical or that he was so self-assured in that "illogicality."[5] "Thoreau is not merely often wrong, but wrong to an incredible degree. . . . He dogmatizes from nothing more solid than his own inspiration. . . . It is difficult not to feel exasperated with him."[6]

Notwithstanding Buranelli's exasperation, the past half century has seen a steady accumulation of scholarship that takes Thoreau seriously as a

1

political thinker. The roots of Thoreau's resurgence in contemporary theory
are more political than intellectual. An inspiration to Martin Luther King
Jr. and the American civil rights movement, Thoreau's theory of civil disobedience captured the attention of political theorists in the 1960s eager to
evaluate the events swirling around them.[7] Hannah Arendt and John Rawls
engaged Thoreau in their own ruminations on civil disobedience, yet in
the end, both denigrated his political significance. Reinterpreting Thoreau's
refusal to pay his poll tax in protest of the Mexican War as a private act
of conscientious refusal aimed at preserving his integrity rather than as a
public act of civil disobedience aimed at transforming public policy, Arendt
and Rawls privatized the meaning of Thoreau's resistance.[8] While Rawls
offered his reinterpretation as a friendly amendment, Arendt characterized
Thoreau's (so-called) politics as morally solipsistic: "[Thoreau] argued his
case not on the ground of a *citizen's* moral relation to the law, but on the
ground of individual conscience and conscience's moral obligation. . . . Thoreau did not pretend that a man's washing his hands of [wrong] would make
the world better. . . . Here, as elsewhere, conscience is unpolitical."[9]

Left to Arendt and Rawls, Thoreau's reemergence in contemporary political theory might have ended as abruptly as it started. Yet Thoreau found
his reader in philosopher Stanley Cavell, whose 1972 *Senses of Walden*
inaugurated a new era of appreciation of Thoreau as a political thinker.
Refuting Arendt's and Rawls's characterization of Thoreauvian civil disobedience as privatistic, Cavell argued that the key to understanding Thoreau's
civil disobedience was recognizing "that the completion of the act was the
writing of the essay which depicts it."[10] In the writing and publication of
"Civil Disobedience," Thoreau achieved the "public address"[11] that—on
Arendt's and Rawls's terms—distinguishes public acts of civil disobedience
from private acts of conscientious refusal. Emphasizing the public purchase
of writing itself, Cavell opened the way to exploring the political purchase
of "words," "sentences," and "portions" in Thoreau's works beyond "Civil
Disobedience."[12]

Moving *Walden* (1854) from the periphery to the center of political
interpretation, Cavell read it as "a tract of political education, education for
membership in the polis."[13] *Walden* is an expression of both "absolute hope"
and "absolute defeat"—hope in freedom's possibilities in postrevolutionary
America, defeat in the face of the pleasure-seeking frivolity that masquerades as freedom in Thoreau's United States.[14] *Walden*, however, seeks to

snatch hope from defeat by making readers capable of seriousness again.[15] It focuses readers' attention on the basic question of modern freedom: What does it mean to have a self, to be human?[16] Cavell wrote of *Walden*, "It would be a fair summary of the book's motive to say that it invites us to take an interest in our lives, and teaches us how."[17] Yet in urging us to take an interest in our lives, *Walden* also urges us to recognize how we fail to live "deliberately," to pursue a life that we have reflectively "weighed," "pondered," and "found good."[18] This realization then spurs us to "press to the limits of experience," to awaken to life itself.[19] Only then, says Cavell's Thoreau, do we become worthy of freedom.

Cavell's brilliant reinterpretation of *Walden* as "a tract of political education" cleared the way for political theorists to further explore Thoreau's political significance. The appearance of two articles in *Political Theory: An International Journal of Political Philosophy* in the early 1980s confirmed Thoreau's rebirth as a serious subject for the field. Nancy L. Rosenblum's 1981 essay, "Thoreau's Militant Conscience," elaborated Thoreau's idea of militancy as "a distinct political stance" and defended his view of antagonism as an essential quality of life.[20] Different in emphasis, though not necessarily in substance, from Cavell's Thoreau, Rosenblum's Thoreau is proto-Nietzschean. Though he adheres militantly to his conscience, that conscience may ultimately lie beyond good and evil:

> For Thoreau conscience was secular, and removed from its original theological meaning, where it had to do with obedience to God—with sin, faith, and doubt. Nor was conscience a matter of conforming one's will to a universal norm, as it had been for Kant. . . . Conscience is a felt experience. . . . Thoreau spoke of an inner voice that is intangible, unspecifiable, and probably evanescent. . . . Conscience has no permanent identifiable content . . . and subjectivity, not universalizability, is its chief recommendation.[21]

Rosenblum's Thoreau defends the wildness of both subjectivity and life; he cheerfully accepts "perpetual antagonism": "However simple this may be . . . it *is* a political view of the world. Its reality is conflict and its chief value is personal power."[22]

George Kateb's 1984 essay, "Democratic Individuality and the Claims of Politics," considered Thoreau (along with Emerson and Whitman) as a representative of a new and distinct form of democratic excellence, an excellence centered on the liberation of human energies, the transcendence of status, and the "acceptance of the dangers and opportunities of being self-conscious creatures, able to see ourselves, see through and around ourselves, and thus able to reject identification with any role or set of conventions."[23] Kateb placed greater stress than Rosenblum did on the moral constraints of Thoreauvian democratic individuality. Right and wrong are objective, not subjective, for Kateb's Thoreau, and uncorrupted common sense is adequate to their discernment. Both Rosenblum and Kateb saw tension between the claims of morality and the claims of life in Thoreau's ethics, but Rosenblum focused on those moments when Thoreau demands the emancipation of life from the dictates of (inherited) morality, while Kateb emphasized how Thoreauvian faithfulness to life ultimately requires respect for the equal rights and dignity of every human being.[24] Together, Cavell, Rosenblum, and Kateb set a broad set of parameters for interpreting Thoreau as a theorist of individuality and democracy. Dispensing with the controversy of *whether* Thoreau's work merits serious attention by political theorists, Cavell, Rosenblum, and Kateb changed the debate to *why* and *how* Thoreau's work is politically significant. This debate continues and is the occasion for this book.

Showcasing eight previously published and eight brand-new essays on Thoreau's political thought, *A Political Companion to Henry David Thoreau* aims both to recap and to advance recent debate on Thoreau as a political thinker. Integrating the work of both emerging and established scholars, the book is divided into four parts.

Part I, "Thoreau and Democracy," centers on the perennial question of whether Thoreau can be accurately described as a democrat. Opening the part is Nancy L. Rosenblum's "Thoreau's Democratic Individualism." Revising her earlier, proto-Nietzschean interpretation of Thoreau, Rosenblum situates Thoreau in the context of early-nineteenth-century, transatlantic romanticism and shows how democratic commitments temper Thoreau's romanticism. Democratic equality and minimum respect for others constrain Thoreau's "impulse to detachment," "transforming his heroic individualism into a distinctively democratic individualism" (15). At the same time, Rosenblum shows how Thoreau puts forward a "distinctively romantic justification" for democracy: democracy is "the political order that best corresponds to the romantic sense of infinite potentiality" (15). Rosenblum thus reconciles the romantic with the democratic Thoreau, showing how the two not only temper but also enrich each other.

Brian Walker's "Thoreau's Alternative Economics: Work, Liberty, and Democratic Cultivation" strengthens the case for viewing Thoreau as a democrat. Reading Thoreau's *Walden* as a "democratic advice book," Walker argues that "Thoreau's central theme is that working conditions in a market democracy can easily undermine liberty and erode autonomy. His goal in *Walden* is to set out strategies by which people can enact their freedom despite working conditions that are likely to threaten their autonomy and well-being" (40). Walker's Thoreau translates the ideal of autonomy into a set of concrete practices by which democratic citizens can resist the encroachment of market forces and the domination inhering in modern labor conditions. Walker therefore demonstrates in detail Thoreau's conviction that freedom's possibilities ought to be democratically accessible.

In contrast, Leigh Kathryn Jenco's "Thoreau's Critique of Democracy" argues against democratic interpretations of Thoreau. Such interpretations, says Jenco, elide Thoreau's fierce critiques of representation, on the one hand, and of majoritarianism, on the other. Jenco's Thoreau insists that the best parts of ourselves cannot be represented; he also insists that the nobility of our souls ought not to be subject to majoritarian dictates. Jenco acknowledges that Thoreau does not positively specify what constitutes a just regime, but she interprets this silence as indicating dissatisfaction with all the available alternatives and as a command to imagine new ones. Complacency about democracy, Jenco's Thoreau warns, "will inhibit the search for better (perhaps more liberal?) possibilities and foreclose any attempt to seek a higher moral ground" (88).

Part II, "Conscience, Citizenship, and Politics," explores how Thoreau imagines America, how he understands liberal democratic citizenship, and how he has been received in contemporary politics. Bob Pepperman Taylor's "Thoreau's American Founding" provides an arresting reading of Thoreau's *A Week on the Concord and Merrimack Rivers* (1849). Taylor reveals how *A Week* represents nineteenth-century New England as a society built on historical battle, bloodshed, and conquest and, more specifically, on the graves of American Indians. Taylor uses this analysis to evoke Thoreau's infrequently noted historical consciousness and his sensitivity to the social and temporal constraints of individual freedom.

George Shulman's "Thoreau, Prophecy, and Politics" situates Thoreau in relation to the American tradition of prophetic speech and narration. Focusing especially on Thoreau's public opposition to slavery, Shulman shows that Thoreau takes up the calling of a prophet, "one who announces, bears witness, and warns," one who "engages a political life he maligns but also dreams of transforming" (128). At the same time, Thoreau makes the American prophetic tradition his own, crafting "two registers of expression to perform a prophetic office . . . the anti-slavery lectures bespeak Puritan (and liberal) idioms of conscience and rights in a jeremiadic form, while *Walden* bespeaks a romantic idiom of rebirth by experiments in nature" (128–29). Intertwined with Shulman's analysis of Thoreau's transformation of American prophecy is a larger meditation on the political danger and promise of prophetic speech for American politics.

My own "Thoreau and John Brown" spotlights Thoreau's public defense of Brown's 1859 attempt to incite a national slave insurrection and evaluates the significance of this defense for our understanding of Thoreau's politics. The 1859 "Plea for Captain John Brown" brings Thoreau's thinking on moral complicity, revolutionary violence, and the ethical significance of mortality into sharp relief and shows that action plays a much more central role in Thoreau's political thought than critics usually acknowledge. I also suggest that the best way to conceptualize Thoreau's politics is as one requiring the public performance of conscience. Thoreau believed that Brown nobly exemplified the translation of conscientious commitment into political action, and Thoreau enacted his own abolitionist commitments by publicly defending Brown as "the most American of us all" (157).

Harry V. Jaffa's "Thoreau and Lincoln" first appeared in 1969, yet his sharp critique of Thoreau remains one of the most penetrating. Contrasting Thoreau with Lincoln, Jaffa demonstrates Lincoln's superior sensitivity to human fallibility and freedom's fragility. Although Thoreau insisted that "action from principle" separates "the diabolical from the divine," he failed to ask the crucial question: "Does the separation of the diabolical from the divine send the diabolical or the divine forth to rule the world? Thoreau's strictures against law and constitutional majority rule can only lead . . . to lawless tyranny" (203). Unlike Thoreau, Lincoln perceived the morality inherent in law's rule. Law not only protects citizens from their bestial nature but also provides the moral education essential for humans who "see through a glass darkly." Furthermore, "the principle of law is that it is not a respecter of persons, and it thereby takes on an attribute of justice. . . . This connection between law and justice, and hence between law and conscience, seems never to be recognized by Thoreau" (185).

William Chaloupka's "Thoreau's Apolitical Legacy for American Environmentalism" deals not with Thoreau himself but with his political reception—specifically, his reception by late-twentieth-century American environmentalism. Earth Day greens gravitated toward Thoreau as they sought symbols for their emerging movement: "What the greens found in Thoreau was an ethical gesture and a romanticism that deeply satisfied them. The Earth Day generation was drawn to Thoreau by his wilderness values and a spiritualism propelled by landscapes" (206). Yet the greens' gravitation toward Thoreau, according to Chaloupka, was politically fatal. Influenced by Thoreau's anti-political values, Earth Day environmentalists failed to have "the explicit conversation about politics that, in retrospect, dearly needed to happen" (206). He observes, "Whereas green commitments could be expressed by gestural protests, conscientious consumerism, and a fairly narrow approach to lobbying and litigating, larger questions of the movement's position toward long-term and large-scale structural change seemed beyond its grasp" (206). Although Chaloupka grants that the reasons for environmentalism's political failures are multiple, he insists that Thoreau's undue influence on the movement counts among them.

Part III of the book, "Reverence, Ethics, and the Self," examines the metaphysical and ethical concerns both informing and issuing from Thoreau's politics. Susan McWilliams's "Thoreau on Body and Soul" shows how Thoreau resists modern conceptions of a unified self and hearkens back to ancient conceptions of human duality in which body and soul conflict. Yet Thoreau's conception of human doubleness is not strictly dualist, for inward and outward life occasionally correspond. "Certain labors of the body may invigorate the spirit; certain spiritual contemplations may elevate the body. . . . Thoreau conceives of a human being who, through disciplined exploration and contemplation of his own nature, discovers himself to be the site of a harmonious, mysterious interplay between matter and spirit" (230). McWilliams, however, insists that Thoreau's quest for harmony is distinct from the modern quest for self-integration and, in turn, self-mastery: "Self-reflection reveals that we must always remain at least partly mysterious to ourselves. . . . The pursuit of self-knowledge . . . begets awareness of self-mystery" (230). Awareness of self-mystery is essential to virtue, for only by acknowledging the self's troublesome nature can one avoid the viciousness that inevitably ensues from projects of mastery, especially political ones.

Christopher A. Dustin's "Thoreau's Religion" argues that Thoreau's worldview is "theological" without being "positively theistic" (257). Understanding Thoreau's religion requires us to resist a dualistic conception of reality opposing nature and divinity. "Those who read Thoreau as either replacing God with nature or locating the divine entirely within it are themselves somewhat hasty in treating nature as conceptually solid ground. They overlook the indefinite nature of Thoreau's nature" (257). Thoreau's "religion" is a way of seeing, a form of communion that reveals how "nature points beyond itself, to a transcendent ground that is neither separable from nor reducible to it" (259). "Thoreau's vision of God as immanent in nature," Dustin concludes, "is incomplete without the moment of transcendence that relates the natural, and the human, to a source lying beyond both" (284).

Jane Bennett's "Thoreau's Techniques of Self" examines Thoreau's project of self-fashioning, focusing especially on the personal precursors of civil disobedience. Rather than asking "What is civil disobedience?" Bennett's Thoreau asks, "What kind of being could be disobedient to civil authority?" (319). Bennett then elaborates eight techniques for forging such a self: "moving inward, idealizing a friend, keeping quiet, going outside, microvisioning, living doubly, hoeing beans, and eating with care" (296). "These exercises are to be practiced daily until they become second nature. Taken as a group, they display how Thoreau's art of the self combines bodily discipline with relaxation of intellect . . . intellectual rigor with flight of fancy" (296).

Thomas L. Dumm's "Thoreau's Solitude" explores the relationship between solitude and derangement in Thoreau's thought. Thoreau claims that "in solitude, we are alone in a sane sense" (326). Yet at the same time, Dumm notes that "solitude's sanity is connected to a kind of derangement, or at least a reckoning of sanity that is not our usual sense of being sane" (326). What connects madness to solitude is the activity of thinking—in which we forget time and place, disregard social convention, talk to ourselves, and imagine ourselves in the company of those who are physically not there. "This is madness," Dumm insists, "but it is a fine madness, a sane madness, a kind of thinking through which we split ourselves wide open in order to touch our wounds, to actually find out whether we exist" (337). Dumm concludes that such madness is essential to human integrity.

Part IV, "Thoreau and Political Theory," situates Thoreau within the classical and contemporary canon of political theory. Melissa Lane's "Thoreau and Rousseau: Nature as Utopia" examines the authors' respective relationships to the utopian tradition of Western thought. Lane argues that while Rousseau's ideas of utopia "fit the standard utopian tradition whereby only a reformed society . . . can produce a good and free person, Thoreau in *Walden* stands that tradition on its head, proposing that individual self-reform is the only path to a reformed society" (341). Thoreau's and Rousseau's later writings also reveal interesting differences in the ways they relate to nature. Although both place a high premium on exploring nature's wildness, "for Rousseau, this remains pure consolation, [while] for Thoreau, it blossoms into a new relationship to the landscape in which the positive meaning of utopia is reclaimed in its etymological sense of topos or place" (342). Interspersed with the comparison of Thoreau and Rousseau on nature as utopia are subtle and stimulating reflections on their contrasting conceptions of law, freedom, and self-government.

Anthony J. Parel's "Thoreau, Gandhi, and Comparative Political Thought" carefully assesses the nature and extent of Thoreau's influence on Gandhi's political thought. Gandhi especially cherished Thoreau's "Walking," "Life without Principle," and "Civil Disobedience," and Parel systematically analyzes how those particular essays impacted Gandhi's thought. Although Gandhi began practicing passive resistance well before he read "Civil Disobedience," Parel shows that Gandhi welcomed Thoreau's essay as a "scientific confirmation" of that practice (385). Parel concludes that it is essential to understand Gandhi on his own terms, not just in terms of his Western influences. Gandhi's satyagraha involves forms of social reform, principled nonviolence, and virtue ethics that extend far beyond Thoreau's influence or anyone else's.

Shannon L. Mariotti's "Thoreau, Adorno, and the Critical Potential of Particularity" offers an arresting interpretation of the parallels between Thoreau's nature writing and the critical theory of Theodor W. Adorno. Both Thoreau and Adorno "identify a critically valuable quality in particular things" (393). Employing a "microscopic gaze" as opposed to an "abstracting idealist gaze," both draw out the world's "nonidentical" qualities "to highlight the illusory harmonies of late modern society" (394). Through this sustained comparison, Mariotti offers an alternative interpretation of the political significance of Thoreau's nature writings: these writings work on us politically by urging us to change "the ways we think and perceive . . . to work against the mainstream social forces that threaten our ability to negate and think against convention" (414). Thoreau seeks to "awaken us to what is violated and lost through the abstract ways of thinking that increasingly characterize modern society" (418).

Andrew Norris's "Thoreau, Cavell, and the Foundations of True Political Expression" assesses the political philosophical significance of Stanley Cavell's 1972 masterpiece of Thoreau interpretation, *The Senses of Walden*. "*The Senses of Walden* is not simply a reading of *Walden* but . . . a reading of it that takes the form of a rewriting of it, a reiteration of its senses or meanings, and hence its perceptions and senses of the world" (424). This reiteration aims to show how *Walden* works to revive our "ability to sense the world," as well as "the society lost in the senses of our degenerate language" (425). Both Thoreau and Cavell seek to regenerate our sense of political possibility by giving new life to the language we use to compose the world; when we as readers collaborate with them as writers to revive language to ever fuller significance, we discover our own power to transform our lives by transforming our lives' very terms. In becoming self-reflexive about how language constitutes us and we constitute it, we also educate ourselves in the nature of both freedom and limitation. Thoreau and Cavell call on us to "actively inherit . . . our language" rather than "passively repeat . . . it," for only through such active inheritance can we achieve the presence to our lives essential to "choosing" itself (435–37).

Together, the sixteen chapters of this volume offer a multitude of reasons to find Thoreau both inspiring and irritating. Thoreau's inspiring and irritating qualities, in fact, collaborate. Thoreau is intent on keeping a certain distance from his reader—from those who embrace his sense as well as those who reject it. Thoreau does not seek to convince his reader so much as to provide an occasion for thinking "*without* bounds; like a man in a waking moment, to men in their waking moments."[25] There must be space between writer and reader for this to occur; the mind of one cannot collapse into the mind of the other. Repelling us even as he charms us, Thoreau creates intellectual agon; within that agon lies the promise of original thought.

# Notes

1. Henry David Thoreau, *Walden,* ed. J. Lyndon Shanley (Princeton, NJ: Princeton University Press, [1854] 2004), 91.

2. Henry David Thoreau, "Resistance to Civil Government" (1849), in *The Higher Law: Thoreau on Civil Disobedience and Reform,* ed. Wendell Glick (Princeton, NJ: Princeton University Press, 2004), 66. "Civil Disobedience" is the better known title of "Resistance to Civil Government," which was first published in 1849 in Elizabeth Peabody's *Aesthetic Papers;* not until 1866 did it appear as "Civil Disobedience" in a posthumous collection of Thoreau's writings entitled *A Yankee in Canada with Anti-Slavery and Reform Papers.* In chapter 6 I refer to the essay as "Resistance to Civil Government"; in this introduction, however, I follow most of the interpreters discussed and call it "Civil Disobedience."

3. Ibid., 74.

4. Vincent Buranelli, "The Case against Thoreau," *Ethics* 67, no. 4 (1957): 266.

5. Vincent Buranelli, "The Verdict on Thoreau," *Ethics* 70, no. 1 (1959): 65. "The Verdict on Thoreau" is a rejoinder to Ralph L. Ketcham's "Some Thoughts on Buranelli's Case against Thoreau," *Ethics* 69, no. 3 (1959): 206–8.

6. Buranelli, "The Case against Thoreau," 262–64.

7. Martin Luther King Jr. credited Thoreau for convincing him that "noncooperation with evil is as much a moral obligation as is cooperation with good." *The Autobiography of Martin Luther King, Jr.,* ed. Clayborne Carson (New York: Warner Books, 1998), 14. See also Martin Luther King Jr., *Stride toward Freedom: The Montgomery Story* (1958), "The Time for Freedom Has Come" (1961), and *Where Do We Go from Here: Chaos or Community?* (1967), in *A Testament of Hope: The Essential Writings and Speeches of Martin Luther King, Jr.,* ed. James M. Washington (San Francisco: HarperSanFranciso, 1986), 429, 486, 164, 620.

8. Hannah Arendt, "Civil Disobedience" (1970), in *Crises of the Republic* (San Diego, CA: Harcourt Brace, 1972), 49–68; John Rawls, *A Theory of Justice* (Cambridge, MA: Harvard University Press, 1971), §§55–56.

9. Arendt, "Civil Disobedience," 60.

10. Stanley Cavell, *The Senses of Walden,* exp. ed. (Chicago: University of Chicago Press, [1972, 1981] 1992), 85.

11. Rawls, *Theory of Justice,* 366.

12. The chapter titles of *The Senses of Walden* are "Words," "Sentences," and "Portions."

13. Cavell, *Senses of Walden,* 85.

14. Ibid., 9.

15. Ibid., 33.

16. Ibid., 53.

17. Ibid., 67.

18. Ibid., 73.

19. Ibid., 74.

20. Nancy L. Rosenblum, "Thoreau's Militant Conscience," *Political Theory* 9, no. 1 (1981): 85.

21. Ibid., 98.

22. Ibid., 106.

23. George Kateb, "Democratic Individuality and the Claims of Politics," *Political Theory* 12, no. 3 (1984): 337, 339.

24. Both Rosenblum and Kateb expanded their treatment of Thoreau in subsequent books. See Rosenblum's *Another Liberalism: Romanticism and the Reconstruction of Liberal Thought* (Cambridge, MA: Harvard University Press, 1987), chap. 5, and Kateb's *The Inner Ocean: Individualism and Democratic Culture* (Ithaca, NY: Cornell University Press, 1992), introduction, chap. 3.

25. Thoreau, *Walden,* 324.

PART I

Thoreau and Democracy

CHAPTER 1

# Thoreau's Democratic Individualism

*Nancy L. Rosenblum*

THOREAU'S FAMOUS AVERSION to ordinary society and his heroic individualism are American variations on familiar romantic themes. Beginning in the late eighteenth century, poets, artists, and political thinkers from Wordsworth and Coleridge to Constant and Mill articulated a unique set of discontents with bourgeois society and with the political arrangements of emerging constitutional democracy. "Romanticism" ushered in the glorification of self-sacrificing militarism against arrant, selfish materialism; the ecstasy of beauty and creativity against mundane happiness; the law of the heart against arid legalism; and utopian visions—from apolitical quietude and withdrawal to hope for total revolution. Put simply, for romantic sensibilities, the world was incommensurate with their sense of infinite, individual potentiality. This chapter is about the inhibitions American democracy imposed on Thoreau, tempering his impulse to detachment and transforming his heroic individualism into a distinctively democratic individualism.

Romanticism's interest for political theorists is heightened if criticism leads to constructive political thought. The standard repertoire of justifications for democracy includes protecting popular interests, moral education through political participation, and democratic deliberation as the ideal mechanism for distributive justice. Thoreau proposed another, distinctively romantic justification: democracy as the political order that best corresponds to the romantic sense of infinite potentiality. For all its failed revolutionary promise and the massive shame of slavery at its heart, Thoreau saw American democracy as the most hospitable order yet devised

for the intense experience and expression of a many-sided self—by potentially innumerable individualists. The inhibitions of democracy both shape
Thoreau's social criticism and enable him to move beyond romantic aversion
and disassociation to positive reconciliation.

## Romantic Aversion and Social Criticism

Thoreau's litanies of discontent with the prosaic, outpourings of ridicule
and disdain, and defiant gestures of isolation and retreat are familiar to
any student of romanticism—English, continental, or American. He shares
the general romantic critical agenda, which entails contrasting heightened
experience and the insufferably mundane. "Wherever a man goes, men will
pursue and paw him with their dirty institutions, and, if they can, constrain
him to belong to their desperate odd-fellow society."[1] The quiet desperation of his neighbors, "always on the limits, trying to get into business and
trying to get out of debt" (*Walden,* 6), struck Thoreau as it has every
romantic—as averse to poetry and philosophy and finally unproductive.
"The twelve labors of Hercules were trifling in comparison with those which
my neighbors have undertaken . . . but I could never see that these men slew
or captured any monster or finished any labor" (*Walden,* 8). Few comments
could be more disdainful of the American belief in the dignity of work and
the public obligation to work. Whereas even Frederick Douglass defined
freedom as industry and the enjoyment of gains—as the very opposite of
the degraded labor of slaves—Thoreau saw slavery of another kind. Those
who were commonly deemed good citizens, he wrote at his most aggressive,
"put themselves on a level with wood and earth and stones. . . . [They] command no more respect than men of straw or a lump of dirt. They have the
same sort of worth only as horses and dogs."[2]

When Thoreau writes "our foe is . . . the all but universal woodenness
of both head and heart, the want of vitality in man,"[3] he says "our," but
"I" and "you" are the dominant pronouns.[4] "It is evident what mean and
sneaking lives many of you live," he writes in *Walden* (6), "seeking to curry
favor . . . lying, flattering, voting, contracting yourselves into a nutshell of
civility, or dilating into an atmosphere of thin and vaporous generosity." His
criticism is accompanied by familiar assertions of romantic exceptionalism.
The thought that "authors are a natural and irresistible aristocracy in every
society, and, more than kings or emperors, exert an influence on mankind"

is nothing new (*Walden*, 103). Neither is Thoreau's affinity for extraordinary souls: "If one listens to the faintest but constant suggestions of his genius, which are certainly true, he sees not to what extremes, or even insanity, it may lead him; and yet that way, as he grows more resolute and faithful, his road lies" (*Walden*, 216). His description of the expressive imperative could have been written by any number of romantics, or by Nietzsche: "I perceive that, when an acorn and a chestnut fall side by side, the one does not remain inert to make way for the other, but both obey their own laws, and spring and grow and flourish as best they can, till one, perchance, overshadows and destroys the other. If a plant cannot live according to its nature it dies; and so a man" ("Resistance," 81).

Nothing makes Thoreau's aversion clearer or is more calculated to *épater la bourgeoisie* than his recurrent attack on domesticity. Anti-domesticity comes in several modes (Byron's Don Juan despises petty contentments, for example), but romantic militarism is the most powerful, whether it takes the form of exhilarating revolutionism or the cult of Bonaparte. Even the conservative Chateaubriand lamented that "the palace of the Tuileries, so clean and soldierly under Napolean, began to reek, instead of the smell of powder, with breakfast odours which rose on every side . . . everything resumed an air of domesticity."[5] Militarism's attraction for romantic sensibilities is clear: war is not work; heroism is not business as usual; the army is a brotherhood of soldiers, which Alfred de Vigny described as a "sacrificial family,"[6] that excludes women, who are held responsible for the breakfast odors Chateaubriand despised.

From his early essay "The Service" to his last essays on John Brown, Thoreau resorts to military terms to describe his self-reliance and detachment from the unabidably prosaic: "You must live within yourself, and depend upon yourself, always tucked up and ready for a start, and not have many affairs" ("Resistance," 78). Of course, in his political tracts, Thoreau's rejection of domesticity serves a specific purpose: by not needing to rely on the government's protection for family and property, he demonstrates the seriousness of his disavowal of political allegiance. But the dominant impetus is romantic aversion to the drearily mundane, and Thoreau's self-distancing from everything domestic is thorough. He entertains no alternative republican vision of the family as a school of civic virtue. He does not single out bourgeois family life for attack or find in the poor any moral relief from the middle-class household's obsession with luxury and consumption. Thoreau's description of John Field's home and family in *Walden* communicates un-relieved revulsion. Instead of the innocent Wordsworthian child, there is a "poor starving brat" and a "wrinkled, sibyl-like cone-headed infant," and there is Field's wife "with round greasy face and bare breast thinking to improve her condition one day; with the never absent mop in her hand, and yet no effects of it visible anywhere" (*Walden*, 204).[7] The sentimental family as haven turns stifling: household echoes haunt, and life "breathes its own breath over and over" (*Walden*, 208). Thoreau will have none of it: "I kept neither dog, cat, cow, pig, nor hens, so that you would have said there was a deficiency of domestic sounds; neither the churn, nor the spinning-wheel, nor even the singing of kettle, nor the hissing of the urn, nor children cry-ing, to comfort one" (*Walden*, 127). And there are no women.[8]

Thoreau's romantic assaults and claims of exceptionalism are repeat-edly offset, however, by the inhibitions of democracy. He confronts Ameri-can democracy as an unalterable social and political reality, but he takes its principal tenets as his own, and democratic equality constrains his disdain and impulse to withdraw. The problem for Thoreau is how to announce his estrangement without adopting an aristocratic ethos, without violating the primary inhibition of democracy by characterizing individuals as constitu-tionally unequal by birth, and without making it impossible to retain the modicum of respect for others without which democracy is pure formalism. It is one thing to call his neighbors "a distinct race from me by their preju-dices and superstitions, as Chinamen and Malays are" ("Resistance," 83) and to feel that "*they* are our Austrias, and Chinas, and South Sea Islands" ("Plea," 121). It is another to indulge romantic exceptionalism in terms of unyielding biological or dispositional differences. Thoreau occasionally crosses the democratic line: differences of constitution, not streams and mountains, "make the true and impassable boundaries between individu-als and between states" ("Plea," 122), for example, or, most threatening to democracy: "not all men can be free, even."[9]

A dizzying internal movement jogs Thoreau's writing—romantic revul-sion and self-distancing, but also backtracking from aloofness and tentative reconciliation in repeated succession.[10] The village Cape Codders are beau-tiful "only to the weary traveler, or the returning native,—or, perchance, the repentant misanthrope," Thoreau writes, leveling and immediately re-tracting the charge of philistinism.[11] His essays are littered with apologetic addenda and jogged by self-conscious halting: "This may be to judge my neighbors harshly" ("Resistance," 83). Hesitations and asides stand alone or are embedded in critical propositions: "When we heard at first that he [John Brown] was dead, one of my townsmen observed that 'he died as the fool dieth'; which, pardon me, for an instant suggested a likeness in him dying to my neighbor living" ("Plea," 118). Rhetorical devices for checking himself form just one element in the larger movement of Thoreau's thought in response to the inhibitions of democracy.

## Responsiveness to the Inhibitions of Democracy: Detachment and Doing Good

There is nothing new about a program of isolation as a condition for imaginative receptivity and creation, and Thoreau is famous for situating himself at some remove from daily society on the "neutral ground" of Walden Pond or Mount Ktaadn. The insights of literary critics who see escapism and displaced political criticism in romantic naturalism are blunted in Thoreau's case, since his political essays were contemporaneous with his writings about nature, and even the latter contain overt social commentary. In any case, no argument has yet been made to justify the assumption, implicit in this widespread charge of "displaced criticism," that a perfectly just or ideal society would undercut the imperative to withdraw to nature or render the experience of undisturbed feeling and immediate unity superfluous. Thoreau represents both his Wordsworthian appreciation of the "indescribable innocence and beneficence of Nature" (*Walden*, 138) and his "hard primitivism," the sublime experience of "vast, Titanic, inhuman Nature," "more lone than you can imagine,"[12] as vital to well-being.[13]

Nonetheless, Thoreau's accounts of his withdrawal to Walden and Ktaadn do hold political interest insofar as they reflect his responsiveness to the inhibitions of democracy. The claim that both Walden Pond and the Concord jail are a "far country" is unremarkable except by contrast—Byron and Shelley were actual expatriates. In this company, Thoreau's romantic orthodoxies are less notable than the fact that he does not allow detachment to fatally separate him from his neighbors. We know that Walden Pond was within range of Concord, and Thoreau remarks on how close the Maine forests are. Both are available to anyone, and neither is more than a partial and temporary retreat.

More important, Thoreau's choice of escape is less hostile than alternative modes of romantic separation from society: the bohemianism of the pseudo-outlaw or the proletariat, the dandyism of an aristocracy of sensibility, Coleridge's elite "pantisocracy," Byronic militancy, Promethean nay-saying, vulgar Nietzscheanism, or Napoleonism. Thoreau did not contemplate the bitter retreat of the wounded soul to a garret or some other scene of martyrdom. There is every difference between being driven mad by the slights of philistines and being drawn to Walden Pond. D. H. Lawrence's thought that "absolutely the safest thing to get your emotional reactions over is NATURE"[14] is confirmed in Thoreau's testament: "The most sweet and tender, the most innocent and encouraging society may be found in any natural object" (*Walden*, 131). The point is precisely that Thoreau does *not* remove to some better company, real or imagined; there is no elite circle of beautiful souls or exclusive republic of letters. He does not indulge in the "soft primitivism" of the South Seas, with its challenge of an ideal community, or create domesticated pastorals; on the contrary, "from the desperate city we go to the desperate country." If Thoreau's declarations of solitude and self-reliance seem to cross the boundary out of democratic society, the affront is modulated, and the way back is kept open. In a dialogue in *Maine Woods*, Thoreau has Mount Ktaadn advise him to return home.

A second instance of the inhibition of democracy at work is the way Thoreau tempers his most provocative exhibition of romantic exceptionalism: his repudiation of the common moral duties that accompany Christian and secular egalitarianism and that were vigorously promoted by the churches and reform societies of New England. His townspeople are devoted in many ways to the good of their fellows, Thoreau observes, but the profession "doing-good" does not agree with his constitution (*Walden*, 73). His references to "benevolent societies" are always ironic, and he calls self-styled reformers the greatest bores of all. He wishes "one at least may be spared to other and less humane pursuits." His defiance borders on the unconditional: "Probably I should not consciously and deliberately forsake my particular calling to do the good which society demands of me, to save the universe from annihilation" (*Walden*, 73).

Thoreau's disclaimer of the obligation to do good turns out to be neither misanthropy nor sheer romantic egotism. He means that too many have made it their mission to mind others' business when they should mind their own; this is Thoreau's definition of a good neighbor and the unexceptional caution behind the observation that "man is the artificer of his own happiness." A more profound point underlies this statement: "Self-emancipation even in the West Indian provinces of the fancy and imagination,—what Wilberforce is there to bring that about?" Thoreau is advising that slavery is a *summum malum*, but liberation per se is not a *summum bonum* (*Walden*, 8). There is none. Absolute injustice does not have a positive counterpart. Emancipation offers little clue to the goods that are valuable or to a well-spent life ("be not *simply* good—be good for something," Thoreau emphasizes). Ordinary philanthropy is premised on an array of assumptions about well-being and a good society that Thoreau found doubtful. "Economy" is his exhaustive assessment of his own "necessaries of life," but they do not hold for everyone, or even for himself for long. Because needs cannot be stereotyped, compassion always rests on untenable ground: "Love for one's fellow-man in the broadest sense" is not true philanthropy (*Walden*, 74).

What is? "Be sure that you give the poor the aid they most need, though it be your example which leaves them far behind" (*Walden*, 75). For Thoreau, the relation between personal life and social reform is the unplanned, unintended effect of heroic individuality. "I want the flower and fruit of a man; that some fragrance be wafted over from him to me" (*Walden*, 27). True philanthropy is the spread of a constant superfluity, which costs the hero nothing and of which he is unconscious: "broadcast and floating in the air," seeds of virtue take root (*Walden*, 164).

This definition of doing good is a retreat from Thoreau's show of indifference to others. Still, it seems to confirm a romantic disregard for ordinary moral duty. There is only the weakest family resemblance to the benign moral influence preached by his friend Bronson Alcott. Thoreau's great man is a force of nature—a meteor, volcano, or vital seed—not defined by his exemplary relation to society, uncommitted to civic virtue or aristocratic service, a philanthropist despite himself.[15] Thoreau seems at his most detached and transcendental here, preoccupied with the ineffable "fragrance" of the hero and genius. But even here, on the subject of the influence of greatness, the inhibitions of democracy are at work. Tortuously but decisively, democratic inhibitions recall Thoreau from imaginative flight to neighborly concern, from exceptionalism to equality.

It is worth considering this dynamic in some detail. Thoreau translated Aeschylus's *Prometheus Bound*, but his heroes, unlike that quintessential romantic rebel, are not gods or supermen. He drew his pantheon of heroes from wide reading in history and literature, but he also found men he likened to heroes among his small local acquaintance: a Native American Penobscot, Joe Polis; the anti-slavery raider John Brown; the Concord woodcutter Alek Therien, a "true Homeric man." Nothing could be farther from Julien Sorel's lament in Stendahl's *The Red and the Black* that greatness has gone from the world and Napoleon's "fatal memory will keep us from ever being happy."[16] Emerson, who wrestled with the same inhibitions of democracy as Thoreau, called his heroes "representative men," but except for Napoleon, Emerson's heroes are all unrepresentative great thinkers.[17] Carlyle's heroes are deliberate men of action, such as Cromwell.[18] Emerson and Carlyle complement each other, Thoreau observes critically: they omit Christ and practical heroes like Columbus, and "above and after all, the Man of the Age, come to be called workingman, it is obvious that none yet speaks to his condition." Carlyle especially exaggerates the heroic in history: "The common man is nothing to him [Carlyle]."[19] The opening passage of *On Heroes* says as much: "The history of what man has accomplished in this world, is at bottom the History of the Great Men who have worked here."[20] The rest are there to be commanded.

Thoreau never doubts that some men are extraordinary, but the inhibitions of democracy ward off the anti-democratic politics of genius that typically follow. There is no natural aristocracy to legislate or govern in Thoreau's political thought. There is no Nietzschean will to power. Thoreau's heroes do not excite erotic attachment, arouse collective passions, cultivate disciples, or inspire the cult of personality and mass mobilization that are often characterized as the political expression of romanticism. Certainly, Thoreau had no use for passive reverence. The hero serves others by showing them what they can be and do. He is an exemplar of individuality. So there is no absolute gap between the extraordinary individual and the rest. Anyone can learn from the spectacle of greatness.

Thoreau brings together romantic heroism and that article of faith shared by every party in America—the possibility of improvement. "We are all great men" is not a fact but a democratic aspiration. Thoreau preserves the necessary modicum of respect and intuitive understanding:

> Most men, even in this comparatively free country, through mere ignorance and mistake, are so occupied with the factitious cares and superfluously coarse labors of life that its finer fruits cannot be plucked by them. Their fingers, from excessive toil, are too clumsy and tremble too much for that. . . . We should feed and clothe him [the common man] gratuitously sometimes,

and recruit him with our cordials, before we judge of him. The finest qualities of our nature, like the bloom on fruits, can be preserved only by the most delicate handling. Yet we do not treat ourselves nor one another thus tenderly. (*Walden*, 6)

The democratic heart of Thoreau's account of heroism and genius follows from his notion of an exemplary life: for greatness to have historical effect, the hero must be recognized. Consent is a powerful democratic inhibition, and we see it operating in Thoreau's essays on John Brown. For Harpers Ferry to be the beginning of the end to slavery, John Brown must be acknowledged as great. Thoreau is apprehensive: "when a noble deed is done, who is likely to appreciate it? They who are noble themselves" ("Last Days," 148). His neighbors are not, and he pleads, "Do yourself the honor to recognize him." Thoreau is palpably relieved when other abolitionists come round to his view of Brown as heroic: "the *living* North, was suddenly all transcendental" ("Last Days," 147).

## Democratic Individualism: Consent and Disobedience

The chief inhibition of democracy operates on Thoreau personally: he cannot "cast his whole influence" without his countrymen's consent, a constraint he accepts as a moral, not just a practical, imperative. Thoreau writes about representative democracy, in which legitimacy depends on popular support. The difficulty he faced was not so much articulating the political promise of independence as he saw it, or knowing what was right, but rather justifying his own standing. He poses this question at the outset of *Walden* and returns to it in his essays: "Who is Thoreau that others should listen to him?" How is it that, speaking for himself ("We commonly do not remember that it is, after all, always the first person that is speaking" [*Walden*, 3]), he can truthfully say he is appealing "from them to themselves"? English and continental romantics did not have this problem. Disappointed with the French Revolution, they could revolutionize literature and adopt political conservatism. Postrevolutionary generations of European romantics could give free rein to aristocratic expressions of genius when repulsed by prosaic affairs and hounded by philistines, boast that their true peers were great souls across the ages, or enjoy the delicious martyrdom of the poet *maudit*.

Thoreau speaks to his fellow citizens with startling directness.[21] He does not soliloquize, or pose as a nightingale singing for his own consolation, or talk to God or to kindred spirits only. He is unwilling to identify with Shelley's unacknowledged legislator. His acute self-consciousness is alien to prophetic speech. Thoreau is not a bard speaking for others; the challenge is precisely how to speak for himself, to them. He does not "wish to quarrel with any man or nation . . . to split hairs, to make fine distinctions, or set myself up as better than my neighbors" ("Resistance," 86). He intends to avoid the mistake of positioning himself too close or too far: "One cannot be too much on his guard in such a case, lest his action be biased by obstinacy, or an undue regard for the opinions of men" ("Resistance," 84). Sheer self-assertion—"giving a strong dose of myself"—will not do.[22] He needs to rely, if not on fellow feeling, then on some common ground.

Thoreau could have attempted to establish his standing on common moral ground, in Tom Paine's terms, say, as men rather than as American citizens, pronouncing the rights of man and the "we" of common sense. This Enlightenment bond assumed universal moral agency, self-evident moral truths, and resistance to tyranny (though not always institutional democracy). Shelley invokes it with "man, equal, unclassed, tribeless, nationless."[23] But Thoreau is averse to radical universal claims and does not appeal to natural rights. He does not imagine that all interests can be harmonized. And the centrality of paradox in his writing challenges Paine's common sense directly.

An alternative course was mapped out by a generation of continental romantics: Humboldt, Schiller, and Constant. All three began with a notion of the development of each individual into "a complete and consistent whole" and soberly considered the political conditions for cultivating individuality.[24] They judged men and women too weak to withstand the exertions of a tutorial state, whether these derived from political absolutism or the rigorous demands of revived civic republicanism. Individuals cannot develop collectively and in public. They offered a romantic justification for liberal, limited government and a severe public-private divide: constitutional bulwarks against official intrusion into personal life ensured self-protective withdrawal. A privileged private sphere and circle of friends constituted the only imaginable context for self-cultivation and expression. Thoreau did not follow Humboldt and Constant in privileging privacy and insisting on vigilant self-protection against the claims of politics.

In contrast, and in response to the inhibitions of democracy, Thoreau addresses his neighbors as citizens of Massachusetts and the United

States, and he speaks to his "countrymen" "practically, and as a citizen" ("Resistance," 64). He finds common ground with readers as democratic individuals. Both elements of "democratic individualism" need emphasizing. Thoreau defines America as a constitutional regime when he opens "Civil Disobedience" with the reminder that American government is a recent tradition dating from the Revolution ("Resistance," 63). With this, he rules out appeal to America's religious tradition and continuity with the chosen people and their city on the hill (even maintaining that the French Jesuits' mission and morals were superior to the Puritans'). Thoreau addresses individuals in their political capacity. Each person is ultimately responsible for the support of political authority that may fatally interfere with his business or make him an agent of injustice. Democracy invites individuals to "cast [their] whole vote, not a strip of paper merely, but [their] whole influence" ("Resistance," 76). Thoreau's point is that American democracy throws individuals back on themselves, for it is equally clear that he is interested in democratic individualism, not collective identity. He does not identify the people or nation, as Wordsworth and Herder did, with a common history and culture. History offers no firm common ground, in his view. Slavery confronts the promise of independence and the rhetoric of liberation with a massive contradiction from the start, which is why Thoreau does not talk of original promises or breaches of compacts. Racial and cultural differences, including the great divide between North and South, ensured that any appeal to the authentic voice of an American people would be in bad faith. *Dred Scott* showed definitively that "the people" officially excluded slaves and freedmen, whom Thoreau explicitly counted as fellow citizens.

To understand the powerful hold democratic individualism had on Thoreau, we must recall that he confronted a host of virulent, systematic ideologies propounding ascriptive inequality—including biblical and scientific racial theories and quasi-romantic assertions of historical and cultural identity and hierarchy. These were not examples of liberal hypocrisy or rare exceptions to a hegemonic liberal-democratic ideology, residual pockets of irrational prejudice. They were powerful, independent forces in American political life. It is bad history and an awful error of moral judgment (to which scholars of romanticism are prone) to assume the existence of a liberal-democratic consensus and to characterize every tension as self-contradiction *within* democratic principles. If the only political categories we recognize are absent feudalism and socialism and pervasive bourgeois liberalism, we are likely to imagine that the inhibitions of democracy operated on Thoreau unconsciously or against his will. We are also likely to underestimate his hesitation to embrace romantic exceptionalism and his impulse to resist the thought that differences are absolute and unbridgeable.

Democratic individualism is Thoreau's common ground. It remains to be shown that although romanticism is tempered, democratic individualism has not lost its romantic resonance altogether. Romanticism is there in his preoccupation with the experience of democracy, of consent and dissent, for men and women personally, particularly in his insistence that democracy means "giving a strong dose" of oneself ("Life," 155). Romantic individualism wants recognition—not only the equal moral recognition that is supposed to accompany the rights of man and citizen but also recognition for one's unique particularity. Thoreau offers himself as an example of what it means to give a strong dose of oneself, and his self-seriousness is a demonstration of true democratic respect for individuality.

Thoreau speaks only from personal experience of government, and only about what attracts his attention. Chattel slavery may be an enormous evil, but it becomes his affair only when it reminds him of "slavery of all kinds" and the need for self-emancipation, or when government tries to make him an agent of injustice—when it is forcibly impressed on him that southern slavery entails slavery in Massachusetts. Not even great political questions are permitted to eclipse his personal perspective on events. No action is right, regardless of whether it is commonly deemed moral, if it is not expressive. That, not political efficacy, is the standard for casting one's whole influence. Thoreau abhorred organizations, for example, and although he did not join the local vigilance committee that aided fugitive slaves, he acknowledged such groups as quasi-governments committed to protecting the weak and dispensing justice. *He* did not attack a federal arsenal. "I quietly declare war with the State, after my fashion" ("Resistance," 84).

## "Comparatively Good" Government and Democratic Reconciliation

Thoreau despised docility. But there is more to democratic individualism than resistance, and political philosophy's single-minded focus on Thoreau as an advocate of civil disobedience is misleading.[25] Opposition is not the defining element of his romantic political thought. Opportunities to cast one's whole influence arise as part of a life in which men and women have other affairs to attend to, Thoreau reminds us. More than once in discussing the anti-slavery movement, he repeats the caution, "I do not think it is quite sane for one to spend his whole life in talking or writing about this matter, unless he is continuously inspired, and I have not done so" ("Plea," 133). This is the same partial, conditional quality that characterizes his detachment and his account of Walden. Thoreau's horizon, with its "own sun and moon and stars, and a little world all to myself" (*Walden*, 130), designates a sphere of aesthetic delight, philosophical contemplation, "epiphanic moments"; it sets his experiences apart from the mundane lives of his disconsolate neighbors and is the emblem of undemocratic retreat. But his self-distancing is measured: "I wish to speak a word for Nature, for absolute freedom and wildness, as contrasted with a freedom and culture merely civil"—only a word.[26] Thoreau always has "several more lives to live" (*Walden*, 323).

In "Slavery in Massachusetts," Thoreau's thoughts move from preoccupation with injustice and regret that "remembrance of my country spoils my walk" to the successful resumption of his consideration of the water lily in nature, "partner to no Missouri Compromise."[27] We know that just as often his thoughts moved in the other direction. And at still other moments, Thoreau "to some extent reckoned himself" among "those who find encouragement and inspiration in the present condition of things, and cherish it with the fondness and enthusiasm of a lover" (*Walden*, 16).

More broadly, then, Thoreau's "little world all to myself" suggests that every standpoint is one among other possible worlds. It evokes diverse and changing horizons. It brings to mind Thoreau's subversive attack on higher law and his anti-foundationalism, his skeptical search for the "hard bottom" in *Walden* (70–71): "Let us settle ourselves, and work and wedge our feet downward through the mud and slush of opinion, and prejudice, and tradition, and delusion, and appearance . . . through poetry and philosophy and religion, till we come to a hard bottom"—all the while confident that the search for a "Realometer" will be disappointed, and finally giving himself over to "fish in the sky, whose bottom is pebbly with stars." Thoreau is no systematic epistemologist, and we do not find an exploration of perspectivism on the order of Nietzsche's. We do, however, get a picture of romantic plenitude and fluid perspectivism and insight into the fact that each entails a corresponding view of democracy.

Thoreau puts the authority of a single standard or standpoint on American democracy in doubt each time he speaks of laws, policies, or political representatives as "comparatively good." America is a "comparatively free country," for example (*Walden*, 6). The U.S. Constitution is "comparatively good," he writes, and so is the railroad that runs through Concord.[28] Thoreau does not intend to compare the relative merits of American institutions to others, actual or ideal. And he takes for granted the divergent evaluations different social groups make of a set of facts: the railroad running through Concord did not have the same significance for the poor Irish immigrants who built it, the southern slaves escaping by it, and those who benefited most from the expanding national economy. The point is that Thoreau's own response to the railroad is alternately disturbed and thrilled, like Marx's estimate of the awesome productive power of modern industry (*Walden*, 116, 118). The comparative mode indicates Thoreau's lack of a single fixed perspective. It invites readers not only to attend to others' standpoints but also to recognize that they assume more than one themselves.

Thoreau's great perspectivist set piece, which appears toward the end of "Civil Disobedience," surveys his shifting orientations toward the U.S. government and Constitution: "Seen from a lower point of view, the constitution, with all its faults, is very good; the law and the courts very respectable" ("Resistance," 86). Thoreau has in mind the obvious advances of representative democracy over monarchy and the way American federalism and separation of powers provide a useful "friction" in the machinery of government. Moreover, the ordinary activities of government are expedient, and Thoreau is happy to pay his highway taxes. Laws may even contribute to private life and virtue: "the effect of good government is to make life more valuable" ("Slavery," 106). From this perspective, citizens accede to authority at no great cost and to real advantage.

Thoreau continues: the state and American government "are even in many respects very admirable and rare things, to be thankful for" ("Resistance," 86). He means that representative democracy is the best design for creating and undoing political authority, because it sets off its partial and conditional character. Elections indicate the dependence of government on the consent of men and women personally and individually, and democracy invites individuals to give a strong dose of themselves. Also "very admirable and rare" is the fact that federal and state constitutions enumerate civil and political liberties. Thoreau was no fond legalist, but he closely followed the judicial treatment of fugitive slaves Thomas Sims and Anthony Burns and insisted that government refused to recognize the dignity of the individual when basic rights of citizenship, among them habeas corpus and due process, were being denied. Massachusetts' personal liberty laws were estimable. Thoreau had his moments of political affirmation.

"But seen from a point of view a little higher, they [the Constitution and government] are what I have described them." Thoreau repeats his "harsh and stubborn and unconciliatory" stand that the Constitution is a proslavery document ("Resistance," 74). From this point of view, withdrawal of allegiance and personal resistance may be felt imperatives. It need not take an injustice like slavery to occasion this harsh view, either; government also inhibits democratic individualism by imposing its discipline on daily life through the militarist conversion of men into "small moveable forts" or by reinforcing the expectation that everyone should engage in the sort of labor that contributes to national economic growth. Thoreau wrote before the rise of the welfare and disciplinary state, but conformity and tyranny of the majority were familiar enough. He knew all about the way individuals unreflectively internalize norms—that is, what leads to self-enslavement and "lives of quiet desperation." Thoreau was inspired to resist when government "fatally interfered with my lawful business" ("Resistance," 107).

Finally, "seen from higher still, and the highest, who shall say what they [the Constitution and government] are, or that they are worth looking at or thinking of at all?" Thoreau can abide the cranking of the machinery of government so long as he does not have to assist in its smooth workings. "Those things which now most engage the attention of men, as politics and the daily routine, are, it is true, vital functions of human society, but should be unconsciously performed, like the corresponding functions of the physical body. They are *infra*-human, a kind of vegetation" ("Life," 178; emphasis in original). Thoreau has his moments of detachment when he practically does not recognize the state.

From this standpoint, Thoreau briefly imagines that democratic government could reciprocate his unconcern by allowing a few of its citizens to live aloof, "not meddling with it, nor embraced by it" ("Resistance," 89). He contemplates a government that admits the need to obtain personal consent for every public measure and allows for individual exemptions from every obligation—not limited to the rare high ground of conscientious objection but whenever an individual's affairs compel disagreement. We should hesitate to see this libertarian vision as a definitive political ideal, however. Thoreau also observes that "to act collectively is according to the spirit of our institutions," and he can imagine government activism and a strong tutorial state. Why should public projects stop with highways, he asks: "New England can hire all the wise men in the world to come and teach her." Villages should "take the place of the nobleman of Europe" and be patrons of fine arts. They should foster magnanimity and refinement (*Walden,* 109). Ordinarily, when a regime is characterized as comparatively good, the question for political theory is what constitutes the best form of government. But Thoreau has no interest in utopia; these suggestions are brief asides. His "higher still" standpoint is neither a foundation for political idealism nor a justification for retirement to his own little world.[29]

For Thoreau, the question is always the same: how much must an individual have to do with democratic government at all? By posing the question and admitting that he sometimes almost does not recognize it at all, Thoreau indicates his ongoing relation to democracy, however tentative and intermittent, and even if government's contribution to well-being is only comparatively important. From the standpoint "higher still, and the highest," he is not prescribing a permanent stoic shift of consciousness within or supersensible transcendence. The point is to refuse to permit res publica to work to the detriment of res privata. Thoreau's answer is clear: He is not wholly taken up with romantic aloofness or contemplative transcendence, with active opposition, moral appreciation, or expedient acquiescence. He assumes all these standpoints on democracy.

When Thoreau designates the perspective from which government is hardly worth thinking about as "higher still," he leaves things in the comparative mode. He parenthetically adds "and the highest" but does not assert that one perspective is better or truer than the rest or that one enlists higher capacities so that the true self is identified with resistance, say, or contemplation. He does not try to willfully center himself by fixing his sights on one horizon or another; nor does he propose that, true or not, one perspective should master the others, if only for the sake of psychological peace or personal integrity. Thoreau accepts sometimes unpredictable and contrary perspectives in himself and acknowledges the fact that some experiences and ends are incompatible and only "comparatively good." Nothing is gained by invoking higher law or plumbing the depths for some integral nature, whether for the purposes of political theory or life; he must exploit the discontinuity of "several lives." These are the grounds on which liberal pluralists such as Isaiah Berlin concede the contribution of romanticism to political theory: it "has permanently shaken the faith in universal, objective truth in matters of conduct, in the possibility of a perfect and harmonious society."[30]

Finally, as the several perspectives Thoreau lays out in "Civil Disobedience" indicate, laws and government not only look different, depending on where he stands, but also excite the exhibition of different aspects of oneself. Despite its injustices and inhibitions, Thoreau sees representative democracy as the political complement of the romantic self, where it can feel at home. He would have agreed with George Kateb that "individuality's meaning is not fully disclosed until it is indissociably connected to democracy."[31]

## Romantic Political Thought

I have argued that Thoreau's romanticism is tempered by the inhibitions of democracy and that, duly constrained, romanticism characterizes his political thought. What is romantic political thought? Since there is no reason to assume an alignment between political opinion and aesthetic sensibility, it cannot be defined in terms of the political ideas writers identified with romanticism happen to adopt. Nor is there any justification for identifying romantic political thought exclusively with revolution, on the one hand, or with conservatism, reaction, or, more accurately, imaginative nostalgia for Catholic medievalism, Hellas, or folk traditions, on the other.[32] Political aspirations are particularly unhelpful in defining romantic political thought in America, where the powerful inhibitions of democracy leave their mark on every variation from utopian communitarianism to Thoreau's democratic individualism.

Whether it is associated with beautiful hierarchy or perfect equality in a community of friends, romantic political thought has the unifying feature of holism. What distinguishes the holism of romantic political ideals from that of philosophical idealists such as Hegel are the peculiar gratifications held out by the former. Romantic holism is aesthetic and psychological rather than metaphysical or sociological. The romantic sensibility can feel at home there because its infinite potentiality is somehow mirrored in political community. The poet may even be an acknowledged legislator. "The true sorrow of humanity consists in this;—not that the mind of man fails; but that the course and demands of action and of life so rarely correspond with the dignity and intensity of human desires," Wordsworth wrote, and romantic political thought is critical of any order that frustrates expressivism and correspondence.[33] When it proceeds beyond criticism, it envisions political community as a setting for romantic plenitude. This is not conventional political theory, of course. Romantic political thought is preoccupied less with justice and institutional design than with the presence or painful absence of complementarity between self and political world. Thoreau's political thought conforms to this rough definition.

Contemporary literary studies of romanticism emphasize the dark underside of holism and of the longing for correspondence between self and world.[34] They point up the fragmented quality of the self, the historical situatedness of the writer, and the way presumably authentic expressions of individuality—including both rebellion and detachment—are socially constituted, deconstructing grandiose romantic claims of "uninfluenced originality" and "creative imagination at once free and unfathomable."[35] Especially for romantic works devoid of explicit social content, critics set out to "expose these dramas of displacement and idealization" and the methods by which "the poem annihilates its own history, biographical and sociohistorical alike, and replaces these particulars with a record of pure consciousness." The "de-transcendentalizing" of Emerson is well under way.[36]

But American romantics, and certainly Thoreau, seem to have anticipated the thrust of these demystifying, unmasking, perspectivist approaches. Consider some of the elements of Thoreau's writing. For instance, the political parameters of where we stand and what we see from there were evident to him: expansion and conquest, dispossession and enslavement govern one's view of American history, government, and culture. Thoreau distinguishes official ideology on the "original" settlement of America and the War of Independence from the stories told by Native Americans and slaves: History "for the most part . . . is merely a story agreed upon by posterity" (*Cape Cod*, 197). The Indian was the native of the New World ("three thousand years deep into time" [*Maine Woods*, 79]), which was not really discovered at all; nor were the Pilgrims the first European settlers ("New England commences only when it ceases to be *New* France" [*Cape Cod*, 183]). And in *Cape Cod*, Thoreau undermines authoritative accounts of property claims based on colonization and dispossession. In "Life without Principle" (167–68), he asserts that even "broad and truly liberal" intellectuals "come to a stand against some institution in which they appear to hold stock" and "continually thrust their own low roof, with its narrow skylight, between you and the sky."

Using the language of classical economics—profit, loss, labor, cost, speculation, and enterprise—Thoreau juxtaposes the promises and actualities of commercial and industrial growth, without subscribing to the competing ideology of republicanism and moral economy.[37]

Thoreau also reflects on the formation of public opinion: "The only book which America has printed, and which America reads," he insists, dismissing the Bible, is the daily newspaper ("Resistance," 100). He parodies elements of popular culture—advice books to young men of the business class on self-improvement, for example—and considers how the increased presence of novels in the literary marketplace will affect the reception of his own work.

Thoreau's writings stand out from the romantic primitivism of his time for their lack of ethnocentrism. And in his vast, systematic, and appreciative reading, he is a thoroughgoing multiculturalist, reading the "scriptures of nations" and avowing the superiority of the Hindu Laws of Menu over the Christian Bible.

Thoreau's scattered references to "former inhabitants" and "borrowing" add up to a series of sensitive reflections on appropriation (*Walden*, 40). And he anticipates reader response: "A man receives only what he is ready to receive, whether physically or intellectually or morally. . . . We hear and apprehend only what we already half know. . . . Every man thus *tracks himself* through life, in all his hearing and reading and observation and traveling."[38]

As for this self, Thoreau reports standing "remote from myself" as a spectator (*Walden*, 135); he is "the scene, so to speak, of thoughts and affections," a "thoroughfare" ("Life," 172). He would rather be a passage for mountain brooks than for town sewers, but he has no illusion of self-control in this matter or even transparent self-understanding. It is not surprising that several of Thoreau's great set pieces are perspectivist riffs on the variability of how things look and what they mean, depending on where we stand, and on the instability of anyone's standpoint, including his own.

The question for contemporary studies of romanticism is whether to leave matters here, with an analysis that portrays expressivism and holism as a reactive longing or romantic ideology, a suspect and inevitably failed pursuit, or whether, this time with fragmentation and constraining contexts

in plain view, to reconfirm romantics' positive efforts at resolution or reconciliation and at political thought.[39] I have argued that Thoreau's "escapist"
transcendence on the one hand and his political resistance on the other are
moments in a comprehensive vision of democracy as a political order that
corresponds to the experience of individuality.

Of course, if holism is thought to require an organic conception of
political community or a sacred or reenchanted order, the judgment is
certain to be that romantic political thought, including Thoreau's, fails. But
romantic holism no more demands these things than it does overarching
metaphysical synthesis or emotional solidarism. It should be enough to
show that a particular political order can be more hospitable than others
to expressivism and can correspond more fully to "dignity and intensity of
desire"—even if what is expressed is the interplay of contrary desires or
perspectives, that is, romantic plenitude rather than underlying unity.

## Notes

Originally published as Nancy L. Rosenblum, "The Inhibitions of Democracy on
Romantic Political Thought: Thoreau's Democratic Individualism," in *Lessons of
Romanticism: A Critical Companion,* ed. Thomas Pfau and Robert F. Gleckner
(Durham, NC: Duke University Press, 1998), 55–75. Copyright 1998 by Duke
University Press. All rights reserved. Used by permission of the publisher. Minor
changes have been made.

1. Henry David Thoreau, *Walden,* ed. J. Lyndon Shanley (Princeton, NJ:
Princeton University Press, 1971), 171; hereafter cited in text.

2. Henry David Thoreau, "Resistance to Civil Government" [commonly referred to as "Civil Disobedience"], in *Reform Papers,* ed. Wendell Glick (Princeton,
NJ: Princeton University Press, 1973), 66; hereafter cited in text as "Resistance."

3. Henry David Thoreau, "A Plea for Captain John Brown," in *Reform Papers,*
120; hereafter cited in text as "Plea."

4. Leonard N. Neufeldt has counted these pronouns in *The Economist:
Henry Thoreau and Enterprise* (New York: Oxford University Press, 1989). Thoreau is chanticleer, awake and alert; his neighbors are stagnant, asleep, little better
than dead. See, for example, *Walden,* 106. I will not pursue the relation Thoreau
sees between anxiety over death and enervation and desperation. One of his most
common accusations is that ordinary men are dead in life, or they might as well
be dead, or they are incapable of dying because they have not lived. Thoreau's
romantic "half in love" with death deserves study.

5. Vicomte Francois Rene de Chateaubriand, *The Memoirs of Chateaubriand,* ed. Robert Baldick (New York: Knopf, 1961), 290.

6. Alfred de Vigny, *Military Servitude and Grandeur* (New York: George Doran, 1919), 107.

7. There is no reason to assume that the emergent sentimental family, with its changing roles for women, was key here; Thoreau boasts self-sufficiency, not paternalism. It is worth noting that (like J. S. Mill) Thoreau had little to say about his mother, though she was active in the cause of anti-slavery reform and Thoreau lived at home most of his adult life.

8. The same abhorrence extended to other intimate attachments. Thoreau was at best mistrustful of romantic love. Friendship was a recurrent theme, but Thoreau preferred to think of friends as goads to self-improvement rather than as "false appreciation," comfort, or pleasure—which is why he would rather honor his friends in thought than keep their company. His yearnings appear to have been homoerotic, confined to his poetry and journals, though his relation to readers has been likened to a homosexual seduction. See Henry Abelove, "From Thoreau to Queer Politics," *Yale Journal of Criticism* 6, no. 2 (1993): 17–27.

9. Henry David Thoreau, "The Last Days of John Brown," in *Reform Papers,* 149; hereafter cited in text as "Last Days."

10. Stanley Hyman's characterization of *Walden* and, by implication, Thoreau's work generally as a movement from individual isolation to collective action is overly simple. See Stanley Hyman, "Henry Thoreau in Our Time," in *Thoreau: A Century of Criticism,* ed. Walter Harding (Dallas: Southern Methodist University Press, 1954), 178.

11. Henry David Thoreau, *Cape Cod,* ed. Joseph J. Moldenhauer (Princeton, NJ: Princeton University Press, 1988), 30; hereafter cited in text.

12. Henry David Thoreau, *The Maine Woods,* ed. Joseph J. Moldenhauer (Princeton, NJ: Princeton University Press, 1972), 64; hereafter cited in text.

13. This is just one example of Thoreau's many-sidedness. The quintessential romanticism described by Charles Taylor as the real world of nature and undistorted human feeling that frees us from the debased, mechanistic world has more than one aspect for Thoreau. See Charles Taylor, *Sources of the Self: The Making of Modern Identity* (Cambridge, MA: Harvard University Press, 1989), 456–57.

14. Quoted in Robert P. Sayre, ed., *New Essays on* Walden (Cambridge: Cambridge University Press, 1992), 1.

15. For a discussion of Thoreau's violent language and toleration of political violence, see Nancy L. Rosenblum, introduction to *Thoreau: Political Writings* (Cambridge: Cambridge University Press, 1996), vii–xxxi.

16. Stendahl, *The Red and the Black,* trans. Lloyd C. Parks (New York: Signet Classics, [1830] 1970), 102.

17. See Judith Shklar, "Emerson and the Inhibitions of Democracy," *Political Theory* 18, no. 4 (November 1990): 601–14. Shklar's article was the model for this section of the chapter, and its heading is borrowed from her.

18. Thomas Carlyle, *On Heroes, Hero-Worship, and the Heroic in History* (Berkeley: University of California Press, 1993), 246.

19. Henry David Thoreau, "Thomas Carlyle and His Works," in *Early Essays and Miscellanies,* ed. Joseph J. Moldenhauer and Edwin Moser (Princeton, NJ: Princeton University Press, 1975), 238, 244–45. What Thoreau took from Carlyle was the militancy of his style, which in Thoreau became a conception of the act of writing. In his extended literary analysis of Carlyle, Thoreau praises the author in martial terms: he "meets face to face," "wrestles and strives," "advances, crashing his way through the host of weak, half-formed, dilettante opinions," and finally "prevails; you don't even hear the groans of the wounded and dying" (ibid., 223–24).

20. Carlyle, *On Heroes,* 3.

21. This contrasts with the view of Stanley Hyman, who sees in Thoreau "the honest artist struggling for terms on which he can adjust to society *in his capacity as an artist*" ("Thoreau in Our Time," 321; emphasis in original).

22. Henry David Thoreau, "Life without Principle," in *Reform Papers,* 155; hereafter cited in text as "Life."

23. Percy Bysshe Shelley, *Prometheus Unbound,* act III, scene 4, ll. 194–95.

24. See Friedrich Schiller, *On the Aesthetic Education of Man, in a Series of Letters* (New York: Ungar, 1974); Benjamin Constant, "The Spirit of Conquest," in *Constant: Political Writings,* ed. Biancamaria Fontana (Cambridge: Cambridge University Press, 1988); Wilhelm von Humboldt, *The Sphere and Duties of Government* (London: Chapman, 1854). J. S. Mill would incorporate this version of romantic political thought in the chapter "Of Individuality" in *On Liberty,* ed. David Spitz (New York: Norton, 1975).

25. George Kateb argues: "The typical politics of the theorized democratic individual is the politics of no-saying." See *The Inner Ocean: Individualism and Democratic Culture* (Ithaca, NY: Cornell University Press, 1992), 103.

26. Quoted in Robert D. Richardson, *Henry Thoreau: A Life of the Mind* (Berkeley: University of California Press, 1986), 225.

27. Henry David Thoreau, "Slavery in Massachusetts," in *Reform Papers,* 108; hereafter cited in text as "Slavery."

28. John Brown understood his own position: "Comparatively, all other men, North and South, were beside themselves" ("Last Days," 278–79). Daniel Webster's defense of the federal consensus over slavery was reprehensible: still, "comparatively, he is always strong, original, and, above all, practical" ("Resistance," 48).

29. This reading differs from the reading of those who see a liberal-democratic

Thoreau: from Vernon Parrington's view that Thoreau revives early Jeffersonian principles; from the host of Thoreauvians, anti-Marxists, and anti-collectivists who present Thoreau as a libertarian; and from those who uphold the "antinomian" theory, according to which major American writers are visionary dissenters. See Vernon Parrington, *Main Currents in American Thought*, vol. 2, *1800–1860—The Romantic Revolution in America* (New York: Harcourt, 1930), 400–414.

30. Isaiah Berlin, "The Apotheosis of the Romantic Will: The Revolt against the Myth of an Ideal World," in *The Crooked Timber of Humanity* (New York: John Murray, 1969), 237.

31. Kateb, *Inner Ocean,* 78.

32. This point is made with regard to German romantics by Carl Schmitt: "Without changing its name and its structure, which invariably remains occasionalist, romantic productivity can be linked to any other object of historical-political reality besides just the legitimate sovereign . . . the king is no less occasional than a colossal revolutionary hero, a bandit, or a courtesan." See *Political Romanticism* (Cambridge, MA: MIT Press, 1986), 123. For a summary of twentieth-century political readings of romanticism ranging from proto-fascist or collectivist to American pluralist readings, see Jon Klancher, "Romantic Criticism and the Meanings of the French Revolution," *Studies in Romanticism* 28 (fall 1989): 480–81. For an account of romantic liberalism, see Nancy L. Rosenblum, *Another Liberalism: Romanticism and the Reconstruction of Liberal Political Thought* (Cambridge, MA: Harvard University Press, 1987).

33. William Wordsworth, "The Convention of Cintra," in *Political Tracts of Wordsworth, Coleridge, and Shelley,* ed. R. J. White (Cambridge: Cambridge University Press, 1953), 192.

34. According to Karl Kroeber, there are few "critics in our time" who do not work from the premise "that art comes into being through injury or dislocation, a fault or fracturing of some kind, either psychological or sociological, perhaps both, and consequently, that the endless interpretability of a work of art is due not to its being a fountain forever overflowing but a *mise en abîme.*" See "Shelley's 'Defense of Poetry,'" in *Romantic Poetry: Recent Revisionary Criticism,* ed. Karl Kroeber and Gene W. Ruoff (New Brunswick, NJ: Rutgers University Press, 1993), 370. The oddity of this useful book is its misleading title—*Romantic Poetry*—since the essays focus exclusively on six canonical English poets.

35. See Thomas McFarland, "Field, Constellation, and Aesthetic Object," in *Romantic Poetry,* 16.

36. See Jerome McGann, *The Romantic Ideology: A Critical Investigation* (Chicago: University of Chicago Press, 1983), 90. McGann has made a much more general claim for all romantic poets: "The grand illusion of Romantic *ideology* is that one may escape such a world through imagination and poetry. The great

truth of Romantic *work* is that there is no escape, that there is only revelation (in a wholly secular sense)" (131). David Perkins argues that the romantic ideology was formed at this time and not in the romantic period itself. See "The Construction of 'the Romantic Movement' as a Literary Classification," *Nineteenth Century Literature* 45, no. 2 (September 1990): 142.

37. For a review of the most recent historical analysis, see Gordon S. Wood, "Inventing American Capitalism," *New York Review of Books,* June 9, 1994, 44–49.

38. Quoted in Richardson, *Henry Thoreau,* 291. Works dealing with the reception of Emerson and Thoreau and the shifting history of the latter's canonization include Michael Meyer, *Several More Lives to Live: Thoreau's Political Reputation in America* (Westport, CT: Greenwood, 1977); Lawrence Buell, "Henry Thoreau Enters the American Canon," in *New Essays on* Walden, 23–52; and Mary Kupiec Cayton, "The Making of an American Prophet: Emerson, His Audiences, and the Rise of the Culture Industry in Nineteenth-Century America," *American Historical Review* 92, no. 3 (June 1987): 597–620.

39. Kateb, in *Inner Ocean,* contends that instead of seeing Emerson as concealing his ideological affinities for possessive or atomistic individualism, one should appreciate him for expanding the typology to include democratic individualism. See Stanley Cavell, *The Senses of Walden* (New York: Viking, 1972), which argues that in response to skepticism, Thoreau produced an American scripture. Sacvan Bercovitch believes that Thoreau contributed to the "contradictory-conciliatory" symbol of America and its sacred mission, which allows for the coexistence of irreconcilable positions. "What makes *Walden* part of the tradition of the jeremiad is that the act of mimesis enables Thoreau simultaneously to berate his neighbors and to safeguard the values that undergird their way of Life." See *American Jeremiad* (Madison: University of Wisconsin Press, 1978), 86. See also Bercovitch, *Rites of Assent: Transformations in the Symbolic Construction of America* (New York: Routledge, 1993), 343n.

CHAPTER 2

# Thoreau's Alternative Economics: Work, Liberty, and Democratic Cultivation

*Brian Walker*

THE CONSTANT CHOICES AND self-direction entailed in meaningful work enliven all our capacities. While strolling through the streets of New York's Upper East Side as people catch their morning taxis, it is hard not to be impressed by their sleekness and fervor—the alert eyes, purposeful movements, and general liveliness of a caste of individuals with invigorating and demanding employment. One great advantage of the modern era is the array of stimulating occupations for those lucky enough to have the taste, capacity, and fortune of birth to find meaningful work. For so many others, work is of another sort: arduous labor, loud machinery, or confinement in some cubicle, unable to leave because aging parents depend on them for support. In its contrasting roles as our foundational source of empowerment and one of our most invasive afflictions, work plays a dominant role in shaping the energies and capacities we bring to our families, our communities, and political action.

The role that work plays has become greater in recent decades. In the United States, the number of hours spent at work each year has increased significantly since the early 1970s. According to the U.S. Bureau of Labor Statistics, women worked an average of 20 percent more in 1996 than in 1973, adding a full 233 hours to their working year, while men added 100 hours to theirs.[1] The proportion of people with very long workweeks has risen significantly in every occupation.[2] There have also been important changes in the quality of work. Corporate downsizing and a shift in organizational structure have made careers much less stable, and there has been a marked rise in contingent work and temporary employment.[3] In America,

the conditions that permitted one to envision a stable career are vanishing for many people.[4] In a society that enshrines labor as a calling, these
transformations in the shape and place of work are likely to have many
far-reaching effects.

Political theorists have long given attention to the fundamental role
that work plays in political life.[5] But very few voices in our tradition discuss
employment from the point of view of the individual laborer attempting to
maintain freedom and equilibrium in relation to the world of work. A major
exception is Henry David Thoreau's *Walden*.[6] Some critics have dismissed it
as the work of a petulant and disaffected romantic individualist, but this is
not an accurate reading of the text.[7] More careful attention reveals *Walden*
to be a carefully constructed study of the tensions between liberty and employment in times of economic change.[8] *Walden* is a rare work of political
theory that asks us to think critically about our relation to the work we do,
and it gives advice as to the strategies and practices we might adopt if we
want to elaborate more flexible responses to the shifting economy of work
in which we find ourselves.

Thoreau's central theme is that working conditions in a market democracy can easily undermine liberty and erode autonomy. His goal in *Walden*
is to set out strategies by which people can enact their freedom despite
working conditions that are likely to threaten their autonomy and well-
being. After a careful reading of *Walden*, we may still be uncomfortable
with many of Thoreau's strategies—his idea of voluntary poverty does not
appeal to everyone—but at least we will no longer underestimate *Walden*'s
complexity and subtlety as a reflection about the preconditions for democratic enactment in market societies.

## *Walden* and Employment

Few political philosophers have made their livings as day laborers. Thoreau
worked as a house painter, mason, land surveyor, gardener, and pencil
maker so that he would have the free time to be a writer, naturalist, and
abolitionist lecturer. His insights about the centrality of employment stem
in part from the strenuous ideal of democracy he absorbed while growing
up in Jacksonian America and in part from his vulnerability as a day laborer
within the swiftly restructuring economy of his time.[9] *Walden* is filled with
references to economic transformations that parallel those of our era in

many ways: a new interconnectedness brought about by the development of transportation infrastructure; diminished distances owing to the growth of railways, canals, and roadways; the rise of newspapers; the increasing power of large corporations; and the swift changes in working conditions brought about by the spread of factory labor.[10] The commercial spirit had taken hold of Concord, as it had so much of the Republic in the postwar period.[11] Thoreau's mother took in boarders, his father ran a struggling pencil manufacturing business, and the family lived in "honest poverty."[12] Thoreau attended Harvard as a scholarship student, but, as Edward Emerson wrote: "The comparatively small amount which it cost to maintain a boy at Harvard . . . was enough seriously to strain the resources of the family."[13]

Given this background, it should not be surprising that Thoreau considered the question of employment to be "the most practically important of all questions." In 1851 he wrote:

> There is little or nothing to be remembered written on the subject of getting an honest living. Neither the New Testament nor Poor Richard speaks to our condition. I cannot think of a single page which entertains, much less answers the questions which I put to myself on this subject. . . . Is it that men are too disgusted with their experience to speak of it? Or that commonly they do not question the common modes? The most practically important of all questions, it seems to me, is how I shall get my living, and yet I find nothing to my purpose in any book. . . . I consider that society with all its arts, has done nothing for us in this respect.[14]

*Walden* was an attempt to fill this lacuna and to explore how citizens forced to fend for themselves in a market democracy might make a living without scotching their liberty.

A careful reading of *Walden* leaves little doubt that employment is the enframing theme of the book. In the opening section, "Economy," in which Thoreau gives reasons for reading his book, he repeatedly underlines the occupational problems facing his fellow residents in Concord. Images of particular forms of employments and their drawbacks crowd the first pages of *Walden* (1–52): Thoreau writes of his fellow citizens in their roles as farmers, teamsters, slave drivers, surveyors, herdsmen, town officers, inspectors, sailors, factory operatives, merchants, masons, housewives, and carpenters. When Thoreau writes of visiting Concord, he speaks primarily of work spaces—of "shops and offices, and fields" (2)—and of the desperation he finds there. The word *labor* and its cognates are mentioned dozens of times in the opening section of *Walden*—seven times on the first three pages alone. When Thoreau wrote a précis of the book to deliver on the lyceum circuit, he first entitled the speech "Getting a Living." There can be little doubt what this book is about.

## Democracy and Employment

Thoreau argues that whatever one may think of the American political system (he calls it "comparatively free" [3]), at the level of everyday work life, it has produced only limited improvement over the feudalisms of Europe. Mortgaged to the banks, deeply in debt, threatened with financial failure, and toiling without cease, the men and women of Concord are, for all their seeming independence, still living as if they were "serfs of the soil" (1–3). "The mass of men lead lives of quiet desperation. What is called resignation is confirmed desperation" (4). Compared with the rest of the world, certainly, America is free, but working conditions consistently reproduce some of the worst aspects of the old tyrannies. Despite the ostensible liberties of the American nation, Thoreau's audience still finds itself "lying, flattering, voting, contracting yourselves into an atmosphere of thin and vaporous generosity" (4). *Walden* is about how the American project of democratization may be seen as blocked and disabled by everyday working conditions.

Thoreau makes four sorts of argument about the tensions among democracy, autonomy, and employment. First, to be free means having time for one's proper pursuits—time to figure out what one wants to do and then go out and do it. Yet earning a living can easily fill up or overshadow the time for such pursuits.[15] "The laboring man . . . has no time to be anything but a machine" (3). Second, there is a tension between work and democratic capacities. Employment conditions frequently entail a "contraction and dilation" (4) of the self, which undermines autonomy and upsets our ability to make the rational calculations necessary for the meaningful enactment of liberty (3, 22, 61). Third, there is also the problem of the narrowing of our choice set. Seeking success in the current work environment means accepting what public opinion values as the best life at any given moment. But individual tastes may well lead people to want a sort of life that differs from the narrow subset their society values and promotes. "The life which men praise and regard as successful is but one kind. Why should we exaggerate any one kind at the expense of others" (12)? Individuals whose tastes or capacities lead them to develop their talents outside of socially approved work paths need strategies to protect their pursuits in the face of socially sponsored exaggerations about what is admirable and what is not. Fourth, a concern with maintaining employment may prevent people from taking principled political positions and thus make them acquiesce in immoral policies. As Thoreau suggests in "Civil Disobedience":

> Practically speaking, the opponents to reform in Massachusetts are not a hundred thousand politicians at the South, but a hundred thousand merchants and farmers here who are more interested in commerce and agriculture than they are in humanity, and are not prepared to do justice to the slave and to Mexico, *cost what it may*.[16]

In *Walden*, Thoreau carefully draws our attention to the fact that he moved to his cabin "on Independence day, or the fourth of July, 1845" (55), and the book is studded with references to the political nature of his explorations of independence and freedom. George Kateb writes of Thoreau and his generation as the intellectual inheritors of the founding; they "disclose its fuller meaning."[17] Thoreau shares with other writers of his time the idea that the republicanism of the founding period established only the institutional preconditions for democracy and liberty and that the real work of creating a democratic culture remains to be done.[18] The founding period opened up a new possibility, but the crucial challenge is to enact democracy, to flesh it out in concrete attitudes, practices, and institutions. People too easily mistake the legal preconditions of liberty for the real thing. Here is how Thoreau puts the problem in "Slavery in Massachusetts":

> Now-a-days, men wear a fool's cap, and call it a liberty cap. I do not know but there are some, who, if they were tied to whipping-post, and could get but one hand free, would use it to ring the bells and fire the cannons to celebrate *their* liberty. So some of my townsmen took the liberty to ring and fire; that was the extent of their freedom; and when the sound of the bells died away, their liberty died away also; when the powder was all expended, their liberty went off with the smoke.[19]

Thoreau is not alone in his belief that we need to think through how we might establish real liberty in the United States. Much of the work of Emerson, Margaret Fuller, George Ripley, Elizabeth Cady Stanton, Walt

Whitman, Bronson Alcott, and other antebellum reformers can be usefully read within this perspective of a hortatory literature of democratic enactment. There is widespread recognition in this era that most of the values democrats take seriously—liberty for all, equality among people, personal autonomy—are very hard to realize in an everyday world long formatted by more hierarchical visions and under working conditions that produce both opportunities and severe challenges.[20] Democratic capacities are fragile and evanescent. They tend to fade from sight amid the bright temptations of everyday life unless they are enacted in concrete practices, strategies, and dispositions. This belief in the evanescence of the central democratic capacities is clearly an echo of republicanism, with its vision of human liberty constantly threatened by the corruptions of power and money and by general inattentiveness.[21] *Walden* is a particularly interesting work within this tradition because of the way it works out the theme of democratic enactment in relation to the economy of everyday life and the trade-offs of work and leisure.

## Democracy and Self-Cultivation

*Walden* is also important because of its focus on individual laborers trying to navigate the dilemmas of their work lives. The book reflects many of the conventions of a broader democratic advice genre that rose to prominence in the antebellum period. In the United States in the 1830s and 1840s, there was a widespread exploration of how citizens might prepare themselves for their new roles as democratic citizens, while as fathers and sons they attempted to orient themselves in a market economy and as mothers they trained future citizens.[22] Bookstores were filled with manuals of advice, young men's guidebooks, periodicals for mechanics, and exemplary biographies of famous Americans such as Ben Franklin and George Washington.[23] The Boston area, in particular, was a center for this movement of democratic self-cultivation, with its popular lyceum lectures, young men's mercantile libraries, evening schools, and literary societies.[24] A wide range of writers advised ordinary Americans how they might give themselves some of the skills and capacities the upper classes counted on as their birthright.[25] The question that guides this literature is how individual citizens might teach themselves the requisite skills to make full use of the new material and political conditions around them. That these writers should stress self-cultivation is not surprising in an era when public education was still the preserve of the upper classes.[26]

Modern scholarship has not been particularly sympathetic to the antebellum literature of democratic self-cultivation. For example, Cayton's influential essay on Emerson stresses elements of social control and class domination within the movement for democratic self-culture. Cayton argues that local boosters and businesspeople in many American cities wanted to maintain moral order among the young men in their employ, and the self-culture movement was a means to inculcate business-friendly values.[27] Cayton's work is typical of much recent scholarship on nineteenth-century moral didacticism in its debunking tone and its unwillingness to see that there might have been something more going on than mere moral indoctrination. Modern middle-class scholars who have had the advantages of a free public education and access to colleges and universities have generally not been very sensitive to the predicaments facing clerks and mechanics who were struggling to rise in society without the benefits of adequate training.[28]

Perhaps another reason for the modern scholarly disdain for this movement (and for writers like Thoreau) is that the focus on the individual in the democratic self-cultivation movement seems to foreshadow the narcissism, privatism, and self-concern detected in our own era by some scholars.[29] Certainly, one can never be too vigilant about the narcissism that individualistic societies tend to engender. But an anachronistic reading of our own reputed insufficiencies into the writers of the Jacksonian era underestimates the important functions democratic self-cultivation plays in periods of social and economic upheaval. Writers of that time were aware that society was transforming from one in which people acquired their social rank by accident of birth to one in which a new mobility was available to most adult white males. The challenges and opportunities of mobility made pressing the questions of self-cultivation and of education in general. Aristocrats had tutors, rhetoric instructors, and a college education to prepare them for the public sphere. How were those born to an average lot to achieve the capacities necessary for full civic participation? We have "no schools for ourselves," Thoreau writes in Walden; "our education is sadly neglected" (71).

Recent scholars also may tend to underestimate the benefits of the self-cultivation literature if they do not recognize the importance of self-preparation in nonaristocratic societies. In market democracies, a great deal is at stake in terms of how dispositions and habits are formed. As

Thoreau shows, the successful practice of self-cultivation can easily mean the difference between a life spent in freedom and a life caught in a spiral of desperation. Aristocrats can rely not only on an elaborate educational infrastructure but also on relatively secure liberties, since they are assigned these freedoms along with their estates and their rank in society. By contrast, the liberties of citizens in a market democracy are often won by their own efforts and capacities. Not all individuals who concern themselves with their dispositions and self-training are narcissistic; for some, it may be a matter of survival or preparation.

As Neufeldt has pointed out, Thoreau's work has deep resonances with the literature of democratic self-cultivation. Thoreau owned a number of "young men's guides," and a passage in the opening section of *Walden* parodies this self-help literature.[30] But *Walden* stands out within the literature on democratic self-culture because it sees democratic citizenship as existing in tension with—rather than supported by—the practices involved in everyday work, business, and enterprise. As Shklar and Wood have shown, the social revolution inaugurated by the founding generation had a radical influence on the way Americans understood the place of labor in life.[31] The attack on aristocracy after the Revolution was cast in terms of an assault on idleness and leisure, and it brought a "heightened appreciation of the significance and dignity of labor."[32] Shklar has argued that the standing of American citizens was, from the beginning, tied up with their status as workers: free democratic citizens neither labored in the degraded conditions of the slave nor loafed in the idleness of the aristocrat. When Thoreau writes in *Walden* of "serfs of the soil," of the need to move from noblemen to "noble villages of men" (72),[33] or of the servility of businessmen who contract and dilate their personalities (4), he is wielding tropes taken from a discourse about aristocracy and slavery that was central to the language of democratization in his day.[34] The radicalism of Thoreau's perspective consists in his suggestion that, far from generalizing access to the liberty and dignity the aristocratic classes enjoyed, everyday working conditions in America might merely be generalizing toiling desperation. This is why *Walden* is a work of democratic advice literature. Thoreau sees the conditions of American employment as the most stubborn obstacle to the enactment of real freedom.

What is *democratic* about democratic self-cultivation? Certainly Thoreau's primary concern is not with encouraging more political engagement and mobilization, as if these were good in themselves. He is, for example, profoundly skeptical about the influence exerted by the unprincipled and easily manipulated voters of Massachusetts on the political and legal life of the state. [35] Ordinary people are too thoroughly submerged in their work worries to exert an autonomous and principled stance on political issues, and to encourage them to be more politically active while they are in such a state would only result in the passage of other problematic laws such as the Fugitive Slave Law or the bills launching war with Mexico. Instead, what Thoreau wants to democratize is the experience of liberty, leisure, and self-cultivation formerly monopolized by the upper classes. This is democratic in the sense that it is premised on the value of the common man, on the idea that all people are equally worthy of ethical concern and development; no longer should only the upper class have a chance at a full life. Self-cultivation and leisure were formerly monopolized by the upper classes, but now these states might be attained by everyday people; this, in turn, would allow them to develop a sense of principle and perhaps resist the manipulations of newspaper editors and jingoistic warmongers. This is the second sense in which Thoreau's is a democratic theory: he assumes that the population at large is voting and exerting a role through public opinion, and he assumes that the question of whether they develop a sense of ethical principle is important in a way it was not when the population at large was less influential in political decision making.

It should be noted that Thoreau does not think all Americans—not even all those who are economically vulnerable—will necessarily need the strategies he sets out. He explicitly exempts from his arguments all those who can, on reflection, describe themselves as well employed, however that might be (10). And some people, he suggests, are so strong and valiant that they will come out well anywhere. To these, he emphasizes, he does not speak (9). Thoreau also excludes from his concern those who have inherited (or dishonestly attained) wealth (164). By exempting from his discussion anyone who feels a comfortable meshing between work and liberty, Thoreau traces out an audience of those who labor *without* a calling, a group rarely addressed within American literature.

## An Experiment in Philosophy

How does one address the predicament of the mass of people who try to enact liberty and their own particular vision of the good without being able to rely on inherited wealth or standing? How might the myriad blessings of our modern technology and productivity be unlocked for the class of people apparently so ill served by modern developments? "I wish to show at what a sacrifice [the advantage of modern civilization] is at present obtained, and to suggest that we may possibly so live as to secure all the advantage without suffering any of the disadvantage" (20). At issue is how those who have trouble getting a living can nonetheless achieve what Thoreau believes he has achieved—namely, the ability to escape misery and desperation—and how they can learn to find "encouragement and inspiration in the present condition," even to the extent of "cherish[ing] it with the fondness and enthusiasm of lovers," as Thoreau says he does (10).

After reviewing a number of the typical occupations of his day, Thoreau introduces the strategy that he believes offers the best alternative to the "enslavements" (4) everyday work life so frequently entails. He suggests that moderns who seek to enact democratic liberty have much to learn from the ancient philosophical schools of various nations. "The ancient philosophers, Chinese, Hindoo, Persian and Greek, were a class than which none has been poorer in outward riches, none so rich in inward" (9). What Thoreau finds particularly attractive in these schools is their strong emphasis on bringing wisdom to bear on the practices of everyday life. "To be a philosopher is not merely to have subtle thoughts, nor even to found a school, but so to love wisdom as to live according to its dictates, a life of simplicity, independence, magnanimity and trust. It is to solve some of the problems of life, not only theoretically, but practically" (9). The "independence" in this passage is important. In developing his democratic experiments outside of schools and other institutions, Thoreau sees himself as returning to a philosophical independence abandoned by many modern philosophers. As Thoreau puts it, "success of great scholars and thinkers is commonly a courtier-like success" (334). The worry that philosophy may be undermined if the working conditions of philosophers become too courtier-like—toadying to superiors, courting public reputation, establishing power blocs, and so on—is part of *Walden*'s general criticism of those forms of life in which participants' stated goals (love of wisdom in philosophy, love of freedom and independence among everyday citizens) are mangled in their enactment and thus are not adequately embodied in the occupations people adopt to realize them. He thinks more "Yankee" shrewdness needs to be applied to resolving the tensions between our higher-order values and the practices of our everyday work lives.

This idea that ancient philosophy might offer the key to modern work predicaments goes back very far in Thoreau's thought. Early in his *Journal* he wrote that "Zeno the Stoic stood in precisely the same relation to the world as I do now. . . . Bred a merchant . . . he strolls into a shop and is charmed by a book by Xenophon and straightaway becomes a philosopher."[36] The key to *Walden* is the way it combines ancient philosophical practices and modern economic calculations to set out a strategy by which citizens can realize their liberty.[37] The seriousness with which the ancient philosophers took the challenge of maintaining their poise in the pursuit of the good, and their willingness to reform the practices of their everyday lives so as to reflect their higher values, become the central attitudes that enable a democratic citizen to reopen the space of freedom at the level of daily life.

Thoreau's description of the philosopher as somebody who solves the "problems of life" may at first reading appear to be a fundamental mis-understanding of ancient philosophy. After all, in the works of Plato and Aristotle, which are the focus of our contemporary curriculum in the field, the philosopher's development of wisdom and insight leads him away from political involvement and creates a marked tension with the political life of the demos. Philosophy is defined in contrast to, and in many ways as an alternative to, everyday democratic life.

Thoreau was a well-trained classicist, one of the best of his genera-tion,[38] but the Harvard curriculum of his day gave less exposure to Plato and Aristotle than to such writers as Cicero and the Hellenistic Stoics, who emphasized a more complex relation between philosophic practice and political life. Thoreau's principal classics teacher, Eliot professor of Greek literature C. C. Felton, encouraged his students to see the close connec-tion between classic literature and the everyday lives of ancient peoples.[39] Moreover, Thoreau's vision of ancient philosophy comprised Chinese texts, such as the *Analects* of Confucius, which are quoted throughout *Walden*,[40] as well as numerous Indian texts, such as the Laws of Menu, the Bhagavad Gita, and the Vedas, all of which emphasize philosophy as a form of advice on how to live as an ordinary householder.[41] All these traditions gave the philosopher a large role in acting as an example and in setting out pathways for others to follow as they confronted the challenges of everyday life.

As many recent scholars have stressed, the relation between the ancient philosopher and the political realm is considerably more complex than
the simple question of whether the philosophically enlightened citizen will
participate in politics.[42] While one strain of ancient thought encouraged a
turn away from political life, another looked on philosophy as ideal training
for public affairs, since it taught how to preserve moral integrity amid the
tumult of political struggle.[43] Philosophers frequently found employment
as tutors and advisers in powerful households, teaching politically involved
citizens how to balance political position, public functions, activities, and
obligations.[44] Given the constant fluctuations and reversals of political life in
the ancient world (in some ways comparable to the fluctuations and reversals
of work life in modern times), the citizen needed to stabilize his desires and
sense of self so as to maneuver with maximum flexibility, to show himself
as capable of ruling, of being ruled in turn, and of holding high office while
resisting the temptations of corruption and immorality.[45]

One reason philosophers came to be seen as fitting advisers to citizens and rulers was that they were versed in exercises by which individuals
learned to bring their passions and desires under control.[46] To operate well
as a citizen or ruler, one had to learn attention, concentration, and resistance
of temptation. None of these capacities is easy for humans to attain, plagued
as they are by anxiety, greed, and fear. Thus, much of the training in the
ancient schools was designed to help people circumvent the temptation of
their passions. For example, the Epicureans formulated various aphorisms
to quell fears and realign the individual with the natural world. One of
these, discussed in Hadot's illuminating book on ancient philosophical
practices, is the so-called *tetrapharmakon*: "God presents no fears, death
no worries. And while good is readily attainable, evil is readily endurable."[47]
Philosophers could teach a range of exercises and strategies to help people
navigate the everyday temptations and obstacles of political life while preserving their moral integrity and political reputation. *Walden* is a modern
revival of this tradition. Thoreau uses the narrative of his experiment at
Walden Pond to show how the resources of ancient philosophy can be used
by those who find themselves vulnerable within the modern market system.
As I show in the next section, the similarity lies not just in general attitude;
the practices and exercises Thoreau sets out in *Walden* are functionally
identical to the techniques found in ancient philosophy.

## Exercises, Strategies, and Replacement Practices

Thoreau advocates a number of exercises and practices as a means of offsetting the forces that threaten autonomy, liberty, and happiness: (1) Thought experiments can clarify our relation to our fundamental needs and thereby counteract anxiety. (2) Maxims can be coined to offset the autonomy-hampering effects of public opinion. (3) Household accounting methods, centered on autonomy, can establish an equilibrium between one's higher-order goods and the practices of everyday life, particularly with regard to the relation between work and leisure. (4) Replacement practices can be developed to encourage individual flourishing while offsetting both economic dependency and social relations of exploitation. (5) Ways of approaching nature and the physical world can be designed to expand and train the self and especially the body, as well as to open up to nature in a way that makes it more than just a tool of human needs. (6) Dietary and sumptuary strategies can be adopted to promote the various goods set out above.

In line with my suggestion that *Walden* is a work about democratic enactment for those facing uncongenial employment choices, these practices and exercises can be separated into two categories. On the one hand are those meant to liberate the time and tranquility needed to elaborate projects expressing one's personal autonomy (practices 1 through 4). On the other hand are those more exclusively tied up with Thoreau's own individual sense of the good life, the particular perfectionistic doctrines to which he adheres. These include the observation of nature by living in a cabin in the woods rather than in a small apartment in the city, and so on.

I make this distinction because each category of practice admits to different degrees of generalizability. Practices in the first group are generally relevant to most citizens who are interested in preserving their freedom under conditions of market democracy. Those in the second group can be interpreted only as reflections of Thoreau's personal tastes and inclinations, such as his dislike of tea or his preference for country living. These are relevant to fewer people compared with the advice Thoreau gives about maintaining liberty in a potentially overwhelming labor environment. Thus, I concentrate primarily on the first category of practices in claiming Thoreau as a philosopher of democratic enactment. They illustrate how Thoreau reformats ancient philosophical practices as elements of a democratic politics of example to address the tension between work and autonomy in market democracies.

## *Thought Experiments to Offset Anxiety*

Thoreau believes that one of the great obstacles to autonomy is anxiety. Self-governance, which is to say the ability to guide ourselves by our own developing sense of the good, requires a certain poise and presence of mind that are easily lost in a complex existence with many cares. For example, worries about long-term economic security can easily lead to a harried life what soon subverts the ends sought through pursuing such security.

Thoreau shows that, for a correct balance of ends and means, our calculus of liberty must take as its base point a well-understood knowledge of our most fundamental physical needs. These play such a large role in our struggle for freedom that Thoreau capitalizes them as if they were deities: "The necessaries of life for man in this climate may, accurately enough, be distributed under the several heads of Food, Shelter, Clothing, and Fuel; for not till we have secured these are we prepared to entertain the true problems of life with freedom and a prospect of success" (7).

In the second half of the "Economy" section, Thoreau guides readers through a set of thought experiments designed to sensitize them to the border between what they do and do not need in terms of fuel, shelter, clothing, and food. These exercises cultivate a disposition to distinguish between what one needs as a physiological organism and what public opinion and habit make one think one needs. An ability to step away from the sense of the socially necessary allows one room for maneuver; one is no longer locked into a set of trade-offs between anxiety-producing complexities and an unrevisable set of goods. An example of Thoreau's strategy here can be found in his section on shelter:

> If one designs to construct a dwelling house, it behooves him to exercise a little Yankee shrewdness, lest after all he find himself in a workhouse, a labyrinth without a clew, a museum, an almshouse, a prison, or a splendid mausoleum instead. Consider first how slight a shelter is absolutely necessary. I have seen Penobscot Indians, in this town, living in tents of thin cotton cloth, while the snow was nearly a foot deep around them, and I thought they would be glad to have it deeper to keep out the wind. (18)

There are numerous noteworthy elements in this passage, but I will point out just a few. Note the parallel between Thoreau's strategy here and the second part of the Epicurean *tetrapharmakon,* which states that the good is readily attainable, and evil is readily endurable. Thoreau tries to remove the sting of autonomy-harming anxiety by stressing that it is easier than we think to get the goods we need to endure even the greatest local evils, which in New England is the winter's cold. Thoreau addresses each of the necessities of life in turn and through a similar set of reflections gives readers a more realistic vision of what they really need and what are luxuries for them (luxuries, that is, if they desire, above all, to maintain their autonomy). Ancient philosophy was replete with such therapies aimed at clarifying our vision of nature so as to release us from potentially harmful passions and anxieties.[48] Thoreau's strategy is the same as the ancient techniques, although Thoreau is careful to cast his arguments in terms of values his audience already holds; for example, he asks why Yankees, who are so shrewd about building machines and forming commercial enterprises, nonetheless permit their own lives to sink into desperation.

Notice also the didactic use Thoreau makes of the Indians. He consistently refers to Native Americans as having managed to work out a relation with the necessities of life that does not force them to lose their liberty—which allows them to live in the realm of stark necessity while being ingenious enough to maintain forms of real richness (19), liberty, and comfort (21). Throughout *Walden,* Native Americans exemplify a population living in relation to the New England climate in a way that allows them to maintain their freedom and happiness without the problems Thoreau sees his fellow countrymen facing.

## Maxims to Offset the Effects of Public Opinion

In the Hellenistic schools and in other ancient philosophical traditions, such as Confucianism and Buddhism, adherents memorized maxims that summed up the complex moral and physical attitudes advocated by their school.[49] These short sayings were then used as guides in daily life, as a source of moral orientation amid constant choices, dilemmas, and stress. Maxims in *Walden* play a similar role. Thoreau is elaborating a new ethos of everyday life, and *Walden*'s place in it is analogous to *Poor Richard's Almanac*'s in the ethos he is calling into question. The maxims in *Walden* sum up and reinforce a particular attitude toward work and time, rendering the ethos into a portable form for use in daily life.

Thoreau employs maxims as a means of stabilizing the new ethos he is developing in the face of a public opinion that continually threatens to upset it: "The cost of a thing is the amount of what I will call life which is required to be exchanged for it" (19). "Money is not required to buy one necessary of the soul" (213). "How can he remember well his ignorance—which his growth requires—who has so often to use his knowledge?" (3). "Simplify, simplify" (60). These maxims are meant to stick in the mind and generate the dispositions that ground the replacement ethos.

Thoreau mirrors Mill in his sensitivity to the autonomy-hampering effects of public opinion in a mass democratic society and to the threats public censure poses to liberty. But Thoreau's economic vulnerability as a day laborer led him to insights Mill missed. Most important is Thoreau's suggestion that the most dangerous influence of public opinion may well be the way it shapes our attitudes as consumers, misleading us into thinking that we can afford things we cannot (not if we want to maintain our autonomy). Public opinion can create autonomy-harming ideas about what our needs truly are. The maxims studding Thoreau's text are designed to help readers remind themselves that, from the perspective of their fragile freedoms, many more items may turn out to be luxuries than they first think.

## An Alternative Household Economics

Thoreau's reflections are based on the assumption that people are forced to be self-supporting but that freedom entails an ability to maintain contact with one's ideals, with what Thoreau terms "proper pursuits" (18). In modern conditions, he suggests, that may be possible only with the most simplified life, since the means by which one gains the resources for a complicated existence are likely to destroy the time and psychic poise needed to keep a firm grip on one's proper pursuits. Thus, individuals who are threatened with a desperation-producing work life may find it useful to revise their basic wants and needs downward.

Thoreau advances a number of formulas and maxims designed to help the individual achieve an acceptable equilibrium between the need to preserve autonomy and the need to gain the necessities of life.[50] Some were cited earlier. But there are also more general algorithms for determining what is affordable if one ranks the maintenance of autonomy as a high priority. One such equation is the following: "The cost of a thing is the amount of what I call life which is required to be exchanged for it, immediately or in the long run" (19). As Richardson has pointed out, Thoreau was a careful reader of the works of Adam Smith, Ricardo, and Say, and the aforementioned formula is a virtual paraphrase of Smith's definition of cost in *The Wealth of Nations*.[51] As Thoreau says in *Walden*, "economics is a subject which admits of being treated with levity, but it cannot be so disposed of" (18). "He must be a great calculator indeed who succeeds" (60). Thoreau gives sample account books for a household economy centered around creating a space for liberty, offering an example of an accounting practice that takes freedom seriously (31–40). He shows how an everyday practice (drawing up the household accounts) can be reformatted as a means of enacting liberty in the daily lives of average citizens.

## A Pattern Book of Practices

Much of *Walden,* and of Thoreau's other work, focuses on the creation of practices that might serve as better means of realizing autonomy than the customary work practices of Concord. *Walden* is a pattern book of replacement practices to help people elude the financial dependency that leads to desperate lives within ostensibly free societies. Much of Thoreau's ingenuity in *Walden* and in his miscellaneous essays is devoted to showing how the entirely banal practices of everyday life—walking, talking with friends, botanizing, reading and writing, doing day labor—can be rethought and reconstructed to enhance autonomy. *Walden* is an attempt to work out an acceptable culture—that is, practices, exercises, and dispositions—that will render poverty livable. Replacement practices aim to make poverty lush rather than barren, thus disclosing it as a position individuals might choose if they felt their liberty threatened by the standard work lives they encountered. Native Americans and ancient philosophers were able to create fully satisfying lives in conditions of great material poverty, and it is not unreasonable to believe that amid the much greater material wealth of bustling America, such savage comforts (21) may be even more easily attainable.[52]

Using the material advantages of our society, we can work out replacement practices that take advantage of any comforts available to us within a position of poverty. The aim is to escape boredom, avoid despair, maintain our financial independence, extend our faculties, and open up a space to express our autonomy. Thoreau's discussion of replacement practices generally follows a standard pattern. After examining the customary way of achieving particular ends, Thoreau explains why the standard practices should be questioned and perhaps rejected. He then offers his own approach and discusses how it enhances autonomy.

A good example is the practice of walking, which Thoreau discusses both in the essay "Walking" and in *Walden*. He concentrates on walking not for exercise or as part of business but in its most banal form—strolling around outdoors with no real purpose in mind: "I think that I cannot preserve my health and spirits, unless I spend four hours a day at least—and it is commonly more than that—sauntering through the woods and over the hills and fields, absolutely free from all worldly engagements"[53]

The customary practice to which Thoreau contrasts his ideal of sauntering is that of staying inside all day—not so much staying inside a building as staying inside the cares and problems of one's work and home life. "Walking" and numerous other passages in Thoreau's works devoted to the benefits of sauntering are really about the relation between labor and leisure and about setting out strategies so that one can work without occluding one's self and sense of the good.

Thoreau also contrasts beneficial walking to the sort of walking during which one ruminates about one's housework or other cares: "Of course it is of no use to direct our steps to the woods, if they do not carry us thither. . . . It sometimes happens that I cannot easily shake off the village. The thought of some work will run in my head and I am not where my body is,—I am out of my senses. In my walks I would fain return to my senses." He argues that walking can be used to regain contact with one's bodily senses and with nature, removing oneself mentally from the world of work. "What business have I in the woods, if I am thinking of something out of the woods?"[54] In Thoreau's work, the exercises that return us to everyday experience are valued because they refresh the faculties and give the self a ballast outside public opinion and standard custom (72–73). This, in turn, allows one to make better judgments about the choices that come up in everyday life. This is but one example of the many replacement practices Thoreau envisions and recounts.

My argument is that something more went on at Walden Pond than mere moral perfectionism. To read *Walden* as nothing more than Thoreau's working out of "private business," his personal attempt to answer the question "How then shall I live?" misses the large sections that are sincere and nonparodistic attempts to write a workable piece of democratic advice literature aimed at those whose liberty is threatened by their employment.

The first five pages and the last five pages of *Walden* are very straightforward about addressing an audience made up of the poor and others whose work lives threaten to subvert their "proper pursuits." One can see *Walden* as a parody of advice literature only if one focuses on a few satirical sections and ignores the harrowing discussion of human toil and desperation in its opening pages. *Walden* is a democratic advice book for the poor and work-weary (1).

## Thoreau's Alternative Economics

In 1851 Thoreau wrote that the question of getting a living is "the most practically important of all questions" because everyone must answer it before going on to explore and then express the possibilities of freedom.[55] The very structure of *Walden* mirrors and reinforces this message. It opens with "Economy," a section in which Thoreau focuses on mundane worries such as employment, food, shelter, and livelihood. But once these self-oriented issues are addressed, he turns to the world outside—the community in Concord and the contemplation of nature. Thoreau is one of the first moderns to develop an idea of the physical environment as an autonomous presence toward which human beings have some accountability, a dialogic partner with its own interests and processes rather than just a tool for human ends.[56] The book may begin with a certain degree of self-concern, but this is just a stepping-stone on the way to a greater objectivity.

The rhetorical conventions of *Walden,* with its quasi-allegorical history of the individual soul's progress from the mundane world of business and self-centered worries to participation in a suprahuman realm beyond, with "new, universal and more liberal laws" (209), link it to other philosophical allegories, such Plato's *Republic.* But in contrast to the philosopher-sage Socrates, who justifies an aristocratic politics of guardianship, the democrat-sage Thoreau illustrates strategies that can make the individual self-reliant.

Perhaps the best way to understand the exercises and practices advocated in *Walden* is to see them as a form of ethical-political athleticism that Thoreau hopes will inspire and liberate others. In the same way that a great athlete can inspire us to great effort and grace, so Thoreau acts out writ-large versions of democratically pertinent skills such as self-direction, the maintenance of ideals, economic awareness, and frugality. He writes frequently of the importance of setting examples, even if they seem dauntingly strenuous: "Be sure that you give the poor the aid they most need, though it be your example which leaves them far behind" (49). An 1851 journal entry reads: "If you would convince a man that he does wrong, do right. But do not care to convince him. Men will believe what they see. Let them see."[57] "Does Wisdom work in a tread-mill? or does she teach how to succeed by her example?"[58] Through recounting his experiments by the pond, Thoreau hopes to inspire his readers to question the choices and decisions they make unthinkingly and perhaps adopt a more rigorous household economics, one that takes their life goals into account. Thoreau reformats the familiar republican vocabulary about preserving liberty through resisting luxury and renders it applicable to the case of individual citizens attempting to make their way as laborers in a modern market economy.

But Thoreau is well aware that the strenuous practices and exercises he advocates will not appeal to all. He carefully includes in *Walden* an episode of failed advice-giving through which he meditates on the stringency of his example. In the chapter "Baker Farm," Thoreau encounters an Irish immigrant and his family in a shack near the pond. The Irishman, John Field, labors day and night for a local farmer hoeing a bog, but he never manages to get ahead. Thoreau summarizes for him an autonomy-oriented household economics based on extreme simplicity:

> John heaved a sigh at this, and his wife stared with arms a-kimbo, and both appeared to be wondering if they had capital enough to begin such a course with, or arithmetic enough to carry it through. It was sailing by dead reckoning to them, and they saw not clearly how to make their port so; therefore I suppose they still take life bravely, after their fashion, face to face, giving it tooth and nail, not having the skill to split its massive columns with any fine entering wedge, and route it in detail;—thinking to deal with it roughly, as one would handle a thistle. But they fight at overwhelming disadvantage,—living, John Field, alas! without arithmetic, and failing so. (134)

Thoreau, it is obvious, is well aware of just how radical his austere household economics will appear to some of his readers.

We might think that Thoreau overestimates the degree of freedom open to people who live in conditions of poverty and does not adequately recognize the predicaments poverty can bring—the way the attainment of freedom is complicated by having to fend for both self and family, for example. We might also find that Thoreau does a poor job of accounting for the importance of cultural capital. Not all poor people have an intact family to rely on, can draw benefit from a Harvard education, and live in a community as vibrant as that of antebellum Concord. To be completely satisfying, Thoreau's alternative economics would have to take all these things into consideration and would have to reflect more articulately on the weight of structures and institutions. Still, no book can do all things, and *Walden* brings considerable illumination to the issues it touches. The book insists that America is "comparatively free" and that strategies to circumvent any disadvantages in its institutions are thus both thinkable and pursuable. Thoreau's strategy is certainly not based on any illusions about the grimness of poverty. Indeed, few northern writers of this time paid as much attention as Thoreau did to the fate of poor laborers, to the people living in human sties by the railroad tracks: "The forms of both old and young are permanently contracted by the long habit of shrinking from cold and misery, and the development of all their limbs and faculties are checked" (22).[59]

Thoreau clearly does not romanticize poverty, but he does refuse to see all poor people as similarly situated with regard to life and choice. He forcibly reminds us by his own example that there is great diversity in the experiences and capacities of poor people, that economic poverty can coexist with widely varying degrees of social capital, and that poverty is not in all cases the worst of afflictions. Thoreau is less likely than some middle-class writers to see poverty as intrinsically and always a barren and liberty-destroying condition.[60] *Walden* questions the automatic connection we make between economic improvement and increased liberty by pointing to groups such as the Native Americans and the ancient philosophers, who maintained liberty in conditions of poverty, and to the workers of Concord, whose freedom often diminished as their economic lives improved. These arguments are not frequently heard in American political thinking.

The best way to read *Walden* is to see it as addressing people of all classes who have talents and tastes that are not adequately mirrored in the lifeways deemed profitable in their time. *Walden* is designed to render readers more sensitive to their choices about the place of work in their lives and about the trade-offs they make between freedom and consumption. Thoreau's strategy of voluntary poverty as a means to achieve liberty and develop one's own projects is designed for people with a strong sense of autonomy who might conceive of projects that cannot be realized through their work. Certainly, not all people have these characteristics. But as social scientists from Weber onward have shown, the modern employment system tends to produce highly disciplined individuals able to eschew short-term comfort in the name of more evanescent goals.[61] The system that produces the sorts of dilemmas Thoreau addresses is also likely to reproduce the forms of character that allow the strategies in *Walden* to make sense to people.

Thoreau's strategies are but one part of the political theory necessary to address the tensions between employment and freedom found in modern democracies. We also need to explain the structural changes in economic and political systems that allow these tensions to persist. But in terms of the immediacy of its advice and its utility for individual citizens, *Walden* is thus far without parallel. In *On Liberty* Mill suggests that it is important for democratic societies to produce individuals who undertake experiments in living and thus serve as generative centers of innovation for their society, illustrating escape routes from the tyranny of majority custom.[62] Thoreau's *Walden* is an exemplary account of one such experiment in living, and one that shows a constant awareness of the exemplary functions of its innovations. It contains an array of practical suggestions that readers might take up as part of their own democratic activities. As a democratic advice book, *Walden* has a proximity to action that contemporary political theory often lacks. Much modern political philosophy is a philosophy of postponement, in the sense that the extension of liberty entails waiting for a collective social actor willing to put radical changes into practice—the proletariat finally coming to consciousness, or a constitutional convention finally being convened and bringing about the redistributions of Rawls's difference principle.[63] The thrust of much modern political theory is to postpone our political activity to some distant day. There is a utility in Thoreau's focus on immediate enactment, on the possibility that we might "adventure on life now" (9), and in his emphasis on showing us how it might be done. Citizens, after all, have to fight for their freedom in the here and now, in the (it is hoped) brief period before the institutional designs of political philosophers and activists are finally realized.

*Walden* also has a number of advantages in terms of understanding democratization in nineteenth-century America. Unlike some European visitors, Thoreau clearly sees the inequalities in the United States in the antebellum period, and he specifically warns against ignoring the poor: "It is a mistake to suppose that, in a country where the usual evidences of civilization exist, the condition of a very large body of the inhabitants may not be as degraded as that of savages. I refer to the degraded poor" (22). Nonetheless, Thoreau refuses to see poverty itself as an affliction and believes that we underestimate the possibility of rendering it tolerable. He also shows great attentiveness to the social and political ramifications of such economic changes as the expansion of the commercial press, the growth of new means of communication and transport, and the development of new forms of labor. Much of his thinking is focused on themes that later writers, such as Habermas,[64] theorize as the colonization of the lifeworld—the expansion of economic and political systems into the dense web of unreflective practices and tacit understandings that make up our customary life.

Thoreau's analyses of this process are neither apocalyptic nor overly optimistic, and his concern throughout is practical. His central goal is to show how the disadvantages of the modern era can be circumvented while its advantages are secured (20). It is this willingness to celebrate the conveniences of a market society and at the same time recognize that the realization of liberty within its conditions requires high levels of imagination, creativity, and self-control that makes *Walden* such an interesting work for democratic theorists in an era of economic restructuring. Thoreau brings serious thought and sustained experimentation to bear on an area of life seldom examined within our tradition—the border between our individual life projects and the means we adopt to make a living. In a time such as ours, which has seen the spread of employment to new populations and a deep restructuring of work conditions, *Walden* may well be one of our most resonant and useful works of political theory.[65]

## Notes

Originally published as Brian Walker, "Thoreau's Alternative Economics: Work, Liberty, and Democratic Cultivation," *American Political Science Review* 92, no. 4 (1998): 845–56. Copyright 1998 by the American Political Science Association. Reprinted with the permission of Cambridge University Press. Minor changes have been made. An earlier version of this chapter was presented at the American Political Science Association meetings in August 1997. I would like to thank the following for their comments: Phillip Abbott, Tom Augst, Lawrence Buell, Blair Campbell, Peter Cannavo, Douglas Crase, Robert Dawidoff, Michael Goodhart,

Douglas Long, Robert Needham, Anne Norton, Daniel O'Neill, Karen Orren, Carole Pateman, Tracy Strong, Victor and Judy Wolfenstein, and the anonymous reviewers.

1. U.S. Bureau of Labor Statistics, "Workers Are on the Job More Hours over the Course of the Year," *Issues in Labor Statistics* (February 1997): 1.

2. Philip L. Rones, Randy E. Ilg, and Jennifer M. Garner, "Trends in Hours of Work since the Mid-1970s," *Monthly Labor Review* 120 (April 1997): 8–10.

3. Richard Belous, *The Contingent Economy: The Growth of the Temporary, Part-Time and Subcontracted Workforce* (Washington, DC: National Planning Association, 1989).

4. Bennett Harrison, *Lean and Mean: The Changing Landscape of Corporate Power in the Age of Flexibility* (New York: Basic Books, 1994), 214–24.

5. See Hannah Arendt, *The Human Condition* (Chicago: University of Chicago Press, 1958); Jon Elster, "Self-Realisation in Work and Politics," in *Alternatives to Capitalism,* ed. J. Elster and K. O. Moene (New York: Cambridge University Press, 1986); Robert Lane, *The Market Experience* (New York: Cambridge University Press, 1991); Karl Marx, *Capital,* vol. 1 (New York: International Publishers, [1867] 1967); James Bernard Murphy, *The Moral Economy of Labor: Aristotelian Themes in Economic Theory* (New Haven, CT: Yale University Press, 1993).

6. Henry David Thoreau, *Walden; or, Life in the Woods* (New York: Dover Publications, [1854] 1995). All in-text citations are to *Walden.*

7. For example, compare Morton and Lucia White's classic description of *Walden* as "a diatribe against the life of the village . . . [by an] isolated individual . . . free of all social attachments" with Thoreau's chapter "The Village," in which he emphasizes that *"every day or two* I strolled to the village to hear some of the gossip . . . which, taken in homeopathic doses, was really as refreshing in its way as the rustle of leaves and the peeping of frogs" and with his comment, "I had more visitors while I lived in the woods than at any other period of my life." Morton White and Lucia White, *The Intellectual versus the City: From Thomas Jefferson to Frank Lloyd Wright* (New York: New American Library, 1962), 41; *Walden,* 108–9 (emphasis added), 93. Thoreau constantly reminds us of his avid taste for society, "for I dearly love to talk" (*Walden,* 53). Or compare the Whites' statement about a "Thoreauvian . . . antipathy to civilization as such" (*Intellectual versus the City,* 155) with Thoreau's comment: "It is asserted that civilization is a real advance in the condition of man—and I think that it is" (*Walden,* 19).

8. The vision of *Walden* as a guidebook for malingerers and political free-riders ignores Thoreau's constant reference to the needs and predicaments of his fellow citizens, his compassion for their plight, and the frequency with which he explores themes central to the democratic theory of the Jacksonian era—liberty and

dependency, serfdom and nobility. An apolitical reading of Thoreau also ignores his political activism and aid to fugitive slaves. See Robert D. Richardson, *Henry Thoreau: A Life of the Mind* (Berkeley: University of California Press, 1986). On the various ways in which political theorists have misread Thoreau and missed the deeper political purpose of his works, see Bob Pepperman Taylor, *America's Bachelor Uncle: Thoreau and the American Polity* (Lawrence: University Press of Kansas, 1996).

9. On economic restructuring in Jacksonian America, see Charles Sellers, *The Market Revolution: Jacksonian America 1815–1846* (New York: Oxford University Press, 1991).

10. See Richard Lebeaux, *Young Man Thoreau* (Amherst: University of Massachusetts Press, 1977); Leonard N. Neufeldt, *The Economist: Henry Thoreau and Enterprise* (Oxford: Oxford University Press, 1989); Sellers, *Market Revolution*. For Thoreau's view on changes in transportation in his time, see *Walden*, 34, 60, 75; on corporations, 17; on factory labor, 16, 22.

11. Gordon S. Wood, *The Radicalism of the American Revolution* (New York: Alfred A. Knopf, 1992), 325–47.

12. Lebeaux, *Young Man Thoreau*, 38.

13. Cited in ibid., 43.

14. Henry David Thoreau, *The Journal of Henry David Thoreau* (Salt Lake City: Peregrine Smith Books, [1906] 1951), 164.

15. For some, of course, work is their proper pursuit, and the dilemma does not arise. Thoreau explicitly exempts such fortunates from his discussion: "I do not speak to those who are well-employed" (*Walden*, 10).

16. Henry David Thoreau, *Civil Disobedience and Other Essays* (New York: Dover, [1862] 1993).

17. George Kateb, *The Inner Ocean: Individualism and Democratic Culture* (Ithaca, NY: Cornell University Press, 1992), 82.

18. Entirely typical of this tradition is a comment by Ralph Waldo Emerson in "Fate": "Nothing is more disgusting than the crowing about liberty by slaves, as most men are, and the flippant mistaking for freedom of some paper preamble like a Declaration of Independence, or the statute right to vote, by those who have never dared to think or act." See Ralph Waldo Emerson, "Fate," in *Essays and Lectures* (New York: Library of America, 1983), 953–54.

19. Henry David Thoreau, "Slavery in Massachusetts" (1854), in *Civil Disobedience and Other Essays*, 22.

20. See the opening chapters of Robert Wiebe, *Self-Rule: A Cultural History of American Democracy* (Chicago: University of Chicago Press, 1995). Also see Merle Curti, *The Growth of American Thought* (New York: Harper and Brothers, 1943), 134–43, 295–317, and Alice Felt Tyler, *Freedom's Ferment: Phases of*

*American Social History to 1860* (Minneapolis: University of Minnesota Press, 1944), 5–22, 47–67.

21. This constellation of concepts has been famously traced in J. G. A. Pocock, *The Machiavellian Moment: Florentine Political Thought and the Atlantic Republican Tradition* (Princeton, NJ: Princeton University Press, 1975).

22. Wood, *Radicalism of American Revolution*, 357.

23. Neufeldt, *The Economist*, 102–5.

24. See Mary Kupiec Cayton, "The Making of an American Prophet: Emerson, His Audiences, and the Rise of the Culture Industry in Nineteenth-Century America," *American Historical Review* 92 (June 1987): 605; Curti, *Growth of American Thought*, 357.

25. See William Ellery Channing, "Self-Culture," in *William Ellery Channing: Selected Writings*, ed. David Robinson (New York: Paulist Press, 1985). There is a good review of the literature of self-culture in Neufeldt, *The Economist*, 23–52, and Curti, *Growth of American Thought*, 355–60.

26. Curti, *Growth of American Thought*, 363ff.

27. Cayton, "Making of an American Prophet," 606–7.

28. Cayton's article is illuminating but one-sided. Her own sources offer an alternative view to the position she sets out. Cayton quotes the clerks and young lawyers of the Cincinnati Literary Society, who describe what they are doing as expanding "the wider culture of our intellectual, moral, and social powers." Cayton, "Making of an American Prophet," 608. They see their effort as the development of their capacities and skills, but Cayton imposes on this straightforward self-description a narrative about outside domination and business boosterism. She pays insufficient attention to the possibility that when the young men said that their literary society was a means to expand their own powers, they knew exactly what they were doing.

29. Christopher Lasch, *The Culture of Narcissism: American Life in an Age of Diminishing Expectations* (New York: Warner Books, 1979); Robert D. Putnam, "Bowling Alone: America's Declining Social Capital," *Journal of Democracy* 6, no. 1 (January 1995): 65–79.

30. Neufeldt, *The Economist*, 103–5.

31. Judith Shklar, *American Citizenship: The Quest for Inclusion* (Cambridge, MA: Harvard University Press, 1991); Wood, *Radicalism of American Revolution*.

32. Wood, *Radicalism of American Revolution*, 277.

33. The passage is worth quoting in full, since it shows how entirely Thoreau shares his generation's vocabulary of democratic preparation and enactment: "As the nobleman of cultivated taste surrounds himself with whatever conduces to his culture,—genius,—learning,—wit,—books,—paintings,—statuary,—music,—

philosophic instruments, and the like; so let the village do,—not stop short at a pedagogue, a parson, a sexton, a parish library and three selectmen. . . . Instead of noblemen, let us have noble villages of men" (*Walden*, 72).

34. Dawson has pointed out that the first English usage of *democrat* was as a term of contrast with aristocrats during the French Revolution, and in that era, it was generalized to refer to all those with anti-aristocratic sentiments. Stuart Dawson, "The Earliest English Usage of the Word 'Democrat,'" *Political Theory Newsletter* 8 (winter 1996): 36.

35. Henry David Thoreau, "Life without Principle," in *Civil Disobedience and Other Essays*, 75–90.

36. Lebeaux, *Young Man Thoreau*, 80.

37. To my knowledge, the only critic who has noted this is Vernon Parrington, *Main Currents in American Thought: An Interpretation of American Literature from the Beginnings to 1920*, vol. 2, *1800–1860, The Romantic Revolution in America* (New York: Harcourt, Brace and World, 1958), 392ff.

38. Robert Sattelmeyer, *Thoreau's Reading: A Study in Intellectual History with Bibliographical Catalogue* (Princeton, NJ: Princeton University Press, 1988), 7.

39. Ibid., 7–8. On Thoreau and the Greek ethical schools, see Richardson, *Henry Thoreau*, 104.

40. Lyman B. Cady, "Thoreau's Quotations from the Confucian Books in *Walden*," *American Literature* 33 (March 1961): 20–32.

41. On the secular focus of Chinese political philosophy, see Roger T. Ames, *The Art of Rulership: A Study of Ancient Chinese Political Thought*, (Albany: State University of New York Press, 1994), 16–22; Herbet Fingarette, *Confucius: The Secular as Sacred* (New York: Harper and Row, 1972), 26–28; and David Hall and Roger Ames, *Thinking Through Confucius* (Albany: State University of New York Press, 1987), 156–92. For a highly illuminating discussion of the Confucian tradition of pragmatic self-cultivation, see Chung-ying Cheng, *New Dimensions of Confucian and Neo-Confucian Philosophy* (Albany: State University of New York Press, 1991), 84–86. On Hindu discussions of philosophy for householders and on Hinduism's influence on Thoreau, see Arthur F. Christy, *The Orient in American Transcendentalism* (New York: Columbia University Press, 1932), 187–233.

42. See Michel Foucault, *Le souci de soi, Historie de la sexualité* (Paris: Editions Gallimard, 1984); Pierre Hadot, *Exercices spirituels et philosophie antique*, 3rd ed. (Paris: Institut d'Etudes Augustiniennes, 1993); Martha Nussbaum, *The Therapy of Desire: Theory and Practice in Hellenistic Ethics* (Princeton, NJ: Princeton University Press, 1994); Paul Rabbow, *Seelenführung: Methodik der Exerzitien in der Antike* (Munich: Kösel Verlag, 1954); and F. H. Sandbach, *The Stoics* (London: Bristol Classical Press, 1989).

43. Foucault, *Le souci de soi;* Sandbach, *Stoics*, 107.

44. Sandbach, *Stoics,* 16–18.

45. Foucault, *Le souci de soi,* 114–15.

46. Rabbow, *Seelenführung,* 112–50.

47. Hadot, *Exercices spirituels et philosophie antique,* 26 (author's translation).

48. See, for example, the magisterial discussion of Lucretius's therapy of the passions in *De Rerum Natura* in Nussbaum, *Therapy of Desire,* 239–79.

49. On maxims in Greek ethical schools, see Hadot, *Exercices spirituels et philosophie antique,* 41. On the role of precepts in Confucianism and Buddhism, respectively, see Arthur Waley, *The Analects of Confucius* (London: George Allen and Unwin, 1938), 51, and T. Griffith Foulk, "Daily Life in Assembly," in *Buddhism in Practice,* ed. D. S. Lopez (Princeton, NJ: Princeton University Press, 1995).

50. William Stull, "Action from Principle: Thoreau's Transcendental Economics," *English Language Notes* 22 (1984): 58–62.

51. Richardson, *Henry Thoreau,* 166–67.

52. "Though we are not so degenerate but that we might possibly live in a cave or wigwam or wear skins to-day, it is certainly better to accept the advantages, through so dearly bought, which the invention and industry of mankind offer. . . . With a little more wit we might use these materials so as to become richer than the richest now are, and make our civilization a blessing. The civilized man is a more experienced and wiser savage" (*Walden,* 25–26).

53. Henry David Thoreau, "Walking" (1862), in *Civil Disobedience and Other Essays,* 50–51.

54. Ibid., 52.

55. Thoreau, *Journal,* 164.

56. Lawrence Buell, *The Environmental Imagination: Thoreau, Nature Writing, and the Formation of American Culture* (Cambridge, MA: Belknap, 1995).

57. Thoreau, *Journal,* 79.

58. Thoreau, "Life without Principle," 79.

59. Nor did most abolitionists draw explicit parallels between wage labor in the North and slavery in the South, as Thoreau did. "I sometimes wonder that we can be so frivolous, I may almost say, as to attend to the gross but somewhat foreign form of servitude called Negro Slavery, [when] there are so many keen and subtle masters that enslave both north and south" (*Walden,* 4). This gives us some idea of the gravity with which Thoreau observed northern work conditions, since such comparisons were usually the stock of pro-slavery discourse in the South. See George Fitzhugh, *Cannibals All! or, Slaves without Masters* (Cambridge, MA: Harvard University Press, [1857] 1960); William J. Grayson, *The Hireling and the Slave* (Charleston, SC: McCarter, 1856).

60. Indeed, Thoreau believes that in some cases, a fear of poverty keeps individuals from adopting a principled political position and leads them to acquiesce

in immoral policies. Adopting poverty may thus be a crucial step toward enacting one's liberty.

61. Max Weber, *The Protestant Ethic and the Spirit of Capitalism,* trans. Talcott Parsons (New York: Scribner's, 1958), 180–83.

62. John Stuart Mill, *On Liberty; with The Subjection of Women and Chapters on Socialism,* ed. Stefan Collini (New York: Cambridge University Press, 1989), 69–70.

63. John Rawls, *A Theory of Justice* (Cambridge, MA: Harvard University Press, 1972), 195–201.

64. Jürgen Habermas, *Theory of Communicative Action,* vol. 2, *Lifeworld and Systems: A Critique of Functionalist Reason,* trans. Thomas McCarthy (Boston: Beacon, 1987).

65. *Walden* is a work of political theory because a central concern is the realization of liberty for citizens of modern market democracies, and it explores this question with frequent references to the language of democratization current in the antebellum period.

# CHAPTER 3

# Thoreau's Critique of Democracy

*Leigh Kathryn Jenco*

Most recent scholarship on Henry David Thoreau's political thought places him firmly within the liberal-democratic camp.[1] There are good reasons for this: Thoreau embodies more famously than any American writer the spirit of freedom and individualism that seems to animate liberal democracy, and his act of "civil disobedience" continues to inspire modern-day political activists to conscientious, public-spirited activity in an affirmation of the democratic way of life.[2] The problem with this interpretation, however, is that it fails to take seriously how deeply Thoreau's numerous and overt criticisms of democracy, and his exhortations to transcend it, are grounded in a deontological moral philosophy that renders impossible the mediation of justice through democratic institutions. This is overlooked even by those commentators who interpret Thoreau's disgust with government and majority rule a bit more literally. Most deny that his political essays provide anything more than an interesting statement of his own personal commitments, whose criteria for legitimacy cannot be applied realistically to society as a whole.[3] In this chapter I instead read Thoreau's political project as an exercise in criticism and make a serious effort to understand Thoreau as he understood himself: as a poet and critic who pointed out with more coherence than is usually acknowledged the incompatibility of representative democracy with his fundamental moral commitments. In so doing, I do not intend to entirely vindicate Thoreau's political views so much as to illuminate his insights about moral and political obligation that remain obscured on a democratic reading; from there, I point to the contribution he can make in accounting for the real but often overlooked costs incurred by democracy.[4]

Thoreau's radical responses to conflicts of political and moral obligation—his controversial support for abolitionist John Brown, his public denunciation of the Fugitive Slave Law, and his refusal to pay the poll tax in protest over the war in Mexico and the slavery issue—are usually interpreted as criticisms meant only to reform the hollowness of contemporary democratic practice. I argue, however, that Thoreau's own explanations for these acts reveal a much deeper concern that the theory and practice of democracy itself, not just democracy in its current manifestation, threaten the commitments that facilitate moral practice in our personal lives. By pointing out that such a system renders our voluntary responsibilities to ourselves and to our neighbors less compelling and meaningful, Thoreau indicts democracy for incurring real costs that, tragically perhaps, cannot be resolved by the system that created them. Thoreau *does* embrace the liberal values he has come to symbolize for many—free expression, civil disobedience, the liberty to follow one's conscience—but he provokes questions about the extent to which these values should or even can survive embedded within a democratic matrix.

His two main points of criticism address the failure of the government to secure true consent and the inadequacy of its representative capability. Thoreau's criticisms are phrased in terms familiar to a democratic conception of government, but this does not mean that he endorses the ideals of the democratic project. Rather, he consistently portrays the democratic regime as a force that polarizes mind and body, disrespects the right in favor of the democratic process, and substitutes offices and institutions for the actions of men. This suggests that democratic readings of Thoreau's work, most prominently those of Nancy Rosenblum and George Kateb, pay insufficient attention to the crucial relationship of his only stated moral obligation, what Thoreau calls the "perception and performance of right," to his political thought. By insisting, moreover, that democracy's liberal variant is capable of assuaging Thoreau's objections because it enables him to be left alone, these thinkers fail to grapple with Thoreau's larger challenge: "Is a democracy, such as we know it, the last improvement possible in government? Is it not possible to take a step further towards recognizing and organizing the rights of man?"[5]

I begin my analysis by situating Thoreau's work within its intellectual and historical context, to make clear the singularity of his approach to politics. I go on to identify his precise criticisms of representative democracy by tying them to more formal categories of political and moral obligation—a vocabulary that helps explain why Thoreau's criticisms of the state are also necessarily criticisms of representative democracy and points the way to more refined definitions of the terms he employs. This leaves me better equipped, in the last section, to sketch a tentative picture of Thoreau's vision for a just polity and to gesture toward the kind of insight into political life we stand to gain from properly understanding Thoreau's political criticisms—criticisms that, though somewhat utopian, remain compelling in their insistence that the best kind of politics maintains the integrity of its citizens' moral commitments.

## Thoreau's Moral Philosophy

Thoreau's essay "Resistance to Civil Government" introduces his most complete model of action from principle: "the perception and performance of right."[6] His pairing of perception and performance implies that one cannot neglect the duty to do what is right any more than one can neglect the duty to ascertain what that right is. Thoreau grounds this morality in an epistemologically obscure higher law, belief in which is a major component of the transcendentalist project initiated by his friend and mentor Ralph Waldo Emerson.[7] Emerson's essays explain higher law as a kind of spiritual symbolism imparted by nature from which man should properly derive his moral understanding. "All things are moral, and in their boundaries changes have an unceasing reference to spiritual nature. . . . [Every change] shall hint or thunder to man the laws of right and wrong, and echo the Ten Commandments."[8]

A major tenet of the higher-law philosophy is that nature refines man's understanding by revealing specific moral truths and disciplines his reason by revealing the holistic correspondence between thought and things. All are fragments of the divine, and each one implies all others and the whole.[9] The higher law directs the outward appearance of nature, and nature itself acts as a metaphor describing an individual's place within the universe and the ongoing and inevitable interaction of substance and concept, body and mind, that manifests within that individual. Again and again in *Walden*—the work in which Thoreau offers his most complete model of a life of principle—he affirms the transcendentalist dependence of moral understanding on the laws made manifest through careful scrutiny of the natural world.[10] "What I have observed of the pond is no less true in ethics," Thoreau observes.

> If we knew all the laws of Nature, we should need only one fact, or the description of one actual phenomenon, to infer all the particular results at that point. Now we know only a few laws, and our result is vitiated, not, of course, by nay confusion or irregularity in Nature, but by our ignorance of essential elements in the calculation. Our notions of law and harmony are commonly confined to those instances which we detect; but the harmony which results from a far greater number of seemingly conflicting, but really concurring, laws, which we have not detected, is still more wonderful.[11]

In Thoreau's mind, the individual is responsible both for uncovering these "higher laws" of nature and for employing them to evaluate and direct his conduct. Disagreements and moral conflicts within a community of people living in accord with these laws are impossible: as nature is harmonized, so too will be the conscientious actions derived from natural observation. The exercise of one's sense of right, if truly in accord with natural, higher laws, is incapable of infringing on the same exercise by someone else. "I perceive that, when an acorn and a chestnut fall side by side, the one does not remain inert to make way for the other, but both obey their own laws . . . till one, perchance, overshadows and destroys the other. If a plant cannot live according to its nature, it dies; and so a man."[12]

Once the individual conscience recognizes this law, its moral authority is binding and irrevocable in all matters. Although a distinction can *logically* be made between the dictates of authority and the requirements of obligation—a terminological hedge many philosophers employ, ironically, to justify a prima facie obligation to obey state laws—Thoreau does not recognize this distinction, because to know the higher law is to recognize an obligation to obey it.[13] This is what Thoreau means by "action from principle."

By emphasizing personal regard for "right" over demands to act for the "common good," Thoreau establishes the individual as the only source of moral authority. This reduces all potentially political obligations to moral ones, an identity that informs his perception of political authority as an extension of the moral authority of *persons*, not rules, laws, institutions, or traditions.[14] He derides the U.S. government for being merely a "tradition," lacking the vitality of even a single living man; it is not the laws of the nation that make men just, but vice versa.[15]

Many commentators on Thoreau have remarked that the inherent subjectivity of Thoreau's conscience-based consent to law cannot sustain universal applicability. Rosenblum asserts that for Thoreau, "conscience has no identifiable content" and as such is unable to "create new social norms or inspire sociable relations."[16] This echoes the usual protest that using one's private conscience as a political guide would result in anarchy or worse, as no justification could be given for public behavior or injurious actions toward other individuals, nor could any vision of a public (i.e., interpersonal) good be conjured.[17] It is important to point out, however, that Thoreau himself brooked no questions on this point. As he understood it, conviction in the higher law would not encourage arbitrary justification for any behavior but instead would present very strict ethical standards that, though accessible only to individuals, could be expected to converge much the same way as he observed the laws of nature do. Although disagreements may arise, Thoreau maintains the somewhat naïve confidence that "the faintest assured objection which one healthy man feels will at length prevail over mankind."[18]

Thoreau's appeal to higher law in making anti-statist arguments actually follows a pattern of political criticism pioneered by many of his contemporaries, who, like Thoreau, believed that the key to reforming society was the reform of individuals. Many of the radical abolitionists with whom Thoreau associated either personally or intellectually subscribed to an ideal of self-government that derived from Puritan antinomianism, which held that both knowledge of and capacity for implementing God's law was implanted in every individual.[19] This doctrine upheld the importance of a personal relationship with God so vehemently that its believers accorded socially directed reform no leverage. These reformers instead promoted an ideal of individual accountability, and some, most famously William Lloyd Garrison, sought to persuade others through the formation of societies and communities organized around these principles. Others promoted more directly political agendas; for example, Beriah Green's "anti-political political theory" advocated the replacement of democratic practice with elitist leadership.[20]

Thoreau is quick to distance himself from these "no-government men" in his essay "Resistance to Civil Government," but apparently for reasons outside of their skeptical attitude toward the state, since—as the essay's title suggests—Thoreau harbors such sentiment himself. Whereas Garrison calls for a repudiation of all earthly authority, Thoreau calls "not for no government, but at once a better government,"[21] which denies not the possibility of a just government but the legitimacy of the present regime. In affirming the *res privata*—insisting that he has "better affairs to attend to" than politics[22] —Thoreau recognizes the importance (and vulnerability) of a private space independent of state or society, and this makes him particularly sensitive to the fact that the planned communities and religious political theories of Garrison and his followers leave no room for a discernible private space or a nonpolitical identity. In the view of these reformers, the government of society is necessarily self-government, and vice versa. Thoreau, in contrast, accepts the need for a government mechanism in order to make his life *less* political. Leaving a minimal governmental machine to clink along relieves individuals of the responsibility of being involved in government at all.

The way Thoreau champions private life is unique even among his fellow transcendentalists, many of whom were unable to find a way out of the paradox that emerged from promoting individual freedom simultane- ously with searching for a perfect community.[23] Thoreau's commitment to a methodologically individualist moral epistemology would be undercut if he followed either the Christian anarchists or the more socially minded transcendentalists in presuming to plan the social order. His organic vision of social and political harmony is more similar to Emerson's, but the same belief in the higher law that provoked such radical political ideas in his pro- tégé amounted in Emerson's case to a kind of faith that things would right themselves.[24] Emerson did criticize democracy, but not on fundamental grounds. Emerson's concern is simply that democracy as it is now practiced does not penetrate the American consciousness as deeply nor motivate it as profoundly as it originally promised to do.[25] Thoreau's outlook is at once more militant and more morally centered. In criticizing the moral damage produced by the democratic process, Thoreau parts company with both contemporary social reformers and his mentor Emerson. In what follows, I show that Thoreau's political thought is best understood as an innovative and unique attempt to expose how democratic institutions inevitably and improperly conflate individual morality with political obligation.

## Thoreau's Criticisms

Thoreau's belief in the moral importance of taking "action from principle" impels him to challenge any political order in which moral authority is vested even partially in another group or individual.[26] His criticisms carry special weight for democracy, since the decision-making prerogative and the moral authority that, according to his higher-law philosophy, rest exclusively in the individual must give way to the expediency of voting and political representation, especially in democracy's more "liberal" forms. Thoreau responds to this moral crisis by committing several acts of "civil disobedience," and his explanations for these acts prompt us to investigate the degree to which the only duty Thoreau articulates—the duty to perceive and perform right—can support political obligations, especially those that representative democracy imposes.

The only government Thoreau recognizes "is that power which establishes justice in the land." By his definition, the government's acts must be consistent with justice, and its mechanism should be constructed to promote it actively. When the state, that organ ostensibly invested with such a power, fails to execute it properly, private citizens are forced to perform its offices. Thoreau in fact identifies the anti-slavery Vigilance Committee as serving just such a purpose.[27] A proper government and the protection of justice are inseparable for Thoreau; one logically entails the other. Under a perfectly just state of the kind Thoreau envisions, acting according to principle would be functionally equivalent to obeying the law. This does *not* imply, however, that the government can or should determine the content of justice, what justice *is,* because we have already seen that such knowledge is accessible only to an individual through the conscientious study of higher law. In fact, to establish what justice is and to enact it through a "life of principle" are an individual's *only* moral duties.[28]

In his political writings Thoreau contrasts this holistic ideal with the reality of the state: he identifies state authority with simple coercive force, which is effective in controlling only the corporeal, not the conscientious, element of the individuals subject to it.

> The State never intentionally confronts a man's sense, intellectual or moral, but only his body, his senses. It is not armed with superior wit or honesty, but with superior physical strength. I was not born to be forced. I will breathe after my own fashion. Let us see who is the strongest. They only can force me who obey a higher law than I. They force me to become like themselves. I do not hear of *men* being *forced* to live this way or that by masses of men. What sort of life were that to live? . . . I am not responsible for the successful working of the machinery of society.[29]

Here Thoreau draws attention to the way the disparity between political and moral obligation is manifested as physical separation and moral displacement. The unilateral use of physical coercion is both necessary and sufficient for the enforcement of political obligations, but this confused reliance on purely physical power is at odds with the holistically perceived higher law that grounds Thoreau's moral duty. Thoreau confronts the reality of his imprisonment using language that indicates how jarring he finds the contrast to be: "I could not help but being struck with the foolishness of that institution which treated me as if I were mere flesh and blood and bones, to be locked up."[30] On this point, Thoreau's act can be interestingly and illuminatingly contrasted to the civil disobedience undertaken by Martin Luther King Jr. and his followers. To King, their protest was a "display": "We would present our very bodies as a means of laying our case before the conscience of the local and national community."[31] For Thoreau, however, presenting only a body as an appeal to conscience is completely antithetical to maintaining the integrity of his moral code. In Thoreau's act of civil disobedience, bodily display is an unnatural consequence of a vicious political system, not a deliberate political statement.[32]

This theme of displacement and separation is replicated in Thoreau's treatment of elections, which he points out *intrinsically* alienate moral actors both from their own conscientiously determined conception of what is right and from their responsibility for arriving at and implementing that conception.

> All voting is a sort of gaming, like chequers or backgammon, with a slight moral tinge to it, a playing with right and wrong, with moral questions; and betting naturally accompanies it. The character of the voters is not staked. I cast my vote, perchance, as I think right; but I am not vitally concerned that that right should prevail. I am willing to leave it to the majority. Its obligation, therefore, never exceeds that of expediency. Even voting *for the right* is *doing* nothing for it.[33]

Thoreau's characterization of *all* voting as a betting game betrays a profound disgust with the participatory requirements constitutive of liberal democracy. He recognizes that majority-determined outcomes wither the vitality of the private conscience because the individual's compliance with rules and procedures he or she had no hand in formulating necessarily disrupts the ongoing process of committing oneself to doing what is right.[34] Even those who actively disagree within the political system represent nothing more than nominal support for their cause, however justified: "A minority is powerless when it conforms to the majority; it is not even a minority then." Its influence is completely undermined when it agrees to abide by the outcome of a vote. Only when conscientious individuals in the minority choose to act as Thoreau has can they become an "irresistible" force by clogging the state mechanism with their true weight.[35]

His remarks go beyond a mere criticism of abuses of the system. Thoreau strikes at the very core principles of democracy, realizing that the sacrifice of an individual's moral interests to the vagaries of representation and voting is moral tyranny. The representatives who make the laws, which, in a democracy, carry the authority of self-rule, are under no obligation to represent their constituents' true interests.[36] As such, the rules they agree on will not and cannot reflect the sense of right that, in Thoreau's mind, is accessible and *meaningful* only to individuals themselves. "Whoever has discerned truth, has received his commission from a higher source than the chiefest justice in the world, who can discern only law. He finds himself constituted judge of the judge."[37]

In his John Brown papers, Thoreau expands his criticism of democracy by taking the representative system to task for its incapacity to acquire anything more than the externals of consent, man's "bodies," not "the noblest faculties of the mind, and the *whole* heart."[38] The distinguishing quality of individuals such as John Brown is precisely that which no system of representation can capture. Thoreau praises him for being a true transcendentalist, "not yielding to whim or transient impulse, but carrying out the purpose of a life."[39] Thoreau's comments point out more than just the violence done to a moral standard when majorities and their proxies are permitted to make binding decisions. For one, representative democracy fails to provide adequate methods of moral redress and frustrates the exercise of moral responsibility by legally prohibiting certain actions that are necessary to satisfy a personal sense of rectitude. But the more far-reaching criticism Thoreau makes with his praise of Brown is that representational democracy presumes to represent that which can never be represented: the most moral individuals among us and, by extension, the moral part of ourselves, "our noble hearts."[40] Brown's act demonstrates even more clearly and definitively than Thoreau's civil disobedience that the "political" obligation under scrutiny here is not a matter of obligation to the polis; rather, it is an obligation to one's moral self, which often implies conflict with political institutions.

## Thoreau's Argument

All of Thoreau's political acts, especially his civil disobedience and his support of John Brown, draw sharp attention to the conflict of moral obligations with political ones. An exploration of the formal distinction between these two kinds of duties then may help by providing a vocabulary and a conceptual apparatus through which Thoreau's moral position can be more systematically articulated. Thoreau himself, of course, did not use such formal language, but I hope this exercise sheds some light on exactly how Thoreau's political criticisms are linked to his moral theory and provides a more complete explanation of how his criticisms can apply to democratic institutions in general, not only to nineteenth-century American democracy in particular.

Contemporary philosophical literature classifies political obligations under the larger heading of institutional (also called positional) duties. John Simmons, following Michael Stocker, identifies positional duties as those connected with a specific office, role, or station: they are tied to the specific requirements attendant to the occupation of a particular position, not to the individuals qua individuals who happen to fill those positions. Such duties, Simmons holds, are morally neutral and can never ground moral requirements. The fulfillment of these obligations is entailed merely by logical requirement.[41] For example, the institutional obligation of promise-keeping implies that one logically "has to" carry through with what has been promised because this is implied in the meaning of the term. It is very important to point out, however, that the actual decision whether to fulfill the promise is derived from an external and independent moral obligation (in Thoreau's case, to realize the precepts of higher law). Thoreau points out the tension that exists between what one feels morally obliged to do and what is required by merely legal (i.e., institutional) obligations when he asks, "Are laws to be enforced simply because they were made? Or declared by any number of men to be good, if they are *not* good? . . . What right have *you* to enter into a compact with yourself that you *will* do thus or so, against the light within you?"[42]

*Moral* duties or obligations, in contrast, exist to establish standards for conduct toward others, independently of any institutional setting or role (although it should be noted that the two duties, institutional and moral, are not always mutually exclusive).[43] All legal and political obligations, then, can be articulated as institutional duties enforced on the populace in their role as citizens of that state, but as such, they carry no moral weight in the absence of a supporting moral obligation.[44] This argument, however, does more than point out the conflict between conscience and law that any act of civil disobedience presumes. Recognizing the limitations on the moral and political justificatory work of each kind of obligation makes Thoreau's call for a better, just government more intelligible, even as he denies his obligation to obey the law and enthusiastically supports the anarchistic militancy of John Brown. Drawing such a distinction between the two kinds of obligations helps us see why Thoreau insists that only the rules of morality, not political institutions or laws, are capable of setting the terms of justice and consent.

For my purposes here, the most relevant insight the distinction between institutional and moral duties yields is this: although institutional obligations may not themselves generate any moral duty, they *do* condition how we expect certain moral duties to be carried out, and in doing so, they form a standard of behavior that must be followed if we wish to uphold certain moral requirements (of justness, fairness, and so forth). This is true because institutional obligations often provide the *specifications*—the socially accepted signals—for how to fulfill moral duties properly. Stocker uses the example of the accepted tradition of allowing the birthday boy or girl an extra piece of cake; violating that tradition on any one occasion would be unjust, because given such a tradition, it would be unfair to deny that particular birthday child his or her extra piece of cake.[45] Bestowing that slice of cake is an institutional act performed "under the auspices" of a particular "constitutive convention," which defines the establishment of that obligation to be (part of) what the act imports or amounts to (fairness, in this case).[46]

In other words, fulfilling the obligation incurred by an institutional act is simultaneously to acknowledge the meaning of the act as provided by the constitutive convention that governs it. This meaning, in turn, may carry with it particular moral obligations. The signification attached to an act of voting in a democracy exemplifies this kind of moral move. The performance of this act signals a willingness—and logically entails a duty—to abide by the results of the election, but the act is also undertaken with the understanding that its performance constitutes "self-government," which in turn embodies a particular idea of justice.

The state is in a very delicate position, then, because by enforcing particular institutional obligations in the name of protecting justice, it risks misrepresenting the pattern of conduct required to fulfill these institutional obligations as part of the individual's *moral* obligation to serve justice. This explains why Thoreau believes that the government is, ideally, just an expedient;[47] allowing it any more leeway gives it power to dictate the understandings that impart meaning to its institutional obligations, which may then overtake the moral values such institutions were originally meant to secure.

Democracy is an especially dangerous threat in this sense because the political obligations particular to it, such as voting and civic involvement, are in fact *intended* to embody a sense of justice: they begin to resemble (and some assert that they actually are) moral obligations.[48] Using the vocabulary of institutional and moral duties, we can articulate Thoreau's criticism of democracy as an indictment of a system that collapses the two kinds of obligations into one, making the intelligibility of "action from principle" impossible to sustain. He is pointing out how the institutional obligation of obedience to the laws democracy enforces has a necessary correlation neither to the constitutive conventions invoked (since, as noted earlier, "voting for the right is *doing* nothing for it," and representation does not really represent what it should be representing) nor to the moral obligation to serve justice that democracy adopts as its goal. Indeed, democracy pretends that voting means consent and that representation means equality; by doing so, it presents as moral duties the institutional obligations that are meant only as expedients to facilitate the fulfillment of those moral duties. "What is the value of any political freedom, but as a means to moral freedom? Is it a freedom to be slaves, or a freedom to be free, of which we boast?" Thoreau asks.[49] It is the disjunction between an action and its intended significance—especially the wide disparity between the way justice must be properly sustained and the democratic institutions meant to secure (and embody) it—to which Thoreau's act of civil disobedience, his vehement opposition to the Fugitive Slave Law, and his elegiac support of John Brown draw attention.

I further argue that Thoreau's departure from the center of social and political life, documented in *Walden*, can be interpreted as a rejection of the legal and political obligations physically imposed through residence in a polity. While at Walden Pond, Thoreau attempts to strip away institutional duty in a restatement of essentials that reinforces his commitment to and recognition of the bare fact of moral duty. His obsession with simplicity and his residence there, well outside of town, can be specifically interpreted as rejections of the convention that popular participation in democracy equals justice. Thus Thoreau is not maintaining, as Rosenblum assumes he must, that "although the pretext of democracy is one cause of civil disobedience it is also what makes it possible to conceive of 'civil' disobedience in the first place."[50] Rather, he denies that democracy can lend any legitimizing influence to his actions at all, however much it may seem that it makes them more convenient.

Consider Thoreau's insistence that the constitutive element of any just regime is consent of the governed. In liberal regimes, consent is usually deduced in one of two ways: either through an assumed acceptance of a hypothetical social contract or through political participation in representative democracy. The former reconciles the fact of man's moral autonomy with the compromises of public life by theoretically positing such autonomy in a "state of nature," before the deliberate creation of society. After the contract takes effect, personal good is relegated to the private sphere and held inferior to the "public good," which now serves as the basis for agreement and therefore dominates political discourse. The logic of majoritarian or representative democracy allows issues of common political interest to be subjected to a tribunal of popular opinion, wherein participation in the voting process comes to stand for the consent of all those governed. The individuals within the polity—whether they voted or not, whether their views won out or not—are then bound by the decisions made by the collective political body.

In both cases, a sense of the common good and one's obligation to promote it serve as the moral basis for the political obligations to which the citizen is subject. The assumption of a common good that morally supersedes all personal good is a central motivation for the construction of the state, and the degree to which the state serves the common good (i.e., is just) is the criterion of its legitimacy.[51] Although disagreements exist over what the common good is and how it should be served, political considerations (i.e., those concerns relevant to the actions and powers of government) must, by definition, reference the prevailing sentiments of common good and phrase its justification in those terms, since it is these (moral) commitments that ground political obligation in the first place. In fact, we can identify one of the primary constitutive conventions of a democracy as the idea that through participation in political decision making citizens serve a notion of the public interest or common good above their personal interests.[52]

Alternatively, George Kateb maintains that Thoreau's call for consent of the governed can be answered by rearticulating democratic practices such as voting and representation not as true expressions of consent but as forms requisite to a legitimate government (which is a government entitled to make laws and policies binding on people in society). Legitimacy (and hence obligation to obey) is assured when the forms and procedures enshrined within the government are such as to provide as much certainty as possible that the state can achieve only those aims that justify its existence and that the governmental mechanism alone can achieve. This legitimation principle is coupled with Kateb's understanding of the U.S. Constitution as a contract between *individuals* that simultaneously specifies the form, powers, procedures, and limitations of that government. Voting citizens "will" the system into being by the electoral procedure. It is a social contract to which all Americans give (rather superfluous) tacit consent.[53] This is a corollary of the argument that justifies democracy by pointing out that it contains the best and most efficient mechanisms available to ensure that a political regime remains responsive to the needs and concerns of its citizens.[54] In this reformulation, the justness of a regime is determined by the extent to which it retains its sensitivity to the true needs of the populace, who are held to "consent" to such a government because the government's practices, presumably, remain within the boundaries of acceptable political and legal conduct.

It should be obvious, however, that Thoreau's version of "consent" departs from all the aforementioned elaborations. Both his sense of justice and his declaration that he "do[es] not wish to be regarded as a member of any incorporated society which [he has] not joined" demand that any institutional obligations be grounded in a true, expressed consent.[55] Simply assuming that a positive evaluation of justice would constitute an act of consent gets the chain of causation backward.[56] For Thoreau, consent, higher law, and acting justly form an identity such that the presence of any one implies the other two: he tells us that a just government is one that has been consented to; one that has been consented to must, by definition, be in accordance with higher law, or else its citizens would not sanction it; and those who consent by reason of its accordance with higher law must, according to Thoreau's double obligation to both perceive and perform right, be leading the just life that such a principle entails (i.e., to agree is to agree to obey). This tripartite identity makes an express act of consent seem superfluous, but it may be possible to lend some coherency to Thoreau's argument here if we return to our discussion of the way constitutive conventions often produce contradictory or unexpected significations for particular acts. We know Thoreau has already rejected typical democratic practices for their demonstrated vulnerability to this kind of manipulation of meaning, but I would like to sketch out a way in which the voluntary assumption of a moral code like Thoreau's may become evident in ways that are discernible as political consent—remembering, of course, that "expressed" consent need not be expressed openly, as long as the act is voluntarily undertaken and recognized as the deliberate assumption of a political obligation.

Because Thoreau criticizes democracy for its irresponsibility in enforcing institutional obligations that are meant to embody justice but do not actually result in justice, he must understand "consent" to mean consent not just to a process but also to an outcome: consent must be given both to the performance of the institutional acts that generate the institutional obligations and to the recognized meaning that fulfillment of the obligation generates under the sanction of the appropriate constitutive convention.

This attitude is borne out by Thoreau's belief that the concatenation of manifold personal interests in society will reflect the diversity-driven harmonization found in nature, over the distortion or homogenization of meanings that a political system must ascribe to the performance of particular acts. "Let everyone mind his own business, and endeavor to be what he was made," he exhorts us in *Walden*.[57] This suggests that, in a social system organized so that the constitutive conventions that govern the meaning of particular acts remain discernible and intelligible to the agents undertaking the pursuant obligations, fulfillment of an implied institutional obligation can be construed as an expression of consent. When the meaning that each act generates is stable and clearly discernible, the agent can evaluate each course of action to see whether the outcome accords with his understanding of higher law. This evaluation is not possible when the meanings of the acts are illegible or contradictory. Consent becomes possible only when one can take real responsibility for the ultimate meanings of institutional acts, and this condition cannot obtain when the outcomes of democratic decision making supplant the morally derived meanings an agent intends.

## Thoreau's Democratic Interpreters

Recasting Thoreau's political critique in this manner calls into question the strongest argument for his democratic status: namely, that the privacy afforded him by a liberal democracy prevents him from lodging any effective critique against it. Both Kateb and Rosenblum interpret Thoreau's embrace of values typically found in a liberal democracy as necessarily (if somewhat critically) supporting the system itself. Kateb positions Thoreau among his fellow transcendentalists, whose "democratic individualism" Kateb sees as both an outcome and an enrichment of representative democracy.[58] He argues, in fact, that the great value of constitutional liberalism lies precisely in its ability to allow individuals to be less involved in political life, which is a goal Thoreau would ostensibly affirm. But when Kateb goes on to insist that the very *process* of constitutional representative democracy promotes and produces a conception of individual dignity and the sphere of action appropriate to that concept of dignity, the irony of Thoreau's critique is obscured. Thoreau is pointing out that these institutions themselves—and the processes that buttress them—violate or render impossible the moral activity that makes private life intelligible to begin with. Kateb's claim that things such as elections and due process contain intrinsic moral value, then, makes a point that Thoreau could not even recognize, much less see as legitimating democracy.[59]

Thoreau's act of civil disobedience in refusing to pay the poll tax deserves careful consideration here, because it openly flaunts the means of redress democracy provides and thus provides a convenient counterexample to Kateb's argument. At the same time, however, there is no denying the act's implicit paradox: even as it aggressively protests the policies undertaken by a democratic regime, it is crucially dependent on the values of free expression and tolerance, which find institutional culmination and security in the procedures of democracy. This tension animates Rosenblum's sophisticated account of Thoreau's political thought, which integrates his militant detachment with the project of liberal democracy. In linking Thoreau to the contemporary romantic movement in Europe, Rosenblum champions him as one of the few romantics wise enough to integrate the personal compulsion to self-development with the needs and virtues of public (and democratic) life.[60] Her argument develops from the conflict she sees in Thoreau's simultaneous embodiment of both radical individualism and romantic sensibility: the former depends on values that, in Rosenblum's opinion, derive their meaning from liberal democracy, "where personal liberty, consent, and resistance have recognized meanings," while the latter "places a premium on noncomformity rather than on moral agreement."[61] The tension is resolved by a stance of "militancy," outwardly manifest in a "heroic individualism" that is both aggressive toward others and detached from public life.[62]

Rosenblum believes that Thoreau's militancy is enough to motivate his political resistance, independent of considerations of conscience, so she ignores the way Thoreau's moral imperatives shape his approach to politics. Because she, like Kateb, conceives of liberal freedoms and democratic institutions as conceptually implicated, Rosenblum cannot account for the degree to which Thoreau sees a commitment to things such as freedom of expression and personal dignity as simply unintelligible when subjected to the vagaries of democratic opinion—even when its evils are diluted by a liberalism that secures what Thoreau most values. Rosenblum insists that "detachment loses both its original temptation and its dramatic force if democracy is not Jacobin but liberal and instead of imposing obligations or demanding loyalties it leaves Thoreau alone."[63] We have already seen, however, that Thoreau indicts democracy—even its liberal variant—for the very reason that it *does* impose obligations, distorting the meaning of citizens' conduct by helplessly implicating the discharge of their duty to obey justice in the outcome of elections or in the legislative choices of representatives. This confusion of meanings leads to a condition in which, ultimately, injustice comes to be called justice: when he is arrested, for example, Thoreau notes the implicit paradox of jail being the appropriate place for a just man in an unjust system.[64] Thoreau goes on to praise John Brown's raid for inspiring the North to go "behind the human law" and return to "original perceptions," to see that "what was called order was confusion, what was called justice, injustice, and that the best was deemed the worst."[65] Thoreau's commentary on this event foregrounds the kind of personal commitment to justice that need not, and should not, reference the distorted sense of justice produced within democratic institutions.

Thoreau's act of state resistance is not a celebration of liberal democracy but rather one part of an ongoing process of challenging and giving new definitions to those terms usually employed to justify it.

## Thoreau's Alternative

Although Thoreau never gives a complete account of his alternative vision, he does suggest a few ways in which typical social practices can be adapted or reconceived to meet the rigorous standards of his moral commitments. I discuss them briefly here in conclusion because they are helpful in comprehending both the importance and the limits of Thoreau's critique of democracy.

Recalling Thoreau's definition of government as "that which secures justice in the land," we must conclude that his vision of justice requires a decentralization of political commitments so radical that they may no longer be recognizably "political" at all. For Thoreau, the proper interpersonal relationship is a form of neighborliness marked by a rhetoric not of community but of commonality[66]—a shared understanding that grounds the constitutive conventions that give sustainable, morally integrated meaning to the fulfillment of institutional obligations.

The distinction Thoreau implicitly draws between legal and moral obligations allows him to reject public life while preserving the private sphere as a domain of fruitful social intercourse. "I deal with men, not offices," Thoreau declares during the narrative of his arrest. Thoreau is not jarred by the dissonance between the political-legal duties such "offices" attempt to discharge and the primacy of independent moral obligation. Any actions with political or other consequences for Thoreau derive exclusively from moral commitments and thus find articulation as obligations to people, not institutions. They are, in that sense, private.[67] The institutional allegiance required by definition for any putative duty to obey the law, *especially* if such a duty is grounded in respect for democratic processes, is fundamentally incapable of finding support from Thoreau's idea of moral duty. Simmons makes the interesting observation that if an absolute monarch makes sacrifices for his subjects, it is conceivable that the personal debts of gratitude owed him might be political obligations, because no separation of private and official capacities is evident.[68] This is the probably the closest model one can find to explain Thoreau's vision of political life: moral obligations replace the legalities originally intended to produce political results, with the paradoxical effect that state-related activity must become personal activity.[69]

This reading turns Kateb's claim about Thoreau's project on its head. To Kateb, Thoreau aims to "politicize the nonpolitical relations of life and thus to democratize them."[70] I contend that Thoreau is engaged in the exact opposite task: *de*politicizing many of the political relations of life to accommodate his moral sensibility. Regardless of what others may claim that liberal democracy promises (e.g., the legal and social capability to be left alone, the possibility for the articulation of public criticism, the fair negotiation of political demands made by individuals and groups, legal guarantees of individual liberties), in Thoreau's understanding, it is no less guilty than monarchy of promoting an authority it cannot morally justify to individuals. More than just a liberal fear of arbitrary power impels Thoreau to champion the private life.

The plea he makes in "Resistance to Civil Government" for the state to treat him "as a neighbor" suggests that Thoreau thinks political actions can and should be advanced much the same as one neighbor appeals to another, trying to win his opinion through persuasion with the full endorsement of his conscience. To Thoreau, the neighborliness ethic seems to stand in for the legal obligations that are often meant to regulate interpersonal conduct. Any other kind of social or political involvement, Thoreau alleges, would be able merely to appropriate one's body, not to establish moral authority. Rosenblum's characterization of Thoreau as so militantly detached that "neighborliness becomes public agon" thus reveals itself to be an overstatement, relying as it does on the premise that Thoreau is a mere exhibitionist, not a moral visionary.[71]

Even those who, like Thoreau, temporarily choose to withdraw their residency still have a universal commitment to treat others and their possessions with this kind of neighborly respect. In *Walden* Thoreau makes a point to borrow a neighbor's ax to fell the trees that would become his cabin on Walden Pond, for the simple reason that "it is the most generous course thus to permit your fellow men to have an interest in your enterprise." Throughout the book he maintains that the *only* kind of social cooperation possible is involved in this effort to "get our living together."[72] The reciprocity of this relationship binds an individual to the community around him without the sacrifice of his moral autonomy. After all, Thoreau explains his willingness to pay the highway tax and to support education in the village as an expression of his desire to be "a good neighbor."[73]

But being neighborly does not necessarily mean maintaining a persistent formal detachment.[74] In addition to insisting on the privacy enjoyed vis-à-vis other people, neighborliness can accommodate social interaction on a personal level, which can secure the kind of privacy enjoyed vis-à-vis the state. The latter kind, of course, is of more direct relevance politically; it sometimes even entails the task of enjoining others to one's cause, a possibility Thoreau took advantage of when he addressed his audience at the Concord Lyceum. The relationships guiding interpersonal behavior that Thoreau elaborates throughout his defense of John Brown are not, as some commentators have assumed, the necessarily alienating commitment to individual principles that Thoreau's civil disobedience embodies.[75] Instead, we again witness a convergence of conscientious interests that, in Thoreau's mind, seems almost inevitable and impels his allegiance to Brown. Commitment to principle does set him apart from the masses, but it also binds him together with the equally conscientious. H. D. Lewis observes that "while the individual must in the least analysis obey his own conscience, yet, as part of his duty to find out what is his duty, there is much in the meantime that he requires to do to correct the limitations of his private point of view," which includes consulting with others who may have more experience or insight.[76] Neighborliness can be seen as one such check on the downward spiral of subjective morality. This may be what Thoreau means by fulfilling "all the duties of neighbors and fellow-men."[77]

In some senses, Thoreau would agree with Michael Walzer that liberal democracy alienates individuals from commonality. But Thoreau's solution is unique in highlighting the dangers of too much political involvement. He calls not for an expansion of political space to accommodate the contestation and negotiation of the content of public good but for more privacy to find one's own good, to reform oneself, to ascribe genuine significance and affect to social relationships—in other words, to more truly "get our living together." The alternative to liberal democracy, Thoreau makes clear, is not communitarianism; social harmony and moral integrity are better sustained when we "succeed alone, that we may enjoy our success together."[78]

It is true, of course, that Thoreau's enthusiastic rhetoric glosses over the sometimes prohibitive difficulty involved in reconciling the demands of political life with those of private morality—a goal already abandoned by many scholars as futile or misguided.[79] But it would be a mistake to assume that the frequently tragic results of our efforts to do so can be unproblematically mitigated by democratic politics, and Thoreau's critique is valuable for precisely its demonstration of democracy's own inability to accommodate all necessary moral commitments. To misinterpret Thoreau's political criticism as sympathetic to democracy, then, is to risk missing the unique contribution he makes to our understanding of political life. Thoreau is showing us what is at stake when democratic legitimacy goes unexamined: the complex relationship of moral loyalties to civic duties is obfuscated, and we remain unable to see or properly gauge democracy's not insignificant side effects, including moral compromise and the elevation of expediency at the expense of justice.

By foregrounding the moral questions that ought to motivate politics, moreover, Thoreau directs our attention away from political institutions and toward the individuals these institutions are ostensibly in place to serve. Thoreau is actually making the surprising observation that, like monarchy or aristocracy, democracy too is a system in which one is unavoidably governed by others, and it is this realization that drives him to a nearly anarchic (but to him, more genuine) form of "self-rule." That such a vision seems utopian does not mean it should not be taken seriously as a criticism of the assumption that democracy is the best we can do. Even if we accept that democracy is the best realistic option at present for the just management of political life, it does not mean that it is unassailable or above criticism. Thus, Thoreau's admission that the U.S. Constitution and the political system it undergirds are "very good" when "seen from a lower point of view" signals not a commitment to democracy but a warning to his readers that their complacency about democracy will inhibit the search for better (perhaps more liberal?) possibilities and foreclose any attempt to seek a higher moral ground. This is because these institutions, "seen from a point of view a little higher . . . are what I have described them; seen from a higher still, and the highest, who shall say what they are, or that they are worth looking at or thinking of at all?"[80] Thoreau's political writings are valuable for the very reason that they help us recognize the trade-offs between liberal freedoms and democratic commitments—moral costs that lie well concealed beneath a mask of practicality.

# Notes

Originally published as Leigh Kathryn Jenco, "Thoreau's Critique of Democracy," *Review of Politics* 65, no. 3 (2003): 355–81. Copyright 2003 by *The Review of Politics*. Reprinted by permission. I thank Danielle Allen, Shelley Burtt, Chad Cyrenne, Jacob Levy, Michael Lienesch, Dimitriy Masterov, and Chris Planer, in addition to the participants of the University of Chicago's Political Theory Workshop and several anonymous readers, for their helpful comments on earlier versions of this chapter. Its writing was made possible in part by a fellowship from the Institute for Humane Studies.

1. Nancy Rosenblum's original interpretation of Thoreau, set forth in her article "Thoreau's Militant Conscience," *Political Theory* 9 (1981): 81–110, is reconciled to a theory of liberal democracy in her book *Another Liberalism: Romanticism and the Reconstruction of Liberal Thought* (Cambridge, MA: Harvard University Press, 1987); however, her introduction to *Thoreau: Political Writings* (Cambridge: Cambridge University Press, 1996) paints him less ambiguously as an unrepentant democrat. George Kateb's book *The Inner Ocean: Individualism and Democratic Culture* (Ithaca, NY: Cornell University Press, 1992) lumps Thoreau with his fellow transcendentalists Ralph Waldo Emerson and Walt Whitman to demonstrate their embodiment of the ideals of modern representative democracy. Recent scholarship by Brian Walker, including chapter 2 of this volume and "Thoreau on Democratic Cultivation," *Political Theory* 29 (2001): 155–89, builds on this theme by reading *Walden* as a "democratic self-help book focusing on the tensions between the political ideal of free self-direction and the unfavorable work conditions that laborers often face."

2. Unfortunately, the term *civil disobedience* has been appropriated to serve a variety of political agendas, ranging from that of Martin Luther King Jr. to Gandhi to Tolstoy to the New Left. The invocation of Thoreau's act and his accompanying essay in these contexts has harnessed both with connotations Thoreau did not intend; mass demonstrations, nonviolent protest, and public demands for governmental reform are perceived as constitutive of and necessary to this type of political action. As I hope this chapter makes clear, Thoreau is better identified with the more solitary and anarchist tradition of civil disobedience emblematized by Antigone's embrace of moral over political law.

3. For the strongest statement of this view, see Vincent Buranelli, "The Case against Thoreau," *Ethics* 67 (July 1957): 257–68. Heinz Eulau, "Wayside Challenger: Some Remarks on the Politics of Henry David Thoreau," in *Thoreau: A Collection of Critical Essays*, ed. Sherman Paul (Englewood Cliffs, NJ: Prentice-Hall, 1962), and Charles A. Madison, "Henry David Thoreau: Transcendental

Individualist," *Ethics* 54 (January 1944): 110–23, agree that his politics ultimately leads to a "blind alley." More sympathetically, Philip Abbott claims that Thoreau's preoccupation with finding his own identity grounds a political ethic that, though compelling, is simply unrealizable by others; see "Henry David Thoreau, the State of Nature, and the Redemption of Liberalism," *Journal of Politics* 47 (1985): 182–208.

4. Before proceeding I should point out that by *democracy* I mean its modern liberal-representative version, because this is the form Thoreau is usually assumed to embrace. This definition, moreover, presents the greatest challenge to my argument, because I also acknowledge that Thoreau's liberalism, coupled with his principled dislike of structured political participation, prohibits him from endorsing other, more thoroughgoing forms—an assumption usually invoked to link Thoreau's political project with representative democratic institutions.

5. Thoreau, "Resistance to Civil Government," in *Political Writings,* 20–21.

6. Although this essay is commonly referred to as "Civil Disobedience," and despite Gandhi's attribution of this term to Thoreau, Thoreau never uses the term in any of his works. When given as a lecture at the Concord Lyceum on January 26, 1848, the essay was titled "On the Relation of the Individual to the State"; its published title (in Elizabeth Peabody's *Aesthetic Papers*) is "Resistance to Civil Government." Only four years after Thoreau's death did the essay assume the title that finally stuck. Since the original (and only authorized) published title suggests that Thoreau's essay placed more weight on examining the responsibilities of an individual in responding to government activity than on the institutionalization of the act as a standard of democratic conduct, I have retained it here. For more on this history, see Wendell Glick's exhaustive textual commentary in *The Writings of Henry David Thoreau: Reform Papers* (Princeton, NJ: Princeton University Press, 1973), 313–21; and Walter Harding, *The Variorum Civil Disobedience* (New York: Twayne Publishers, 1967), 59n1.

7. Edward Madden identifies the major elements of transcendentalism as "German romanticism [via Coleridge], a distinction between Reason and Understanding, a basic optimism about human nature, and a general commitment to intuitionism as a theory of knowledge." See Edward Madden, *Civil Disobedience and Moral Law in Nineteenth-Century American Philosophy* (Seattle: University of Washington Press, 1968), 8.

8. Ralph Waldo Emerson, "Nature," in *The Selected Writings of Ralph Waldo Emerson,* ed. Brooks Atkinson (New York: Modern Library, 1950), 23.

9. Madden, *Civil Disobedience and Moral Law,* 88. This synergy was first explicated by Theodore Parker in his *Discourse of Matters Pertaining to Religion* (Boston: Rufus Leighton Jr., 1859), bk. 2, chaps. 6–8. For a more detailed philo-

sophical history of transcendentalism, see Harold Clark Goddard, *Studies in New England Transcendentalism* (New York: Hillary House Publishers, 1960).

10. See, for example, Henry David Thoreau, *Walden,* in *Walden and Other Writings,* ed. Joseph Wood Krutch (New York: Bantam Books, 1962), 320, 325, 339. Far from embodying the duplicitous combination of violent antagonism and moral innocence that Rosenblum (*Another Liberalism*) perceives Thoreau's militant conscience as forcing on the natural world, nature stands most prominently in Thoreau's works as a manifestation of the higher law. See note 12 below.

11. Thoreau, *Walden,* 319. Thoreau's essay "The Natural History of Massachusetts" was commissioned by Emerson to explore how the concrete particulars of nature could yield principles of the general and universal. In that essay Thoreau notes, "The merely political aspect of the land is not very cheering; men are degraded when considered as the members of a political organization." See *The Transcendentalists: An Anthology,* ed. Perry Miller (Cambridge, MA: Harvard University Press, 1950), 324–25.

12. Thoreau, "Resistance," 14. Rosenblum, "Thoreau's Militant Conscience," 94, cites this passage as evidence of Thoreau's celebration of competition and antagonism in nature. I think it is more reasonable to assume (especially in the context of Thoreau's other nature writings and the beliefs of his fellow transcendentalists) that his mention of the trees is a simple reiteration of his conviction that nature impels all the elements within it, especially and including man, to "obey their own laws."

13. He does not, however, recognize a political obligation as a necessarily moral obligation. The distinction between political and moral obligations is dealt with more fully later in this chapter.

14. Thoreau, "Resistance," 10, 13, 17. Here and throughout the chapter I use the term *politics* and all its derivatives simply to identify that which involves, or exists as a condition of, the institution and affairs of government.

15. Ibid., 1–2.

16. Rosenblum, "Thoreau's Militant Conscience," 98, 100–101.

17. See Michael Walzer, *Obligations: Essays on Disobedience, War, and Citizenship* (Cambridge, MA: Harvard University Press, 1970), 129: "For what is lost when morality becomes 'merely personal' is . . . the sharing of moral knowledge, the sense of Another's presence, the connection of the individual to a universal order." He denies that a subjective sense of right can involve any meaningful sense of responsibility (22). However, I fail to see why a methodologically individualist understanding of values precludes moral interactions with others or how a conviction in a higher, "universal" order or law can possibly relieve one of moral responsibility.

18. Thoreau, *Walden,* 265, 267. This sentiment is echoed throughout his other works, such as "Slavery in Massachusetts," in *Political Writings,* 127.

19. For more details on Thoreau's association with the abolitionist movement, see Frank Sanborn, *The Life of Henry David Thoreau* (Boston: Houghton Mifflin, 1917), 466–69; Wendell Glick, "Thoreau and Radical Abolitionism" (Ph.D. diss., Northwestern University, 1950); John C. Broderick, "Thoreau, Alcott, and the Poll Tax," *Studies in Philology* 53 (October 1956): 612–26.

20. An exhaustive survey of these reformers and the variety of political programs they formulated can be found in Lewis Perry, *Radical Abolitionism: Anarchy and the Government of God in Antislavery Thought* (Ithaca, NY: Cornell University Press, 1973), 36–45, 174. For a focus on transcendentalist movements, see Richard Francis, *Transcendental Utopias: Individuality and Community at Brook Farm, Fruitlands, and Walden* (Ithaca, NY: Cornell University Press, 1997).

21. Thoreau, "Resistance," 2.

22. Ibid., 9.

23. Francis, *Transcendental Utopias,* x. Francis portrays Thoreau's mission as a replacement of the totality with an individual, and he interprets Thoreau's hut at Walden Pond as symbolic of the fundamental unit of his community (227).

24. Emerson repeatedly expresses confidence that the laws of nature act persistently to bring humanity back to the moral track. See especially his essay "Compensation," in *Selected Writings,* 174.

25. For example, Emerson complains that the political candidates currently running for office "have not at heart the ends which give to the name of democracy what hope and virtue are in it" ("Politics," in *Selected Writings,* 428). In his journals Emerson derides Thoreau's radicalism and criticizes his refusal to admit of concerted moral action: "If I knew only Thoreau, I should think cooperation of good men impossible. Must we always talk for victory, and never once for truth, comfort, and joy?" (quoted in Madden, *Civil Disobedience and Moral Law,* 90).

26. William Earle, "Some Paradoxes of Private Conscience as a Political Guide," *Ethics* 80 (1970): 306, rightly identifies it as a question of *moral* resolution to a moral conflict between public law and private conscience. See also Robert Paul Wolff, *In Defense of Anarchism* (New York: Harper and Row, 1976), 18–19.

27. Thoreau, "A Plea for Captain John Brown," in *Political Writings,* 151.

28. Thoreau acknowledges the need to give the government penal power but seems to believe that those who violate the higher law will recognize the justice in their punishment: "The murderer always knows that he is justly punished" (ibid., 156).

29. Thoreau, "Resistance," 14.

30. Ibid., 13.

31. Martin Luther King Jr., "Letter from Birmingham City Jail," reprinted in

Hugo Bedau, *Civil Disobedience: Theory and Practice* (New York: Pegasus, 1969), 74. In his acceptance speech for the Nobel Peace Prize, King phrases this display of bodies in religious terms: the protesters are "witnesses to the truth as [they] see it" (quoted in Carl Cohen, *Civil Disobedience* [New York: Columbia University Press, 1971], 40).

32. In "Civil Disobedience," in *Crises of the Republic* (New York: Harcourt Brace Jovanovich, 1969), 60, Hannah Arendt dismisses Thoreau's actions as inherently unpolitical because they are private actions taken merely to free himself from evil. The basis for her judgment is the equation of conscientious action with mere opinion separated from the bodily action that would have public consequences. However, Thoreau intended his act to demonstrate that only private conscientious action can avoid the false dichotomy between body and mind; taking action according to the rules and laws of the public realm alienates one's mindful moral responsibility from the body it inhabits.

33. Thoreau, "Resistance," 6.

34. H. D. Lewis notes the agreement among moral philosophers that virtue must be cultivated, meaning its practice must be habitual and ongoing. See "Obedience to Conscience," *Mind* 54 (1945): 227–53.

35. Thoreau, "Resistance," 11. In "A Plea for Captain John Brown" (*Political Writings*, 152), Thoreau asks quite simply, "When were the good and brave ever in a majority?"

36. Wolff, *In Defense of Anarchism*, 29. See also Thoreau, "Slavery in Massachusetts," 132.

37. Thoreau, "Slavery in Massachusetts," 128.

38. Thoreau, "A Plea for Captain John Brown," 150.

39. Ibid., 140.

40. "The few who talk about his vindictive spirit, while they really admire his heroism, have no test by which to detect a noble man, no amalgam to combine with his pure gold. They mix their own dross with it" (ibid., 149).

41. See J. R. Cameron's "'Ought' and Institutional Obligations," *Philosophy* 46 (October 1971): 320.

42. Thoreau, "A Plea for Captain John Brown," 156.

43. Although all moral obligations rely on certain necessary preconditions for their realization (e.g., most require the presence of another sentient being), these preconditions do not ground their reasons for fulfillment. Michael Stocker, "Moral Duties, Institutions, and Natural Facts," *Monist* 54 (1970): 610.

44. John Simmons, *Moral Principles and Political Obligations* (Princeton, NJ: Princeton University Press, 1979), 17, 24. See also Peter Singer, *Democracy and Disobedience* (Oxford: Clarendon Press, 1973), 3: "Our ultimate obligation to obey the law is a moral obligation and not a legal obligation. It cannot be a legal

obligation, for this would lead to an infinite regress—since legal obligations derive from laws, there would have to be a law that says we must obey the law. What obligation would there then be to obey this law?"

45. Stocker, "Moral Duties," 611.

46. Cameron, "'Ought' and Institutional Obligations," 311.

47. John Simmons would agree with this assessment, noting that there are certain positive moral duties, such as securing justice, that may sometimes require us to perform the obligations attached to various institutional roles simply because that is the most (or sometimes the only) efficient way of discharging those duties. See "External Justifications and Institutional Roles," in *Justification and Legitimacy: Essays on Rights and Obligations* (Cambridge: Cambridge University Press, 2001), 95.

48. For an overview of this debate over the moral duty of political obligations, see J. Roland Pennock and John Chapman, eds., *Nomos XII: Political and Legal Obligation* (New York: Atherton Press, 1970), xvi–xviii. As already noted, George Kateb believes that the legal and political procedures of constitutional democracy (and, we may infer, the obligations required to sustain them) have intrinsic moral worth; see *Inner Ocean,* 57.

49. Thoreau, "Life without Principle," in *Political Writings,* 117.

50. Rosenblum, *Another Liberalism,* 105–6.

51. Hanna Pitkin, "Obligation and Consent—I," *American Political Science Review* 59 (1965): 990–99, contends that both Locke and Joseph Tussman advance consent theories that do not ground obligation in consent but really see the arrangement as an obligation to consent to a (just) government; this means that one's political obligation is derived not from an incidence of contract but from a judgment of the justness of the government. Two responses to Wolff's *In Defense of Anarchism* echo Arendt's argument in "Civil Disobedience" that the issue at stake in consent theory is less the security of moral autonomy than the protection of a sense of the common good: Robert F. Ladenson, "Legitimate Authority," *American Philosophical Quarterly* 9 (1972): 335–41, contends that the authority of the state is grounded in respect for its service of the unanimously agreed-upon "good." Lisa Perkins, "On Reconciling Autonomy and Authority," *Ethics* 82 (1972): 114–23, follows Socrates in asserting that obedience to laws is grounded in a duty to preserve the conditions that make the good possible.

52. For instance, see Arendt, "Civil Disobedience," 85; Joseph Tussman, *Obligation and the Body Politic* (New York: Oxford University Press, 1960), 10. Michael Walzer, in *Obligations,* elaborates a version of consent wherein obligations are grounded in promises made to other people, so that obligation begins with membership in a group; the state is a primary authority whose obligations may nevertheless conflict with those of a secondary group (7, 10, 21). But since Thoreau

certainly did not phrase his obligation to higher law in terms of group member-ship, the same criticisms he implicitly levels against the collectivism of democratic "consent" apply here.

53. Kateb, *Inner Ocean*, 114, 120, 173.

54. This is Don Herzog's argument in *Happy Slaves: A Critique of Consent Theory* (Chicago: University of Chicago Press, 1997), 205–13. He notes that re-sponsiveness does not itself imply consent, but a list of regimes we intuit as resting on consent would consist of the responsive ones. Moreover, given that true volun-tary consent is difficult to establish, he suggests that it may be more important to respect the autonomy of all individual people under a political regime that could take consent as its foundation than to worry about securing the consent itself.

55. Thoreau, "Resistance," 13.

56. See Thoreau, "A Plea for Captain John Brown," 151; Thoreau, "Resistance," 20. This is very similar to the argument made by A. John Simmons on behalf of John Locke. Simmons maintains that Locke intended expressed consent and that any attempts to reconcile his theory to reality by formulating approximations to this consent (e.g., through the radical participationism of Herzog or the hypotheti-cal contractarianism of John Rawls) miss the point entirely. See *On the Edge of Anarchy: Locke, Consent, and the Limits of Society* (Princeton, NJ: Princeton University Press, 1993), 74–78.

57. Thoreau, *Walden*, 345.

58. Kateb, *Inner Ocean*, 78.

59. Ibid., 57–64. I should note that my argument with Kateb extends only to his characterization of Thoreau as a democrat, not to his arguments about the value of constitutionalism and representative democracy, which I find otherwise fascinating and persuasive.

60. See Rosenblum, *Another Liberalism;* Rosenblum, "Thoreau's Militant Conscience." Her later views concerning Thoreau's commitment to representative democracy are considerably less ambivalent; see her introduction to *Political Writ-ings*, xxix–xxx.

61. Rosenblum, "Thoreau's Militant Conscience," 83.

62. Rosenblum, *Another Liberalism*, 103.

63. Ibid., 92.

64. Thoreau, "Resistance," 10.

65. Thoreau, "The Last Days of John Brown," in *Political Writings*, 164–65.

66. Robert D. Richardson Jr., "The Social Ethics of Walden," in *Critical Es-says on Henry David Thoreau's* Walden, ed. Joel Myerson (Boston: G. K. Hall, 1988), 244.

67. Even his abolitionism was less directly political than one might imagine. Alfred Tauber insightfully observes that Thoreau's indignation over slavery arises

more from the fact that *his* rights are being threatened, not the slaves'. See *Henry David Thoreau and the Moral Agency of Knowing* (Berkeley: University of California Press, 2001), 191.

68. Simmons, *Moral Principles and Political Obligations*, 190.

69. Walker ("Thoreau on Democratic Cultivation," 180–83) relates Thoreau's doctrine of advice giving to the concept of continuity between everyday activity in the local sphere and in the rest of the political sphere, which is precisely the way Thoreau seems to envision political activity in the ideal state. It is unclear from his article, however, what, for Walker, constitutes Thoreau's endorsement of democratic institutions as such, other than Thoreau's gestures in *Walden* toward a universal capacity for self-cultivation. For a similar argument about Thoreau's tactics and purpose, see Elliot M. Zashin, *Civil Disobedience and Democracy* (New York: Free Press, 1971), 60.

70. Kateb, *Inner Ocean*, 40.

71. Rosenblum, *Another Liberalism*, 114.

72. Thoreau, *Walden*, 135, 138.

73. Thoreau, "Resistance," 17.

74. This is Rosenblum's claim in *Another Liberalism*, 64. She also asserts that to Thoreau, neighbors are simply irritants who provide the friction necessary to maintain a militant conscience (113).

75. See, for instance, ibid., 153.

76. Lewis, "Obedience to Conscience," 244.

77. Thoreau, "Resistance," 21. Such a characterization may lend some support to the "community consciousness" that many commentators read into Thoreau's social criticism in *Walden*. See, for example, Richard Drinnon, "Thoreau's Politics of the Upright Man," in *Walden and Civil Disobedience: Authoritative Texts, Background, Reviews, and Essays in Criticism*, ed. Owen Thomas (New York: W. W. Norton, 1966), 416.

78. Thoreau, "Paradise (to Be) Regained," in *Reform Papers*, 42.

79. See, for example, Tussman, *Obligation and the Body Politic*, 18, 25–31; Michael Walzer, "Political Action: The Problem of Dirty Hands," *Philosophy and Political Affairs* 2 (1973): 160–80.

80. Thoreau, "Resistance," 18.

# PART II

# Conscience, Citizenship, and Politics

CHAPTER 4

# Thoreau's American Founding

*Bob Pepperman Taylor*

I cannot bear to be told to wait for good results, I pine as much for good beginnings.
—Thoreau, "Reform and Reformers"

It is remarkable how closely the history of the apple-tree is connected with that of man.
—Thoreau, "Wild Apples"

IN HIS "DIVINITY SCHOOL Address," Emerson declares, "The old is for slaves,"[1] and in a talk delivered at Dartmouth College a month later, he claims that the "perpetual admonition of nature to us, is, 'The world is new, untried. Do not believe the past. I give you the universe a virgin today.'"[2] Emerson teaches us to turn away from what he sees as our confining traditions, customs, and histories; to make a clean break with the past; to invent a fresh, new, and free reality. This is the message of his first book, *Nature,* which concludes by encouraging the reader, "Build, therefore, your own world."[3] It is also a message of "Self-Reliance," where Emerson scolds us, saying, "I am ashamed to think how easily we capitulate to badges and names, to large societies and dead institutions."[4] The freedom Emerson seeks is a freedom beyond history because, in his view, history gives us only thoughtless prejudice and habit, both enemies of an authentic independence.

It is tempting to think that Thoreau shares this understanding of freedom with Emerson. In "Walking," for example, Thoreau writes, "Above all, we cannot afford not to live in the present. He is blessed over all mortals who loses no moment of the passing life in remembering the past."[5] Here, as when he writes in his *Journal* that he wishes "to get the Concord, the Massachusetts, the America, out of my head and be sane a part of every day,"[6] nature appears to play the role suggested by Emerson: it is a refuge from society in the fullest sense of the word. Nature allows us to escape our daily affairs and human contacts. Indeed, it allows us to escape the human world altogether, not only our contemporaries but also our predecessors and all the institutions, practices, and beliefs that bind the present to the past. The free individual who is ready for a walk is a solitary who escapes society in the shelter of nature.

Because Thoreau is commonly thought to subscribe to this Emersonian perspective, interpreters of Thoreau's political thought have predictably observed that such an orientation is less than promising for thinking about social and political life. Jane Bennett worries that "Thoreau acts as if one could exempt oneself from public life."[7] In the same vein, John Patrick Diggins writes, "Obsessed with his own salvation, Thoreau called upon others to withdraw from society and thereby become oblivious to all that is general and public."[8] Perhaps the most critical of all, C. Roland Wagner accuses Thoreau of a selfish childishness: "Thoreau's uncompromising moral idealism, despite its occasional embodiment in sentences of supreme literary power, created an essentially child's view of political and social reality. Because his moral principles were little more than expressions of his quest for purity and of hostility to any civilized interference with the absolute attainment of his wishes he was unable to discriminate between better and worse in the real world."[9] Bennett, Diggins, Wagner, and many others like them, are right to believe that *if* Thoreau holds an understanding of nature and freedom similar to that found in Emerson's writings, we cannot expect a social and political commentary of any real sophistication or significance. In this event, it is easy to think that Thoreau is little more than a self-absorbed egoist.

There are good reasons to believe, however, that Thoreau's views are significantly different from Emerson's on these matters. In fact, these differences can be dramatically illustrated by looking at Thoreau's first book, *A Week on the Concord and Merrimack Rivers.* In this work Thoreau immerses himself in American colonial history, specifically investigating the relationship between Indian and European settlers. Far from encouraging us to escape our past, to cut ourselves off from our social legacies and the determinative facts of our collective lives, Thoreau provides us with a tough, revealing look at the historical events and conditions and struggles that gave birth to contemporary American society. When Thoreau and his brother travel up the Concord and Merrimack rivers, nature does not give them "the universe a virgin." On the contrary, they find a social world within this nature that is filled with crime, violence, heroism, and the tragedy resulting from the conflict of dissimilar social orders.

A *Week* has rarely been taken seriously (or considered at all) by those interested in Thoreau's political ideas. It is often viewed, by Thoreau's admirers and critics alike, as a rather tedious series of seemingly unrelated observations, thoughts, and ideas all tied together by a young, preachy, self-preoccupied Thoreau. Melville, who thought it was a terrible and self-indulgent book, wrote to Hawthorne that he planned to satirize it with a work entitled "A Week on a Work-Bench in a Barn."[10] One of Thoreau's friendliest biographers, Henry S. Salt, concludes that the book is "vague, disjointed, and discursive; and is, moreover, almost arrogant in its transcendental egoism."[11] What could such an unbearably "transcendental" book have to do with politics? Even those (mainly literary) critics who are friendly toward the work describe it as concerned primarily with private issues, such as Thoreau's response to his brother's death.[12]

One recent biographer, Robert D. Richardson, breaks with these common views when he writes, "A *Week* has strong, if frequently overlooked, social themes: friendship, settlement, Indian life, oriental law."[13] I agree but would make the case even more forcefully: what is thought of as a painfully personal and apolitical book is actually a sophisticated meditation on the realities and consequences of the American founding. Once we are in a position to appreciate the degree to which Thoreau, unlike Emerson, accepts the necessity of locating our choices and freedoms within social contexts and historical time, we have taken the first step toward a reevaluation of the quality and significance of Thoreau's political thought as a whole.

Thoreau begins his book with the following sentence: "The Musketa-quid, or Grass-ground River, though probably as old as the Nile or Euphrates, did not begin to have a place in civilized history, until the fame of its grassy meadows and its fish attracted settlers out of England in 1635, when it received the other but kindred name of CONCORD from the first plantation on its banks, which appears to have been commenced in a spirit of peace and harmony."[14] Out of respect for historical chronology, Thoreau presents

the Indian before the English name for the river. The river itself and, by
implication, the native inhabitants are of ancient lineage, while "Concord"
and the people responsible for this name are relative newcomers.[15] In the
second sentence of text, Thoreau explains that the Indian name is actually
superior to the English, since it will remain descriptively accurate as long as
"grass grows and water runs here," whereas "Concord" will be accurate only
"while men lead peaceable lives on its banks"—something obviously much
less permanent than the grass and flowing water. In fact, the third sentence
indicates that "Concord" has already failed to live up to its name, since the
Indians are now an "extinct race."[16] Thoreau wastes no time in pointing out
that regardless of the "spirit of peace and harmony" that first moved the
whites to establish a plantation on this river, relations between the natives
and the settlers soon exhibited very little concord indeed.

In these opening sentences, Thoreau presents us with an indication of
a primary motivation for his trip down the Concord and Merrimack rivers:
he hopes to probe the nature of the relationship between Indian and white
societies and to consider the importance of this relationship for understanding our America.[17] Joan Burbick, one of the few to recognize the primacy
of the political theme underlying Thoreau's voyage, writes that in this book
Thoreau "tries to forge the uncivil history of America."[18] We know the end
of the story already: one "race" annihilates the other. Part of Thoreau's intention is to not let us forget this critical truth about our society, to remind
us that our founding was as bloody and unjust as any, try as we might to put
this fact out of sight and tell alternative tales about our past. As the book
progresses, however, we see that another intention is to explain the complexity and ambiguity of the historical processes that led to and beyond this
bloody founding. The history Thoreau presents is "uncivil" in two senses:
first, and most obviously, it is about violent, brutal, uncivil acts; second, it
is not the official or common self-understanding the nation wants to hold.[19]
Thoreau's journey is not aimed only at personal self-discovery, despite the
obvious importance of that theme. On the contrary, the opening sentences
and the problems they pose suggest that Thoreau is first and foremost interested in a project of discovery for the nation as a whole, the success of
which will depend on looking carefully at the relationship between settler
and native. The project of self-discovery is to be accomplished within the
context of this larger social history. Thoreau's personal and more private
ruminations are set quite literally between ongoing discussions of events

from the colonial life of New England. We are never allowed to forget for very long that our contemporary private lives are bounded by, and in some crucial sense defined within, the possibilities created by this earlier drama of Indian and colonist.

When Thoreau and his brother cast off from Concord on Saturday afternoon, a number of friends are present along the riverbank to wish them well. The two brothers, however, refuse to return the waves and shouts: "We, having already performed those shore rites, with excusable reserve, as befits those who are embarked on unusual enterprises, who behold but speak not, silently glided past the firm lands of Concord."[20] There is a noticeable silence throughout this book, marked by the complete absence of dialogue. The narration is entirely reflective and contemplative, and when human interactions are recorded, even those between Thoreau and his brother, they are presented impersonally, as if by a detached observer. Once on the river, Thoreau is not so much relaying a series of personal events and interpersonal interactions—such would best be conveyed by talk among individuals—as he is interested in gaining a distance from the intensely personal in order to assume the appropriate position from which to observe and tell the stories of the larger society. His is an "unusual enterprise" and an ambitious one, precisely because it requires a subordination of the intensely personal nature of his experience to a greater project of social discovery and evaluation. The brothers, in fact, immediately and symbolically assume the role of their forebears. Although they refuse to return the greetings of their friends, they "did unbend so far as to let our guns speak for us, when at length we had swept out of sight."[21] This military salute is only appropriate as they move from the established Concord of their generation back in time to the original settlement of the region, in that they now let their guns do their speaking for them.[22]

The first landmark they pass is the remains of the North Bridge, where the first battle of the Revolution was fought. Thoreau pauses long enough to give a poem or two and to remind the citizens of Concord that the Revolution was fought and won by patriots of greater courage than is now routinely exhibited in Concord.

> Ah, 't is in vain the peaceful din
> That wakes the ignoble town,
> Not thus did braver spirits win
> A patriot's renown.[23]

This, however, is not the end but the beginning of their journey of discovery of America's origins. The Revolution, with its heroes, principles, noble deeds, and ideals, is the story we like to tell of our founding. But Thoreau floats by the remains of this event, and he and his brother are off to more remote but more revealing regions and times.

It is not until the next day that they have enough distance from the America of the Revolution to return to the theme of the settlement of New England by Europeans. On Sunday morning they find themselves in sparsely populated country: "For long reaches we could see neither house nor cultivated field, nor any sign of the vicinity of man."[24] They are now far enough from the world of contemporary America that it is possible for them to discover earlier times when the fate of the new civilization was still unsettled, when white settlements were themselves new, untested, and unsure of their future. Thoreau introduces these white incursions into the "howling wilderness" quite gently, much as the whites themselves might want them portrayed.[25] He and his brother pass the village of Billerica, a town of "ancient" character that is "now in its dotage."[26] It is a living illustration of a European village that has experienced an almost complete life cycle and is thus useful as a representative of its kind. With the initial settlement came the bells to call the faithful to worship on the Sabbath; these bells can still be heard, sometimes as far away as Concord. Thoreau thus equates the founding and perpetuation of this colonial town with the attractive, pastoral symbol of church bells. But Thoreau refuses to move on without hinting at the very different reality these bells represent for the Indian. They ring so loud that it is "no wonder that such a sound startled the dreaming Indian, and frightened his game, when the first bells were swung on trees, and sounded through the forest beyond the plantations of the white man."[27] This comment is brief and understated, but Thoreau rightly suggests that even something as seemingly innocent and pious as the church bells of the white settlers represents an ominous development for the native. The noise is new to the landscape, unusual and startling. It apparently will have significant material consequences as well, since it is capable of "frightening" the Indian's game and thus threatening the economic foundation of his mode of life. There has as yet been no overt violence nor, as far as we know, evil intention on the part of the new settlers. But even if we grant that the first "plantation" along the river was "commenced with a spirit of peace and harmony," the seemingly innocuous religious habits of the white settlers will threaten the foundations of the Indian's world.

We see, then, that the interaction between whites and Indians does not have to be self-consciously or overtly hostile for the consequences to be dramatic, harmful, even murderous to the Indians. The whites bring their religion and their economic institutions as well. The white "buys the Indian's moccasins and baskets, then buys his hunting-grounds, and at length forgets where he is buried and ploughs up his bones."[28] Even if the economic transactions between white and Indian are "consensual" and contain no threats or fraud, the result is disastrous. The Indian's entire social order is undermined through its contact with white forms of property ownership and commerce. The end is annihilation and, perhaps the worst consequence of such annihilation, the loss of memory. When the Indians die, we do not even remember, or care to remember, where they are buried.[29]

The compulsion of white society is to continually plow more and more of the land, and the memory of a dying people will not be allowed to intrude on economic progress. "The white man's mullein soon reigned in Indian cornfields, and sweet-scented English grasses clothed the new soil. Where, then, could the Red Man set his foot?"[30] Nowhere, of course. It does not require individually and personally malicious behavior to threaten the survival of a people. What is at work here is the clash between dramatically different and incompatible modes of life. The forces are impersonal and deadly. "We talk of civilizing the Indian, but that is not the name for his improvement." His "improvement" is possible only in his traditional life, in which he engages in an "intercourse with nature" that admits "of the greatest possible independence of each."[31] This life is simply not available once the wilderness has been tamed by European agriculture. "If we could listen but for an instant to the chant of the Indian muse, we should understand why he will not exchange his savageness for civilization. Nations are not whimsical. Steel and blankets are strong temptations; but the Indian does well to continue Indian."[32] But if he does remain Indian, where is he to "set his foot"? To retain his identity is to face a certain death. Thoreau's observations here are similar to William Cronon's in his ecological history of New England: "A people who loved property little had been overwhelmed by a people who loved it much."[33] As agriculture replaces hunting, the hunter becomes obsolete, irrelevant, extinct. As Thoreau writes in his *Journal,* "A race of hunters can never withstand the inroads of a race of husbandmen."[34]

In the remainder of "Sunday," two significant passages address the relationship of white settlers and Indians. In the first, Thoreau quotes extensively from Gookin regarding John Eliot's conversion of Indians at a place on the Merrimack where the natives traditionally gather to fish.[35] Eliot succeeds in converting a sachem named Wannalancet (about whom Thoreau has more to say later), among others. The final paragraph of this passage simply observes that "Pawtucket and Wamesit, where the Indians resorted in the fishing season, are now Lowell, the city of Spindles and Manchester of America, which sends its cotton cloth round the globe."[36] For Thoreau, the conversion of these Indians is clearly just a step in the process of displacing and destroying them, replacing them with manufacturing towns and economic development.

The final discussion of white-Indian relations in "Sunday" moves again from religion to economics. Thoreau tells the story of Wicasuck, a large and desirable island owned by the Indians. In or around 1663, the son of an Indian chief was jailed for a debt owed to one John Tinker. The jailed man's brother, Wannalancet (who was not yet a Christian), arranged for the sale of Wicasuck Island to raise the revenue needed to pay the debt. The General Court, apparently feeling that the sale took place under some sort of duress or coercion, voided the transaction and returned the island to the Indians in 1665. Later, Thoreau tells us, the land was granted to a white man, Jonathan Tyng, as a reward for maintaining a garrison against the Indians during King Philip's War. This took place "after the departure of the Indians in 1683."[37]

There are a number of interesting elements in this story. First, it appears that the Indians were the recipients of something fairly close to justice when the General Court returned the island to them. This alone gives a somewhat hopeful quality to the tale. Yes, certain whites unscrupulously attempted to take the land from the Indians, but they were foiled, at least in this case, by the independence and integrity of the white judicial system. Second, however, overt hostilities between Indians and colonists broke out in 1675 with King Philip's War. We learn later[38] that Wannalancet, on the advice of his father, Pasaconaway, refused to participate in this war and withdrew from the region. Thoreau tells us that the Indians did not leave the island until 1683; this is important, since it suggests that when they did leave, it was for reasons other than military hostilities, since King Philip's War was concluded by 1678. It apparently was not the overt threat of arms that drove the Indians from this land (land that quickly became a prize for a white Indian fighter). On the contrary, it appears that the social processes generated by the religious and economic differences Thoreau has discussed throughout the chapter made it impossible for the Indian to find a place to "set his foot." Even though a certain kind of justice had been granted the Indians, they were still unable to retain their grip on the land. Not even religious conversion (Wannalancet was converted by Eliot in 1674) was able to produce a lasting accommodation between the two communities. Christians or not, Wannalancet and his people were forced from a favored place. "Sunday" thus ends with a very pessimistic assessment of the compatibility of two radically different ways of life and the conflict and misery that appear to be the inevitable result when such social orders crash against each other.[39]

Although these processes of conflict and struggle may begin, as it were, "on the sabbath" (and, Thoreau seems to be saying, let us assume for the sake of argument that they do)—in an environment where there are good intentions on the parts of all the players—it is just a matter of time before they spill over into overt acts of violence. And this is exactly what happens in the next chapter, "Monday," which begins with an account of the "famous Captain Lovewell," a man of mythic and heroic reputation who is said to be the son of "an ensign in the army of Oliver Cromwell." He lived a life of biblical span, finally dying at the age of 120 at the hands of the Indians he fought throughout his life in the New World.[40] In his final raid, Lovewell leads a small group of men into a successful engagement with a far more numerous enemy, but the price of victory is very high. Most of Thoreau's discussion of the event is a gruesome account of the fate and agonies of the wounded white survivors.

Although the details of the physical suffering experienced by these men as they attempt to find their way back home are horrific, Thoreau presents them in such a manner that we are not allowed to forget the context in which they suffered. He quotes a ballad, for example, that praises the "wounded good young Frye, Who was our English Chaplin." The ballad continues, "He many Indians slew, / And some of them he scalped while bullets round him flew."[41] Thoreau lets us know that Frye, who would be left by his fellows to die of his wounds alone in the wilderness,[42] is a fierce, even vicious character who risked his life to scalp his victims. Barbarism and savagery are certainly not absent from the colonists' ranks. As Thoreau would write in his *Journal* years later, "Savage meets savage, and the white man's only distinction is that he is the chief."[43] Similarly, after telling of the men's ordeal after the battle, Thoreau observes that there is no record of the wounded Indians and how they suffered in their attempt to return home.[44] The fight with the Indians has taken a terrible toll on these white men, but at least we have a memory of their suffering, unlike that of their native counterparts. Finally, Thoreau suggests that not only the bodies of these soldiers have been tormented and crippled. As the example of the scalping chaplain suggests, the soldiers' hatred of Indians has disfigured their moral characters as well. Their leader, Captain Lovewell, is himself the embodiment of hatred for the Indian: "It is stated in the History of Dunstable, that just before his last march, Lovewell was warned to beware of the ambuscades of the enemy, but he replied, 'that he did not care for them,' and bending down a small elm beside which he was standing into a bow, declared 'that he would treat the Indians in the same way.' This elm is still standing, a venerable and magnificent tree."[45] The ironically named Lovewell is consumed by this hatred, while the elm flourishes.

Thoreau's understanding of these events is complex and ambivalent. There is a good deal of dry criticism in his discussion, but there is real sympathy as well. We are left thinking, on the one hand, that these men get roughly what they deserve and, on the other, that no human beings deserve the torments they experience. But even more pointed is Thoreau's contrast between these men of Lovewell's generation and Thoreau's own contemporaries: "Our brave forefathers have exterminated all the Indians, and their degenerate children no longer dwell in garrisoned houses nor hear any war-whoop in their path. It would be well, perchance, if many an 'English Chaplin' in these days could exhibit as unquestionable trophies of his valor as did 'good young Frye.'"[46] There are two crucial points here. First, although the hatred these men felt and the crimes they committed were enormous, it is simply not true that they were without moral virtues. They were loyal and brave to a degree that few of our contemporaries even aspire to. Second, all the descendants of these white settlers enjoy a peace and stability that are taken for granted and are the direct result of the actions of these earlier colonists. Thoreau's casual journey down the Concord

and Merrimack rivers would be unimaginable in an earlier age, when peace
was not possible between whites and Indians. Thoreau's reflections, this
very book, and the criticisms it includes of American society are utterly dependent on these original murderous acts of founding. Far from exempting
himself from the implications of the story he tells, Thoreau situates himself
right in the middle of it. He is nothing if not the offspring of these "brave
forefathers."[47]

Thoreau returns to Lovewell later in "Monday," repeating the story of
his long life.[48] And if this is not enough, Thoreau explains that during the
various Indian wars, the Indians spared him "on account of his kindness to
them."[49] Lovewell's death in battle would not come until 1725, but prior to
this, he apparently led a charmed life, the life of a noble soldier respected
even by his enemies. Thoreau uses Lovewell as the mythic thread to tie
other stories and characters together. He mentions that it is Lovewell's
house that Mrs. Dustan reaches when fleeing her Indian captors[50]—a
story he does not tell in full until "Thursday," late in the book. It is through
Lovewell that we first learn about Farwell (who was present at Lovewell's
final battle), and it is to Farwell that Thoreau now turns. A year before his
death, Farwell is involved in a campaign to rescue two settlers who were
captured by Indians and taken to Canada. Soon after their capture, a party
of ten rescuers rushes foolishly into an ambush. Only one, Farwell—the
only member of the rescue party to warn against this method of pursuit—
survives.[51] Farwell lives another year, only to die from wounds received
while fighting with Lovewell.

Thoreau concludes this passage with the following comments:

> These battles sound incredible to us. I think that posterity will doubt if such
> things ever were; if our bold ancestors who settled this land were not strug-
> gling rather with the forest shadows, and not with a copper-colored race of
> men. They were vapors, fever and ague of the unsettled woods. Now, only a
> few arrow-heads are turned up by the plough. In the Pelasgic, the Etruscan,
> or the British story, there is nothing so shadowy and unreal.[52]

Again, Thoreau is contrasting our current reality with the historical realities
on which it is built. The destruction of the Indians makes their original
existence hard to imagine, and the deeds of the settlers in response to the
presence of the Indians are thus equally incredible. But even though these

brutal facts seem shadowy and unreal to us, Thoreau reminds us that they are nonetheless the facts of our collective life. As distant as such fear, violence, and killing seem from our everyday experiences, Thoreau does not let us forget that they were once all present in plenty along the banks of our rivers.

In "Sunday" Thoreau discusses some of the original sources of conflict between the Indians and the settlers, and in "Monday" we find these conflicts bursting into brutal, genocidal violence. There is violence in the stories Thoreau has yet to tell, but in the remaining days of the week, Thoreau will, on the whole, dwell less on it. Most of the remaining references to the relationship between Indian and settler are brief comments, intended primarily to reinforce what has already been detailed in "Sunday" and "Monday." Thus, for example, in "Tuesday" Thoreau points to a wood where Farwell escaped from Indians. Thoreau's point is only to remind the reader of the contrast between the present and the past: "It did not look as if men had ever had to run for their lives on this now open and peaceful interval."[53] And again, at the beginning of "Wednesday," Thoreau juxtaposes the success of the town of Bedford, famous for its "hops and for its fine domestic manufactures," with "some graves of the aborigines."[54] In a longer and poignant passage in "Wednesday," Thoreau contrasts the fate of Pasaconaway and his son Wannalancet with that of a local white hero, John Stark. Thoreau tells us that Pasaconaway is believed to have lived 120 years, implying that he is as deserving of heroic status as the 120-year-old Lovewell. Thoreau also praises Stark, a hero in the French and Indian Wars as well as the Revolution, and suggests that he is deserving of the monument built for him in Manchester, overlooking the Merrimack: "Who is most dead,—a hero by whose monument you stand, or his descendants of whom you have never heard?" But Thoreau ends the passage by reminding us of Pasaconaway and Wannalancet: "The graves of Pasaconaway and Wannalancet are marked by no monument on the bank of their native river."[55] In passages like this, the discussion of the relationship between Indians and colonists is a reminder of issues Thoreau has already explored, ambivalence he has already expressed, rather than a presentation of new issues or ideas.

Some of the remaining stories, however, introduce new complexities into our understanding of these relationships. In "Tuesday" Thoreau tells of three violent incidents between Penacook and Mohawk Indians along the Merrimack, occurring between 1670 and 1685.[56] It is clear that even though the hostilities between these two tribes may or may not have ancient roots, these specific events take place in a context in which the Penacooks are increasingly aligned with the colonists: we learn later that Pasaconaway had advised his Penacooks as early as 1660 to make peace with the white settlers.[57] And two of these three confrontations, one of which is an assault on Wannalancet's son by a group of Mohawks,[58] occur after Wannalancet's conversion to Christianity. Thus, the white settlement of the land produces obvious conflicts with the native peoples, and the indigenous peoples are themselves increasingly divided by the white presence. And, lest we forget, the Indians are just as capable of fratricide as the whites are.

Or consider the story of the relationship between Wawatam and Henry the fur trader found in Thoreau's long discourse on friendship in "Wednesday." Thoreau uses this as an illustration of how friendship can transcend the barriers of tribe and culture. "If Wawatam would taste the 'white man's milk' with his tribe, or take his bowl of human broth made of the trader's fellow-countrymen, he first finds a place of safety for his Friend, whom he has rescued from a similar fate."[59] After escaping many dangers, Henry and Wawatam eventually manage to spend a happy winter together. But Henry is forced to leave his friend in the spring in order to "avoid his enemies," that is, Indians who continue to hate him for being English and who wish to kill and consume him to gain courage for future battles with the colonists. The friends never meet again. So the message is clear: even this ideal friendship is limited by the broader sets of relationships within which these individuals live. Friendship may transcend the cultural gulf between Indian and white, but it is ultimately unable to overcome the contemporary context of warfare between the English and Chipeway societies.

The last and perhaps most powerful of the major tales of Indians and colonists is the Hannah Dustan odyssey in "Thursday." Dustan is taken from childbed by attacking Indians, sees "her infant's brains dashed out against an apple-tree," and is held captive with her nurse, Mary Neff, and an English boy, Samuel Lennardson. She is told that she and her nurse will be taken to an Indian settlement, where they will be forced to "run the gauntlet naked." To avoid this fate, Dustan instructs the boy to ask one of the men how best to kill an enemy and take a scalp. The man obliges, and that night Dustan, Neff, and Lennardson use this information to kill all the Indians—two men, two women, and six children—except for a "favorite boy, and one squaw who fled wounded with him to the woods." They then scuttle all the canoes except the one needed for their escape. They flee, only to return soon thereafter to scalp the dead as proof of their ordeal. They then manage to paddle the sixty or so miles to John Lovewell's house and are rescued. The General Court pays them fifty pounds as bounty for the ten scalps, and Dustan is reunited with her family, all of whom, except the infant, have survived the attack. Thoreau ends the story by telling us that "there have been many who in later times have lived to say that they had eaten of the fruit of that apple-tree," the tree upon which Dustan's child was murdered.[60]

Striking as it is, many of the themes of this story are repetitive of what has come before; it is a powerful return to the material from the opening chapters, primarily the violence in "Monday." Thus, Thoreau starkly conveys the grotesque violence on both sides of the conflict, and he concludes here, as he does earlier, that we are the beneficiaries, even the products, of theses terrible events—it is we, of course, who have "eaten of the fruit of that apple-tree."

But this story is different, too. Most obviously, it is a story in which women and children, traditional noncombatants, play a crucial role. The brutality in the Lovewell campaigns is between men who voluntarily assume the roles of warrior and soldier. The brutality in the Dustan story is aimed primarily at those who are most innocent, children. And this brutality, like that among male combatants, is not confined to one side. The Indians murder Dustan's infant, but she, in turn, methodically kills six children and attempts to kill the seventh (the "favorite boy" was a favorite within his own family, not to Dustan). In addition, this murder of children is conducted not only by men but also by women and children. The violence and hostility between Indian and settler have reached a point where all traditional restraints have vanished, where the weakest are fair game and all members of the community are combatants. Here, not in the Revolution, is the climax of the American founding. In this climax all colonists and Indians, even women and children, are implicated, and the entire family of Indians, not just the male warriors, is systematically killed off. This frenzy of violence, of escalating atrocity and counteratrocity, of total war, is the natural culmination of the processes Thoreau has been describing throughout the book. The Dustan story represents the victory of the colonists and the final destruction of the Indians. Thoreau is returning down the river to his home, as Dustan had to hers 142 years earlier. His investigation into the nature of the American founding, his "uncivil history," is mainly complete.

The image of the apple tree returns in "Friday" at two critical points. First, Thoreau tells of Elisha, a "friendly Indian" in the service of Jonathan Tyng (the recipient of Wicasuck Island), who was killed "by his own race in one of the Indian wars."[61] Although the exact location of his grave has been forgotten (like the graves of all the Indians Thoreau tells us of), a great flood in 1785 left an indentation in the earth that was believed to mark the spot. This place, too, has since been forgotten, but there is an apple tree—"Elisha's apple tree"—that stands in the neighborhood of where the grave must be. Elisha, like Dustan's infant, died at the foot of an apple tree and is remembered by the fruit the tree continues to bear. Not only white blood has borne fruit.

Second, Thoreau directs our attention back to these stories in the final sentences of the book, the last of which, describing the brothers' landing at Concord, reads: "And we leaped gladly on shore, drawing it up, and fastening it to the wild apple-tree, whose stem still bore the mark which its chain had worn in the chafing of the spring freshets."[62] In case we need yet another reminder, the tree that has grown out of the violence and conflict described throughout the book is the tree in our own hometown, to which we anchor our own peaceful, mundane, and unheroic lives.

In November 1851, more than two years after the publication of *A Week*, Thoreau declares in his *Journal*, "And this is my home, my native soil; and I am a New-Englander."[63] Thoreau is acutely aware of his rootedness in New England culture and society and the impossibility of separating his own battles and concerns from the human environment that produced him. This alone should make us skeptical of Quentin Anderson's claim that Thoreau joins Emerson and Whitman in denying "the shaping character of the past," that he, like they, does not wish to see his life as a story in which other people figure.[64] Thoreau's first book confirms this skepticism by clearly illustrating his break with the Emersonian understanding of moral self-reliance. Although Anderson's claims about Emerson have a great deal of power, Thoreau, in contrast, is plainly insisting that we cannot escape our society and our past. In *A Week*, Thoreau is not so much a disciple of Emerson as he is assuming the decidedly un-Emersonian role of an American Machiavelli. He is unafraid to look honestly at the terror and inhumanity of our political founding; he understands and conveys this terror clearly. But this does not lead him to a simple moral revulsion or paralysis or denial of the degree to which he too is implicated in this history. On the contrary, the point is made again and again that for better or worse, our collective fates are played out within the context of this founding drama: "Our fates at least are social. Our courses do not diverge; but as the web of destiny is woven it is fulled, and we are cast more and more into the centre."[65]

Consider Thoreau's use of the Hannah Dustan story as a climax of a historical process set in motion by the collision of incompatible societies. He is appalled by the events, but he also understands that they are the culmination of huge political conflicts that are greater than the individual players. It is instructive to contrast this analysis with Cotton Mather's simple praise of Dustan as a colonial heroine and with Nathaniel Hawthorne's shrieking condemnation of her when he calls her "this awful woman," "a raging tigress," and "a bloody old hag" because her victims were primarily children.[66] Thoreau's analysis is considerably more shrewd than either Mather's or Hawthorne's, and Thoreau resists the temptation of either of these simpler and much less satisfactory moral responses.

Thoreau's conclusions about our political interconnectedness are built on a hard-boiled and realistic political analysis combined with a notable moral subtlety. As we have seen, Thoreau believes that the forms of life represented by Indian and colonist are simply and irrevocably incompatible; the structure of each requires a mode of production and a social organization that make it impossible to accommodate the other. This argument is compelling, but more importantly, it illustrates the degree to which critics such as Diggins are mistaken when they accuse Thoreau of being "innocent of the nature of power, ignorant of the realities of social change, and indifferent at times to the spectacle of human suffering."[67] Much of the story Thoreau tells in *A Week* is an impersonal and terrible one in which individuals are swept up by the much greater flow and brutality of history. There is room for heroism and virtue within this story, but the hero's freedom is limited by the historical cards he or she has been dealt. Pasaconaway is forced by the superiority of colonial power to seek peace with the whites, but he is also a heroic, inspired, and wise leader of his people. Lovewell is a courageous soldier who rightly deserves our admiration for his martial heroism, but he is also a man twisted by the hatred engendered, nurtured, and inflamed by the struggle between white and Indian. Both these men are caught in a whirlwind of conflict, hatred, and violence that eventually spins out of control (as represented in the frantic and indiscriminate violence of the Dustan story). But both retain an essential human freedom and dignity within this struggle that they do not control. Far from having, in Bennett's phrase, an "aversion to thinking about power,"[68] Thoreau presents in A Week a meditation on the nature, extent, and limitations of such power. Thoreau's conclusions resist both a heroic denial of impersonal power and a fatalistic submission to it. Instead, he suggests a more sophisticated understanding of the possibilities and limitations of human freedom in the face of power.

Throughout his writings, Thoreau is committed to a view of human nature that transcends, in essential ways, the limitations of history. Thus, he is devoted to classical literature (as he argues in A Week, the Iliad is among the greatest books ever written),[69] and he firmly believes that truth, heroism, and virtue are universal attributes found in great individuals in all historical settings. But we also know, in light of the conflict between Indian and colonist, that different social orders produce significant, sometimes unbridgeable, gulfs between people.[70] Even when individuals are able to overcome cultural differences and experience each other as related and equal human beings, such as the friends Henry and Wawatam, it is not surprising that great social pressures sometimes intervene to pull them apart.[71] Despite such profound barriers, Thoreau succeeds in suggesting the common failures and virtues of the players in these stories. White set-tlers can be as vicious as "savages," and they frequently are (the only two episodes of scalping in A Week are performed by a white chaplain and by white women and a child). And just as there is an inclination toward evil in both communities, there is a common possibility for virtue. Thoreau insists on the heroic status of the Indian: Lovewell is not the only hero to live, like Moses, 120 years, and Pasaconaway is just as deserving of a monument as John Stark. Despite the differences between the white and Indian ways of life, the virtues of courage, loyalty, and humanity are recognizable as "natural," as containing essential qualities and potentials for members of both communities, the foundations of a universal humanity. "All men are children, and of one family. The same tale sends them all to bed, and wakes them in the morning."[72] Thoreau is committed to this overriding humanism and the moral freedom it implies, but in no way does this blind him to the power of culture and different modes of life and the complexities that cultural differences raise for his view.

Rejecting any historical determinism that would deny our freedom and thus our moral responsibility, and also rejecting an extreme Emersonian libertarianism that denies the realities of our history, Thoreau rightly promotes an understanding of our moral choice that is bounded and constrained by our social inheritance. In this context, Thoreau observes early in *A Week* that "conscience really does not, and ought not to monopolize the whole of our lives, any more than the heart or the head. It is as liable to disease as any other part."[73] This comment may be surprising to those who have looked for Thoreau's political ideas only in "Civil Disobedience," where conscience appears to hold a privileged and solitary authority.[74] But here Thoreau is well aware of the potential pitfalls of conscience, a radically individualized sensibility and will. An absolute and untempered appeal to conscience is just as dangerous as untempered appeals to love or reason, and any satisfactory morality will have to appeal to all three. The project of *A Week* is, in large part, to provide some of the knowledge we need to develop an appropriate moral relationship with our nation. Such a relationship must be based on a love that is not blind to the harsh realities of our history. It must be based on a reasonable evaluation of the possibilities available to us.[75] And we must not allow our consciences, in response to the evil we find in our own social—and personal—fabric, to prevent us from making a kind of peace with the world we are part of. "It is not worth the while to let our imperfections disturb us always."[76] This is not a call for moral blindness, fatalism, or disinterest. On the contrary, it is a call for a moral realism that nonetheless maintains a sharp and critical eye on the society around it. Thoreau's argument is a rejection of any simplistic moralism that appeals to only one side of our understanding, one way of knowing. Instead, he is promoting a morality that appeals to our reason, our conscience, and our love and that critically embraces the world despite its flaws.

A number of passages in *A Week* are similar to those found in Thoreau's more familiar political works. He alludes to his night in jail and says, "I do not wish, it happens, to be associated with Massachusetts, either in holding slaves or in conquering Mexico. I am a little better than herself in these respects."[77] He says that he loves mankind but hates the "institutions of the dead un-kind."[78] He satirizes a soldier that he and his brother pass while hiking: "Poor man! He actually shivered like a reed in his thin military pants, and by the time we had got up with him, all the sternness that becomes the soldier had forsaken his face, and he skulked past as if he were driving his father's sheep under a sword-proof helmet."[79] And, as noted earlier, he doubts the courage and heroism of his own generation, fearing that "generally speaking, the land is now . . . very barren of men."[80] All these comments are similar to those found in "Civil Disobedience" and elsewhere, but in the context of the rest of A Week, we are able to appreciate the degree to which they do not represent the simple moral arrogance of an antisocial egoist. Thoreau knows very well the limitations history places on us. But he also believes, as we have seen, that we are left a healthy space for moral freedom and action, and it is this freedom that he believes American citizens have abandoned. The soldiers he criticizes here and in "Civil Disobedience" are morally repugnant not because they are soldiers but because they are soldiers who appear to have no martial virtue.[81] Such virtue has limits and moral blindness, but it at least has moral courage and commitment. Likewise, the Indian and white men who struggled so terribly at the nation's founding were, for all their excesses, individuals who took their moral characters seriously, unlike the increasingly complacent contemporary state and society on which it is built. Thoreau wants us to be both appalled and inspired by the history he tells. Only then will we break the cycle of moral cowardice and lethargy from which he believes we suffer.[82]

In "Concord River," the first chapter of A Week, Thoreau says that along the banks of the Concord you will find "greater men than Homer, or Chaucer, or Shakespeare, only they never got time to say so; they never took to the way of writing."[83] The story he tells is both real and mythic, an attempt to capture in our American setting truths akin to those found in that greatest of books, the Iliad. Thoreau notes, "Our own country furnishes antiquities as ancient and durable, and as useful, as any."[84] A Week is written to inspire us to two heroic tasks: to face up to the truths of our past, and to recapture a moral inspiration from that past on which we can build the courage and commitment to reform our contemporary society. It is not that we should become modern Indian fighters; rather, we must discover the moral resolve that inspired the founders and direct this resolve toward combating current moral evils, such as slavery and imperialism. The problem facing our nation, Thoreau suggests, is not primarily moral error. On the contrary, it is moral fear and indifference.[85] Our Iliad, the founding that Thoreau presents, is an attack on what he sees as our moral deterioration. "The past is only so heroic as we see it."[86] Thoreau's "uncivil history," paradoxically, functions as both shocking revelation and moral inspiration.

Nancy Rosenblum claims that "Thoreau declared his country lost."[87] In reality, however, Thoreau is deeply involved in exploring what he sees as the possibilities before the nation. Far from abandoning hope, Thoreau is committed to considering the ways in which New England and all of America might be reformed to develop a more vigorous and respectable moral character. Thoreau's investigation of the real American founding in *A Week* is only a first step in a critical analysis of the American political community. In Thoreau's major mature writings, he continues to study what he understands to be America's shaping environments, precedents, and values, with the aim of encouraging and directing the growth of a more legitimate and admirable polity and reclaiming what he takes to be the promise of American political life.

## Notes

Originally published as Bob Pepperman Taylor, *America's Bachelor Uncle: Thoreau and the American Polity* (Lawrence: University Press of Kansas, 1996), chap. 2. Copyright 1996 by the University Press of Kansas. All rights reserved. Reprinted by permission. Minor changes have been made.

    1. Ralph Waldo Emerson, "Divinity School Address," in *Essays and Lectures*, ed. Joel Porte (New York: Library of America, 1983), 88.
    2. Ralph Waldo Emerson, "Literary Ethics," ibid., 101.
    3. Ralph Waldo Emerson, *Nature*, ibid., 48.
    4. Ralph Waldo Emerson, "Self-Reliance," ibid., 262.
    5. Henry David Thoreau, *Excursions*, ed. Joseph J. Moldenhauer (Princeton, NJ: Princeton University Press, 2007), 220.
    6. Henry D. Thoreau, *The Journal of Henry D. Thoreau*, ed. Bradford Torrey and Francis H. Allen (Boston: Houghton Mifflin, 1949), 9:208.
    7. Jane Bennett, *Thoreau's Nature* (Thousand Oaks, CA: Sage, 1994), 132.
    8. John Patrick Diggins, "Thoreau, Marx, and the 'Riddle' of Alienation," *Social Research* 39 (winter 1972): 581.
    9. C. Roland Wagner, "Lucky Fox at Walden," in *Thoreau in Our Season*, ed. John H. Hicks (Amherst: University of Massachusetts Press, 1967), 130–31.
    10. Walter Harding, *The Days of Henry Thoreau* (New York: Alfred A. Knopf, 1966), 253.

11. Henry S. Salt, *The Life of Henry David Thoreau,* ed. George Hendrick, Wilene Hendrick, and Fritz Oehlschlaeger (Urbana: University of Illinois Press, 1993), 68.

12. "*A Week* is his [Thoreau's] attempt to immerse himself in the river of time in order to recover from time his greatest loss." H. Daniel Peck, *Thoreau's Morning Work* (New Haven, CT: Yale University Press, 1990), 11. "The central concerns of *A Week* [are]—death and a brotherhood that transcends death." Linck C. Johnson, *Thoreau's Complex Weave* (Charlottesville: University Press of Virginia, 1986), 52. "The toughest, most disturbing problem with which Thoreau struggled to come to terms in *A Week*—frequently in an indirect, subterranean, unconscious manner—centered around the painful loss of his brother." Richard Lebeaux, *Thoreau's Seasons* (Amherst: University of Massachusetts Press, 1984), 4.

13. Robert D. Richardson, *Henry Thoreau* (Berkeley: University of California Press, 1986), 171.

14. Henry David Thoreau, *A Week on the Concord and Merrimack Rivers,* in *A Week on the Concord and Merrimack Rivers; Walden, or, Life in the Woods; The Maine Woods; Cape Cod* (New York: Library of America, 1985), 7.

15. Thoreau follows a similar strategy in his "Huckleberries" lecture when he argues for use of the Indian rather than the Latin names for huckleberries, out of respect for those who knew them first and best. "I think that it would be well if the Indian names, were as far as possible restored and applied to the numerous species of huckleberries, by our botanists—instead of the very inadequate—Greek and Latin or English ones at present used." Henry David Thoreau, *Huckleberries,* ed. Leo Stoller (Iowa City: Windhover Press of the University of Iowa and the New York Public Library, 1970), 5, 20.

16. "To an extinct race it was grass-ground, where they hunted and fished, and it is still perennial grass-ground to Concord farmers, who own the Great Meadows, and get the hay from year to year." Thoreau, *A Week,* 7.

17. Linck Johnson, one of the foremost students of Thoreau's composition of *A Week,* points out Thoreau's deepening interest in the conflict between Indian and colonist as the book evolves. Johnson, *Thoreau's Complex Weave,* 135.

18. Joan Burbick, *Thoreau's Alternative History* (Philadelphia: University of Pennsylvania Press, 1987), 33.

19. H. Daniel Peck writes, "He [Thoreau] is sensitive to the way in which the historical record, through self-serving distortion and omission, can destroy vital elements of the past. He feels this with special force in relation to the American settlers' treatment of the Indians" (*Thoreau's Morning Work,* 17).

20. Thoreau, *A Week,* 15.

21. Ibid.

22. Peck (*Thoreau's Morning Work*, 17) observes that Thoreau appears to be reluctant to cast off on this journey, and it is with some difficulty that he floats beyond the "familiar meadows" of Concord. This is not surprising, since the "unusual enterprise" on which he is embarking will take him far from the safe and comforting moral ground of the histories we tell in our everyday lives.

23. Thoreau, *A Week*, 16.

24. Ibid., 37.

25. Ibid., 41. Thoreau later notes that this "howling wilderness" was experienced quite differently by the native inhabitants: "the primeval forest . . . ; to the white man a drear and howling wilderness, but to the Indian a home, adapted to his nature, and cheerful as the smile of the Great Spirit" (264).

26. Ibid., 41.

27. Ibid., 42.

28. Ibid., 44.

29. As Peck writes, "lacking a written history of their own, the Indians have in effect fallen out of human memory" (*Thoreau's Morning Work*, 18).

30. Thoreau, *A Week*, 44.

31. Ibid., 46.

32. Ibid., 47.

33. William Cronon, *Changes in the Land: Indians, Colonists, and the Ecology of New England* (New York: Hill and Wang, 1983), 81. Cronon has much to say about the incompatibility of the European and Native American understandings of property, wealth, and production in this brilliant study; see especially chapter 4.

34. Thoreau, *Journal*, 1:445. Robert Sattelmeyer points out that while writing *A Week*, Thoreau "conceived of the Indians largely as a race either extinct or on its way to extirpation." Robert Sattelmeyer, *Thoreau's Reading* (Princeton, NJ: Princeton University Press, 1988), 102. Historian Robert Wiebe writes that it was common in the early nineteenth century for white Americans to think of the Indian as already vanished: "In the white mind's eye, which saw the future in the present, Native Americans slipped out of focus. 'Yet they have vanished from the face of the earth,' one eastern gentleman sighed as early as 1825, '—their very names are blotted from the pages of history.' Fated to die, dying, soon to die, already dead blurred into a single vision of Native American elimination not just as inevitable but as natural." Robert H. Wiebe, *Self-Rule* (Chicago: University of Chicago Press, 1995), 87. Thoreau certainly believed that the Indian stood very little chance against the onslaught of white society, but it is precisely the blotting of "their very names . . . from the pages of history" that he protests in this work.

35. Thoreau, *A Week*, 66–67.

36. Ibid., 68.

37. Ibid., 90.

38. In "Wednesday," ibid., 206.

39. It is interesting to note that Tyng's legacy fails to clarify the proper ownership of Wicasuck Island. Thoreau comments that as they sail by the island on their return down the river, a boatman asks them about it, explains that it is currently disputed property, and suspects that Thoreau and his brother have a claim upon it (A Week, 291). Apparently, the history of the island will not allow for an unambiguously just claim to it. As Thoreau observes in Cape Cod, "I know that if you hold a thing unjustly, there will surely be the devil to pay at last" (in A Week; Walden; Cape Cod, 878).

40. Thoreau, A Week, 96–97. See page 129 for a slightly different biographical sketch.

41. Ibid., 97.

42. A revisionist poet denies this abandonment and, as Thoreau says, "assigned him company in his last hours" (ibid., 98).

43. Thoreau, Journal, 12:124.

44. Thoreau, A Week, 99.

45. Ibid.

46. Ibid., 97.

47. Discussing the passage in "Civil Disobedience" in which Thoreau says he does "not wish to be regarded as a member of any incorporated society which I have not joined," Stanley Cavell makes the following observation: "The joke very quickly went sour. In particular, he could not name society or the government as such, because he knows he has somehow signed on." Even though Thoreau finds association with the government shameful, he nevertheless "recognizes that *he* is associated with it, that his withdrawal has not 'dissolved the Union' between ourselves and the state, and hence that he is disgraced. Apparently, as things stand, one cannot but choose to serve the state; so he will 'serve the state with [his conscience] also, and so necessarily resist it for the most part.'" Stanley Cavell, *The Senses of Walden* (San Francisco: North Point Press, 1981), 83–84.

48. Thoreau, A Week, 129.

49. Ibid.

50. Ibid., 130.

51. Ibid., 134–35.

52. Ibid., 136.

53. Ibid., 161; see also 179.

54. Ibid., 193.

55. Ibid., 206.

56. Thoreau also mentions open warfare between Penacooks and Mohawks; see ibid., 201.

57. Ibid., 206.

58. Ibid., 178–79.

59. Ibid., 224. Henry's story is quite extraordinary. As he tells it, he escaped death in a massacre of English by Chipeway Indians at Michilimackinac, partly through his own efforts and good luck, and partly through the efforts of his friend Wawatam. Henry says the Indians cooked and ate a broth made from their victims, which they believed would give them courage. After saving Henry, Wawatam eats, in Henry's presence, a bowl of human broth containing a hand and a large piece of flesh—from men Henry had just been held captive with. For a full account of this relationship, see Alexander Henry, *Travels and Adventures* (Rutland, VT: Charles E. Tuttle, 1969), 73–152.

60. Thoreau, *A Week*, 262–64.

61. Ibid., 290.

62. Ibid., 319.

63. Thoreau, *Journal*, 3:95.

64. Quentin Anderson, *Making Americans* (New York: Harcourt Brace and Jovanovich, 1992), 182, 230.

65. Thoreau, *A Week*, 215.

66. See Robert F. Sayre, *Thoreau and the American Indians* (Princeton, NJ: Princeton University Press, 1977), 52. Hawthorne tells the Dustan story in "The Dustan Family," first published in 1836 and reprinted in Nathaniel Hawthorne, *Hawthorne as Editor*, ed. Arlin Turner (Port Washington, NY: Kennikat Press, 1941), 131–37; see especially 136–37.

67. Diggins, "Thoreau, Marx, and the 'Riddle' of Alienation," 582.

68. Bennett, *Thoreau's Nature*, 89.

69. Thoreau, *A Week*, 75. The *Iliad* is the only book Thoreau keeps on his table at Walden. See Thoreau, *Walden*, in *A Week; Walden; Cape Cod*, 402.

70. Thoreau notes in his *Journal* (4:400) that Indians measure time by winters and moons, while whites measure summers and days, suggesting significant differences in the thought and experience of these two cultures.

71. Henry's account of his friendship with Wawatam suggests that even in this ideal relationship, seemingly sanctioned by the gods (the Great Spirit told Wawatam of Henry in a dream), there is a fair amount of room for ambiguity and inequality. For example, Henry notes that Wawatam assumed the roles of both brother and father to him. See Henry, *Travels and Adventures*, 73–76, 152. Thoreau is therefore well aware of both the possibilities for overcoming social barriers in discovering a common humanity and the complexities (even ignoring intrusions by other individuals or groups) of any such relationship.

72. Thoreau, *A Week*, 49. Consider this more negative formulation of the same idea that nature is an equalizer across cultures and history: "There might be seen here on the bank of the Merrimack, near Goff's Falls, in what is now the

town off Bedford, famous 'for hops and for its fine domestic manufactures,' some graves of the aborigines. The land still bears this scar here, and time is slowly crumbling the bones of a race. Yet, without fail, every spring, since they first fished and hunted here, the brown thrasher has heralded the morning from a birch or alder spray, and the undying race of reed-birds still rustles through the withering grass. But these bones rustle not. These mouldering elements are slowly preparing for another metamorphosis, to serve new masters, and what was the Indian's will erelong be the white man's sinew" (ibid., 193–94).

73. Ibid., 60.

74. "Must the citizen ever for a moment, or in the least degree, resign his conscience to the legislator? Why has every man a conscience, then? I think that we should be men first, and subjects afterward." Henry D. Thoreau, *Reform Papers*, ed. Wendell Glick (Princeton, NJ: Princeton University Press, 1973), 65.

75. Robert Sayre suggests that Thoreau's discussion of reformers, and how they annoy him so, is based on what he takes to be their ignorance of "the true state of things." (See *A Week*, 102–4, for Thoreau's comments.) At least part of their ignorance is of the "uncivil history" presented in this book, and its implications for meaningful reform. Sayre, *Thoreau and the American Indians*, 38.

76. Thoreau, *A Week*, 60.

77. Ibid., 105.

78. Ibid., 106.

79. Ibid., 256.

80. Ibid., 208.

81. "The mass of men serve the state thus, not as men mainly, but as machines, with their bodies. . . . In most cases there is no free exercise whatever of the judgment or of the moral sense; but they put themselves on a level with wood and earth and stones, and wooden men can perhaps be manufactured that will serve the purpose as well. Such command no more respect than men of straw, or a lump of dirt." Thoreau, "Civil Disobedience," in *Reform Papers*, 66.

82. "There is nothing to redeem the bigotry and moral cowardice of New-Englanders in my eyes." Thoreau, *Journal*, 11:326.

83. Thoreau, *A Week*, 9.

84. Ibid., 204.

85. "There are nine hundred and ninety-nine patrons of virtue to one virtuous man." Thoreau, "Civil Disobedience," 69.

86. Thoreau, *A Week*, 238.

87. Nancy L. Rosenblum, "Thoreau's Militant Conscience," *Political Theory* 9 (February 1981): 92.

CHAPTER 5

# Thoreau, Prophecy, and Politics

*George Shulman*

THE IMAGINATION AND practice of an "American nationhood" have
been tightly bound both to ideas of democracy and to white supremacy,
and political actors and theorists in American history have repeatedly used
prophetic language to retie, or try to untie, this knot. On the one hand,
racial domination and imperial power are still authorized in the name of
redeeming a chosen people from a corruption linked to "alien" ways. But
on the other hand, the great critical voices in American politics have used
prophetic language to transform prevalent racial practices and enlarge the
democratic imagination. My work treats prophecy as a distinctive genre of
political theory and as a language that is especially important in American
politics. This chapter examines the political dangers and resources of this
language by focusing on Henry Thoreau's practice of prophecy.

## Prophecy

To invoke *prophecy* is to face a problem of definition at the outset, for scholars argue about how to define *prophecy* or what marks a *prophet,* and different views of prophecy yield different views of its relationship to politics.
We can safely say that prophecy is a social practice that appears in many
cultures. Modern commentators link the practice to shamanism, ecstatic
vision, charismatic authority, political demagoguery, and social criticism
and depict prophets as those whose social role is to address a community by
mediating the larger realities that condition its existence and choices. But
prophecy is also a changeable and contested practice. After all, there was

profound conflict between those who worked for the royal house of Israel (call them "house prophets") and voiced a warrior god's unconditional support for it and those now canonized as *the* prophets, who voiced a god of justice that holds the monarchy and nation to account. People revise the practice of prophecy and argue about whose and which words to endow with (or to recognize as having) authority. Simon and Garfunkel sing "the words of the prophets are written on subway walls and tenement halls" to signal how prophecy still surrounds us, as we still count some voices while ignoring others—at our peril.

Rather than assert a fixed definition, I treat prophecy both as an "office" whose practice is open to revision and as a language whose meaning has been and can be resignified. In the Bible and since, it is the office assumed by those "called" as *messengers* who announce, as *witnesses* who testify, as *watchmen* who forewarn to forestall, as *singers* who lament. In each regard, prophecy mediates between a community and powerful realities it does not understand or control; in each regard, prophets make claims about the difficulties and fateful decisions of a community they address and seek to *redeem*. European and American romantics (from Blake and Shelley to Emerson and Whitman) thus enact a kind of secularization as they place "the poet" in the office of the prophet as one who announces, bears witness, warns, and redeems. But in cultures bearing biblical traces, *prophecy* also names a literary and political *genre* of speech, with characteristic—but not fixed—narrative forms and tropes, cadences of speech, registers of voice. William Blake, Friedrich Nietzsche, and American literary artists and social critics—from Frederick Douglass and Henry Thoreau to Allen Ginsberg, Martin Luther King, and James Baldwin—thus take on and revise not only an office but also a genre.[1]

What characterizes this genre? The substance of biblical prophecy is criticism of idolatry, social injustice, and monarchical power, but as a genre, prophecy tells a story about a chosen people who stray from their founding covenant and first principles, which once redeemed them from captivity in Egypt. Prophets thus seek what they call a *turn*, translated as *repentance*, by which Hebrews can *reconstitute* themselves as a community. The genre inaugurates profoundly resonant tropes of captivity, founding, and corruption, of covenant and marriage, of fidelity, adultery, and recommitment, of repentance and purifying rebirth. In these terms, prophets (from Amos, Micah, and Hosea to Isaiah, Jeremiah, and then Jesus) frame and narrate the fateful choices that constitute, endanger, and redeem the community they at once invoke and reenvision. From the perspective of political theory, biblical prophecy addresses the character and fate of the whole, as well as the constitutive power of choice and action. As Martin Buber argues, before exile to Babylon, prophets do not "decree a fate" but "demand a decision" concerning the commitments and practices that constitute community. Their critique of "idolatry," indeed, is that the worship of other gods is linked to imperial power, state centralization, priestly rule, and gross social inequality, whereas a people ruled only by god establish relations of relative social equality and nonrule amongst themselves. Idolatry is a political regime, not a philosophical mistake, and obeying god is not ritualized worship but attending to justice and resisting idolatry. Biblical prophecy thus stands in profound tension with the state, "religion," and law; in contrast to these reified forms of worldly authority, prophecy enjoins what Weber calls "the ethical righteousness of the deed."[2]

But the centrality of god's sovereign authority, and hostility to other countervailing attachments, also entitles Carl Schmitt to draw from prophecy the idea that "decision" is the constitutively political act, by defining both the sovereign and the enemy. The biblical genre thus bears a vexed relation to democratic politics: its populist and antinomian registers of voice are democratic resources, but dangerous, because prophecy lacks an Aristotelian dimension, an explicit valuation of ongoing political life. After all, biblical prophets invoke god's authority to provoke contest about pervasive practices long deemed legitimate, not to defend a pluralism of valid truths and worthy goods.

## Prophecy in America

We can see this danger as American elites recurrently use prophetic language to sacralize liberal origins, justify racial domination, and authorize imperial expansion. From the center, not the margins, prophecy voices the national or communitarian face of liberalism, linking the redemption of a special American promise to a politics that purifies the social body of impulses, practices, and peoples signifying corruption. For Sacvan Bercovitch, the problem with prophecy exceeds the exclusion it justifies, for the "jeremiad" is a "prescribed ritual form" that "contains" social criticism by always orienting it toward origins it continually reauthorizes. As jeremiads voice criticism in the name of founding values a people betray, critics enact

a "ritual of consensus" that only replenishes the hegemony of liberal principles and a national frame for politics: "The dream that inspired them to
defy the false Americanism of their time compelled them to speak their
defiance as keepers of the dream." For Bercovitch, Americans can confront
the limits of liberalism and nationalism on democratic possibility only by
*relinquishing* prophecy, to accept themselves as a profane nation among
others, fated to politics.[3]

Bercovitch rightly recognizes the hegemonic weight of prophetic language as it is often used, but he inadvertently repeats the very containment
he denounces. As I argue here, Thoreau is one of several American critics
who use prophecy in counterhegemonic ways. They attack white supremacy
and the idea of race as an idolatrous system, and in relation to it, they are no
more pluralist than biblical prophets; at issue for them is complicity in domination, not openness to difference. Seeing that liberal freedom is founded
by a racial state of exception, and seeking to end it, these critics repeatedly
draw on prophecy to voice aspects of politics occluded by a focus on rights,
procedures, deliberation, or plurality. Forging a critical relationship toward
the liberal axioms, national frame, and origin story dominating American
politics, they use prophecy to advance an agonal, not a communitarian or
consensual, view of politics and on behalf of democratic projects. Still, does
the prophetic genre preclude advancing claims in a *political* way?[4]

This is not only a theoretical or a historical question: as prophetic language joins Thoreau's abolitionist civil disobedience to his later embrace of
John Brown's violence, so evangelical Christianity and post-9/11 crusades
against terror turn political theorists away from "prophecy" to reaffirm
liberal constitutionalism, varieties of pluralism, norms of deliberation, and
the sanctity of private rights. Yet these genres of political theory always fail
to address white supremacy or imperial violence, which recurrently compel
critics toward prophecy as a genre, despite its risks. In the current crisis in
the American Republic, then, might counterprophecy be needful, despite
being dangerous? With this question in mind, I turn to Thoreau's practice
of prophecy.

## Thoreau and Prophecy

To link Thoreau and prophecy to politics goes against the grain of Thoreau
scholarship. Thoreau himself asserts his overt hostility "to what is called

politics," as he puts it. His anti-slavery lectures seem to invoke god and conscience to juxtapose "moral" (i.e., principled) and "political" (i.e., expedient) responses to injustice. Likewise, *Walden* seems to respond to social imprisonment by devaluing political action for the sake of personal rebirth in nature and poetic apprehension of reality. As he moves from conscientious personal resistance to escape into nature, and then to glorification of John Brown's self-sacrificing violence, he seems trapped between withdrawal from and solitary action to redeem a social world he always sees as essentially corrupt. His synergy of the moral and the aesthetic seems to underwrite a masculinized individualism and anti-politics that signal not nonconformity but hegemonic liberalism.[5]

In my alternative reading, Thoreau is hostile to "what is *called* politics" because being political, in the terms and channels provided by his regime, makes him an agent of slavery and imperial expansion. He is haunted by these "facts," as he calls them, outraged that enfranchised men deny them, and worried about the "penalty" of domination and its disavowal. Denouncing complicity in this slaveholding and imperial regime, he seeks to reconstitute it. He "speaks practically and as a citizen" in "Civil Disobedience" and addresses *Walden* to his "neighbors," because he must believe, even as he despairs of believing, that a "wise minority" can serve a political role. What is that role?

My first claim is that Thoreau takes up and revises the idea that prophecy is the office of those who announce, bear witness, and warn, to address and incite the constitutive and fateful choices of a community they "serve" by their opposition. He uses prophetic tropes to announce "the facts" of injustice—of constitutive exclusion—that "those bred in the school of politics" disavow, and to warn of and forestall the (self) destructive consequences of this conduct. He thus speaks as a witness: partly, he says what he sees and stands against it; partly, he testifies to capacities for judgment and action he calls "action from principle" to show people they can act otherwise; and partly, he bears witness to the faith by which he cultivates the agency he models. Taking up the calling of one who announces, bears witness, and warns, he engages a political life he maligns but also dreams of transforming.

My second claim is that he crafts two registers of expression to perform a prophetic office: each bears witness against captivity by demonstrating a contrary practice of life, but the anti-slavery lectures bespeak Puritan (and liberal) idioms of conscience and rights in a jeremiadic form, while *Walden* bespeaks a romantic idiom of rebirth by experiments in nature. Thoreau's speech and action thus reflect his investment in but also struggle with a Protestant language that Kierkegaard calls a "religion for adult men."[6] Surely Thoreau's anti-slavery lectures signal his indebtedness to a tradition— from Luther and Calvin to abolitionism, Eugene Debs, and Martin Luther King Jr.—that entails a gendered language of theistic authority, moral autonomy, and personal conscience, of calling, service, and redemption. Joining personal identity and collective purpose, this idiom argues that we always serve authority; it depicts captivity and freedom in terms of which authority we choose to orient by, and it links individual conversion to collective redemption. Yet as *Walden* links Protestantism to worldly asceticism, "the slavedriver within," resentment, and racism, so his experiment in nature seeks antidotes in nontheistic practices of poetic imagination. But how do these registers of prophecy engage the illiberal exclusions that enable liberal politics? How do they relate to one another? And does Thoreau's prophetic practice malign (in moral and aesthetic terms) the impure actuality of politics?[7]

## Thoreau's Anti-Slavery Jeremiads

"Civil Disobedience" and "Slavery in Massachusetts" frame in time the political context of *Walden* and reveal the Protestant register of prophecy with which that text struggles. Both lectures are organized by prophetic questions: By what authority is our action oriented, and what purposes does it serve? With whom do we identify, and on what basis? What constitutes the redemption that can deliver us from captivity, atone for our crimes, and make good on our founding promises? Both lectures manifest a prophetic presumption that Thoreau's peers need to be alerted and aroused. At their core is the claim that "they who have been bred in the school of politics fail now and always to face the facts."[8] What facts?

First, the United States is an ex-colonial and formally democratic but slaveholding and imperial republic. Second, enfranchised northern men support chattel slavery and war: "Practically speaking, the opponents to a reform in Massachusetts are not a hundred thousand politicians at the South, but a hundred thousand merchants and farmers here . . . I quarrel not with far-off foes, but with those who, near at home" sustain a slave system.[9] Third, those who are "*in opinion* opposed to slavery and to the war" are led by "undue respect" for the authority of majorities and constitutional law to become the "most conscientious supporters" of the regime and the "most serious obstacles to reform" ("Civil Disobedience," 69, 65, 72). Since slavery and war are democratically authorized and protected by the authority of constitutionalism, he bears witness to a fourth fact: "Whatever the human law may be, neither an individual nor a nation can ever commit the least injustice against the obscurest individual without having to pay a penalty for it" ("Slavery," 96). Those who "disapprove of the character and measures of a government" but "yield to it their allegiance" pay the "penalty" of another kind of servitude:

> The mass of men serve the state . . . not as men mainly, but as machines, with their bodies. They are the standing army, and the militia, jailers, constables. . . . In most cases there is no free exercise of the judgment or of moral sense; but they put themselves on a level with wood and earth and stones. . . . Yet such as these even are commonly esteemed good citizens. Others, as most legislators, politicians, lawyers, ministers, and office holders, serve the State chiefly with their heads; and, as they rarely make any moral distinctions, they are as likely to serve the devil, without intending it, as God. A very few, as heroes, patriots, martyrs, reformers in the great sense . . . serve the State with their consciences also, and so necessarily resist it for the most part; and they are commonly treated by it as enemies. ("Civil Disobedience," 72, 66)

What is commonly esteemed good citizenship is a conscientious reification by which people subordinate the "free exercise of judgment" and become thoughtless bodies. In Puritan terms, citizenship severed from "the moral sense" is a covenant of works, a diabolical "outward service" by which people would save but in fact lose their souls. Politically, a "common and natural result of undue respect for law" is a mass of men marching "to the wars against their wills, aye, against their common sense and consciences" ("Civil Disobedience," 65). In 1854, undue respect means that people invest authority in judges, not in themselves as citizens exercising judgment and acting in concert. They judge according to precedent rather than "establish a precedent for the future" ("Slavery," 97): "It is to some extent fatal to the courts, when the people are compelled to go behind them . . . but think of leaving to it any court . . . to decide whether more than three millions of people, in this case, a sixth part of the nation, have the right to be freemen or not! ("Slavery," 97–98).

Thoreau seeks a political not a legal decision: "I would much rather trust to the sentiment of the people" ("Slavery," 97). He seeks political dialogue and decision in public meetings he calls "a true congress" ("Slavery," 99), but majority rule remains an issue because it displaces responsibility: "When the majority shall at length vote for the abolition of slavery, it will be because they are indifferent to slavery, or because there is little slavery left to be abolished by their vote. They will then be the only slaves" ("Civil Disobedience," 70). To defer in time means to abdicate now: "If the majority vote the devil to be God, the minority will . . . obey the successful candidate, trusting that some time . . . they may reinstate God." Serving that majority, the minority become "tools" rather than "men" ("Slavery," 103).

To resist the servitude he attributes to undue respect for the authority of legal precedent, majority rule, and representative government, Thoreau invokes the authority his culture claims to lodge in god, conscience, and equality as a principle, as well as in the idea of active and embodied consent. His purpose is to unsettle—not simply reject—liberal constitutionalism and the broader filiopiety it bespeaks. That is why he goes after Daniel Webster, who does not ask what "it behooves a man to do here in America to-day with regard to slavery" but accepts it as "part of the original compact"; he cannot say the compact is itself "the evil" because he is "not a leader but a follower. His leaders are the men of '87" ("Civil Disobedience," 88, 74, 87). But "all men are partially buried in the grave of custom, and of some we see only the crown of the head above ground. Better are the physically dead, for they more lively rot."[10]

In prophetic terms, Thoreau announces the captivity citizens impose on others, and he bears witness to its "penalty," the political entombment they impose on themselves. He names the servitude he attributes to idolatry (or conscientious reification) as "undue respect," but he also bears witness to the capacity for choice and action that might (re)animate deadened men and an entombed social body. This rebirth enacts an alternative filiopiety that goes behind the compact and fathers of 1787 to revolutionary fathers and to Puritans cast as rebels, not founders.

He invokes and demonstrates the idea of active and embodied consent, which he links to making, not following, precedent. But since consent has authorized war and slavery, his return to origins also emphasizes a faculty of judgment he calls both a "moral sense" and a constitution "written in your being" by god ("Slavery," 103). A capacity to judge inheres in human beings and enables people to resist the constitution written by subjection to worldly authorities. To obey our "divine" constitution is to utter "sentences" that both name and "sentence" any "enactment or custom of men" ("Slavery," 98). Citizens must perform this office if they are not to become mechanical or inanimate. "But just in proportion as I regard this as not wholly a brute force, but partly a human force . . . I see that appeal is possible, first and instantaneously, from them to the Maker of them, and secondly, from them to themselves" ("Civil Disobedience," 85). He denaturalizes the reification that makes relations among men become (like) relations among (brute and inanimate) things. In turn, to enact "the moral sense" is to exemplify "action from principle": "The perception and performance of right,—changes things and relations; it is essentially revolutionary, and does not consist wholly with anything which was. It not only divides states and churches, it divides families; aye, it divides the individual, separating the diabolical in him from the divine" ("Civil Disobedience," 72).[11]

As "all change for the better, like birth and death . . . convulse[s] the body," so "the perception and performance of right" signifies the rebirth of adults and revolution in the social bodies they constitute ("Civil Disobedience," 74, 72). Thoreau thus claims, paradoxically, to renew a cultural legacy, for he also appeals to men as bearers of a specific history in which theist faith, personal conscience, and political consent are avowedly linked to liberty. If self-declared sons emulate the creativity and initiative of Puritan and revolutionary fathers, they can re-member the judgment and action severed by constitutional piety, regenerate their own authority, and create rather than repeat precedent. Thoreau begins with himself as a minority of one, but his point is to create "corporation[s] of conscientious men" whose embodied action is a "counter friction" to the machinery of power. Such associations can be instrumentally effective: a "minority is powerless while it conforms to the majority" but "irresistible when it clogs [the machine] by its whole weight" ("Civil Disobedience," 65, 74, 76).[12]

We should name the danger in these arguments. It is not that Thoreau speaks a "moral" language to condemn slavery, for no self-evident political action follows from the claim that slavery is "wrong," as the difference between Lincoln and abolitionists attests. The question is how he conceives and practices his notion of "the right." One obvious danger is his splitting of the subject into brute-diabolical or manly-divine aspects: by this masculinized individualism, "moral sense" names a pure "inside" threatened by contamination from culture "outside" it, and a higher authority threatened by lower passions related to material interest or expediency. Just as putting anything higher than this authority is to be unmanned, made a brute or slave, so obeying it redeems the human from the death-in-life of "life without principle." By this idealized image of integral moral agency, Thoreau would overcome his own sense of weakness and address the docility of his peers, but only after misconceiving interdependence and making "what is political" wholly ignoble. So he fumes, "We are not a religious people, but we are a nation of politicians" ("Slavery," 99). Hannah Arendt thus sees him protecting the purity of self and principle, not the worldly freedom of citizens; to Lincoln, such abolitionism takes no account of historical circumstance or of a plurality of opinions and interests that requires "politicians" (or people in their capacity as citizens) to accept impurity because they must *build* consensus. The result of investing in (moral) purity is monologue and violence.[13]

But Thoreau claims to "speak practically and as a citizen" at the outset of "Civil Disobedience." He believes he is making a political argument when he declares that "this people must cease to hold slaves, and to make war on Mexico, though it cost them their existence as a people," for grievous injustice imposes great costs and risks ("Civil Disobedience," 64, 68). To those who fear that an anti-slavery politics invoking "the right" will ignite violence, he says, "But even suppose blood should flow. Is there not a sort of blood shed when the conscience is wounded? Through this wound a man's real manhood and immortality flow out, and he bleeds to an everlasting death. I see this blood flowing now" ("Civil Disobedience," 77). Thoreau worries about spiritual death by self-betrayal and passivity; rectifying injustice means risking mortal life and a mortal national existence. As Baldwin later reckons "the price of the ticket,"[14] Thoreau warns that the "cost" of freedom *is* profound conflict if people do not agree about fundamental ideals or how to practice them. To dismiss conscientious politics because it risks violence is to enshrine the order founded by the last act of violence.

He can be said to speak as a citizen because he addresses neighbors who "in opinion" are opposed to slavery: what can be done now? He calls for "minority action" immediately because slavery is an egregious injustice and because its nationalization jeopardizes the freedom of northern citizens. Indeed, their guilty passivity is a political fact his action must address: he shows that they bear conflicting loyalties (to majority rule and conscience, for example) that cannot be reconciled but must be ranked; only a different ranking of authority will enable them to end both the wrong and the passivity they sustain. By demonstrating his own ranking, he politicizes the issue of authority at the center of prophecy and politics, and he displays the judgment and minority action that, he claims, can make a worldly difference.

"Unjust laws exist: shall we be content to obey them, or shall we endeavor to amend them, and obey them until we have succeeded, or shall we transgress them at once?" ("Civil Disobedience," 72–73). In most cases he agrees with Lincoln that we should follow constitutional procedure and electoral politics, but he depicts a crisis, a state of exception, and calls for a decision. Men can "serve the devil, without intending it, as God," and "obstinacy" is a danger, but he remains committed to "the perception and performance of right" by "corporations with a conscience" ("Civil Disobedience," 84, 72, 65). As Arendt recognizes in Tocqueville but not Thoreau, "association" transforms conscience into public opinion and action oriented toward world building.[15] Addressing what action would be effective when the majority does not oppose slavery, Thoreau himself is trying to shift a northern consensus about what is right and what is practical.

He does not call "action from principle" political, but it addresses injustice, calculates the costs of loyalty to conflicting authorities, takes (and demands) responsibility for the consequence of private as well as public actions, and, by provoking neighbors to self-reflection and speech, both invites solidarity to create power and clears a space for dialogue where none had been. In Puritan terms, he is refusing (not endorsing) the separation of grace and works. Rooting the moral sense in a body acting in social space and historical time, he demands the personal responsibility whose absence makes covenants the tomb of spirit, not its worldly testament. Call this a 1960s reading of Thoreau, whose joining of moral witness, personal autonomy, and embodied action made him an exemplar at a moment when imperial war and racial apartheid also compelled critics and citizens to relocate action in concert outside "what is called politics." In the shadow of Max Weber, who cast constitutionalism and popular sovereignty as ideologies that authorize violent and bureaucratic regimes, we should not so hastily dismiss Thoreau's effort to embody antinomian critique in a beloved community.[16]

Conflict about the 1960s still fuels arguments about Thoreau. Is the problem the regime he faces, or his unrealistic expectations, his moralistic anger at neighbors who must fail him, and thus his self-imposed marginality? Rather than inventing expectations and imposing them on others, I think, he affirms expectations they already profess as public truths. Rather than making neighbors abject or guilty, he politicizes a despair they already voice in private. Rather than showing inappropriate anger at a world that has failed him, perhaps he is right to be enraged about slavery and complicity in it, even as he binds his anger by faith in human capacities for judgment and action.

His voice is strident, and since he is holding others to account, they feel defensive; they accuse him of lacking the authority to judge them or unmask what seems to be his claim to a superior moral position. But his judgments are those of a peer and a witness, not a father. He does not invent the facts he laments, the standards he invokes, or the cross they constitute; he does intensify the contradiction others live, but only to show its penalty and how to resist it. He creates rhetorical distance, but he speaks words that are "common" in the sense of ordinary and shared, and he uses an everyday encounter with a tax collector to open and symbolize dialogue about personal and political responsibility.

Peter Euben's view of Socrates is apt here: "By chastening fellow citizens for not living up to their own ideals, while subjecting those ideals to critique and reinterpretation," he would "reestablish the conditions of political deliberation and moral discourse." If Thoreau's political practice is to bear witness—against injustice and to the generative power of action from principle, against what Stanley Cavell calls "conspiracies of silence" and to the transfiguring power of speech—his authority partly rests on his ability to honor the meaning of his words in his action, but it rests finally with those he calls neighbors and fellow citizens, who may not recognize themselves or their situation, language, or capacities in his testimony.[17]

He thus suffers the pathos of every prophetic witness: he stands here and can do no other, but he also must endure the freedom of those he addresses, who coauthor a fate he cannot control and from which he is not exempt. "If I could convince myself that I have any right to be satisfied with men as they are, and to treat them accordingly, and not according, in some respects, to my requisitions and expectations of what they and I ought to be, then . . . I should endeavor to be satisfied with things as they are and say it is the will of God" ("Civil Disobedience," 85).[18] In some respects, *Walden* is the effort to become "satisfied with things as they are." It offers the "highest" perspective by which to resist the self-loathing, rage, and despair that Thoreau links to the office of prophecy in an unjust world.

## *Walden* and Prophecy

Drawing on the cultural idiom of militant Protestantism, Thoreau's anti-slavery lectures radicalize jeremiadic dissent; he openly risks "the nation" to contest the slavery that has constituted American freedom. He does not philosophically justify his critique of slaveholding liberalism but cultivates resistance to it by his example. Invoking origins both in racial violence and in the "action from principle" he calls "essentially revolutionary," he depicts "freer and less desponding spirits" forging political bonds on "the more free and honorable ground" of the jail, standing with Mexicans, Indians, and fugitive slaves against the state ("Civil Disobedience," 72, 76). The difference between his abolitionist prophecy and *Walden,* then, is not that he turns from militancy and jail to nature. Rather, he develops a different register of cultivation to resist white supremacy and despairing docility among the enfranchised.[19]

Partly, Thoreau believes his 1846 act of resistance and his 1848 lecture about it failed to foster neighbors who link citizenship to resistance rather than to subjection. Still committed to this goal, he takes up but revises the poetry of regeneration in nature that has justified liberal nationalism. His experiment in cultivation and myth-making is readily—but mistakenly—seen as escaping from or merely mirroring the political world, as if he replenishes (not confronts) the imperial poetry of nature's nation, to repeat (not overcome) its devaluation of political bonds. Indeed, his textual experiment is a parable of reconstituting citizens and community by redoing a history he depicts as a violent and self-destructive failure. Yet his *Walden* persona also revises the abolitionist register of his anti-slavery voice. Moving from judgment of the world to participation in its creation through acts of poetic imagination, he seeks a supplement and antidote to prophecy as militant judgment, even while giving poesis a prophetic meaning.

Cavell's *The Senses of Walden* persuasively shows Thoreau engaging rather than fleeing society and politics. To work through the "key words" in his culture—cost, spending, accounts, earning, consenting, choosing, civilized, savage, wild—he also assesses the practices in which they gain their meanings. Cavell's Thoreau thereby redoes biblical prophecy in a nontheistic way: he shifts from the authority of god to the authority of language but still tells a story of voluntary imprisonment, self-betrayal, and despair overcome by mourning our losses and recommitting to our words and to one another.[20]

That story begins with "the outward condition" of those "said to live in New England."[21] Thoreau depicts those circumstances as created by their labors, which he casts as a form of slavery: "It is hard to have a southern overseer; it is worse to have a northern one; but worst of all is when you are the slave-driver of yourself" (*Walden*, 7). Making Protestant conscience the link between worldly slavery and worldly asceticism, Thoreau depicts his peers' labors as self-mortifying forms of "penance," sacrificial rituals that promise redemption but divide the self and entomb it in a world of deadened things (*Walden*, 4). Addressing a nation haunted by specters of enslavement, he bears witness against captivities his peers do not count as real or name as experience. Giving voice to the "quiet desperation" of those who believe they are trapped, who live by "fate" because they do not live by "faith," he also bears witness to their capacity to live otherwise (*Walden*, 8, 5, 9). Thoreau uses the example of building a house and growing beans to model other ways to "labor" and to "spend" their lives (*Walden*, 5–7). The beans signify how "men," rather than "tobacco, slaves and operatives," could be what they cultivate, the "staple production" of their labors; the house signifies rebuilding community as a dwelling and remaking citizens to inhabit it ("Life," 176–77).

The question of authority remains crucial in this parable of refounding: What and whom do we endow with authority? How did Thoreau gain the sense of authority by which he now speaks? On the assumption that already formed adults require estrangement from convention to achieve their own authority, he positions himself at a rhetorical distance from those he calls his neighbors. But the sense of authority that makes him a stranger in relation to these neighbors, and a "sojourner" in relation to what they call civilization, is achieved only by "fronting"—naming and assessing—the legacy and language, assumptions, practices, and stories he shares with them (*Walden*, 3, 90). Narrating his own experiment in judging what to affirm and reject from the legacy his neighbors also inherit and take inside, he confronts not only their criteria for making such decisions, not only their key words and practices, but also ingrained dispositions of despair or faith that project a world that is fated or open to possibility.

His story of a personal "accounting" is thus a *political* parable of coming to terms with their "constitution," to clear "more free and honorable ground" and dispositions for acting otherwise (*Walden,* 91, 73; "Civil Disobedience," 76). But how and why does Thoreau use an idea of *poetry* to revise the register of voice in his anti-slavery lectures? Surely, his epigraph shows him assuming a prophetic public office: "I do not mean to write an ode to dejection, but to brag as lustily as chanticleer in the morning, if only to wake my neighbors up." But why take on the persona of chanticleer, and to what purpose would he awaken his neighbors?

For Thoreau, the cockerel signals his poetic transformation of prophecy. Prophets say what they see and stand against it by inhabiting, albeit never fully, a persona or office from which they utter divine sentences they do not author but make their own. In contrast, Thoreau emphasizes the experiential, imaginative, and formative elements in language: abolitionist witnessing becomes a poesis that recognizes the constitutive power of imagination to "instill and drench" reality with meaning. Rejecting the plain speech of Protestant literalism, he embraces the multivocality and "obscurity" of what he calls "extra-vagant" language, while depicting a universe that answers our conceptions (*Walden,* 324–25). By crafting his prophetic persona as a cockerel, he also shifts from the "dejection" he associates with sin, judgment, and repentance to an arousal and natality he associates with dawn, which signals his faith that possibility is wired into (human) nature (*Walden,* 84).

> The note of this once wild Indian pheasant is certainly the most remarkable of any bird's, and if they could be naturalized without being domesticated, it would soon become the most famous sound in our woods, surpassing the clangor of the goose and the hooting of the owl. . . . [To] hear the wild cockerels crow . . . drowning the feebler notes of the other birds,—think of it! It would put the nations on the alert. Who would not . . . rise earlier and earlier every successive day of his life, till he became unspeakably healthy, wealthy, and wise? This foreign bird's note is celebrated by the poets of all countries along with the notes of their native songsters. All climates agree with brave Chanticleer. He is more indigenous even than the natives. His health is ever good . . . his spirits never flag. (*Walden,* 184)

Here Thoreau links prophecy to poetry in a song that puts nations on alert, even as he plays with the ways such singers are both "native" and "foreign" to those they address. He contrasts cockerels to owls—the voice of philosophy

—whose wisdom is melancholy because belated and retrospective and whose "Oh-*o-o-o-o that I had never been born!*" speaks the despairing lament of Silenus. "I rejoice that there are owls" to voice "the stark twilight and unsatisfied thoughts that all men have," he states, but *he* imitates the cockerel, who acclaims "expectation of the dawn" (*Walden,* 124–25, 90).

> There is something suggested by [the cockerel] that is a newer testament—the gospel according to this moment, a brag for all the world, healthiness as a spring burst forth. The merit of this bird's strain is its freedom from all plaintiveness . . . when I hear a cockerel crow . . . I think to myself, there is one of us well, at any rate, and with a sudden gush return to my senses.[22]

To what reality does the cockerel awaken us? By announcing dawn he declares the passing of time, which means irreversible loss as each moment passes, and our life with it. To awake to time is to "return to my senses," to the impressionable and willful particularity Philip Roth calls "human stain,"[23] and so to the carnal separateness that makes us at once strangers and "kindred" (*Walden,* 62, 3). Since only by acknowledging this separateness can others be(come) real to us, the cockerel awakens us from utter loneliness (because no reality is outside) to the reality of others and our shared life in language. Thoreau imagines "words addressed to our condition exactly, which, if we could really hear and understand, would be more salutary than the morning or spring to our lives," because the cockerel's announcement of passing time includes not only loss but also dawn, symbolizing capacities in (human) nature to awaken and begin anew (*Walden,* 107). Since "morning is when I am awake and there is a dawn in me," and "to be awake is to be alive," so "moral reform is the effort to throw off sleep" (*Walden,* 90). To say "the present was my next experiment" is to experiment in becoming present to, or acknowledging, realities we have disavowed (*Walden,* 84).[24]

If you do not live in time, you are "said to live." And if you are not in your acts and in your body, where are you? Like any prophet, Thoreau begins with loss and makes us wretched, provoking grief, eliciting mourning, but to enable change: "Our moulting season, like that of the fowls, must be a crisis in our lives. The loon retires to solitary ponds to spend it. Thus also the snake casts its slough, and the caterpillar its wormy coat, by an internal industry and expansion" (*Walden,* 24). Shedding an old skin is partly the internal industry of counting as real what we have forgone, wasted, or disavowed. But mourning brings morning, renewed (faith in) capacity to change. "We must learn to reawaken and keep ourselves awake . . . by an infinite expectation of the dawn," for one "who does not believe that each day contains an earlier, more sacred, and auroral hour than he has yet profaned, has despaired of life" (*Walden,* 90, 89).

Thoreau is personally invested in the persona of the cockerel, but he also insists on the political importance of a prophecy without plaintiveness, because he links freedom to dawn, not to dusk. Unlike prior "prophets and redeemers," whose "cast-off griefs" consoled only our fears, he trumpets "a simple and irrepressible satisfaction with the gift of life," as symbolized by the dawn (*Walden,* 78, 77). By the image of the cockerel he identifies newness and possibility with potency and generativity, "bragging lustily" about the gifts he bears. "It is not by compromise, it is not by a timid and feeble repentance that a man will save his soul and *live* at last. He must *conquer* a clear field, letting Repentance & Co. go."[25] Indeed, "the greater part of what my neighbors call good I believe in my soul to be bad, and if I repent of any thing it is very likely to be my good behavior" (*Walden,* 10). He thus "reverences" what he calls "the wild" as well as "the good," suggesting a necessary tension between morality and life (*Walden,* 210).[26]

Thoreau's narrator identifies with the cockerel to overcome (his own) melancholy, envy, propriety, and despair. He crafts a persona:

> If I seem to boast more than is becoming, my excuse is that I brag for humanity rather than for myself; and my shortcomings and inconsistencies do not affect the truth of my statement. Notwithstanding much cant and hypocrisy . . . for which I am sorry as any man . . . I am resolved that I will not through humility become the devil's attorney. (*Walden,* 49–50)

He rhetorically distances himself from dejection and resentment to confront and relinquish them, not to enact or rationalize them. But like his prophetic forebears, he deploys appearances in a rhetorical project with political purposes: to demonstrate the "faith" by which people must live if they are to be(come) free.[27]

Accordingly, the prophetic poet declares the dawn not just anywhere but to a specific political community whose self-declared errand into the wilderness has promised freedom while producing slavery and violent dispossession of native peoples. How can he not compose an ode to dejection? If he awakens his neighbors to this history and, like biblical forebears, insists that it be remembered, not forgotten or disavowed, to what possibilities does he awaken them? Whereas Cavell's prophetic Thoreau refounds the conditions of language as such, by "returning" people to the authority not of god but of ordinary language, my Thoreau "roots" this project in "native" ground, an American ordinary of racialized violence and national myths about wild(er)ness.

Identifying his voice with a "once wild Indian pheasant" called chanticleer, he uses the myth of wilderness to critically restage how declarations of independence have juxtaposed god and nature, civilized and savage, native and foreign, (European) heir and (nonwhite) outcast, domesticated settlement and untamed wildness. His experiment does not occur in private or by finding a prediscursive nature but through the language he shares with those he calls his neighbors. He proceeds not alone but in the company of Puritans, savages, and fugitive slaves he recovers in the woods; they haunt his neighbors but "people" his solitude and inspire his perspective on the purposes and labors by which his neighbors "are said to live." By using the office of the poet to retell the stories his neighbors tell themselves about themselves, he at once revises prophecy and aspires to make what Norman Mailer calls "a myth sufficiently true to offer a life adequately large."[28]

On the one hand, he redoes a history he depicts as a violent and self-destructive failure, but for those who must work this soil, "declaring independence" and withholding consent remain crucial tropes and first principles, a democratic practice to invoke and sustain or revive. By claiming to begin "by accident" on July 4, he signals that personal and political identity are not divinely guaranteed but contingent on action (*Walden*, 84). Identity is an accident and without meaning, unless we give it one. Against imposed, passively inherited, or reified forms of identity, which he attributes to slavery or bad faith, he makes political community into a project. As accidents of birth, self and nation are artifacts created in action, contingent and mortal. Such an identity lives not in rest but only as enacted in time, subject to loss, failure, change.

On the other hand, to demonstrate this idea, he takes seriously the wilderness myth, to revise it. In prophetic (and Puritan) terms, wilderness names a space of transformation and possibility—of betrothal, covenant, and new beginnings—so also one of contingency, decision, and terror. Thoreau thus says he goes to the woods to "front" the "essential facts of life" by an experiment in building a house and hoeing beans (*Walden*, 90). One experiments in housing rather than entombing the spirit, the other experiments in relating the cultivated and the wild, and both signify citizenship as a practice of cultivation and world building. By retelling a myth of wilderness, therefore, he is not escaping but reinhabiting a history of settlement and domination, to redeem it by redoing it.

If he uses dawn to signify capacities for renewal in (human) nature, he uses spring as a metaphor to *embody* culture by making form giving and shape shifting part of nature. Signifying on a muddy hillside in spring, he depicts recurring, grotesque, and violent transformation. Awed by flowing mud and emerging foliage, he depicts the "creation of Cosmos out of Chaos" in the creative emergence of forms (*Walden*, 313). As "the lumpish grub in the earth" is transformed into the "airy and fluttering butterfly," so the "very globe continually transcends and translates itself, and becomes winged in its orbit" (*Walden*, 306–7). Inwardly driving all forms—including human institutions—are energies "somewhat excrementitious in [their] character," which "suggest that Nature has some bowels, and there again is the mother of humanity" (*Walden*, 308). Struck that man "is but a mass of thawing clay," he announces, "there is nothing inorganic" (*Walden*, 307–8).

> The earth is not a fragment of dead history . . . but living poetry like the leaves of a tree, which precede flowers and fruit,—not a fossil earth, but a living earth; compared with whose great central life all animal and vegetable life is merely parasitic. Its throes will heave our exuviae from their graves. You may melt your metals and cast them into the most beautiful molds you can; they will never excite me like the forms which this molten earth flows out into. And not only it, but the institutions upon it, are plastic like clay in the hands of the potter. (*Walden*, 309)

Whereas the God of Isaiah and Jeremiah declares himself the potter who is (therefore) entitled to smash his creations in frustration at their recalcitrant agency, Thoreau imagines mother earth generating forms from within and calls human beings to become "indwellers" who "build" self and world from inside out (*Walden*, 46–47). Institutions and cultures could be such "forms," produced by reverent "labors." Or rather, any faith, practice, or institution will fail to retain our assent if it is merely external or abstract; if dwellings become tombs, frozen like "winter," we must initiate "the crisis in our lives," which he depicts as a thawing spring, to undergo a moulting of dead skin. In such a crisis, Thoreau undertook the experiments by which he earned and fashioned the faith he now announces, a faith that a redemptive capacity for renewal is part of nature—and in humans as "part and parcel of nature" ("Walking," 49).

Generative capacities for form giving and world building are "larval," not unconditioned, so Thoreau concludes *Walden* by repeating the story of a "strong and beautiful bug which came out of the dry leaf of an old table" in a farmer's kitchen. "Who does not feel his faith in a resurrection and immortality strengthened by hearing of this? Who knows what beautiful and winged life, whose egg has been buried under many concentric layers of woodenness in the dead dry life of society," may gnaw its way out of this "well-seasoned tomb" to "enjoy its perfect summer life at last!" No mere lapse of time can assure this beginning, however. "Only that day dawns to which we are awake." But always, "there is more day to dawn. The sun is but a morning star" (*Walden*, 333).

By making a this-worldly prophecy through poetic imagination, Thoreau fashions a countercultural ethos, and models ideal readers, to resist worldly asceticism, the "staple production" of what Tocqueville rightly calls "a Puritan and trading nation."[29] As Emerson reads prophets as poets—"the religions of the world are the ejaculations of a few imaginative men"[30]—so Thoreau imagines a creative force within (human) nature; as prophecy becomes poesis, prophets become cockerels announcing not doctrine but dawn, not moral law and its penalty but capacities for renewal, not divine providence but the richness of life. The poet as prophet seeks not a personal god but a world (and body) made holy by poetic imagination. Casting life in such libidinal and aesthetic terms, he would temper the resentment and despair entailed by his intense attachment to justice. But his faith—that possibility is written into (human) nature—is vulnerable to charges of false prophecy, in the sense of projecting (not revealing) meaning, and so of giving false comfort.

Melville could be referring to Thoreau when he says, "Say what some poets will, nature is not so much her own ever-sweet interpreter as the mere supplier of that cunning alphabet where by selecting and combining as he pleases, each man reads his own lesson." Melville refuses visions of universal innocence because human evil bespeaks depravity in nature: "All deified nature absolutely paints like the harlot, whose allurements cover nothing but the charnel-house within." That is why Ahab's effort to get at the truth of reality—by striking through the "pasteboard mask" of visible appearances—results in apocalyptic self-destruction.[31]

Like Ahab, Thoreau does undertake a quest to experience the "truth" of reality, but to heal resentment and to restore trust in the appearances Ahab devalues as mere pasteboard. Cavell thus reads Thoreau turning from despair, skepticism, and metaphysics to the ordinary. The redemption in that turning is symbolized by spring and enacted by experiments in building and cultivating. But surrendering to those experiences and undertaking those experiments require a kind of faith—which Melville refuses, and whose real dangers he dramatizes. He thus writes a great novel warning against redemptive projects, whereas Thoreau's *Walden* is a seminal effort to recast the myth of wilderness regeneration in politicizing ways.[32]

His critical retelling is seminal because it inaugurates a second register of prophecy, an ecstatic, libidinal, and aesthetic voice that narrates not jeremiads about betrayed first principles but stories of rebirth from a death-in-life. It does not reject but reworks myths of a "new" world, imagined both as an overcoming of white supremacy and as an overcoming of what William Carlos Williams calls "the spiritually withering plague" of duality.[33] Thoreau believes the myth he revises is "sufficiently true," because in it, racial domination, worldly asceticism, and political captivity—as well as human capacities for action and self-overcoming—become "facts" we deny at great cost. He hopes his myth "offers a life adequately large," because experiments in "fronting" these facts open our purposes and practices to question and revision, because such experiments change participants and the world in ways not knowable in advance, because such changes put what people know and assume at risk, and because such risks ennoble their bearers.

But his mythic vision cannot bear the redemptive burden he invests in it. The cockerel announces the dawn, but Thoreau awakens every day to the slavery and violence authorized or allowed by his neighbors. Delivered a month before *Walden* appeared in print, his "Slavery in Massachusetts" lecture is no enraptured portrait of "somewhat excrementitious nature" but a denunciation of people dwelling "*wholly within* hell" because they have allowed the nationalization of slavery ("Slavery," 106). Nature, or poetic projects to cultivate "freer and less desponding spirits" who stand against slavery and the state, do not free him from or console him for political reality. "I am surprised to see men going about their business as if nothing had happened." Don't they know that "all beneficent harvests fail as you approach the empire of hell?" ("Slavery," 107). Undergoing a devaluation of life that no person can escape and no enterprise can redeem, he rejects pastoral compensation. "I walk toward one of our ponds, but what signifies the beauty of nature when . . . both the rulers and the ruled are without principle?" Politics is inescapable: "It is not an era of repose. We have used up all our inherited freedom." To "save our lives, we must fight for them" ("Slavery," 108).

Still, he concludes the lecture by meditating on the water lily: "It is the emblem of purity . . . as if to show us what purity . . . can be extracted from, the slime and muck of the earth. . . . I shall not so soon despair of the world for it, notwithstanding slavery, and the cowardice and want of principle of Northern men." The flower is "extracted" from the slime, but the lily also signifies how "the sweet, and pure, and innocent, are wholly sundered from the obscene and baleful" ("Slavery," 108). Indeed, "Slavery and servility have produced no sweet-scented flower . . . for they have no real life: they are merely a decaying and a death, offensive to all healthy nostrils. We do not complain that they *live,* but that they do not *get buried.* Let the living bury them; even they are good for manure" ("Slavery," 109). In spring, the "bowels" of earth are a "somewhat excrementitious" womb of living forms, linking larval and winged life, joining what he "wholly sunders" in his slavery lecture. He cannot fold slavery into a poetry of rebirth in the way he folds excrement and death into his story of spring. Slavery (and servility) cannot be redeemed, for they produce no valuable fruit; they yield the blessing of more life only if and as we bury them.

Four years later, John Brown exemplifies the virtuous action that, by bury-ing servility, enables Thoreau to appreciate the sweetness of the lily. Against the advice of Republican Party activists and many abolitionists, he orga-nizes several events to defend Brown. Voicing what he calls the "sublime" meaning of Brown's deed, his speech so effectively refutes the prevailing view that Brown is a madman and fanatic that he initiates a transformation of northern opinion, which in turn leads southerners to infer the necessity of secession.[34] It is beyond the scope of this chapter to analyze that speech and its impact, but key questions about it condense my view of Thoreau's use of prophecy.

The key question is, how are we to relate Thoreau's support of John Brown to the two registers of his prophecy? Partly, Thoreau sees in Brown the power in the democratic orthodoxy and abolitionist fundamentalism that he disrupts and troubles by his literary "experiment" but that remain crucial to his life and ongoing political labors. He feels a kinship to Brown because he has always worked around the flame of prophecy, we might say, and now he uses his artfulness to defend its value. Indeed, it seems likely that prophetic conceptions of "action from principle" sustain his fear that literary art is "just words," impotent to bury slavery, while despair about the power of language compels him to celebrate (in staggeringly artful and politically resonant words) Brown's example. His reduction of literary art to passivity is enacted by idealization of Brown as a man of action, but years of literary labor "in the wilderness" have prepared *him* to write this eulogy. Still, by artfully defending Brown's moral integrity as artless faith in action, he rejects—or betrays—*Walden*'s artfully ironic distancing from moralism. It is as if failure to embody his persona of masculinized heroism, so linked to slavery's nationalization, drives him to embrace Brown, whose martyrdom appears to close the gap between art and life.

But Thoreau's defense of Brown warrants political, not only psychological, analysis, for surely the political space for dialogue has closed down. As Frederick Douglass also argues, the nationalization of slavery and the failure of party politics to resolve the conflict make insurrectionary violence necessary. African American commentary has always paralleled Thoreau's view of necessity and principle: only war could and did end slavery, and Brown warrants praise not as a crazy martyr trying to free slaves but as a sober citizen risking himself to redeem a white republic from its constitutive origin in slavery. Depictions of Brown—as fanatic fundamentalist or heroic citizen—still mirror the color line constituting "democracy in America."

That generative and haunting division impels Thoreau to prophecy as a language of and for politics. Assuming the office of prophecy to reconstitute a white republic, he sees the value and not only the risk in a democratic fundamentalism we are inclined only to fear. But he also dreams of transforming prophecy—and thereby politics—by poetry. To be sure, he cannot sustain a poeticized prophecy under the pressure of circumstances that seem to render language impotent, and his politicized myth of wild(er)ness and transformation is not sufficiently true, now, to offer a life adequately large. But his idea of transforming prophecy by poetry, and politics by both, remains a legacy worth cultivating today.

# Notes

Excerpted from George Shulman, *American Prophecy: Race and Redemption in American Political Culture* (Minneapolis: University of Minnesota Press, 2008), chap. 2. Copyright 2008 by the Regents at the University of Minnesota. Reprinted by permission. Revisions have been made. This chapter was first presented at the American Political Science Association annual meeting in 1996.

1. I navigate between interpretations of prophecy as necessarily theistic, which reifies prophecy once and for all, and secularizing or nontheistic "translations" of prophecy, which make it too elastic a category.

2. Martin Buber, *The Prophetic Faith* (New York: Harper and Row, 1949), 102. The other seminal accounts of biblical prophecy are Abraham Heschel, *The Prophets* (New York: Harper and Row, 1958), and Max Weber, *Ancient Judaism* (New York: Free Press, 1952). See also Herbert Schneidau, *Sacred Discontent* (Berkeley: University of California Press, 1976).

3. Sacvan Bercovitch, *The American Jeremiad* (Madison: University of Wisconsin Press, 1978), 35. Whereas Louis Hartz and Perry Miller argue that liberalism buries Puritanism, Bercovitch argues that the jeremiad as a rhetorical form pressures critics to replenish liberal hegemony in ways that he illustrates by contrasting Emma Goldman to Eugene Debs. But for the "left Puritan" critics who rework jeremiads, the great danger is marginality. Cf. Robert Bellah, *The Broken Covenant: American Civil Religion in a Time of Trial* (New York: Seabury, 1975); Michael Sandel, *Democracy's Discontent: America in Search of a Public Philosophy* (Cambridge, MA: Belknap Press, 1996); Cornel West, *The Cornel West Reader* (New York: Basic Books, 1999).

4. Thoreau models how prophetic critics often connect the two major critiques of liberalism, which had been severed since Tocqueville: the mobile freedom of some is premised on the subordination of racialized others, so that fluidity generates homogeneity, not independence, among the enfranchised. When Thoreau denounces "slavery in Massachusetts," he rightly twins the white supremacy and conformity that haunt and mock celebrations of American freedom.

5. "What is called politics is comparatively something so superficial and inhuman that, practically, I have never fairly recognized that it concerns me at all." Henry David Thoreau, "Life without Principle," in *Reform Papers*, ed. Wendell Glick (Princeton, NJ: Princeton University Press, 1973), 177; hereafter cited in text as "Life." On Thoreau's anti-politics, see Leo Marx, *The Machine in the Garden* (New York: Oxford, 1964); George Kateb, *The Inner Ocean: Individualism and Democratic Culture* (Ithaca, NY: Cornell University Press, 1992); Jane Bennett,

*Thoreau's Nature: Ethics, Politics, and the Wild,* new ed. (Lanham, MD: Rowman and Littlefield, 2002).

6. Quoted in Eric Erikson, *Young Man Luther* (New York: Norton, 1962), 71.

7. Obviously, the Protestant and romantic are related: Harold Bloom calls romanticism "severely displaced Protestantism." See Bloom's *The Anxiety of Influence* (New York: Oxford University Press, 1997), 152. See also Perry Miller, "From Edwards to Emerson," in *Errand into the Wilderness* (Cambridge, MA: Harvard University Press, 1956), chap. 8.

8. Henry David Thoreau, "Slavery in Massachusetts," in *Reform Papers,* 91; hereafter cited in text as "Slavery."

9. Henry David Thoreau, "Civil Disobedience," in *Reform Papers,* 68; hereafter cited in text.

10. Henry David Thoreau, *A Week on the Concord and Merrimack Rivers,* ed. Carl F. Hovde, William L. Howarth, and Elizabeth Hall Witherell (Princeton, NJ: Princeton University Press, 2004), 132.

11. "The question is not whether you or your grandfather, seventy years ago, did not enter into an agreement to serve the devil, and that service is not accordingly now due; but whether you will not now, for once and at last, serve God,—in spite of your own past recreancy, or that of your ancestor,—by obeying that eternal and only just CONSTITUTION which He, and not any Jefferson or Adams, has written in your being" ("Slavery," 103). Human judgment does not implement morality as a divine command. Rather, "among human beings, the judge whose words seal the fate of a man furthest into eternity, is not he who merely pronounces the verdict of the law, but he, whomever he may be, who, from a love of truth, and unprejudiced by any custom or enactment of men, utters a true opinion or *sentence* concerning him. He it is that *sentences* him. Whoever has discerned truth, has received his commission from a higher source than the chiefest justice in the world, who can discern only law. He finds himself constituted judge of the judge" ("Slavery," 98). He discerns and utters truth not because he receives a revelation from god but because he obeys a "constitution" that enables him to utter "sentences."

12. As Jonathan Schell says of the Polish Solidarity movement: "its simple but radical principle" is "to start doing things you think should be done and start being what you think society should become." If "the journey and the destination are the same," action in the name of democracy must not be "degraded by brutality, deception, or any other disfigurement." As "corporations with a conscience" assume that means are ends in the making and create power where none had been, so Thoreau says, here "is peaceable revolution, if any such is possible" ("Civil Disobedience," 65, 76). See Jonathan Schell, introduction to Adam Michnik, *Letters from Prison and Other Essays* (Berkeley: University of California Press, 1985), xvii.

13. See Hannah Arendt, "Civil Disobedience," in *Crises of the Republic*

(New York: Harvest, 1972); Harry V. Jaffa, *Crisis of the House Divided* (Chicago: University of Chicago Press, 1982); Eileen Kraditor, *Means and Ends in American Abolitionism* (New York: Vintage, 1969).

14. James Baldwin, *The Price of the Ticket: Collected Nonfiction, 1948–1985* (New York: St. Martin's Press, 1985).

15. Hannah Arendt, *On Revolution* (New York: Penguin), 2006.

16. See Max Weber, "Politics as a Vocation," in *From Max Weber: Essays in Sociology*, ed. H. H. Gerth and C. Wright Mills (New York: Oxford University Press, 1946), 77–128. Sheldon Wolin distinguishes democracy as a form of rule or regime linked to constitutionalism and democracy as episodic insurgency. Whereas Thoreau sustains this tension until the nationalization of slavery turns him decisively against constitutionalism, so Wolin now offers a gothic account of an inherently anti-democratic constitutionalism. See Wolin's "Fugitive Democracy," in *Democracy and Difference: Contesting the Boundaries of the Political*, ed. Seyla Benhabib (Princeton, NJ: Princeton University Press, 1996), 31–45.

17. Peter Euben, *The Tragedy of Political Theory: The Road Not Taken* (Princeton, NJ: Princeton University Press, 1990) 206; Stanley Cavell, *The Senses of Walden*, exp. ed. (Chicago: University of Chicago Press, 1992). Despite parallels, Socratic and prophetic understandings of criticism and citizenship differ greatly.

18. Thoreau always negotiates different perspectives: "Seen from a lower point of view, the Constitution, with all its faults, is very good . . . even this State and this American government are, in many respects, very admirable and rare things, to be thankful for, such as a great many have described them; but seen from a point of view a little higher, they are what I have described them; seen from a higher still, and the highest [point of view], who shall say what they are, or that they are worth looking at or thinking of at all?" ("Civil Disobedience," 86).

19. "What shall a State like Virginia say for itself at the last day" if "tobacco and slaves" are its "staple productions? What ground is there for patriotism in such a State?" Instead, "when we want culture more than potatoes, and illumination more than sugar-plums, then the great resources of a world are taxed and drawn out, and the result, or staple production, is not slaves nor operatives, but men—those rare fruits called heroes, saints, poets, philosophers, and redeemers" ("Life," 177).

20. Cavell, *Senses of Walden*, passim.

21. Henry David Thoreau, *Walden*, ed. J. Lyndon Shanley (Princeton, NJ: Princeton University Press, 2004), 4; hereafter cited in text.

22. Henry David Thoreau, "Walking," in *Civil Disobedience and Other Essays* (New York: Dover 1993), 173; hereafter cited in text.

23. Philip Roth, *The Human Stain* (New York: Houghton Mifflin, 2000).

24. "Becoming present to" is Cavell's beautifully condensed expression of

Thoreau's project. Not coincidentally, Arendt ends *On Revolution* by posing politics as a redemptive practice against Silenus. Politics is not *the* privileged site of the natality Thoreau links to dawn, but "action from principle" names that possibility.

25. *Autumn from the Journal of Henry D. Thoreau,* ed. H. G. O. Blake (Boston: Adamant Media Corporation, 2005), 10.

26. Thoreau would "impart his courage not his despair," for "it is rare that we are able to impart wealth to our fellows, and not surround them with our own cast off griefs. . . . Even the prophets and redeemers have consoled the fears rather than satisfied the free demands and hopes of man! We know nowhere recorded a simple and irrepressible satisfaction with the gift of life." Henry David Thoreau, "Reform and the Reformers," in *Reform Papers,* 191–92.

27. Is his persona "false" because it disavows whatever contradicts brave experiment and natality? Does it thus reflect a masculinized individualism that disavows weakness and interdependence? Then the tropes by which he "arouses" neighbors sustain conformity. But if his persona models an estrangement adults need to refound community, he does not disavow despair or dependence so much as give one voice and the other an avowedly political form.

28. Norman Mailer, *Presidential Papers* (New York: Berkeley Medallion, 1963), 210.

29. Alexis de Tocqueville, *Democracy in America,* 2 vols. (New York: Vintage, 1990), 2:201.

30. Ralph Waldo Emerson, "The Poet," in *Emerson Essays: First and Second Series,* ed. Douglas Crane (New York: Vintage, 1990), 279.

31. Herman Melville's Ishmael, quoted in Michael Rogin, *Subversive Genealogy: The Politics and Art of Herman Melville* (New York: Knopf, 1983), 106.

32. Like Ahab, Thoreau imagines working through "prejudice, and tradition, and delusion and appearance . . . till we come to a hard bottom . . . which we can call *reality*" (*Walden,* 97–98). For Melville, that reality is a charnel house, and culture is our only defense against it, a fragile artifice we must not unmask. For Cavell, that reality is the ordinary, to which Thoreau returns us.

33. William Carlos Williams, *In the American Grain* (New York: New Directions, 1956), 111, 136.

34. Henry David Thoreau, "A Plea for Captain John Brown," in *Reform Papers,* 125.

CHAPTER 6

# Thoreau and John Brown

*Jack Turner*

## Harpers Ferry, 1859

ON SUNDAY NIGHT, October 16, 1859, John Brown and eighteen of his followers invaded Harpers Ferry, Virginia, and seized control of the federal armory.[1] Hoping to ignite a slave insurrection that would spread throughout the South, Brown intended to use the arsenal's weapons to arm both mutinous slaves and dissident whites in a guerrilla war of liberation. When it came time for the raid, however, Brown both overestimated the support he would receive from slaves in northern Virginia and underestimated the speed with which government authorities would mobilize against the insurrection. Local militia wrested control of the town from Brown by midday Monday. Trapped in the armory, Brown tried to negotiate his way out. Colonel Robert E. Lee, commander of federal forces at the scene, refused all offers short of unconditional surrender. By Tuesday morning, marines prepared to force their way in to take Brown, his sons, and their coconspirators dead or alive. One of Brown's prisoners observed that in the face of the siege, "[Brown] was the coolest and firmest man I ever saw. . . . With one son dead by his side, and another shot through, he felt the pulse of his dying son with one hand and held his rifle with the other."[2] After Brown rejected Lee's final order to surrender, the marines battered down the door and stormed the armory, killing two of Brown's lieutenants but taking Brown alive.

In the ensuing weeks, Brown stood trial for murder, conspiracy to incite the slaves to rebel, and treason against Virginia. As news of the drama spread, passions flared both north and south. Although most northerners condemned Brown, many expressed admiration for his anti-slavery convictions and his extremity in living them. For southerners, however, Brown's raid was the latest evidence of a "Black Republican" conspiracy against slavery.[3] On October 31, the Virginia jury found Brown guilty of all charges; two days later, the judge sentenced him to hang. At his sentencing, Brown explained himself:

> I see a book kissed here which I suppose to be the Bible, or at least the New Testament. That teaches me that all things whatsoever I would that men should do to me, I should do even so to them. It teaches me, further, to "remember them that are in bonds as bound with them." I endeavored to act up to that instruction. . . . I believe that to have interfered as I have done—as I have always freely admitted I have done—in behalf of His despised poor, was not wrong, but right. Now, if it is deemed necessary that I should forfeit my life for the furtherance of the ends of justice, and mingle my blood further with the blood of my children and with the blood of millions in this slave country whose rights are disregarded by wicked, cruel, and unjust enactments—I submit; so let it be done![4]

Taking the Golden Rule as his standard, Brown defended his right to "interfere" with slavery. If such interference resulted in violence on either the slaveholders' heads or his own, so be it. So long as slavery exists, it is just that the blood of the free mingle with the blood of the enslaved.[5] Brown's serenity in the face of execution evinces a certain Socratic virtue, albeit in a Calvinist guise: the choice of moral principle over mortal longevity, of moral right over mortal life.[6]

## Concord, 1859

Among the most vocal of Brown's admirers in Harpers Ferry's wake was Henry David Thoreau. On October 30—one day before the jury's verdict and three days before the judge's sentence—Thoreau mounted the platform in Concord Town Hall and delivered "A Plea for Captain John Brown."[7] Knowing, however, that Brown would be most valuable to the anti-slavery cause as its most recent martyr,[8] Thoreau's plea was not for Brown's life: "I *almost fear* that I may yet hear of his deliverance, doubting if a prolonged life, if *any* life, can do as much good as his death" (137). Thoreau pleaded instead for Brown's memory: "I am here to plead his cause with you. I plead . . . for his character,—his immortal life" (137). Hauntingly, Thoreau spoke of Brown throughout the "Plea" in the past tense, as if the execution had already occurred.[9] Incensed that northern reformers had failed to rally to the old Calvinist's side, Thoreau worried that Brown would be lost to either infamy or oblivion after the trial ended and the execution was carried out.[10] The memory of Brown, however, could have great value not only for the anti-slavery cause but also for American democracy generally. What distinguished Brown were not simply his principles, since others voiced and shared them, but rather his readiness to live those principles. In "Resistance to Civil Government" (1849), Thoreau wrote, "This American government,—what is it but a tradition, though a recent one, endeavoring to transmit itself unimpaired to posterity, but each instance losing some of its integrity? It has not the vitality and force of a single living man; for a single man can bend it to his will."[11] Brown's willingness to confront slavery on its own violent terms, however, had bent the American government to his will. Even though his insurrection had failed, Brown's actions and their aftermath were escalating the sectional conflict, making compromise less tenable and thus making disunion more likely. This is not to say that either Thoreau or Brown could have predicted that the raid on Harpers Ferry would precipitate both disunion and emancipation; it is to say, however, that both Thoreau and Brown could perceive how one person's actions could create an atmosphere of crisis conducive to slavery's destruction. Brown possessed a force and vitality that Thoreau believed the American government and most of the American people lacked. In John Brown, Thoreau saw a personification of principled action that American citizens would do well to emulate.[12]

Exploring the meaning of John Brown in Thoreau's moral imagination, this chapter also analyzes the relationship among conscience, character, and action in Thoreau's political thought. Because Thoreau's knowledge of Brown was imperfect, the distinction I draw between Brown himself and Thoreau's imagining of him is crucial. Thoreau either did not know or did not trust the full story of Brown's actions in "Bleeding Kansas" in 1856. As slave- and free-state settlers terrorized each other in the newly opened Kansas territory, Brown personally supervised the massacre of five southern sympathizers in retaliation for an earlier massacre of six free-state men.[13] Walter Harding insists that had Thoreau known of

Brown's participation in the massacre at Pottawatomie, "he might never have endorsed him and might [even] have been convinced of his insanity."[14] Imperfect knowledge aside, Thoreau's imagining of Brown still sheds light on Thoreau's ideas of conscience, character, and action. Thoreau's public exaltation of Brown provides a window into Thoreau's thinking on action especially, for as it celebrates Brown's actions, the "Plea" itself constitutes a dramatic political act. Political action by Thoreau was not unprecedented. His refusal to pay his poll tax in 1846 and his willingness to go to jail as a result were incontestably political; his sojourn at Walden can also be viewed as a political performance.[15] Yet the "Plea for Captain John Brown" is unique for two reasons: because of its bearing on the most immediate political issue of the day and because—unlike when the tax collector stepped in Thoreau's path—Thoreau himself set the process of protest into motion. Biographer Robert Richardson recalls that in the aftermath of Harpers Ferry, "public opinion [in Concord] began to harden against Brown, and Thoreau . . . decided to make a public speech to right the imbalance. As Brown acted, so he must act now. . . . The selectmen would not have the town bell rung, so Thoreau rang it himself."[16] The image of Thoreau ringing the bell to gather the townspeople for his speech reveals the act's self-initiated nature. More than any other action in his lifetime, Thoreau's public defense of John Brown was a premeditated projection of himself into political affairs.[17]

Political action is a pivotal issue in Thoreau's philosophy because of how his theory of moral obligation implicates it. In "Resistance," Thoreau states:

> It is not a man's duty, as a matter of course, to devote himself to the eradication of any, even the most enormous wrong; he may still properly have other concerns to engage him; but it is his duty, at least, to wash his hands of it, and, if he gives it no thought longer, not to give it practically his support. If I devote myself to other pursuits and contemplations, I must first see, at least, that I do not pursue them sitting upon another man's shoulders. I must get off him first, that he may pursue his contemplations too. (71)

The passage seems to confirm Hannah Arendt's denigration of Thoreau as a philosopher of private conscience—one who refuses to dirty his hands with injustice but also with the politics needed to make the world more just.[18] Thoreau allows individuals to dedicate themselves fully to private pursuits even if great wrongs exist that admit of public remedy; so long as one is not complicit in public wrong, one may preserve one's energies for oneself and withhold them from the world.[19] At the same time, the negative duty to avoid complicity may entail a positive duty to take part in politics. Before one can enjoy private life unencumbered by public affairs, one must make sure that one's freedom and self-cultivation are not parasitic on the freedom and self-cultivation of others.[20] In an unjust world, this usually requires positive political action. Because Brown's raid reminded Thoreau of the ways his location in a slave-sanctioning polity implicated him in slavery, Thoreau acted dramatically in the wake of Harpers Ferry.

Political theorists who have studied Thoreau have traditionally denied that he has a positive politics.[21] They emphasize his aversion to political parties and organized reform movements and underscore the negativity of his politics of "no-saying."[22] In this chapter, I refute these theorists by bringing the "Plea for Captain John Brown" into the interpretive foreground. The "Plea" shows that Thoreau has a positive politics—a politics of *performing conscience.* The performance of conscience before an audience transforms the invocation of conscience from a personally political act into a publicly political one. The aim of the performance is to provoke one's neighbors into a process of individual self-reform that will make them capable of properly vigilant democratic citizenship and conscientious political agitation. Only by provoking self-reform in his fellow citizens can Thoreau hope for the sole type of political incorporation he finds acceptable: "a corporation of conscientious men" ("Resistance," 65). To an extent, I build on Nancy Rosenblum's suggestion that, for Thoreau, "public life [is] life in public, a life of exhibitionism . . . a scene for 'giving a strong dose of myself.'"[23] At the same time, I enlarge her suggestion and illustrate the politics of performing conscience in greater detail.[24] One advantage of performing conscience as a conceptualization of Thoreau's politics is that it encompasses both the negatively political and the positively political moments of his career. Allowing that even the most unmistakably negative political acts can possess positive performative political valence, performing conscience best captures Thoreau's ideal model of political action. Through close analysis of the "Plea," we see why and how Brown's deeds at Harpers Ferry inspired Thoreau's words at Concord Town Hall, and gain a fuller view of the role of action in Thoreau's moral and political imagination.

## "The Most American of Us All": Brown in Thoreau's Moral Imagination

In Henry Thoreau's eyes, John Brown was a consummate American citizen. Early in the "Plea," Thoreau states:

> He was by descent and birth a New England farmer, a man of great common sense, deliberate and practical as that class is, and tenfold more so. He was like the best of those who stood at Concord Bridge once, on Lexington Common, and on Bunker Hill, only he was firmer and higher principled than any that I have chanced to hear of as there. . . . They could bravely face their country's foes, but he had the courage to face his country herself, when she was in the wrong. (112–13)

Thoreau begins by emphasizing Brown's agrarian roots. Although this seems a morally neutral description, Thoreau may be attributing to Brown the agrarian virtue and independence celebrated by both Locke and Jefferson. Thoreau then compares Brown to the patriots of Lexington, Concord, and Bunker Hill, as if to say that he retains the spirit of independent freeholding and the willingness to take up arms in defense of liberty that inspired the heroes of 1775 and 1776. In the end, however, Thoreau places Brown on a higher moral plane than the original patriots. What Thoreau most admires about Brown is his willingness to hold not simply America's enemies to moral account but America itself. In Thoreau's eyes, democratic citizens must have the capacity for self-criticism, both personal and national. Though it would be wishful thinking to hold up the self-righteous Brown as a paragon of personal self-criticism, he nevertheless fulfills his role in the project of national self-criticism.

In his impressive capacity for critical citizenship, Brown ceases to be a mere American patriot to Thoreau and earns an even higher appellation: "a transcendentalist above all, a man of ideas and principles. . . . Not yielding to a whim or transient impulse, but carrying out the purpose of a life" ("Plea," 115). In identifying Brown as a transcendentalist, Thoreau places him alongside himself and Emerson in the effort to draw out the moral and intellectual implications of political independence.[25] Brown's contribution to this project, however, is not intellectual but active: he exemplifies the translation of moral commitment into political action and reminds his fellow citizens of the necessity of doing so. As Emerson said, "John Brown was an idealist. He believed in ideas to that extent, that he existed to put them all into action. He did not believe in moral suasion;—he believed in putting the thing through."[26] In synchronizing commitment and action, Brown epitomizes "purposeful life," the kind of life to which all democratic individuals should aspire. Later in the "Plea," Thoreau insists:

> I wish I could say that Brown was the representative of the North. He was a superior man. He did not value his bodily life in comparison with ideal things. He did not recognize unjust human laws, but resisted them as he was bid. For once we are lifted out of the trivialness and dust of politics into the region of truth and manhood. No man in America has ever stood up so persistently and effectively for the dignity of human nature, knowing himself for a man, and the equal of any and all governments. In that sense he was the most American of us all. (125)

Thoreau's identification of Brown as "the most American of us all" is a radical utterance, surely one that shocked his audience. Brown saw himself as a "passionate outsider,"[27] and his state of alienation from the American polity exceeded even Thoreau's. Knowing this, however, Thoreau aims to reduce his audience's sense of distance from Brown. To make Brown's radicalism intelligible and respectable, Thoreau inserts him into a political lineage that extends back from the present to the American Revolution to the Puritan Revolution in the age of Cromwell ("Plea," 111–15).[28] By showing Brown to be at bottom a genuine New Englander, an authentic American, Thoreau encourages his audience to regard Brown as a fellow and not as an alien.[29] Yet Thoreau's identification of Brown as "the most American of us all" also works in a subversive second direction. Even though Thoreau often derided America as a land of slavery, commercialism, Manifest Destiny, moral numbness, and fear of freedom, he worked continuously in his writing to effect both a spiritual transformation of America as a polity and an interpretive transfiguration of America as an idea.[30] In the "Plea," Thoreau's portrait of Brown progresses from a description of him as a patriot to an exaltation of him as a transcendentalist. The order of this progression and its consummation in Thoreau's designation of Brown as "the most American of us all" are not coincidental, for they track precisely the transformation of American citizenship Thoreau wishes to effect. Thoreau wants reflexive nationalism, a form of groupthink, to yield to liberal democratic idealism—one against which citizens can evaluate both their own actions and those of the state. Thoreau's redescription of Americanism through the figure of Brown is a vehicle for encouraging this transformation in his fellow citizens' political postures. If Thoreau can convince his audience that Brown's qualities are consummately American, he will have persuaded them not only to view Brown with sympathy but also to enact their own patriotism through an embrace of Brown's moral idealism.

If we examine the sentences leading up to Thoreau's identification of Brown as "the most American of us all," we find four elements to Brown's consummate Americanism. First, Brown "did not value bodily life in comparison with ideal things." Consummate Americanism, in Thoreau's eyes, demands attachment to something beyond bodily life. Viewed in light of the history of liberalism, this is a controversial claim: the tradition of rights-based individualism and toleration proceeds, in part, from the Levellers' and Hobbes's commitment to protecting bodily life from arbitrary monarchs and civil war and Locke's desire to protect bodily life from religious war and persecution. Yet here Thoreau suggests that there are times when it is appropriate to sacrifice bodily life for ideal things. If we can construe Thoreau, as George Kateb does, as one of the last true inheritors of the American founding and thus of the rights-based individualist tradition, then the founding premise of rights-based individualism—the preservation of bodily life—exists only so that it can be transcended.[31] In other words, rights-based individualism ultimately holds that life is valuable only insofar as it is a life of liberty.[32] Yet once life and liberty are secured, the life of the free intellect discloses truths worth dying for. Rights-based individualism can countenance the sacrifice of life for principle insofar as the sacrifice is reflective and voluntary. As opposed to the truths that motivate self-sacrifice in the era of religious war, these truths are individually arrived at and may be secular in character. Although it is true that Brown's ideology is ultimately Calvinist, Thoreau believes his attachment to the ideal over the corporeal can still instruct an increasingly worldly and pluralist America.

The second element of Brown's consummate Americanism is his refusal to recognize "unjust human laws" and his resistance to them. Here Thoreau praises a certain moral perceptiveness that, when extricated from its religious context, displays a Socratic excellence. American citizenship requires resistance to the all-too-common conflation of legal and political authority with moral authority.[33] In monarchical regimes that claimed divine sanction for the laws and justified themselves through the doctrine of divine right, this precise conflation occurred in the minds of both the monarch and the populace. The rise of social-contract theory, however, demystified legal and political authority and separated them from moral authority. Still, postmonarchical peoples have not fully recovered from the habit of seeing laws as having their own morality by mere virtue of the fact that they are laws. Yet Brown sees moral justice and earthly law as separate entities that frequently contradict each other. Moreover, Brown separates himself from idle abolitionists by taking the obligation to resist injustice so seriously that he resists it actively. In contrast to Thoreau himself, whose resistance to the Mexican War took the form of noncooperation, Brown resists the slave regime by positively facilitating slavery's destruction.

After praising Brown's active resistance of unjust laws, Thoreau writes, "For once we are lifted out of the trivialness and dust of politics into the region of truth and manhood." At first it seems that Thoreau is rebuking politics in favor of truth. But there is an alternative reading. Rather than rebuking politics carte blanche, Thoreau is pointing out how the politics of slavery in the United States compromises truth's pursuit. Debate over the morality of slavery is resisted. Far too often, defenders of slavery preempt a discussion of its moral dimension by asserting its constitutionality. The truth-evading tendencies of the slave regime find their way into institutional practices: Congress's gag rule on anti-slavery petitions, for instance, or the Fugitive Slave Law's provision for twice the fee for federal commissioners who sent alleged runaways back into slavery instead of setting them free.[34] When politics evades the slavery question, when it postpones decision on slavery's morality through compromise after compromise, politics becomes trivial. The trivialness of politics entails costs not only to morality but also to democratic character: moral evasion both necessitates and intensifies the dulling of the moral senses, the atrophy of the critical capacities necessary for democratic citizenship. But notice that Thoreau ascribes not only "trivialness" but also "dust" to current politics. Is Thoreau's equation of politics and dust mere rhetorical flourish? Or is he saying something more substantive about politics in pre-emancipation America? Would it go too far to suggest that dust is a figure for death and that Thoreau is portraying politics divorced from ideals and principles as a form of death?

Recall the significance of dust in the Bible. Although God initially makes man from dust, dust takes on a fatal meaning when Adam and Eve defy his authority. For "dust thou *art*," God declares, "and unto dust shalt thou return."[35] The trope recurs throughout the Old Testament, especially dramatically in Ecclesiastes: "All go unto one place . . . all turn to dust again."[36] Dust is time, mortality, and contingency, and it opposes eternity, immortality, and truth. Perhaps we can interpret Thoreau's equation of amoral politics with death as an expression of his sense that amoral politics is a second Fall, an expression of power without principle that widens the gap between time and eternity.[37]

Yet the equation of death and politics also operates on a more local register. Indeed, the political sanction of slavery in the United States had mortal consequences. The slave who resisted his slavery risked physical death at the hands of his master, with no protection or redress from the state. The slave who submitted to his slavery risked spiritual death, a resignation to suffering so great that he imperiled his capacity to assert freedom. Any politics that refuses to confront the immorality of slavery is thus not only anemic but also complicit in the physical and spiritual death wrought by the slave system. Nowhere does Thoreau confront the relays between pre-emancipation politics and death more powerfully than in the following passage in which the slave ship stands for the ship of state:

> The slave-ship is on her way, crowded with its dying victims; new cargoes are being added in mid ocean; a small crew of slaveholders, countenanced by a large body of passengers, is smothering four millions under the hatches, and yet the politician asserts that the only proper way by which deliverance is to be obtained, is by "the quiet diffusion of the sentiments of humanity," without any "outbreak." As if the sentiments of humanity were ever found unaccompanied by its deeds, and you could disperse them, all finished to order, the pure article, as easily as water with a watering-pot, and so lay the dust. What is that that I hear cast overboard? The bodies of the dead that have found deliverance. That is the way we are "diffusing" humanity, and its sentiments with it. ("Plea," 124)

Thoreau suggests that whether its representatives will admit it or not, the American state contains four million slaves in the hull and countless others in the wake. Although the small crew is most directly responsible for the ship's course and operation, the large body of passengers has the power to overtake the crew, open the hatches, and let the slaves rise to the deck, yet it does not exercise it. One interesting aspect of the metaphor is that the liberation of the slaves requires activity and not merely passive resistance on the part of the passengers. Presumably the crew already controls the ship's course, supplies, and rations, making passive resistance by the passengers insufficient to the task of freeing the slaves in the hold. Yet the passage as a whole is unmistakably condemnatory, suggesting that Thoreau now thinks passive resistance so inadequate to the evil of slavery as to be frivolously self-indulgent. Passive resistance is no longer enough to eradicate complicity, and if the eradication of complicity is morally imperative, then action becomes the order of the day. Insofar as Americans postpone action, however, they facilitate the varieties of death that constitute racial slavery, silently assisting in the casting of humanity overboard.

Thoreau thus calls on Americans to recognize their own complicity in slavery and seize the moment for abolition. If one takes seriously the third element of Brown's consummate Americanism—a stance for the dignity of human nature—the recognition of such complicity should follow. A test of one's respect for human dignity is the extent to which one interrogates oneself to see whether one is complicit in the suffering of others. A further and more important test is the extent to which one seeks to effect positive change after discovering one's complicity. Respect for human dignity, by this view, entails not only sensitivity to the suffering of others and a cultivated disposition to relieve it but also the refusal to fool oneself, the determination to militate against those distancing mechanisms in the human psyche that allow us to evade moral responsibility for the bodies and souls of others.

But the sense of responsibility that follows from such self-interrogation has an outlet insofar as one realizes the fourth element of Brown's consummate Americanism—the confidence that the individual is "the equal of any and all governments." In realizing this, the individual's moral agency becomes commensurate with her moral responsibility. To see oneself as "the equal of any and all governments" is to revive one's sense of the fundamental role of individual consent and conscience in the life and legitimacy of democracy, to accept one's part as an ultimate constituent of democratic governance and a final judge of state law, policy, and action. Brown's consummate Americanism encourages political action by fostering an awareness of oneself as potentially and legitimately *agent*,[38] a belief that one has the right to act against the government and not merely be acted upon. Thoreau and Brown renew our sense that we are not only free to shape the future of the polity but sometimes obliged to do so.

## The Question of Violence

Thoreau's exaltation of Brown as a consummate American has its complications. Brown's effort to liberate America's slaves depended on violence,
which raises the question of whether his effort to impose morality entailed
immorality. Brown believed in Old Testament justice and admired Paul's
Epistle to the Hebrews, which said, "almost all things are by the law purged
with blood; and without shedding of blood [there] is no remission [of sin]."[39]
Brown's and Thoreau's comfort with the use of violence, however, may be
more philosophically nuanced than its Old Testament connotations suggest. Although Brown did not use the language of political theory to justify
himself—that is, terms such as *active resistance* or *revolutionary violence*—
he used one term at his sentencing that may encapsulate a philosophical
defense.

Recall that at his sentencing Brown said, "I believe that to have interfered as I have done in behalf of [God's] despised poor, was not wrong, but
right."[40] The operative word is *interfere*. What does the use of this word imply? Perhaps it is the sense that it is not violence but interference that is the
defining moment of slave liberation. More precisely, the defining moment is
when the liberator—literally or figuratively—stands between the slave and
his master and enables the slave to walk into freedom. The master then has
the choice either to resist the liberation with violence or to let the slave go.
From the liberator's perspective, the slaveholder has no right to resist the
slave's liberation due to the evil of slavery itself. If, however, the slaveholder
does resist, both the liberator and the slave have the right to use violence
to ensure liberation; for the slave, it is tantamount to self-defense, and for
the liberator, it is tantamount to aiding someone who acts in self-defense.
Violence, therefore, is only consequential and is not itself integral to the act
of liberation. And if violence is a consequence, it is a consequence brought
on by the slaveholder himself.[41]

Whether or not this conjectured theory of interference accurately
reconstructs Brown's thinking on the matter, passages from the "Plea" suggest that it does accurately reconstruct Thoreau's: "It was [Brown's] peculiar
doctrine that a man has a perfect right to interfere by force with the slaveholder, in order to rescue the slave. I agree with him" (132). Elsewhere in the
"Plea," Thoreau shows that he understands *interference* precisely to mean
to "step" or "stand" between oppressor and oppressed, enabling the latter to

claim his rightful freedom (132, 129).[42] Thoreau also explicitly defends one of the theory's essential presuppositions—that one must judge the moral acceptability of violence by a standard of natural morality and not positive law. Scathingly he derides those who object to Brown's raid out of reflexive alarm at the idea of men employing violence without law's sanction, those who "think that the only righteous use that can be made of Sharps' rifles and revolvers is . . . to hunt Indians, or shoot fugitive slaves" (133). To those repulsed by the killing of slaveholders, Thoreau remarks, "They who are continually shocked by slavery have some right to be shocked by the violent death of the slaveholder, but no others. Such will be more shocked by his life than by his death" (132–33).

May liberators use violence to occasion interference? In other words, may liberators use violence in the course of standing between the slave-holder and the slave? Like most moral matters, it depends on specifics. A liberator may use violence, for example, to overcome an overseer guarding a slave quarters. In this case, the overseer is guarding against both the slaves' escape and the liberator's interference and thus is preemptively using violence or the threat of violence to maintain an injustice. In such cases, the liberator may use violence preemptively, but only if he can confidently assume his interference would be violently resisted.

May liberators wound or kill the guards at a federal armory to seize weapons for a slave insurrection? Strictly speaking, the theory of interference would not justify this. The guards of the armory keep government weapons, not slaves, and thus are too far removed from the actual captivity of slaves for their killing to be easily justified. But what if a liberator could confidently assume that the armory's weapons would be used to put down a legitimate insurrection against slavery? One could interpret the theory of interference as justifying an attack on the armory in this instance, for it would be a case of liberators "standing between" the slaves' fight for free-dom and the political apparatus that enforces the slaveholders' alleged right to property in men and women. The theory of interference blends into a right to revolution. As Thoreau says in the "Plea":

> When a government puts forth its strength on the side of injustice, as ours to maintain Slavery and kill the liberators of the slave, it reveals itself a merely brute force, or worse, a demoniacal force. . . . It is more manifest than ever that tyranny rules. . . . There sits a tyrant holding fettered four millions of slaves; here comes their heroic liberator. This most hypocritical and diabolical

government looks up from its seat on the gasping four millions, and inquires with an assumption of innocence: "What do you assault me for? Am I not an honest man? Cease agitation on this subject, or I will make a slave of you, too, or else hang you." (129)

When a government "puts forth its strength on the side of injustice," it diminishes its claim to recognition. Thoreau denounces the U.S. government as a tyranny precisely because it puts the force of, say, the arsenal at Harpers Ferry on the side of the slaveholder instead of the slave. Thoreau pronounces his view of the right to revolution in "Resistance":

> All men recognize the right of revolution; that is, the right to refuse allegiance to and to resist the government, when its tyranny or its inefficiency are great and unendurable. . . . If one were to tell me that this was a bad government because it taxed certain foreign commodities brought to its ports, it is most probable that I should not make an ado about it. . . . All machines have their friction. . . . But when the friction comes to have its machine, and oppression and robbery are organized, I say, let us not have a machine any longer. In other words, when a sixth of the population of a nation which has undertaken to be the refuge of liberty are slaves . . . I think that it is not too soon for honest men to rebel and revolutionize. (67)

When the government becomes a gross abettor of injustice—when it organizes rather than outlaws the "oppression and robbery" that are racial slavery—it loses its claim to respect.[43]

Thoreau states his final analysis on the question of violence toward the end of the "Plea": "I do not wish to kill nor to be killed, but I can foresee circumstances in which both would be by me unavoidable. We preserve the so-called 'peace' of our community by deeds of petty violence every day" (133). Thoreau sees violence as deeply interwoven in the fabric of American society, perhaps even all societies. The proof lies in everyday sights: "the policeman's billy . . . the jail . . . the gallows . . . the chaplain of the regiment" ("Plea," 133). Yet in the American polity these everyday sights of violence are doubly significant: they point to a larger violence that constitutes the national polity. The so-called peace between the North and South is preserved by the former's acquiescence in the maintenance of the latter's slave system.[44] The white North guarantees military assistance to the white South in cases of slave insurrection and agrees to capture and return all fugitive slaves; in return, the South promises union, tranquility, and commerce. The price of peace is therefore northern agreement to act violently against slaves on occasions of rebellion or escape.[45] "The United States have a coffle of four millions of slaves . . . and Massachusetts is one of the confederated overseers," Thoreau declares ("Plea," 130). He refuses, however, to comply with this violence just by virtue of its political constitutionality. As a citizen not of the nation but of the world, he will judge the appropriateness of government action. If the government's violence threatens his life and liberty or the life and liberty of others, he will resist, violently if necessary. Thus Thoreau implies a contingent willingness to kill or be killed when forced by his government to assist, for example, in the suppression of a slave insurrection.

Thoreau's views on violence demonstrate the vigor of his conceptions of individual judgment and agency. Because they upend conventional reformist inhibitions—such as the need to work within established institutions and the commitment to nonviolence—he expands the scope of conceivable human action and equalizes the power of the individual with that of the state by ending the latter's monopoly on legitimate violence. Confrontation with institutional injustice becomes viable, not only because the people have legitimate recourse to violent means but also because such recourse weakens the state's ability to intimidate the public and make its own power seem inexorable. Democratizing the power to judge the legitimacy of violent resistance is inescapably hazardous, but it is also a cornerstone of liberal self-government, for it limits the state's ability to impose itself on the citizenry without adequate justification and therefore chastens the state to stay within its bounds.

## Knowing How to Die

Decrying the United States as a tyranny, Thoreau shows outrage toward his government's pretensions of innocence. Mockingly, he imagines and impersonates the government's response to Brown, his followers, and his sympathizers: "'What do you assault me for? Am I not an honest man?'" ("Plea," 129). Part of what enrages Thoreau is the willful self-deceit he sees not only in individual political leaders but also among his fellow citizens. We all bear some measure of responsibility for the suffering of the slave, he suggests, for we all tolerate the government that enforces the slaveholders' "right." The "Plea for Captain John Brown" is thus a natural continuation of his earlier anti-slavery works "Resistance to Civil Government" and "Slavery in Massachusetts" (1854).[46] The "Plea," however, goes to new and more powerful extremes. Like the earlier works, "Plea" reminds its readers that insofar as they tolerate an immoral institution for the sake of political unity and civil peace, they enslave their consciences and thus themselves. Thoreau nicely captures this idea when, in his impersonation of the government, he says, "Cease agitation on this subject, or I will make a slave of you, too, or else hang you" ("Plea," 129). What is ironic about the government's ultimatum is that the choice it offers is barely a choice: individuals must choose between the enslavement of their bodies and the enslavement of their minds. How is it possible not to be a slave in these circumstances? The answer, says Thoreau, is by knowing how to die.

When the government issues its ultimatum to the individual, it offers not two but three choices: (1) cease agitation, (2) become a slave, or (3) be hung. In choosing among mental enslavement, bodily enslavement, and death, most people consider the first two alternatives the only viable ones, and most of the time, they choose the first to avoid the humiliation that comes with the second. But for Thoreau, enslavement of the mind is even less becoming the democratic individual than enslavement of the body. At the same time, he does not urge his fellow citizens to choose physical slavery over mental slavery but rather to reject both. When faced with the ultimatum—an ultimatum that in many ways encapsulates the idea of sovereignty to which rights-based individualism is hostile—Thoreau urges his fellow citizens to follow John Brown and choose death over enslavement of either kind. Of Brown's raid, he says:

> This event advertises me that there is such a fact as death,—the possibility of a man's dying. It seems as if no man had ever died in America before, for in order to die you must first have lived. I don't believe in the hearses and palls and funerals that they have had. There was no death in the case, because there had been no life. . . . I hear a good many pretend that they are going to die;—or that they have died. . . . Nonsense! I'll defy them to do it. They haven't got life enough in them. . . . Only a half dozen or so have died since the world began. . . . But be sure you do die, nevertheless. Do your work, and finish it.[47] If you know how to begin, you will know when to end. ("Plea," 134)

Here Thoreau relates the task of dying to the task of leading a purposeful life. In his eyes, Brown led such a life because he chose intellectual and moral integrity over mortal longevity. Thoreau appreciates the extent to which the choice of moral principle over mortal life shakes the foundations of the state, for it denies the state the basic means of instilling docility in subjects: the threat of death. Thus Socrates, Jesus, and John Brown— three men whose integrity and moral vision their polities could not safely countenance—all have to count in Thoreau's unnamed "half dozen or so [that] have died since the world began," for all three suffered public deaths that were part and parcel of their public lives. In Thoreau's words, they were men who "in teaching us how to die, have at the same time taught us how to live" ("Plea," 134).

Thoreau's idea of "purposeful death" enhances his conceptions of human agency and action. Thus he bids his neighbors, "be sure you do die, nevertheless. Do your work and finish it. If you know how to begin, you will know when to end." This rhetorical conflation of endings and beginnings subtly suggests that a mortal ending can constitute an ethical or political beginning. Thoreau suspects that the end of Brown's life has the potential to spawn a new American beginning—of intensified national discussion of slavery and its hostility to democracy, of escalated conflict between the sections and within them, of a public enlivened with renewed moral seriousness and passion. Brown's actions could initiate a national political awakening. What Americans will do with their newfound wakefulness is unknown, but the possibilities are interesting. Arendt is better known than Thoreau for equating *action* with *beginning:* through action, she says, humans interrupt the natural process of mortality, the inevitable course of biological decay, and remind themselves that "though they must die, [humans] are not born in order to die but in order to begin."[48] When death is but the result of decay, the individual succumbs to the biological life process, failing to transcend it. But when the individual dies in the active pursuit of a public good and ideal end, she rises above the biological process onto the stage of human affairs and opens the possibility that her end—through its purposefulness, publicity, and potentially inspirational quality—can be a beginning.[49]

Thoreau's call to purposeful death and purposeful life is thus both existential and moral. It is also political insofar as it enables the only form of political incorporation Thoreau finds morally acceptable—a "corporation of conscientious men" ("Resistance," 65). Although Socrates, Jesus, and Brown are the exemplars of purposeful life culminating in purposeful death, it is unfair to say that Thoreau expects each of his fellow citizens to act in kind. Thoreau's humbler and more abiding hope is to loosen the human attachment to the mortal and the material and to inspire his fellow citizens to take themselves seriously enough to place the ethical at the center of their lives. Thoreau states his moral and political aim in desperate terms when he says, "We aspire to be something more than stupid and timid chattels, pretending to read history and our bibles, but desecrating every house and every day we breathe in" ("Plea," 117). Or, as he writes more exaltedly in "Resistance to Civil Government," "Action from principle,—the perception and performance of right,—changes things and relations; it is essentially revolutionary, and does not consist wholly with anything which was. It not only divides states and churches, it divides families; ay, it divides the *individual,* separating the diabolical in him from the divine" (72). Moral action is the pinnacle of conscious living because it requires the successful exercise of one's ability to perceive right, the formation of an intention to act accordingly, and the successful translation of that intention into action over and against one's baser instincts. Moral action consummates self-mastery in one particular worldly moment and leaves a mark—thus its quality of being "essentially revolutionary." The revolution occurs in the individual who grows stronger each time she triumphs (to paraphrase Lincoln) over the lesser angels of her nature. The revolution also occurs in the world, since moral action defies commonly accepted but essentially immoral conventions. In moral action one can "improve the nick of time, and notch it on [one's] stick . . . [one can] stand on the meeting of two eternities, the past and the future, which is precisely the present moment."[50] Moral action marks the present by departing from the habits of the past as well as by excluding crude calculations of future utility.[51] To live by any precept other than "action from principle,—the perception and performance of right" is thus to forgo one's chance and renounce one's ability to act on the world in the noblest and most definitively human way. Morally consequential action from anything other than moral principle desecrates the human condition, Thoreau insists. But does his vindication of action from principle open into a vindication of politics?

## Performing Conscience

Thoreau values and encourages public acts that take a stand for moral right against immoral law and spark wonder in their audience at the powers of individual agency, especially moral agency. Thoreau himself felt moral awe at Brown's words and deeds and despaired when his neighbors did not feel the same. But insofar as his neighbors felt an aesthetic awe in the face of Brown's actions, hope was not lost for their conversion to a morally appreciative view of him. What I mean by *aesthetic* awe is the sense of having one's imagination captured by a story, spectacle, or scene, notwithstanding one's negative or positive judgment of its moral nature. Aesthetic awe is the state of having one's attention held by an object. The moral and political value of Brown's act derived not simply from its aim of liberating the slaves, which it ultimately failed to achieve, but additionally from the spectacular way it demonstrated conscientious moral commitment. The act's aesthetic quality enabled it to hold the attention of the public even in the face of reflexive condemnation by political authority and majority opinion. But because it remained a focal point of public consideration—precisely because the act was vivid and gripping—it enabled thinkers like Thoreau to use it as a pivot for public moral conversation. Thoreau could seize upon the aesthetic awe Brown's action provoked and attempt to transform it into moral appreciation. Throughout the "Plea" Thoreau translates what appear to be Brown's madness and vanity into evidence of virtue, and through his comparison of Brown to Christ, he suggests that the practice of virtue always appears vain and mad in the eyes of a corrupt society ("Plea," 129–30, 136–37). Thoreau works in the "Plea" to make Brown morally comprehensible, and he believes that if his audience can see through Brown's initial strangeness and recognize his moral qualities, this very act of reinterpretation will both signal and accelerate a transformation of their moral natures.

The primary value of Brown's action in Thoreau's mind was therefore not instrumental but instructional.[52] In "The Last Days of John Brown" (1860), a lecture read nine months after the "Plea," Thoreau insists that the memory of Brown instructed Americans how to be transcendentalists, how to live for principle.[53] "He has liberated many thousands of slaves, both North and South," Thoreau declared. "They seem to have known nothing about living or dying for a principle," but now they have witnessed it in spectacular form (149). Describing the effect the last six weeks of John Brown's life had on the North, Thoreau said:

> The North, I mean the *living* North, was suddenly all transcendental. It went behind the human law . . . and recognized eternal justice and glory. Commonly, men live according to a formula, and are satisfied if the order of the

law is observed, but in this instance they, to some extent, returned to original
perceptions. . . . They saw that what was called order was confusion, what was
called justice, injustice, and that the best was deemed the worst. This attitude
suggested a more intelligent and generous spirit than that which actuated our
forefathers, and the possibility, in the course of ages, of a revolution in behalf
of another and an oppressed people. ("Last Days," 147)

Forcing Americans to consider the difference between earthly law and
eternal justice, Brown catalyzed Americans into critical thinking and compelled them to consider the various ways that injustice masquerades as law
and justice is made illegal.[54] Despite Brown's neo-Calvinist faith and his
conception of himself as an instrument of God, his example educated his
countrymen in mature moral agency, in the readiness to brave moral choice
and live according to educated moral perception rather than inherited legal
formula. Moreover, Brown showed America how it could transcend the
greatness of its founding generation and thus cease living in abject worship of it: whereas the Republic's founders defended liberty and principle
only on their own behalf, Brown defended them on behalf of a despised
people. In so doing, he achieved a freedom greater than political freedom;
he achieved moral freedom. He transcended the egoistic impulse to defend
principle only when one's own interests are at stake.

Public action that expresses and inspires an individual's recovery of
moral agency is the form of political action Thoreau admires most. It may
be the only form of positive political action he would gladly endorse. Therefore, it seems that for politics to be worthwhile, it must be politics in theatrical form on a grand scale, politics as democratic morality tale, politics that
puts individualist virtues on display.[55] At the same time, the performance
of conscience need not always be as preconceived as either Brown's raid or
Thoreau's "Plea." Although Thoreau did not initially intend his act of civil
disobedience in 1846 to be a political performance, his decision to lecture
and write about it converted this personal act of no-saying into a positively
political act of self-exhibition; the self-exhibition became political as soon as
Thoreau sought to use his experience to influence the ethical and political
dispositions of his fellow citizens.[56] Conscientious refusal became public
statement through the artistic re-creation of the act of refusal and public
meditation on its significance. Through art, Thoreau converted conscience
into politics. Artists may feel reluctance about the politicization of their

endeavors, but insofar as art affects self and the constitution of self affects democratic politics, art inevitably contains political potential.[57]

Critics may argue that artistic and performative forms of public engagement are not properly political because they precede the legislative processes and democratic institutions wherein policies are set and laws are made. Moreover, the violent form of Brown's action flouted both the rule of law and the essential constitutional purpose of "insuring domestic tranquility," making Thoreau's endorsement of a politics of spectacular performance suspect. Yet Thoreau believed that in a democracy, what manner of selves we are ultimately determines the laws and policies we make ("Resistance," 65, 89; "Slavery," 98). Self-formation is therefore a political activity, and our humdrum civic spaces—town halls, town squares, the free press—are politically most powerful when they are venues for performative conscientious expression and thus potential sites for self-reformation. As for the hesitation we rightly feel about taking Brown's raid as our text for determining the meaning of conscientious democratic citizenship, it is crucial to note that violence itself is not essential to any of the four elements of Brown's consummate Americanism: (1) valuation of the ideal over the corporeal, (2) the ability to perceive unjust laws and resistance to them, (3) a stance for the dignity of human nature, and (4) a belief that the individual is "the equal of any and all governments." Notwithstanding the fact that the first element overturns the Hobbesian belief that the preservation of biological life is paramount, this does not have to lead to a devaluation of the lives of one's political opponents; when joined with the third element, it can, in fact, promote a willingness to risk one's life on behalf of others. Martin Luther King Jr. possessed all four elements of Brown's consummate Americanism, yet the devaluation of the corporeal encouraged him only to "lay his body down" for the rights of others.[58] What is more, King sponsored a politics of performing conscience that provoked moral and aesthetic awe in his audiences while promoting the principle of nonviolence.[59] Although Thoreau's politics of performing conscience does not exclude violence, it does not need violence to be effective. The question of whether violence is permissible depends on whether all other means to defend the rights of others have been exhausted. In Thoreau's judgment, John Brown's raid came at a time when there was no hope of destroying American slavery except by bloodshed. Brown's clear-eyed recognition of this fact, and of the obligation it imposed on him to delay action no longer, won him Thoreau's admiration. Brown's performance of conscience with arms chastened Thoreau into performing his with words; Thoreau, in turn, hoped that words could make Brown into a model of liberal democratic idealism.[60]

# Notes

Originally published as Jack Turner, "Performing Conscience: Thoreau, Political Action, and the Plea for John Brown," *Political Theory* 33, no. 4 (August 2005): 448–71. Copyright 2005 by Sage Publications Inc. Reprinted by permission. With the benefit of retrospection, and in light of new scholarship, I have substantially revised the original article. For their help, encouragement, and advice on different versions, I thank Lawrie Balfour, Eric Beerbohm, Jane Bennett, Eduardo Cadava, Jillian Cutler, Patrick Deneen, Thomas Dumm, Michael Frazer, Denise Gagnon, Eddie Glaude, William Howarth, George Kateb, Stephen Macedo, Susan McWilliams, Barry O'Connell, Melvin Rogers, Simon Stow, Cornel West, Stephen White, and Alex Zakaras.

1. I relied on two biographies of Brown to reconstruct Harpers Ferry and its aftermath: Stephen B. Oates, *To Purge This Land with Blood: A Biography of John Brown*, 2nd ed. (Amherst: University of Massachusetts Press, [1970] 1984), chaps. 18–20; David S. Reynolds, *John Brown, Abolitionist: The Man Who Killed Slavery, Sparked the Civil War, and Seeded Civil Rights* (New York: Knopf, 2005), chaps. 13–14.

2. Oates, *To Purge This Land,* 299–300; Reynolds, *John Brown,* 327. The observer was Colonel Lewis W. Washington (great-grandnephew of George Washington), who was taken captive during the raid.

3. Oates, *To Purge This Land,* 310–24; Reynolds, *John Brown,* 335–47.

4. "John Brown's Last Speech to the Court, November 2, 1859," in *A John Brown Reader,* ed. Louis Ruchames (London: Abelard-Schuman, 1959), 126. Cf. Oates, *To Purge This Land,* 327; Reynolds, *John Brown,* 354.

5. Lincoln thus echoed Brown when he said in his second inaugural address (1865), "If God wills that [the Civil War] continue, until all the wealth piled by the bonds-man's two hundred and fifty years of unrequited toil shall be sunk, and until every drop of blood drawn with the lash, shall be paid by another drawn with the sword, as was said three thousand years ago, so still it must be said, 'the judgments of the Lord are true and righteous altogether.'" In *Lincoln: Speeches and Writings, 1859–1865,* ed. Don E. Fehrenbacher (New York: Library of America, 1989), 687.

6. See Plato, *Apology,* in *The Last Days of Socrates,* trans. Hugh Tredennick and Harold Tarrant (London: Penguin, 1993), 37–67.

7. Henry D. Thoreau, "A Plea for Captain John Brown" (1859), in *The Higher Law: Thoreau on Civil Disobedience and Reform,* ed. Wendell Glick (Princeton, NJ: Princeton University Press, 2004); hereafter cited in the text as "Plea." Thoreau read the lecture twice more after this occasion—in Boston on November 1 and in Worcester on November 3. For a fuller view of Thoreau's personal and literary relationship to Brown, see Walter Harding, *The Days of Henry Thoreau: A Biography,* rev. ed. (Princeton, NJ: Princeton University Press, 1992), 415–26; Robert B. Richardson, *Henry Thoreau: A Life of the Mind* (Berkeley: University of California Press, 1986), 370–73.

8. Brown shared this conviction. See Oates, *To Purge This Land,* 319, 335–36; Reynolds, *John Brown,* 370, 381.

9. For discussion of the literary significance of this fact, see Andrew Taylor, "Consenting to Violence: Henry David Thoreau, John Brown, and the Transcendent Intellectual," in *The Afterlife of John Brown,* ed. Andrew Taylor and Eldrid Herrington (New York: Palgrave Macmillan, 2005), 89–105.

10. For more details about Thoreau's immediate response to Harpers Ferry, see—in addition to the biographies of Thoreau cited above—Oates, *To Purge This Land,* 318–19, and Reynolds, *John Brown,* 344–47.

11. Henry D. Thoreau, "Resistance to Civil Government" (1849), in *Higher Law,* 63; hereafter cited in text as "Resistance." Based on a lecture entitled "The Rights and Duties of the Individual in Relation to Government," which Thoreau delivered in 1848, "Resistance" was first published in 1849. Not until it appeared posthumously in 1866 in *A Yankee in Canada with Anti-Slavery and Reform Papers* did the essay acquire the title "Civil Disobedience," by which it is better known today. See Nancy L. Rosenblum's introduction in *Thoreau: Political Writings* (Cambridge: Cambridge University Press, 1996), xii.

12. For an analysis of how Thoreau's radical response to Brown fell in line with those of the most prominent African American leaders of his day, see Bob Pepperman Taylor, *America's Bachelor Uncle: Thoreau and the American Polity* (Lawrence: University Press of Kansas, 1996), 110–12.

13. See Oates, *To Purge This Land,* chap. 10; Reynolds, *John Brown,* chap. 7.

14. Harding, *Days of Henry Thoreau,* 418. Reynolds (*John Brown,* 221–33) argues that, given the wide circulation of the story of Brown's murderous actions at Pottawatomie, especially in the days and weeks immediately following the raid, Thoreau had to have known of the event. Though Reynolds may be right that Thoreau had heard of Pottawatomie, that does not necessarily mean he *trusted* the story. Pro-slavery propaganda was rampant in both the years leading up to

Harpers Ferry and the days and weeks immediately following it; Thoreau may have regarded the story of Pottawatomie as one more piece of it.

15. See Stanley Cavell, *The Senses of Walden,* exp. ed. (Chicago: University of Chicago Press, [1972, 1981] 1992), 85; Nancy L. Rosenblum, *Another Liberalism: Romanticism and the Reconstruction of Liberal Thought* (Cambridge, MA: Harvard University Press, 1987), 104, 112, 116–17; Taylor, *America's Bachelor Uncle,* chap. 5; Brian Walker, "Thoreau's Alternative Economics: Work, Liberty, and Democratic Cultivation," *American Political Science Review* 92, no. 4 (1998): 852–54 (revised and reprinted as chapter 2 of this volume).

16. Richardson, *Henry Thoreau,* 370.

17. As Rosenblum (introduction to *Political Writings,* xxii) says, "Thoreau was never more consumed by a political event."

18. Hannah Arendt, "Civil Disobedience" (1970), in *Crises of the Republic* (New York: Harcourt Brace, 1972), 60.

19. On the right *not* to be political in Thoreau, see Rosenblum, *Another Liberalism,* 103; Nancy L. Rosenblum, "The Inhibitions of Democracy on Romantic Political Thought: Thoreau's Democratic Individualism," in *Lessons of Romanticism: A Critical Companion,* ed. Thomas Pfau and Robert F. Gleckner (Durham, NC: Duke University Press, 1998), 68 (revised and reprinted as chapter 1 of this volume); Jane Bennett, *Thoreau's Nature: Ethics, Politics, and the Wild,* new ed. (Lanham, MD: Rowman and Littlefield, 2002), 132; Leigh Kathryn Jenco, "Thoreau's Critique of Democracy," *Review of Politics* 65, no. 3 (2003): 362 (revised and reprinted as chapter 3 of this volume).

20. This leads me to reject Rosenblum's contention in *Another Liberalism* that Thoreau's "vision of good neighbors does not pretend to be harmonious. It is an anomic and amoral Nietzschean vision, and there is good reason to think he would have accepted the consequences of personal freedom gained at the expense of others" (114). Cf. Brian Walker, "Thoreau on Democratic Cultivation," *Political Theory* 29, no. 2 (2001): 183; Len Gougeon, "Thoreau and Reform," in *The Cambridge Companion to Henry David Thoreau,* ed. Joel Myerson (Cambridge: Cambridge University Press, 1995), 196. For an extended analysis of the inverse relationship between self-reliance and complicity in Emerson's thought, see Jack Turner, "Emerson, Slavery and Citizenship," *Raritan* 28, no. 2 (2008): 127–46.

21. See especially George Kateb, *The Inner Ocean: Individualism and Democratic Culture* (Ithaca, NY: Cornell University Press), 100–105; Bennett, *Thoreau's Nature,* 133.

22. Kateb, *Inner Ocean,* 87–89, 100–105; George Kateb, *Patriotism and Other Mistakes* (New Haven, CT: Yale University Press, 2006), 268; Bennett, *Thoreau's Nature,* 9.

23. Rosenblum, *Another Liberalism,* 116. My account also bears affinity to Walker's portrayal of Thoreau as a "philosopher of democratic enactment . . . a democratic politics of example" ("Thoreau's Alternative Economics," 851; see chapter 2).

24. In her first published essay on Thoreau, Rosenblum dedicates a section to Thoreau's writing on Brown to illustrate Thoreau's idea of "militancy." She uses the Brown lectures to enunciate Thoreau's *amoral* vision of "antagonism as a way of life." See Nancy L. Rosenblum, "Thoreau's Militant Conscience," *Political Theory* 9, no. 1 (1981): 93–97. My analysis differs from Rosenblum's in that I focus precisely on the *moral* lessons Thoreau draws from Brown.

25. On the transcendentalist effort to declare moral and intellectual independence, see Kateb, *Inner Ocean,* chap. 3; George Kateb, "Democratic Individuality and the Meaning of Rights," in *Liberalism and the Moral Life,* ed. Nancy L. Rosenblum (Cambridge, MA: Harvard University Press, 1989), 183–206.

26. Ralph Waldo Emerson, "Speech at a Meeting to Aid John Brown's Family—18 November 1859," in *Emerson's Antislavery Writings,* ed. Len Gougeon and Joel Myerson (New Haven, CT: Yale University Press, 1995), 119.

27. John Stauffer, *The Black Hearts of Men: Radical Abolitionists and the Transformation of Race* (Cambridge, MA: Harvard University Press, 2001), 15.

28. On the significance of the comparison to Cromwell, see Reynolds, *John Brown,* 164–66, 229–32.

29. As Taylor notes, Thoreau works to "reattach [Brown] to recognizable coordinates," to root him in a shared history and geography ("Consenting to Violence," 97–98; see also 95, 99, 105).

30. See Cavell, *Senses of Walden,* 78–88.

31. Kateb, *Inner Ocean,* 82.

32. Sharon R. Krause astutely points out that the preference for liberty over life was an essential tenet of the liberalisms of both Frederick Douglass and Martin Luther King Jr. See her *Liberalism with Honor* (Cambridge, MA: Harvard University Press, 2002), 147–48, 175.

33. Cf. "Plea," 136: "Are laws to be enforced simply because they were made? or declared by any number of men to be good, if they are *not* good?" For the decoupling of political authority from morality as a distinctively Socratic enterprise, see Dana Villa, *Socratic Citizenship* (Princeton, NJ: Princeton University Press, 2001), chap. 1.

34. See the entries for "Gag Rule" and "Fugitive Slave Law" in *The Reader's Companion to American History,* ed. Eric Foner and John S. Garraty (Boston: Houghton Mifflin, 1991), 436–37, 432–33.

35. Genesis 3:19 (King James Version).

36. Ecclesiastes 3:20. Cf. Job 4:19 and 34:15.

37. For a meditation on the relation among prophecy, time, and eternity in both Brown's and Thoreau's imaginations, see Lewis Hyde, "Henry Thoreau, John Brown, and the Problem of Prophetic Action," *Raritan* 22, no. 2 (2002): 125–44.

38. Krause, *Liberalism with Honor,* ix.

39. Hebrews 9:22. Cf. Oates, *To Purge This Land,* 61, which discusses Henry Highland Garnet's use of Hebrews 9 and Brown's admiration of Garnet.

40. "Brown's Last Speech to the Court," 126.

41. See Louis Menand, "John Brown's Body," *Raritan* 22, no. 2 (2002): 57; Stauffer, *Black Hearts of Men,* 26–27. Henry Highland Garnet sketched a view of violent resistance similar to the theory of interference I articulate here in "An Address to the Slaves of the United States" (1843), in *The Heath Anthology of American Literature,* 4th ed., ed. Paul Lauter et al. (Boston: Houghton Mifflin, 2002), 1905. For Garnet's influence on Brown, see Oates, *To Purge This Land,* 61; Reynolds, *John Brown,* 103. Reynolds also convincingly shows that Brown understood the relation between master and slave to be "a state of war," allowing the slave to defend himself by any means necessary (104, 251).

42. Thoreau's theory of violent resistance is thus far more generalizable and nuanced than Jason P. Matzke suggests in "The John Brown Way: Frederick Douglass and Henry David Thoreau on the Use of Violence," *Massachusetts Review* 46, no. 1 (2005): 62–75.

43. "The only government I recognize . . . is that power that establishes justice, never that which establishes injustice" ("Plea," 129).

44. As Thoreau says famously in "Resistance," the state's "very Constitution is the evil" (74).

45. For Massachusetts citizens' explicit objection to ratification of the Constitution on precisely these grounds, see Consider Arms, Malichi Maynard, and Samuel Field, "Reasons for Dissent," *Hampshire Gazette,* April 1788, in *The Complete Anti-Federalist,* ed. Herbert J. Storing and Murray Dry (Chicago: University of Chicago Press, 1981), 4:26.

46. Henry D. Thoreau, "Slavery in Massachusetts" (1854), in *Higher Law;* hereafter cited in text as "Slavery."

47. Thoreau here echoes Brown's own sentiments. In the midst of Bleeding Kansas, he advised a comrade, "Take more care to end life well than to live long." Reynolds, *John Brown,* 200; cf. 202.

48. Hannah Arendt, *The Human Condition,* 2nd ed. (Chicago: University of Chicago Press, [1958] 1998), 246.

49. Ibid., 246–47.

50. Henry David Thoreau, *Walden,* ed. J. Lyndon Shanley (Princeton, NJ: Princeton University Press, [1854] 2004), 17.

51. See Bennett, *Thoreau's Nature*, 3: "Human action is action without the benefit of foresight, without, that is, knowledge of the long chain of events that one's act is about to engender." On "marking the present," see Cavell, *Senses of Walden*, 9–10, 61; Thomas L. Dumm, *A Politics of the Ordinary* (New York: New York University Press, 1999), 67.

52. See Rosenblum, "Thoreau's Militant Conscience," 105.

53. Henry D. Thoreau, "The Last Days of John Brown" (1860), in *Higher Law*; hereafter cited in text as "Last Days."

54. Thoreau's understanding of higher law and natural morality remains a source of controversy in the literature. Jenco grounds Thoreau's moral philosophy in what she characterizes as Emerson's understanding of "a kind of spiritual symbolism imparted by nature from which man should properly derive his moral understanding. . . . A major tenet of the higher law philosophy is that nature refines man's understanding by revealing specific moral truths, and disciplines his reason by revealing the holistic correspondence between thoughts and things. All are fragments of the divine, and each one implies all others and the whole" ("Thoreau's Critique of Democracy," 358; see chapter 3). Rosenblum, however, insists that Thoreau's emphasis on the wildness of nature commits him to a belief in the evanescence of "higher laws" ("Inhibitions of Democracy," 63, 66; see chapter 1). Because he assumes in his practical ethics that there are acts (e.g., slavery) that offend "eternal justice," I read Thoreau as believing in a natural order of justice existing beyond convention. This belief, however, is qualified by his sense that human perception is imperfect and that nature is continually disclosing itself—which means that our readings of higher law should be animated by a sense of contingency and subjected to continual reevaluation and revision.

55. Cf. Rosenblum, *Another Liberalism*, 117: "Democracy is transformed into a scene of continuous declarations of independence, a spectacle of heroic self-display."

56. As Cavell writes, "the completion of the act was the writing of the essay which depicts it" (*Senses of Walden*, 85).

57. On the relationship among art, sensibility, temperament, and politics in Thoreau, see Bennett, *Thoreau's Nature*, 105–7; Walker, "Thoreau on Democratic Cultivation," 159–60, 179–83.

58. See Martin Luther King Jr., "Letter from Birmingham Jail" (1963), in *Why We Can't Wait* (New York: Signet Classics, 2000), 66–67.

59. For King's references to nonviolent protest as a "dramatization" of injustice, see *The Autobiography of Martin Luther King, Jr.*, ed. Clayborne Carson (New York: Warner Books, 1998), 177, 190, 349.

60. As Kateb writes, "The word and the act need each other, and they form together one memorable deed" (*Patriotism and Other Mistakes*, 267).

# CHAPTER 7

# Thoreau and Lincoln

*Harry V. Jaffa*

THOREAU IS THE PATRON saint of the American tradition of civil disobedience. I speak of an American tradition because this nation was born in virtue of what we all hold to be a legitimate rebellion against established authority—a rebellion legitimate according to the "laws of Nature and of Nature's God." "They only can force me," writes Thoreau—referring to moral force as distinct from physical force—"who obey a higher law than I." So saying, he invokes a tradition older even than the American, calling to mind the words of Socrates to the court of Athens in Plato's *Apology of Socrates*:

> I should have done something terrible, O men of Athens, if when the commanders whom you chose to command me, both at Potidaea and at Amphipolis and at Delium, had stationed me, and I remained there like anybody else, and ran the risk of death, but when the God gave me a station, as I believed and supposed, commanding me to spend my life philosophizing, and examining myself and others, then I were to desert my post, whether through fear of death or anything else whatever.[1]

Political philosophy, from Socrates to Jefferson, taught that there is a principle of obligation higher than that of the human authorities of political communities and that in a conflict between the higher and the lower, the higher takes precedence. The American Revolution was fought on the premise that such a precedence dissolved the obligations the rebellious colonists once owed to the British Crown and that the very right by which they withdrew their allegiance enfranchised them to institute a new government that "to them shall seem most likely to effect their safety and happiness." But is not the same dissatisfaction the founding fathers of the American government felt with the British Crown a source of legitimacy for revolt against the government they founded, when dissatisfaction against it burgeons? Thoreau, like Socrates, confronts what he believes to be an unjust democracy. Those who would abolish slavery ought not "wait till they constitute a majority of one," he says. "I think it is enough if they have God on their side, without waiting for that other one."[2]

Many Americans today take pride in the fact that Thoreau was the acknowledged teacher of Gandhi and that the lessons learned by Martin Luther King from Gandhi are, in a sense, lessons come home to the land of their birth. Thoreau writes:

> Cast your whole vote, not a strip of paper merely, but your whole influence. A minority is powerless when it conforms to the majority; it is not even a minority then; but it is irresistible when it clogs by its whole weight. If the alternative is to keep all just men in prison, or give up war and slavery, the State will not hesitate which to choose.[3]

It is not difficult to discern in these words the inspiration of Montgomery and Birmingham and, ultimately, of the Civil Rights Acts of the 1960s. Nor is it unlikely that these same words inspired many of the protesters against the Vietnam War. Thoreau has contributed phrases of undying eloquence to the cause of resistance to oppression, as well as a device of immeasurable political power in the technique of passive resistance. It is the work of this chapter to examine the import of some of these phrases, and of the technique, within the context of Thoreau's thought. I also attempt to deepen our understanding of that thought by placing it within the context of the American political tradition from which it derives so much of its meaning. Is "resistance to civil government," as Thoreau propounds it, an instrument more likely to be serviceable to good causes than to bad? There is no good thing that cannot be misused, but how good a thing is Thoreau's teaching in "Civil Disobedience"?

The essay begins by Thoreau "heartily" accepting the motto, "That government is best which governs least." "Carried out," he continues, "it finally amounts to this, which also I believe,—'That government is best which governs not at all.'"[4] But a little later, Thoreau says he speaks "practically, and as a citizen, unlike those who call themselves no-government men."

In that capacity he asks for "not at once no government, but *at once* a better government." "Let every man," he continues, "make known what kind of government would command his respect, and that will be one step toward obtaining it."[5] Is Thoreau an anarchist? If so, in what sense? Does he think of anarchy as the best condition of human society, but to be obtained only at the end of a kind of evolutionary process, as did many other nineteenth-century thinkers, including Karl Marx? Or does he think of anarchy as an ever-present positive force, always existing side by side with government and from time to time interfering with government to compel the abandonment of some of its evils? There can be no question but that the best human condition, according to Thoreau, is one in which there is no coercive power of man over man and the work of society is carried on by voluntary cooperation. That is the kind of "government" men will have "when they are prepared for it."

There is a similarity between Thoreau's attitude toward government and St. Paul's toward marriage: both institutions are seen as lesser evils necessitated by the blind strength of human passions. (Thoreau, incidentally, remained celibate throughout his life; one wonders whether the views expressed in *Walden* could have been held by a man for whom the married state was a vocation.) One might address a similar question to Paul and Thoreau: Is the Kingdom of Heaven—or the best government which governs not at all—only within each man, as a higher standard by which the superior are to govern themselves and judge and admonish others? Or is it something objectively to be fulfilled here, in a messianic era yet to come?

In the peroration of Abraham Lincoln's "Temperance Address," given on Washington's birthday 1842, we can see the extent to which the Pauline conception of the Kingdom of Heaven had entered the utopian thought of the time and had made utopian ends the direct aim of political reform movements:

> And what a noble ally is this [the temperance revolution], to the cause of political freedom. With such an aid, its march cannot fail to be on and on, till every son of earth shall drink in rich fruition, the sorrow-quenching draughts of perfect liberty. Happy day, when, all appetites controlled, all passions subdued, all matters subjected, *mind,* all conquering *mind,* shall live and move the monarch of the world.[6]

Lincoln himself privately mocked this utopianism and was distressed at the fanaticism it implied. But there can be no doubt that such utopianism and fanaticism motivated much of the nineteenth-century reform movements, radical abolitionism and temperance prominent among them. Nor can there be much doubt that Thoreau was among those who believed that such a vision of the absolutely best human condition constituted the true principle of political action. *Walden* is above all a political work, devoted to showing how the life according to nature is a life of emancipation from superfluous desires (and hence from government) and therefore one that eliminates the causes both of war and of slavery.

James Madison in Federalist No. 51, when he considers that such constitutional devices as separation of powers rely on base human motives, observes:

> It may be a reflection on human nature, that such devices should be necessary to control the abuses of government. But what is government itself, but the greatest of all reflections on human nature? If men were angels, no government would be necessary. If angels were to govern men, neither external nor internal controls on government would be necessary.[7]

We thus see a kind of agreement between Thoreau and Madison (as well as with Marx) that government is an evil. But for Madison, it must always be a necessary evil, while for Thoreau (as for Marx), it is an evil that the progress of mankind must eventually make superfluous. Thoreau's man of conscience leads the way toward "no government," no less than Marx's proletariat leads the way toward the classless society and the withering away of the state.

Having exhorted every man to make known what kind of government would command his respect—a strange exhortation, considering the high respect in which slavery was held by so many of his fellow citizens—Thoreau proceeds to let it be known that the government commanding his respect is one in which not majorities but conscience decides. "Can there not," he asks, "be a government in which majorities do not virtually decide right and wrong, but conscience? . . . Must the citizen ever for a moment . . . resign his conscience to the legislator?"[8] Thoreau here strangely confuses the acceptance of majority rule with the abdication of conscience—a confusion made plausible by his belief that it is the function of majorities (or, a fortiori, any government) to decide right and wrong. But the function of government in the American political tradition has always been that of deciding how to secure (or implement) certain rights—to life, liberty, and the pursuit of happiness. The existence of these rights, as we all know, is regarded as a self-evident truth, so there can be no question whether one is conscientious in seeking their fulfillment.

It is widely held, moreover, that matters of conscience, properly so called, are beyond the province of government. Jefferson, in Query XVII of *Notes on Virginia*, writes:

> The error seems not sufficiently eradicated, that the operations of the mind, as well as the acts of the body, are subject to the coercion of the laws. But our rulers can have no authority over such natural rights, only as we have submitted to them. The rights of conscience we have never submitted, we could not submit. We are answerable for them to our God. The legitimate powers of government extend to such acts only as are injurious to others.[9]

Thus the traditional understanding of conscience refers primarily, though not exclusively, to opinions as distinct from actions and to our relations with God rather than with men. Government, from this perspective, is first of all a means whereby we provide ourselves with security against injury, whether from enemies abroad or criminals at home. For this there must be collective action and, therefore, government.

The anarchist, of course, denies that collective self-defense is a true necessity of human life. For him, the motives that cause men to commit aggression against other men are themselves caused, directly or indirectly, by government. To abolish the need for police and armed forces, one must abolish police and armed forces. This is certainly the inference to be drawn from the famous lines on soldiers in "Civil Disobedience":

> Now what are they? Men at all? or small moveable forts and magazines, at the service of some unscrupulous man in power? . . . Such command no more respect than men of straw, or a lump of dirt. They have the same sort of worth only as horses and dogs.[10]

There is no suggestion here that armed force is sometimes necessary to protect the innocent from malefactors. The view that government—and its ultimate expression in armed force—is dehumanizing has as its corollary the view that man by nature, man apart from government, is good. But for those who believe that the requirement of armed protection is a consequence of human nature, the adoption of such protection cannot be intrinsically hostile to the demands of conscience, however grave the problems of conscience that arise because of it.

To abide by majority rule does not mean resigning our consciences. It means, rather, that we have, as citizens, surrendered our natural freedom to act independently so that we may have the cooperation of other men who have equally surrendered their natural freedom to act independently. We have made a bargain with others, and as honest men, we have a duty to keep that bargain—so long as good faith is kept with us. Jefferson, in the Declaration of Independence, in his indictment of the British Crown, gives a detailed argument why the American people are conscientious in dissolving their political bonds with Great Britain. Whether good faith is indeed being kept with us—whether the "us" be a majority or a minority—seems a large enough political sphere for conscience, without conscience usurping the whole province of law and government, as Thoreau demands.

But why, it may be asked, should the majority principle be the one to decide the common concerns of fellow citizens? The answer is that unanimity is impossible, and the majority principle is the only direct reflection of the original equality of natural rights of the members of the political association. It is *not* the case that the majority are permitted to rule because, as Thoreau says, "they are physically the strongest." That would be necessarily true only if all men were equal in physical strength, which they are not. It is the equality of natural *right* that supplies the moral ground of the majority principle. In the last paragraph of the essay, Thoreau says, "There will never be a really free and enlightened State, until the State comes to recognize the individual as a higher and independent power, from which all its own power and authority are derived, and treats him accordingly." *But the principle of the equality of all men and its corollary, the requirement of the consent of the governed, affirmed in the Declaration of Independence, mean precisely that.* However imperfectly the United States may have implemented these principles, their recognition constituted an epoch in the history of the world, and Thoreau seems not to appreciate that fact at all. What Thoreau seems to want is a "State" in which nothing is ever done without the concurrence of every single member. But were such a state possible, it would be unnecessary. Such agreement could prevail only among angels—and were men angels, government would be unnecessary.

Majority rule is a necessary but by no means a sufficient substitute for unanimity. The Constitution is a massive device for instilling qualitative safeguards into the practical operation of the quantitative rule of the majority. Thoreau's strictures against majority rule are related to his greater scorn for the Constitution.

Thoreau denies that there is any general duty to obey law. "The only obligation which I have a right to assume," he says, "is to do at any time what I think right."[11] In one sense, of course, that is a mere truism. But *most* of us think it is *usually* right to obey the law, without considering in *every* instance whether the law squares with the dictates of conscience apart from law. For example, one might read the transcript of a criminal trial and conscientiously disagree with the verdict of the jury, but this does not impose a duty to do violence to that verdict or to overthrow the jury system. One might still think, as most of us do, that the jury system, with all its faults, is the best system possible, in an imperfect world, for administering criminal justice. Moreover, the view that there is a general obligation of obedience to law does not forbid us to participate in revolution against an established government, nor does it forbid us to disobey a particular lawful enactment even in a regime we regard as just. According to Thoreau, however, the very presence of conscience requires the disavowal of every presumption in favor of law as a guide to human behavior. Conscience and law, as used by Thoreau, are simply incompatible.

"It is truly enough said," declares Thoreau, "that a corporation has no conscience; but a corporation of conscientious men is a corporation *with* a conscience. Law never made men a whit more just; and, by means of their respect for it, even the well disposed are daily made agents of injustice."[12] In his desire to have conscience abolish both law and government from a good society, Thoreau distinguishes a corporation of conscientious men, a corporation *with a* conscience, from a corporate conscience. But is it a distinction that corresponds with any real difference? For example, if men engage their faith to each other—as fellow citizens are supposed to do—that if one is attacked the others will come to his defense, do they not, for certain purposes, thereby constitute a corporation? And is it not a sufficiently conscientious corporation by the mere fact that it exists (if it really does) to implement the natural right of every man to defend himself? Do we not properly distinguish the principle of such a corporation from that of one like a pirate ship or a pirate nation, which associates for the sake of collective aggression on the rights of others? Does not respect for law, in the first instance, imply respect for civil society, properly so called, as distinct from a band of robbers? Although we may call by the name of "law" the collective rules of any regime, it belongs of right to those regimes that are directed, however imperfectly, to lawful ends. Thoreau's characterization of the "State" as a kind of abstract entity, indifferent to the different ends among men and among collectivities of men, is an unreal abstraction from political life as we know it.

If there may be men who are conscientious, in the sense of being committed to one another for the lawful end of mutual protection, must they not have means to implement their agreement? How shall they decide each one's contributions in money and in personal service to the cause of their common defense? Let us suppose their government is, for reasons already suggested, based on majority rule. Would it not be wrong to decide separately what each man—for example, Henry David Thoreau—should pay? Might not even conscientious men in an assembly be influenced by Thoreau's eccentricities to assess him more than his fair share? Is it not better to employ *laws* rather than *decrees* to levy taxes on *classes* rather than *persons*? Is it not better, for example, to levy a sales tax to be paid by anyone who purchases, or an income tax to be paid at preestablished rates by anyone with taxable income? Similarly, is it not better that men be drafted into the armed services by rules laid down in advance, so far as possible, rather than at the pleasure even of a majority? Laws may not be perfect, and their practical administration may require some discretionary judgment, but the principle of law is that it is not a respecter of persons, and it thereby takes on an attribute of justice. The rule of the majority by law is better than majority rule by discretion or decree. This connection between law and justice, and hence between law and conscience, seems never to be recognized by Thoreau. Thoreau's doctrine of the supreme right of conscience not only is impractical, it also undermines the morality it purports to invoke.

Thoreau is far from being the isolated individualist his eloquence sometimes conjures. His teaching is, notwithstanding its exaggerations, in the main current of the popular political opinions of his day. The secret of his power may be explored in relation to the motto with which the essay "Civil Disobedience" begins. "That government is best which governs least" has echoed through the corridors of American history. When President John F. Kennedy, in his inaugural address in 1961, said that we should ask not what our country can do for us but what we can do for our country, he was evoking one implication of that aphorism. Richard M. Nixon more evidently evoked another when, in his speech accepting the Republican nomination for the presidency in 1968, he said that America had grown great not because of what government had done for the people but because of what the people had done for themselves. And so Thoreau writes:

> This government never of itself furthered any enterprise, but by the alacrity with which it got out of its way. *It* does not settle the West. *It* does not educate. The character inherent in the American people has done all that has been accomplished; and it would have done somewhat more, if the government had not sometimes got in its way. . . . Trade and commerce, if they were not made of India rubber, would never manage to bounce over the obstacles which legislators are continually putting in their way.[13]

Thus we see Thoreau lending authority to those today regarded as being on the "right" of the political spectrum in their opposition to government interference with business or education, as we have seen him in a similar relationship to those regarded as being on the "left" in their opposition to the government's use of armed force.

"That government is best which governs least" is commonly thought to have originated with Jefferson, although no one has ever found it among his writings. It seems to have first appeared as the motto of the *United States Magazine and Democratic Review*, a journal founded in 1837 at the very apogee of the Jacksonian movement and designed to strengthen and perpetuate the fighting faith of the party, now that the retirement of the hero was at hand. The first issue of the *Review* contains an essay explaining the principles of the editors and incorporating an extended explanation of the famous slogan. The main thrust of the essay is to strengthen faith in the mass of the people for self-government, while acknowledging that minorities have rights that are not always recognized by majorities "flushed with triumph and impelled with strong interests." But the conflict between the majority and minority rights is not, the essayist holds, intrinsic to democracy; the conflict arises from an imperfect understanding of its true theory. Democratic republics have hitherto, he says, been

> administered on ideas and in a spirit borrowed from strong governments of the other forms. . . . It is under the word *government* that the subtle danger lurks. Understood as a central consolidated power, managing and directing the various interests of the society, all government is evil, and the parent of evil. A strong and active *government* . . . is an evil, differing only in degree and mode of operation, and not in nature from a strong despotism.[14]

Then he declares, "The best government is that which governs least." The grand reason is that "no human depositaries can, with safety, be trusted with the power of legislation upon the general interests of society."[15] But if *no* human depositaries can be entrusted, how are the general interests of society to be attended to? The solution to this riddle can be found in a thesis closely resembling that of the famous "invisible hand" of Adam Smith. But now it has been generalized to include not only the marketplace but also society at large. Indeed, the laws governing man in society are now seen as but particular applications of more general, universal laws. The principle of *inertia* in physics has its parallel in the *voluntary principle* of society. The sole necessary connection between the internal polity of society and of government is the administration of justice.

> Afford but [this] single nucleus . . . and, under the sure operation of this principle, the floating atoms will distribute and combine themselves, as we see in the beautiful natural processes of crystallization, into a far more perfect and harmonious result than if government, with its "fostering hand" undertake to disturb, under the plea of directing, the process.[16]

It is apparent that Thoreau's belief in the beneficence of human nature apart from government is a particular instance of a widespread nineteenth-century conviction of the beneficence of nature in general, whose laws the progress of science was steadily revealing. The enlightened adaptation of man to nature will result from the diffusion of the knowledge of nature, and this diffusion will explode the superstitions that have so long enslaved men—among them the superstition that government has to organize and direct the general interests of society and coerce men to do what it is in their interest to do.

The eighteenth-century antecedent of this view may be seen in Thomas Paine's *Rights of Man*, published in 1791 with Jefferson's endorsement. In chapter 1 of book 2, Paine says:

> Great part of that order which reigns among mankind is not the effect of Government, and would exist if the formality of Government was abolished. [It is the] mutual dependence and reciprocal interest which man has upon man, and all the parts of a civilized community upon each other. . . . The landholder, the farmer, the manufacturer, the merchant, the tradesman, and every occupation, prospers by the aid which each receives from the other,

and from the whole. . . . In fine, society performs for itself almost everything which is ascribed to Government.[17]

And again, "The more perfect civilization is, the less occasion it has for Government, because the more it does regulate its own affairs and govern itself." One can reformulate Paine's thought into the Jacksonian dogma of Thoreau's day by saying that civilization perfects itself in direct proportion to government's being prevented from interfering with it; that the incentive to perfection is weakened or corrupted by the presence of government and strengthened in its absence.

The affinity of Paine and Jefferson—at least as far as abstract theories are concerned—is well known. The struggle occasioned by the Alien and Sedition Acts led to the Kentucky and Virginia Resolutions, which laid down the political dogmas that were to dominate American party rhetoric for the next two generations. "It would be a dangerous delusion," wrote Jefferson in the Kentucky Resolutions of 1798, "were a confidence in the men of our choice to silence our fears for the safety of our rights; that confidence is everywhere the parent of despotism—free government is founded in jealousy, and not in confidence; it is jealousy and not confidence which prescribes limited constitutions, to bind down those whom we are obliged to trust with power." With reference to the obnoxious Alien Act, Jefferson declaimed, "Let him say what the government is, if it be not a tyranny, which the men of our choice have conferred on our President, and the President of our choice assented to."[18] Thus is expressed in its classic form the Jeffersonian and Jacksonian creed that combines faith in the people with distrust of their representatives, especially in the government of the United States. After the victory of the Republicans in 1800, this was further expressed in the memorable lines of Jefferson's inaugural address, when he said that the "one thing more" needed to make us a happy and prosperous people was "a wise and frugal government, which shall restrain men from injuring one another [and] shall leave them otherwise free to regulate their own pursuits of industry and improvement, and shall not take from the mouth of labor the bread it has earned." "This," said Jefferson, "is the sum of good government."[19]

To this point, it might appear that Thoreau merely represents an eccentric radicalization of the Jeffersonian viewpoint that government is at best a necessary evil and that it is usually a great deal less necessary than commonly supposed. But Jefferson, and Jackson after him, saw in the Constitution the great ark of the covenant that restricts government as much as possible to its proper sphere. Thoreau, in contrast, holds the Constitution in contempt, as the very symbol of the law that causes men to abandon conscience. But even this difference is less in substance than in appearance. Jefferson and Jackson expressed their reverence not simply for the Constitution but for the Constitution very strictly construed, the Constitution as a device for limiting the sphere of government.

Jefferson and Jackson are today considered strong presidents, but they were strong presidents opposed in principle to active government. They saw themselves as tribunes of the people, protecting the people from the aristocratic corruptions of government. In his purchase of Louisiana, the crowning achievement of his presidency, Jefferson himself believed he had performed an action unauthorized by the Constitution. But he believed it to be something critically necessary to the safety of that severely limited form of government in which he so believed. Thus he confided not in the Constitution but in the people, who would ratify what he had done after the fact.

Similarly, Jackson saw in his vetoes of bills for internal improvements and of the bill to recharter the Bank of the United States a vindication of the people against those who, equally with himself, were their constitutional representatives. Thus did the tribune, or the people's champion, theory of the presidency originate, a conception of an office in some sense outside the Constitution whose exercise, even if in conflict with the letter of the Constitution, would enable the true Constitution to prevail.

Thus Thoreau's call to civil disobedience is, at the least, an apolitical or anti-political analogue to Jefferson's and Jackson's supraconstitutional constitutionalism. Thoreau summons the phalanxes of the conscientious, enjoining the righteous to clog the machinery of government, to compel the "State" to give up war and slavery, even as Jefferson and Jackson acted in crises ultra vires, in defense of, and in the name of the people.

In the secularized radical Protestantism of his day—the quasi-religious Protestantism of unitarianism and transcendentalism—Thoreau's individualism, like Emerson's, is a species of antinomianism, seeing the individual under the grace of conscience emancipated from the lower law of the merely political order, and helping to elevate that order by defying it. It is, I have argued, a kind of eccentric coordinate of the Jacksonian hero worship (Thoreau himself was an admirer of Carlyle), which saw its idol slaying the dragons of oligarchy and aristocracy. It was in full accord with the popular opinion of the day—and appealed to the prejudice in favor of that opinion—that government is something evil, while the people are essentially good.

Yet there was—and is—within the American political tradition another opinion, both popular and philosophical, that holds nearly the opposite. It is perhaps an oversimplification to say that the leading doctrines of the Federalist Papers were governed by the assumption that people are evil and government is good. Both Hamilton and Madison saw man apart from government as not in society or civilization but in a state of nature very like that described by Hobbes. Although the government they recommended differed widely from the monarchy preferred by Hobbes, it was nonetheless conceived, like Hobbes's, mainly in terms of overcoming the ills of human nature, for which society, apart from good government, possessed no remedy.

Yet despite the formal opposition of these two great theses—the one insisting on human depravity by nature and the goodness of government, the other insisting on human goodness by nature and the inherent depravity of government—there is a point of agreement. I have already alluded to it in citing Madison's aphorism that if men were angels, no government would be necessary. Notwithstanding the Madisonian assumption that men cannot be angelic, there is a tacit admission that, in the best case imaginable—even if that case be impossible—there is no government. Madison thus makes a concession to human desire or aspiration going back at least as far as Plato's *Republic*. There, Socrates, in constructing in speech the perfect city, asks to be excused from proving that what he proposes is possible and invites his interlocutors to consider, at first, only whether it is desirable.

Whether the *Republic* intends to set forth the human condition that is most desirable, even if impossible, or whether it intends to set forth the condition that is both most desirable and possible, we need not here inquire. Suffice it to say that it has been taken in both senses within the tradition of the Christian West, and a form of Platonism has motivated messianic reform movements within that tradition. Lincoln's apocalyptic vision, in the "Temperance Address," of the perfect (albeit passionate) conquest of passion by reason is at once an evocation of the rule of philosopher-kings and of the rule of the Kingdom of God. It is curious that Lincoln refers to this perfect regime as both the culmination of the political revolution based on equal human rights and the *monarchy* of all-conquering mind. This monarchy resembles that of the Heavenly City promised by divine revelation, since it implies what is at once the perfection and the extinction of authority. The rule of love or pure reason or both transcends authority because it directs men toward what they above all desire. By abolishing all impediments to consummation, it is the perfection of liberty. But a state of perfect liberty, even if in accord with the dictates of authority, can no longer be understood as a state under authority. Hence it must be a state of "no-government."

In Plato's *Republic,* justice is defined as everyone doing only that work for which they are by nature best fitted. By doing that one work, one may carry to perfection the art of doing it well. One's capacity for one's work and one's devotion to it may then be fully equal to each other. Although the guardians, the ruling class, will be set over the shoemakers, they will not tell the shoemakers how to cobble. The *Republic* is essentially a community of craftsmen in perfect harmony because each craftsman abstains from the other's craft. This abstention is assured by the very thing that makes each a craftsman: since the free practice of his own craft is the consuming passion of his soul, perfect cooperation is secured not by coercion but by the form of consciousness that makes one a craftsman. The harmony of the workman and his work ends the tension between private ends and the common good, thus ending everything today called "alienation." The *Republic,* in this respect, is the ultimate source of those anarchist-syndicalist theories of the nineteenth and twentieth centuries that see in the voluntary cooperation of workers (or craftsmen or guilds) the solution to the problem of authority in society. This is the *Republic* seen as the perfection of its communism and egalitarianism of the sexes, prior to the introduction of the philosopher-kings.

But in the *Republic,* one may recall, the rule of philosopher-kings is introduced not as an end but as a means of bringing into actual existence the perfect communist regime already sketched. By the nineteenth century, however, it seemed to many who had (however indirectly) accepted Plato's premise of the desirability of such a regime that its actualization might be easier than he had supposed and that, indeed, the abolition of private property and the introduction of equality of rights would be a sufficient condition for that actualization. Implicit in this judgment, however, was the taking over of the role of philosophy by different aspects of modern science.

Modern craftsmanship has scientific know-how infused into it; philosophy in the form of modern science has descended from the clouds of sterile metaphysics and entered the cities as fruitful technology. Craftsmanship has indeed been subdivided now into capital and labor—capital embodying technology, as distinct from mere tools. The improvement on Plato concerning the feasibility of the best regime arises from the perception that, in the *Republic*, the perfect cooperation of the craftsmen is assumed rather than demonstrated and that, in point of fact, it is not spontaneous because it is not intrinsic to their craftsmanship. That a man's whole soul can by nature be absorbed in cobbling (or restricted to any other single function) is a myth. The shoemakers and all the other artisans are, in the final analysis, kept in their places by lies, noble and not so noble.

But the knowledge of nature that informs the modern machinery of shoemaking is the same as that which underlies all other forms of efficient material production, including that by which the universe itself has come to be. The world is now unmediated by myth, and all stand in the same relationship to it; there can be no permanent basis for class distinctions. All may be freed by communism from an invidious alienation from the means of production, all may be freed by technology from an invidious alienation from the means of consumption, all may be freed by science from an invidious alienation from nature. Slavery, intemperance, otherworldly religion, coercive government—all become superfluous when society becomes thoroughly rational. This, I believe, conveys the outline of that transformation in the radical political thought of the nineteenth century by virtue of which Madison's hypothetical preference for a society of "angels" became the nonhypothetical ground for demanding that such a society be made actual. One can easily understand why, once the conviction arose that such a society was possible, there should be a belief in a categorical imperative to bring it into actual existence.

The foregoing has been intended as a characterization not of any particular thought of Thoreau's but rather of the milieu in which it flourished. It was the same milieu in which the numerous communist societies of mid-nineteenth-century America flourished, along with numerous radical reform movements—to abolish slavery, to abolish strong drink, to reform the prison system, to bring about full equality of rights for women, to abolish war, and many others. No one reading the *Communist Manifesto* of Marx and Engels together with "Civil Disobedience," both of them composed at about the same time, can fail to perceive the same temper—a temper indicating that the total reform of society is, or should be, near at hand. This milieu is still the ground of the politics of the revolutionary "New Left," a Left that is actually more than a century old, as we realize when we understand that Thoreau, perhaps even more than Marx and Engels, is one of its authentic heroes.

The tradition of obedience to law in the United States is at best an ambiguous one. The most obvious reason for this was given at the outset of this chapter: the United States annually celebrates its revolutionary origins, its withdrawal of allegiance from a system of law on the grounds of natural right. These grounds indicate that the laws of nature and nature's God take precedence over any positive human law. The sense of obligation to law has long focused on the Constitution, most obviously because the Constitution is the supreme law of the land, and it invites respect because of this supremacy.

Yet the very circumstance that makes the Constitution supreme encourages certain tendencies toward civil disobedience. The supremacy of the Constitution is a supremacy over all public officials, state or national, legislative, executive, or judicial. In theory, any act in conflict with the Constitution is null and void. To challenge a public act, however, it is frequently necessary to violate it in order to secure a test of its legality in the courts. Hence disobedience to lawfully constituted authorities may be an act of respect for the Constitution.

The supremacy of the Constitution is a very practical matter: the nature of American federalism—the diversity of its political jurisdictions and their overlapping character—is such that American public law would tend toward chaos if there were no final arbiter, no final authority. The final arbiter of American public law is usually the Supreme Court of the United States. The qualification *usually* is in recognition of the fact that questions regarding the law cannot always be tried in the courts. The word *arbiter* is in recognition that, at any given time, the Supreme Court is the deciding body. But the authority of the Court is the authority of the Constitution, and if the sense of the political community of the United States differs with the Supreme Court as to the meaning of the Constitution, the authority of the Court will not stand, and future Courts will interpret the Constitution in a manner more consistent with the sense of the community.

But suppose the community itself is divided? It is, of course, normal that any community should be divided into majority and minority. However, the acceptance of majority rule by the minority (or minorities), on the one hand, and the acceptance by the majority of the minority's right not to be coerced in certain matters, on the other hand, depend on a prior understanding of the relationship of majority rule to minority rights. "All too will bear in mind this sacred principle," said Jefferson in his first inaugural address, "that though the will of the majority is in all cases to prevail, that will, to be rightful must be reasonable; that the minority possess equal rights, which equal laws must protect, and to violate which would be oppression."[20]

The Constitution, as every schoolboy knows, is in certain respects a bundle of compromises. To interpret the Constitution, one must make a judgment as to what are mere expedients and what are dictates of principle. For example, if the Warren Court was correct in its opinions on the subject of apportionment, the U.S. Senate must be the most malapportioned legislative body in the country, and its existence can be justified only as the merest expedient. In contrast, if one sees the Senate as an institution designed to secure a certain equality of the states within the Union, to the end that national majorities be distributed as well as amassed, the Senate can be viewed as a wise or principled expedient. It may be seen as one of those expedients designed to induce reasonableness in the majority and to protect those equal rights the minority possesses, the violation of which would be oppression.

The most fundamental of all the compromises the Constitution of 1787 exhibited, and the source of the most undoubted mere expedients, was that which treated the Negro slaves both as persons and as things. The population that determined the representation of each state in the lower house of Congress was arrived at by adding to the whole number of white persons three-fifths of all others, exclusive of Indians. There is an anomaly in the very idea of a three-fifths person. But in the so-called fugitive slave clause (the words *slave, slavery,* and *Negro* do not occur in the original Constitution), it is said that all persons held to labor or service under the laws of any of the states, escaping into another state, shall not be discharged from such service or labor, but shall be returned to the person to whom the service or labor is due. By this clause, the government of the United States was committed to assisting in enforcing the laws of the slave states. These laws treated Negro slaves as chattels—that is, mere movable property—although in certain respects, such as responsibility for most felonies, they were also regarded as human persons. By its indirect incorporation of state law, the U.S. Constitution undoubtedly treated Negro slaves as both human persons and nonhuman chattels.

Therefore, when the Fifth Amendment commanded that no person should be deprived of life, liberty, or property, except by due process of law, the Constitution commanded two absolutely contradictory things: that no slave owner be arbitrarily deprived of his chattel, and that no Negro be arbitrarily deprived of his liberty. But when conflict arose, which of these two conflicting imperatives represented the "real" Constitution?

It is against this background of difficulty that respect for law—above all, the supreme law, the law of the Constitution—must be examined. Everyone knows that the greatest cause of social and civil conflict, and hence of law-lessness, in the United States has been racial difference. But this is not mere racial difference such as that which has existed in many times and many places. This is racial difference in the presence of the great commitment to the proposition "that all men are created equal."

Thoreau saw no problem: If the Constitution sanctions slavery, disobey it. If the Union includes slave states, secede. But Abraham Lincoln, in his Springfield Lyceum speech of 1838, saw the matter differently. The turmoil racking the country then was similar to that of the 1960s. Then the question concerned the American Negro's transition from slavery to legal freedom. In the 1960s it concerned his transition from legal freedom to social and political equality. Lincoln foresaw even then that terrible forfeits might be exacted for the abolition of slavery.

The first quality of the Lyceum speech that immediately sets it in a different genre from Thoreau's essay is that it is *political*. It is an oration by a rising young Whig member of the Illinois legislature. It deals with a matter deeply agitating the country at large, and it displays a special sensitivity to the impact of that matter on the south-central Illinois city of Springfield. That community, like most others in southern Ohio, Indiana, and Illinois, was populated by families, like the Lincolns, who had migrated across the Ohio River from slave states. Such families usually preferred to live on free soil, to get away from slavery. But it was more often the degrading competition of Negro slave labor, rather than the moral obliquy of slavery itself, to which they objected. Many still had family ties southward, and they resented any condemnations of slavery that implicated their kinsmen. Moreover, they feared abolitionism as much as they feared the extension of slavery, and for much the same reason: either would bring them into unwanted contact with Negroes.

The rise of abolitionist agitation in the 1830s led the Illinois legislature, in January 1837, just a year before the Lyceum speech, to pass resolutions denouncing abolitionism. Six weeks after these resolutions, a protest against them appeared in the journal of the House, signed by Dan Stone and A. Lincoln, representatives of Sangamon County. It declared that "the institution of slavery is founded in both injustice and bad policy, but that the promulgation of abolition doctrines tends rather to increase than abate its evils."[21] It is of some interest that those six weeks between the time the majority resolutions passed and the time Lincoln and Stone entered their dissenting views was the same period when the two representatives of Sangamon County brought to a climax their successful maneuvers to remove the state capital from Vandalia to Springfield—a logrolling operation that was perhaps the high point of Lincoln's career in the state legislature. Politicians are certainly permitted to have convictions of their own, but the expression of those convictions must not be deeply offensive to the people they represent. Lincoln's rhetorical maxim was that a drop of honey catches more flies than a gallon of gall. Certainly, the abolitionists at this time were profoundly galling, even to most shades of anti-slavery opinion.

Some six weeks before the Lyceum speech, on November 7, 1837, the lynching of abolitionist editor Elijah Lovejoy had occurred at nearby Alton, Illinois. This event hung like a pall over both Lincoln and his audience. The extraordinary tact with which Lincoln treated his own and his audience's complex reaction to this ambiguous event accounts for much of the complexity of the speech.[22]

Today the tendency is to regard Lovejoy, like John Brown, as a genuine witness to the cause of freedom. Yet Lincoln had no great sympathy for either man. Brown he regarded as a mere fanatic who brooded over slavery until he became demented with the notion that he had a divine mission to extirpate it. To Lincoln, Brown accomplished little—after the murder of a number of innocents—besides his own destruction and that of his followers. To Thoreau, in contrast, John Brown was an authentic Carlylean hero, a prophet, a martyr, and a saint. An ultimate judgment on the wisdom of Lincoln and Thoreau would require judgments on the respective contributions of Lincoln and Brown to the ultimate emancipation of the slaves. Lincoln's attitude toward the murder of Lovejoy must have been influenced not only by his belief that Lovejoy's denunciations of slavery and slave owners were doing more to strengthen pro-slavery than anti-slavery feelings but also by the fact that Lovejoy was as violently anti-Catholic as he was anti-slavery.

The abolitionist movement had its roots in the evangelical Protestantism of the day. In today's parlance, it was emphatically "waspish." The same roots produced the temperance movement, which also was mainly Protestant. The Irish were objects of antagonism both for their supposed addiction to whiskey and for their popery (not to mention their tendency to march down the gangplanks directly to the polls, under the guidance of Democratic politicians), and Lovejoy was against them for both reasons. But the Irish were also violently anti-Negro, for they, as the lowest class of white labor, were in competition with Negroes. It was the Negroes who, before the Civil War, built the southern railroads, as it was the Irish who built the railroads of the North. But the problem of civil liberty in the antebellum United States was not a problem of Negro slavery alone—it was a problem of discrimination based on race, religion, and nationality together.

In the period between 1854 and 1860, the anti-slavery movement was muddled by the fact that the Know-Nothings flourished side by side with the Republicans, and both movements were, to a great extent, competing for the same votes. In 1856 the anti-Democratic vote was divided between Frémont, the Republican candidate, and Fillmore, who was nominated both by the Know-Nothing (or American) Party and by the remnant of the Whig Party. It was this division of the Free-Soil vote that enabled Buchanan to be elected. In 1855 Lincoln gave his private opinion of the Know-Nothings to his old friend Joshua Speed, who had moved to Kentucky:

> I am not a Know-Nothing. That is certain. How could I be? How can any one who abhors the oppression of negroes, be in favor of degrading classes of white people? Our progress in degeneracy appears to me to be pretty rapid. As a nation, we began by declaring that *"all men are created equal."* We now practically read it "all men are created equal, *except negroes."* When the Know-Nothings get control, it will read "all men are created equal, except negroes, *and foreigners, and Catholics."* When it comes to this I should prefer emigrating to some country where they make no pretence of loving liberty—to Russia, for instance, where despotism can be taken pure and without the base alloy of hypocrisy.[23]

Yet in 1860, so important was the Know-Nothing vote to the Republicans that Lincoln refused to make any public denial of association with them. In considering the letter to Speed, one must be struck not only by the vehemence of Lincoln's views but also by the fact that he felt compelled to make such a disavowal. So close was the affinity of Know-Nothingism and the anti-slavery movement that even such a close personal friend as Speed could not be certain where Lincoln stood. There is a remarkable resemblance between the political currents that carried the anti-slavery movement forward in the 1850s—currents that included some of the noblest and some of the basest passions American politics exhibits—and those that brought "law and order" to the fore in the latter 1960s. The good and the bad are closely intertwined politically, making the problem of political persuasion a delicate one.

Lincoln sympathized with Lovejoy's anti-slavery feelings, but he disagreed strongly with his anti-Catholicism and anti-foreignism. He certainly believed in Lovejoy's constitutional right to freedom of speech, but he did not believe that one could properly claim the protection of the Constitution in one respect and then disregard the Constitution in other respects. This is what the abolitionists did when they denied the validity of the provisions for the rendition of fugitive slaves or when they denied the limitations on federal power to interfere with slavery in the states. In the Lyceum speech, Lincoln is not making a bid for partisan electoral support, as he would do in 1858 and 1860. But he provides a remarkable example of his capacity for leadership in his diagnosis of a grave problem and in the manner in which he discriminates the point on which conscience and prudence might agree.

The Lyceum speech begins by announcing as its subject "the perpetuation of our political institutions."[24] This would also be the theme of the Gettysburg Address twenty-five years later. Lincoln then goes on to remind his listeners of their great good fortune to be citizens of the United States: of their material prosperity, of their comparative immunity from foreign dangers, of the fact that they have inherited nearly all these blessings, having "toiled not in the acquirement or establishment of them." At the heart of these blessings, however, is a "government . . . conducing more essentially to the ends of civil and religious liberty, than any of which the history of former times tells us." Thus, whereas Thoreau looks forward to an apocalyptic vision of uncoerced men of conscience freely associating in a regime of pure virtue, Lincoln looks back toward the despotism and religious persecution from which "a political edifice of liberty and equal rights" has freed us, and rejoices. Whereas Thoreau feels the intolerableness of a system that permits slavery and unjust war, Lincoln warns against the spirit of lawlessness abroad in the land, a spirit that may in time lead to the overthrow of these free institutions. As we have seen, Lincoln is keenly aware of the fact that the fear and hatred engendered by slavery and racial difference are the principal causes of the mob violence sweeping the land, but he makes little direct reference to the fact, preferring to find neutral ground on which he can unite his audience in the contemplation of the dangers into which their own conflicting passions might be leading them. After reviewing the terrible scenes of mob violence, Lincoln comments, "Its direct consequences are, comparatively speaking, but a small evil; and much of its danger consists, in the proneness of our minds, to regard its direct, as its only consequences." The lynching of gamblers or of murderers is in itself no matter of necessary regret. But once the habit of taking the direct way with the guilty is adopted, what is to prevent its being extended to the innocent? Presently, the lawless in spirit, encouraged by the example of those who smugly believe they can dispense with the forms of law in dealing with malefactors, "make a jubilee" of the suspension of the operations of legal government.

Lincoln deals subtly and elaborately with the distinction between the direct and indirect consequences of what might be called, somewhat inaccurately, "innocuous lawlessness." There is the obvious point that those who, in their self-righteous indignation, lynch undoubted malefactors cannot easily be made to believe they are endangering the innocent. To persuade the individuals in a lynch mob (whether at the moment they form part of the mob or at some other time) that they might be mistaken in their victims is not easy. Lincoln makes this point but lays more stress on the next one, namely, that toleration of "justifiable" lynchings eventually supplies the pretext for general assaults on personal safety and property. The distance from this to the death of constitutional liberty is not so great as might be supposed, and most of the Lyceum speech is directed at warning against this danger. When "good men . . . who love tranquility, who desire to abide by the laws, and enjoy their benefits . . . seeing their property destroyed; their families insulted . . . become tired of, and disgusted with, a Government that offers them no protection," the turning point is at hand. It is at this juncture that the danger of the demagogue becomes acute.

Lincoln cites the three great destroyers of republics according to the tradition of his day: Alexander, Caesar, and Napoleon. But we cannot help thinking of Hitler and Mussolini, both of whom induced street rioting to precipitate the crises that brought them to power. In the crunch, they used the middle-class fear of lawlessness as a means of installing regimes from which the very idea of law was rooted out in favor of the iron fist of dictatorship. And this fist was brought down without discrimination on erstwhile supporters as well as former foes. Lincoln, it seems, anticipated with something like clairvoyance the typology of the process by which twentieth-century dictatorships were established on the ruins of constitutional government.

Lincoln is, in the Lyceum speech, directly addressing the very people whose unwitting defection from the forms of law might bring about constitutional crisis. In the most remarkable passage of the speech, he warns that the demagogic destroyer who "thirsts and burns for distinction . . . will have it, whether at the expense of emancipating slaves, or enslaving freemen." Lincoln here, as elsewhere, appears to display a curious neutrality between pro-slavery and anti-slavery positions. In part, this reflects the ambiguity in the feelings of his audience. Yet the select committee of the Illinois legislature that had reported the anti-abolitionism resolutions the year before also deeply deplored "the unfortunate condition of our fellow-men, whose lots are cast in thraldom in a land of liberty and peace." But it is also true that, throughout his life and until the very moment he issued the final Emancipation Proclamation, Lincoln was profoundly opposed to the uncompensated emancipation of the slaves. And that is what the abolitionists (as distinct from Free-Soilers) stood for—Thoreau among them.

Abolition at a stroke would destroy a vast body of invested capital. It would throw the economic cost of emancipating the slaves entirely on those who, by the accident of the moment, held title to the slaves. It would unnecessarily exacerbate the feelings of those whose goodwill and assistance would, of necessity, be integral to the process of social reconstruction that would follow emancipation. Slavery was woven into the economic life of the entire nation, and the guilt for its presence must be allocated among all, North and South, who were implicated in it. That was always Lincoln's conviction. Northern ship owners had made fortunes in the foreign slave trade before 1809. Their descendants were carrying slave-produced cotton to Europe now. The mills of the North were spinning it and weaving it; railroads were moving it; banks were financing it; stores were selling it;

and every household in the land was consuming it. Many a northern free state that had arranged for the emancipation of slaves within its boundaries had allowed owners to sell their slaves in the South rather than actually emancipate them. Were those who bought so much more guilty than those who sold that the entire burden should fall on the buyers alone? Not a man, woman, or child who was free in the antebellum United States did not share in the product of the unrequited toil of the slaves. The injustice of uncompensated emancipation, Lincoln thought, was of the kind practiced throughout history by designing demagogues who would set class against class by offering to despoil one for the benefit of the other, and end up destroying the liberties of all. The zeal of the reformer may well be indistinguishable from that of the would-be tyrant. Lincoln's thesis is that our tendency to regard direct consequences as if they were the only consequences provides the opportunity for tyranny by both the mob and the demagogue.

The Lyceum speech does not, in any programmatic sense, provide a solution to the problem it describes. The only solution mentioned by Lincoln is that reverence for the Constitution and the laws become the political religion of the nation. Lincoln is well aware of the defects in the American political system—above all, those connected with slavery and the Negro. He is careful to mention that bad laws may exist and that grievances may be intolerable. Yet the alternative to the constitutional means for rectifying evils is unconstitutional. This would mean adopting a remedy that may in the end be as bad as, if not worse than, the disease. A free society that tolerates slavery is under a reproach from its own principles and may undertake to make freedmen of slaves. A society in which no man is free, and from which the principle of freedom has been banished, offers no reproach to slavery and has no principle of reform.

Thoreau and Lincoln both consider the question of unjust laws. Lincoln says they should be obeyed until they can be changed by legal means, "if not too intolerable." With this exception, Lincoln's argument touches Thoreau's thesis. However, Lincoln continues, "There is no grievance that is a fit object of mob law." The question becomes, does the justification for civil disobedience in extreme cases also justify the organization of a minority to clog and, by its whole weight, force the majority to bow to its will?

Thoreau calls on the government—by which he means the constitutional majority—to "cherish its wise minority." Of course, in substance, this is what representative government, as distinct from direct democracy, is supposed to do. But why should a self-appointed "wise minority" outside of government be entitled to an obedience that Thoreau denies to the minority chosen constitutionally by the majority? As for the ways provided by law, says Thoreau, "They take too much time, and a man's life will be gone."[25] But the time required for constitutional decisions reflects the inborn difficulty of infusing rationality into political decisions and then securing widespread consent. On the one hand, Thoreau wishes to have no decisions by society to which everyone has not consented—that is the essence of his anarchism—but on the other hand, he demands that society bow to its wise minority.

Lincoln's call for a "political religion" is a recognition that, as Aristotle says, law itself has no power to persuade other than the power of habit. It is habit that forms character, and the rule of law presupposes the character of law-abidingness. A regime in which law rules becomes more lawful by reason of its legality; this may sound like a tautology, but it is founded on the perception that every habit grows by repetition of the activity from which the habit first arose. Lincoln recognizes the possibility of intolerable grievances even under a good government. But he believes that the more the rule of law takes effect, the less the possibility that such grievances will exist, because the more people will respect the processes by which reform takes place. Thoreau's approach, setting conscience against law rather than enlisting it on the side of law, corrupts the very process by which reason replaces force in arbitrating human differences.

Lincoln's call to make reverence for the Constitution and the laws the political religion of the nation is a recognition that a merely utilitarian view of the value of freedom and free institutions can never induce the sacrifices necessary for their preservation. The crucial sacrifices are not those required by war—of blood and treasure. The dearest sacrifices are those of self-love and obstinate opinion, which tend to dominate a free society at peace. Lincoln begins the Lyceum speech by indicating the relationship between a relative immunity to foreign danger and the violence sweeping the country in 1838. He is aware, as is Madison in Federalist No. 10, that human nature embodies a propensity to violent faction, which is particularly manifest when that nature is emancipated from arbitrary government and from myths that induce in everyone the same opinions and passions. Lincoln agrees with Aristotle (as does Madison) that man separated from law is not divine but bestial. Yet he disagrees with the opinion to which Madison gives countenance, that government is a reproach to human nature. As Aristotle and Lincoln see it, government is required not only to overcome the ills of human nature but also to give scope to the good. However rhetorical Madison's concession to the superiority of a state of anarchy, he implies there is a human condition imaginable better than that of the best regime imaginable. But government is needed not only to prevent harm but also to achieve good. Friendship, says Aristotle, is better than justice. But friendship does not arise in a vacuum. The conditions under which men become friends are those that the political community provides. Outside the political community, there is neither the leisure nor the activity for men to discover friendship.

Thoreau demands life according to principle. But principle, as he sees it, is something asocial, something that is as inconsistent with friendship as with justice under law. "Action from principle . . . changes things and relations," he writes. "It is essentially revolutionary, and does not consist wholly with any thing which was. It not only divides states and churches, it divides families; aye, it divides the *individual,* separating the diabolical in him from the divine."[26]

But the question must be asked, does the separation of the diabolical from the divine send the diabolical or the divine forth to rule the world? Thoreau's strictures against law and constitutional majority rule can only lead to rule not by a "wise minority" but to lawless tyranny. Lincoln's solution is to subject the diabolical to the divine, by moral education and the rule of law, in a regime dedicated not to any minority, wise or unwise, but to the proposition that all men are created equal.

## Notes

Originally published as Harry V. Jaffa, "Reflections on Thoreau and Lincoln: Civil Disobedience and the American Tradition," in *On Civil Disobedience: American Essays, Old and New* (Chicago: Rand McNally Public Affairs Series, 1969), chapter 3. Subsequently reprinted in *The Conditions of Freedom: Essays in Political Philosophy* (Claremont, CA: Claremont Institute, 2003), chapter 6. Reprinted by permission. Minor changes have been made.

1. Plato, *Apology of Socrates,* 28d 10ff. (author's translation).

2. Henry David Thoreau, *Walden and Civil Disobedience,* ed. Owen Thomas (New York: W. W. Norton, 1966), 232.

3. Ibid., 233.

4. Ibid., 224.

5. Ibid., 225.

6. *The Collected Works of Abraham Lincoln,* ed. Roy P. Basler (New Brunswick, NJ: Rutgers University Press, 1953), 1:279.

7. *The Federalist Papers,* ed. Clinton Rossiter (New York: Signet Classics, 2003), 319.

8. Thoreau, *Walden and Civil Disobedience,* 225.

9. *The Complete Jefferson,* comp. Saul K. Padover (New York: Tudor Publishing Company, 1943), 675.

10. Thoreau, *Walden and Civil Disobedience,* 226.

11. Ibid., 225.

12. Ibid.

13. Ibid., 224–25.

14. *Social Theories of Jacksonian Democracy,* ed. Joseph L. Blau (New York: Liberal Arts Press, 1954), 26–27.

15. Ibid.

16. Ibid., 28.

17. *Common Sense, The Rights of Man, and Other Essential Writings of Thomas Paine* (New York: Signet Classics, 2003), 270.

18. *Complete Jefferson,* 133.

19. Ibid., 386.

20. Ibid., 384.

21. *Collected Works of Lincoln,* 1:75.

22. I provide a comprehensive analysis of this masterpiece in chapter 9 of *Crisis of the House Divided: An Interpretation of the Issues in the Lincoln-Douglas Debates,* new ed. (Chicago: University of Chicago Press, [1959] 1982); here I can only touch on some of its leading features.

23. *Collected Works of Lincoln,* 2:323.

24. The full speech is at ibid., 1:108–15.

25. Thoreau, *Walden and Civil Disobedience,* 231–32.

26. Ibid., 230–31.

# CHAPTER 8

# Thoreau's Apolitical Legacy for American Environmentalism

*William Chaloupka*

> As for taking Thoreau's arm, I should as soon take the arm of an elm tree.
> —Ralph Waldo Emerson, *Journals*

TO UNDERSTAND THOREAU'S impact on contemporary environmentalism, it helps to recognize that when the Earth Day greens found him, Thoreau's reputation as a literary and political figure was still in flux. Other famous writers in the canon of American literature are sometimes understood in terms of their early, middle, or late periods—reflecting the detailed sense of a writer's thought that emerges after decades or even centuries of examination. But with Thoreau, we find no important distinctions between his early and late writings. What we do find, however, are distinctive channels his influence traveled on its way to contemporary environmentalism. This is not Thoreau's fault; it is an artifact of the historical path his legacy took.

There have been several Thoreaus—a shifting cast of characters made multiple not by any error or indecision on Thoreau's part or by a discernible maturation of his thought but by the historically contingent way those several Thoreaus emerged. It would be erroneous to say that he anticipated an environmental movement; he was more than a little ambivalent about "movements." Still, contemporary American environmentalism constitutes one of Thoreau's most important recent audiences, both in the sense that the greens renewed interest in Thoreau and in terms of the remarkable influence his work had on the movement.

Environmentalism emerged in the context of the proliferation of movements that followed the civil rights and anti–Vietnam War efforts.

Environmentalism was as distinct from its conservationist roots as feminism was from the suffragettes. The green mixture was unprecedented—at one moment radical, then conservative; indebted to science and nature but also capable of a particular spiritualism; deeply engaged in the public world but ambivalent about politics. In each of these ways, the Thoreau the environmentalists discovered seemed to speak directly to them.

What the greens found in Thoreau was an ethical gesture and a romanticism that deeply satisfied them. The Earth Day generation was drawn to Thoreau by his wilderness values and a spiritualism propelled by landscapes. As Earth Day greens responded to Thoreau's integrity, independence, and attentiveness to nature, they were also willing to embrace a predecessor who had rejected the American polity and whose political views were often immature and even contradictory. Several choices and conditions eventually blocked environmentalism from the explicit conversation about politics that, in retrospect, dearly needed to happen. Whereas green commitments could be expressed by gestural protests, conscientious consumerism, and a fairly narrow approach to lobbying and litigating, larger questions of the movement's position toward long-term and large-scale structural change seemed beyond its grasp. In this respect, among others, the movement reflected Thoreau's influence when it should have worked to overcome it.

This chapter first examines the several Thoreaus available to the Earth Day generation and then analyzes the fateful symbolic and political choices the greens made at the outset of their movement. Later sections examine the consequences of the greens' appropriation of Thoreau—consequences that have often worked to the movement's disadvantage.

## The Several Thoreaus

Thoreau's work had little impact during his lifetime. As influential as his mentor Emerson became, the transcendentalists hardly constituted a nationally significant intellectual or political movement. Despite sponsors such as Emerson, Hawthorne, and Greeley, Thoreau's career as a speaker and writer remained on a surprisingly small scale, and it sustained him only because his need for money was legendarily slim. Emerson understood the lack of ambition or even social skills in his protégé: "Thoreau wants a little ambition in his mixture. . . . Instead of being the head of American engineers, he is captain of a huckleberry party."[1]

Thoreau's reputation waned after his death. In *Thoreau's Ecstatic Witness,* Alan Hodder traces the trajectory of that reputation.[2] Although Thoreau's death was widely reported, the demise of his legacy began immediately, with Emerson's eulogy, which was published in the *Atlantic Monthly* in August 1862. While acknowledging Thoreau's great gifts, Emerson stressed his friend's apparent eccentricities. A couple of years later, the influential critic James Russell Lowell characterized Thoreau "as a man with so high a conceit of himself that he accepted . . . his defects and weaknesses of character as virtues and powers peculiar to himself."[3] Lowell is still quoted on Thoreau's character, sometimes even by Thoreau's advocates.[4] As Hodder summarizes, although "friends rallied to Thoreau's defense, it would be decades before the damage done by Lowell's salvos could be entirely repaired."[5] In short, despite famous literary friends and a substantial body of work, Thoreau's influence emerged later and in an idiosyncratic fashion that resonates with his own character.

Later in the nineteenth century, Houghton Mifflin (the successor to Thoreau's original publisher) released Thoreau's journal and generally promoted his importance, but its approach, as Hodder explains, domesticated Thoreau as a nature writer, "effectively sidelin[ing] the political dimension of his writings in the United States for almost a generation."[6] As the twentieth century began, John Macy and Vernon Louis Parrington embraced what they saw as Thoreau's critique of capitalism's voracious expansionism and nascent consumerism, setting the stage for subsequent appropriations of Thoreau by the Left.[7] Not until 1941, however, did Thoreau secure a place in the nineteenth-century canon of literary figures, with his treatment in F. O. Matthiessen's *American Renaissance.* [8]

Matthiessen, a central New Criticism figure, set the tone of America's understanding of Thoreau for a quarter century. Matthiessen argued against limiting Thoreau to his nature writing: "Thoreau has not ordinarily been approached primarily as an artist. His first disciples tended to think of him as a naturalist, with the result that later scientists have criticized him for his want of severe method and his crotchety inaccuracies. He gave enough warnings against this interpretation. He said that he did not want too exact knowledge: the poet and the botanist look very differently at the same object."[9] Matthiessen appreciated Thoreau's ability to function within a contradiction, but he clearly wanted to push Thoreau's legacy in the political direction: "Though he often talked in paradoxes, he was still more explicit in warning readers against taking *Walden* as a reformer's manual. Yet his vitality as a revolutionary is still unexhausted."[10]

Quickly dispensing with Emerson's apolitical or conservative reading ("Thoreau was in his own person a practical answer, almost a refutation, to the theories of the socialists"[11]), Matthiessen credited Thoreau as a "chief basis" for Gandhi's passive resistance and identified Thoreau's "natural direction" as "left-wing individualism."[12] Matthiessen did not address the obvious paradox of "left-wing individualism" in his early-twentieth-century context; not until the emergence of the New Left a quarter of a century later did leftists begin to see individualism and Marxism as compatible. Matthiessen also may have given Thoreau too much credit for political approaches Gandhi developed. Still, Matthiessen identified Thoreau as a critic with a somewhat narrow but crucial target: "Thoreau's radical value does not lie in his gestures of protest, the shock of [which] was cushioned by his circumstances. . . . His contribution to our social thought lies in his thoroughgoing criticism of the narrow materialism of his day."[13]

In short, Matthiessen promoted Thoreau's voluntary simplicity as his work's core, ignoring that Thoreau based this claim more on his love of natural settings, his Stoic critique of materialism, and his crabby complaints about bourgeois Concord than on anything faintly resembling Marxism. This was how Matthiessen, writing from the secular Left, appropriated Thoreau without being troubled by the latter's obvious spiritualism and individualism. It is a generous reading: when Matthiessen praised Thoreau for "not want[ing] that freedom [of life without encumbrances] for his private self alone," he conflated Thoreau's hope for social transformation via transcendental spiritualism with an emergent political position, despite ample evidence of Thoreau's reluctance to engage politically.[14] These are thin reeds on which to base a political reading of a canonical figure. Matthiessen put Thoreau into the American canon but left room for other Thoreaus to emerge.

While Matthiessen was refining Thoreau's meaning for scholars and intellectuals, *New Yorker* writer E. B. White revived Thoreau for a broader (if still elite) audience.[15] White's reading of Thoreau was deliberately sophisticated: "There is hardly a paragraph of *Walden* which does not seem humorous to me."[16] White brought Thoreau to a specific American audience, one characterized more by the *New Yorker*'s recreational woodsiness than by anything as raw as Thoreauvian wilderness. White's Thoreau was an explicitly literary figure: "Henry Thoreau has probably been more wildly misconstrued than any other person of comparable literary stature. He got a reputation for being a naturalist, and he was not much of a naturalist. He got a reputation for being a hermit, and he was no hermit. He was a writer, is what he was."[17]

White understood the limits of the uses others were beginning to find for Thoreau's writings in the 1940s (Matthiessen is not mentioned but seems to be the referent):

> Because of a few crotchety remarks [Thoreau] made about the factory system and because of his essay on civil disobedience, he is one of the early Americans now being taken up by Marxists. But not even these hard-working Johnnies-come-lately can pin him down; he subscribed to no economic system and his convictions were strong but disorderly. What seemed so wrong to him was less man's economy than man's puny spirit and man's strained relationship with nature—which he regarded as a public scandal. Most of the time he didn't want to do anything about anything—he wanted to observe and to feel.[18]

White understood that Thoreau's accomplishment was specifically literary, even gestural. If there was any plane of transformation at play in White's Thoreau, it was spiritual or perhaps cultural. But White's strong voice did more than simply recapture Thoreau from the leftists; perhaps more important, he gave his Thoreau a cultural position and sensibility, albeit a somewhat ironic one, given Thoreau's own antipathy for bourgeois society. White's Thoreau has an elite New Englander's sense of class and love of natural retreat. Although the *New Yorker* would be important to the emergence of American environmentalism (specifically by publishing Rachel Carson), this was hardly Earth Day environmentalism's political base.

White and Matthiessen deployed somewhat different Thoreaus, even though they both contributed to his canonical status. Ironically, they both recognized yet another Thoreau, one that would emerge even more forcefully with the rise of contemporary environmentalism. Matthiessen was closest to White in his acute observation that Thoreau's engagement with nature was most powerful when it addressed landscape. This may have been Matthiessen's attempt to discount Thoreau's transcendentalism, but it also foreshadowed an important subsequent reading. Commenting on *A Week on the Concord*, Matthiessen read Thoreau's aim as neither spiritual nor primarily naturalist: that aim was "not just to suggest the diffused radiance that stimulated him, but to present by minute notations the record of a whole scene."[19] Matthiessen noted that Thoreau understood that "we are not wholly involved in Nature," as a naturalist might argue.[20] Instead, Thoreau's best insights involved landscape, "most akin to the tradition of the pioneer settlers, who had regarded the lonely wilderness with awe that could mount to terror."[21]

Long before the Earth Day era, Americans had accorded nearly mythical status to the pastoral, agrarian origins of the national character. Matthiessen understood that Thoreau's sense of the moral value of landscape shifted the American pastoral so that it could inspire terror as well as positive versions of awe. The transformation of the pastoral ideal that Thoreau initiated and John Muir elaborated actually had much in common with the landscape painting of the nineteenth century. Historian Roderick Nash—whose promotion of wilderness was enormously important to contemporary environmentalism—drew this connection, citing landscape painter Thomas Cole's *The Oxbow:* "Cole's divided canvas implied the idea Henry David Thoreau accepted as axiomatic: man's optimum environment is a blend of wilderness and civilization."[22]

Nash proposed that Thoreau was not writing about nature as much as wildness and that Thoreau's project (consistent with the landscape painter's own, separate project) intended to alter the moral narrative associated with the American landscape: "Previously most Americans had revered the rural, agrarian condition as a release both from wilderness and from high civilization. They stood, so to speak, with both feet in the center of the spectrum of environments. Thoreau, on the other hand, arrived at the middle by straddling. He rejoiced in the extremes, and, but keeping a foot in each, believed he could extract the best of both worlds."[23] In short, Thoreau was not simply promoting nature as an issue or a cause. His project was to reanimate the American pastoral origin myth with a moralistic drive and a broader, more dynamic narrative. As Nash explained, this was the Thoreau that inspired Muir and then the modern wilderness movement. In this way and others, Thoreau's moralism reflected his century's moralism.

In the post–World War II era, yet another Thoreau emerged. As the success of Gandhi's and Martin Luther King's application of nonviolent civil disobedience became more widely understood and appreciated, the Left's deployment of Thoreau shifted dramatically from the path Matthiessen had charted. Mulford Q. Sibley's seminal *The Quiet Battle,* published in 1963, called "Civil Disobedience", "one of the great classics of non-violent civil disobedience."[24] Writing about the Montgomery bus boycott, King recalled having read and "reread . . . several times" Thoreau's "On Civil Disobedience" in the 1940s as a student at Morehouse.[25] The actions of the civil rights movement "are outgrowths of Thoreau's insistence that evil must be resisted."[26] King also reported that he "began to think about Thoreau's" essay when planning the Montgomery bus boycott: "What we were preparing to do in Montgomery was related to what Thoreau had expressed. We were simply saying to the white community, 'We can no longer lend our cooperation to an evil system.'"[27] King's praise of Thoreau was careful and narrow, crediting him with the idea of noncooperation with evil, but not going as far as Sibley. With his appeal to conscience and distinction between just and unjust laws, King moved beyond Thoreau's anarchism. King's narrow endorsement nevertheless informed post–Earth Day readings of Thoreau.

Matthiessen had managed to elevate Thoreau to the literary canon, but his political reading could not really persist, other than to help put Thoreau vaguely on the Left. With the emergence of the New Left and a new "humanist" reading of Marx, American intellectuals and scholars no longer needed to find "stand-ins" for Marx in their attempt to evade McCarthyist attacks. At the same time, Sibley's disobedient Thoreau was thin, summoned out of a need to give practitioners of this new mode of political action a venerable heritage. Even the complaints about Thoreau's character by Emerson and others had been largely forgotten by the 1960s. That era's encounter with Thoreau could therefore be remarkably fresh. Accordingly, the various elements of American society found different Thoreaus, with little resistance to their readings. The interaction of Thoreau and American environmentalism, to which I turn next, was not tempered by a lengthy tradition of Thoreau readings or even a dominant reading against which contemporary environmentalists could rebel.

## The Earth Day Generation

In the usual origin story of contemporary environmentalism, Earth Day was supposed to rescue the conservation movement from its debilitating elitism. In 1970, while some of the most radical aspects of the 1960s had begun to experience setbacks and frustrations, still other components were spinning off from the core civil rights and anti-war nexus. Radical and populist feminist and gay rights movements emerged. Earth Day signaled a similar emergence of an environmental movement clearly distinct from its predecessors. Whereas the Wilderness Society (which led the way in passing the Wilderness Act in 1964) was still benefiting from the endowment left by its founder, Bob Marshall, and whereas John Muir pursued a specifically elite strategy (inviting luminaries to visit Yosemite, since they could afford such a sojourn and might help with preservation), Earth Day was supposed to be populist. Enter the green multitude.

Of course, it did not work out that way. Even though environmental concerns captured public attention as never before, a few short years later, William Tucker branded the environmentalists as elitist, white, and amenity driven.[28] Tucker's critique stuck like glue.[29] Environmentalists found it surprisingly hard to deflect that critique, which grew as their critics learned the refined art of resentment politics that would eventually become the core strategy of the emerging new conservatism.

The post–Earth Day environmentalists were baffled and offended by criticisms such as Tucker's. These activists knew that their origins and sympathies resided with the 1960s movements. It proved hard for the movement to acknowledge that whereas other movements were thoroughly progressive, the environmentalists had at least a whiff of the conservative about them. As an emerging social movement (along with the civil rights, feminist, and gay liberation movements), environmentalism seemed to be part of a leftist phalanx. But the new movement's interaction with their Thoreau's anti-industrialism, pastoralism, and cultural nervousness about the American middle class all encouraged a cultural conservatism embedded within the ostensibly progressive green identity. Although this issue of ideology was largely ignored, signs of it emerged now and then. Environmentalists such as EarthFirst! founder Dave Foreman would slyly suggest that they were conservatives, since they were pursuing conservation.[30]

Green nervousness about middle-class culture and the economic life of the industrial age sounded like traditional European conservatism. Several green cultural themes were borrowed from the Right. Conservation was often an elite concern; "health food" was associated with cultural conservatives, including the Mormons; and opposition to additives such as fluoride was originally a conservative issue. (Stanley Kubrick's *Dr. Strangelove* is probably now remembered as much for the ultraconservative General Ripper's concern about pollutants as for its fictionalization of Henry Kissinger.) Muir was a nemesis of Progressive leader Gifford Pinchot, and elite conservationists such as Teddy Roosevelt and Bob Marshall, if not ideologically conservative, were more closely aligned with Republicans than with the liberals or leftists of their day. Characteristically, concern about the negative aspects of change has been a conservative position in Western cultures.

Consider the rift between greens and labor, fought almost continuously since Earth Day. The American Left had always positioned itself as "progressive," confident about prospects for the future and eager to incorporate the American middle class (or, in the case of organized labor, to have its membership join that middle class). Factory life was a problem to be fixed, not a moral evil. The same was true of pollution and ugly neighborhoods. The city mattered more than the countryside. Pinchot was the Progressives' "environmentalist." Muir, far closer to Thoreau, was something else. If not for the political Right's need to make alliances with the corporate world, Thoreau could have been perceived as a conservative, with his gestural anti-government stance, ruralism, individualism, and pastoralism. He could have been Rush Limbaugh's hero rather than David Brower's.

The environmental movement's reluctance to confront its own elite, conservative, moralist, pastoral, and white composition contributed to the odd political history environmentalism has compiled. As greens developed a political position, they established themselves as advocates for nature. Speaking for nature inured greens to the sort of political debate that might have dealt with the contradictory—radical and conservative—impulses implied by post–Earth Day environmentalism. *Nature* is such a powerful term in Western political discourse that it seemed to settle too many political discussions prematurely. Skirting the difficult questions politics can raise, environmentalists reenacted their Thoreau's trajectory. In doing so, contemporary greens set themselves up for a resentful counterattack that has been massively successful. Environmentalists largely settled for what they could get in enclave localities or in court, living off elaborations of laws passed in a mad rush after Earth Day—a rush that was over by the early 1970s.

The Earth Day generation's encounter with Thoreau drew heavily from the transcendental Thoreau, who found inspiration in the New England landscape but was exasperated by politics. Earth Day culture was similarly exasperated by politics, and many of those in the movement thought they could skip over the political phase by claiming to channel the voice of nature. That movement learned its disdain for politics from its hero. The transcendentalist Thoreau had a thorough disdain for the political world, even though he worried terribly about some political issues, especially slavery. His spiritualism and his writing—a clearly social act—sought to resolve that tension, promising a transformation that would circumvent the political world he found so hopeless.

Thoreau's rejection of politics was intentional. Although he was active in Concord's Underground Railroad and spoke out—sometimes quite dramatically—on the issue of slavery, Thoreau never joined an anti-slavery organization.[31] The reluctance to embrace social reform was not incidental but carefully theorized. As Thoreau biographer Walter Harding summarized it:

> So far as Thoreau was concerned, [reformers] went at things backwards. They believed that if they succeeded in reforming society, society would then reform the individual. Thoreau, true Transcendentalist that he was, believed that all reforms must begin with the individual. So long as the individual was corrupt he would find ways and means of corrupting even the most ideal society, but if the individual were truly reformed from within, he would lead the good life in society.[32]

As early as 1844, Thoreau put his individualism—even on the intensely political topic of slavery—into print, praising abolitionist Nathaniel P. Rogers over the better-known William Lloyd Garrison for the former's individualistic approach to the struggle over slavery. Rogers advocated dissolving anti-slavery societies as impediments to the actions of individual abolitionists.[33] According to Harding, Rogers "believed the only possible solution was the reformation of mankind" and "feared that Garrison's plans would lead to the institutionalizing of the anti-slavery societies themselves and argued that a utopian society could be achieved only through self-reformation of each individual in a society."[34]

Considering the institutional cataclysm the fight over slavery produced, Thoreau's thoughtful and deliberate pursuit of such a position makes him either a mystic (as he called himself in a note to the American Association for the Advancement of Science, declining consideration for membership)[35] or an anarchist, a possibility obvious enough in his proclamation, "My thoughts are murder to the State."[36] Some notion of social and political change inheres in each of these possibilities, to be sure. At one level, Thoreau's unquestionable commitment to transcendentalism answers the mystic or anarchist question; he thought individual ethical transformation must precede political progress, so he combined the two. Post–Earth Day greens absorbed Thoreau's individualism completely; private acts of consumption (buying healthy foods or a solar water heater or a bicycle) were presumed to be political acts. Of course, that could be the case, but as an unquestioned assumption, green individualism posed great political risks.

Thoreau's approach to civil disobedience forms part of his political argument as well, both because it informed a culture of protest in the 1960s and because any such position involves insights into ethics, public life, government, and myriad other political questions. But Gandhi and King understood that civil disobedience is not decisive on its own as an individualist, ethical action detached from politics (except for its impact on individuals). Their movements elaborated a notion of campaign—with its incumbent sense of goals, constituencies, and so forth. As Thomas Dumm has noted, Gandhi elaborated the notion of accepting punishment as an element of his ethical politics, but Thoreau did not get far enough into the topic to decide whether his night in the Concord jail was punishment.[37]

At the start of "Civil Disobedience," Thoreau takes his hard stance in vividly polemical terms: "'That government is best which governs not at all'; and when men are prepared for it, that will be the kind of government which they will have."[38] But as usefully polemical as that gesture is, it is unsatisfying as political argument. What sense are we to make of a government that aspires not to govern? And what prepares citizens for that situation, if not some collective endeavor? Thoreau's point is that government's role is predictably pernicious: "Witness the present Mexican war, the work of comparatively a few individuals using the standing government as their tool; for, in the outset, the people would not have consented to this measure."[39] So government will wither away when we are prepared for it, but in the meantime, government can positively block our preparations.

As has often been noted, there is a maturity here, as Thoreau distances himself from the standard American hymn of deference to institutions that govern in the name of the popular will: "The government itself, which is only the mode which the people have chosen to execute their will, is equally liable to be abused and perverted before the people can act through it."[40] Thoreau anticipates the critique of government that would emerge with the development of the social sciences a half century later: "The people must have some complicated machinery or other, and hear its din, to satisfy that idea of government which they have."[41] But we are soon disappointed. Thoreau has rushed to give government such a fixed identity and function that his political analysis veers toward confusion: "Governments show . . . how successfully men can be imposed on, even impose on themselves, for their own advantage."[42] At this point, readers might well find themselves wishing that Thoreau had spent fewer hours with the classical poets and a few more hours with, say, his fellow romantic Rousseau, whose analysis of the tensions faced by governments that rule on behalf of the popular will is deservedly canonical.

Soon enough, of course, Thoreau relaxes back into something not so distant from liberalism. He asks for "a better government" and is clear about how such an improvement would emerge: "Let every man make known what kind of government would command his respect, and that will be one step toward obtaining it."[43] He invokes the well-known tensions among majority rule, conscience, and justice. Then he skips along, insulting the very people he hopes will rise above their inherent limitations: "The mass of men serve the State . . . , not as men mainly, but as machines, with their bodies."[44] Such persons lack judgment and moral sense, putting "themselves on a level with wood and earth and stones. . . . They have the same sort of worth only as horses and dogs."[45] So, in political terms, it is not only the state that has a rigidly fixed identity; so too do the citizens on whom hopes for changing the state depend. Exasperated with both organized politics and the capacity of individual humans, Thoreau has nowhere to go except toward assertion of his own moral position.

Of course, much of "Civil Disobedience" is straightforwardly polemical. Appealing to "honest men," Thoreau complains about the excuses deployed by those who, at some level, know that slavery is wrong. For some, solving the moral problem seems too expensive or too damaging to commerce or too complicated, compared with other policy debates of the day. Or it seems impossible, since voting is futile, given the power of those forces that resist change.[46] Given this complexity, how is one to act?

As for himself, Thoreau simply has better things to do than to solve this difficult puzzle. In the paragraph after he memorably advises, "let your life be a counter friction to stop the machine," Thoreau simply jumps over an opportunity to elaborate how civil disobedience might work when he addresses what efforts at redress through legal channels are required before one is justified in breaking an unjust law. Later elaborations of civil disobedience have been emphatic on this point: it is an integral and routine part of the justification for righteous lawbreaking that one first exhaust the ostensibly available opportunities for redress. Not so for Thoreau: "As for adopting the ways which the State has provided for remedying the evil, I know not of such ways. They take too much time, and a man's life will be gone. I have other affairs to attend to."[47]

## Political Culture

Two of the best recent studies of Thoreau address his cultural-political importance for Americans and reroute his politics. Toward the end of *America's Bachelor Uncle: Thoreau and the American Polity*, which attempts (and accomplishes) a reclamation of Thoreau, Bob Pepperman Taylor argues that the principal weakness of Thoreau's views is his naturalism—which is precisely what contemporary environmentalism admires in him and inherits from him:

> The true weakness of Thoreau's views is . . . his naturalism, his belief that the American landscape can provide an alternative source of inspiration, can teach a way of life that encourages the moral independence required by democratic citizens. . . . For Thoreau, nature first teaches us our independence, then controls and moderates this independence within proper boundaries. There is no reason for us to believe, however, that our experience of nature will necessarily function in the way Thoreau hopes it will.[48]

Taylor also points out that we can see from Thoreau's own arrogance "that the moral autonomy he seeks is not always or necessarily compatible with the sense of reverence and humility he also desires."[49]

Taylor wants Americans to understand Thoreau as an important political theorist, and he is explicit about what he wants his Thoreau to do. Taylor's Thoreau deploys nature-related arguments to intervene in American culture: "The role of nature in *Walden* is essentially political: it is the means by which Thoreau proposes to break the chain of conventional wisdom that prevents us, in his view, from seriously doubting the necessity or the desirability of the status quo, or imagining an alternative.[50] For Taylor, Thoreau's notion of nature should play a rather confined role; it helps shock us out of the conventional wisdom without necessarily legitimizing a cadre of believers who would hope to govern in its name.

In *Thoreau's Nature: Ethics, Politics, and the Wild,* Jane Bennett also tries to find a niche for Thoreau in the canon of American political thought. Bennett's Thoreau crafts "the self as a nonconformist" in genuinely political ways and directs it toward a nature far more heterogeneous and relational than has usually been understood.[51] This reading of Thoreau is not alien to the environmental movement's treatment of him. Influential *New York Times* environmental reporter Phillip Shabecoff published a widely read history of the contemporary environmental movement in 1993. Shabecoff credits Thoreau with sounding "many of the leitmotifs of modern environmentalism," specifically, "as the spiritual founder of the modern crusade to preserve what is left of our wilderness."[52] He accurately identifies Thoreau's role in putting wilderness at the center of contemporary environmentalism, an emphasis that is still sometimes controversial. In political terms, Shabecoff seems most interested in Thoreau's anticipation of "some of the causes and methods of today's radical environmentalists," citing *A Week on the Concord* on the protection of animals and as presenting "what may be the first reference to the possibility of ecosabotage" when Thoreau urges the use of "a crowbar against that Billerica Dam" due to its interference with local aquatic life.[53] Nonetheless, having surveyed the range of ideas that might be traced back to Thoreau, Shabecoff identifies a different central contribution:

> The central issue addressed by Thoreau . . . was embodied in the question of how life ought to be lived and what gives meaning to life. These are fundamental themes of environmentalism, although today's environmental leaders tend to shunt them aside in the heat and tumult of their endless trench warfare against the powerful forces that threaten both human health and the natural world.[54]

Culture is a central if ambivalent feature of American environmentalism. On the one hand, the movement's scope is extraordinary and probably contributes to the durability of green commitments. Perhaps more than any other contemporary American movement, environmentalism identifies positions on a wide range of activities: food, recreation, procreation, health, work, transportation, energy, aesthetics, attitudes toward animals, a range of ideological positions on commerce, rights, progress, technology, and more. On the other hand, the heavy reliance on nature-related arguments and a tendency toward moralism make environmentalism universalist and thus inhospitable to identity politics, with its inherent pluralism. Identity initiatives have worked better for the movement's adversaries, who cite their identity as miners or loggers, for example, and taunt their green adversaries as "owl lovers" or "granolas."

In a way, Thoreau anticipates the politicization of identity; resisting the society that prevents one from enacting one's vision of "the good life" is an appropriate—and perhaps the best—political activity. Thoreau is the prototypical ethical actor, in the best sense of that term. But there is a risk inherent in this position, and Thoreau demonstrates that danger. While arguing for a "care for the self" (to appropriate Michel Foucault's phrase), Thoreau also advances a moralism that undermines his ambition to promote ethical transformation. As historian Robert Dorman reminds us, "As a boy his schoolmates called Thoreau by the nickname 'Judge,' a reflection (according to his biographers) of his innate stoicism and solemnity. [Thoreau] seemed a born moralizer."[55]

## Nature

A movement that speaks for nature, that hears its voice, would be expected to have a coherent and systematic canon. And, as expected, environmentalism has waged few internal battles over "the correct line" or the appropriate epistemological or ethical basis of the movement. Instead, the internal green battles tend to be tactical, between, say, big green and the grass roots. But at the core, strategic level, greens have built a unanimity that aspires to Thoreau's level of self-certainty, to his level of adamance. To speak convincingly for nature, greens needed a clean and compelling "origin story." The movement needed a history that got around the fact that Western politics was formed largely by a struggle over the political control of the authority-granting legitimacy nature could lend, a struggle that has continued more or less throughout Western civilization.

Environmentalism was hardly the first to claim nature's voice, but with some help from Thoreau, the movement actually managed to maneuver itself into a position to make that claim. Oddly enough, to meet the need for a distinctive origin story, the green solution (again, learned from Thoreau) was to separate humans from nature, based on the unique ability of human civilization to alter nature. People threaten nature but can also save it. Nature might inspire a person, but that person is separate from nature. This perilous position then doubled back to grant authority from nature to those people who claim the green perspective.

Given that intellectual setting, greens sought a strong naturalist voice. That role was only indirectly or unsatisfactorily filled by most of the canonical figures, who pointed toward unalloyed elitism and romanticism (Muir and Marshall), biochemistry (Carson), and updated woodsy mysticism (Aldo Leopold). In Thoreau, the movement found a figure from the American literary canon who—due to the awkward trajectory of his literary legacy—was available for a fresh, green reading. As I suggested at the start of this chapter, post–Earth Day greens found a Thoreau little related to the Thoreaus identified earlier by Emerson and White. Even the civil disobedient Thoreau claimed by King and Gandhi was not really the same as the environmentalists' Thoreau. Matthiessen's urge to push Thoreau leftward resonated with participants in the new environmental movement, but they did not rush, as Matthiessen had, to impose a politics on the apolitical Thoreau.

As I discussed earlier, there were ample warnings against a naturalist reading; Thoreau resisted the naturalist label and seems better described as engaging landscapes and pastoralism. Still, *Walden* encouraged greens to read Thoreau for his naturalism (rather than in a cultural or political context). The transitional environmentalism that emerged at Earth Day found precisely what it needed in Thoreau: a cranky yet often sociable and charismatic invitation to hit the trail and announce an affinity for nature. Thoreau's civil disobedience was a political plan for the hopeless, and even though most Earth Day constituents exhibited a rather speculative optimism, they were not, in fact, a particularly hopeful lot after the disappointments of the anti-war movement and before the elaboration of identity politics. The environmental movement tended toward absolutism and utopianism, and in both respects, Thoreau's moralism was helpful. But whereas Gandhi and King built a political strategy on Thoreau's apolitical gesture, the environmental movement eschewed those helpful correctives and veered from dismal jeremiad to a huge ambition—the very reconfiguration of the contemporary world—fueled by the appropriation of nature, long one of the West's most potent political figurations. The lack of political argument that charmed White perfectly matched the contradictory, conflicted, and still powerful new environmental movement.

Thoreau's spiritualism also cut another way in the hands of a counter-culture prone to a dismal sense of foreboding and powerlessness, as well as a spiritualism that sometimes veered toward resentful moralism. As critical as Thoreau was of the American bourgeoisie, his spiritualism was closer to middling American Christianity than he would admit. It is composed by the moralism of the New England jeremiad, reworked for transcenden-talism, underscored by a dose of scientism. As influential environmental philosopher J. Baird Callicott summarizes, "While Thoreau's philosophy is hardly Calvinist or even Christian, his temperament is thoroughly Puritan. He was celibate, vegetarian, abstemious, ascetic, self-righteous, judgmental. At points it seems that wild nature serves Thoreau more as a bearing for criticizing his fellow citizens than as something valuable in itself."[56]

Some environmentalists focused more on Thoreau as a defender of lo-calism—of the importance of a commitment to a specific "place" as a locale for political activity in a rapidly changing world. "Place" had the advantage of being less global and absolute, with an appeal to the notion of commu-nity that, in the Earth Day era, had not yet been conceded to the political Right. Environmentalists adopted the slogan "Think globally, act locally," emphasizing the importance of appreciating and protecting important local sites. But "place" had its limits, too. It was susceptible to the NIMBY (not in my backyard) mentality, as well as the related charge that environmental-ism was merely advocating a class-based amenity program. Critics such as geography theorist David Harvey also complained about the intellectual incoherence of place-related claims. "The intimacy of many place-based accounts—Thoreau's famous and influential exploration of Walden being an exemplary case—yields only limited natural knowledge embedded in ecological processes operating at a small scale."[57]

In short, the romantic association with place, often featured in the bioregionalist wing of environmentalism, depends on an unhealthy green reliance on a rhetoric of nature—an overly romantic nature confused about scientific ecology and other markers of the "real." Even worse, "place" risks conflating environmentalism with its recreational component. Once these risks were noticed (and environmentalism's critics were quick to notice), complaints about special pleading and frivolous romanticism were sure to follow.

Compared with other proponents of the ethical, Thoreau leaves him-self unprotected from potential collapse into the role of moralizer. Too often, Thoreau seems to present an ethical model primarily for the purpose of generating an opportunity to moralize. This is the source of the rigidity that, eventually, so annoyed Emerson. And the tension persists: with their commitment to universality, scientism, and arguments from nature, contemporary environmentalists continually risk arrogance, moralism, and charges of authoritarianism. Sanctimonious scolding is a perilous political posture. Although it certainly presents a focused, ethical model, it always risks offending its audience with its judgmental superiority. As King and Gandhi understood, taking this position while also hoping for positive political change requires adept and careful attention to politics.

The way to negotiate a way through this set of risks is explicitly political. Here again, contemporary greens wrestle with Thoreau's legacy, which does not provide happy political precedents, unless one borrows civil disobedience and swiftly flees from Thoreau to build a political apparatus around it, which is what Gandhi and King did. Thoreau cannot be blamed for the greens' problem with politics, but the Thoreau the greens found did nothing to discourage an apolitical approach. Blame must be shared; the greens found a Thoreau who helped them avoid solving the problems inherent in his position—problems the greens were susceptible to, whether or not they ever found Thoreau. Thoreau gave contemporary environmentalism a promising ethical model, but one fraught with the risk that it would collapse into moralism, in ways that were potentially disastrous in social and political terms.

Ultimately, Thoreau's "strong but disorderly" convictions found their audience. Disoriented by politics, Earth Day–era environmentalists tended toward the grand gesture on behalf of claims powerful enough to seriously engage the world. Those early greens did not fit in their world any better than Thoreau did in his, and they appreciated him for what they shared. Environmentalists were blocked from an effective politicization of their movement: blocked by the very enormity of the reforms they habitually proposed; blocked by their own elitism, which took a while to process; blocked by their own combination (shared with Thoreau) of science and mysticism. The flood of theory that emerged in the decade around Earth Day—by Arne Naess, Murray Bookchin, Barry Commoner, the Club of Rome (the Meadowses et al.), Paul Ehrlich, and others—did not solve this puzzle.[58]

The present dilemma of American environmentalism might well be understood as the long-delayed consequence of having been founded on such an odd and, finally, deficient political model. The payback was long delayed for several reasons. There was much to do in the interim, fighting wilderness and wildlife issues, articulating the pollution model into a concern about toxic waste and then global warming, arranging a culture of healthiness, and so on. All of this was done on an ad hoc basis, with much more effort given to science than to political thought. The very breadth of the environmental claim ensures that there will never be a shortage of work to do. But there was also the remarkable and confounding backlash that wound from Reagan to Bush II. That development, at least, should have reminded greens that there was unfinished work, that some political dimension had to be added to the actual legacy inherited from Thoreau. Alas, a movement thus founded was hardly prepared to respond.

Although the multiple Thoreaus that made it to Earth Day probably caused some political trouble for the greens, they also attested to Thoreau's vivid literary accomplishment. The multiple Thoreaus left room for other theorists to rescue Thoreau from the environmentalists and to find in him the potential for a new kind of American political thought, which describes Bennett's and Taylor's projects. Environmentalists no longer need the naturalist and moralist Thoreau; in the decades since Earth Day, they have been creating their own contemporary models. The crucial turn is one away from naturalism, with its attendant risks, and toward politics, with the potential for negotiations around the political sense the movement still needs to make of itself.[59] Environmentalists have political work to do, figuring out what to do about the profound backlash that leaves the United States, a century after the Scopes monkey trial, with perhaps less confidence in natural science than it had when Clarence Darrow strode the earth. An environmental movement that understands Thoreau's legacy as decidedly mixed could yet confront its political situation.

# Notes

1. Ralph Waldo Emerson, *Journals* (Boston: Houghton Mifflin, 1910), 7:228, quoted in Walter Harding, *The Days of Henry Thoreau* (New York: Knopf, 1965), 299.

2. Alan D. Hodder, *Thoreau's Ecstatic Witness* (New Haven, CT: Yale University Press, 2001), 6–9.

3. Editor Walter Harding, an important midcentury Thoreau biographer, writes that we "must accept this as Lowell's final judgment of Thoreau, for it was this essay which he chose to appear in his collected works." See James Russell Lowell, "Thoreau," in *Thoreau: A Century of Criticism*, ed. Walter Harding (Dallas: Southern Methodist University Press, 1954), 44. The Lowell essay was reprinted from the *North American Review* (October 1865): 597–608.

4. See Bob Pepperman Taylor, *America's Bachelor Uncle: Thoreau and the American Polity* (Lawrence: University Press of Kansas, 1996), 2.

5. Hodder, *Thoreau's Ecstatic Witness*, 7.

6. Ibid., 8.

7. Ibid., 9, citing John Macy, *The Spirit of American Literature* (New York: Doubleday, Page, 1913), and Vernon Louis Parrington, *Main Currents in American Thought* (New York: Harcourt, Brace, 1929).

8. F. O. Matthiessen, *American Renaissance: Art and Expression in the Age of Emerson and Whitman* (London: Oxford University Press, 1941), discussed in Hodder, *Thoreau's Ecstatic Witness*, 9, 309, 310.

9. Matthiessen, *American Renaissance*, 76.

10. Ibid., 76–77.

11. Emerson quoted ibid., 77.

12. Ibid.

13. Ibid., 77–78.

14. Ibid., 79.

15. For evidence of Thoreau's influence on White, see Robert L. Root Jr., *Critical Essays on E. B. White* (New York: G. K. Hall, 1994).

16. E. B. White, "Preface," *A Subtreasure of American Humor*, ed. E. B. White and Katharine S. White (New York: Coward-McCann, 1941), xvi.

17. E. B. White, "The Individualist" (1949), in *Writings from the* New Yorker: *1927–1976*, ed. Rebecca M. Dale (New York: HarperCollins, 1990), 39.

18. Ibid., 39–40.

19. Matthiessen, *American Renaissance*, 162.

20. Ibid.

21. Ibid., 163.

22. Roderick Nash, *Wilderness and the American Mind*, 3rd ed. (New Haven, CT: Yale University Press, 1982), 81.

23. Ibid., 94.

24. Mulford Q. Sibley, *The Quiet Battle: Writings on the Theory and Practice of Non-violent Resistance* (Boston: Beacon Press, 1963), 25.

25. Martin Luther King Jr., *The Autobiography of Martin Luther King, Jr.*, ed. Clayborne Carson (New York: Warner, 1998), 14, excerpted from King, *Stride toward Freedom: The Montgomery Story* (New York: Harper and Row, 1958).

26. Ibid.

27. Ibid., 54.

28. William Tucker, *Progress and Privilege* (Garden City, NY: Anchor/Doubleday, 1982). Originally published as "Environmentalism and the Leisure Class," *Harper's*, December 1977, 49–56, 73–80.

29. Although environmentalists and others roundly criticized Tucker for inaccuracies and faulty logic, the appearance of the article—featured on the cover of *Harper's* in the late 1970s as conservatives strove to identify viable political positions on a range of liberal issues—had significant impact. Tucker's book was widely and often positively reviewed in prominent venues, including the *New York Times Book Review, Wall Street Journal, Los Angeles Times, Natural History, Boston Globe, Science, New Republic,* and *Business Week.* Of course, between the essay's first appearance in 1977 and the book's publication in 1982, the conservative position on environmental issues was set by Ronald Reagan's successful campaign for the presidency and the subsequent appointment of such controversial figures as James Watt. On Tucker's reception, see William J. Bennetta, "Progress and Privilege: A Book about Environmentalism Meets the Press," *Environmental Management* 8, no. 6 (November 1984): 455–62.

30. In one case, legendary among radical greens, at an EarthFirst! road blockade, Dave Foreman encountered a logger who drove a truck into him and dragged him some distance before screaming, "You dirty communist bastard! Why don't you go back to Russia!" Foreman replied, "But, Les, I'm a registered Republican." Susan Zakin, *Coyotes and Town Dogs: EarthFirst! and the Environmental Movement* (New York: Viking, 1993), 257.

31. Harding, *Days of Thoreau,* 316–19.

32. Ibid., 319.

33. Ibid., 120, 201–2.

34. Ibid., 201–2.

35. Ibid., 291.

36. Henry D. Thoreau, "Slavery in Massachusetts," in *The Higher Law: Thoreau on Civil Disobedience and Reform,* ed. Wendell Glick (Princeton, NJ: Princeton University Press, 2004), 108.

37. Thomas L. Dumm, remarks on the "Thoreau and His Political Legacy" panel at the Western Political Science Association meeting, Las Vegas, NV, March 8, 2007.

38. Henry D. Thoreau, "Resistance to Civil Government," in *Higher Law,* 63.

39. Ibid.

40. Ibid.

41. Ibid., 63–64.

42. Ibid., 64.

43. Ibid.

44. Ibid., 66.

45. Ibid.

46. Ibid., 69–70.

47. Ibid., 74.

48. Taylor, *America's Bachelor Uncle,* 127.

49. Ibid., 128.

50. Ibid., 90.

51. Jane Bennett, *Thoreau's Nature: Ethics, Politics, and the Wild,* new ed. (Lanham, MD: Rowman and Littlefield, 2002), xx.

52. Philip Shabecoff, *A Fierce Green Fire: The American Environmental Movement* (New York: Hill and Wang, 1993), 52.

53. Ibid., 53; Roderick Nash, *The Rights of Nature* (Madison: University of Wisconsin Press, 1989), 167.

54. Shabecoff, *Fierce Green Fire,* 54.

55. Robert L. Dorman, *A Word for Nature: Four Pioneering Environmental Advocates, 1845–1913* (Chapel Hill: University of North Carolina Press, 1998), 54.

56. J. Baird Callicott, "That Good Old-Time Wilderness Religion," in *The Great New Wilderness Debate,* ed. J. Baird Callicott and Michael P. Nelson (Athens: University of Georgia Press, 1998), 390.

57. David Harvey, *Justice, Nature & the Geography of Difference* (Oxford: Blackwell, 1996), 3.

58. Arne Naess, "The Shallow and the Deep, Long-Range Ecology Movement: A Summary," *Inquiry* 16 (1983): 95–100, which expanded on arguments dating to 1973; Murray Bookchin, *Our Synthetic Environment* (New York: Harper and Row, 1974); Barry Commoner, *The Closing Circle: Nature, Man, and Technology* (New York: Knopf, 1971); Donella H. Meadows, Dennis L. Meadows, Jorgen Randers, and William H. Behrens III, *The Limits to Growth* (New York: Universe Books, 1972); Paul R. Ehrlich, *The Population Bomb* (New York: Ballantine, 1968).

59. See, for example, Bruno Latour, *Politics of Nature: How to Bring the Sciences into Democracy* (Cambridge, MA: Harvard University Press, 2004); John M. Meyer, *Political Nature: Environmentalism and the Interpretation of Western Thought* (Cambridge, MA: MIT Press, 2001); Andrew Biro, *Denaturalizing Ecological Politics: Alienation from Nature from Rousseau to the Frankfurt School and Beyond* (Toronto: University of Toronto Press, 2005).

PART III

Reverence, Ethics, and the Self

CHAPTER 9

# Thoreau on Body and Soul

*Susan McWilliams*

> There was never yet philosopher
> That could endure the toothache patiently.
> —William Shakespeare, *Much Ado About Nothing*

HENRY DAVID THOREAU was plagued by bad teeth. They started falling out when he was twenty-one years old, and they occupy a considerable place in his journals. "Here I have swallowed an indispensable tooth," he reports on August 27, 1838, "and so am no whole man, but a lame and halting piece of manhood." Thoreau writes that the loss of the tooth has left him paralyzed—"I believe if I were called at this moment to rush into the thickest of the fight, I should halt for lack of so insignificant a piece of armor as a tooth"—and his frustration is palpable:

> I am conscious of no gap in my soul, but it would seem that now the entrance to the oracle has been enlarged, the more rare and commonplace the responses that issue from it. I have felt cheap, and hardly dared hold up my head among men, ever since this accident happened. Nothing can I do as well and freely as before; nothing do I undertake but I am hindered and balked by this circumstance. . . . One does not need that the earth quake for the sake of excitement—when so slight a crack—produces an impassable moat.

"Verily," Thoreau concludes, "I am the creature of circumstances." Still, he adds, one must sometimes proceed in spite of circumstances. "Let the lame man shake his leg, and match himself with the fleetest in the race," and "if you are toothless . . . open your mouth wide and gabble never so resolutely."[1]

In this reflection, written almost a decade before he took to the shores of Walden Pond, Thoreau's preoccupation with the human self—an embodied mind, a mindful body—is already evident. Indeed, questions about body and soul recur throughout Thoreau's corpus, in both his published and unpublished writings. They are central questions for Thoreau because contemplation of the human self must precede, or underlie, a contemplation of the possibilities of human self-governance. And the issue of human self-governance, as so many have observed, lies at the heart of Thoreau's enterprise.

Ultimately, Thoreau's conception of the self, and therefore Thoreau's conception of self-governance, turns on a complicated sense of human "doubleness." Humans are "double-edged blades," self-conscious creatures of body and soul.[2] This notion of doubleness harks back to the ancient tradition of seeing humans as dual—and thus as flawed—creatures who resist philosophical integration. He thus resists certain modern views of the self, such as Hobbes's rational man or Locke's Enlightenment man, which presume a unified human animal.[3]

Yet Thoreau's doubleness rests on more than a strict dualist framework, for he also believes that "the outward and the inward life correspond."[4] Certain labors of the body may invigorate the spirit; certain spiritual contemplations may elevate the body. And it is the truly successful man—albeit "the rarest success"—who learns to support his body and his spirit "by one & the same means," who recognizes that both the body and the soul have moral status.[5] Said differently, Thoreau conceives of a human being who, through disciplined exploration and contemplation of his own nature, discovers himself to be the site of a harmonious, mysterious interplay between matter and spirit. Toward that end, human beings have a certain degree of transcendent power; following Emerson, Thoreau sees a "lurking divinity of nature"—in George Kateb's words—in the human animal.[6] But self-reflection reveals that we must always remain at least partly mysterious to ourselves. "I do not know why we should be styled 'misters' or 'masters,'" Thoreau writes. "We come so near to being anything or nothing" and are inwardly "indefinite."[7] The pursuit of self-knowledge—the kind of pursuit in which Thoreau engages in *Walden*—ultimately begets awareness of self-mystery.[8] So although on the surface the pursuit of self-knowledge seems to resemble a project of mastery, since both involve aspirational rejections of the status quo, they are radically opposed endeavors. Projects of mastery, for Thoreau, are predicated on a fundamental illusion: the illusion that humans can change or ignore the troublesome nature of the self.

Thus, for Thoreau, self-government lies within human capacity, but its realization is tricky and embattled, for self-government depends on individuals committed to the pursuit of a certain kind of truth, individuals willing to honestly investigate themselves. These individuals must recognize, along with Thoreau, that "our whole life is startlingly moral" yet still not fully within our grasp. In human life, "there is never an instant's truce between virtue and vice."[9] Politics, as a conventional human form, is caught in the same battle, tempted by vice in the same way individuals are. And Thoreau sees a modern political world in which the pursuit of truth is often compromised by the embrace of projects of mastery, a political world in which the fundamental truths of human mystery and human morality are readily obscured.[10] Modern political life, then, tends toward a politics of vice. For Thoreau, the only way to mitigate this tendency is to reinvigorate ancient understandings of the human animal, to point people back to wonder at human mystery and thus undermine modern conceits about the human condition. Thoreau's plea for a revolution in government is no less than a plea for a revolution in his fellows' understanding of their selves. "There are various tough problems yet to solve," he writes, "and we must make shift to live, betwixt spirit and matter, such a human life as we can."[11]

## Double(ness) Trouble

Thirteen years after his first mandibular meditation, Thoreau asserts, "If I have got false teeth, I trust that I have not got a false conscience."[12] Throughout his corpus, Thoreau makes recourse to such a notion of human doubleness, in which the spirit stands apart from the body. "However intense my experience," he writes, "I am conscious of the presence and criticism of a part of me, which, as it were, is not a part of me, but spectator, sharing no experience, but taking note of it; and that is no more I than it is you."[13] Human thought seems distinct from human action, for one can contemplate one's physical doings—even one's physical being—from a distance:

> See how I can play with my fingers! They are the funniest companions I have ever found. Where did they come from? What strange control I have over them! *Who* am I? What are they?—those little peaks—call them Madison, Jefferson, Lafayette. What is *the matter*? *My* fingers ten, I say.[14]

The spirit and the body may stand not just in positions of difference but also in positions of estrangement. "I stand in awe of my body," Thoreau writes on Mount Ktaadn, "this matter to which I am bound has become so strange to me."[15]

Moreover, both the spirit and the body have claims on the human animal; one does not necessarily govern the other. "I found in myself, and still find, an instinct toward a higher, or, as it is named, spiritual life, as do most men, and another toward a primitive rank and savage one," Thoreau writes, having just felt the "thrill of savage delight" as he considered seizing a woodchuck and sinking his teeth into it. "I reverence them both. I love the wild not less than the good."[16] This is a fascinating statement, since if his wildness is worthy of Thoreau's reverence and love, it has a kind of goodness as well. But Thoreau refuses to collapse the distinction between the unreflective bodily exertions that constitute "wildness," in this case, and the reflective judgment that constitutes "good." Even if the "wild" or the bodily has a claim on human life—which means that sometimes one yearns to rip apart a woodland creature, and sometimes one actually does so—and even if those impulses are worthy of reverence by virtue of being part of the self, they are separate from a more thoughtful, spiritual good. "A true *humanity*, or account of human experience" encompasses both unreflective action and active reflection.[17] At different times one trumps the other. (Although Thoreau is known for his articulation of conscience-based resistance and action, he is disarmingly honest about the fact that his wild desires sometimes dominate his hours: "Sometimes I like to spend my day more as the animals do," hunting and fishing and rolling about in the woods.)[18] This is part of what it means to be human; both are necessary components of human life and experience. But one should not collapse the two, for in collapsing the wild and the good, the body and the soul, one loses a sense of the conflicts and tensions that define human life and experience. And someone who collapses that distinction is likely to act with little goodness at all.

Indeed, central to Thoreau's critique of his own civilization is that it has an enervating way of collapsing the body and the soul. "We think that that *is* which *appears* to be."[19] The social preoccupation with fashion, for instance, suggests the belief that a change in outfits is equivalent to a change in purpose. "We don garment after garment, as if we grew like exogenous plants by addition without."[20] His tailor, he says, "does not measure my character, but only the breadth of my shoulders, as it were a peg to hang the coat on."[21] In such an environment, men learn to behave less like men and more like coat racks. In such a society, a scarecrow could have power; if dressed according to the fashion of the day, "who would not soonest address the scarecrow and salute it?"[22] In such an environment, humans become habituated to the delusion that new enterprises "require new clothes, and not rather a new wearer of clothes."[23] In such an environment, any transformation or change in human life becomes nearly impossible; only the illusion of transformation or change exists. This is a critique that takes a central role in *Walden's* final paragraphs:

> We think that we can change our clothes only. It is said that the British Empire is very large and respectable, and that the United States are a first-rate power. We do not believe that a tide rises and falls behind every man which can float the British Empire like a chip, if he should ever harbor it in his mind. Who knows what sort of seventeen-year locust will next come out of the ground?[24]

Before any true improvement in human life or governance is viable, humans must understand themselves to be creatures of both outward matter and inward spirit, where one cannot be neglected in favor of the other.

But if thinking is distinct from doing, and both thought and action have trumping rights in human life, the human condition may in fact be a kind of "tragedy."[25] That human beings are creatures of this kind of doubleness means that "we are double-edged blades." As such, "every time we whet our virtue the return stroke straps our vice." "Where," wonders Thoreau, "is the skilful swordsman who can give clean wounds, and not rip up his work with the other edge?" Human life is a story of "incessant tragedies."[26] In fact, the tragic condition is a definitively human one, one that proceeds from the possibility—the necessity—of acting against our intellectual or spiritual judgment. Humans have a hand in their own fate, which makes human fate tragic, as Walter Hesford has explained, "whereas the hard fate of dumb creatures is more pathetic than tragic."[27] Each human has the ability to be complicit in his or her own fall.

Humans may also be complicit—and more than complicit—in the falls of others. Thoreau's comment on the "incessant tragedies" of human life comes between two stories about animals he and his brother John have killed: the pigeon they just killed for lunch, and the squirrels they killed for dinner the night before. Humans regularly do violence to nonhuman ani-

mals, and casually so. Thoreau and his brother had watched as those squirrels "frisked so merrily in the morning," then "skinned and embowelled"
them. That would have been criminal enough—"who could commit so great
a crime against a poor animal, who is fed only by the herbs which grow
wild in the woods?"—but then they decide that eating the squirrels would
be disgusting, so they throw away the bodies and boil some rice instead.
Thoreau laments, "O me miserable!"[28] Though he knows that all animal
life ends in a fall, Thoreau sees in man's flesh eating a carnality that deems
souls separate from—or secondary to—bodies. In fact, he jokes that men
tend to choose not to eat squirrels but to eat sheep or oxen, "whose souls
perchance are not so large in proportion to their bodies."[29] Of course, since
the soul-to-body ratio is not a standard calculation in the human choice of
what to eat, Thoreau underscores the extent to which humans are capable
of making (almost literally!) soulless judgments.

The tragic nature of doubleness is perhaps best or most strikingly made
manifest in humans' relations with one another. As Thoreau puts it, "This
doubleness may easily make us poor neighbors and friends sometimes."[30]
For human creatures, it is simple to behave with aloofness or apathy toward
others, even when those others demonstrate a need for immediate action
or help. "I *may* be affected by a theatrical exhibition; on the other hand, I
*may not* be affected by an actual event which appears to concern me much
more." Because body and soul have their separations, and because we humans can effectively stand "beside" ourselves, we are capable of acting as if
we have great concern for matters that are relatively distant from us, while
acting with neglect for those things closest to us. "By a conscious effort of
the mind we can stand aloof from actions and their consequences; and all
things, good, and bad, go by us like a torrent."[31] Arising from an internal disconnection of body and soul, doubleness allows for broader disconnection
in human affairs. For Thoreau, as Lawrence Buell describes, "the possibility
of drawing back at any moment from the experience to an immense critical
and emotional distance remains."[32]

Thoreau's political speeches and writings, particularly on the question
of slavery, tend to reflect his frustration with the detached doubleness of his
fellows along these lines. When, in 1854, Thoreau perceives ambivalence
among citizens in Massachusetts about the forced return of Anthony Burns,
a fugitive slave from Virginia, he lambastes them for action unaffected by
actual and proximate events:

> I had thought that the house was on fire, and not the prairie; but though several of the citizens of Massachusetts are now in prison for attempting to rescue a slave from her own clutches, not one of the speakers at that meeting expressed regret for it, not one even referred to it. It was only the disposition of some wild lands a thousand miles off, which appeared to concern them.[33]

Thoreau goes on to say that he is "surprised to see men going about their business as if nothing had happened."[34] "Talk of a divinity in man!"[35] That his fellows are going about their business can mean one of two things. First, they might *know* that something disturbing has happened, and they choose to go about their business as if it had not, thus illustrating the possibility of detaching thought from action. Second, they might *not know* that something disturbing has happened—they might not recognize the moral import of the Burns case—thus demonstrating the possibility of acting without thinking at all, the possibility of moral dumbness. Thoreau sees in the human animal a pervasive tendency toward detachment between thought and deed, between knowledge and action. This is a central problem of conventional political life.

Given that assessment of human doubleness and its effects, it is reasonable for Thoreau to argue in "Resistance to Civil Government" that "it is not a man's duty, as a matter of course, to devote himself to the eradication of any, even the most enormous wrong."[36] If, as a matter of course, one cannot expect action to reflect better judgment, one cannot argue that men have a "duty" to function otherwise; one can only argue, as Thoreau does, that if men are going to wash their hands of concern for a great wrong, they should try not to be complicit in it. It may be *desirable* for men to act against what they know to be a great wrong, and it may be frustrating when they do not. But given that the human constitution begins in savagery, and given that man "never completely over[comes] this part of his nature," with its "tendencies toward self-indulgence, self-centeredness, pride, and complacency," it would be futile to attempt to derive a morally sensitive version of human nature from the notion of duty.[37] To do so would be to ignore the basic difficulty of political life. "Compassion is a very untenable ground."[38] (As Thoreau puts it elsewhere, "I warn you, mothers, that my sympathies do not always make the usual phil-*anthropic* distinctions.")[39]

Thoreau's conception of the human as dual thus rejects modern theoretical conceptions of a well-formed, unified individual. For Thoreau, within a single moment in a single body, you may "experience an interval

as between one life and another—a greater space than you ever traveled."[40]
It therefore becomes untenable or inadequate to speak as if "the self is
not a problem," to join in the basic assumptions of the Cartesian model.
(As Peter McCormick has pointed out, "Descartes' system of radical doubt,
culminating in the famous *cogito ergo sum,* may have shocked the devout
by questioning the existence of God, but it never questioned the existence
or identity of the self that thought.")[41] Thoreau can make no such confident
assumptions about the human animal; in fact, his meditations on doubleness
often culminate in radical and stark self-questioning: "*Contact! Contact!
Who* are we? *where* are we?"[42] "*Who* am I?"[43]

Thoreau thus challenges political theories predicated on unproblematic,
unified models of the individual. His conception of the self contains an implicit critique of the social-contract model, which depends on the notion of
rational individuals who are not only aware of their desires but also inclined
to act on them with some degree of purposefulness. This is not Hobbes's
rational man, whose action is, by definition, always directed toward what is
desired, toward one's internally perceived good.[44] Nor is it Locke's "natural"
individual, whose actions derive from the desire to control one's destiny
through the exercise of reason.[45] (In part, this explains why Thoreau has a
famously more difficult relationship with government than do individuals in
Hobbes's or Locke's formulations, although something superficially similar
to a social-contract theory underwrites his argument in "Resistance to Civil
Government.")[46]

Also for Thoreau, it would be senseless to develop a political theory
dependent on "rational and mutually disinterested" actors even as an ideal
type, as in John Rawls's formulation.[47] To formulate an "ideal human" in
this way is to formulate a creature who is not recognizably human, whose
conditions do not speak to the central truth—and the central problem—of
human life, particularly at the relational or political level.[48]

Thoreau's basic apprehension of the human animal, then, harks back to
certain ancient understandings of human beings as resisting philosophical
integration. That there are ancient overtones in Thoreau's thought should
not be surprising; certain classical writings seem to have dominated his
intellectual life. In fact, Thoreau—the same Thoreau who regards sugar
as a luxury—brings with him to Walden Pond a copy of the *Iliad,* one of
a set of classical works that he turns to time and again.[49] He values those
ancient texts, he told a Concord audience in 1851, because of their embrace

of wildness in humanity. The ancients, he believes, rightly portrayed human greatness as deriving from a primordial vitality that cannot be categorized, rationalized, or constrained.[50]

Along those lines, Thoreau accepts the pre-Socratic formulation that "mind, *nous,* is separate from all of the things of which it also is a part," a view that develops into a vision of the mind conflicting with the body.[51] As such, the human condition veers toward tragic outcomes. Thoreau subscribes to the view of the ancient tragedians, as Peter Euben formulates it, that human nature is twofold in this way: "This man of unparalleled intelligence is a creature of the wild." Doubleness defines human action and makes it problematic.[52] Just as for the Greeks, Thoreau demands an "account of man in conflict with himself."[53]

## You Can't Spell Globe without Lobe

But critically, Thoreau's concept of human doubleness is not a concept of strict or unmitigated duality. Body and soul are not perfectly distinct. "The outward and the inward life correspond," he writes to H. G. O. Blake. "The outward is only the outside of that which is within."[54] Put another way: "Packed in my mind lie all the clothes / which outward nature wears."[55] Though Thoreau takes doubleness to be the human estate, he does not ignore the fact that, in Jonathan Lear's formulation, "minds must be embodied."[56] In other words, though mind and body have their separations, they are still tangibly connected. As such, Thoreau extends his investigation to the character of the relationship between human matter and human spirit.

It is nature that suggests to Thoreau the ways in which the physical and extraphysical dimensions of life are fungible, if not coextensive. On a hillside next to Walden Pond, Thoreau describes a stirring scene: "I am affected as if in a peculiar sense I stood in the laboratory of the Artist who made the world and me,—had come to where he was still at work, sporting on this bank, and with excess of energy strewing his fresh designs about." After this arresting introduction, in which he carefully places humans and the natural world on equal ground, Thoreau describes the dripping and shifting and thawing of streams in the morning. The whole process "is somewhat excrementitious in its character, and there is no end to the heaps of liver lights and bowels, as if the globe were turned wrong side outward." To Thoreau, "this suggests at least that Nature has some bowels, and there again is mother of humanity."[57] The globe is like an animal body, internally "a moist thick *lobe,* a word especially applicable to the liver and lungs and the *leaves* of fat." In the gooey physicality of the phenomenon, he draws parallels to the human form: the watery paths form like blood vessels, and its channels are arteries; the softened sand is "like the ball of the finger"; "in the silicious matter which the water deposits is perhaps the bony system, and in the still finer soil and organic matter the fleshy fibre or cellular tissue."

> What is man but a mass of thawing clay? The ball of the human finger is but a drop congealed. The fingers and toes flow to their extent from the thawing mass of the body. . . . Is not the hand a spreading *palm* leaf with its lobes and veins? The ear may be regarded, fancifully, as a lichen, *umbilicaria,* on the side of the head, with its lobe or drop. The lip (*labium,* from *labor* (?)) laps or lapses from the sides of the cavernous mouth. The nose is a manifest congealed drop or stalactite. The chin is a still larger drop, the confluent dripping of the face. The cheeks are a slide from the brows into the valley of the face, opposed and diffused by the cheek bones.

The relation between the human body and the body of the world demonstrates itself not only in a physical similarity but also in the whole language of nature: internally, it is "λειβω, *labor, lapsus,* to flow or slip downward, a lapsing; λοβος, *globus,* lobe, globe; also lap, flap and many other words," while "*externally,* a dry thin *leaf,* even as the *f* and *v* are a pressed and dried *b.*"[58] In this rendering of the connection between man and earth, as Philip Gura has said, "the deepest layers of language, of man's very articulation, reinforce this knowledge."[59] "What is man," Thoreau asks, "but a mass of thawing clay?"

Yet if the globe is a laboring bodily mass, in its most viscous and glutinous processes like a human body, it is still something more. The leaves of fat are the prototype for "the overhanging leaf" and for "the feathers and wings of birds," which "are still drier and thinner leaves." So, by the labors of the globe, "you pass from the lumpish grub in the earth to the airy and fluttering butterfly. The very globe continually transcends and translates itself, and becomes winged in its orbit."[60]

What is perhaps most crucial about this passage is Thoreau's complication of the relationship between matter and spirit. In it, animal matter—animal matter of the lowest or most earthbound sort—comes to have a kind of spiritual dimension. "Heaven is under our feet as well as over our heads."[61] In its living processes, "the spontaneous language of nature," to use Leo Marx's formulation, supplies "value and meaning."[62]

The implication for human life is apparent. If the globe, a thawing and oozing animal body, is capable of transcending and translating itself through physical action, then the human, a nearly identical thawing and oozing animal body, is capable of transcending and translating itself by the same actions. The "common vital impulse" that is shared in human and other natural forms points toward the possibility of self-generated change or elevation.[63] "The body, then, for Thoreau, is a conduit between spirit and matter."[64] Nature teaches that bodies themselves may be the vehicles for transcendence.

There may be an even more striking political implication born in this moment. After Thoreau speaks of the globe's own transformation, he concludes that "the whole tree itself is but one leaf, and rivers are still vaster leaves whose pulp is intervening earth, and towns and cities are the ova of insects in their axils."[65] He suggests, in doing so, that civilized human society has a place in the natural formulation of self-cultivating transcendence. As John Pipkin notes, this is the "closest that Thoreau ever comes . . . to subsuming the human and natural landscapes under one model."[66] In other words, it is not just humans as individual beings or bodies that contain the capacity for higher change; human "towns and cities" are also latent with this possibility.

Accordingly, Thoreau marvels at "the unquestionable ability of man to elevate his life by a conscious endeavor."[67] This conscious endeavor takes two primary forms, both of which proceed from assumptions that blur the line between body and soul. First is the notion that through certain types of *cultivation* of his bodily life, a human may elevate his spiritual or moral state. Second is the notion that the *contemplation* of one's own bodily nature may lead to a kind of spiritual redemption.[68]

"Who knows but if men constructed their dwellings with their own hands, and provided food for themselves and families simply and honestly enough, the poetic faculty would be universally developed?"[69] Thoreau believes he knows the answer to this question; in well-acknowledged ways, *Walden* is a "pattern-book of practices" designed to connect seemingly banal physical exertions to experiences of greater meaning.[70] But more specifically, Thoreau is interested in the cultivation of a particular kind of physical exertion: artful and purposeful work. Work is "in the higher sense a discipline," one that might "be elevating a ladder, the means by which we are translated":

> How admirably the artist is made to accomplish his self-culture by devotion to his art! The wood-sawyer, through his effort to do his work well, becomes not merely a better wood-sawyer, but measurably a better *man*. Few are the men that can work on their navels,—only some Brahmins that I have heard of. To the painter is given some paint and canvas instead; to the Irishman a hog, typical of himself. In a thousand apparently humble ways men busy themselves to make some right take the place of some wrong, if it is only to make a better paste-blacking,—and they are themselves *so much* the better morally for it.[71]

Here, Thoreau draws a connection between the purposeful cultivation of one's physical labors and the development of a higher spiritual state. The art of labor and the labor of art are superior to intellectualism, for both their inputs and their outcomes are tangible. "We are all sculptors and painters, and our material is our own flesh and blood and bones," he writes.[72] A painter can take a blank canvas and some jars of oil and transform them into a picture of enduring beauty that affects other human souls. So would Thoreau have us envision our lives: take the materials you are given and transform them; in doing so, you will be transformed by them. Such a life of work and commitment, reminiscent of Emerson's notion of "vocation," is not a static endeavor but rather an "unfolding," a process of discovery.[73]

Thoreau's radical reconception of work as art, or as cultivation, leads him to suggest that in all parts of human life, to proceed with bodily purpose is to invoke a spiritual purpose; "every walk is a sort of crusade."[74] One learns by developing an "art of life" in which tangible practice informs the spirit or intellect.[75] If a scholar is wise, he says, "he will confine the observations of his mind as closely as possible to the experience or life of his senses," and "his thought must live with and be inspired with the life of the body."[76] Thus, for Thoreau, the most troubling kind of men are those "of ideas instead of legs, a sort of intellectual centipede that made you crawl all over"; in other words, traditional intellectuals have the equation backward.[77] "Our resolution is taking root or hold on the earth then, as seeds first send a shoot downward which is fed by their own albumen, ere they send one upward to the light."[78] Mind and soul are enhanced through cultivated engagement with the world; thought should not proceed without reference to experience, without something to hold on to.

At the same time, Thoreau argues that the *contemplation* of one's bodily nature is a vital component of self-cultivation. One's intellectual energies are properly directed to one's tangible aspects. He lauds the "Hindoo lawgiver" who "teaches how to eat, drink, cohabit, void excrement and urine, and the like, elevating what is mean."[79] To take one's embodiment seriously is to take oneself seriously—one's whole self, warts and liver and excrement and all. Contemplating matter gives that matter a spiritual status. It also complicates one's understanding of that matter. As Brian Walker has noted, Thoreau's love of physical cultivation is not unconditional; by contemplation, he wants people to "put the work of cultivation in perspective" and "see it as more morally complicated than we at first would think."[80] Thoreau, writes Buell, is not "about ascending to a spiritual state in which the body is left behind, but about reforming the bodily life . . . so that even the seemingly ignobler functions are purified."[81] It is something for a man, says Thoreau, "to practise some new austerity, to let his mind descend into his body and redeem it, and treat himself with ever increasing respect."[82]

All these endeavors point, ultimately, to the possibility that the human individual can develop ever more refined harmonies of body and soul. This is the standard set by nature. "What Nature is to the mind she is also to the body," he writes. "As she feeds my imagination, she will feed my body."[83] Following the model of nature, humans can aspire to be that "rarest success" who supports body and soul "by one & the same means," who achieves self-synchronization.[84] That is, Thoreau conceives of a human being who, through disciplined exploration and contemplation of his own nature, discovers himself to be the site of a harmonious interplay between matter and spirit. Toward that end, human beings have a certain degree of transcendent power.

The ancient overtones of Thoreau's thought—the notion that "a good body [is] the necessary correlative of the good soul"—ring through this trajectory of thought as well.[85] Here, though, Thoreau's turn toward ancient political thought bears a decidedly Stoic influence. The Stoics were ever present in Thoreau's mind; he had decided as a young man that the Stoics, particularly Zeno, apprehended the world as he did.[86] And though he seems to have had little systematic or formal training in Stoic thought, as Robert Sattelmeyer notes, "Thoreau's notion of the ideal relation between philosophy and life is perhaps best represented by the Stoics," about whom he always commented approvingly.[87]

Like the Stoics, Thoreau wants to resist a strict or impenetrable dualism while preserving the basic insights of the dualist model. He too turns to the corporeality of nature as a model for thinking about human possibility and asserts, along Stoic lines, that "the capacity to act and be acted upon" is possessed only by what is corporeal in nature.[88] Thus, Thoreau ascribes to the human body a moral standing in which actions of the body can themselves be spiritually transformative. But whereas the Stoics would proceed to use this understanding as a means to collapse the distinction between body and soul altogether—the Stoics moved toward the conclusion that the soul itself *is* matter—Thoreau continues to assert that the body is merely a channel for the spirit. Human bodies are worthy of reverence—each is a "temple" where worship may happen, and for that, each has value—but they themselves are not the objects of worship.[89]

## Body Building(s)

Thoreau understands that bodies, like temples and other material things, set limits on spirit and thought. "Thinking about the body is both exhilarating and sobering for the thinker," Leon Kass reminds us. It is exhilarating for the thinker "because it shows the possibility of a more integrated account of his own psychosomatic being"—demonstrating how the body prepares him for "the active life of thought and communication." But it is sobering "because it shows him the limits on the power of thought to free him from embodiment, setting limits on thought understood as a tool for mastery."[90]

To a degree, Thoreau's plea for self-development and the pursuit of truth through the cultivation of labor and the contemplation of body looks suspiciously like a project of progress or mastery. Both, after all, are aspirational models posited against the status quo. Both promise transformation. But Thoreau ultimately aims to teach humans to come to terms with their own embodiment and thus the limits of human transformation. Some of his most shocking formulations of the relationship between mind and matter—"Shall I not have intelligence with the earth? Am I not partly leaves and vegetable mould myself?"—deflate the hubristic human aspiration to transcend the corporeal.[91] One must try to harmonize body and soul because the soul has its home in the body. The body is the human circumstance, the contingent set of material facts within which intellect and spirit operate. One must pay attention to the possibilities offered within a given material circumstance, but one must also pay attention to the fundamental limitations of that circumstance. Bodily limitation is definitive. Humans are mortal, after all, as Thoreau says almost cheekily in *Cape Cod:* "It is hard to part with one's body, but no doubt, it is easy enough to do without it when once it is gone."[92]

Thoreau strips away the illusion that we can completely master or go beyond certain bodily limits. Our bodies preclude us from operating in all spaces at all times; for three months out of every year in New England, for example, "the human destiny is wrapped in furs."[93] When he proclaims that "no dominion of nature is quite closed to man at all times," he is also suggesting that no dominion of nature is ever completely *open* to man, either.[94] Likewise, when he asserts, "my head is hands and feet," he intimates not only that his head is the location for his exploratory capacity but also that his head is inextricably subsumed within his body.[95] Embodiment constrains human action; there is a limit to the transcendentalist notion of always being able to transcend boundaries. For Thoreau, there is no Emersonian vision of a "kingdom of man over nature" in which an "advancing spirit" forges a path to a world in which "evil is no more seen."[96]

Thoreau's model of self-cultivation also underscores the extent to which we human beings must remain at least partly mysterious to ourselves, and the permanence of this mystery is perhaps the enduring human truth. "At the same time that we are earnest to explore and learn all things, we require that all things be mysterious and unexplorable."[97] This is nowhere more true than in the region of the self. "Direct your eye sight inward, and you'll find / A thousand regions in your mind / Yet undiscovered."[98] For Thoreau, this remains true no matter how much inward attention one has already paid.

In fact, it seems that the more a human reflects on his nature, the more he comes to sense its mysteries. It is no coincidence that Thoreau ends *Walden* with the notion that "the life in us is like the water in the river."[99] This sentiment echoes one of Thoreau's unpublished poems: "I was born upon the banks, River, / My blood flows in thy stream, / And thou meanderest forever / As the bottom of my dream." For Thoreau, identification with the water is identification with a "mystical entity," as Allen Beecher Hovey has noted.[100] The water in a river is something we can possess only in infinitesimally small bits. Water falls through our hands, resisting our best efforts to contain it. It is always moving, so that no single snapshot or image of it is like another. Even when one considers a river from a fixed point, the river itself shifts, restricting and limiting the possibilities of sustained examination.[101] Although contemplation of the water in a river provides moments of solace, it forces us to ask a continual stream of questions. Where does the water come from? Will it ever stop flowing? How high or low might it get? Having come to the end of his many experiments, Thoreau's apprehension of human life is that it is fundamentally mysterious, eluding a perfect grasp. The attempt at self-mastery begets awareness of self-mystery.

Accordingly, Thoreau posits his own experiments as not only distinct from but also opposed to projects of human mastery. "I do not know why we should be styled 'misters' or 'masters,'" Thoreau writes; "we come so near to being anything or nothing" and are inwardly "indefinite."[102] As Emerson would reflect, "The meaning of Nature was never attempted to be defined by him."[103] Thoreau defends the reality of an "undetermined, if poetic, existence" in which there is always an underlying "uncertainty" about humanity.[104] Our ultimate truth is an ultimate mystery.

Thoreau thus finds much to criticize in the civilization of which he is a part. He has deep suspicions about scientific enterprises and claims of progress precisely because they tend to downplay the mystery of existence that is also its most fundamental truth. As David Robinson writes, although Thoreau "understood and used science with increasing sophistication, he remained alert to its potential power to obscure the very thing that is presumably illuminated":

> "The mystery of the life of plants is kindred with that of our own lives," he wrote in 1859, adding this cautionary proviso: "The physiologist must not presume to explain their growth according to mechanical laws, or as he might explain some machinery of his own making. We must not expect to prove with our fingers the sanctuary of any life, whether animal or vegetable. If we do, we shall discover nothing but surface still."[105]

Science, for Thoreau, is involved only at the apparent level of things. The more it attempts to explain and thus control, the less it in fact knows.

Thoreau sees this kind of misguided pursuit of mastery not just in scientific pursuits but also in the fabric of daily American habits. Robert Kuhn McGregor recalls:

> People had deluded themselves into believing themselves separate from the rest. . . . By domesticating plants and animals, humankind had set itself up as

"the lord of the fowl and the brute." But there was a price for this domination: "Birds certainly are afraid of man. They [allow] all other creatures—cows and horses, etc.—excepting only one or two kinds, birds or beasts of prey, to come near them, but not man. What does this fact signify? Does it not signify that man too, is a beast of prey to them? Is he, then, a true lord of creation, whose subjects are afraid of him, and with reason? They know very well that he is not human, as he pretends to be."[106]

This appetite for domination and mastery, which Thoreau sees evidenced not only in the domestication of animals but also in the destruction of New England's forests and the wanton slaughter of wild creatures, demonstrates a society that is lost in surface and appearance.

But nowhere is Thoreau's hostility toward the modern project more evident than in his biting criticisms of technophilia and its underlying perfectionist assumptions. Reviewing J. A. Etzler's *The Paradise within the Reach of All Men, without Labour, by Powers of Nature and Machinery*, Thoreau laments the present science, which thinks "not that man will always be the victim of circumstance" but that someday man "shall indeed be the lord of creation." Through the development of machinery, "thus is Paradise to be Regained, and that old and stern decree at length reversed. Man shall no more earn his living by the sweat of his brow." To that notion, Thoreau replies:

> In fact no work can be shirked. It may be postponed indefinitely, but not infinitely. Nor can any really important work be made easier by co-operation or machinery. Not one particle of labor now threatening any man can be routed without being performed. It cannot be hunted out of the vicinity like jackals and hyenas. It will not run. You may begin by sawing the little sticks, or you may saw the great sticks first, but sooner or later you must saw them both.[107]

As H. Daniel Peck has observed, "The 'restless, nervous, bustling, trivial Nineteenth Century' had obscured . . . nature's centrality to human life." Therefore, "what was needed was a reorientation, or repositioning, of the self toward the world."[108] At the heart of Thoreau's project is an attempt at that reorientation.

The skeleton of Thoreau's enterprise, the framework on which all else hangs, is his rejection of modern notions of the human self and a return to more classical understandings. The failure of modern politics lies in the modern habit of neglecting and obscuring human self-knowledge. That self-knowledge—the knowledge that we each are constrained and mysterious—remains unapprehended by a culture won over by the illusion of its own mastery. So moderns mistake apparent changes for substantive ones and technological improvement for human improvement. Thoreau's fellows, he thinks, are doing so much rearranging of the furniture.

Modern citizens have been lured, via a habituated faith in the possibility of dominion and mastery, into the notion that change can be sudden and radical, that within short periods of time, "the whole face of nature shall be changed"—or can be changed.[109] Against such seductive fantasies, Thoreau cautions: "Revolutions are never sudden."[110] Revolutions and other transformations depend first on a kind of moral reform that is *not* apparent. It is inward, and even if it is cataclysmic on the inside, it may not seem so on the outside. (Contrary to Shakespeare's assertion, Thoreau is a philosopher who cultivates patience with a toothache.) For Thoreau, true revolution does not depend on the dramatic and apparent changes that science or technology offers; rather, true revolution depends on a kind of humane progress that happens through the transformation of individual souls over time, who then subtly or dramatically transform their broader environs.[111] As Richard Groff writes:

> Could new external patterns bring about a change of heart in man, or make him happier, or in any important sense better off? Thoreau doubted it. He believed that only a spiritual rebirth in the individual could bring this about. . . . An essential difference between the social reformer or political agitator and the prophet is that the former, in looking for his first convert, starts off eagerly down the road, while the latter sits down quietly to confront—himself.[112]

Such change does not have the appeal of being glamorous or easy, but it has the advantage of being truly transformative in the long term. "It is men who have got to make the law free," Thoreau instructs, by freeing themselves from even their cherished and instituted illusions.[113] Thoreau's is not a call to retreat from political life but rather a call to reform it from within by grappling with the hard facts of body and soul: the fact that embodiment imposes constraints on human possibility and that an unfathomable mystery of existence imposes constraints on human knowledge. Thoreau counsels: look inward first, and learn. We humans cannot be perfect masters, even of ourselves. Still, "there are various tough problems yet to solve, and we must make shift to live, betwixt spirit and matter, such a human life as we can."[114]

We humans must make do with a series of imperfect possibilities defined by our constraints. Ultimately, humans are limited by time. Thoreau says that when contemplating Jesus' teaching that "heaven and earth shall pass away, but my words shall not pass away," he "draw[s] near to him."[115] The greatest possibility for human transcendence, perhaps, lies in the one method by which human minds and spirits can find each other, unconstrained by bodies: in written form. As Stanley Cavell argues, in *Walden*, Thoreau is invested in the possibility of creating "sacred text," in the possibility that writing can take him "just far enough" away from others "to be seen clearly." Thoreau recognizes that "writing is a labor of the hands," the kind of labor that yields a material crop.[116]

Consider Thoreau's statement: "If we would enjoy the most intimate society with that in each of us which is without, or above, being spoken to, we must not only be silent, but commonly so far apart bodily that we cannot possibly hear each other's voice in any case." By this standard, as he notes, the spoken word is insufficient.[117] The written word, however, may be sufficient:

> There is a memorable interval between the spoken and the written language, the language heard and the language read. The one is commonly transitory, a sound, a tongue, a dialect merely, almost brutish, and we learn it unconsciously, like the brutes, of our mothers. The other is maturity and experience of that; if that is our mother tongue, this is our father tongue, a reserved and select expression, too significant to be heard by the ear, which we must be born again in order to speak.[118]

If moral reform, and therefore political reform, is silent and inward and patient, it depends on written words for the sustenance and nourishment of camaraderie. Descending inward into the cave of the self is only the first step in the pursuit of knowledge, and it is a solitary one. Committing that pursuit to the page is how we begin to help others ascend, slowly and haltingly and with all our imperfections, toward a better life.

## Notes

I extend my profound thanks to my research assistant at Pomona College, Andrew

Carlson. Our conversations deeply informed the arguments I make here, and any true insight in this chapter is probably his. In addition, Tom Dumm, Shannon Mariotti, Anthony Parel, and Jack Turner provided helpful reflections on an earlier draft, and Amanda Shapiro gave this piece its final polish.

1. Henry David Thoreau, *Journal*, vol. 1, *1837–1844*, ed. Elizabeth Hall Witherell et al. (Princeton, NJ: Princeton University Press, 1981), 53.

2. Henry David Thoreau, *A Week on the Concord and Merrimack Rivers*, ed. Carl F. Hovde et al. (Princeton, NJ: Princeton University Press, 1980), 224.

3. Ruth Lane speaks of Thoreau contra Hobbes and Locke in this fashion. See "Standing 'Aloof' from the State: Thoreau on Self-Government," *Review of Politics* 67, no. 2 (spring 2005): 294–95. Lane moves from these points of analysis to a claim that Thoreau's view of the human self is multiple, uncultivated, and "prematurely postmodern." Though she acknowledges that Thoreau seems to adhere to a "classical psychology" of body and soul, she argues that he embraces a model of open personality in which human roles "may represent dimensions of the individual self's *definition of its own community* of needs and purposes" (296). Lane's claims on this point are intriguing, although I think she downplays the many possible nuances and complications of a basically classical framework. It is to those nuances and complications that this chapter attends.

4. Henry David Thoreau, *Letters to a Spiritual Seeker*, ed. Bradley P. Dean (New York: W. W. Norton, 2004), 35.

5. Ibid., 57.

6. George Kateb, *The Inner Ocean: Individualism and Democratic Culture* (Ithaca, NY: Cornell University Press, 1992), 170. Robert D. Richardson Jr. describes the ways in which Emerson's thought—particularly in *Nature*—shaped Thoreau's sense of a divinity in nature. See his *Henry Thoreau: A Life of the Mind* (Berkeley: University of California Press, 1988), 19ff.

7. Thoreau, *Letters,* 89.

8. One might also view Thoreau's time in Walden as its own kind of exercise in self-mastery. The quest for self-knowledge—the quest to know the self as well as one can—may begin from the desire to master the self. But for Thoreau, anyone who has truly achieved some measure of self-knowledge will be dominated by feelings not of self-mastery but of self-mystery. Even if a search for self-knowledge is predicated on the aspiration to self-mastery, that aspiration will, in the end, be undermined by the more powerful awareness of self-mystery.

9. Henry David Thoreau, *Walden*, ed. J. Lyndon Shanley (Princeton, NJ: Princeton University Press, 1971), 218.

10. In Thoreau's writings on slavery—quite literally a system of mastery—this

critique is evident. See Jack Turner, "Performing Conscience: Thoreau, Political Action, and the Plea for John Brown," *Political Theory* 33, no. 4 (August 2005): 456ff (revised and reprinted as chapter 6 of this volume).

11. Thoreau, *A Week,* 73–74.

12. Henry David Thoreau, *Journal,* vol. 3, *1848–1851,* ed. Robert Sattelmeyer et al. (Princeton, NJ: Princeton University Press, 1991), 218.

13. Thoreau, *Walden,* 135.

14. Thoreau, *Letters,* 158.

15. Henry David Thoreau, *The Maine Woods,* ed. Joseph J. Moldenhauer (Princeton, NJ: Princeton University Press, 1972), 71.

16. Thoreau, *Walden,* 210.

17. Ibid., 211.

18. Ibid., 210. George Kateb argues that Thoreau and Emerson understand there to be different kinds of wildness, some more worthy of reverence than others: "Good democratic wildness must face up to bad democratic wildness." See *Patriotism and Other Mistakes* (New Haven, CT: Yale University Press, 2006), 270. I also draw on Kateb's discussion of the idea of conscience in Thoreau: "Conscience is taking with the utmost seriousness what everyone professes, and many fail to take seriously. . . . One often has to fight hard against one's conscience, and almost as often defeats it. It has to be touched to live" (264). Kateb points out that for Thoreau, conscience is not an individual, atomized, or subjective standard; it is "thinking, thoughtfulness, anyone's not only his, that can establish the very nature of obligation and the existence of a particular obligation" (263). At the same time, Nancy Rosenblum argues that Thoreauvian conscience itself is wild. As she writes in *Another Liberalism: Romanticism and the Reconstruction of Liberal Thought* (Cambridge, MA: Harvard University Press, 1987), 107: "[Thoreau's] conscience is a purely personal voice that does not necessarily speak consistently or in terms of rules. . . . Personal inspiration takes priority over reason, and conscience is more like the law of the heart than like rectitude. . . . This openness to irrationality marks Thoreau's distance from Kantian conscience."

19. Thoreau, *Walden,* 96.

20. Ibid., 24.

21. Ibid., 25.

22. Henry David Thoreau, *Journal,* vol. 2, *1842–1848,* ed. Robert Sattelmeyer (Princeton, NJ: Princeton University Press, 1984), 211.

23. Thoreau, *Walden,* 23.

24. Ibid., 332.

25. Ibid., 135.

26. Thoreau, *A Week,* 223–24.

27. Walter Hesford, "'Incessant Tragedies': A Reading of *A Week on the Concord and Merrimack Rivers*," *ELH* 44, no. 3 (autumn 1977): 515–16.

28. Thoreau, *A Week*, 224.

29. Ibid., 225.

30. Thoreau, *Walden*, 135. This chapter does not discuss Thoreau's understanding of the potential tragedies of human friendship; for a brief but compelling analysis of this topic, see Norman Jacobson, "'Damn Your Eyes!' Thoreau on (Male) Friendship in America," in *Friends and Citizens: Essays in Honor of Wilson Carey McWilliams*, ed. Peter Dennis Bathory and Nancy L. Schwartz (Lanham, MD: Rowman and Littlefield, 2001), 123–29. Here it is also worth noting the conspicuous absence of sex and sexuality in Thoreau's writing—an absence that has not received too much critical attention. Mary Elkins Moller treats this subject as well as anyone in *Thoreau in the Human Community* (Amherst: University of Massachusetts Press, 1980), 113ff., and in "Thoreau, Womankind, and Sexuality," *ESQ: A Journal of the American Renaissance* 22, no. 3 (1976): 123–48.

31. Thoreau, *Walden*, 134–35.

32. Lawrence Buell, *The Environmental Imagination: Thoreau, Nature-Writing, and the Formation of American Culture* (Cambridge, MA: Belknap Press of Harvard University Press, 1995), 378.

33. Henry David Thoreau, "Slavery in Massachusetts," in *Reform Papers*, ed. Wendell Glick (Princeton, NJ: Princeton University Press, 1973), 91.

34. Ibid., 107.

35. Thoreau, *Walden*, 7.

36. Henry David Thoreau, "Resistance to Civil Government," in *Reform Papers*, 71. I include a discussion of this quotation in particular because it has received disproportionate scholarly attention, as Turner points out in "Performing Conscience."

37. Wilson Carey McWilliams, *The Idea of Fraternity in America* (Berkeley: University of California Press, 1973), 291.

38. Thoreau, *Walden*, 318. It is this kind of comment that leads some commentators, most notably Richard Bridgman, to call Thoreau a pessimist or melancholic. Thoreau's response, I am sure, would be that it is not pessimistic or melancholic to report the truth of human nature. See *Dark Thoreau* (Lincoln: University of Nebraska Press, 1982).

39. Thoreau, *Walden*, 212.

40. Thoreau, *Journal*, 3:218.

41. Peter McCormick, "The Concept of the Self in Political Thought," *Canadian Journal of Political Science* 12, no. 4 (December 1979): 701.

42. Thoreau, *Maine Woods*, 71.

43. Thoreau, *Letters*, 158.

44. See Thomas Hobbes, *Leviathan*, ed. J. C. A. Gaskin (Oxford: Oxford University Press, 1996).

45. See John Locke, *Two Treatises of Government*, ed. Peter Laslett (Cambridge: Cambridge University Press, 1988).

46. For instance, Thoreau says, "To be strictly just, [the government] must have the sanction and consent of the governed" ("Resistance to Civil Government," 89). But as Kateb has articulated, Thoreau "invokes the moral necessity that the people be governed only by their consent, but immediately renders that idea as individual consent." Moreover, that individual consent must be *continuous*—that is, Thoreau does not neglect the fact that an individual's allegiances and reasons and desires may rightly shift over time—and "even one's enfranchisement in the system of elections isn't enough for the reality of individual continuous consent." Moreover, "morality is binding apart from anyone's consent. Consent has nothing to do with the authority of moral principles: I am not free to decide whether or not I will do right" (*Patriotism and Other Mistakes*, 252, 267).

47. John Rawls, *A Theory of Justice*, rev. ed. (Cambridge, MA: Harvard University Press, 1999), 12.

48. Miriam Galston has argued, convincingly, that there is in fact a particular kind of "Rawlsian dualism" that sees political thought as parallel to metaphysical or other "comprehensive" forms of thought. Of course, even if one allows for dualism of this sort, it collapses the political into a single or unified category; for Rawls, "doubleness" is not properly a problem within politics. See "Rawlsian Dualism and the Autonomy of Political Thought," *Columbia Law Review* 94, no. 6 (October 1994): 1842–59.

49. See Ethel Seybold, *Thoreau: The Quest and the Classics* (New Haven, CT: Yale University Press, 1951), 14. Seybold lists the following ancient authors and texts as those Thoreau spent the most time with: Homer; Orpheus; the Greek lyrists, particularly Anacreon and Pindar; Aeschylus's *Prometheus Bound* and *Seven Against Thebes*; Plutarch's *Lives* and *Morals*; Jamblichus's *Life of Pythagoras*; Porphyry's *On Abstinence from Animal Food*; Sophocles' *Antigone*; Aristotle; Theophrastus; Aelian; Herodotus; and Strabo. Of the Latin authors, she says, he read Virgil, Horace, Persius, Ovid, and the "agricultural writers": Cato, Varro, Columella, and Palladius (15–16).

50. See Roderick Nash, *Wilderness and the American Mind*, 4th ed. (New Haven, CT: Yale University Press, 2001), 88.

51. Bennett Simon, *Mind and Madness in Ancient Greece: The Classical Roots of Modern Psychiatry* (Ithaca, NY: Cornell University Press, 1978), 159. For an extended—though perhaps overblown—discussion of this and other dualist no-

tions in ancient Greece, see P. F. M. Fontaine, *The Light and the Dark: A Cultural History of Dualism,* vol. 2 (Amsterdam: J. C. Geiben, 1987).

52. J. Peter Euben, *The Tragedy of Political Theory: The Road Not Taken* (Princeton, NJ: Princeton University Press, 1990), 102–3. As Euben notes, it is no coincidence that Oedipus—*oi-dipous*—comes from the combination of *oi,* an expression of grief, and *dipous,* which means two-footed. Doubleness is the source of the problem.

53. Simon, *Mind and Madness in Ancient Greece,* 163.

54. Thoreau, *Letters,* 35.

55. Thoreau, *A Week,* 294.

56. Jonathan Lear, *Open Minded: Working Out the Logic of the Soul* (Cambridge, MA: Harvard University Press, 1998), 85.

57. Thomas Dumm has a charming discussion of "Thoreau's shit" in *A Politics of the Ordinary* (New York: New York University Press, 1999), 88–89.

58. Thoreau, *Walden,* 306–9.

59. Philip T. Gura, "Henry Thoreau and the Wisdom of Words," *New England Quarterly* 52, no. 1 (March 1979): 52.

60. Thoreau, *Walden,* 306–7.

61. Ibid., 283.

62. Leo Marx, *The Machine in the Garden: Technology and the Pastoral Ideal in America* (London: Oxford University Press, 1964), 249.

63. John S. Pipkin, "Hiding Places: Thoreau's Geographies," *Annals of the Association of American Geographers* 91, no. 3 (September 2001): 530.

64. Footnote to Thoreau's *Letters,* 247.

65. Thoreau, *Walden,* 307.

66. Pipkin, "Hiding Places," 530.

67. Thoreau, *Walden,* 90.

68. For an excellent reflection on the role of cultivation in Thoreau's thought, see Brian Walker, "Thoreau on Democratic Cultivation," *Political Theory* 29, no. 2 (April 2001): 155–89.

69. Thoreau, *Walden,* 46.

70. Brian Walker, "Thoreau's Alternative Economics: Work, Liberty, and Democratic Cultivation," *American Political Science Review* 92, no. 4 (December 1998): 852 (revised and reprinted as chapter 2 of this volume).

71. Thoreau, *Letters,* 94–95.

72. Thoreau, *Walden,* 221.

73. See George Kateb's illuminating discussion of Emerson's notion of "vocation" in *Emerson and Self-Reliance* (Thousand Oaks, CA: Sage Publications, 1995), 153, 162–72.

74. Henry David Thoreau, "Walking," in *Thoreau: Collected Essays and Poems*, ed. Elizabeth Hall Witherell (New York: Library of America, 2001), 225.

75. Thoreau, *Walden*, 51.

76. Henry David Thoreau, *Journal*, vol. 6, *1853*, ed. William Rossi and Heather Kirk Thomas (Princeton, NJ: Princeton University Press, 2000), 6–7.

77. Thoreau, *Walden*, 152.

78. Thoreau, *A Week*, 108.

79. Thoreau, *Walden*, 221.

80. Walker, "Thoreau on Democratic Cultivation," 161.

81. Buell, *Environmental Imagination*, 392.

82. Thoreau, *Walden*, 222.

83. Thoreau, *Letters*, 41.

84. Ibid., 57.

85. G. Lowes Dickinson, *The Greek View of Life* (Garden City, NY: Doubleday, Doran, 1931), 142.

86. See Seybold, *Thoreau*, 30.

87. Robert Sattelmeyer, *Thoreau's Reading: A Study in Intellectual History* (Princeton, NJ: Princeton University Press, 1988), 29.

88. See A. R. C. Duncan, "The Stoic View of Life," *Phoenix* 6, no. 4 (winter 1952): 129ff.

89. Thoreau, *Walden*, 221.

90. Leon R. Kass, *Toward a More Natural Science: Biology and Human Affairs* (New York: Free Press, 1985), 295.

91. Thoreau, *Walden*, 138.

92. Henry David Thoreau, *Cape Cod*, ed. Joseph J. Moldenhauer (Princeton, NJ: Princeton University Press, 1988), 10.

93. Henry David Thoreau, "A Winter Walk," in *Collected Essays and Poems*, 106.

94. Ibid., 103.

95. Thoreau, *Walden*, 98.

96. Ralph Waldo Emerson, "Nature," in *Nature and Selected Essays*, ed. Larker Ziff (New York: Penguin Books, 1982), 81.

97. Thoreau, *Walden*, 317.

98. Ibid., 320.

99. Ibid., 332.

100. Allen Beecher Hovey, *The Hidden Thoreau* (Beirut: Catholic Press 1966), 62.

101. See H. Daniel Peck, *Thoreau's Morning Work: Memory and Perception in* A Week on the Concord and Merrimack Rivers, *the Journal, and* Walden (New

Haven, CT: Yale University Press, 1990), 22ff. See also the final lines of Norman Maclean's *A River Runs through It* (Chicago: University of Chicago Press, 1976), 104: "Eventually, all things merge into one, and a river runs through it. The river was cut by the world's great flood and runs over rocks from the basement of time. On some of the rocks are timeless raindrops. Under the rocks are the words, and some of the words are theirs."

102. Thoreau, *Letters*, 89.

103. Ralph Waldo Emerson, *The Journals and Miscellaneous Notebooks of Ralph Waldo Emerson,* vol. 10, *1847–1848,* ed. Merton M. Sealts Jr. (Cambridge, MA: Harvard University Press, 1973), 471.

104. James McIntosh, *Thoreau as Romantic Naturalist: His Shifting Stance toward Nature* (Ithaca, NY: Cornell University Press, 1974), 299–300.

105. David M. Robinson, *Natural Life: Thoreau's Worldly Transcendentalism* (Ithaca, NY: Cornell University Press, 2004), 180; the quotation is from Thoreau's journal.

106. Robert Kuhn McGregor, *A Wider View of the Universe: Henry Thoreau's Study of Nature* (Urbana: University of Illinois Press, 1997), 181–82.

107. Henry David Thoreau, "Paradise (To Be) Regained," in *Reform Papers,* 24, 36, 39–40.

108. Peck, *Thoreau's Morning Work,* 127.

109. Thoreau, "Paradise (To Be) Regained," 19. This is Thoreau's quotation from Etzler's book.

110. Henry David Thoreau, "Reform and the Reformers," in *Reform Papers,* 195.

111. D. A. Hamlin makes an argument along these lines in terms of the writings of Kurt Vonnegut. He argues that writers—especially prophetic writers—often understand revolution in the long term. His argument, I think, applies to Thoreau's way of understanding change and revolution. See "The Art of Citizenship in the Graduation Speeches of Kurt Vonnegut," in *Democracy's Literature: Politics and Fiction in America,* ed. Patrick J. Deneen and Joseph Romance (Lanham, MD: Rowman and Littlefield, 2005), 191–206.

112. Richard Groff, *Thoreau and the Prophetic Tradition* (Alhambra, CA: Manas Publishing Company, 1961), 36.

113. Thoreau, "Slavery in Massachusetts," 98.

114. Thoreau, *A Week,* 73–74.

115. Ibid., 73.

116. Stanley Cavell, *The Senses of Walden* (New York: Viking Press, 1972), 14, 11, 27. Cavell argues that for Thoreau, the written word must take preeminence over the spoken word "until the nation is capable of serious speech again" (33). I

would argue, though, that Thoreau understands written words to have *under all circumstances* a connective capacity that speech does not, since in writing one separates words from the body. In putting words down on paper, they develop a physical presence apart from the body of the writer or the thinker.

117. Thoreau, *Walden*, 141.

118. Ibid., 101.

# CHAPTER 10

# Thoreau's Religion

*Christopher A. Dustin*

> For most men, it seems to me, are in a strange uncertainty about [life], whether it is of the devil or of God, and have *somewhat hastily* concluded that it is the chief end of man here to "glorify God and enjoy him forever."
> —Thoreau, *Walden*

## Through a Glass Darkly

"ENVIRONMENTAL SAINT," "pastoral hermit," "pantheistic philosopher and religious contemplative"—these are only a few of the labels applied to Thoreau that suggest he was a religious thinker. Among Thoreau's contemporaries, Emerson was not alone in insisting that although he "used in his writings a certain petulance of remark in reference to churches and churchmen," he was actually "a person of . . . absolute religion."[1] More recent commentators have arrived at the same conclusion. Lawrence Buell describes "the religiocentric inquest into the correspondence between the natural and the spiritual" as central to Thoreau's environmental projects.[2] For Buell and others, any understanding of Thoreau as a naturalist, literary artist, or social critic must also take account of the "devotional" calling without which he thought "nothing great was ever accomplished."[3] Thus, while granting that Thoreau was "a highly accomplished and ambitious writer," Alan Hodder echoes Emerson in asserting that "a dispassionate reader of his journals, his letters, *Walden*, or *A Week* can hardly deny that he was an irreclaimably religious person as well."[4]

These very texts should move us to consider, however, whether such a conclusion is (as Thoreau says) "somewhat hastily" reached. The question itself may be hastily posed. In his journal entry for June 23, 1840, Thoreau remarks, "We Yankees are not so far from right, who answer one question by asking another. . . . A true answer will not aim to establish anything, but rather to set all well afloat."[5] In posing the question of Thoreau's religion, one could proceed by settling on the meaning of terms and showing that his thought satisfies those definitions (one could "establish" his religiosity), or one could allow his writing to do what it does so effectively: "to set all well afloat." Emerson famously observed that although Thoreau's life was intimately connected with nature, "the meaning of Nature was never attempted to be defined by him."[6] This did not prevent Thoreau from "speaking a word" for it. His unwillingness to define nature followed from the meaning he saw it as having. The same may be said, I believe, of Thoreau's religion. He himself says as much in the concluding chapter of *Walden:* "The words which express our faith and piety are *not definite;* yet they are significant and fragrant like frankincense to superior natures."[7]

In what follows, I argue that Thoreau's vision is fundamentally theological. This is not to say that his thinking is positively theistic. In approaching the question of Thoreau's religiosity, I am not primarily concerned with establishing his position on the existence of a transcendent or personal God. Thoreau is no more a positivist about religion than he is about anything else. Indeed, this very point is crucial to understanding his religiosity. "The wisest man," he writes, "preaches no doctrines; he has no scheme; he sees no rafter, not even a cobweb, against the heavens. It is clear sky."[8] Thoreau's religious view sits within his overall vision of nature. This does not mean that he reduces the divine to the natural, nor does it make him a pantheist. Those who read Thoreau as either replacing God with nature or locating the divine entirely within it are themselves somewhat hasty in treating nature as conceptually solid ground. They overlook the indefinite nature of Thoreau's nature.

Given the difficulty of coming to terms with Thoreau's religiosity, it is tempting to interpret the religious expressions used by and about him as mere metaphors or rhetorical gestures. We know that terms such as *prophecy* or *pilgrimage, reverence* or *redemption,* can be detached from their strictly religious meaning. But we may overlook the fact that when these terms are being used in the conventionally religious sense, they are *already* being used as metaphors. An original meaning underlies their conventional appropriation—one that is more experientially concrete. Instead of using religious language in a way that is less strictly religious, a departure from the conventional meaning might serve to reconnect such language to its original source. Although Thoreau may seek to express his faith in terms that are not definite, he never uses words loosely. On the contrary: "He would be a poet . . . who nailed words to their primitive senses . . . who derived his words as often as he used them" and "transplanted them to his page with earth adhering to their roots."[9]

This is not to say that Thoreau's etymologically faithful use of language necessarily expresses a distinctly religious faith. In the "Sunday" chapter of *A Week on the Concord and Merrimack Rivers*, he performs just such a derivation, nailing down a sense of the religious that provides the basis for what sounds like a critique:

> In the latter part of the seventeenth century, according to the historian of Dunstable, "Towns were directed to erect 'a cage' near the meeting-house, and in this all offenders against the sanctity of the Sabbath were confined." Society has relaxed a little from its strictness, one would say, but I presume that there is not less *religion* than formerly. If the *ligature* is found to be loosened in one part, it is only drawn the tighter in another.[10]

In making this observation, Thoreau places himself among the "offenders against the sanctity of the Sabbath": "As we passed under the last bridge over the canal . . . the people coming out of church paused to look at us from above, and apparently, so strong is custom, indulged in some heathen-ish comparisons; but we were the truest observers of this sunny day."[11] If Thoreau is "observant," this passage suggests, it is from a standpoint outside the religious. He is in no way caged, but rather set afloat.

It is this critical voice that is most prominent in readings such as those of Robert D. Richardson Jr. On Richardson's reading, although "Walking" may begin and end with a movement toward the Holy Land (and is underwritten by a religious derivation of the verb *to saunter*), it remains a "pointedly secular" essay.[12] Thoreau's invocation of "wildness" as a source of salvation is, for Richardson, a parodic statement of faith ("I believe in the forest, and in the meadow, and in the night in which corn grows") or a call to conversion from the "religion of God" to the "religion of nature."[13] Thoreau's outlook, focused as it is on that "great awakening light" to which the final passage of "Walking" looks forward, is (for Richardson) that of a "secular luminist," concerned with the wonders not of the invisible but of the visible world.[14]

With regard to the theme of awakening that figures so prominently in *Walden*, Richardson argues that although the experience Thoreau describes may be a "spiritual" one, it incorporates no theological elements. It is religious only "in the broadest sense of the word."[15] When Thoreau says that he "got up early and bathed in the pond" and calls this "a religious exercise, and one of the best things [he] did," he means it.[16] He is, as he says, "a sincere worshipper of Aurora," and he bathes, as we sometimes say, "religiously" (as a regular practice). What this signifies for Richardson, however, is nothing like baptism; it is "an awakening to daily renewal, *not* to eternal redemption."[17] In Richardson's view, Thoreau "was not interested in a religion that strove to redeem man from this world, or to raise him above it." If anything, Thoreau strove to reverse the sort of dualism—between the visible and the invisible, this world and the next—that Christianity seems (to Richardson) to presuppose. The foundation for Thoreau's sense of reverence was "his recognition that the divine is to be found in the natural world," as opposed to the "supernatural."[18]

All this demonstrates how variously Thoreau can be interpreted. It is not just the interpreters who are responsible. Thoreau's own role in his enigmatic self-presentation is widely recognized.[19] But even if the experience of reading Thoreau is always that of seeing through a glass darkly, these refracted interpretations help focus the question: what is the nature of that "one true vision" Thoreau seeks to communicate, which he likens to a communication "with the gods"?[20]

Thoreau's religion, I argue, is rooted in a way of seeing.[21] This way of seeing is essentially a form a *communion*. The communion Thoreau seeks through his engagement with the natural world is a realization of (what he calls) "moral freedom." It is reverential and redemptive in ways that we fail to understand if we think such notions presuppose a dualistic conception of reality. Thoreau's vision of nature points *beyond* nature, to a divinely creative source. As such, it incorporates a form of religious transcendence that is seldom recognized. As Thoreau sees it, nature points beyond itself, to a transcendent ground that is neither separable from nor reducible to it.

## Faithfulness to the Earth: One Day Out of *A Week*

Richardson's claim that the language Thoreau uses to express his religious ideas "turns to Hindu, Chinese, and above all Greek religion to the pointed exclusion of Christianity"—that he "does not use or suggest the language of redemption"—is not entirely accurate.[22] Thoreau's use of such language should not be overlooked. At the same time, we cannot overlook the proto-Nietzschean strain in Thoreau's rejection of all life-denying ideals.[23] As Zarathustra exhorts, "I beseech you! Remain faithful to the earth, and do not believe those who speak to you of otherworldly hopes! . . . To sin against the earth is now the most dreadful thing, and to esteem the entrails of the unknowable higher than the meaning of the earth."[24] Thoreau's declaration that he "went to the woods because [he] wished to live deliberately" and that he "did not wish to live what was not life" can be read in this light. The aim of Thoreau's experiment is, as he professes, "to live deep and suck out all the marrow of life, to live so sturdily and Spartan-like as to put to rout all that was *not* life . . . to drive life into a corner, and reduce it to its lowest terms, and, if it proved to be mean, why then to get the whole and genuine meanness of it."[25] Such rhetoric seems to steer us not toward but away from transcendent realities or a heavenly realm of meaning and value. This, it seems, is the conclusion Thoreau reaches in his reflections on Walden Pond: "Nature has no human inhabitant who appreciates her. . . . Talk of heaven! Ye disgrace earth."[26]

However "deliberate" these sayings may appear, they are not dispositive.[27] Thoreau's statements of or about religious faith are often dialectical, in that what is said or suggested in one place is seemingly canceled or negated in another. Thus, in *Walden's* opening chapter, Thoreau complains that "we now no longer camp as for a night, but have settled down on earth and forgotten heaven. . . . We have built for this world a family mansion and for the next a family tomb."[28] One might be overly hasty in relying on passages in which Thoreau expresses his thoughts in explicitly religious terms. But then, one might also be overly hasty in citing passages such as this from his journal (October 1842): "I feel that I draw nearest to understanding the great secret of my life in my closest intercourse with nature. There is a reality and health in (present) nature; which is not to be found in any religion. . . . I suppose that what in other men is religion is in me love of nature." Nature, it appears, can furnish something religion cannot—the kind of "health" that Nietzsche associates with faithfulness to the earth, as opposed to those "otherworldly hopes" that would sicken us and it. Thus, we might conclude that Thoreau simply rejects religion in favor of a return to nature. What Thoreau actually says, however, is not that simple. Nature offers not just reality and health but also illumination, the understanding of a "great secret" that Thoreau approaches only in his "closest intercourse" with nature—that is, when nature is "present" to him, and he to it. Even in that moment of presence, however, the promise is not entirely fulfilled; the great secret remains a secret, for even then, Thoreau does not *arrive* at this understanding but draws "nearest to" it. Nature's promise, moreover, is not strictly opposed to the religious, for what "*in other men* is religion" is not necessarily (and perhaps not at all) the religious as such. The critique keeps the promise of an authentic religiosity alive. It is this that is "not to be found" in "any religion."

What exactly is missing? The precise focus of Thoreau's complaints about religion, and about Christianity in particular, is hard to determine. In the opening chapter of *Walden,* Thoreau laments:

> Our manners have been corrupted by communication with the saints. Our hymn-books resound with a melodious cursing of God and enduring him forever. One would say that even the prophets and redeemers had rather consoled the fears than confirmed the hopes of man. There is nowhere recorded a simple and irrepressible satisfaction with the gift of life, any memorable praise of God.[29]

What is missing is not just a greater love for nature but a more memorable praise of God. Just as the "next world" deserves better than the building of a tomb, the religious should do more than simply console our worldly fears. Here again, Thoreau wants to see a greater hope confirmed—an "irrepressible satisfaction" with "*the gift of life*" and its "secret."

It is not the religious as such, Thoreau suggests, but our conventional adherence to it that is corruptive. Our "communication with the saints" is not a true communion. Any religion is corrupt when it is disconnected from life. Restoring that connection involves more than simply returning to nature, for as Thoreau constantly reminds us, our communication with nature is as prone to corruption as our communication with the saints:

> Men nowhere, east or west, live yet a *natural* life, round which the vine clings, and which the elm willingly shadows. Man would desecrate it by his touch, and so the beauty of the world remains veiled to him. He needs not only to be spiritualized, but *naturalized,* on the soil of the earth. . . . We need to be earth-born as well as heaven-born.[30]

Thoreau's "natural" life is not set against the religious as the only authentic alternative. The question of an authentic naturality mirrors the question of an authentic religiosity. We can experience both the natural and the religious in detachment from life. To separate either from its source—the "gift," or "secret"—is to "desecrate" it. Such desecration is associated with a "veiled" or impoverished vision, with a failure to see. But then, it is the *same source* to which the viewer of nature and the religiously observant person is called to return. In this way, Thoreau suggests, life itself might be reconsecrated. This requires that we be earth-born as well as heaven-born—naturalized and spiritualized "on the soil of the earth." Thoreau's point is not that we should forsake our heavenly aspirations but that heavenly aspirations not bound to the earth are not heavenly enough: "What is this heaven which they expect, if it is no better than they expect? Are they prepared for a better than they can now imagine?"[31]

Recall Thoreau's own Sunday observances in *A Week*, where he seems to set himself adrift from the religious rather than allow himself to be bound by it. Although the Latin *religens* does suggest a kind of bondage, Thoreau does not simply reject this but tries to restore it to its original sense. Strictly speaking, the opposite of *religious* (*religens*) is *negligent* (*negligens*), and Thoreau is not negligent. He is a diligent observer. Of what? The answer to this question emerges most clearly in *Walden*. The Latin *religens* is closely tied to the Greek *alegein*—"to reverence"—and it is in *Walden* that Thoreau's reverential vision is most fully developed. It is in *A Week*, however, that Thoreau's struggle with the religious comes to the surface. What is expressed there is not simply the repudiation of religion in favor of a return to nature but a hope that religion itself can be religiously as well as naturally redeemed. The sense of the religious that Thoreau hopes to re-store is not merely etymological. Where *religion* is concerned, the linguistic root itself—the very source of the word—suggests a kind of rootedness that conventional usage tends to neglect. The corruption Thoreau senses in our "communication with the saints" can be traced to our ignorance of that to which the religious ought to attach us—of the living source the etymologi-cal source intimates.

The people Thoreau sees coming out of church are not neglecting nature in favor of the divine. They are neglecting both: "It seems to me that the god that is commonly worshipped in civilized countries is not at all divine, though he bears a divine name, but is the overwhelming authority and respectability of mankind combined. Men reverence one another, not yet God."[32] The fundamental problem with "most men's religion" is not the "ligature," Thoreau goes on to say, or the sense in which it is binding. The problem lies in their vision of that to which they are bound and in the nature of their attachment. That which "*should* be its umbilical cord connecting them with divinity" is instead "like the thread which the accomplices of Cylon held in their hands when they went abroad from the temple of Minerva, the other end being attached to the statue of the goddess. But frequently, as in their case, the thread breaks, and they are left without an asylum."[33] The thread that binds us to our religious idols offers the same material (and mechanical) assurance as the mansion, the tomb, and the cage. This form of attachment is tenuous at best and ultimately false, since it does not attach us to the divine. This is the kind of bondage, with its essentially false promise, that Thoreau rejects. The metaphor of the umbilical cord (from the Latin *umbilicus,* referring to the navel, but also to the center or "middle" of our bodies) is no less physical, but here the connection is organic. It draws us toward something—like the "great secret" to which Thoreau refers—but also draws upon it. It is in this way, Thoreau suggests, that religion *should* bind us. The religious should not merely secure us to one another or to the world, where such security serves merely to console our fears rather than confirm our hopes. It should connect us with the very sources of life. It should attach us, centrally, to that "gift."

The idea that religion should draw us closer to a "great secret" illuminates what Thoreau sees as irreligious about positive religious doctrine. The religious should derive from the same source as the natural. Cut off at the root, it is essentially lifeless, a mere "scheme": "Most people with whom I talk . . . have their scheme of the universe all cut and dried,—*very* dry, I assure you, to hear, dry enough to burn, dry-rotted and powder-post, methinks . . . an ancient frame with all its boards blown off."[34] The people Thoreau is addressing here are those for whom "Father, Son, and Holy Ghost, and the like" are "everlastingly settled." When called to "examine [their] authority," they will see not that there is no basis for religious belief but that its true authority, or source, has been underrated. When positive doctrine frames our faith, the religious itself suffers a fall:

> Your scheme must be the frame-work of the universe; all other schemes will soon be in ruins. The perfect God in his revelations of himself has never got to the length of one such proposition as you, his prophets, state. Have you learned the alphabet of heaven, and can count three? Do you know the

number of God's family? Can you put mysteries into words? Do you presume
to fable of the ineffable? Pray, what geographer are you, that speak of heaven's
topography? Whose friend are you that speak of God's personality?[35]

Thoreauvian religiosity does not bind us to an ascetic ideal, or what
Nietzsche would describe as the "idols" of Christianity. To enframe the
"frame-work of the universe"—to render an account of God's self-revelation
—is to underestimate its perfection. When we presume to speak authorita-
tively of a "personal" God, we neglect the very transcendence that makes
divine revelation worthy of reverence. The "propositions" that express our
faith and piety are definite, whereas God's sayings are essentially indefinite.
To frame the divine in these terms—to believe that we can comprehend it
with our "schemes"—is to put our own authority in place of God's. This is
what moves Thoreau to say that "the god that is *commonly* worshipped . . .
is not at all divine," or that, in adhering to conventional dogmas, "men reverence one another, not yet God." Although Thoreau's repudiation of religious
doctrine may lead some to conclude that he was a spiritual rather than
an essentially religious thinker, such a conclusion is premature. Thoreau's
critique of religious doctrine is that it is *not properly religious.* The mystery
"put into words"—or "framed" as positive doctrine—is no longer seen, or
truly revered, as a mystery.[36]

## Fabling the Ineffable: Thoreauvian Communion

A truly religious author, Thoreau suggests, would put mysteries into words
without betraying their mystery. By expressing his faith and piety in terms
that are "not definite," Thoreau presents himself as such an author. He
strives to remain faithful to what he sees, even as he seeks to communicate
it. If Thoreau is a better *theographer* than those who presume to know the
number of God's family, it is because he is also a better *geographer.* His
earthly experience organizes his theological vision. The latter is inscribed
within the former:

> God did not make this world in jest, no, nor in indifference. . . . I love the
> birds and the beasts because they are mythologically in earnest. I see that
> the sparrow *cheeps,* and flits, and sings adequately to the great design of the
> universe, that man does not communicate with it, understand its language,
> because he is not at one with nature.[37]

To see the world as divine creation, one must communicate with that creation. One must commune, or be "at one," with nature. Only then can one communicate, or put into words, what one sees (and hears). Just as we cannot comprehend the divine with our schemes, we cannot understand "the great design of the universe" by distancing ourselves from or enframing it in objective terms. In the same way that the sparrow sings *to* a divine source, our fables must acknowledge, and express, nature's ineffability. Our language must keep faith with the language we seek to understand. It is not enough to speak "about" the mysteries of nature. If our mythologizing is to be as earnest as that of the birds and the beasts, we must participate in the mystery their language bespeaks.

The idea of a Thoreauvian "communion" with nature is one that must be handled with care. Here again, his expressions seem to work against themselves. The "Solitude" chapter of *Walden* begins with Thoreau's description of that "delicious evening, when the whole body is one sense, and imbibes delight through every pore."[38] Shortly thereafter, however, he describes what sounds like a radically different mode of experience:

> With thinking we may be beside ourselves in a sane sense. . . . We are not wholly involved in Nature. I may be either driftwood in the stream, or Indra in the sky looking down on it. I . . . am sensible of a certain doubleness by which I can stand as remote from myself as from another. However intense my experience, I am conscious of the presence and criticism of a part of me, which, as it were, is not a part of me, but spectator.[39]

Focusing on passages such as this, Hodder points to a "dissociative" vision as the defining feature of Thoreau's religious experience. On his reading, such episodes of "contemplative detachment and disjunctive perception" are key to an understanding of Thoreauvian religiosity.[40]

Hodder's contention that "the religious philosopher" is one who assumes "the detached position of . . . witness and onlooker" is, however, one that Thoreau himself calls into question.[41] Though "with thinking" he may be "beside" himself, he also yearns for those moments when his "whole body" becomes "one sense"—moments when what he sees is thoroughly "imbibed." Such experiences move him to declare: "I go and come with *a strange liberty* in Nature, *a part of herself.*"[42]

Are Thoreau's religious "ecstasies" a matter of contemplative detachment or of sensory participation? Here again, we must read him dialectically.

Thoreau's ode to "Solitude" is not simply a declaration of independence. It points to a tension that relates freedom to a deeper form of dependence. The "doubleness" Hodder emphasizes may be linked to an experience of freedom. But it is grounded in a moment of absorption—an immersion in, or oneness with, nature and with oneself—that Thoreau associates with freedom of a stranger sort.[43] This stranger freedom is the aim of Thoreau's "Walking":

> Of course it is of no use to direct our steps to the woods, if they do not carry us thither. I am alarmed when it happens that I have walked a mile into the woods bodily, without getting there in spirit. . . . It sometimes happens that I cannot easily shake off the village. The thought of some work will run in my head and I am not where my body is,—I am out of my senses. In my walks I would fain return to my senses.[44]

Here, Thoreau refers to a kind of "thinking" that drives us *out* of our senses and thereby prevents us from reaching our goal. We are not where our bodies are. What is it, then, that Thoreau seeks? Not a dissociative vision but a freedom that reunites him, both physically and spiritually, with himself and the natural world. This is not an experience that just happens, Thoreau suggests. It takes work—a kind of work that differs from the alienated labor of the village. This is what Thoreau describes as the original "business" of walking. His "sauntering" toward the "Holy Land" is no mere rhetorical gesture. It involves an engagement with the earth that is missing from the mystical detachment Hodder describes.

Thoreau's communion with nature is both an engaged seeing and a realization of freedom. But if such communion is freeing, is the nature of the religious not essentially binding, even for Thoreau? The language of "Walking" suggests a communion Thoreau would celebrate both bodily and "in spirit," but does the experience that draws him into the woods necessarily entail the divine? Whether it points to a transcendent ground is a question Thoreau himself is frequently moved to ask:

> What is that other kind of life to which I am continually allured? which alone I love? Is it a life for this world? . . . Are our serene moments mere foretastes of heavenly joys gratuitously vouchsafed to us as a consolation? or simply a transient realization of what might be the whole tenor of our lives? . . . Sometimes we are clarified and calmed healthily . . . not by an opiate, but by some unconscious obedience to the all-just laws, so that we become like a still lake

of purest crystal, and . . . our depths are revealed to ourselves. All the world
goes by us and is reflected in our depth. Such clarity! . . . We live and rejoice.
I awoke to a music which no one about me heard. Whom shall I thank for it?
. . . I feel my Maker blessing me.[45]

Is "that other kind of life" a heavenly or a natural one? Is it "a life for *this*
world" as opposed to some *other* world? As I hope to show, Thoreau's account of the communion he experiences reflects not an agnosticism but a
vision of nature *and* the divine that neither a dualistic scheme nor a collapse
of one into the other can articulate. The freedom he experiences in nature
and the binding nature of the religious appear to be at odds only insofar as
we fail to appreciate what he sees as the strangeness of both.

## The Religious Sources of Moral Freedom

Thoreau characterizes the freedom to which he would "fain return"—the
freedom realized through communion—as a "strange" liberty. In "Life
without Principle," he poses the question, "What is the value of any political freedom, but as a means to moral freedom? Is it a freedom to be slaves,
or a freedom to be free, of which we boast? We are a nation of politicians,
concerned about the outermost defenses only of freedom. . . . We tax ourselves unjustly. There is a part of us which is not represented."[46] Whereas
"political" freedom is more commonly understood and more commonly
achieved, "moral" freedom is strange, Thoreau suggests, as is the part of us
that remains unrepresented even when our liberties are outwardly secured.
Although much of Thoreau's writing constitutes a critique of the (merely) politically free life, *Walden* explores freedom's stranger dimensions. Thoreau's
stay at Walden Pond has been described as an "experiment in freedom."[47]
But the question remains: what makes it an experiment in *moral* freedom?
A large part of the freedom Thoreau seeks to achieve by moving to Walden
can and should be represented in "political" terms. The return to nature,
as a removal from culture, is not necessarily a transcendence of the political.[48] It is political freedom taken to the extreme, perhaps, but not to what
Thoreau sees as its true end.

With what kind of liberty does Thoreau "go and come" in nature, if it
is not merely political? What is the ground, or source, of the moral freedom
for which political freedom is but a means? A comparison with Kant is
helpful here. The Kantian distinction between heteronomy and autonomy

seems to correspond to Thoreau's distinction between a "freedom to be slaves" (where freedom is governed by self-interest) and a "freedom to be free" (where freedom is genuine self-determination). The latter is possible, Kant argues, only through obedience to the moral law. For Kant, however, the moral law is determined by reason as opposed to nature. Nature cannot constitute the grounds of moral freedom. It is only through conformity to the laws of reason that one's autonomy is established.[49]

There is a part of us, Thoreau says, that is not represented by a freedom that is merely political. Although political participation can secure a kind of autonomy, such freedom is still heteronomous. Though outwardly unconstrained and politically self-determined, inwardly we are not fully ourselves. "Our sills are rotten," as Thoreau puts it: "We select granite for the underpinning of our houses and barns; we build fences of stone; but we do not ourselves rest on an underpinning of granitic truth, the lowest primitive rock."[50]

Such foundational imagery suggests a further comparison with Kant. But it is on this point that crucial differences emerge. For Thoreau, this "primitive rock" is not supplied by a reason that functions in opposition to or frees us from nature. Nature itself provides the stuff of which moral freedom is made. Thoreau's metaphor suggests not only that moral freedom rests on something other than a purely rational foundation but that it is ultimately grounded in something deeper than any foundation we ourselves set down. We may cut and lay the sills for our houses, but the "underpinning of granitic truth" on which Thoreau would have us establish our autonomy is not among the things we "build." The lowest primitive rock is not a foundation that a moral agent furnishes for himself. Thoreauvian moral freedom draws on a source outside the self. But it is not heteronomous in the Kantian sense. Neither is it autonomous, in the sense of the will's being "a law to itself." To rest ourselves on this underpinning is to make ourselves whole, but it is not a purely *self-determining* act. This is what makes it strange. We owe our wholeness—our being fully ourselves—to something that is and is not other than us.

The strangeness goes even deeper than this. One could draw an important contrast between Kant's foundational moral reason and Thoreau's appeal to "conscience."[51] It is on the latter, one might argue, that moral freedom properly rests. One could further argue that the language Thoreau uses, in appealing to conscience, introduces a religious orientation that Kantian morality seems to exclude.[52] George Kateb is right to observe that Thoreauvian conscience is not a purely individual or self-determining standard.[53] But neither does it take the place of that "lowest primitive rock." Thoreau's discussion of conscience in "Resistance to Civil Government" forgoes foundational imagery in favor of a different metaphor:

> They who know of no purer sources of truth, who have traced up its stream no higher, stand, and wisely stand, by the Bible and the Constitution, and drink at it there with reverence and humility; but they who behold where it comes trickling into this lake or that pool, gird up their loins once more, and continue their pilgrimage toward its fountain-head.[54]

The metaphor of the "source," in the way Thoreau invokes it, is as physical as the foundational one. Their philosophical implications, however, are very different. In this passage, Thoreau suggests that conscience is not a basis on which moral freedom "rests." Appealing to conscience is not a matter of "standing" but of "tracing"—as in tracing a river to its source. One might still regard conscience as supplying the content of moral freedom, in the same way that the source supplies water to the stream. But Thoreau does not explicitly identify conscience with those "purer sources of truth." What is philosophically significant about the experience of tracing a river to its source is that such sources cannot finally be identified. Those who arrive at "this lake or that pool" might mistake these for the source, until they discover where a stream comes "trickling into" them, at which point they must "continue their pilgrimage." The appeal to conscience involves a search for what must ultimately constitute the sources of conscience itself. The object of this search is, as Thoreau would say, "indefinite." Such sources are metaphysically (as well as physically) elusive, or strange. We no sooner point to them than they point beyond themselves to their own mysterious source.

Although *Walden* plays extensively with foundational imagery, a preoccupation with "sources" lies at the heart of it. This preoccupation is itself the source of Thoreau's theological vision. What Kant finds in reason alone, Thoreau discovers in a redemptive vision of "wildness"—a vision realized through participation in or communion with the natural world.

## Revering Nature: Thoreau's Redemptive Vision

"I found in myself," Thoreau tells us in *Walden*, "and still find, an instinct toward a higher, or, as it is named, a spiritual life, as do most men, and another toward a primitive rank and savage one, and I reverence them both."[55] Thoreau seems to point to a kind of dualism here, between a "higher life" and the freedom associated with "wildness and adventure." But while he marks the difference between them, it is not their separateness that he emphasizes. As he says, he reverences them both. "I love the wild not less than the good," he goes on to say. Does he love it more? What is truly worthy of reverence, he suggests, is the interpenetration between them. For thus spoke the "notes of the flute" to John Farmer:

> Why do you stay here and live this mean moiling life, when a glorious existence is possible for you? Those same stars twinkle over other fields than these.—But how to come out of this condition and actually migrate thither? All that he could think of was to practise some new austerity, *to let his mind descend into his body and redeem it.*[56]

We might read this alongside a passage from "Walking," where Thoreau laments our tendency to "hug the earth:" "How rarely we mount! Methinks we might elevate ourselves a little more. We might climb a tree, at least."[57] While Thoreau draws a contrast between heaven and earth, the distance we must cover in "elevating" ourselves is not a distance that separates them. To climb a tree (the revelatory experience Thoreau goes on to describe, for which he says he was "well paid"[58]) is not to leave the earth behind. To mount successfully, one must "hug"—or hold tight to—the tree. So it is that Thoreau would "take rank hold on life and spend [his] day more as the animals do," yet the "true harvest" of his daily life is "somewhat intangible and indescribable as the tints of morning or evening."[59] It is an "intangible" harvest, but like any real harvest, it is drawn from the earth. This is what Thoreauvian communion promises to yield: "Nature is reported," he notes in his journal, "not by him who goes forth [merely] as an observer, but *in the fullness of life.* To such a one she rushes to make her report."[60] It is one thing for us to direct our steps to the woods, Thoreau warns, and another for them to "carry us thither." All too often, we are not where our bodies are.[61] As Thoreau "returns to his senses," the mind descends while the body is raised up. Here again, our earthly experience (the "rank and savage" life) is not left behind; nor is heaven (that "higher" life) simply brought down to earth. To "migrate thither" (toward the heavenly) is to see the earth itself as "elevating." It is in this way, Thoreau suggests, that both body and mind are "redeemed." To "go forth . . . in the fullness of life" is to be fully ourselves.

In theological terms, redemption seems to presuppose a fallenness of some kind—of human beings or nature or both. Redemption is restoration or "atonement"—reconciliation or, literally, a "setting at one." Redemption can also refer to a kind of exchange (from the Latin *redemire*, "to buy back"). In what sense does Thoreau seek redemption? To what, exactly, are our bodies (and souls) restored? If the point is simply that we must return to nature to restore the fullness of our being, then it is unclear why Thoreauvian redemption would refer us to any sort of divine ground.

For Thoreau, it is never a question of "simply" returning to nature. He sees a parallel between nature's aspirations and our own: "The soil, it appears, is suited to the seed, for it has sent its radicle downward, and it may now send its shoot upward with confidence. Why has man rooted himself thus firmly on the earth, but that he may rise in the same proportion into the heavens above?"[62] Thoreau's vision is often characterized by simultaneous upward and downward movements. What he describes is not just the coming together of minds and bodies but an orientation toward heaven and earth that is, or ought to be, "radical" in both directions. Nature is not simply what is "earth-bound." Like the seed, it penetrates (sends its roots) more deeply *into* the earth, and on that basis rises above it. Neither of these movements is "exchanged" for the other. They must, rather, be "set at one." Our fallenness consists in our failure to *see* this—not merely to observe it, but to live that vision in the realization that we shall rise to the same extent that (or "in the same proportion" as) we are rooted. But then nature's aspirations are not merely parallel with or symbolic of our own. Thoreauvian communion celebrates the coincidence between them. When nature is observed "in the fullness of life," it is restored to itself and its own transcendent ground. It is then, Thoreau says, that nature is truly "reported." Thoreau comes to this realization in *A Week:* "The eyes were not made for such grovelling uses as they are now put to and worn out by, but to behold beauty now invisible. May we not *see* God?" To see God, Thoreau suggests, our eyes must penetrate all the more deeply into the visible world:

> There is only necessary a moment's sanity and sound senses, to teach us that *there is a nature beyond the ordinary.* . . . We live on the outskirts of that region. . . . Let us wait a little, and not purchase any clearing here, trusting that richer bottoms will soon be put up. It is but thin soil where we stand; I have felt my roots in a richer ere this.[63]

To "return to our senses" is not merely to observe nature and to stop thinking about our business in town. Even then, we may fail to see what is before our eyes: though we reach the deepest part of the forest, we remain on the outskirts. "It is but thin soil" that we see. To behold nature in its richness— to participate in the fullness of life—is to see "a nature beyond the ordinary." To see in this way is not to look *beyond nature,* nor is it merely to look *at* it. There is a sense of the beyond, Thoreau suggests, that is part and parcel of nature itself.

"To such a one" who stands on or is rooted in this richer ground, Thoreau suggests, nature herself "rushes to make her report." Thoreau's daily harvest is, as he says, "somewhat indescribable." For Kant, the grounds of moral freedom are rationally determined and can be articulated in the form of a principle. Thoreau's declaration that he went to the woods because he wished to live deliberately sounds like a call to a more principled way of living. But again, the Thoreauvian imperative to "simplify" our lives is less simple than it sounds, for we must also address the question of what we are simplifying. As he originally puts it (in the journal entry from which the passage in *Walden* is drawn): "I wish to meet the facts of life—the vital facts, which were the phenomena or actuality the Gods meant to show us—face to face. And so I came down here. Life! who knows what it is?"[64]

This is a question one might hope to answer in a determinate way. Thoreau himself seems to express such a hope. Kant speaks of a fundamental "respect" for the moral law. Thoreau often voices a respect for the lawful regularities of nature as sources of moral as well as scientific truth.[65] Richardson identifies this as one of the primary lessons Thoreau learns from his Walden experiment. Moved by the discovery that law pervades nature, Thoreau recognizes the wholeness underlying seemingly isolated phenomena. The way natural phenomena respect certain laws brings forth a corresponding respect from the attentive observer of them. In accepting the laws of nature, Richardson suggests, Thoreau "accepted nature." In accepting nature, "he accepted not only himself, but things beyond himself."[66]

On this reading, the laws of nature turn out to be moral laws, displacing conventional obligations, on the one hand, and lifeless principles, on the other. Thoreau's awareness of them brings him to an attitude he expresses in religious terms. The freedom he describes is grounded not merely on a "respect" for the laws of nature, however, but on a reverence for them.

Kantian respect (in German, *Achtung*) involves attention to or observance of the kind of law that ought to govern our conduct. Having respect for the moral law is like respecting a limit or boundary. But Thoreau does not merely "attend" to the lawful regularities he observes in nature or accept the limits they impose. The lawfulness of nature points to something deeper—not to a determinate principle that must be observed but to a source for which he is fundamentally thankful:

> There can be no very black melancholy to him who lives in the midst of Nature and has his senses still. There was never yet such a storm but it was Aeolian music to a healthy and innocent ear. . . . While I enjoy the friendship of the seasons I trust that nothing can make life a burden to me. The gentle rain which waters my beans and keeps me in the house to-day is not drear and melancholy, but good for me too. Though it prevents my hoeing them, it is of far more worth than my hoeing. If it should continue so long as to cause the seeds to rot in the ground and destroy the potatoes in the low lands, it would still be good for the grass in the uplands, and, being good for the grass, it would be good for me.[67]

The goodness of the storm that nourishes the grass but causes the seeds to rot is a goodness (or "worth") that transcends utility. Although the inconvenience of the gentle rain is ultimately beneficial, the storm is not, since in watering the beans it has destroyed them. But to assume that the rain's benefit to the upland grasses may yet ensure a profitable harvest is to miss the point. Observing this, Thoreau writes:

> Sometimes, when I compare myself with other men, it seems as if I were more favored by the gods than they, beyond any deserts that I am conscious of; as if I had a warrant and surety at their hands which my fellows have not, and were especially guided and guarded. I do not flatter myself, but if it be possible they flatter me.[68]

Thoreau sees that, in being good for the grass, the rain may yet be good for him. In what sense? Not in the sense that it may benefit his neighbors too, making them all equally blessed (by an abundant crop of hay, for example). If the benefit is his alone, this is because it is drawn not from whatever else the grass might be good for but from what he "senses"—or sees—as the underlying goodness of nature itself. Thoreau says that he *seems* to be divinely favored, and the fact that he is not positive is important. If he is divinely favored, that favor takes the form not of outward security but of the guidance offered only to one who takes joy in "the friendship of the seasons" and the ineluctable cycle of growth and decay—one whose joy remains undiminished even as the gentle rain becomes a destructive flood. The sense of guardedness such guidance provides (the sense of being favored "beyond any deserts") is very different from the "outermost defenses" that mark the distinction between political and moral freedom. A belief in the ultimacy of such security is what Thoreau's divine guidance (or "surety") guards against. If Thoreau is "guided and guarded," it is not by a defensive boundary, or limit. He is inwardly guarded—his autonomy is secured—by an openness to what nature promises. Only insofar as the rain is good for the grass, Thoreau says, is it good for him. It is by identifying with nature that he is able to recognize its underlying goodness.

There is more to Thoreau's "acceptance" of nature than an awareness of the lawful regularities and interconnectedness of natural phenomena. The enlightenment he describes does not come to one who merely observes and records; it comes to one who *"lives in the midst of Nature and has his senses still."* To "live in the midst of nature" is not merely to respect but to *participate in* what one sees. Although Thoreau sees nature as regular and lawful, specific laws of nature cannot furnish the grounds of moral freedom, for he ultimately sees *through* them to something else—to a deeper ground that they only partially reveal.[69]

This is where Thoreau's reverence for the laws of nature takes on its religious meaning. It is drawn from precisely that which guards against his being positively assured of divine favor. In etymological terms, the meaning of *reverence* derives from an experience of awe (the Latin *re-ueriri* means "to feel fear again") and is allied to the English *wary.* The wariness that is akin to awe is not just a form of skepticism. Nature's laws *can* be observed and recorded, Thoreau thinks. Much of his work at Walden Pond consists in doing just that. But it is not their objective determinacy that makes them objects of reverence, for they are determinable only in light of an absolute wholeness of things, the grounds for which remain essentially indeterminate. Any laws we record can only intimate these grounds; they can never supply them:

> If we knew all the laws of nature, we should need only one fact, or the description of one actual phenomenon, to infer all the particular results at that point. Now we know only a few laws, and our result is vitiated, not, of course,

by any confusion or irregularity in Nature, but by our ignorance of essential elements in the calculation.[70]

No *known* law can reveal the sense in which nature as whole is ultimately lawful or harmonious. Such a vision lies beyond the horizon of any natural or moral science:

> Our notions of law and harmony are commonly confined to those instances which we can detect. . . . The particular laws are as our points of view, as, to the traveler, a mountain outline varies with every step, and it has an infinite number of profiles, though absolutely one form. Even when cleft or bored through it is not comprehended in its entirety. . . . What I have observed of the pond is no less true in ethics.[71]

For Thoreau, the laws of nature do not furnish models for the conduct of life so much as intimations of the sources of life itself. They do not point directly upward (to some higher application of them) so much as downward, to a terrestrial or even subterranean light that shows through them and ultimately reflects the divine. The grounds of moral freedom are here on earth, or, rather, they issue *from* the earth—just as the "thawing sand and clay" flow out of the "deep cut" through which Thoreau passes on his way to the village: "Thus it seemed that this one hillside illustrated the principle of all the operations of Nature."[72] Thoreau traces "the gift of life" neither to a supernatural source, in Richardson's sense, nor to a source that is purely natural. His search does not simply lead him back to the earth, nor does it lead directly to an idea of God as the intelligent author of the "all-just laws" to which he confesses his "unconscious obedience." It leads to a source that is both deeper and higher than either of these.

"Even when cleft or bored through," Thoreau says, nature "is not comprehended in its entirety." *Wildness* is the word Thoreau uses to refer not to nature in its entirety, for that would imply a static conception, but to the creative source within it. Just as it is a mistake to confuse Thoreau's *wildness* with *wilderness*, it is also a mistake to identify *wildness* with the *natural*. Thoreau refers to the wild less frequently and more exclusively than he does to nature. Wildness, for Thoreau, is a quality or essence *within* nature. To understand wildness by identifying it with nature is to risk objectifying both. For the same reason, we should beware of distinguishing between wildness "out there" (in the natural world) and a wildness "internal" to the self.[73] To do so means that we fail to understand the participatory nature of

Thoreau's vision. For Thoreau, wildness is never simply "out there" in nature (any more than nature itself is simply "out there"). Wildness is nature's own inwardness. Wildness is what the self communes with.

Jane Bennett is right when she characterizes Thoreauvian wildness as both indestructible and indefinable—as the unstable ground of nature's "indeterminacy and excessiveness." But something is missing from the view of wildness she goes on to develop. Wildness is not just a "remainder" or "surplus" that always escapes our attempts to conceptualize or domesticate nature.[74] On Bennett's reading, wildness is that "element of heterogeneity" —of plurality and immanent antagonism—that Thoreau is (supposedly) seeking in nature. As that which "eludes human reckoning," it runs counter to our expectation that nature can be seen as a complete, harmonious, or self-sufficient whole. It is "an ideal that articulates the experience of being 'part and parcel' of one's surroundings even as those surroundings exceed full comprehension." Bennett's Thoreau lives in this tension: he "idealizes living in intimacy with one's surroundings [but] also loves the Wild, that which makes complete intimacy impossible."[75]

It is not as clear to me as it is to Bennett that Thoreau's invocation of wildness stands in the way of his seeing the world as divine creation. Nor is it antithetical to the wholeness he seeks. Thoreau looks at nature, Bennett writes, "and for moments finds himself . . . inextricably enmeshed within a vast web of life extending beyond his powers of cognition and imagination."[76] It is precisely this, I argue, that furnishes the grounds for his communion with it.[77] As he writes in his journal for June 22, 1853, "I long for wildness, a nature which I cannot put my foot through . . . where the hours are early morning ones, and there is dew on the grass, and the day is forever unproved, where I might have a fertile unknown for a soil about me." There is more to wildness, or to the fundamental indeterminacy of nature, than an epistemo- logically disruptive otherness. The question remains: what is it about nature that "exceeds" or places it "beyond" our comprehensive schemes? The point is not that nature must have a determinate essence that accounts for its excessive quality but that its wildness (in Thoreau's view) cannot ultimately depend on us and our ability, or inability, to comprehend it. Wildness points to what is unaccountable in nature—not just to its (negative) potential to resist understanding but to a positive potentiality, or power. There is more to it than what is "left over" from any given account. Its very excessive- ness argues against its being reduced to a mere remainder. Wildness—as manifest in nature's superabundance—is not simply that which lies outside of or is resistant to our explanatory systems. It is more than what we cannot understand. To "long for wildness," in Thoreau's terms, is to approach (or draw nearer to) the *source* of nature's excessiveness—"a *fertile* unknown." In "Walking," Thoreau says that "life consists with wildness. The most alive is the wildest."[78] Wildness is not simply life. It points to that from which life springs. And this is neither fully comprehensible nor fully communicable. To see nature as wild is to see it, fundamentally, as creation. This is what Thoreau longs to participate in, or commune with.

On my reading, we must interpret Thoreauvian wildness in metaphysical and not just epistemological terms. The very physical way Thoreau presents it demands this interpretation. Bennett is right in saying that wildness is not a "foundation" for Thoreau. The reason he cannot put his foot through it is not because of its firmness but because of its excessive depth. It is not "thin soil" but "impermeable and unfathomable," like the swamps to which Thoreau is drawn.[79] But if wildness is not a foundation, it does not follow that nature must dissolve into (what Bennett calls) a "heteroverse." The mountain that "varies with every step" has, in reality, "*absolutely* one form." Though it may exhibit "an infinite number of profiles" to the detached observer, it has an "entireness" the true seer, or communicant, can discern. Its oneness cannot be grasped "even when cleft or bored through." If nature is not a self-sufficient whole for Thoreau, it is because the source of its unity—the source of creation—does not lie entirely within it. It is as transcendent as it is immanent.

This moment of transcendence is an essential component of Thoreau's vision of nature. Wildness is not a replacement for God, in Thoreau's view. As a revelation of nature's own indeterminate ground, it becomes his point of contact with the divine.

## Fathoming the Infinite: Reflective Transcendence

In winter, Thoreau's "morning work" consists, first and foremost, not of bathing but of finding water, though, "after a cold and snowy night it needed a divining rod to find it."

> I cut my way first through a foot of snow, and then through a foot of ice, and open a window under my feet, where, kneeling to drink, I look down into the quiet parlor of the fishes, pervaded by a softened light as through a window

of ground glass, with its bright sanded floor the same as in summer; there a perennial waveless serenity reigns as in the amber twilight sky, corresponding to the cool and even temperament of the inhabitants. Heaven is under our feet as well as over our heads.[80]

We should not overlook Thoreau's figurative reliance on a "divining" rod and the kneeling attitude he is so careful to describe. More significant, though, is the nature of his looking—the structure of his vision and what it takes in. Were he to be more precise, Thoreau might have said that heaven is *under* what is under our feet. What is directly under his feet is a firm but ephemeral foundation of ice that allows him to see into the pond in a way he otherwise could not. To see what there is to see, however (to "imbibe" these waters), he must penetrate the ice, cutting through the foundation to reveal what is beneath it. In seeing more deeply, he discovers a "waveless serenity" that transcends seasonal change. He sees a vision of heaven.

It is no accident that such revelations—or tangible reflections of the divine—occur most often in those settings where water mediates between earth and sky. Whether on a greater or lesser scale, Thoreau is struck by their luminosity. But it is not just the play of light that makes water more than a metaphysical symbol for Thoreau. In its very substance, water makes visible the mysteriousness of the source he seeks.[81] Water is not just a source of life. There is life in it. At the same time, bodies of water (like all living bodies) have a source that can be traced but never ultimately fathomed. Walden Pond, too, issues from the earth. But where, exactly, does it come from? This, together with the pond's precise depth, is something Thoreau enthusiastically seeks to determine. He "was desirous to recover the long lost bottom of Walden Pond," and so he "surveyed it carefully" and methodically, arriving at a formula for calculating the deepest point in any pond: "It is remarkable how long men will believe in the bottomlessness of a pond without taking the trouble to sound it. But I can assure my readers that Walden has a reasonably tight bottom at a not unreasonable, though at an unusual, depth. I fathomed it easily."[82]

What, exactly, has he "fathomed"? "I am thankful," he says, "that this pond was made deep and pure. . . . While men believe in the infinite some ponds will be thought to be bottomless."[83] Having measured the depth, does he no longer "believe"? Walden has no inlet or outlet, no stream running into or out of it. Being spring fed, its waters flow from the bottom of the pond itself. Its source lies within it. The pond itself seems "free" or autonomous in a way that moves Thoreau ceaselessly to wonder. Although he succeeds in locating its bottom, he cannot really fathom its source, which lies deeper than any depth he can "reasonably" measure. It is this belief in the infinite that Thoreau has taken the trouble to sound:

> At the same time that we are earnest to explore and learn all things, we require that all things be mysterious and unexplorable, that land and sea be infinitely wild, unsurveyed and unfathomed by us because unfathomable. We can never have enough of Nature.[84]

"We can never have enough of Nature," he says, but not in the sense that *we* are never satisfied with the resources nature provides and are therefore bent on using it up (though that is certainly true). For Thoreau, we can never have enough of nature because nature itself is "bottomless." Our earnestness to explore it and the requirement that it be "unexplorable" do not stand in opposition, as we might picture reason in relation to its limits or to faith. It is the earnestness to explore that deepens our belief in the infinite, for it is in the infinite that the sources of natural phenomena are ultimately seen to lie.

For Thoreau, the "requirement" that nature be grounded in something like a divine mystery does not follow merely from our being infinitely desirous of it. The sense in which our "belief in the infinite" might be mistaken is different from that in which any of our calculations might be wrong. Insofar as every pond must have a physical bottom, its depth can be measured. But no such bottom is absolutely firm. It is, Thoreau says, but "reasonably tight." It has its own depth. This is what our desire to get to the bottom of nature can and should reveal. It is important that Thoreau's earnest desire to determine Walden's precise depth is linked to the question of its source. Those who do not "take the trouble to sound" this are negligent. Their "belief in the infinite" falls short of religious belief. Thoreau's explorations reveal the sense in which any reasonable measurement can never determine the source of what we are trying to measure. Walden's source cannot be identified with its (reasonably tight) bottom. But the same is true of any "bottom" we may arrive at. To measure the depth is *never* to fathom the source. The source of the requirement that nature be unfathomable lies within nature itself. This is what Thoreau discovers, in sounding the depths of what others merely believe.

We cannot fathom the source of Walden's or of our own autonomy, because nature always points beyond itself. Moral freedom does not involve a mere "acceptance" of nature as lawfully determined, any more than it involves the acceptance of a rationally (or naturally) determined self. Its grounds cannot be measured or surveyed; its bounds cannot be set. But although the sources of life cannot be comprehended, or merely "respected" as a limit, such wildness can and ought to be revered. Here again, Thoreau expresses an attitude of faith:

> We need to witness our own limits transgressed, and some life pasturing freely where we never wander. . . . I love to see that Nature is so rife with life that myriads can be afforded to be sacrificed and suffered to prey on one another; that tender organizations can be so serenely squashed out of existence like pulp,—tadpoles which herons gobble up, and tortoises and toads run over in the road; and that sometimes it has rained flesh and blood! . . . The impression made on a wise man is that of universal innocence. Poison is not poisonous after all, nor are any wounds fatal.[85]

How does this differ from a Nietzschean faithfulness to the earth? The Nietzschean vision (or one interpretation of it ) would have us live and die *only* for the earth, renouncing the idea that there can be any grounds for salvation beyond this endless sacrifice of "flesh and blood." Such "natural" processes are, in this view, all there is. Our autonomy and their "innocence" are secured only by our willing acceptance of them and by our renunciation of all transcendent ideals. It is on these earthly grounds that life is supposedly affirmed.

Thoreau's vision is "higher" because it penetrates more deeply into these earthly grounds. "We need the tonic of wildness," he writes, "to wade . . . in marshes where the bittern and the meadow-hen lurk."[86] What Thoreau loves to see in nature—wildness—is not just a universal cycle of sacrifice and suffering by which it is riven but the superabundance of life with which it is "rife." "Where do we want most to dwell near to?" he asks. Not to the meetinghouse or any of the places "where most men congregate," but rather *to the perennial source of our life,* whence in all experience we have found that to issue, as the willow stands near the water and sends out its roots in that direction."[87] For the very reason that "we can never have enough of nature," natural processes are not all there is. Life is truly affirmed when we are moved to wonder about *its* source. This is what casts the whole of nature in a redemptive light. Precisely where we dwell matters little, for "nearest to all things is that power which fashions their being. *Next* to us the grandest laws are continually being executed. *Next* to us is not the workman whom we have hired, with whom we love so well to talk, but the workman whose work we are."[88]

In urging us to dwell in closest proximity to "the perennial source of our life"—to commune with wildness by "wading" in it—Thoreau expresses more than a mere acknowledgment or acceptance of nature's essential indeterminacy. It is tempting to think that when Thoreau speaks a word for nature, "wildness" has the *last* word—that, in his view, this is all nature ultimately is. But his expressions typically reach beyond this. The "power" in nature is, for him, the intimation of a source that lies deeper even than the wildness of the swamps. These intimations of a divine being—"the workman whose work we are"—are expressed in ways that are not definite, to be sure, but are nonetheless expressions of faith. For Thoreau, this is the form of expression that genuine faith requires.

## Thoreau's Horizonal Eschatology

So far as I know, Thoreau's vision has never been described as eschatological.[89] Many of his "visions" are, however, surrounded by an eschatological horizon that is more than just rhetorical. Eschatological visions need not be sharply dualistic or otherworldly. They may describe transcendent realities continuous with yet distant from our own, offering redemptive possibilities within our present experience. An *eschatology* is, in the original sense, a *logos* of the *eschata*—of what is "outermost," "utmost," "farthest," or "remotest," of that which lies at the edges of space and time as they are commonly experienced, or the "end" of life as we know it.[90] As fables of the ineffable, eschatological accounts look to "the beyond." They *may* point to what lies "on the other side" (to a reality separate from this one), or they may describe regions of being that are vitally linked to those we inhabit, regions to which we might conceivably journey or that we might even see from where stand.

For Thoreau, such visions do not detach us from ourselves. They return us to our senses. They transfigure and transform. They point not to separate regions but to transcendent dimensions of being. Although they do suggest a kind of doubling, their structure is not so much dualistic as horizontal. Their luminosity is like that of the visible horizon. They do not mark a definite limit beyond which we may eventually pass; they reflect a limitlessness we can never fully grasp.

Thoreau's "morning work" is conducted within such a horizon. "The morning," Thoreau says, "is the awakening hour." But we do not simply awaken "in" the morning (for then the true morning is past), nor does the morning simply follow the night. Each morning, Thoreau suggests, points to its own awakening and hence to a morning that preceded it, not as a separate point in time but as a source from which we may continue to draw. This is what gives Thoreau's work (of body and of mind) its sacramental quality:

> That man who does not believe that each day contains an earlier, more sacred, and auroral hour than he has yet profaned, has despaired of life. . . . To him whose elastic and vigorous thought keeps pace with the sun, the day is a perpetual morning. It matters not what the clocks say or the attitudes and labors of men. Morning is when I am awake and there is dawn in me.[91]

In contrast to the man who does not see that every sunrise originally arises from a source deeper than the material exchange of night and day (the man who has "despaired of life"), he who rejoices in that immeasurable morning of all mornings (who does his work at *this* time, which is not a time at all but is eternal) will dwell nearer to that "perennial source" that transfigures his daily life and work.

For Thoreau, Walden itself becomes the primary source of these reflective revelations. In a passage that recalls the "myth of the true earth" from Plato's *Phaedo,* he arrives at the following observation:

> A field of water betrays the spirit that is in the air. It is continually receiving new life and motion from above. It is intermediate in its nature between land and sky. On land only the grass and trees wave, but the water itself is rippled by the wind. I see where the breeze dashes across it by the streaks or flakes of light. It is remarkable that we can look down on its surface. We shall, perhaps, look down thus on the surface of the air at length, and mark where a still subtler spirit sweeps over it.[92]

Unlike Plato, whose myth appeals to the appearance of stability (the permanence of earthly beings compared with the fluctuating nature of undersea life), for Thoreau, it is the changeable nature of the pond's surface—its very naturalness, or animation—that intimates a "new life and motion" that all of nature (and he himself) receives "from above." Like the ripples that Thoreau so carefully observes, it is a "subtler" spirit that he sees. It sweeps over the whole of creation, not with the metaphysical force of a Platonic form or of a God whose being is rationally posited, but with a penumbral presence that makes it all the more visible.[93]

"The life in us is like the water in the river," Thoreau writes in *Walden's* penultimate paragraph. "It may rise this year higher than man has ever known it, and flood the parched uplands. . . . It was not always dry land where we dwell."[94] The rain that destroyed the lowland crops has now consumed the entire earth (it is a flood, one might say, of biblical proportions). So it is that *"the life in us"* is ultimately affirmed. The prospect of its rising, however, is not deferred to some Last Day when this life (or this world) is exchanged for the next. "It may rise *this year*." The redemptive moment consists not in the redirection of our vision from one region of being to another (from the natural to the supernatural) but in our seeing more deeply into that which is dawning in the present.[95] *Walden's* last words are, in this sense, eschatological: "I do not say that John or Jonathan will realize all this; but such is the character of that morrow which mere lapse of time can never make to dawn. The light which puts out our eyes is darkness to us. Only that day dawns to which we are awake. There is more day to dawn. The sun is but a morning star."[96]

## Seeing God in a Sandbank

Thoreau's writings are replete with visions like the ones I have described. They are often highly particularized, stemming from a subtlety of observation that distinguishes Thoreau's insights from those of his fellow transcendentalists. There is a redemptive yearning in Thoreau. It is a yearning, first and foremost, for presence. This moment of presence, however, is at the same time a moment of transcendence—just as "each day" is seen to derive from, and share in, a "more sacred" and eternal source: "We should be blessed if we lived in the present always, and took advantage of every accident that befell us, like the grass which confesses the influence of the slightest dew that falls on it. . . . In a pleasant spring morning all men's sins are forgiven."[97] "While such a sun holds out to burn, the vilest sinner may return," Thoreau is moved to sing. "Through our own recovered innocence, we discern the innocence of our neighbors." To participate in the presence of nature—to experience it in the fullness of life, and to experience the fullness of life in it—is to keep pace with the "perpetual morning" that makes every hour an "awakening" hour or a renewal of life. To "confess the influence" of nature's "every accident" is to draw on the indeterminate source that invites us to be born again at every present moment.

If the sun alone can redeem us—if a spring morning is sufficient for "recreating the world"—what distinguishes Thoreauvian presence from the pantheism commonly ascribed to him? The forgiveness he mentions seems to come as a natural gift. Our innocence is recovered—the "savor of holiness" is discerned—when divinity is seen as immanent in nature. This, it seems, is Thoreau's version of grace.

Divine immanence, however, is only half the story. If "the jailer does not leave open his prison doors" on such a morning, Thoreau says, it is not because he has failed to see that the morning is itself divine. It is because he does not "obey *the hint* which God gives" him.[98] The return to innocence is not achieved by simply opening one's eyes to what is present in nature, nor is divinity as readily available as Thoreau's alleged pantheism would suggest. Thoreau's vision of God as immanent in nature is incomplete without the moment of transcendence that relates the natural and the human to a source lying beyond both. To "take advantage of every accident that befell us"—to experience the spring morning as a "re-creation"—one must participate in a revelation that transcends the here and now. One has to become "completely lost," Thoreau suggests, or rather "turned around," without ceasing to be where one is. Only then does one "appreciate the vastness and strangeness of Nature" and come to recognize, in the utter contingency of those accidents, the "solid" but immeasurable bottom that is their source.[99] "Not til we are lost," in this sense, "do we begin to find ourselves, and realize where we are and the infinite extent of our relations."[100]

"To sin against the earth is now the most dreadful thing," Zarathustra says, "and to esteem the entrails of the unknowable higher than the meaning of the earth." Thoreau locates the entrails of the unknowable *in* the meaning of the earth and thus esteems or "reverences" them both. But this does not make him a pantheist. His theological vision is more sophisticated. Nietzsche would have us "remain faithful to the earth" and "not believe those who speak of otherwordly hopes." In Thoreauvian terms, one cannot remain faithful to the earth without entertaining a hope in the mystery that surrounds the sources of life. Without this redemptive horizon, our faith in the earth (our very affirmation of life) is superficial. Conversely, without faith in the earth, our religiosity is cut off from life. Thoreau renounces the otherworldly—in its dualistic version—and thereby professes his faith in the eternal presence of the divine:

> Men esteem truth remote, in the outskirts of the system, behind the farthest star, before Adam and after the last man. In eternity there is indeed something true and sublime. But all these times and places and occasions are now and here. God himself culminates in the present moment, and will never be more divine in the lapse of all the ages. And we are enabled to apprehend at all what is sublime and noble only by the perpetual instilling and drenching of the reality that surrounds us.[101]

God is not present in nature such that the divine is simply what is "now and here." What Thoreau calls the "gift" of life is a form of grace, but the recovery of innocence calls for a kind of redemptive work in which we and nature participate together. It is not without effort that Thoreau would "return to his senses." It is only by a *perpetual instilling and drenching of the reality that surrounds us*" that we apprehend the divine.

As he walked on the railroad, Thoreau says, he would "wonder at the halo of light" around his shadow and "would fain fancy [himself] one of the elect."[102] The penumbra that surrounds our shadows may go unseen by us. Though "constant," Thoreau observes, "it is not commonly noticed." A penumbra issues from a sunlike body, recalling Plato's (indirect) vision of the form of the Good. In Thoreau's vision, the sunlike body is also our own. We share in a divine light. As it did for Plato, this light issues from a transcendent source—not a transcendent "being" but something that, as Plato suggests, is beyond being.[103] For Thoreau too, the signs of our "election" point to a source that is ontologically indeterminate. But whereas Plato would forsake the shadows for the sun, Thoreau's penumbral vision holds them together. We do not "apprehend" it by looking directly toward the sun. The penumbra is a revelation we participate in only by "drenching" ourselves in the reality that surrounds us.

Spring is overflowing with these moments of active communion, where the full presence of nature points to a transcendent source of light and of life:

> I have penetrated to those meadows on the morning of many a first spring day . . . when the wild river valley and the woods were bathed in so pure and

bright a light as would have waked the dead, if they had been slumbering in their graves, as some suppose. There needs no stronger proof of immortality. All things must live in such a light. O Death, where was thy sting? O Grave, where was thy victory, then?[104]

Here again, such a vision—such faith—is given only to one who "penetrates" what is seen. Of course, there is at least one instance when, rather than penetrating nature's inwardness, Thoreau finds that it miraculously comes to meet him. In that sudden "springing into existence" in the thawing sand and clay, he feels the presence of "the Artist who made the world and me," who is "still at work . . . with excess of energy strewing his fresh designs about."[105] It is, he says, "as if the globe were turned inside outward." What flows from this portion of earth is nature as a whole, the unfolding of leaves, the formation of blood vessels, the "sources of rivers." Caught up in this vision, Thoreau is moved to ask: "What is man but a mass of thawing clay?"[106] This is not a rhetorical question (as if it were clear to Thoreau that our own sources can be reduced to the basic laws of matter). What, after all, is a mass of thawing clay? If we "look closely," he says, and think more deeply, we shall see that it is not fundamentally material or fully determinate. In exhibiting "the principle of all the operations of Nature," the thawing clay provides evidence, once again, of an unfathomable source—evidence, we might say, of "things unseen."[107] This vision of wildness does not merely relate us to the earth; it shows how "the very globe continually *transcends* . . . itself."[108] It is the kind of vision, Thoreau suggests, in which we realize "the infinite extent" of our relations.

So it is that as nature points back ever more deeply into itself, to a source that transcends it, "the life in us" is seen, by Thoreau, as inherently resurrectional. This is what "the first sparrow of spring" announces:

The year beginning with younger hope than ever! . . . What at such a time are histories, chronologies, traditions, and all written revelations? The brooks sing carols and glees to the spring . . . the grass-blade . . . streams from the sod into the summer, checked indeed by the frost, but anon pushing on again, lifting its spear of last year's hay with the fresh life below. It grows as steadily as the rill oozes out of the ground. It is almost identical with that, for in the growing days of June, when the rills are dry, the grass blades are their channels, and from year to year the herds drink at this perennial green stream, and the mower draws from it betimes their winter supply. So our human life but dies down to its root, and still puts forth its green blade to eternity.[109]

# Notes

Earlier versions of this chapter were presented at the October 2006 meeting of the Society for Nature, Philosophy, and Religion and at the College of the Holy Cross. I am grateful to Bruce Foltz and Joseph Lawrence for their responses. I also thank Denise Schaeffer, James Kee, Jack Turner, and Susan McWilliams for their careful readings of a later draft. Their comments and suggestions were illuminating and helpful.

1. Ralph Waldo Emerson, "Thoreau," in *Lectures and Autobiographical Sketches* (Boston: Houghton, Mifflin, 1883), 477–78.

2. Lawrence Buell, *The Environmental Imagination* (Cambridge, MA: Harvard University Press, 1995), 128–29.

3. Emerson, "Thoreau," 478.

4. Alan Hodder, *Thoreau's Ecstatic Witness* (New Haven, CT: Yale University Press, 2001), 3.

5. All quotations from Thoreau's journal are from *The Journal of Henry D. Thoreau* (New York: Dover Publications, 1962).

6. Emerson, "Thoreau," 471.

7. Henry David Thoreau, *Walden, or Life in the Woods* (Boston: Beacon Press, 2004), 304 (emphasis added).

8. Ibid., 70.

9. Henry David Thoreau, "Walking," in *Excursions* (Boston: Houghton, Mifflin, 1863), 194.

10. Henry David Thoreau, *A Week on the Concord and Merrimack Rivers* (Princeton, NJ: Princeton University Press, 1980), 64 (emphasis in original).

11. Ibid., 63.

12. Robert D. Richardson Jr., *Henry Thoreau: A Life of the Mind* (Berkeley: University of California Press, 1986), 226.

13. Ibid., 269.

14. Ibid., 226, 50.

15. Ibid., 174.

16. Thoreau, *Walden*, 83.

17. Richardson, *Henry Thoreau*, 174.

18. Ibid., 193–94.

19. See, for example, Buell, *Environmental Imagination*, 371–84; Hodder, *Thoreau's Ecstatic Witness*, 218–49.

20. Thoreau, *A Week*, 140.

21. Thoreau's resistance to religious ideology and to institutional (or sectarian) religious life leads Hodder to suggest that "religion [for Thoreau] was experiential

or it was nothing" (*Thoreau's Ecstatic Witness*, 20). It would be a mistake, however, to conclude that Thoreau's religion is *nothing more* than a mode of experience, for then it becomes difficult for us to recognize him for what Hodder thinks he is—namely, "an essentially religious" and not just a "spiritual" writer (3).

22. Richardson, *Henry Thoreau*, 174.

23. Richardson draws several parallels between Thoreau's outlook and Nietzsche's (see ibid., 165, 191–94, 226). On the comparison between Thoreauvian and Nietzschean "ideals," see also Jane Bennett, *Thoreau's Nature: Ethics, Politics, and the Wild*, new ed. (Lanham, MD: Rowman and Littlefield, 2002), 28–29, 108–13.

24. Friedrich Nietzsche, *Thus Spoke Zarathustra*, trans. Walter Kaufmann (New York: Viking Press, 1966), 13.

25. Thoreau, *Walden*, 85 (emphasis added).

26. Ibid., 188.

27. This may be true of Nietzsche's sayings as well, but that is a subject for another essay.

28. Thoreau, *Walden*, 34.

29. Ibid., 73.

30. Thoreau, *A Week*, 379–80.

31. Ibid., 379.

32. Ibid., 65.

33. Ibid., 78 (emphasis added).

34. Ibid., 69–70.

35. Ibid., 70–71.

36. See also the passage in *A Week* (72) where Thoreau suggests that if the New Testament were to be properly (as opposed to "outwardly") received and truly read, it would be "foolishness and a stumbling block" to "Christians, no less than Greeks and Jews." This call for a more authentic religiosity that will redeem rather than replace collective or institutionalized faith is echoed in *Walden*: "What avails it that you are Christian, if you are not purer than the heathen, if you do not deny yourself more, if you are not *more religious?*" (207).

37. Thoreau, *Journal*, March 31, 1852.

38. Thoreau, *Walden*, 122.

39. Ibid., 128.

40. Hodder, *Thoreau's Ecstatic Witness*, 5, 246.

41. Ibid., 232.

42. Thoreau, *Walden*, 122 (emphasis added).

43. Thoreauvian "doubleness" is itself an important but difficult theme. Different interpretations are offered by Bennett (*Thoreau's Nature*, 30–31) and Susan McWilliams (chapter 9 of this volume). My aim here is not simply to collapse this

doubleness (a move McWilliams smartly warns against) but to resituate it. In my view, Thoreauvian communion works through the doubleness of both the communicant (Thoreau) and that with which he communes. It not only redeems the spectator but also returns nature to itself.

44. Thoreau, "Walking," 168–69.

45. Thoreau, *Journal*, June 22, 1840.

46. Henry David Thoreau, "Life without Principle," in *The Higher Law: Thoreau on Civil Disobedience and Reform*, ed. Wendell Glick (Princeton, NJ: Princeton University Press, 2004), 174.

47. See Richardson, *Henry Thoreau*, 151.

48. This is essentially Stanley Cavell's argument in *The Senses of Walden* (Chicago: University of Chicago Press, 1992). George Shulman argues along similar lines in chapter 5 of this volume, as does Bennett in *Thoreau's Nature*. I agree with this argument, as far as it goes. On my reading, however, the implications of Thoreau's conception of moral freedom are more fundamentally religious than these interpretations suggest.

49. In his *Grounding for the Metaphysics of Morals*, trans. James Ellington (Indianapolis: Hackett, 1981), Kant argues that "a free will and a will subject to moral laws are one and the same" (49). A free will is an autonomous will, one that has "the property of being a law to itself." The world of nature is, for Kant, essentially heteronomous. Our moral freedom is dependent on reason's ability to rise above nature.

50. Thoreau, "Life without Principle," 168.

51. See, for example, Nancy Rosenblum's discussion of the difference between Thoreauvian conscience and Kantian moral reason in *Another Liberalism: Romanticism and the Reconstruction of Liberal Thought* (Cambridge, MA: Harvard University Press, 1987), 107.

52. I am grateful to Susan McWilliams for drawing my attention to this point.

53. See note 18 of McWilliams's chapter 9. See also George Kateb, *Patriotism and Other Mistakes* (New Haven, CT: Yale University Press, 2006), 263–64.

54. Henry David Thoreau, "Resistance to Civil Government," in *Higher Law*, 88.

55. Thoreau, *Walden*, 197.

56. Ibid., 208–9 (emphasis added).

57. Thoreau, "Walking," 210.

58. The passage continues thus: "I found my account in climbing a tree once. It was a tall white pine, on the top of a hill, and though I got well pitched, I was well paid for it, for I discovered new mountains in the horizon which I had never seen before,—so much more of the earth *and* the heavens" ("Walking," 210; emphasis added).

59. Ibid., 203.

60. Thoreau, *Journal*, July 2, 1852 (emphasis added).

61. In *Cape Cod*, Thoreau seems to say the opposite, as McWilliams argues in chapter 9. We are always where our bodies are, Thoreau reminds us, until we die, at which point they are easily parted with. See *Cape Cod* (Princeton, NJ: Princeton University Press, 1988), 10. This is not the only place where Thoreau seems to contradict himself. But the two ideas are not at odds. In one sense, of course, we *are* always where our bodies are. But we can also be—and often are—estranged from them. Even in life, Thoreau suggests, we can be more dead than alive. For Thoreau, not to be "where his body is" is to be estranged from himself both physically and spiritually. Thoreauvian communion celebrates not only a return one's senses but also a restoration to "the fullness of life."

62. Thoreau, *Walden*, 13.

63. Thoreau, *A Week*, 382–83 (emphasis added).

64. Thoreau, *Journal*, July 6, 1845.

65. See, for example, the "Friday" chapter of *A Week*, especially 363.

66. Richardson, *Henry Thoreau*, 317.

67. Thoreau, *Walden*, 124.

68. Ibid.

69. If Thoreau is inclined to view the New Testament as "too moral" (see *A Week*, 73), it is because it seems to harbor a devotion to determinate laws that, given the nature of its vision, it ought to transcend: "Absolutely speaking, Do unto others as you would that they should do unto you, is by no means a golden rule, but the best of current silver. An honest man would have but little occasion for it. It is golden not to have any rule in such a case."

70. Thoreau, *Walden*, 272.

71. Ibid.

72. Ibid., 289.

73. See, for example, Bennett, *Thoreau's Nature*, 31.

74. Ibid., xxii–xxvii, 52.

75. Ibid., 25–26, 52–53, 59.

76. Ibid., 52.

77. Bennett argues that the proper relationship to "the Wild" is neither one of exploration nor one of engagement. It is not a relationship of "intimacy" or "depth" but a matter of "coming up to the edge" or "fronting" (ibid., 35). In "Walking," Thoreau calls on us to "bring our sills up to the very edge" of the swamp (187), but the swamp is not identical with its "wildness." Nor do I think it is right to say that the word Thoreau typically uses to describe our encounters with wildness is the verb *to front*. On this point, compare Frederick Garber, *Thoreau's Redemptive Imagination* (New York: New York University Press, 1977), 46.

78. Thoreau, "Walking," 187. Note that Thoreau does not say (simply) that wildness "consists in" life.

79. Ibid., especially 188–89. Here, I think Bennett mistakes what Thoreau sees in the "wildness" of these swamps. "Dark, slimy, malodorous," she writes, "the swamp is the other to socially privileged values of enlightenment, clarity, cleanliness" (*Thoreau's Nature*, 55). But it is not just (or even) "the rank and revolting power of the swamp" that matters to Thoreau. What he calls attention to, in "Walking," is not its subversive potential but its fertility. When Thoreau would have us "bring our sills up to the very edge of the swamp," it is not so we may learn to "tolerate the complexity and ambiguity in . . . Nature" (as Bennett suggests), but so we may draw nearer to the creative source it expresses. Thoreau describes these swamps as "dismal" (that is, "to the citizen"), but he makes no mention of their being messy or smelling bad. It is their "darkness," "thickness," and "interminability"—the unfathomability of the source—that he seeks in order to "re-create" himself.

80. Thoreau, *Walden*, 266.

81. Thoreau does talk about natural features (including Walden Pond itself) as "symbols." But it is not merely a "correspondence" between the natural and the spiritual that he sees in them (as Buell suggests). It is a substantial interpenetration. McWilliams (in chapter 9 of this volume) has some important and interesting things to say about Thoreau's "identification" with water as a "mystical entity." The focus of her analysis is on the extent to which, for Thoreau, human beings must remain mysterious to themselves. On my reading, the mystery Thoreau locates in the depths of the self derives from the kind of mystery he locates in his attempt to measure the depth of Walden Pond. It is a literal derivation, insofar as the word *de-rive* refers, originally, to the experience of drawing water from a stream. In my view, the mystery that lies at the bottom of the pond is the metaphysical source of the mystery that lies at the bottom of the self.

82. Thoreau, *Walden*, 268.

83. Ibid., 269.

84. Ibid., 297.

85. Ibid., 297–98.

86. Ibid., 297.

87. Ibid., 126 (emphasis added).

88. Ibid., 127. Cavell proposes a decisively nontheological reading of this passage. "The workman whose work we are—which some may call God," is, on his reading, "that in ourselves, or that aspect of ourselves, whom the writer calls the indweller" (*Senses of Walden*, 106). The "indweller" makes his appearance in the "Economy" chapter. The "workman" to whom Thoreau refers in this passage is invoked in "Sounds." On my view, Cavell's reading underestimates Thoreau's

more fully developed vision of that "power which fashions [our] being," or the significance of the indweller's participation in, and communion with, wildness.

89. The final chapter of Michael West's *Transcendental Wordplay* (Athens: Ohio University Press, 2000) is titled "Scatology and Eschatology." Its primary focus, however, is on the former, and it does not attach any deeply religious meaning to the eschatological language Thoreau uses. Etymologically, scatology and eschatology do not share a common root, though I propose that Thoreau's eschatological vision is derived from his earthly one (in his reflections on the sandbank, for example).

90. See Andrea Wilson Nightingale, *Spectacles of Truth in Classical Greek Philosophy* (Cambridge: Cambridge University Press, 2004), 141–42.

91. Thoreau, *Walden*, 84.

92. Ibid., 178.

93. Compare this passage in *A Week* (382): "When the common man looks into the sky . . . he thinks it less gross than the earth, and with reverence speaks of 'the Heavens,' but the seer will in the same sense speak of 'the Earths,' and his Father who is in them." On my reading of this passage, the Thoreauvian seer sees beyond what is conventionally referred to as "the heavens" (and the Father who is in them) to what Plato would call the true heaven. Unlike Plato, however, he does not arrive at this vision by separating himself from the (true) earth.

94. Thoreau, *Walden*, 311.

95. This is why I am less comfortable than others in characterizing Thoreau's religious outlook as a "prophetic" one. One might assume that prophecy and eschatology would go hand in hand, but Thoreau's eschatological vision does not incorporate the predictive dimension that prophecy seems to entail.

96. Thoreau, *Walden*, 312.

97. Ibid., 294.

98. Ibid. (emphasis added).

99. As previously noted, Thoreau's preoccupation with sources, and their unfathomability, is not entirely without "foundational" moments. Thus, in the "Conclusion" to *Walden*, he says that "there is a solid bottom everywhere"(309). But we should take note of the way in which he concretizes the point. The "argument" is set in a swamp that a traveler hopes to negotiate. A boy assures him that it has a "hard bottom," but when he sinks, the boy informs him that he has "not got half way to it yet." It is significant, I think, that he has not got *even halfway*. It suggests that such "foundations," for Thoreau, are as unfathomable as the sources he would have us trace. The "solid bottom" and that which "exceeds" it coincide. This, I believe, is as close as we dare come to naming Thoreau's God.

100. Thoreau, *Walden*, 162.

101. Ibid., 91.

102. Ibid., 190.

103. See, for example, Plato's *Republic,* 509b.

104. Thoreau, *Walden,* 296–97.

105. Ibid., 285–88. It is "wonderful," Thoreau says. It is, of course, from the Latin *mirari* ("to wonder") that *miracle* is derived.

106. Ibid., 287.

107. See Hebrews 11:1: "Faith is the substance of things hoped for, the evidence of things unseen."

108. Thoreau, *Walden,* 287.

109. Ibid., 290–91.

CHAPTER 11

# Thoreau's Techniques of Self

*Jane Bennett*

Every man is the builder of a temple . . . to the god he worships. . . . We are all sculptors and painters, and our material is our own flesh and blood and bones.
—Thoreau, *Walden*

When I ask for a garment of a particular form, my tailoress tells me gravely, "They do not make them so now." . . . When I hear this oracular sentence, I am for a moment absorbed in thought, emphasizing to myself each word separately that I may come at the meaning of it, that I may find out by what degree of consanguity They are related to me, and what authority they may have in an affair which affects me so nearly.
—Thoreau, *Walden*

## The They

IN THIS CHAPTER I examine Thoreau's project of self-fashioning, a project designed to weaken the voice of the They within him. Thoreau admits to an initial attraction to this voice, which announces what is normal, though he considers this an ignoble attraction and works hard to overcome it. The first step in this process is to become alienated from this internalized voice and to make it an object of suspicion; the second step is to mark the specific occasions during which one's susceptibility to it is greatest. For Thoreau, these occasions are political ones, times when he is called on to be a good citizen. In "Resistance to Civil Government," he notes this special vulnerability to the They when it speaks on behalf of the respectable, taxpaying public:

I do not wish to . . . set myself up as better than my neighbors. I seek rather, I may say, even an excuse for conforming to the laws of the land. I am but too ready to conform to them. Indeed I have reason to suspect myself on this head; and each year, as the tax-gatherer comes round, I find myself disposed to review the acts and position of the general and state governments, and the spirit of the people, to discover a pretext for conformity.[1]

There are many reasons why the They is so seductive. Human action must proceed without the benefit of foresight: to obey the They is to diffuse some of the anxiety generated by this fact. Fears about the wisdom or efficacy of one's action are soothed by the great body of convention: They do it this way, and so shall I. Social and intellectual conformity, that vertiginous fall into the norm, also provides a sense of closure: it answers the question What ought I to do? quickly and definitively.

But it is only under conditions of uncertainty, Thoreau believes, that individuality forms. Only in a setting that surprises and is in some significant way unfamiliar can Thoreau live deliberately, with full consciousness of "Where I Lived and What I Lived For." Describing his experience on the lecture circuit, Thoreau notes that "ordinarily, the inquiry is, Where did you come from? or, Where are you going?" But there "was a more pertinent question which I overheard one of my auditors put to another once—'What does he lecture for?' It made me quake in my shoes" (*Reform Papers*, 168). Only an examined life is worth living; only a periodically shaken self is worth being.

If a deliberate life is the richest and most noble,[2] and if conformity is both attractive to mortal Americans and fatal to an intensely experienced life that is one's own and none other, then the most pressing project becomes finding ways to be caught off guard, to be quaked, surprised, and estranged from one's usual psychological, intellectual, and social landscapes. Extraordinary measures must be taken to disrupt the state of dependence on others, to jar oneself away from the They. "We need to be provoked,—goaded, like oxen, as we are, into a trot." The task is to locate and then regularly expose oneself to wild sites and sights, to maximize opportunities for shock and disorientation, for "not till we have lost the world, do we begin to find ourselves."[3] As a substitute for the dulling comfort provided by a conventional identity, Thoreau seeks the sublime experience of a "universe," of a self capable of fleeting moments of unity with Nature: "Would it not be worthwhile," wonders Thoreau, "[to] be native to the universe?"[4]

I describe Thoreau's quest as a series of eight techniques: moving inward, idealizing a friend, keeping quiet, going outside, microvisioning, living doubly, hoeing beans, and eating with care. These exercises are to be practiced daily until they become second nature. Taken as a group, they display how Thoreau's art of the self combines bodily discipline with relaxation of intellect, and how it mixes intellectual rigor with flight of fancy.

## Moving Inward

Like Thoreau, Hegel is fascinated by the process through which a self becomes an "I." His *Phenomenology of Spirit* is presented as a virtual replica of that process. A brief account of Hegel's discussion of "Lordship and Bondage" serves to introduce the first of Thoreau's techniques of self, a mental exercise one might call "moving inward."

Hegel argues that lordship, or a social order of domination, is a fatally flawed strategy for developing individual self-consciousness because it precludes what is implicitly sought by every struggling "I": recognition by another whose own struggle qualifies him to confirm one's own progress toward subjectivity. Though neither master nor slave can articulate this, mutual recognition is fundamental to an identity as a free and self-determining being: "Self-consciousness exists . . . when, and by the fact that it so exists for another; that is, it exists only in being acknowledged."[5]

The slave, though hardly to be envied, does have a small advantage when it comes to self-consciousness: in the product of his labor he glimpses his (reflected) subjectivity. The master, in contrast, does not work; what is worse, he insists on surrounding himself with beings who are, by his own definition, mere slaves, unfit to confirm him as a reflective being. The master's "victory" over the slave fails to afford the master the possibility of mutual affirmation or reciprocal recognition of personhood. The master is thus unable to define and refine thoughts that are peculiarly his own. For Hegel, to become an individual is to be psychologically, intellectually, and morally interdependent with others; subjectivity and intersubjectivity are coterminous.

Thoreau presupposes much of what Hegel says about mutual recognition, but Thoreau's version of the story emphasizes its conformist implications. Intersubjectivity is a condition of possibility of the I *and* the They.

Neighbors, acquaintances, and fellow citizens are functionaries—of gossip, moralism, prejudice, and platitude. They are not only carriers of the They-world; they also activate and strengthen the They in oneself. Too often, Thoreau fears, to relate to others is to latch on to what is familiar in them; too often, the feeling of satisfaction accompanying mutual recognition is the ignoble pleasure of closure: the They in them smoothly gliding toward and finally merging with the They in oneself.

"I love society as much as most," says Thoreau, "and am ready enough to fasten myself like a bloodsucker for the time to any full-blooded man that comes in my way" (*Walden*, 140). Sociality, although a powerful human predisposition, is also the way of parasites. Thoreau seeks only "full-blooded"—that is, strong and independent—hosts, but even these are "in [his] way." One's fellows too easily function as neighbors—close by, they close in and intrude. "Exclude such trespassers from the only ground which can be sacred to you," warns Thoreau (*Reform Papers*, 172).[6]

That "ground" is inward, with its rivers of past experience, hills of desire, fields of imagination. Thoreau's remedy for the gold fever plaguing his contemporaries is to turn the spade inward ("is not our *native* soil auriferous?"), to "separate . . . from the multitude," and to journey not to the West but to the center: "Inward is a direction which no traveller has taken. Inward is the bourne which all travellers seek and from which none desire to return" (*Reform Papers*, 165, 164, 193). This personal interior is a rich mix of the familiar and the Wild: beloved memories, concrete desires, and vivid dreams exist alongside half-forgotten events, indeterminate longings, and obscure or protean images.

Wild versus domestic, like I versus They, is an animating contrast for Thoreau. Domesticity is a state of mind appropriate to and evoked by ordinary social intercourse, civilized manners, civic or political organization. All that is conventional, standard, and predictable is "domestic." Domesticity, dwelling with the They, is necessary, and Thoreau aims not to eradicate it but to avoid an existence wholly dominated by it.

The wildness of anything consists in its capacity to inspire extraordinary experiences, startling metaphors, unsettling thoughts. "The most alive is the wildest. Not yet subdued to man, its presence refreshes him."[7] Wildness is the unexplored, unexpected, and inexplicably foreign dimension of anything. It is more easily "fronted" out-of-doors, but it resides even within the self: "It is vain to dream of a wilderness distant from ourselves. There is none such. It is the bog in our brain and bowels, the primitive vigor of Nature in us, that inspires that dream."[8]

The terrain of other selves too is diverse and Wild, but the magnetic force of the They makes others tend to function as trespassers (who run in packs and flatten the landscape):

> In proportion as our inward life fails, we go more constantly and desperately to the post office. You may depend on it, that the poor fellow who walks away with the greatest number of letters . . . has not heard from himself this long while. (*Reform Papers*, 169)

So look not to the Hegelian other but to the wildness and roughness within, for one's self can be less familiar than another's. "Follow your genius closely enough and it will not fail to show you a fresh prospect every hour" (*Walden*, 112).

*Genius* is one of Thoreau's terms of art. He uses it to point to those thoughts that come unannounced, those that we do not have because they have us—we are struck by them.[9] Our Genius is "winged thoughts" and "like birds . . . will not be handled" (*A Week*, 339). Such thoughts are "free" and "awake"; they are not reducible to something we have learned or heard from another. They are thoughts that engage instead in "celestial relations":

> When I am stimulated by reading the biographies of literary men to adopt some method of educating myself . . . —I can only resolve to keep unimpaired the freedom and wakefulness of my genius. I will not seek to accomplish much in breadth and bulk and loose my self in industry but keep my celestial relations fresh. (*Journal*, 2:357)

Dreams, too, are an internal source of the Wild. They offer a counter-reality, they go beyond the limits of acceptable or decent behavior, and they have the power to challenge or make strange the formations of the waking world. In dreams "we have a more liberal and juster apprehension of things, unconstrained by habit, which is then in some measure put off, and divested of memory, which we call history" (*A Week*, 58). Thoreau writes of one such dream in his journal, of a "mountain in the easterly part of our town (where no high hill actually is)." He does not remember its contents very clearly, only that he "shuddered" on his way up the mountain, that it was "unhandselled, awful, grand," and that "you are lost the moment you set foot there . . . thrilled" (*Journal of HDT*, 10:141–42).

## Idealizing a Friend

The typical effect of human interaction, then, is to "give each other a new taste of that old musty cheese that we are"(*Walden*, 136). On rare occasions, however, other humans—those who are not "spoiled by being so civil and well disposed"—can have an inoculative effect against the They. To enter into a relationship with those possessing "some provoking strangeness" is to engage in "Friendship," the second technique of self (*Journal*, 3:322).[10]

A friend can foster individuality not only as a source of wildness but also as a locus for one's most divine thoughts. In friendship each party becomes the site in which the other invests his or her highest aspirations. A friend is the actual object around which one may spin the threads of one's ideals; it is the person to whom one might write:

> I love thee not as something private and personal, which is *your own*, but as something universal and worthy of love, *which I have found*. O how I think of you! You are purely good,—you are infinitely good. (*A Week*, 271)

A "Friend is that one whom I can associate my choicest thought" (*A Week*, 271), one "who could bear to be so wonderfully and beautifully exaggerated every day."[11]

The choice of a friend is not something one deliberately plans. It is, rather, the spontaneous identification of one in whom it is possible to invest one's ideals. One has a nose for friends; one is instinctively drawn to them. The example Thoreau gives is Wawatam, who befriends Henry the fur trader after affirming that Henry is "the white brother whom he saw in his dream" (*A Week*, 274–75).

Thoreau describes this investment of one's own ideals in another as simultaneously treating the other as what he or she, the other, aspires to be (*A Week*, 259). This is the case even if the two friends do not share the same set of ideals. Thoreau's point, I think, is that this act of idealization is contagious: putting a friend on an ethical pedestal inspires the friend to refine and perfect his or her own thoughts and to raise his or her own expectations from the actual to the ideal. Friends interact (or opt to postpone or forgo interaction) to elevate the expectations each has about the other and about the self. Friends can add nothing to each other; they can, however, help each other look inward in the right way, to become "two solitary stars" (*A Week*, 288).

Thoreau prefers not to elaborate the attributes of this "stardom," and he usually eludes the question of what makes "higher" thoughts higher, privileging the act of idealization over the content of the ideals (as his own ideal of individuality demands). But of course, standards of value permeate his texts: individuality over sociality, the heroic over the conventional, the Wild over the domestic, a deliberate life over one asleep, valor over politeness, nobility over the common, an expansive outlook over a parochial one.[12] Thoreau is such a wonderful rhetorician, his use of exaggeration, puns, parody, strained metaphors, oxymoron, paradox, and indirection is so artful that it is tempting to focus exclusively on him as a literary figure. Henry Golemba, who compares Thoreau's approach to deconstruction, does this when he argues that "reform, along with the theme of nature, provides fine material to weave into his text. Nature is not distinct from civilization, nor is reform possible, but they can make a fine story, can supply a good read."[13] But my Thoreau is interested in more than a good read. He is also an artist of the self. His rhetorical devices, even when they have the effect of displaying the ambiguity and indeterminateness of language, are part of this endeavor.

Take, for example, Thoreau's claim that friends are "solitary stars." Readers of this discussion in *A Week* will find that "stardom" is not anything an individual chooses it to be. When another functions as the locus of one's noblest and most "refined" thoughts, it is not only the process of idealization that Thoreau values but also the experience of spirituality, material simplicity, utopian imagination, and social skepticism that this process enables. Thoreau does not wish to deflate the high, the good, the elevated, the divine by specifying too closely their content, but the semantic content of these terms is not completely fluid.

Friends tap into or insert into (this too Thoreau leaves unspecified) the extraordinary or "divine" in each other, so their bond is not really personal or exclusive. The "very superfluity and dispersed love" involved in friendship is, says Thoreau, "the humanity which sweetens society, and sympathizes with foreign nations; for though its foundations are private, it is in effect, a public affair and a public advantage, and the Friend, more than the father of a family, deserves well of the state" (*A Week*, 277). Friendship is Thoreau's alternative to neighborliness and citizenship as models for intersubjective relations.

The friendship of which Thoreau speaks is, however, a peculiar *kind* of union: the mingling of one's *ideals* with the perceived persona of another. Thoreau notes that this union is unlikely: "Perhaps there are none charitable, none disinterested, none wise, noble, and heroic enough, for a true and lasting Friendship" (*A Week*, 277). The "perhaps" is Thoreau's public act of encouragement, for privately he admits that friendship, as the union of two souls, as the "annexing [of] another world to mine," never actually occurs (*Journal*, 3:18). In *deed* it is absent. Friendship exists only as an ideal; its home is the imagination. Thoreau comes closest to it with his sister, "the stream of whose being unites with your own without a ripple or a murmur." But he dares not speak of this to her and can mention his love at all only with a nervous coda: "O Do not disappoint me" (*Journal*, 3:17, 18).

Thoreau sees only "too plainly—that if I degraded my ideal to an identity with any actual mortal whose hand is to be grasped there would be an end to our fine relations" (*Journal*, 3:19). Actual friendship is always a "vestige," "flitting like a summer cloud," "a rumor," a "mirage," a "fabled shore none ever reach, no mariner has found our beach" (*A Week*, 261, 262). William Bronk argues that this elusive quality derives from the fact that Thoreauvian friendship is always after the fact, retroactively constituted:

> To embody friendship without losing its essential quality was extremely difficult. . . . Sometimes it seemed best not to attempt at all to express one's love but to depend upon it to express itself in some unexpected way. . . . Thoreau knew how some distant gesture or unconscious behavior that we remember will suddenly speak to us. . . . Friendship was often, then, a remembered thing. . . . It was therefore not to be thought of as defined in time and place by the presence of a friend or even by a particular relationship.[14]

Both to be a friend and to be challenged by one requires that one is already somewhat inured to the call of the They. The other practices by which one crafts oneself into a sojourner (we have so far considered only one of these—looking inward) must be established or must at least have taken root *prior to* friendship, for friends approach each other as "continent," that is, disciplined, individuals:

> The Friend is some fair floating isle of palms eluding the mariner in Pacific seas. Many are the dangers to be encountered, equinoctial gales and coral reefs. . . . But who would not sail through mutiny and storm . . . to reach the fabulous retreating shores of some continent man? (*A Week*, 262)

## Keeping Quiet

Another shift in emphasis from Hegel's tale of self-consciousness to Thoreau's story concerns the role of discourse. According to Hegel, an I is made in the course of *mutual discussion,* where both those terms are coequal in value. Mutuality: I acknowledge your subjectivity by responding to you in ways that you recognize as partly your own, and you do the same for me; I then adjust my self-conception in response to the picture of me that you have presented, and you do the same; I then respond to the new version of you that confronts me, and you do the same. Discussion: these acknowledgments, recognitions, and responses are linguistic; by articulating or expressing thoughts (simultaneously one's own and those born from the words of another), one helps bring them more fully into existence.

Although Thoreau has very little good to say about mutuality, he shares Hegel's belief in the constitutive or productive power of linguistic expression: the act of writing is one of the means by which Thoreau inculcates in himself a sense of independent individuality. And writing about Nature can do this as well as induce in the writer a certain experience of wholeness with a "universe." This is not to say that linguistic expression is, for Thoreau, a specially privileged technique of self. More exclusively somatic practices—walking, hoeing, surveying, and so forth—are equally important to him. One might say that while discourse is an element in Thoreau's project of creating a sojourner, the relationship of discourse to this self is somewhat more tenuous and more attenuated than it is in Hegel's account. The very act of expressing one's thoughts *to another* is fraught with the danger of conformity; language lends itself more readily to "the generalized voice of convention, of one's region or circumstance," than to new or wild ideas.[15]

Thoreau prefers writing to speech because it affords more distance between persons,[16] but silent reflection is even better:

> The Friend responds silently through his nature and life. . . . The language of Friendship is not words but meanings. It is an intelligence above language. (*A Week,* 273)

> There are times when we have had enough even of our Friends, when we begin inevitably to profane one another, and must withdraw religiously into solitude and silence, the better to prepare ourselves for a loftier intimacy. Silence is the ambrosial night in the intercourse of Friends. (*A Week,* 272)

Note that solitude and silence are an "intelligence above language" and offer a "loftier intimacy" than mutual discourse. But what would such a nonlinguistic experience be like? Bronk describes this silence as a "way toward knowing because it cuts us off from the safely usual patterns of thought and behavior" and puts us where there is "nothing known and no way to know. . . . Silence is the world of potentialities and meanings beyond the actual and expressed, which the meanness of our actions and the inter- pretations put upon them threatens to conceal."[17] Thoreau alludes to some spiritual feeling, a tranquillity or sense of fullness perhaps.

Linguistic expression is worrisome to Thoreau because language is an indiscriminate transmitter: it lets through what is "hostile or indifferent" to friendship (gossip, prejudice, platitudes) as easily as what is "kindred and harmonious" (eccentric ideas, one's genius, wildness, the particularity of the self). Despite the perpetual possibility of misunderstood words, discourse is still an all-too-clear conduit for the They.

Silence and reserve are keys to friendship, as is the willingness to sur- round oneself with a layer of sheer space. "I have found it a singular luxury to talk across the pond to a companion on the opposite side. In my house we were so near that we could not begin to hear" (*Walden*, 141). Physical distance allows thoughts to emerge and to be sent and received, somewhat removed from the fray of conventional truths as well as biological desires. "If we speak reservedly and thoughtfully, we want to be further apart, that all animal heat and moisture may have a chance to evaporate" (*Walden*, 141).[18] Emerson sees Thoreau as a cold man, observing that he, Emerson, would just as soon think of taking the arm of an elm tree as think of taking Thoreau's arm. Bronk notes that Thoreau would have been pleased at this comparison. "It seems," writes Bronk, that "the greatest kindness that we know, is to leave each other alone, to respect one another's integrity, to meet with the grace and dignity of elms and only then to link arms."[19]

The mutual recognition commended by Hegel takes place through (nonenslaving) social relations. Thoreau's friendship, with its emphasis on strangeness, reserve, and silence, is a counter to the human tendency toward social entanglement. Why do one's fellows rarely invigorate individuality and instead instantiate the They? Because, Thoreau suggests, humans are in general insufficiently *other* to one another.[20] It is too easy to see what is familiar in an other of "one's own kind," and familiarity breeds conformity. Thoreauvian individuality requires surprise even more than mirroring;

it insists on a greater diversity of experiences than that available among humans—even friends—alone.

## Going Outside

The techniques of Thoreauvian individuality include not only solitary self-examination, putting another on a pedestal and preserving a certain auditory and spatial distance, but also a carefully modulated relationship with the outdoors, with the things there that elude and exceed human reckoning. Nature is a thing "equally glorious with the most inward experience" (*Journal of HDT,* 4:313). Writing from the banks of the Concord River, Thoreau notes that "there was no recognition of human life in the night . . . we sat up, kept wide awake by the novelty of our situation" (*A Week,* 40). Nature is a vital part of the quest to cut oneself loose from the They, for a time.

Thoreau suggests that we be like the "anchorite," one who withdraws from the known world but withdraws in order to find a more suitable background.[21] The term is from the Greek *anachorein,* "to withdraw"; from *ana* and *chorein,* "to make room"; from *choros,* "place":

> All our lives want a suitable background. They should at least, like the life of the anchorite, be as impressive to behold as objects in the desert, a broken shaft or crumbling mound against a limitless horizon. Character always secures for itself this advantage, and is thus distinct and unrelated to near or trivial objects, whether things or persons. (*A Week,* 46)

The ideal relationship to the land, like relations among friends, preserves and defends an element of distance. The "friendliness" of Nature is "unaccountable," and therein lies its peculiar value (*Walden,* 132). Thoreau's model here is the Native American: "The Indian's intercourse with Nature . . . admits of the greatest independence of each. If he is somewhat of a stranger in her midst, the gardener is too much of a familiar. There is something vulgar and foul in the latter's closeness to his mistress, something noble and cleanly in the former's distance" (*A Week,* 56).

## Microvisioning

How does the Indian achieve *independent* intercourse? How can one enmesh oneself with Nature without domesticating it and thereby destroying its value, its wildness? Thoreau is alert to this dilemma and to the possibility of escaping it only sporadically. He understands those buoyant occasions as a function of a peculiar kind of observation of the outdoors. This gaze, which engages the "nobler faculties" that "in our daily intercourse with men . . . are dormant and suffered to rust," is a simple concentration on one particular spot at one particular moment. Thoreau states: "I have stood under a tree in the woods half a day at a time, and yet employed myself happily and profitably there prying with microscopic eye into the crevices of the bark or the leaves or the fungi at my feet" (*A Week,* 267, 300). I call this fifth technique of self microvision.[22]

The "home-staying, laborious native of the soil"—as Thoreau refers to himself after hoeing beans all summer—pays attention first and most closely to his immediate surroundings (*Walden,* 157). "Nature will bear the closest inspection," he writes in "The Natural History of Massachusetts," and "she invites us to lay our eye level with the smallest leaf, and take an insect view of its plain."[23] Thoreau's October 29, 1857, journal entry is a good example of this detail-centered microvision:

> I see evidently what Storer calls the little brown snake (*Coluber ordinatus*), driven out of the grass of the meadow by the flood. Its head is raised to the surface for air, and it appears sluggish and enfeebled by the water. Putting out my paddle, it immediately coils about it and is raised into the boat. It has a distinct pale-pink abdomen, slightly bluish forward. Above it is pale-brown, with a still lighter brown stripe running down the middle of the back, on each side of which is a line of dark-brown spots about an eighth of an inch apart, as the two lines are also an eighth of an inch apart. This snake is about one foot long. I hold it in my hand, and it is quite inoffensive. (*Journal of HDT,* 10:139–40)

To practice microvision on Nature is to transform it into something beautiful, sublime, and wild.

> We can never have enough of Nature. We must be refreshed by the sight of inexhaustible vigor, vast and Titanic features. . . . We need to witness our own limits transgressed, and some life pasturing freely where we never wander. (*Walden,* 318)

Thoreau trains his gaze on the native soil of Concord, with faith that "the perception of surfaces will always have the effect of miracle to a sane sense" (*Journal of HDT,* 4:313).

No method nor discipline can supersede the necessity of being forever on the alert. What is a course of history, or philosophy, or poetry, no matter how well selected, or the best society, or the most admirable routine of life, compared with the discipline of looking always at what is to be seen? Will you be a reader, a student merely, or a seer? (*Walden,* 111)

Microvision can also be applied to less pastoral objects. Although Thoreau complains about the locomotive, whose "panting . . . interrupts my dreams," close observation of this most contrived object too may reveal something strange and invigorating: "I am refreshed and expanded when the freight train rattles past me," he says in *Walden,* "and I smell the stores which go dispensing their odors all the way from Long Wharf to Lake Champlain, reminding me of foreign parts, of coral reefs, and Indian oceans, and tropical climes and the extent of the globe" (119).

Microvision is not only a specifying observation—"O the evening robin . . . ! If I could ever find the twig he sits upon! I mean *he;* I mean *the twig*" (*Walden,* 312)—but also a detached or cool observation, a "fingering" of the scenery rather than a probing or systematic study (*Reform Papers,* 22). "I must let my senses wander as my thought, my eyes see without looking. . . . Be not preoccupied with looking. Go not to the object; let it come to you. . . . What I need is not to look at all, but a true sauntering of the eye" (*Journal of HDT,* 4:351).

Thoreau's rejection of "looking" shares much with Nietzsche's criticism, in *Twilight of the Idols,* of "objectivity":

In an attitude of hostile calm one will allow the strange, the *novel* of every kind to approach one first—one will draw one's hand back from it. To stand with all doors open, to prostrate oneself submissively before every petty fact, to be ever itching to mingle with, *plunge into* other people and other things, in short our celebrate modern "objectivity," is bad taste, is ignoble *par excellence.*[24]

Both Thoreau and Nietzsche are preoccupied with the problem of conformity; both valorize the extraordinary; both afford distance a key *ethical* role; both seek to resuscitate pagan sensibilities as counters to Christian ones. And yet in each of these instances, their tones differ.

In the quotation just cited, Nietzsche tells us to wait for the strange in a "hostile" calm, while Thoreau is more likely to suggest a patient, receptive, and alert calm. This difference may be traced to the greater emphasis Nietzsche places on struggle or the agon. Thoreau's inward exploration confronts a wildness more sublime than abysmal or chaotic and that calls more for awe than for will to power: Thoreau is less wary of "transcendentalizing" his subject. Nietzsche would be highly critical of Thoreau's very privileging of inwardness, with its link to the idea of a "soul" or "living kernel." Thoreau's invocation of this core self is taken up later in the chapter, where I consider whether Thoreau's call to look "in" must mean that he assigns a prediscursive or given status to what is "seen."

A second difference between the two thinkers concerns religion. Nietzsche's rejection of Christianity is more relentless and thorough than is Thoreau's. It is true that Nature, especially as it appears in Thoreau's essay "Ktaadn," is no loving father's creation and that Thoreau "almost always preferred to seek in Greek and Roman religion rather than in Christianity for his religious ideas, terms, and emotions."[25] But the voice of Christian ethics can be heard clearly in his reform papers, especially in "Life without Principle," the John Brown defenses, and "Slavery in Massachusetts."

Consider, as a final example of their rhetorical and philosophical differences, the question of "distance." Here is Nietzsche:

> "Equality," a certain actual rendering similar of which the theory of "equal rights" is only the expression, belongs essentially to decline: the chasm between man and man, class and class, the multiplicity of types, the will to be oneself, to stand out—that which I call *pathos of distance*—characterizes every *strong* age.[26]

For Nietzsche, the distance among us is a "chasm"; for Thoreau, it is something less dreadful. Nietzsche is, moreover, more willing to *rank* than is Thoreau: failure to acknowledge the chasm and willingness to endorse "equality" are symptoms of *decline* and *weakness*. Thoreau says there is something "vulgar" and "foul" in closeness, but more often he prefers to *distract* us from our desire to intermingle than to condemn it overtly. He does so by holding before us alternative objects of affection: when we get too close to humans, he dangles the ideal of friendship; when we love society too much, he offers Nature; when we begin to want to merge with Nature, he invokes the alluring Wild. Whereas Nietzsche ranks and judges, Thoreau invites, cajoles, and distracts.[27]

# Living Doubly

In terms of sheer volume, Thoreau's writing contains more reportage than poetry. Richardson notes that in 1852 Thoreau began, "systematically and in earnest, the vast project of keeping track of every stage of every plant in town, the project that would culminate in 1860 and 1861 in the great charts he would then assemble, large sheets of paper on which he recorded days of a month in a column down the left-hand side and years from 1852 to 1860 . . . across the top."[28] Even *Walden*, Thoreau's most theorized book, displays his mania for "the orderly accumulation of details."[29] An accountant not only of his household budget but also of the natural economy, Thoreau, prefiguring Heidegger's critique of "enframing," strives to note the world without attempting to capture it, to describe detail in a way that displays how the world always fades into an indefiniteness that exceeds our best capacity for inventory.[30]

Despite this, the sojourner is not to be a dispassionate being. When Thoreau hoes beans, raises a house, chops wood, hikes, bakes bread, and makes a better pencil, he does so enthusiastically and with feeling. The poet shares the text with the detached scribe:

> I only know myself as a human entity; the scene, so to speak, of thoughts and affections; and am sensible of a certain doubleness by which I can stand as remote from myself as from another. However intense my experience, I am conscious . . . of a part of me, which . . . is not a part of me, but spectator, sharing no experience, but taking note of it. (*Walden*, 135)

The sojourner on his way, then, is simultaneously a recording spectator and a very particular self with a series of specific passionate responses. Thoreau's prose, in which the reporting mode alternates with the poetic, mirrors this duality.[31]

Thoreau is *double* in that he is both a subjective agent with the potential for submersion in intense personal experience and an objective agent capable of recording, with minimal mediation, the facts of Nature.[32] He is both a chanticleer of sentiment and a chronicler of data—and there is even a sense in which the latter enhances the former, for the sojourner is rewarded for microvision with a heightened sense of individuality. But the doubleness of which Thoreau speaks also refers to the fact that he is both a self-conscious agent and a mere object. "He" is acutely conscious of and can articulate his interior thought, his character, his dual capacity for experience and spectation. But also, "he" is something that does not think at all but stands by as an object among others in Nature, as an object for contemplation. The self-conscious, reflective I-Thoreau moves in tandem with the it-Thoreau that stands "as remote from myself as from another."

The sojourning self, then, is doubly double. Through the doubleness of experience and observation, the sojourner finds him- or herself enmeshed with Nature; through the doubleness of subjecthood and objecthood, the sojourner reflexively engages him- or herself. These doublings suggest that, for Thoreau, a "native" is no simple or primitive self but a highly complex identity composed of so many parts that an internal coordinating agency is needed. Thoreau describes the precariousness of this identity in a letter to Blake: "The self constantly fluctuates, sometimes looming large, at other times almost vanishing. Suddenly I can come forward into the utmost apparent distinctness, and speak with a sort of emphasis to you; and the next moment I am so faint an entity and make so slight an impression, that nobody can find the traces of me."[33]

The sojourner requires a coordinating agency, but the self prior to the application of Thoreauvian techniques does not include one. It includes only "genius" and the imprint of the They. Genius, as the locus of internal wildness, confounds expectations; it cannot perform the orderly coordination of an identity made up of diverse parts. The They, in contrast, can order, but only at the price of the diversity of parts. Thoreau thus appoints "character" to head the multiple self: "A man's peculiar character appears in every feature and in every action. . . . Character is plenipotentiary and despotic. It rules in all things" (*Journal*, 3:5).

Thoreau's descriptions of character often present it as an essence—as a true self or "meat" in contrast to a merely social presentation or "shell":

> It is the vice but not the excellence of manners, that they are continually being deserted by the character; they are cast-off clothes or shells, claiming the respect which belonged to the living creature. You are presented with the shells instead of the meat. . . . The man who thrusts his manners upon me . . . introduc[es] . . . me to his cabinet of curiosities when I wished to see himself. (*Reform Papers,* 175)[34]

Thoreau chastises those who act "as if we were all husk and shell, with no tender and living kernel to us" (*Reform Papers,* 175).[35] He also writes of character as something beyond conscious control: a man's "influence is the result of his entire character—both that which is subject and that which is superior to his understanding—And what he really means or intends it is not in his power to explain or offer an apology for"; "manners are conscious. Character is unconscious" (*Journal*, 2:45, 3:195).

But I do not take these claims as evidence that Thoreau views character as something simply given to individuals. Rather, character is *made* by one who aspires to become individual.[36] Thoreau's presentation of character as an essential self is designed to allow the sojourner to *forget* the artful quality of his or her identity.[37] Such claims are examples of Thoreauvian transcendentalizing—that is, his practice of presenting a fiction useful to the production of individuality as a truth. It is a truth in that it is part and parcel of (his vision of) Nature. Character is an artifice that, if properly constructed and maintained, functions as if it were always there. Character displaces both the authentic self and the They-self. The sojourner is individual because he or she posits a core of self that renders the sojourner whole, much as a magnet attracts metal pieces of various shapes and functions without destroying the integrity of any of them.

If "Character is Genius settled or established" (*Journal*, 2:37), then the key question becomes, how does that establishment occur? If the purported "center" of the self "may and perhaps oftenest does lie entirely aside from us, and we are in fact eccentric" (*Correspondence*, 298–99), what are the means by which the self is realigned and character formed?

## Hoeing Beans

Character building requires a certain orientation to human and nonhuman others. Thoreau's comment about the anchorite (discussed earlier) is useful in specifying the relationship between these orientations and the notion of "character." Let us examine this comment a second time:

> All our lives want a suitable background. They should at least, like the life of the anchorite, be as impressive to behold as objects in the desert, a broken shaft or crumbling mound against a limitless horizon. Character always secures for itself this advantage, and is thus distinct and unrelated to near or trivial objects, whether things or persons. (*A Week*, 46)

Thoreau repeats the claim that character requires distance from "near or trivial objects." One goes to the desert to escape the order imposed by the They. But he also adds that the anchorite is "impressive"—as impressive, however, as a "broken" shaft and a "crumbling" mound. What is impressive about these things? Or, to put the question more aptly, what do they impress upon us? They leave us, I think, with the idea of partialness (a *broken* shaft) and temporariness (a *crumbling* mound). To be like the anchorite, then, is to place oneself against the backdrop of a limitless horizon in order to become impressed with one's incompleteness and transitoriness. To be like the anchorite is to see that one lacks anything to shore oneself up with; it is to see that to escape the They is to disintegrate. This realization is an "advantage" for character, in that it is a precondition of the will to craft a new center of gravity, to insert into the fertile and uneven mix of one's inward ground a magnetic core. And this is where another important means of character formation comes in: what Thoreau describes as "making invidious distinctions with his hoe" (*Walden,* 161).[38]

The "living kernel" or "character," like the beans Thoreau grows at Walden, requires a "small Herculean labor" of daily toil "from five o'clock in the morning til noon" (*Walden,* 155, 161). Thoreau describes this labor as "sedulous": diligent, active, constant in application to the matter in hand, assiduous, persistent. Whereas Thoreau expresses disdain for politics and business as "nothing but work, work, work" (*Reform Papers,* 156), his orientation toward repetitive labor also has another side. In another letter to Blake, the same phrase—"work, work, work"—recurs, this time to much different effect. Surely, "work, work, work" is stupid motion, says Thoreau, but properly exercised, it is also integral to the finer, nobler pursuit of self-individualization. Repetitive work here appears as part of the process of forming in oneself a hard core of individuality: "Is it not imperative on us that we do something, if we only work in a treadmill? And indeed, some sort of revolving is necessary to produce a centre and nucleus of being" (*Familiar Letters,* 221).

We are like shellfish in this regard. "There are so many layers of mere white lime in every shell to that thin inner one so beautifully tinted. . . . With him [the shellfish], too, it is . . . 'Work,—work,—work!'" Work is, Thoreau tells Blake, an existential necessity, a condition of being: "We must heap up a great pile of doing, for a small diameter of being." We are the same here as the muskrat: "The other day I opened a muskrat's house. It was made of weeds, five feet broad at base, and three feet high, and far and low within it was a little cavity, only a foot in diameter, where the rat dwelt. It may seem trivial, this piling up of weeds, but so the race of muskrats is preserved" (*Familiar Letters,* 222, 221).

Thoreau's criticism of business as monotonous busywork, then, exists alongside his conviction that work such as the hoeing of beans is integral to the task of building an individualized self capable of social criticism. Thoreau knows all too well the necessity of his implication in the political and economic structures he lambastes. The glorious moments of escape from the They are themselves launched from a base of diligent and painstaking, even mind-numbing work.

To grow character, one must cast the weeds aside in favor of those thoughts, ideals, images, and inclinations specific to the idiosyncratic experience that is one's own life. One must "level . . . whole ranks of one species, and sedulously cultivat[e] . . . another" (*Walden,* 161). Diligent hoeing is required because the inward ground supports the more prolific and hardy They-seedlings as well as I-life. There is, however, a serious problem involved in this cultivation of character: mixed in with the They-weeds are the weeds of one's genius—the thoughts, ideals, images, and even instinctual drives that, though internal, are also alien, surprising, and wild, bearing no discernible relation to one's unique life experience. The farmer's very gaze, if too intense or lingering, will uproot their precious wildness before the hoe even hits them. Reflection appropriates and familiarizes. How can one avoid doing to one's "genius" what "neighbors" and "citizens" would do—namely, domesticate, digest, or declaw it?

Thoreau is surely alert to the problematic relation between the deliberate, self-conscious individual and the Wild. For example, the verb he chooses to describe their meeting is *to front.* This is Thoreau's favorite verb for confronting, for being up at the very edge against something. It is what one does when faced with the elements of essential wildness."[39] "To front" the Wild is not to "explore" it, for that implies a relationship of depth: too much intimacy and not enough shock value. Even the more standard *confront* is inappropriate, not simply because it is too aggressive but also because aggression itself is too *engaged,* as the *con,* or "being with," prefix suggests. Come up to the edge of the Wild, face-to-face, says Thoreau, no more and no less.

> The frontiers are not east or west, north or south, but wherever a man *fronts* a fact, though that fact be his neighbor, there is an unsettled wilderness be-

tween him and Canada, between him and the setting sun, or, further still, between him and *it*. (*A Week*, 304)

And in "Walking" he advises home builders to "bring your sills *up to the very edge*" of an "impervious and quaking swamp" (*Excursions*, 227–28; emphasis added).

But the tension between his ideal of a deliberate life and his ideal of a wild life—what I take to be the central tension driving his work—is not wholly resolved by "fronting," which is but one of the coping strategies Thoreau employs. In other places he finds comfort in the thought that the Wild is indestructible, that complete domestication is impossible because every act of organization engenders elements that escape it: he who "grew fast and made infinite demand on life, would always find himself in a new country or wilderness" (*Excursions*, 226); or, "these continents and hemispheres are soon run over, but an always unexplored and infinite region makes off on every side from the mind, further than to sunset, and we can make no highway or beaten track into it, but the grass immediately springs up in the path" (*A Week*, 359).

These passages suggest that wildness is not a definable entity but the shadow of humanity's brave but relentless quest to domesticate life, a quest that Thoreau knows himself to be implicated in. Wildness is the remainder that always escapes taxonomies of flora and fauna or inventories of one's character or conscience; it is the variation in the woods that remains no matter how many times one walks them; it is the distance never bridged between two humans, no matter how well acquainted.[40] Thoreau here presents Nature as a fund of inspirational images cheerfully reconstituting itself just outside the border of any concept used to describe it. Wildness is thus partly constituted by a consciously cultivated *longing for it*, a longing Thoreau seeks to evoke in himself and his readers and put to ethical effect.[41] "I shall never find in the wilds of Labrador any greater wilderness than in some recess in Concord, i.e. than I import into it" (*Journal of HDT*, 9:43). That the wilderness is in some sense a domestic product does not mean that there is nothing Other or Wild about it.

Another of Thoreau's responses to the tension between reflection and wildness, the tack he takes in "The Bean-Field," is to hoe leisurely, relaxedly, to refrain from overcultivating the soil. Thoreau hoes alone, for example, and uses only the simplest hand tools so that his weeding remains imperfect and not wholly efficacious. *His* bean field has the special status of being "the connecting link between wild and cultivated fields; as some states are civilized, and others half-civilized, and others savage . . . my field was, though not in a bad sense, a half-cultivated field" (*Walden,* 158).

Thoreau is troubled by the element of offense—the *invidiousness*—in his distinction between beans and weeds. His sweat has made "the earth say beans instead of grass," but "what right had I to oust johnswort and the rest, and break up their [the woodchucks'] ancient herb garden?" "Should I not rejoice also at the abundance of the weeds whose seeds are the granary of the birds?" (*Walden,* 157, 155, 166). Golemba describes Thoreau's misgivings like this:

> As soon as he begins to make the simplest distinctions, he not only raises havoc with the environment that he generally loves, but he creates distinctions that lead to hatreds, even to roasting a Mexican on a spit and devouring him with relish. And this author, who seemed to make such clear distinctions between a noble, rustic, independent "I" in "Economy" and the multiform failures of civilization, reveals that all distinction, even the "most noble and inspiring" ones, are unfair and artificial, if not fatal.[42]

For Golemba, the fact that Thoreau hears the strains of military marches in town while hoeing is further evidence of his acknowledgment of the violence within his pastoral act of cultivation. "Sometimes," Thoreau says, "I felt as if I could spit a Mexican with a good relish,—for why should we always stand for trifles?—and looked round for a woodchuck or a skunk to exercise my chivalry upon" (*Walden,* 161). I concur with Golemba on this point, but my Thoreau retains his commitment to hoeing, despite misgivings. My Thoreau acknowledges injustice and falsity as elements within his discriminations and valuations, but these elements neither exhaust these practices nor counsel him to abandon them. Hoeing, like idealization, *requires* the invidious hoe.

This difference in interpretation can be traced in part to a difference in focus between Golemba and me. My Thoreau is "political" in the sense of consciously engaging in practices that mold a particular kind of self. Golemba's Thoreau is primarily a rhetorician whose "beans" to be cultivated represent not a self in the making but a language rich with ambiguity. Golemba's Thoreau views "order, structure, and coherence" as acts of violence against the play of language. My Thoreau is a diligent worker who no more hopes for "a nondiscriminating reading experience" than for a self without a character.[43]

## Eating with Care

Thoreau's cannibalistic urge with regard to the Mexican raises the need for techniques to govern the individual's relation to appetite. In "Chastity and Sensuality" Thoreau argues that the mental discipline of weeding must be coupled with a careful regulation of bodily functions: "A man's social and spiritual discipline must answer to his corporeal" (*Early Essays*, 275). Such regulation bespeaks a "reverent" attitude or attentiveness toward the body: "In earlier ages, in some countries, every function was reverently spoken of and regulated by law . . . the Hindoo lawgiver . . . teaches how to eat, drink, cohabit, void excrement and urine, and the like" (*Walden*, 221).

Thoreau makes a famous statement at the beginning of the chapter "Higher Laws" in *Walden:*

> As I came home through the woods with my string of fish, . . . I caught a glimpse of a woodchuck stealing across my path, and felt a strange thrill of savage delight, and was strongly tempted to seize and devour him raw; not that I was hungry then, except for that wildness which he represented. (210)

What troubles Thoreau about this episode is not, as many commentators suggest, the wildness of the object of his desire—to be hungry for wildness is most laudable—but the raw, indiscriminate, or undisciplined quality of this desire. He is not fascinated by the woodchuck but wants only to consume it. Fascination would require that one respect a certain distance, exercise a certain restraint. Thoreau's urge that evening is not (as it is later, through his words) mediated by the imagination. The sojourner, in contrast, eats in such a way that does "not offend the imagination." Thoreau, for the most part, refrains from "animal food, or tea, or coffee, etc.; not so much because of any ill effects which I had traced to them," but because "it appeared more beautiful to live low and fare hard." To "practice some new austerity, to let his mind descend into his body and redeem it," is to treat one's self "with ever increasing respect" (*Walden*, 215, 214, 222).

It is important to note that Thoreau makes a sharp distinction between sensuality (appetite for food, drink, and sex) and sensibility. Clearly, the senses hold an esteemed place within his ethic; it can even be said that Thoreau's texts are designed as "a medium capable of forming and altering perception, in which the 'formation of the sense' chiefly takes place."[44] Thoreau seeks to forge a new sensibility, one ever alert to the details of one's surroundings—but sensuality is a drug that *dulls* the senses: "In the student sensuality is a sluggish habit of mind" (*Walden*, 220). "For Thoreau cold water remains the drink of drinks, although here, too, restraint must be exercised. 'Any excess,' he writes, '—to have drunk too much water, even, the day before—is fatal to the morning's clarity.'"[45]

An appetite may be powerful, but it is never sharp: an ax can fell a tree, but it cannot pull huckleberries from their stems. *Continence* is Thoreau's name for one of the techniques that harness or channel the gross passions: "the generative energy, which, when we are loose, dissipates and makes us unclean, when we are continent invigorates and inspires us" (*Walden*, 219). Invigorates us toward what end? Toward an alertness to the world in its glorious specificity. Inspires us to do what? To imagine the world as a beautiful universe.

If hoeing is the discipline of the mind, continence is hoeing applied to the body. It too involves sedulousness, and it too has a unifying or centering effect on the self: the term comes from the Latin *continere*, "to hold together," "to press parts into a whole"; in geography, a continent is a continuous body of land, of a whole piece. Thoreau signals the link between the practices of hoeing and continence by using the same imagery: hoeing is "a small Herculean labor"; continence requires avoiding "uncleanness, and all the sins, work[ing] earnestly, though it be at cleaning a stable" (*Walden*, 221).

Thoreau's religious vocabulary here—"Man flows at once to God when the channel of purity is open" (*Walden*, 220)—provokes a comparison with another advocate of continence: St. Augustine. Like Thoreau, Augustine argues that bodily desires must be disciplined if the self is to achieve a certain coherence: "Certainly it is by continence that we are brought together and brought back to the One, after having dissipated ourselves among the Many."[46] And like Thoreau, Augustine couples continence with a kind of inwardness—although Augustine's practice of confession differs in significant ways from Thoreau's self-exploration. A brief discussion of these differences will help clarify Thoreau's position.

The purpose of Augustinian confession is to identify those thoughts and beliefs that are polluted by lust, those ideas and images that are the product of the body and its unregulated quest for feeling. These crudities are sin. To confess them is to take the first step toward remaking the self in the (anticorporeal) image of the Christian God. Whereas Thoreau distinguishes between the sensual and the sensible, Augustine tends to reject them both. Augustine seeks to live not in doubleness but in pure spirit. His continence involves not only fasting and chastity but also the minimization of sense perception and memory.

For Augustine, continence requires confession because the self is a cloudy pool that must be purified before it is ready to receive God. The confessing self is under an injunction to probe its most remote nook and cranny. Even dreams are sites for investigation:

> Certainly you command me to restrain myself from *the lust of the flesh, the lust of the eyes,* and *the ambition of the world.* . . . But there still live in that memory of mine . . . images . . . which . . . come . . . in sleep.[47]

As we have seen, self-examination is also central to Thoreauvian individuality. One directs one's microgaze on one's interior landscape as well as on the countryside, and the sojourner shall experience a correspondence between these two fields: "I . . . see a crimson cloud in the horizon. . . . This red vision excites me . . . makes my thoughts flow—and I have new and indescribable fancies" (*Journal,* 4:222).[48] The self capable of civil disobedience must be in touch with its character, that moral center or conscience within. But as we have also seen, contact that is too relentless or thorough threatens to harm one's genius. Thoreau's inward exploration must avoid the inquisitorial zeal of Augustinian confession, for the Wild must be treated at a distance, or else it ceases to be an object of fascination and becomes something to "devour."

Augustine's ideal self, like Thoreau's, is an arduous achievement. Using the same agricultural metaphors as Thoreau, Augustine calls his confessional quest "hard labor, hard labor inside myself, and I have become to myself a piece of difficult ground, not to be worked over without much sweat."[49] We do not find in Augustine, however, Thoreau's warning against overcultivation of the soil. Given Augustine's harshness toward the pleasures of the body, too much "weeding" hardly appears to be a danger. Thoreau fears that excessive intellectual discipline reduces the richness of sense experience and thus deprives him of opportunities for transcendentalizing. The white water lily symbolizes for Thoreau this creative potential: "what purity and sweetness reside in, and can be extracted from, the slime and muck of earth" (*Reform Papers,* 108). Sensory experience does not, it seems, harbor this potential for Augustine.

Augustine and Thoreau both speak of an inner core of identity: for Augustine, it is the "soul"; for Thoreau, "character." Augustine's confession

purifies a preexisting core; Thoreau's hoeing helps form one. The Augustinian "soul" lacks both the artificiality and the wildness that together mark
Thoreauvian "character." The soul, albeit divine, is marred by a sin that is
not specific to an individual but common to humanity, a sin that separates
humans from the creator. Although Thoreau speaks too of a shamefulness in
our nature, his formulation does not match Augustine's vilification of human
nature. For Thoreau, the "inferior and brutish" components of our nature are
best described in a language of "perhaps," "I fear," and "to some extent":

> Perhaps there is none but has cause for shame on account of the inferior and
> brutish nature to which he is allied. I fear that we are such gods or demigods
> only as fauns and satyrs, the divine allied to beasts . . . and that, to some
> extent, our very life is our disgrace. (*Walden*, 220)

Surely it is difficult to channel the "generative energy" of the beast
within ("from exertion come wisdom and purity; from sloth ignorance and
sensuality" [*Walden*, 220]), but humans have within themselves all the resources to do so: the ability to look inward, to gaze out, to idealize a friend, to
distinguish between the They and the I. The sojourner requires something
outside, but it is Nature rather than divine grace. The unreconstructed self
on which the sojourner applies his or her techniques of individuality has a
susceptibility for nobility that the sinful creature Augustine describes does
not. Thoreau's Nature, having less subjectivity than Augustine's God (just
how much Thoreau's God has remains obscure), throws the bulk of responsibility for self-cultivation on each particular individual-in-the-making.

Although Thoreau makes generous use of Christian imagery throughout his writing, he draws also on Eastern religions (e.g., the Laws of Menu)
and Greek mythology. An example of the latter is his use of the term *devil*:
friendship is rare and sporadic because "every one has a devil in him" (*A
Week*, 284). This devil refers to those aspects of the self that, though not
necessarily beastly, conflict with the priorities, desires, or tendencies of
one's friend. It refers also to extravagant emotions and thoughtless urges, to
intemperateness within the self: "It is proof of a man's fitness for Friendship
that he is able to do without that which is cheap and passionate" (*A Week*,
274). But even these cheap and passionate dimensions are not placed within
an Augustinian framework of "sin" or "flesh" or "concupiscence." Indeed,
Thoreau's conception of nobility is downright pagan:

> Friendship . . . consists with a certain disregard for men and their erections,

the Christian duties and humanities, while it purifies the air like electricity. . . . We may call it an essentially heathenish intercourse, free and irresponsible in its nature, and practicing all the virtues gratuitously. It is not the highest sympathy merely, but a pure and lofty intercourse . . . which . . . does not hesitate to disregard the humbler rites and duties of humanity. . . . When the Friend . . . forgets his mythology, and treats his Friend like a Christian . . . then Friendship ceases to be Friendship. (*A Week*, 276)

## Building the Sojourner

Thoreau's sense of the great psychological appeal of domesticity explains his wariness of social life and collective projects. It is why he says in "Resistance to Civil Government" that the best government is one that governs not at all. It is why he moves into the public realm only sporadically and negatively—for instance, to dissociate himself from slavery or to pronounce in lectures his rejection of a life without principle. Many have turned to Thoreau because of an interest in civil disobedience; they look to him for insight into how citizens might protest unjust forms of state power.

My Thoreau, however, takes one down a somewhat different path—to reflection into the type of self capable of an act of conscientious dissent and into the processes through which that individual may come into being. "Thoreau anchors public affairs in private ones, and he returns the word 'economy' to its original Greek sense of 'household management' or 'domestic arrangements.'"[50] The question is not What is civil disobedience? but What kind of being could be disobedient to civil authority?[51] The tools and techniques by which Thoreau seeks to erect such a being include, as we have seen, a kind of inwardness or solitude that enables one to resist the allure of conventional wisdom and the comfort of conformity. What is required is a periodic withdrawal from social intercourse; episodes of self-induced aphasia (or, at the very least, a wariness of language and a heightened respect for silence and distance); an awareness of the wildness or genius within; the investment of one's highest hopes and ideals into the person of a friend; "work, work, work" to build character and to render bodily appetites sublime; and microvision, the deliberate and keen attention to the minutiae of the material world, a sensitivity to *that* robin, *this* twig. When practiced in concert, such exercises open the self to the Wild and help it to resist the lure of the They.

# Notes

Originally published as Jane Bennett, *Thoreau's Nature: Ethics, Politics, and the Wild,* new ed. (Lanham, MD: Rowman and Littlefield, 2002), chap. 2. Copyright 2002 by Rowman and Littlefield Publishers, Inc. Reprinted with permission. Minor changes have been made.

1. Henry David Thoreau, "Resistance to Civil Government," in *Reform Papers,* ed. Wendell Glick (Princeton, NJ: Princeton University Press, 1973), 86; hereafter, quotations from this volume are cited in text.

2. Thoreau does not attempt to demonstrate, in any logical or scientific sense, the moral priority of "individuality" (better described as the self-understanding of a sojourner). Instead, he seeks to draw out the reader's attraction to free thinking, to induce a will to wildness and a revulsion for blinking mindlessness through an artistic linking of mutually referential metaphors. These include "They," "inwardness," "Nature," "character," "genius," "deliberateness," and "principle." That Thoreau chooses this mode of persuasion is, to my mind, laudable; it is for me a mark of honesty and an acknowledgment of the element of contingency, even arbitrariness, in any moral vision. But for those who seek a more foolproof foundation for moral claims, Thoreau's ethic may appear to be a group of assertions "banded together, as usual one leaning on another, and all together on nothing, as the Hindus made the world rest on an elephant, the elephant on a tortoise, and the tortoise on a serpent, and had nothing to put under the serpent" (*Reform Papers,* 169).

3. Henry David Thoreau, *Walden,* ed. J. Lyndon Shanley (Princeton, NJ: Princeton University Press, 1973), 108, 171; hereafter cited in text.

4. Henry David Thoreau, *Familiar Letters,* ed. F. B. Sanforn (New York: AMS Press, 1968), 187; hereafter cited in text.

5. G. W. F. Hegel, *Phenomenology of Spirit,* trans. A. V. Miller (Oxford: Oxford University Press, 1977), para. 178.

6. Thoreau seems to have followed his advice, as this statement by Emerson suggests: "Thoreau goes to a house to say with little preface what he has just read or observed, delivers it in a lump, is quite inattentive to any comment or thought which any of the company offer . . . , nay, is merely interrupted by it." See *The Complete Works of Ralph Waldo Emerson* (Boston: Houghton Mifflin, 1903–1904), 9:34.

7. Henry David Thoreau, *A Week on the Concord and Merrimack Rivers,* ed. Carol F. Hovde, William L. Howarth, and Elizabeth Hall Witherell (Princeton, NJ: Princeton University Press, 1980), 114; hereafter cited in text as *A Week.*

8. Henry David Thoreau, *The Journal of Henry David Thoreau,* 14 vols., ed.

Bradford Torrey and Francis H. Allen (Boston: Houghton Mifflin, 1949), 9:43; hereafter cited in text as *Journal of HDT*.

9. All selves are so visited, according to Thoreau. But "poets" or "men of Genius" are those who know how to make something of these visitors. They know how to "grasp and confront the thought" and insert it into *words:* "I think that an important difference between men of genius or poets and men not of Genius—is in the inability of the latter to grasp and confront the thought that visits them. It is too faint for expression or even conscious impression—What merely quickens or retards the blood in their veins—and fills their afternoons with pleasure they know not whence—conveys a distinct assurance to the finer organization of the poet." Henry David Thoreau, *Journal*, 4 vols., ed. John C. Broderick et al. (Princeton, NJ: Princeton University Press, 1981–1992), 2:247–48; hereafter cited in text. See also *A Week*, 339–40.

10. Thoreau also speaks of a friend as something wild in the sense of inexplicable: "I could tame a hyena more easily than my Friend. He is a material which no tool of mine will work" (*A Week*, 283–84).

11. Henry David Thoreau, *Early Essays and Miscellanies*, ed. Joseph J. Moldenhauer and Edwin Moser, with Alexander C. Kern (Princeton, NJ: Princeton University Press, 1975), 272; hereafter cited in text as *Early Essays*.

12. Thoreau's relation with friends "implies such qualities as the warrior prizes; for it takes a valor to open the hearts of men as well as the gates of castles. It is . . . a heroic sympathy of aspiration and endeavor" (*A Week*, 274).

13. Henry Golemba, *Thoreau's Wild Rhetoric* (New York: New York University Press, 1990), 193. The preceding list of rhetorical devices is also from Golemba. Golemba acknowledges that "although [Thoreau] might often sound Derridean, he balked at the thought that language may be nothing more than Pyrrhic play" (9). But despite this disclaimer, Golemba tends, I think, to overplay Thoreau's tolerance for ambiguity.

14. William Bronk, *The Brothers in Elysium: Ideas of Friendship and Society in the United States* (New Rochelle, NY: Elizabeth Press, 1980), 33.

15. Ibid., 47.

16. "The language heard . . . is commonly transitory, a sound, a tongue, a dialect merely. . . . [The language read] is the maturity and experience of . . . a reserved and select expression, too significant to be heard by the ear" (*Walden*, 101).

17. Bronk, *Brothers in Elysium*, 47.

18. Thoreau wrote to Mrs. Emerson, whom he considered a friend, "It was a pleasure to go away from you . . . as it apprised me of my high relations and such a departure is a sort of further introduction and meeting. Nothing makes the earth seem so spacious as to have friends at a distance; they make the latitudes and

longitudes" (*Familiar Letters,* 76). And on June 22, 1851, Thoreau wrote in his journal: "I find that I postpone all actual intercourse with my friends to a certain real intercourse which takes place commonly when we are *actually* at a distance from one another" (*Journal,* 3:273).

19. Bronk, *Brothers in Elysium,* 27.

20. Roger Scruton makes a quite different argument for the moral value of difference in *Sexual Desire* (New York: Free Press, 1986).

21. "The best society, the richest discourse with an-other, is found between the solitary self and nature—this is the essential point of *Walden* throughout." H. Daniel Peck, *Thoreau's Morning Work* (New Haven, CT: Yale University Press, 1990), 135.

22. Richardson notes that Thoreau "was interested in the art of seeing. At the start of 'Sunday' in *A Week on the Concord and Merrimack Rivers* he would talk about objects that required 'a separate intention of the eye.'" See Robert D. Richardson Jr., *Henry David Thoreau: A Life of the Mind* (Berkeley: University of California Press, 1986), 53.

23. Henry David Thoreau, *Excursions and Poems* (New York: AMS Press, 1968), 107; hereafter cited in text as *Excursions.*

24. Friedrich Nietzsche, *Twilight of the Idols,* trans. R. J. Hollingdale (New York: Penguin, 1983), 65.

25. Richardson, *Henry David Thoreau,* 50.

26. Nietzsche, *Twilight of the Idols,* 91.

27. For a reading of Nietzsche that draws from him an ethic of "agonistic respect" for life as "the abyss and the abundance" and thus draws Nietzsche and Thoreau closer together, see William Connolly, *Political Theory and Modernity,* 2nd ed. (Ithaca, NY: Cornell University Press, 1993), and *Identity/Difference* (Ithaca, NY: Cornell University Press, 1991).

28. Richardson, *Henry David Thoreau,* 271.

29. Ibid., 346.

30. See Martin Heidegger, *The Question Concerning Technology,* trans. William Lovitt (New York: Harper, 1977).

31. "The scientist and the artist-poet were equally congenial to him, and his own best work partook of both. 'Every poet has trembled on the verge of science,' he noted in mid-July [1852]" (Richardson, *Henry David Thoreau,* 272). Richardson makes the argument throughout his biography that Thoreau's penchant for classification is not in tension with his idealism or transcendentalism: "In the late 1840's he began to assemble data on such things as the height of the river, not because he was becoming unimaginative, but because he had enough imagination to see what kinds of fresh generalizations were possible through statistics" (227).

32. Thoreau mentions this kind of doubleness again in a journal entry for April 2, 1852. There it is described not as a simultaneous state but as experienced over a lifetime: one side, "susceptibility" to feelings about Nature, exists in youth; the other, "discrimination," is characteristic of adulthood: "How few valuable observations can we make in youth— What if there were united the susceptibility of youth with the discrimination of age. Once I was part and parcel of Nature—now I am observant of her" (*Journal*, 4:416).

33. Henry David Thoreau, *The Correspondence of Henry David Thoreau*, ed. Walter Harding and Carl Bode (Westport, CT: Greenwood Press, 1974), 125; hereafter cited in text as *Correspondence*.

34. See also *Journal*, 3:159.

35. This theme also appears in his critique of the obsession with making a living: "Commonly, if men want anything of me, it is only to know how many acres I make of their land—since I am a surveyor. . . . They never will go to law for my meat; they prefer the shell" (*Reform Papers*, 155). Some of Thoreau's themes—the superiority of frugality and simplicity, an ambivalence toward social life—recall Rousseau. Using language that is remarkably Rousseauian, Thoreau describes Walden as an attempt "to show at what a sacrifice this advantage [civilization] is at present obtained, and to suggest that we may possibly so lie as to secure all the advantage without suffering any of the disadvantage" (*Walden*, 32). Thoreau, like Rousseau, is looking for a way to "combine the hardiness of . . . savages with the intellectualness of the civilized man" (*Walden*, 13). Thoreau believes that this combination requires solitary encounters with wildness and the universe, whereas Rousseau views the hardy intellectual as the product of a virtuous community where "each one, uniting with all, nevertheless obeys only himself and remains as free as before" (*On the Social Contract* [New York: St. Martin's, 1978], 53). Both speak of an inner core of identity that is sullied by civilization. The status each assigns to such claims, however, may not be the same.

36. I am torn between this interpretation of Thoreau and one that reads him as leaving open the question of whether "character" finds its genesis in God, bestower of souls, or in humans, makers of poetry.

37. Thoreau's art of forgetting and the epistemological status he assigns to his key terms are themes in my *Thoreau's Nature: Ethics, Politics, and the Wild*, new ed. (Lanham, MD: Rowman and Littlefield, 2002), chap. 3.

38. My discussion of the invidiousness of Thoreau's hoeing owes much to Golemba's *Thoreau's Wild Rhetoric*, chap. 4.

39. Frederick Garber, *Thoreau's Redemptive Imagination* (New York: New York University Press, 1977), 46.

40. In "Walking," Thoreau says, "There is in fact a sort of harmony discover-

able between the capabilities of the landscape within a circle of ten miles' radius, or the limits of an afternoon walk, and the threescore years and ten of human life. It will never become quite familiar to you" (*Excursions,* 211–12).

41. Eric Sundquist also notes, "Thoreau's subtle alertness to the fact that the . . . figures of his own writing . . . turn him into an entrepreneur who corrupts his Edenic property at the same time he advertises its value." See "'Plowing Homeward': Cultivation and Grafting in Thoreau and the *Week*," in *Henry David Thoreau,* ed. Harold Bloom (New York: Chelsea House, 1987), 101. But Sundquist underplays the self-generating nature of wildness. And so he reads Thoreau as cognizant of doing "violence" to Nature by writing it.

42. Golemba, *Thoreau's Wild Rhetoric,* 201–2.

43. Ibid., 202. Elsewhere in Golemba's text, he acknowledges that, despite Thoreau's deconstructive fascination with words, he remains a moralist: "However, the agony of his rhetoric is that he could not revel in chaos. Possible readings might be infinite, but some order must exist to structure infinity. The random stars must be made to seem a zodiac. . . . Although he might often sound like the most radical postmodern theorist, he could never quite convince himself that a text without principle was any more desirable than a 'Life without Principle'" (187). I do not think Thoreau ever tried to convince himself of this.

44. Jeffrey Steele, *The Representation of the Self in the American Renaissance* (Chapel Hill: University of North Carolina Press, 1987), 45. Also: "Thoreau dramatizes the sensuous appropriation of reality. He focuses, in other words, upon ontology—the art of living, of being" (45).

45. Kenneth Allen Robinson, *Thoreau and the Wild Appetite* (New York: AMS Press, 1957), 16.

46. Augustine, *Confessions,* trans. Rex Warner (New York: Mentor, 1963), 236. See also William E. Connolly, *The Augustinian Imperative* (Thousand Oaks, CA: Sage Publications, 1993).

47. Augustine, *Confessions,* 237.

48. See also Perry Miller, *The American Transcendentalist* (Baltimore: Johns Hopkins University Press, 1957), 69.

49. Augustine, *Confessions,* 226.

50. Robert Richardson Jr., "Social Ethics of *Walden*," in *Critical Essays on Thoreau's Walden,* ed. Joel Myerson (Boston: G. K. Hall, 1988), 239.

51. This question throws a different light on the practice of civil disobedience and generates a new set of questions: Given Thoreau's understanding of the relationship of the individual to society, to friends, and to Nature, what are the prospects today for the formation of sojourners? Are Thoreauvian techniques of self adequate to challenges posed by contemporary forms of power? What happens

to friendship in a world where solitude and retreat involve great hardship or require great sums of money? Can "the environment" continue to play the role of Nature whose wildness invigorates and disrupts the They? Can the sojourner flourish in a world where Walden is a $2.5 million state erosion-control and beautification project that includes construction of a path around the pond?

# CHAPTER 12

# Thoreau's Solitude

## Thomas L. Dumm

> I have a great deal of company in my house; especially in the morning, when nobody calls.
> —Thoreau, "Solitude," in *Walden*

THE DISTINCTION BETWEEN loneliness and solitude, it is said, turns on the state of mind of the person who is alone. In loneliness, we feel a sense of isolation, that we are cut off from others in a way that makes us bereaved, lost, without a proper bearing in the world. Isolation leads to desolation, a sense that the world itself has been abandoned. The aloneness of loneliness is destructive to our souls. But in solitude, we are alone in a sane sense, Thoreau says, able to console and counsel ourselves. Yet the difference between these two states of existence is not as simple as it seems, for solitude's sanity is connected to a kind of derangement, or at least a reckoning of sanity that is not our usual sense of being sane. A clue to this connection between madness and sanity lies in the relationship of desolation to isolation, in the struggle we engage in to avoid the loss of our souls to the desert of loneliness. I do not want to reach any final conclusion concerning what it means to be alone in a sane sense. Instead, I explore how we might think about this sense of madness that informs Thoreau's sense of sanity. In parsing that relationship between madness and sanity as Thoreau understands it, we might gain a better grasp of his achievement of solitude. Moreover, we might begin to get a better sense of the enduring importance of his thought for our times. The rise of a modern psychology has limited our understanding of both madness and sanity. Thoreau, however, offers something else, something that touches on the experience of both in a way that might provide us with a renewed appreciation of an ancient sense of solace that is still available to us in these times of trouble.

## Being Poor

At the beginning of *Walden* Thoreau explains, "I should not obtrude my affairs so much on the notice of my readers if very particular inquiries had not been made by townsmen concerning my mode of life, which some would call impertinent, though they do not appear to me at all impertinent, but, considering the circumstances, very natural and pertinent. Some have asked what I got to eat; if I did not feel lonesome; if I was not afraid; and the like."[1] The purpose of his book is to answer pertinent questions, and these first questions are paramount. The townspeople's questions to Thoreau concern hunger, lonesomeness, fear, and other phenomena that may be related to them in one way or another. Their questions prompt his test of experience, which is what he calls his experiment in living. The book itself forms the core of his response to the citizens of Concord, a town he considers one of the most important places in the world and, in fact, a surrogate for the world itself. If Thoreau successfully answers the questions of his townsmen, he will provide an answer for all those who wish to live.

Thoreau also suggests, "Perhaps these pages are more particularly addressed to poor students" (259). Poor students may be those who are lacking in money, but they are also people who are unable to learn from others and must instead learn from themselves. Although some readers will read him only partially, "accept such portions as apply to them" (259), poor students will be able to learn from him more completely because, paradoxically, they will not be his students at all; instead, they will descend to meet him in his woods and carry with them their own experiences. Poor students form Thoreau's community—those he will be able to teach, and those from whom he may learn. They might be considered American scholars who, despite their seeming prosperity, do not have what they need to assuage their hunger, to overcome their loneliness and fear. They are his poor, in answer to the question famously posed by Emerson in "Self-Reliance": "Are they *my* poor?" Whereas Emerson claims that there is a class of people by whom he may be bought and sold, to whom he belongs, who constitute his poor, for Thoreau, poor students are those who learn to refuse both buying and selling. The poor student will remain poor so as to be a proper student, and he will stay in the company of his peers, those who know how to be poor as well as he does. How he is able to reach this state of being is in large part the point of *Walden.*

This experiment, the experience of confronting the basics of life, provides Thoreau with a way of thinking that is grounded in the activity of the everyday, stripped to its essentials, simplified, so as to provide the possibility for living life, for becoming who he is. It is a way of life that is thoughtful, deliberate, in the sense of being willfully expressive of freedom. He writes, "Some of you, we all know, are poor, find it hard to live, are sometimes, as it were, gasping for breath" (262). The test at Walden Pond is to determine how hard life is so as to evaluate whether it is worth living. To gasp for breath is to lack inspiration, the vital breath that allows one to advance beyond the illusions of conformity. Such a person is dying instead of living. It is a most common experience. In an extremely lengthy sentence he writes:

> It is very evident what mean and sneaking lives many of you live, for my sight has been whetted by experience; always on the limits, trying to get into business and trying to get out of debt, a very ancient slough, called by the Latins *aes alienum,* another's brass, for some of the coins were made of brass; still living and dying, and buried by this other's brass; always promising to pay, tomorrow, and dying today, insolvent; seeking to curry favor, to get custom by how many modes, only not state-prison offenses; lying, flattering, voting, contracting yourselves into a nutshell of civility, or dilating into an atmosphere of thin and vaporous generosity, that you may persuade your neighbor to let you make his shoes, or his hat, or his coat, or his carriage, or import his groceries to him; making yourself sick, that you may lay up something against a sick day, something to be tucked away in an old chest, or in a stocking behind the plastering, or, more safely, in the brick bank; no matter where, no matter how much or how little. (262)

Here Thoreau not only acknowledges a condition afflicting his most important readers. He also describes the most important experience he has shared with his readers. When he writes "for my sight has been whetted by experience," he is not referring to his observation of others' experience. These experiences—the meanest, most self-abnegating, most alienating; the common division of labor; the connection between manners and commerce; the loss of a sense of self—are all *his* experiences and have been his as only he can know them. For his sight to be whetted by experience suggests that it has deepened his vision, sharpened it.[2] The very length of the sentence illustrates how important it is to him, for Thoreau is a careful writer, and for him to devote such a lengthy sentence to this subject is his way of underscoring the concentrated power of this alienation and its force on his insight.

Thoreau's practical failures were many. The school he founded with his brother failed, and it is hard to imagine him as a schoolteacher, given his stubborn rectitude. He had admirers but few friends. Those friendships he had were prickly and contentious. Few of his contemporaries read his writings, and were it not for Emerson and the *Dial*, the work of Thoreau and some of the other Concord eccentrics might never have seen the light of day. Emerson himself thought Thoreau a failure of sorts, one who did not fulfill his promise, who chose to lead huckleberry parties instead of men and women. (But to understand the importance of those huckleberry parties, see Shannon Mariotti's chapter 15 in this volume.) He also gasped for breath, finally succumbing to consumption in 1862.

*Walden* is a testament of his struggle, his attempt to fulfill the contract he made with his townspeople to tell them of his experiment, to explain to his poor students how they might properly be poor, to present himself as an exemplar of joining and rejoining society. For Thoreau, resignation, a life of enslavement to one's possessions, is a token of despair; it is the sleepwalking through life of those who never get to the heart of living, neither its meanness nor its sublimity. He contrasts that form of resignation to what he terms necessary resignation, which one does only after assessing the outside limits of what life can offer. This reckoning provides a true understanding of the fullest sense of life, one that has to be stripped to its minimum requirements. To test the limits of life, to intensify and simplify, to intensify by simplifying, to determine for himself the meanness or sublimity of life itself—those are his reasons for going to the woods. And his return to society, to lead other lives, is his re-signing, on his own terms, of the social contract he earlier resigned from.[3]

Solitude is the fruit of this struggle to achieve a fuller sense of life. In solitude Thoreau is sane, better able to reckon the costs of his resignation. He is not alone and desperate but shares the company of those who are able to ask his questions and answer them for themselves. But it remains for us to meet him on his terms, to explore the fine madness that informs this deeper sanity.

# Birds

Thoreau's chapter on solitude is framed by two gestures, both made in reference to the value of the company of others. In what might be called a typical Thoreauvian paradox, the first sentence of "Visitors" (the chapter that follows "Solitude") presents a strange endorsement of the social. There he claims, "I think I love society as much as most, and am ready enough to fasten myself like a bloodsucker for the time to any full-blooded man that comes in my way" (390). Like many of his sentences, we can read this one several ways—as a testament of his reckoning of the extent to which anyone loves society, for it is not clear that he thinks anyone likes society; as a confession of his desire to be with a full-blooded man, for he clearly wishes to find someone as awake as he is; or as a description of the impulse to socialize as emerging from a vampire-like, or at least parasitic, desire to live off the vitality of others, which is the despair of those who have never lived life, those who are not awake, those who are the walking dead.

If this passage from "Visitors" frames an exit from solitude into the riot of the social, the conclusion of the chapter "Sounds" frames an entrance into solitude by providing a sustained celebration of the absence of certain sounds from his home in the woods. The most important of these absent sounds is that of the cock crowing:

> I am not sure that I ever heard the sound of cock-crowing from my clearing, and I thought that it might be worth the while to keep a cockerel for his music merely, as a singing bird. The note of this once wild Indian pheasant is certainly the most remarkable of any bird's, and if they could be naturalized without being domesticated, it would soon become the most famous sound in our woods, surpassing the clangor of the goose and the hooting of the owl. . . . No wonder that man added this bird to his tame stock—to say nothing of the eggs and drumsticks. To walk in a winter morning in a wood where these birds abounded, their native woods, and hear the wild cockerels crow in the trees, clear and shrill for miles over the resounding earth, drowning the feebler notes of other birds—think of it! It would put nations on the alert. Who would not be early to rise, and rise earlier and earlier every successive day of his life, till he became unspeakably healthy, wealthy and wise? (378–79)

Stanley Cavell suggests that Thoreau is uncertain about hearing the cockerel because "the sound is so familiar and frequent to his ear, and at once faint and so unmistakable, that he is not sure it is a heard sound, i.e., that it comes from the outside. But then you may find yourself conjecturing whether one is quite sure one hears, or knows, the sound of one's own voice."[4] To hear the sound of one's own voice, one must be talking to oneself, a prelude to questioning one's existence. (At the same time, we cannot actually hear our own voices without the aid of technology. Our mouths cannot speak directly into our ears, as we can speak into our neighbors' ears. Thus the sounds of our voices on a recording are always different from the sounds of us talking to ourselves. Furthermore, insofar as the mediation of technology distorts the sounds of our voices, we *never* hear ourselves as others hear us.) Existence itself becomes a question for those of us who listen for the sound of our own voices.

Both questions—suggesting that we might be able to imagine we do not exist at all—can be read as expressions of the skepticism of Descartes. For Descartes, a key question is whether we as individuals or the world itself exists. Our proofs of existence—the presence of others to whom we speak, the sound of our own voices—ultimately fail us, and we fall back on the very thought of our doubt. Thus, famously, the *cogito* itself consists of the proof of our existence. "I think, I am." But if our thought is mad, then what? (The famous controversy between Michel Foucault and Jacques Derrida concerning Descartes centers on this question: whether madness should be given the same status as dreaming in presenting a challenge to the testing of reality.) Thoreau's response to skepticism is to understand his thought as a practical activity that occurs between the natural and the cultivated, in the arena of the wild.

Thoreau says that for the cockerel's sound to become famous, and thus provide a social assurance that we would be able to hear it, the bird would have to be "naturalized without being domesticated." What does Thoreau mean by this? To be naturalized suggests being attuned to nature, to be one with it. When placed in opposition to the idea of being domesticated —which suggests tamed, comfortable in the company of humans, and humans comfortable with it—naturalized seems to mean being wild. But this does not quite exhaust the idea underlying the term, for the cockerel is descended from a once wild breed of bird. The passage does not suggest a return to the wild, for something already wild cannot return to wildness. A retention of wildness, or the latent wildness of the cockerel, raises the possibility that naturalization may be a way of continuing to be wild in the context of domestication, and it may provide a clue to Thoreau's embrace of the cockerel as a bird he admires.

An alternative or complementary idea is that Thoreau wishes to make the cockerel a harbinger of citizenship, for to be naturalized is to become a citizen of the land one inhabits. To be domesticated means to be subjected to the social forces of conformity, to live a desperate life that is no life for a proper citizen, a free person. The fame of the cockerel's sound suggests the full awakening of man, a proper claim for citizenship being wakefulness. But even more, wakefulness is a form of godliness. "To be awake is to be alive. I have never yet met a man who was quite awake. How could I have looked him in the face?" (343). To look a fully awake man in the face is to look into the face of a god, to risk one's existence for a glimpse at divinity. This is what Thoreau whets his sight to do.

The cockerel, as Cavell notes, is preceded by the owl for Thoreau, the traditional bird of philosophy that flies at dusk. Thoreau hears a strain in the call of the screech owl, a voice that cries, "*Oh-o-o-o-o that I never had been bor-r-r-n!*" The call of the screech owl represents a mortification, and more generally, the voices of all owls "represent a stark twilight and unsatisfied thoughts which all have" (376–77). The contrast with the cockerel could not be more extreme—it is day and night. But that is also his point. The night precedes the dawning of the day. The screech owl echoes the ancient wisdom of Silenus, taken from Sophocles' *Oedipus at Colonus*, that it is best never to have been born, and it is second best to die young.[5]

In the original preface to *History of Madness*, Michel Foucault writes:

> In our time, the experience of madness is made in the calm of a knowledge which, through knowing it too much, passes it over. But in the movement from one experience to the other, the passage is made through a world without images or positivity, in a sort of silent transparency that allows a great immobile structure to appear, like a wordless institution, a gesture without commentary, an immediate knowledge; this structure is neither that of drama nor of knowledge; it is the point at which history freezes, in the tragic mode that founds it and calls it into question.
>
> At the centre of this attempt to re-establish the value of the classical experience of madness, in its rights and its becoming, there is therefore a motionless figure to be found; the simple division into daylight and obscurity,

shadow and light, dream and waking, the truth of the sun and the power of midnight. An elementary figure, which only accepts time as the indefinite return of a limit.[6]

Foucault's description of the motionless figure can serve as the template for another such elementary figure, one that accepts time as the indefinite return of a limit—namely, Thoreau at Walden Pond. Thoreau's compression of time, his quest for a glimpse of eternal truths, his melding of beans and tropes, his testing of the value of living by greeting an earlier and earlier dawn in himself, and the heroic nature he surrounds himself with all attest to a fine madness, fully aware of its rights and its becoming. The relationship of this madness—an experience that is not quite nameable, or, as he puts it, "wordless"—to the sanity one may come to realize is the problem Thoreau struggles with throughout *Walden,* but the struggle reaches a peak in his chapter on solitude.

## A Slight Insanity of Mood

It is important to remember that one of the pertinent questions Thoreau is asked is whether he ever feels lonesome at Walden. His most immediate answer is straightforward:

> I have never felt lonesome, or in the least oppressed by a sense of solitude, but once, and that was a few weeks after I came to the woods, when, for an hour, I doubted if the near neighborhood of man was not essential to a serene and healthy life. To be alone was something unpleasant. But I was at the same time conscious of a slight insanity in my mood, and seemed to foresee my recovery. (382–83)

Explaining why he suffers this mood and describing his overcoming of it are the subjects of his chapter on solitude. His hour of doubt concerning the need for the near neighborhood of man is a moment of crisis for Thoreau. His largest claim for his experiment is to be present in his present. He writes, "In any weather, at any hour of day or night, I have been anxious to improve upon the nick of time, and notch it on my stick too; to stand on the meeting of two eternities, the past and the future, which is precisely the present moment; to toe that line" (272). Here, he gives that idea of presence his full attention. Hence, Thoreau's awareness of the weather helps him overcome his insanity of mood:

> In the midst of a gentle rain while these thoughts prevailed, I was suddenly
> sensible of such sweet and beneficent society in Nature, in the very pattering
> of the drops, and in every sound and sight around my house, like infinite
> and unaccountable friendliness all at once like an atmosphere sustaining me,
> as made the fancied advantages of human neighborhood insignificant, and I
> have never thought of them since. (383)

This insight is in keeping with his observation, "There can be no very black
melancholy to him who lives in the midst of Nature and has his senses still"
(382).

But it is not as if this nature is pastoral, at any far remove from the
worlds of human being. Although Thoreau is able to foresee a recovery from
this insanity because his sensibility is expanded by his contact with a world
wider than the neighborhood of man, his repose within this wider horizon
is still deeply human. How this tension between the natural and the human
is negotiated is a key to understanding his sense of solitude.

In the first place, Thoreau's sense of space is crucial to his realization of
a wider horizon. Space, for him, is a question of perspective:

> There is commonly sufficient space about us. Our horizon is never quite at our
> elbows. The thick wood is not just at our door, nor the pond, but somewhat is
> always clearing, familiar, and worn by us, appropriated and fenced in some
> way, and reclaimed from Nature. (381)

The horizon is formed by our contact with nature, yet there is an antagonism between ourselves and nature, an appropriation by the human, if
only through the casting of our eyes on the horizon itself. Nonetheless, our
contact with each other is mediated through an immeasurable distance that
lies between us:

> This whole earth which we inhabit is but a point in space. How far apart,
> think you, dwell the two most distant inhabitants of yonder star, the breadth
> of whose disk cannot be appreciated by our instruments? Why should I feel
> lonely? Is not our planet in the Milky Way? . . . What sort of space is that
> which separates a man from his fellows and makes him solitary? I have found
> that no exertion of the legs can bring two minds much nearer to each other.
> (384)

It is not the fact of space, then, but the sort of space we choose to
inhabit that separates a man from his fellows. Whether we are in the town

or the country matters not in this regard. What counts instead is the sort
of space we are in. And this is a space in which time and place fall away,
a space of awakening. "Any prospect of awakening or coming to life to a
dead man makes indifferent all times and places," he writes (385). Such an
indifference to place is the first and final fact about space for Thoreau. To go
to the woods, to move away from the society of men, is not the point, except
for the sake of the metaphors, the new materials, they may provide. What
matters is to awaken, to have the dawn inside oneself.

Indifference to place is one thing, but what about indifference to time?
Cavell claims that Thoreau's discussion of the present is his open admission
of his path to mysticism, his way of showing us how we are to be awakened,
to have the dawn in us, and how improving on the nick of time necessarily involves a writing of the moment, a moment writing.[7] This idea is
verified by Thoreau's description of his experiment. "The present was my
next experiment of this kind, which I propose to describe more at length,
for convenience, putting the experience of two years into one" (337). His
writing of the present, then, is the experiment of *Walden,* a compression
of two years into one, an intensification of time, designed to illuminate the
power of being present in our present.

The coming to life of a dead man also carries with it at least two very
disturbing associations—one of resurrection, and hence of divinity, and the
other of reanimation or zombification. In this sense, indifference to time
and place may lead one to two political extremes—the sovereignty of a god,
on the one hand, and the status of a neo-morph, the quintessentially modern
version of *homo sacer,* on the other.[8] Thoreau attempts to rise above both
extremes by endeavoring to become human, a state that lies between:

> I only know myself as a human entity; the scene, so to speak, of thoughts
> and affections; and am sensible of a certain doubleness by which I can stand
> as remote from myself as from another. However intense my experience, I
> am conscious of the presence and criticism of a part of me, but spectator,
> sharing no experience, but taking note of it; and that is no more I than it is
> you. (386)

Doubleness, a standing away from oneself, enables the movement away from
the state of insanity even as one is able to incorporate it through spectator-
ship. This return to a vision that is whetted, sharpened, by experience and
yet is not part of that experience, that is perhaps objective—no more I than

you—is indeed close to what Foucault calls the indescribable experience of madness.

Thoreau recognizes this mad element of objectivity, Cavell notes, in his praise of the loon.[9] This madness finds expression in "Solitude" when he writes, "I am no more lonely than the loon in the pond that laughs so loud, or than Walden Pond itself" (388). This is yet another double-edged sentence, and because it comes after he notes that his moment of loneliness was accompanied by a slight mood of insanity, his invocation of the loon and the pond itself suggests a deeper madness underwriting his solitude than the fleeting sense to which he refers more directly. Becoming animal, becoming thing, he is metamorphosed, inhabiting the metaphors he lives by.

For Thoreau, the relationship of sanity to loneliness and society presents itself as an inversion of the normal. The normal itself is a kind of death or insanity, but the society of others remains a part of experience. One of his most complex formulations of this inversion is the following paragraph:

> I have heard of a man lost in the woods and dying of famine and exhaustion at the foot of a tree, whose loneliness was relieved by the grotesque visions with which, owing to bodily weakness, his diseased imagination surrounded him, and which he believed to be real. So also, owing to bodily and mental health and strength, we may be continually cheered by a like but more normal and natural society, and come to know that we are never alone. (387)

How might we understand this passage? The story of a man being lost in the woods may be understood as an allegory, evoked throughout *Walden*, for how we become lost in our words. In language, one may become lost, enfeebled, starved, and subjected to grotesque imagination. But our recovery involves a less extreme version of the same vision. We must always be talking to ourselves but also imagining ourselves in the company of others. This passage may be thought of as a reformulation of Emerson's advice to treat the men and women as if they are real, for perhaps they are. But it admits of more, of the essential weakness of the body, the neediness that prevents us from a fuller awakening.

To reach this dreamlike state of being entails thinking. "With thinking we may be beside ourselves in a sane sense," he writes (385). The thinking that Thoreau suggests we do involves a forgetfulness of time and place, a removal from the constraints and bonds of the social. Thoreau here is evocative of his poor teacher Emerson, who reminds us in his essay "Intellect" that "the intellect goes out of the individual, floats over its own personality, and regards it as a fact, and not as *I* and *mine*. He who is immersed in what concerns person or place cannot see the problem of existence. This the intellect always ponders."[10] The scholar in the hive of Cambridge, the carpenter working on a bench, the farmer hoeing weeds—each is outside of him- or herself, each is engaged in thinking. In all this activity we are talking to ourselves, inventing ourselves as our most essential companions, becoming objects of interest to ourselves.

This is madness. But it is a fine madness, a sane madness, a kind of thinking through which we split ourselves wide open in order to touch our wounds, to actually find out whether we exist. Such a madness is essential to our very being. How else are we to live with ourselves and one another and remain true to who we are?

## Notes

1. Henry David Thoreau, "Economy," in *Walden*, in *The Portable Thoreau*, ed. Carl Bode (New York: Penguin, 1982), 258–59. Subsequent references to *Walden* are cited in text.

2. I have often, and I think mistakenly, imagined Thoreau otherwise, as being divorced from despair or of having come to understand despair by what he has observed in others. (Is this a sense that others share?) Whose poor student has he been? What are we failing to see? How has our sight not yet been whetted by our experience? What are we to do to sharpen our sight? Perhaps this optics, a deepened vision of the bottom of the pond viewed through a hole in the ice on the surface, or a measuring of the depth of the pond itself, provides a metaphor for the sort of vision we are to sharpen.

3. For a fuller discussion of Thoreau's sense of resignation, see Thomas L. Dumm, "Resignation," *Critical Inquiry* 25, no. 1 (autumn 1998): 56–76.

4. Stanley Cavell, *The Senses of Walden*, exp. ed. (Chicago: University of Chicago Press, [1981] 1992), 38.

5. See Hannah Arendt, *On Revolution* (New York: Penguin, [1963] 1990), 281. For a discussion of this passage, see George Kateb, *Hannah Arendt: Politics, Conscience, Evil* (Totowa, NJ: Rowman and Allenheld, 1984), 1–2.

6. Michel Foucault, *History of Madness*, ed. Jean Khalfa, trans. Jonathan Murphy and Jean Khalfa (New York: Routledge, 2006), xxxiv.

7. Cavell, *Senses of Walden,* 9.

8. See Giorgio Agamben, *Homo Sacer,* trans. Daniel Heller-Roazen (Stanford, CA: Stanford University Press, 1998).

9. Cavell, *Senses of Walden,* 42.

10. Ralph Waldo Emerson, "Intellect," in *Emerson: Essays and Lectures,* ed. Joel Porte (New York: Library of America, 1983), 417.

PART IV

Thoreau and Political Theory

CHAPTER 13

# Thoreau and Rousseau: Nature as Utopia

*Melissa Lane*

> Man is born free, and everywhere he is in chains.
> —Rousseau, *On the Social Contract*

> What is it to be born free and not to live free?
> —Thoreau, "Life without Principle"

BOTH ROUSSEAU AND THOREAU understand freedom as independence, and both these quasi-romantic thinkers are preoccupied by the question of the human and social relation to nature.[1] Rousseau's major constructive works—*Emile* (1762), *Social Contract* (1762), and the novel *Julie, or the New Héloise* (1761)—explore the ways in which education, politics, and the family could variously reshape the self to achieve a social analogue of the standard of natural independence and freedom identified in his *Discourse on the Origin and the Foundations of Inequality among Men* (1754). One hundred years later, Thoreau's major constructive work, *Walden* (1854), rejects the claim that social agency is necessary to reshape the self, arguing instead that one can live the good life on one's own resources if one lives economically and independently of society; in this quest, living in nature serves as both instrument and metaphor. Using the language of utopianism, a language that has been widely applied to construe both writers' significance for political thought, one can say that whereas Rousseau's various models fit the standard utopian tradition whereby only a reformed society (even if it is only a society of two, as in *Emile*) can produce a good and free person, Thoreau in *Walden* stands that tradition on its head, proposing that individual self-reform is the only path to a reformed society.[2]

Yet there is another, less familiar comparison to be made between these two figures.[3] In their later writings, both develop a romantic celebration of nature that charts a very different relationship to nature and utopia from that in their constructive works.[4] There we can compare Rousseau's *Reveries of a Solitary Walker* (written in 1776–1778 and published in 1782) and Thoreau's later writings, beginning with "Walking" (a lecture first delivered as "The Wild" on April 23, 1851) and encompassing his post-*Walden* journals and late manuscripts.[5] (Of course, the division between works and periods cannot be absolute, and there are remarks in later works that echo those in earlier ones, and vice versa.) Each thinker's later writings differ importantly in emphasis from his constructive writings, sharing a preoccupation with the value of exploring nature in the wild, especially through botany.[6] For Rousseau, this remains pure consolation, but for Thoreau, it blossoms into a new relationship to the landscape in which the positive meaning of utopia is reclaimed in its etymological sense of topos or place. In both cases, the later works help us appreciate and shed light on the earlier works, while moving in a new direction. I summarize these comparisons in the following list and label them with Greek words coined here to parallel *utopia*. Whereas we have come to use *utopia* to signify the good society or city, in fact, this tradition as engaged in Rousseau's constructive works is better called *upolia* (literally, "the good city") to capture its civic dimension, a vision that contrasts with Thoreau's constructive aim of *uidia*, or "the good individual life" (from the Greek *idiotēs*). Rousseau's *Reveries* turn instead to the ideal of a good day or a brief stretch of time, which I term *uhemeria* (literally, "the good day") or *uchronia* ("the good time"). Although Thoreau shares this celebration of the good day in his later writings, he also invents a new and more literal sense of *utopia* as "the good place," the landscape where politics must be situated and to which it must be subordinated. The remainder of the chapter discusses each of these elements in turn.[7]

| Rousseau | Thoreau |
|---|---|
| Constructive Works: *utopia* in the traditional sense of *upolia* (the good city) | Constructive Works: *uidia* (the good individual life) |
| Late Works: *uhemeria* (the good day), or more generally, *uchronia* (the good time) | Late Works: *uhemeria* (the good day), but also *utopia* in the literal sense (the good place) |

## The Constructive Texts

Rousseau and Thoreau strikingly, and similarly, depart from one central aspect of the utopian tradition stretching from Plato to More and subsequent interpreters.[8] Plato, his followers, and two of the major Hellenistic schools suggest that for a city to be ideal, it has to abolish the divisive institution of the household. The city is a site of commonness and communality, the achievement of which is obstructed by the family and private property, which constitute the household. In the words of a leading student of the subject, the Platonic utopia was "a city without the household," the Cynic way was "a life without the household," and the Stoic utopia was "a world without households."[9] Yet both Rousseau and Thoreau abandon the hostility to the household that characterizes this central strand of the utopian tradition. They countenance the household as a possible—and, for Thoreau, even necessary—site of political relevance.

Rousseau affirms the possibility of reforming the household in his novel *Julie, or the New Héloise,* where the estate of Wolmar (Julie's husband) constitutes a sort of miniature affective utopia. But there is no suggestion that reforming the household is the path to, or a building block for, a larger civic and political utopia. The *Social Contract* does not prescribe hundreds of freely associating patriarchs, or patriarchal estates, as sufficient to establish a legitimate polity. Its citizens will be allowed households, but this will not make them citizens; their transformation into citizens requires the general will to establish and transform the body politic. Indeed, Rousseau has already insisted in the *Encyclopédie* that *"l'économie domestique,* ou *particulière,"* or the economy of the household, must be sharply distinguished from *"l'économie générale,* ou *publique,"* or political economy.[10] And he goes so far as to remark in *Emile* that "forced to combat nature or the social institutions, one must choose between making a man or making a citizen, for one cannot make both at the same time."[11]

Thoreau goes even further in the revaluation of the household and its economy, drawing on but also challenging and transforming a rival tradition of *œconomia* stemming from Xenophon, which focuses not on politics but on the household per se. While insisting on the critical importance of a "rigid economy" for the individual—"Economy" is the title of the first chapter of *Walden*—Thoreau dispenses with *œconomia*'s traditional constituents of money, property, and family. He announces that the economy of the individual's living establishment has no need for money or property beyond a cabin (built on Emerson's land: ownership, too, is unimportant) and a few tools.[12] Instead of prescribing ways of increasing wealth, as did the classical works of *œconomia,* Thoreau's economics prescribes ways to prevent the drive for wealth from consuming mental and spiritual independence.[13] And one key path to this aim is to recover, in some form, the independence of a life in nature as opposed to the settled households of civilization. "Men have become the tools of their tools," he laments, drawing this contrast: "The man who independently plucked the fruits when he was hungry is become a farmer; and he who stood under a tree for shelter, a housekeeper. We now no longer camp as for a night, but have settled down on earth and forgotten heaven." The world itself, the natural world and the intimations of the spiritual world it brings, has been shut out and forgotten in this settled, "comfortable" civilization: "We have built for this world a family mansion, and for the next a family tomb." These domestic comforts must be abandoned if true independence is to be achieved.[14]

Yet despite sharing this significant revaluation of the household, the two thinkers take very different views of the relationship between the household and society. Rousseau's constructive utopias come in various shapes, sizes, and relations to nature, all of them depending on the standard of natural independence, in which needs equate to capabilities and psychological self-sufficiency is preserved, but this is achieved within social contexts designed to render otherwise oppressive dependence benign.[15] The *Social Contract* achieves this through the artificial transformation of man into citizen by the wise legislator; *Emile,* through the preservation of natural independence in the society of two between a boy and his wise tutor; *The New Héloise,* through the preservation of natural emotional independence in the context of the family in the small society of the estate belonging to the wise Wolmar.[16] Yet in all these solutions to human self-division, Rousseau adheres to the traditional view of utopia as a social project. He shares this approach with the Greek republican lineage, and it is embraced as well by the Puritan and nonconformist utopian communities established in the United States: one must change society to create a new individual.[17] That is why I identify Rousseau's constructive works with utopia in the traditional, Greek-derived understanding of the *upolia,* or good city (taken here in the broadest sense of a community of at least two).

Thoreau turns this theory of utopia on its head. For him, the way to make good individuals is not to reform society. Rather, individuals must make themselves good; only then do they have a chance of making a good—or at least tolerable—society. But in any case, the fundamental question is of the good life.[18] Thus Thoreau inverts the traditional utopian understanding of the relationship between society and the individual. He is undoubtedly influenced by the Puritan commitment to the holy society, the millennialism ingrained in the American historical imagination, and the tiny utopian outposts dotted across New England. The last include ventures founded by friends, such as Bronson Alcott's Fruitlands, and the progressive Raritan Bay Union School founded in the 1850s by abolitionists Theodore Weld and Angelina Grimké (which Thoreau visited and described as a "queer place").[19] He is certainly aware of the appeal to spiritual recovery in nature in the Second Great Awakening; many revivalist meetings were held in fields.[20] But he does not see the path of social reform as primary. Instead, he posits the individual household and life, or *uidia,* to be the primary ingredient of utopia, not its derivative. *Walden* has been called a "community of one," but as another critic rightly observes, "one man does not make a community, even a utopian community."[21] There is an infinite difference between a political society, or polis (as writ large by Rousseau in the *Social Contract* or small in the relationship between Emile and his tutor), and a so-called community of one. *Uidia* is a certain kind of solitary life: a heroic life of self making and world making. This is not the solipsistic solitude of a man "obsessed with his own salvation" alone.[22] Thoreau is committed to making himself an exemplar for others, and he spends his life exhorting and provoking them to change (discussed in more detail later). But the good life he models *for* others does not involve an engagement *with* others as a foundation of its goodness. Neighborliness, though Thoreau occasionally extols it and recounts his various visitors, is incapable of remaking one's life without the individual economics, and attunement to nature, at the heart of *Walden*'s "experiment in living."[23]

These different solutions arise from different diagnoses of what is wrong with the social state. Both Rousseau and Thoreau hold that social existence imposes false necessities. According to Rousseau, we desire luxury because our anxious craving for outside approval—rooted originally in the physical and sexual division of labor, which soon became a division of psychic labor as well—inflates our natural desires. Once spurred by *amour-propre,* or the competitive need for self-esteem (which contrasts with simple self-preservation, or *amour de soi*), human nature at once de-velops and degenerates. Runaway and perverse desires are uncontainable without a strong exertion of law, education, or authority to reshape them from the beginning. But Rousseau is not optimistic about the chances of that occurring. There is no natural path from our history of degeneration to utopia; this would require a drastic social intervention and transformation by a legislator, a tutor, or a wise, aristocratic paterfamilias.

For Thoreau, as for Rousseau, opinion and dependence constitute the shackles of society, which is why both seek freedom as independence. Thoreau, however, rejects the psychology of internalization on which Rous-seau bases his analysis of *amour-propre*. For Thoreau, only habit and the false perception of necessity—"mere ignorance and mistake"—bind us to the social.[24] The extent of disagreement is measured in Thoreau's claims that "the civilized man is a more experienced and wiser savage" and that "inside the civilized man stands the savage still in a place of honor."[25] He sees civilization as a superficial veneer that can be stripped off if we only muster the will to do so. To Thoreau, we are externally corrupted but still, in crucial respects, the same as savages ("Every genuine thing retains this wild tone—which no true culture displaces").[26] To Rousseau, we are internally corrupted and so no longer savages.

Strikingly, both men reject the notion of a fatal original sin: Thoreau has been called "the ultimate Pelagian," whereas Rousseau, controversially, puts the account of evil as originating in human moral freedom, a sort of Pelagianism, in the mouth of his character Saint-Preux in *Julie*. According to Saint-Preux, Wolmar insists that the existence of evil indicates "deficiency of power, of intelligence, or of goodness in the first cause," but Saint-Preux argues that "the origin of physical evil lay in the nature of matter, and that of moral evil in man's freedom."[27] Yet for Rousseau, this free choice of evil has deep historical roots in real social choices, even if not in a single Adamic fall. Thoreau, however, rejects history as well as fate, attacking the tendency to blame current woes on the past: "A man will not need to study history to find out what is best for his own culture."[28] For Rousseau, the depth of our corruption by society is tragic and, like tragedy, historically rooted and so not easily undone (only to be overcome or, in reverie, temporarily escaped); for Thoreau, our muddled vision is inexplicable, so the best strategy against it is the comic. If we can see and avoid this danger, then society is not tragic but pathetic and sometimes bathetic: "Thus men invite the devil in at every angle and then prate about the garden of Eden and the fall of man."[29]

For Rousseau, almost all civilized people are doomed to psychological misery unless some utopian solution can be imposed—and the conditions for doing so are difficult and in most places impossible. For Thoreau, individual self-discipline should be enough. He prescribes "a stern and more than Spartan simplicity of life and elevation of purpose."[30] The reference to Sparta nicely measures the difference between the two thinkers. For Rousseau, the Spartans are firmly in the ancient past, an ideal but anachronistic model of social unity (*Emile* recounts with awe the tale of a Spartan mother who sent five sons into battle; the first question she asked the messenger was not whether they had survived but whether the war had been won).[31] For Thoreau, in contrast, a Spartan life has no social prerequisites; it is the life of voluntary individual simplicity open to anyone with sufficient will.[32] Even when Thoreau asserts that "the mind can be permanently profaned by the habit of attending to trivial things," this is not an indelible permanence, for he immediately proffers its remedy: "by wariness and devotion to reconsecrate ourselves."[33]

Here we come to a crucial difference in the two thinkers' attitudes toward law and freedom, epitomized by the epigraphs of this chapter: are we actually in chains, or simply not choosing to "live free"? For Rousseau, being born free is a natural human condition that is violated by the unjust social pacts enslaving men everywhere. The social problem for Rousseau is fundamentally a problem of unjust laws. Because man is born free but is everywhere in chains, the correct response is to take "men as they are, and laws as they can be."[34] This is why Rousseau's great constructive projects of the *Social Contract, Emile,* and *New Héloise* fall in the broad tradition of utopianism: they envision a wholly new society in which, and only in which, humans can be (made) happy, virtuous, and, crucially for Rousseau, free. Law—or its analogues education and estate management, in the smaller societies—must be the starting point, not the end result, of the formation of good communities and so of good individuals.

In contrast, free birth for Thoreau applies not only to a natural condition but also to the special condition of the American birthright of civil as well as natural liberty. So the law is not the source of unfreedom for most men (though it is, of course, the source of unfreedom for slaves; on

Thoreau's anti-slavery writings, see Jack Turner's chapter 6 in this volume). Rousseau dares to say that the old world needs to be remade but sees this as demanding a wholesale social change from above, whether at the microcosm or macrocosm level in society. Thoreau is trying to live up to the promise of the New World by calling on individuals to make their world anew; as I argue at the end of this chapter, for Thoreau, the New World means independence more profoundly than it means democracy. So in contrast to Rousseau's exploration in the *Social Contract* of what laws "can be," Thoreau announces in "Slavery in Massachusetts" that "the law will never make men free; it is men who have got to make the law free."[35] This is the *uidia* solution. Man has to reform himself, in contrast to the vain hope of transforming society and so the individual from above.

So in Rousseau's constructive works, the notion of nature is that of human nature, and law is the solution to transforming it. In *Walden*, Thoreau's relation to nature is more complicated. He suggests that the way to escape false necessity and to recover a sense of ourselves through economy is to go back to nature and live according to it, not according to civilized standards. Nature offers a new and asocial standard, such as in its exemplification of innocence and of chastity, which bridges the wild and the good: "The moral aspect of nature is a disease caught of man—a jaundice imported into her—To the innocent there are no cherubim nor angels."[36] Yet even here, the primary focus is on using such natural standards to remake human nature. Nature serves as a yardstick and a resource for human effort, and although its radical and alien integrity is often glimpsed, its invocation is primarily hortatory and for edification.[37]

The task of remaking human nature is conceived in *Walden* as an act of heroism. The activity of clearing a space of consciousness in which to create the world is heroic: it is solitary combat that, in triumphing over nature—whether by written account or by domination in farming— displays the force of a natural phenomenon. The continual epic references in *Walden*—the battle of the ants portrayed as Roman civil war, the "Homeric or Paphlagonian" woodcutter, the "small Herculean labor" Thoreau carries out in the bean field—all serve to establish Thoreau as the hero over and against the spectator roles to which his neighbors allow themselves to be limited.[38] In *Walden*, the individual must both triumph over nature and reidentify himself with it, separating himself from a corrupt society in the cause of remaking himself according to an independent standard able to judge and indict it.

If the *uidia* of *Walden* is Hectorian, it is also hectoring. Thoreau conceives his task to be that of the prophet: he calls *Walden* a scripture, one of the race of holy books that may be "more salutary than the morning" for our lives.[39] (Nor does Thoreau have any of the qualms about the instability and impurity of the written word, as compared with the oral word, that Derrida explores in Rousseau's prose.[40] For Thoreau, the spoken language is impermanent and animal, while the written language is "a reserved and select expression, too significant to be heard by the ear, which we must be born again in order to speak."[41]) Thoreau is never inclined to hide his light under a bushel; as he declares to his journal at age twenty-five, "I would fain communicate the wealth of my life to men."[42] His writing, and indeed his living, is conceived not as personal or private but as suitably public for others' improvement: "Truth and a true man is something essentially public not private. . . . By living the life of a man is made common property."[43] Notice, however, that Thoreau's determination to give his fellows "a strong dose of myself" refers to the professional obligations he undertakes as a lecturer, not, as has been suggested, to the general demands of democracy.[44] I return to whether his commitments are "democratic" later. Here, it is suffices to note that Rousseau too conceives his task in the constructive works to be like the great prophet-lawgivers—Moses, Solon, Numa, Lycurgus. But unlike Thoreau, he does not seek to inspire his readers to heroism. His constructive thought is directed not to making individuals unique but to making them happy and equal and free by means of a healing authority.

## The Turn to Naturalist Pursuits: Consolation versus the Landscape

Rousseau and Thoreau change their tone, and their preoccupations, in their naturalist works (specifically, the *Reveries* for Rousseau; his journal from about 1850, late lectures, and late manuscripts for Thoreau, although in Thoreau's case, this turn has earlier intimations and is also expressed in the latter, and late-redacted, parts of *Walden*). Both become accomplished botanists who delight in nature: Thoreau calls "walking" the activity of the "saunterer," and Rousseau names himself the "solitary walker."[45] Both deride medical approaches to nature. Rousseau says they "tarnish the colour of the meadows," and Thoreau criticizes the invalid who drinks herb tea rather than living according to the seasons, "for all Nature is doing her best each moment to make us well. She exists for no other end."[46] Both of them celebrate the experience of an episodic and transitory absorption in nature (named here *uhemeria,* "the good day," or more generally, *uchronia,* "the good time"). Yet despite sharing this love of naturalist exploration, the two disagree on the meaning of such immersion in nature. Rousseau's public-mindedness gives way to an insistence on private consolation from which there is no path to public reform; Thoreau largely abandons the hectoring demand for heroism from his readers in favor of a gentler invitation to situate themselves and their polis inside a natural landscape and to accept with gratitude the plenitude nature there bestows. Thus for Rousseau, the nature of the constructive works, in which human liberation is a social enterprise, means that communing with nature can at best be consolation, not a social solution. Thoreau, in contrast, retains a faith in the power of individual action, though softening it from the self-mastery of *Walden* to the acceptance and gratitude we see in his later works. In both cases, the later works help us appreciate and shed light on the earlier works.

Rousseau's *Reveries* canvasses a range of motives for writing, virtually all of which refer solely to himself. He proclaims himself to have been relieved of the burden of social responsibility he executed in his earlier, constructive texts by the persecution that has driven him out of society. The derision and defamation showered on him exonerate him from any concern for social welfare; henceforth his fellows can and will be nothing for him.[47] So the *Reveries* is a new kind of text, different from the social address and purpose of the *Confessions,* which had been written "to display to my kind a portrait in every way true to nature."[48] He is writing now to benefit not others but himself.

In a paragraph of the *Reveries,* Rousseau explores the possible purposes such writing might serve—to "take the barometer readings of my soul," to re-create former pleasures by using writing to "double the space of my existence."[49] Personal consolation, not social reform, is the purpose of the *Reveries,* and Rousseau proposes no path from the former to the latter. It is not even meant to be exemplary—Rousseau contends that reverie is unwise for most men, given their socially inflated needs. His uniqueness is not presented as a model for emulation. Whereas in *Walden* Thoreau presents himself as a hero to inspire others to be equally heroic, and in the late writings as a saunterer whom others would benefit from emulating or accompanying, in the *Reveries* Rousseau presents himself as a uniquely unfortunate man, with a uniquely natural heart, whom others should acknowledge as unique rather than seek to imitate.

Thus the purpose of the *Reveries* is explicitly stated as the search for temporary personal consolation. This is the fallacy in recent attempts to recover Rousseau's reveries for deep ecology.[50] Nature has no privileged status for Rousseau but is only one of several possible paths to his real interest, which is emotional independence. Although Rousseau enjoys losing himself in the surface of nature (I discuss his botanizing later), nature is only one of several possible sources of reverie, and he values the reverie of a lost sexual partnership in the Tenth Walk even more highly than the pastoral charms of the island of St. Pierre described in the Fifth Walk: the lost sexual partnership is described as "that one short time in my life when I was myself, completely myself, unmixed and unimpeded, and when I can genuinely claim to have lived."[51] What is important is not the experience of nature or sex per se, but rather the experience of freedom and independence achieved in each. Indeed, nature is so far from being essential (and Rousseau's conception of reverie so far removed from deep ecology) that he declares, "I have often thought that in the Bastille, and even in a dungeon with not a single object to rest my eyes on, I could still have dreamed pleasantly."[52] The value of the lost sexual union with Madame de Warens is this: "I was perfectly free, or better than free because I was subject only to my own affections and did only what I wanted to do."[53] What matters most is not the content of any given reverie but rather the sense of being "self-sufficient like God," freed even from the trammels of time, as "the present runs on indefinitely but this duration goes unnoticed, with no sign of the passing of time."[54] Finally, these sentiments are experienced as well or better in the recall of reverie or the reading of his composed *Reveries* as in the original experience itself; this is what Jean Starobinski identifies as "the prospect of *ecstasy*, repeated indefinitely through reading."[55] Far from being identical with deep ecology, Rousseau's solipsistic account of reverie is its polar opposite.

For Rousseau, then, the overriding purpose of immersion in nature is emotional solace and consolation. For Thoreau, its purpose—described in the journal entry for September 7, 1851, in which he declares watching to be "the way to spend a day"—is quite different.[56] His commitment to watchfulness in time aims to "find God in nature," echoing Emerson's schematic program in his essay "Nature."[57] But now it is infused with a Humboldtian and Darwinian commitment to knowledge of the natural world as the path to knowledge of the (divine) whole.[58] Thoreau's purpose is knowledge and a higher understanding. Although he never ceases the search for emotional consolation, particularly after the devastating loss of his brother John in 1842, he seeks it through patient and careful investigation, through wakefulness rather than through blissful Rousseauian forgetfulness. (Indeed, Rousseau's failure to find a higher moral law in nature was attacked by one of his earliest critics, the Jesuit Louis-Bertrand Castel, who defended a view of "naturalisme" as including and leading to an understanding of God—a sort of anticipation of the path to transcendence taken by Thoreau.)[59]

Such different purposes lend a different coloration to their views of botany, knowledge, and time. Although Rousseau recommends the pursuit of botany as part of reverie, he sees this not as a key to the understanding of nature but rather as an activity deliberately confined to the pleasant surface of nature. Plants are the visible surface of nature, the "clothing and adornment of the earth." They are available to the unaided eye without expense or effort, with no need to probe or postulate any deeper level of reality, in contrast to the unpleasant toil that the study of minerals or anatomy requires. ("What a terrible sight an anatomy theatre is! Stinking corpses, livid running flesh, blood, repellent intestines, horrible skeletons, pestilential vapours!")[60]

Thus for Rousseau, the study of botany is not intended to generate any strong program of knowledge of the kind needed to rebut the Pyrrhonian skepticism about the relationship between appearance and reality and the impossibility of knowing reality that, in its reformulation by Montaigne, so troubled Rousseau. It is only in his "Moral Letters," written in a purported address to Sophie d'Houdetot and haunted by Montaigne, that he fully expresses the enormity of this skepticism. There Rousseau admits to an "awful doubt" grounded in the imprisonment of our sensory faculties (we do not feel the real weight of gravity or the blood circulating within us) and the impossibility of knowledge.[61] Summing up the limitations of our senses and so our knowledge, Montaigne had declared that "our vision is reduced to the length of our nose."[62] Like Montaigne, Rousseau indicts our reason as well as our senses, since reason relies on the senses, which are so easily fooled even about size and touch: "We know nothing, dear Sophie, we see nothing; we are a troop of blind men, thrown out by chance in this vast universe," and in short, "we have no certain notion of anything."[63]

But if Rousseau bows under the same doubt as Montaigne, he is unable to accept his predecessor's equable willingness to live with it. Savaging human presumption is no pleasure for Rousseau as it is for Montaigne; Rousseau longs for human dignity in the universe, even while saying grimly that we are and must appear ridiculous. The solution to which Rousseau's doubt drives him is a renunciation of the possibility of knowledge—understood as knowledge beyond appearances, resulting from investigation—but also an insistence on the possibility of happiness. Our senses and reason were given to us to secure happiness, not knowledge. When we use them to investigate nature, "they are insufficient, they fool us."[64] But if we use them only to preserve ourselves, they will be dependable; we may be misled as to the outside world, but never as to our own happiness (we can achieve emotionally independent self-preservation, and so happiness, without speculative knowledge). Hence we can be at home in nature. Montaigne had denied that nature is an unjust stepmother, meaning that she provides for us adequately; Rousseau affirms in the *Reveries* that she is a true mother indeed.[65] We must give up any drive for knowledge, any natural object whose study requires effort or penetration, to take consolation in those aspects of nature available to us on the surface, without strain. This is why Rousseau shrinks back from the horrifying sights of the anatomy theater and cries out instead to the flowers, streams, woods, and glades, to nature circumscribed to the pleasing and pastoral alone. The "study" he applauds in the *Reveries* must be understood within the context of this peculiar response to skepticism. It is a purely ruminative study, involving a comparison of appearances and delight in perceptions, but no attempt to base rational deductions on those flimsy foundations, in contrast to the investigation of the reality behind appearances that Thoreau pursues. For Rousseau, the "effortless pleasure" of botany alone among cognitive activities escapes the constraining calculus of cause and effect, truth and lying, labor and suffering; it enables those few who are able to pursue it with a pure heart to be at home in nature without strain or transformation.[66]

Unlike Rousseau, Thoreau is not fearful of depths or investigation. In *Walden* he glorifies digging below the surface as a way of getting to reality—the famous passage in which he measures the depth of Walden Pond is meant as a cure for the skepticism based on a false longing for metaphysical depths—and constructs the text of bottoms and foundations.[67] He aims to establish a distinction between reality and appearance that will hold firm both materially and morally. The bottom is "a place where you might found a wall or a state," and this is something anyone can do: "there is a solid bottom every where."[68] Thoreau feels skepticism as a loss of compass and responds to it by establishing a bottom; Rousseau feels it as the absurdity of human pretensions in the universe and responds to it by substituting feeling—in which we are not ridiculous—for knowledge.

In *Walden* Thoreau sometimes expresses a peculiar conception of knowledge, such as his insistence that he has built his cabin on a previously unoccupied site: "I am not aware that any man has ever built on the spot which I occupy. Deliver me from a city built on the site of a more ancient city, whose materials are ruins, whose gardens cemeteries."[69] Satisfying knowledge, it seems, is available only by making something from scratch. Here he sets out to create the world in order to know it. Solitude functions to exclude the other who could disturb this balance. Immediately after the reflection just quoted, Thoreau repopulates the woods that he has just cleansed of human presence: "With such reminiscences I repeopled the woods and lulled myself asleep."[70] He is oriented in nature here only by projecting it on a self-made foundation.

But there are already hints in *Walden* of a less solipsistic, more cosmic kind of knowledge: "Not till we are lost, in other words, not till we have lost the world, do we begin to find ourselves, and realize where we are and the infinite extent of our relations."[71] Elsewhere Thoreau extends the trust in nature expressed in *Walden* ("I think that we may safely trust a good deal more than we do. . . . Nature is as well adapted to our weakness as to our strength") to a trust in the knowledge it is possible to gain of nature's whole interrelated and infinite workings.[72] He expresses this specifically in, among other ways, his active interest in the indigenous population. The posture of solipsistic foundation that he plays with, at times, in *Walden* must be juxtaposed with his awareness elsewhere in that text, and in other texts, of Amerindian displacement as the fundamental condition for the independence of New England.[73] Thus in some moods he relaxes the requirement of a tabula rasa for the landscape:

> I love that the rocks should appear to have some spots of blood on them. Indian blood at least—to be convinced that the earth has been crowded with

men—living enjoying suffering—that races past [sic] away have stained the rocks with their blood—That the mould I tread on has been animated—aye humanized. I am the more at home. I farm the dust of my ancestors—though the chemists [sic] analysis may not detect it—I go forth to redeem the meadows they have become.[74]

Here Thoreau can tolerate the peopling as well as the studying of the world; he does not need the purity of the tabula rasa to enable him to understand nature.[75]

Yet it is not only knowledge of the natural world, and the divinity revealed within it, that Thoreau seeks in his naturalist writings. It is also a new understanding of the "landscape" of which both individuals and society are but a part, and against the background of which they must come to understand themselves as partial. This is heralded earlier in Thoreau's career in his 1842 journal: "How little matters it all men have built and delved there in the valley, it is but a feature in the landscape."[76] This presages a new understanding of the relation between nature and utopia: the valley—by which Thoreau means city and civilization—is to be understood as subordinate and as decentered in a greater natural whole. The same line of thought is developed in "Walking" in 1851:

Man and his affairs, church and state—and school, trade and commerce, and manufactures and agriculture—even politics, the most alarming of them all,—I am pleased to see how little space they occupy in the landscape. Politics is but a narrow field, and that still narrower highway yonder leads to it.[77]

Thus politics—the city—is not the whole of human existence. It must be put in (decidedly minor) proportion in relation to the natural world.

This perspective on both nature and politics generates a distinctive set of emotional and cognitive attitudes toward nature. Preeminent among these attitudes are gratitude, love, and freedom: the love and enjoyment of pursuits in nature as leisure rather than commerce, and gratitude for the munificence of nature, which provides freedom as both leisure and independence. Characteristic of this attitudinal complex is the setting of human affairs—in particular, social and political institutions—into a definite and limited perspective. As Thoreau writes in his journal, "Some rarely go outdoors—most are always at home at night—very few indeed have stayed out all night once in their lives—fewer still have gone behind the world of humanity—seen his institutions like toad-stools by the way-side."[78]

Although human affairs are not central, they benefit from the plenitude and leisure available in nature. Thoreau declares in a late manuscript that "the very earth itself is a granary and a seminary."[79] This is not nature as opposed to civilization but nature as the context or home for civilization, in which it belongs, a context of plenitude from which we may learn and to which we must be grateful.

Thoreau's greatest image of the leisure and freedom afforded by nature to its chastened and somewhat dwarfed human inhabitants is that of berrying, or huckleberry picking. Shannon L. Mariotti remarks in chapter 15 of this volume how the physicality of berrying transforms perception; here, our focus is on the experience of leisure and thus the independence and self-sufficiency it provides. Berrying is a free gift from nature, "a pastime, not a drudgery," an original type of leisure in nature that we can still experience. Thoreau dramatically equates the independence afforded by summer berry picking with that achieved on the first of August, the anniversary of Britain's 1834 emancipation of the slaves in the West Indies, which was widely celebrated throughout antebellum New England. Thoreau names this "the anniversary of Emancipation in New England," twinning the emancipation of legal slaves with the emancipation from dependence and slavishness for all.[80] In berrying, we are emancipated from the need to buy food, from the need to spend our lives in slavish pursuits; we are free to enjoy our natural livelihood.

Thoreau establishes a further parallel between berrying and a chastened politics when he observes that the "natural rights" to huckleberrying have been lost in England and the Continent already.[81] Only Americans, who can still go berry picking, can find the perfect independence as self-sufficiency that Thoreau (and indeed, Rousseau) seeks. The bounty of nature is incompatible with slavishness and exploitation; it is compatible only with independence and self-sufficiency on the part of each individual. Speaking of the "true fruit of Nature," in both metaphorical and literal senses, he warns (in a remark anticipated in *Walden*) that "no hired man can help us to gather that crop."[82] No one else can do that for an individual who desires to preserve independence; in relation to nature, one must be independent and self-sufficient: "you who taste these berries are a god" (recall Rousseau's assertion that, in reverie, one is "self-sufficient like God").[83] And as a god, one is innocent as well as independent, so the rejection of original sin noted in the 1855 journal is reiterated: "[Berrying] is a sort of sacrament, a communion,—the *not* forbidden fruits, which no serpent tempts us to eat."[84]

Notice that Thoreau talks similarly about leisure for certain farmers as for berry pickers. For example, just as berrying is a pastime and not a drudgery, so he speaks of the farmer Minot doing "nothing (with haste and drudgery)—but as if he loved it."[85] His point, then, cannot be to draw a strict line between wild, untouched nature and civilization. Although he talks of wanting "absolute Freedom and Wildness" as opposed to freedom that is "merely civil,"[86] he also talks of any relation to nature—whether farming or berrying—as potentially affording the same leisure. It is important to preserve the wild, especially in the context of the dramatic deforestation of the Concord area in Thoreau's lifetime. But we can experience nature, and the gratitude and delight it inspires, even in and around a well-organized settlement of civilization.[87]

Within this landscape, we do have some civic tasks. Thoreau acknowledges a need for government but insists that it is not worth our conscious attention: the functions of government are "vital functions of human society, but should be unconsciously performed, like the corresponding functions of the physical body. They are *infra*-human, a kind of vegetation."[88] (Note Thoreau's scorn for the vegetable state for which Rousseau's *Reveries* yearn.) Ideally, the state should accept this subordinate place, as already stated in the conclusion of "Resistance to Civil Government" (1849):

> I please myself with imagining a State at last which can afford to be just to all men, and to treat the individual with respect as a neighbor; which even would not think it inconsistent with its own repose, if a few were to live aloof from it, not meddling with it, nor embraced by it, who fulfilled all the duties of neighbors and fellow-men. A State which bore this kind of fruit, and suffered it to drop off as fast as it ripened, would prepare the way for a still more perfect and glorious State, which also I have imagined, but not yet anywhere seen.[89]

Earlier in that essay, Thoreau criticizes those statesmen who "speak of moving society, but have no resting-place without it."[90] There he is speaking metaphorically about principles. But the late writings constitute a similar image, offering a resting place not in the sense of absolute Archimedean principles but in the sense of a place for actual rest. Leisure has political significance because it allows us to recall our relation to nature and the subordinate position of politics in the landscape.

The truly utopian task lies not in the city but in the landscape as a whole: "We are all schoolmasters, and our schoolhouse is the universe."[91] (Recalling the hectoring tone of *Walden,* Thoreau characteristically makes his readers the teachers rather than the pupils.) Having earlier insisted that the good individual must precede the good society, Thoreau here steps outside and beyond that debate by acknowledging the need to begin by establishing one's sense of place, putting both self and polity into severe proportion while gaining for them the plenitude of leisure. Whereas Rousseau's attempts to remake human nature give way to an attempt to lose himself in nature and forget the political altogether in *uchronia,* Thoreau's later vision of nature as *utopia* teaches that utopia must return to its original meaning and recover the meaning and value of our place in the natural world as the setting for a suitably chastened politics.[92] If nature serves both Thoreau and Rousseau as a moral yardstick, it becomes a refuge for Rousseau, while it modulates for Thoreau from a gladiatorial arena to an all-encompassing environment. The flight to nature can bear many political meanings. It need not signify a mere rejection of the political; it can also yield a reformulation of its boundaries and significance.

Thus the naturalist writings shed new light on the question of whether Thoreau is a political thinker, as memorably denied by Hannah Arendt. Arendt's attack on Thoreau for heeding, and caring for, only his "unpolitical" individual conscience, rather than joining in a corporate political judgment as a citizen, deals only with "Resistance to Civil Government."[93] Although I do not evaluate that text here, I have argued that a full assessment of Thoreau's politics requires an understanding of his changing views of the place of politics in nature. But that still leaves the question of the nature of his politics. Partly in response to Arendt, George Kateb and Nancy Rosenblum have pioneered the reading of Thoreau as a "democratic individualist" who is committed, at least provisionally and for his own purposes, to representative democracy.[94] Mariotti, too, repeatedly imputes a concern with democracy to Thoreau, claiming that he wants to cultivate "more truly democratic citizens," to "reach toward a more truly democratic polity," and that "he sees these critical practices as opening up more democratic possibilities."[95] Likewise, George Shulman suggests in chapter 5 of this volume that Thoreau's concern with prophecy must be understood in the context of democratic culture,[96] while Brian Walker argues in chapter 2 that *Walden* belongs to the genre of "democratic advice book."[97] Against such claims,

Leigh Kathryn Jenco, in chapter 3, argues that Thoreau's concern with "action from principle" leads him to criticize democratic majoritarianism and representation for embodying legal claims potentially opposed to genuine moral demands.[98]

Absent a full evaluation of the writings on resistance and "action from principle," it is impossible to settle the question of whether Thoreau is a democratic thinker. Certainly, he does not sing praises to democracy, as Whitman does. It is notable that although he certainly plays on the language of voting and representation, forms of the word *democracy* appear only twice in any of Thoreau's works collected in the Cambridge *Political Writings* volume; compare the thirteen or so references to *democracy* in Rosenblum's introduction to that volume.[99] This does not prove that democracy is not a fruitful category to discuss his thought (it is at least a category he used at times, unlike the category of utopia used to organize this chapter), but it suggests that to assimilate him too readily to Whitman or even Emerson on democracy may be to fail to register a significant difference in the pattern of his thought and prose. For all their commonalities, a gulf divides Thoreau's commitment to independence and the uses of individuality from Whitman's ecstatic democratic odes. This chapter has argued that the language and meaning of freedom as independence afford an illuminating account of Thoreau's writings, as well as those of Rousseau, and should frame any evaluation of his politics, including the vexed question of their democratic character.

In this respect, Thoreau's own language may be said to be the child not of 1787 or 1828 (the year of Andrew Jackson's election) but of 1776. In *Walden*, Thoreau proclaims himself "more independent than any farmer in Concord" and evaluates his occupation as day-laborer as "the most independent of any."[100] The New World is, for Thoreau, the land promising independence, the same psychological standard of self-sufficiency that Rousseau finds has vanished in the corruption of the old. Such independence raises a political question, however, if it is meant to be independence not only for one but for all, as it certainly is for Thoreau, the preacher and prophet. But independence does not demand interpersonal interaction, even though it may set itself up as a model for others. It is the politics of the lonely beacon, not the convivial bonfire.

As noted earlier, *Walden*'s insistence on *uidia* must be read in the light of Thoreau's simultaneous and incessant insistence on addressing a public

that he exhorts to emulate him. Thoreau says little about the lineaments of a
society made up of independent and economical figures, except to mention
briefly—without filling in—the idyll of "a still more perfect and glorious
State" for which such a society of independent figures can pave the way.
From his naturalist writings, we can sketch in the further importance of
the independence secured by the plenitude and leisure that can be enjoyed
in nature, as bulwarks against an excessively dependent or oppressive social
condition. If independence is to be secured, *uidia* must become *utopia*
while maintaining the psychic enjoyment of *uchronia*. These approaches
to the good individual and the good society replace the traditional role and
meaning of utopia as *upolia*. Instead of starting from the good society, let
alone the democratic polity, Thoreau's conception of independence affords
each person a relationship to nature and the self that would dispense with
the traditional route to utopia altogether.[101]

# Notes

This chapter owes its inception to the incomparable teaching of Judith N. Shklar,
with whom I first studied Rousseau and American political thought, and to the
provocative model of Stanley Cavell's and George Kateb's reflections and teachings on Thoreau. Professor Shklar was the adviser of my undergraduate disserta-
tion, cited in note 16, and I would like to dedicate this chapter to her undimmed
memory. Katrina Gulliver and Mary-Rose Cheadle of the Centre for History and
Economics, King's College, Cambridge, provided helpful research assistance.
Participants in the Gresham College–School of Advanced Study Symposium
on Utopia in London (May 2007), the Cambridge University Reading Group in
American Intellectual and Cultural History (October 2007), and the conference
"Men and Citizens: Nature, Foundations and Challenges of Citizenship," Centre
for History and Economics, King's College, Cambridge (July 2008), offered helpful
discussions of previous drafts. I am particularly grateful to the anonymous readers
of this volume for their comments, to Michael Sonenscher for sharing his erudite
knowledge of Rousseau, and to Jack Turner for his similar knowledge of Thoreau,
combined with stimulating and precise editorial advice.

1. The comparison between Rousseau and Thoreau was briefly made by Stanley Cavell, *The Senses of Walden* (San Francisco: North Point Press, [1972] 1981),
87, remarking on their understandings of society as conspiracy, and by Frederick
Garber, *Thoreau's Redemptive Imagination* (New York: New York University Press,
1977), on their understandings of nature. More recently, it has been advanced

in the context of appropriating both for deep ecology in an article by Joseph H. Lane Jr. (see note 4). On romanticism in Rousseau, see, for example, Peter Gay, "Reading about Rousseau: A Survey of the Literature," in *The Party of Humanity: Essays in the French Enlightenment* (New York: Knopf, 1963). On romanticism in Thoreau, see Perry Miller, *Nature's Nation* (Cambridge, MA: Harvard University Press, 1967); Michael Gilmore, *American Romanticism and the Marketplace* (Chicago: University of Chicago Press, 1985); Daniel Walker Howe, *Making the American Self: Jonathan Edwards to Abraham Lincoln* (Cambridge, MA: Belknap Press of Harvard University Press, 1997) (Howe calls Thoreau a "Romantic religious perfectionist" [244]); and important work by Nancy Rosenblum, especially *Another Liberalism: Romanticism and the Reconstruction of Liberal Thought* (Cambridge, MA: Harvard University Press, 1987), and chapter 1 of this volume. The nonstandard relationships of both authors to romanticism are indicated, for example, by Leon Chai, *The Romantic Foundations of the American Renaissance* (Ithaca, NY: Cornell University Press, 1987), who classes Rousseau's *Reveries* as "pre-Romantic" (2) and omits Thoreau and Whitman from the main theme, seeing their relationship to romanticism as "mediated through the vision of Emerson" (7). It is this sort of uneasiness of classification that I indicate in the term *quasiromantic.* I am grateful to Michael O'Brien for helpful discussions of the meaning of, and literature on, American romanticism.

2. Neither thinker uses the term *utopia* himself. I introduce it here (following a large literature, especially on Thoreau), with the variations noted, as a neat way to capture the changing significance of their stances for political philosophy. Thoreau is more central to most studies of utopia than is Rousseau (but see Judith N. Shklar, *Men and Citizens: A Study of Rousseau's Social Theory* [Cambridge: Cambridge University Press, 1969], 8–12). The fullest discussion is Andrea Bollinger, *Henry David Thoreaus "World of Full and Fair Proportions": Gesellschaftskritik, Sozialreform und Utopie in Neuengland* (Bern: Peter Lang, 1995), who argues that the peaceful revolution of self-reform in *Walden,* heralding an existentialist kind of liberal utopia that contrasts with the "holy utopia" of Puritanism, becomes impossible to maintain with the rise of controversy about slavery and is abandoned in favor of political action in the later writings on John Brown (244). Exceptionally, a chapter is devoted to Rousseau, but only passing mention is made of Thoreau, in Frank E. Manuel and Fritzie P. Manuel, *Utopian Thought in the Western World* (Cambridge, MA: Harvard University Press, 1979). By using the term *utopia,* however, I do not mean to prejudge how applicable or possible an author believes a particular model to be. The term *constructive work* is my own heuristic to signal works in which the author advances some sort of arguably utopian model, as opposed to works that have a less directive or focused ambition.

3. This is an exercise in comparison and contrast, not a claim of influence.

There is no mention of any work by Rousseau in Robert Sattelmeyer, *Thoreau's Reading: A Study in Intellectual History with Bibliographical Catalogue* (Princeton, NJ: Princeton University Press, 1988), nor of any work by Montesquieu. Thoreau is not interested in constitutional questions. However, as Sattelmeyer shows, Thoreau was well read in certain French literature, in particular Victor Cousin's "eclectic" introduction to the history of philosophy, and he was familiar with other French thinkers such as Fénelon (28) and Constant (20), though probably not the then little-known lecture on the ancients and the moderns. Cousin's book would have acquainted Thoreau with the then widely held critical view of Rousseau as an Epicurean and a Hobbist, hostile to the idealist themes that Cousin and his American followers such as Emerson and Orestes Brownson (Thoreau's teacher at Harvard) found compelling in German transcendental philosophy and its English exponents such as Coleridge and Carlyle.

4. This is the appropriate object of comparison, contrary to the opinion of Joseph H. Lane Jr., "Reveries and the Return to Nature: Rousseau's Experience of Convergence," *Review of Politics* 68 (2006): 474–99, who argues for the similarity of Thoreau's *Walden* and Rousseau's *Reveries*. To treat these two texts as similar misunderstands their purposes and natures and indicates a deafness to the difference between heroic self and world remaking and the search for personal consolation. As I show, the more relevant (though still divergent) comparator to Rousseau's *Reveries* is Thoreau's later and more committedly naturalist writing, although the temporal boundary is not stark: he continued to work on *Walden* after the 1851 turn in "Walking," and there is much continuity in his preoccupations as well as a change in emphasis. See Sharon Cameron, *Writing Nature: Henry Thoreau's Journal* (New York: Oxford University Press, 1985), 25–26.

5. The editions and translations quoted in the text are as follows. For Jean-Jacques Rousseau: *On the Social Contract*, trans. Judith R. Masters, ed. Roger D. Masters (New York: St. Martin's Press, 1978); *The First and Second Discourses, Together with the Replies to Critics, and Essay on the Origin of Languages*, ed. and trans. Victor Gourevitch (New York: Harper and Row, 1986); *Reveries of the Solitary Walker*, trans. Peter France (Suffolk: Penguin, 1979); *The Confessions of Jean-Jacques Rousseau*, trans. J. M. Cohen (Harmondsworth: Penguin, 1985); *Emile*, trans. Allan Bloom (New York: Basic Books, 1979); and the French texts for the above as well as "Lettres Morales" (for which I provide my own translations) and "[Discours sur] L'économie politique" (quoted in French) in *Oeuvres complètes*, 4 vols., gen. ed. Bernard Gagnebin and Marcel Raymond (Paris: Gallimard, 1959–1969). For Henry David Thoreau, the authoritative Princeton University Press editions (not yet completed) are used to the extent possible: *Excursions*, ed. Joseph J. Moldenhauer (2007; including "Walking"); *A Week on the Concord and Merrimack Rivers*, ed. Carl F. Hovde et al. (1980); *Reform Papers*, ed. Wendell

Glick (1973; including "Resistance to Civil Government," "Life without Principle," "Slavery in Massachusetts," and "A Plea for Captain John Brown"); *Walden*, ed. J. Lyndon Shanley (1971); and *Journal*, vols. 1–8, gen. ed. John C. Broderick (1981–2002), volumes cited by Roman numerals. For the last, when the Princeton text has not yet been published, I cite *Journal*, 14 vols., ed. Bradford Torrey and Francis H. Allen (Salt Lake City: Peregrine Smith Books, 1984), volumes cited by Arabic numerals. For the late Thoreau manuscripts written in 1858–1861: *Wild Fruits*, ed. Bradley P. Dean (New York: W. W. Norton, 2000); and "The Dispersion of Seeds," in *Faith in a Seed: The Dispersion of Seeds, and Other Late Natural History Writings*, ed. Bradley P. Dean (Washington, DC: Island Press/Shearwater Books, 1993), 21–173. Rather than refer to the posthumous selections and publications of Thoreau's natural history essays "Wild Apples," "Autumnal Tints," and "Huckleberries," I refer to them in Dean's *Wild Fruits*. Likewise, rather than refer separately to the essay "The Succession of Forest Trees," published in 1860 in both the *New York Tribune* and *Transactions of the Middlesex Agricultural Society*, I cite the manuscript from which it was taken, "The Dispersion of Seeds." For information of publication and provenance, I found the following overview useful: Ronald Wesley Hoag, "Thoreau's Later Natural History Writings," in *The Cambridge Companion to Henry David Thoreau*, ed. Joel Myerson (Cambridge: Cambridge University Press, 1995), 152–70.

6. The discussion of Rousseau's later work refers to the *Confessions* (completed in 1770) and the *Reveries* (begun in 1776), but it excludes the uneven, repetitive, and vitriolic text *Rousseau, Judge of Jean-Jacques: Dialogues* (written in 1775).

7. As has often been noted, the *u* in Thomas More's coinage of *utopia* is a privative, so that *utopia* means "no place" and fits with the other puns More makes in *Utopia* (1516), such as the river Anyder, named by the Greek for "waterless." See Thomas More, *Utopia*, ed. George M. Logan and Robert M. Adams (Cambridge: Cambridge University Press, 1989), especially 5n9. However, it has become widely and traditionally interpreted as the ideal society (playing on the typographically and possibly aurally similar *eu*, or "good," in Greek). My coinages play on this traditional interpretation of *utopia*.

8. On the distinctiveness of this tradition, see Eric Nelson, *The Greek Tradition in Republican Thought* (Cambridge: Cambridge University Press, 2004).

9. Doyne Dawson, *Cities of the Gods: Communist Utopias in Greek Thought* (Oxford: Oxford University Press, 1992); these are the titles of chaps. 2–4. Coined by More in the sixteenth century, the term *utopia* was obviously not used by Plato or other ancients any more than by Rousseau or Thoreau, but I follow Dawson, among others, who adopt it in discussing ancient thought. See also Melissa Lane, "Plato, Popper, Strauss, and Utopianism: Open Secrets?" *History of Philosophy Quarterly* 16, no. 2 (1999): 119–42.

10. Rousseau, "Économie politique," *l'Encyclopédie*, vol. 5, November 1755; *Oeuvres complètes*, vol. 3, 241–78, quoting from 277. On Enlightenment conceptions of "economy," both domestic and political, see Christophe Salvat, "Les articles 'Œ\Économie' et leurs désignants," *Recherches sur Diderot et sur l'Encyclopédie* 40–41 (2006): 107–26.

11. Rousseau, *Emile*, 39; see also Shklar, *Men and Citizens*, 5.

12. The exclusion of money from the list of "necessaries" (*Walden*, 329) is noted by Richard J. Schneider, "*Walden*," in *Cambridge Companion to Thoreau*, 92–106, at 98.

13. An instructive discussion of *Walden*'s strategies of economy is provided by Brian Walker in chapter 2 of this volume, although I question below his claim that these strategies are best conceived as deliberately "democratic." See also Gilmore, *American Romanticism*.

14. All quotations are from Thoreau, *Walden*, 37.

15. For Rousseau, the self-sufficiency that matters is purely psychological; that others meet one's bodily needs is no objection so long as this does not introduce any psychological dependence (so the Wolmar estate is self-sufficient because it can rely on servants to grow produce and do all the necessary work). Compare Thoreau's sense of self-sufficiency, which is in no way compromised by the fact that Emerson owns the land on which the cabin at Walden Pond stands, or by the dinner parties he attends and laundry services he regularly obtains from friends and family in Concord; he simply decrees that ownership and menial assistance (not to mention familial and friendly companionship) are irrelevant to emotional and material independence. Contrast the ideal of Bronson Alcott's Fruitlands utopian society, which aspired to divide labor and leisure equally, although this noble aim was scuppered by a persisting sexual division of labor.

16. The conception of these diverse projects as parallel is articulated in the precursor of this chapter: Melissa Sharon Lane, "The Flight to Nature as a Mode of Social Critique: A Study of Rousseau and Thoreau" (AB diss., Harvard University, 1988), stored and cataloged in the Harvard Archives. A similar conception is articulated in terms of Rousseau's multiple "archetypes" in Joseph H. Lane Jr. and Rebecca R. Clark, "The Solitary Walker in the Political World: The Paradoxes of Rousseau and Deep Ecology," *Political Theory* 34 (2006): 62–94; George Armstrong Kelly, "A General Overview," in *The Cambridge Companion to Rousseau*, ed. Patrick Riley (Cambridge: Cambridge University Press, 2001), 8–56; and Shklar, *Men and Citizens*.

17. The claim that one must change society in order to create a new individual does not preclude the possibility of a few exceptional individuals arising, spontaneously, within the existing society. This is countenanced by Plato in his discussion of the "natural philosophers" in *Republic* VI (see especially 485a–487a) and by Rous-

seau in his celebration of his own natural goodness and innocence in *Confessions*, qualities that make possible his later *Reveries*. But for neither thinker is the need to transform society to make the vast majority of people happy and good negated by these few exceptions. On this issue in Plato, see Melissa Lane, "Virtue as the Love of Knowledge in Plato's *Symposium* and *Republic*," in *Maieusis: Essays in Ancient Philosophy in Honour of Myles Burnyeat*, ed. Dominic Scott (Oxford: Oxford University Press, 2007), 44–67.

18. I am grateful to John Thompson for the latter formulation.

19. Quoted in John L. Thomas, "Antislavery and Utopia," in *The Antislavery Vanguard: New Essays on the Abolitionists*, ed. Martin Duberman (Princeton, NJ: Princeton University Press, 1965), 240–69, at 263. On the Puritan "holy society" and its influence on Thoreau, as well as his distancing of himself from it, see Bollinger, *Thoreaus "World of Full and Fair Proportions*," 29–60, 236n4.

20. I am grateful to Gideon Mailer for this suggestion.

21. The first quotation is from Robert S. Fogarty, *All Things New: American Communes and Utopian Movements, 1860–1914* (Chicago: University of Chicago Press, 1990), 24; the riposte is from Krishan Kumar, *Utopia and Anti-Utopia in Modern Times* (Oxford: Basil Blackwell, 1987), 82, remarking that this makes Thoreau at once the epitome and the *reductio ad absurdum* of American utopianism in its traditional sense.

22. As John Patrick Diggins contends he is in "Thoreau, Marx, and the 'Riddle' of Alienation," *Social Research* 39 (1972): 571–98, at 581, quoted by Bob Pepperman Taylor, *America's Bachelor Uncle: Thoreau and the American Polity* (Lawrence: University Press of Kansas, 1996), 16. Taylor rejects the idea that Thoreau agrees with Emerson in viewing nature as "a refuge from society."

23. To put it another way, on this reading, Thoreau should not count as what Wilson Carey McWilliams, *The Idea of Fraternity in America* (Berkeley: University of California Press, 1973), calls a "fraternal" thinker. McWilliams, however, uses the idea of utopia in connection with fraternity rather oddly, speaking of "the old liberal utopia" as "a world of total private liberty" that is "blind to the nature of communion" yet seeks to "blot out separate identity" of each individual ego (620).

24. Thoreau, *Walden*, 6.

25. Ibid., 40; Thoreau, *A Week*, 345.

26. Thoreau, *Journal*, April 21, 1852, IV:479.

27. The phrase "the ultimate Pelagian" is from Howe, *Making the American Self*, 248. Michael Sonenscher called my attention to what one might consider Rousseau's Pelagianism, in the form of an advocacy (by the character Saint-Preux) of the views of the Jesuit Luis de Molina. Saint-Preux asserts that "God could do anything, except create other substances as perfect as his own and affording evil no purchase" (pt. V, letter 5, 595). Rousseau defends the theological content of his

novel (though playfully attributing some independence to Saint-Preux) in a 1761 exchange of letters with Chrétien-Guillaume de Lamoignon de Malesherbes, who was seeking changes to the work being published in Amsterdam to make it acceptable to the French authorities. See Rousseau to Malesherbes (March 10?, 1761), in *Correspondance complète de Jean Jacques Rousseau,* vol. 8, ed. R. A. Leigh (Geneva and Madison: Institut et musée Voltaire and University of Wisconsin Press, 1969), 237 (letter 1350), 119–20 (letter 1298), 132–33 (letter 1303, rejecting "cette mutilation" [132] as unnecessary for a "Roman genevois" to accept [133]). For background, see Victor Gourevitch, "The Religious Thought," in *Cambridge Companion to Rousseau,* 193–246.

28. Thoreau, *Walden,* 205. There is much of interest in Joan Burbick, *Thoreau's Alternative History: Changing Perspectives on Nature, Culture, and Language* (Philadelphia: University of Pennsylvania Press, 1987), which argues that Thoreau invents an "uncivil history" (1), based on nature, to counter American progressivist accounts. Burbick draws on both *Walden* and the later writings to make her case. Yet the invention of a new kind of natural history does not contradict the condemnation of history as an explanation of human nature or fate, which is such a significant a part of *Walden.* In contrast, Bernard Rosenthal, *City of Nature: Journeys to Nature in the Age of American Romanticism* (Newark: University of Delaware Press, 1980), takes the rejection of the external American narratives of history and religion, in favor of a mythic and religious private world that is within one's own power to perceive and construct, to be central to American romantics (including Thoreau).

29. Thoreau, *Journal,* November 5, 1855, 8:8.

30. Thoreau, *Walden,* 92.

31. Rousseau, *Emile,* 40.

32. Strikingly, he later calls the violent abolitionist John Brown "a man of Spartan habits" in "A Plea for Captain John Brown," in *Reform Papers,* 111–38, at 115.

33. Thoreau, "Life without Principle," in *Reform Papers,* 155–80, quoting from 173.

34. Rousseau, *On the Social Contract,* 46; the Thoreau epigraph is from "Life without Principle," 174.

35. Thoreau, "Slavery in Massachusetts," in *Reform Papers,* 91–110, quoting from 98.

36. Thoreau, *Journal,* August 1, 1841, I:315. On chastity, see *Walden,* 219–20.

37. *Walden's* purpose and rhetoric in these respects often differ even from the closely related journal passages, as discussed by Cameron, *Writing Nature,* 22–24.

38. Thoreau, *Walden,* 229–30 (ants), 144 (woodcutter), 155 (Herculean labor). The epic aspects of these encounters is noted by Schneider, "*Walden,*" 101.

39. Thoreau, *Walden,* 107. On Thoreau as prophet, see George Shulman's chapter 5 in this volume.

40. See Jacques Derrida, *Of Grammatology,* trans. Gayatri Chakravorty Spivak, corrected ed. (Baltimore: Johns Hopkins University Press, 1997).

41. Thoreau, *Walden,* 101.

42. Thoreau, *Journal,* March 26, 1842, I:393. It is interesting to note Thoreau's anxious concern with the circulation and sales of his books, described in Gilmore, *American Romanticism,* 9–10, 50–51. But in reading the shift in tone in the latter part of *Walden* as due to an attempt to avoid the commodification of his work (15), Gilmore misses its relationship to the naturalist turn described in this chapter.

43. Thoreau, *Journal,* August 8, 1852; V:289–90.

44. Thoreau, "Life without Principle," 155. In chapter 1, Rosenblum mischaracterizes this passage—in which Thoreau is describing his response to paid invitations to lecture—as "his insistence that *democracy* means 'giving a strong dose' of oneself" (emphasis added).

45. Evidencing his new devotion to naturalist studies, from mid-November 1850, Thoreau began to carefully date his notebooks, according to Dean, introduction to *Wild Fruits,* ix–xvii, at ix–x. Also demonstrating his late naturalist commitment is his active engagement with Darwin's writings both before and after the publication of *The Origin of Species* in 1859 (Darwin was well known from the publication of his *Beagle* journal in 1839). See Robert D. Richardson Jr., "Introduction: Thoreau's Broken Task," in *Faith in a Seed,* 3–17, at 11–14, and Laura Dassow Walls, *Seeing New Worlds: Henry David Thoreau and Nineteenth-Century Natural Science* (Madison: University of Wisconsin Press, 1995).

46. Rousseau, *Reveries,* 110; Thoreau, *Journal,* August 23, 1853, 5:395.

47. Rousseau, *Reveries,* 27.

48. Rousseau, *Confessions,* 17.

49. Rousseau, *Reveries,* 33, 34.

50. J. H. Lane and Clark, "Solitary Walker"; Lane, "Reveries."

51. Rousseau, *Reveries,* 153–54.

52. Ibid., 90.

53. Ibid., 154.

54. Ibid., 89, 88.

55. Jean Starobinski, *Jean-Jacques Rousseau: Transparency and Obstruction,* trans. Arthur Goldhammer (Chicago: University of Chicago Press, 1988), 361, emphasis in original; first published as *Jean-Jacques Rousseau: La transparence et l'obstacle* (Paris: Gallimard, 1971).

56. Thoreau, *Journal,* September 7, 1851, IV:54. The importance of this passage is identified and well explained in Dean, introduction to *Wild Fruit,* xi–xii.

57. Emerson's "Nature" was published in 1836, during Thoreau's senior year at Harvard, and deeply influenced the younger man.

58. The Humboldtian and Darwinian connections are discussed extensively

in Walls, *Seeing New Worlds*. Contrasting Thoreau with the "rational holism" of Emerson and Coleridge, she identifies the younger man as an "empirical holist," usefully noting similar terms coined to identify this complex stance in Thoreau by Robert Richardson ("practical transcendentalism"), in Humboldt by Margarita Bowen ("thinking empiricism"), and in Darwin by Gillian Beer ("romantic materialism") (133–34).

59. The Abbé (Louis-Bertrand) Castel published a pamphlet attacking the "Second Discourse" titled "L'homme moral oppose à l'homme physique de M. R°°°" in Toulouse in February 1756, reprinted in *Collection complete des oeuvres de J.-J. Rousseau, citoyen de Genève*, ed. P. Moultou and P.-A. du Peyrou (Geneva: Société Typographique, 1782). He argues, for example, that "la societé est le fondement de tout; elle est naturelle et de la première nature" (221). I owe my knowledge of Castel to Michael Sonenscher. See also the discussion of Castel in John T. Scott, "The Theodicy of the Second Discourse: The 'Pure State of Nature' and Rousseau's Political Thought," *American Political Science Review* 86, no. 3 (1992): 696–711, at 699–700.

60. Rousseau, *Reveries*, 108, 114.

61. The letters are quoted in my translation from *Oeuvres complètes*, vol. IV; see Second Letter, IV:1087, and Third Letter, IV:1094.

62. Michel de Montaigne, "Of the Education of Children," in *The Complete Works of Montaigne*, trans. Donald M. Frame (London: Hamish Hamilton, 1958), 106–31, at 116.

63. "Nous ne savons rien, chère Sophie, nous ne voyons rien; nous sommes une troupe d'aveugles, jettés à l'aventure dans ce vaste univers" (Third Letter, IV:1092). "Nous n'avons nulle notion certaine de rien" (Third Letter, IV:1096).

64. "Ils sont insuffisans, ils nous trompent" (Third Letter, IV:1093).

65. Montaigne, "Apology for Raymond Sebond," in *Complete Works*, 318–457, at 333; Rousseau, *Reveries*, 112.

66. Rousseau, *Reveries*, 116.

67. I see no basis for Rosenblum's claim in chapter 1 that this is actually a "skeptical" passage in which Thoreau is "confident that the search for a 'Realometer' will be disappointed."

68. Thoreau, *Walden*, 98, 330.

69. Ibid., 264.

70. Ibid.

71. Ibid., 171.

72. Ibid., 11.

73. Taylor, *America's Bachelor Uncle*, 15–34, especially 16–17, shows that this preoccupation already strongly shapes *A Week*, written in the course of a decade

following the canoe trip in 1839 and published in 1849; see also Brian Walker, "Thoreau on Democratic Cultivation," *Political Theory* 29 (2001): 155–89, at 161.

74. Thoreau, *Journal*, March 4, 1852, IV:375–76.

75. See Shulman's chapter 5 of this volume.

76. Thoreau, *Journal*, undated (transcribed in 1842), I:406. Lawrence Buell, "Thoreau and the Natural Environment," in *Cambridge Companion to Thoreau*, 171–93, at 182, discusses Thoreau's interest in what the literature has termed "landscape aesthetics," as linked to the work of William Gilpin and John Ruskin.

77. Thoreau, "Walking," 185–222, quoting from 191–92.

78. Thoreau, *Journal*, April 2, 1852, IV:420.

79. Thoreau, *Faith in a Seed*, 151.

80. Both quotations are from *Wild Fruits*, 54. I am grateful to Jack Turner for discussion of the 1834 Declaration.

81. Thoreau, *Journal*, August 6, 1858, 11:78–79; see also Mariotti's chapter 15 in this volume.

82. Thoreau, *Wild Fruits*, 235. In *Walden*, a few sentences at the beginning of the chapter "The Ponds" anticipate this concern with huckleberrying and the free and independent livelihood it affords, but Thoreau does not develop its political significance.

83. Thoreau, *Wild Fruits*, 52; Rousseau, *Reveries*, 89.

84. Thoreau, *Wild Fruits*, 52.

85. Thoreau, *Journal*, October 4, 1851, IV:116.

86. Thoreau, "Walking," 185.

87. These complexities are noted, but Thoreau's appropriation for environmentalism (not deep ecology) is still defended, in Buell, "Thoreau and the Natural Environment." Contrast Rosenthal, *City of Nature*, 220, who is puzzled by "the same man equating the city with the swamp [in a letter to Harrison Blake dated August 9, 1850], who in 'Walking' would proclaim the much-quoted phrase, 'in Wildness is the preservation of the World.'"

88. Thoreau, "Life without Principle," 178 (emphasis in original).

89. Thoreau, "Resistance to Civil Government," in *Reform Papers*, 63–90, quoting from 89–90.

90. Ibid., 86–87.

91. Thoreau, *Wild Fruits*, 238.

92. Walls, *Seeing New Worlds*, 249, calls this hybridity, making Thoreau into a sort of postmodern, or as she puts it, "'nonmodern.'" Her account risks diminishing his focus on perspective, on subordinating and settling the social and political in contraposition to the greater unity of nature. But this caveat should not blind us to her stunning description of Thoreau's late attitude as a surveyor, tracing "an

interactive field of possibilities, regeneration even of land laid waste, succession rather than apocalypse, in a land constituted by history and preparing in the present the mold—not the determinate stamp, but the yeasty wild compost—for its own future. Indeed, if 'the preservation of the World' is in the Wild, it is in the wild seen not as a demarcated zone but as a sustainable process" (252).

93. Hannah Arendt, "Civil Disobedience," in *Crises of the Republic* (Harmondsworth: Penguin, 1973), 43–82, quoting from 50.

94. See especially George Kateb, "Democratic Individuality and the Claims of Politics," in *The Inner Ocean: Individualism and Democratic Culture* (Ithaca, NY: Cornell University Press, 1992), 77–105; Rosenblum, *Another Liberalism* and chapter 1 of this volume. Their trajectories on this question seem to have crossed. Kateb has become more skeptical of Thoreau's political-democratic commitments in his latest work, "Wildness and Conscience: Thoreau and Emerson," in *Patriotism and Other Mistakes* (New Haven, CT: Yale University Press, 2006), 245–71, where he avers that, for Thoreau and Emerson, "anarchy is their highest hope" (251) and speaks of their "overall political skepticism" (253). In contrast, Rosenblum's early insistence on a "tension" between Thoreau's "radical individualism" as a "social conscience in a democracy" and his "romantic soul" (in "Thoreau's Militant Conscience," *Political Theory* 9, no. 1 [1981]: 81–110, at 83) has given way to her confident assertion of his "democratic individualism" in her chapter in this volume. For Kateb, the democratic aspects of Emerson, Thoreau, and Whitman include their attack on social and institutional conventions and their insistence on limited government—even, in Thoreau's drastic aspiration, to a government that does as little as possible: "That government is best which governs not at all" ("Resistance to Civil Government," 63). Yet it is not clear why either of these should necessarily be democratic in character: one of the greatest attacks on convention ever made was launched by Plato, who was no democrat, while the most eloquent insistence on limited government in recent decades has been F. A. von Hayek, only instrumentally and contingently a democrat. Admittedly, as Kateb observes, even Whitman ultimately sees democracy as instrumental to the project of developing the soul: "It is not that democracy is of exhaustive account, in itself. Perhaps, indeed, it is (like Nature) of no account in itself. It is that . . . it is the best, perhaps the only, fit and full means, formulater, general caller-forth, trainer for the million . . . for immortal souls" (*Inner Ocean*, 85, quoting Whitman, *Democratic Vistas*). Yet for Whitman, democracy is constitutive as a means to this end, as a form of relationship—the relationship of political participation, and the more fundamental relationship of equality and nonservility on which participation is grounded. For Thoreau, it is not the fact of equality but its uses that matter; he is indifferent to positionality, to the agon of admiration and disdain in which democratic citizens struggle with one another for esteem (an agon stretching back to the competitive roots of Athenian democracy). Likewise, the subtle lineaments of the "inhibitions" of democracy that

Rosenblum traces in Thoreau do not establish a democratic purpose at the heart of his thought.

95. See Mariotti's chapter 15 in this volume.

96. Shulman's argument hinges on Thoreau's claim in "Resistance to Civil Government" that "a corporation of conscientious men is a corporation *with* a conscience." He does not recognize that Thoreau seems to be referring to a remark attributed to Edward, first Baron Thurlow and Lord Chancellor of England (1731–1806): "Did you ever expect a corporation to have a conscience, when it has no soul to be damned, and no body to be kicked?" The story has been widely quoted; see John C. Coffee Jr., "'No Soul to Damn: No Body to Kick': An Unscandalized Inquiry into the Problem of Corporate Punishment," *Michigan Law Review* 79, no. 3 (1981): 386–459, at 386n1. Thurlow's challenge has been taken up by modern organizational theorists to argue that conscience (moral reasoning and action) can emerge from within the organization itself. Thoreau's riposte to Thurlow's challenge, in contrast, is to insist that the conscience of an individual or individuals within the group is enough. Whereas modern proponents of organizational ethics look to ethics as an emergent property of the whole, Thoreau sees it as a function of the individual. So Shulman's slight misquotation matters: he speaks of Thoreau's aim being to create "corporations of conscientious men," as if this were set out by Thoreau as a goal; in fact, Thoreau speaks in the singular of "a corporation of honest men" not creating but merely analyzing the condition of a corporation (an organized body) to point out that its conscience must derive from the consciences of the individuals within it.

97. That Thoreau is aware of such advice books does not establish that his relationship to them is not satirical. One might argue that he rejects advice that would entrench one in social conformity and success in favor of a heroic standard of individual self-development.

98. Jenco must be right when she observes that "Thoreau's criticisms are phrased in terms familiar to a democratic conception of government, but this does not mean he endorses the ideals of the democratic project," to show that the latter requires further argument. However, her own case fails to take the measure of Thoreau's claim in "Resistance to Civil Government" (64) to be speaking "practically and as a citizen." That claim may be better indexed to the occasion and the provocation for that specific work.

99. Nancy L. Rosenblum, introduction to *Thoreau: Political Writings* (Cambridge: Cambridge University Press, 1996), vii–xxxi.

100. Thoreau, *Walden,* 56, 70.

101. At proof stage, I saw Zev Trachtenberg, "The Exile and the Moss-trooper: Rousseau and Thoreau on Walking in Nature," in *The Nature of Rousseau's Rêveries: Physical, Human, Aesthetic,* ed. John C. O'Neal (Oxford: Voltaire Foundation, 2008), 209–22, with which I broadly agree.

# CHAPTER 14

# Thoreau, Gandhi, and Comparative Political Thought

*Anthony J. Parel*

THOREAU PLAYED A significant role in Mahatma Gandhi's intellectual life from 1907 to about 1920. He was one of five who had a lasting impact on Gandhi. Writing to a disciple in 1931, Gandhi stated: "'Hero' means one worthy of reverence, a god, so to say. In the political field, Gokhale [1866–1915] holds that place for me. The persons who have influenced my life, as whole and in a general way, are Tolstoy [1828–1910], Ruskin [1819–1900], Thoreau [1817–1862] and Rajchandbhai [1868–1901]."[1] He first read Thoreau in 1907 in South Africa, when an unidentified friend sent him a copy of "The Duty of Civil Disobedience."[2] He found the essay "to be so convincing and truthful" that he began to read more of Thoreau. His early readings included *Walden* and Henry S. Salt's biography of Thoreau.[3] In September 1907 Gandhi published a paraphrase of "The Duty of Civil Disobedience" in a two-part series in his Durban weekly newspaper, *Indian Opinion;* it was later published as a pamphlet.[4] Thoreau was, for him, the model par excellence for the early practitioners of satyagraha. He exhorted his followers to resist unjust laws to the last and be "so many Thoreaus in miniature."[5] In particular, they were to imitate his sincerity and sense of commitment. "The great Thoreau said that one sincere man is more than a hundred thousand insincere men. We want to know how many of us are sincere."[6] Likewise, "The great Thoreau has said that a worthy cause should not be deemed lost, that it is bound to triumph, so long as there is at least one sincere man to fight for it."[7]

In November 1907 Gandhi put Thoreau on the reading list he had prepared to guide those entering an essay competition on the topic "The Ethics of Passive Resistance." "It [the essay] should contain an examination of Thoreau's classic, 'The Duty of Civil Disobedience,' Tolstoy's works—more especially *The Kingdom of Heaven Is within You*—and it should give Biblical and other religious authorities and illustrations and also the application of the *Apology of Socrates* to the question. The essay should give illustrations from modern history in support of the doctrine."[8] In 1908, during his incarceration in South Africa, Gandhi read "the essays of the great Thoreau," and he saw his own imprisonment as a verification of Thoreau's dictum that in a tyrannical state, jail is the only place for a just man.[9]

In March 1910 he paid Thoreau a high compliment by mentioning him in the preface to the English translation of *Hind Swaraj,* his fundamental work. "Whilst the views expressed in *Hind Swaraj* are held by me, I have but endeavored humbly to follow Tolstoy, Ruskin, Thoreau, Emerson and other writers, besides the masters of Indian philosophy."[10] In addition, two of Thoreau's works, "The Duty of Civil Disobedience" and "Life without Principle," were included in the famous appendix I of *Hind Swaraj.* It contained a list of twenty works—six by Tolstoy, two by Ruskin, and one each by Plato and Mazzini. The readers of *Hind Swaraj* were advised to study these twenty works if they wanted to gain a deeper understanding of its philosophy. Ever since, Thoreau has remained a permanent part of the broader field of Gandhi studies. In 1911 Gandhi urged Maganlal Gandhi, his deputy at Phoenix Ashram near Durban, to read Salt's biography of Thoreau.[11] He further urged him "to copy out a sentence from Thoreau occasionally" and publish it in *Indian Opinion.*[12]

In 1915, the year Gandhi returned to India for good, he took Thoreau with him. Throughout 1916, we are told, "The Duty of Civil Disobedience" was read every evening in Sabarmati Ashram in Ahmedabad.[13] By 1919 "The Duty of Civil Disobedience" was on a new reading list he had prepared for his followers in India—a list that included works by Plato (*The Apology*), Ruskin, and Tolstoy as well. However, Thoreau was singled out for special treatment: in March 1919 Gandhi published *Satyagraha Leaflet No. 1,* entitled "Extracts from 'The Duty of Civil Disobedience,' by Henry Thoreau, Schoolmaster of Massachusetts, dated 1849."[14] All those involved in the new Gandhian movement in India were expected to read this Thoreau digest—about one-quarter of the original text.

Although his interest in Thoreau was focused on "The Duty of Civil Disobedience," it was not limited to it. As noted earlier, "Life without Principle" was honored by its inclusion among the twenty works in appendix I of *Hind Swaraj*. And Thoreau's essay "Walking" came up for interesting comments in some of his other writings.

In this chapter I give a brief account of Gandhi's interest in these three writings, followed by an assessment of Thoreau's impact on his thought. I conclude with comments on the broader implications of the Gandhi-Thoreau encounter for political philosophy in general and comparative political philosophy in particular.

## "Walking"

According to Robert Richardson, "Walking" is Thoreau's "central essay," just as *Walden* is his "central book."[15] Walking, for Thoreau, is more than just a physical activity. It is a means of experiencing "wildness" or "absolute freedom," contrasted with "freedom and culture merely civil." The opening lines of the essay make this point clear: "I wish to speak a word for Nature, for absolute freedom and wildness, as contrasted with a freedom and culture merely civil—to regard man as an inhabitant, or part and parcel of Nature, rather than member of society."[16] Man the walker, not the rider, is the authentic representative of Thoreauvian humanity. The walker constitutes "the fourth estate, outside of the Church and State and People."[17] It is only when we get away from the institutions of society and retreat into our inner self that we experience true freedom. Not only are absolute freedom and civil freedom put in oppositional terms, but the importance of the political seems to be downgraded. Politics, he remarks, is "but as the cigar smoke of a man."[18] "Life consists with wildness. The most alive is the wildest."[19] And "all good things are wild and free."[20] There is something "servile," he writes, "in seeking after a law which we may obey." Although there is no harm in *studying* such laws, "a successful life knows no law." In support of this view, he invokes the Advaita doctrine of absolute freedom as treated in the *Vishnu Purana:* "That is active duty . . . which is not for our bondage; that is knowledge which is for our liberation: all other duty is good only unto weariness; all other knowledge is only cleverness of an artist."[21]

Although Gandhi found this essay "highly thought-provoking,"[22] on closer inspection, it appears he had a different conception of what walking means. He was, of course, a famous walker—as demonstrated by the

241-mile Salt March of 1930. His walking staff has become as integral to his public image as his loincloth. First of all, he looked on walking as a means of maintaining physical health: walking is, as he put it, "the prince of exercises."[23] He believed there existed a link between the habit of taking long walks and that of producing excellent writing. He invoked Thoreau's authority to support his belief: "According to him the writings of one who refuses to leave his house on the excuse of lack of time and who undertakes no physical activity, are bound to be anemic like himself. Speaking of his own experience, he says that when he wrote his best books he was doing his longest walking. He thought nothing of walking four or five hours at a stretch."[24] Though walking is "the best exercise," to take advantage of it, one has to walk "six miles at a stretch in the morning and again in the evening. The walking should be done briskly, at a speed of four miles an hour. Thoreau used to walk for eight hours daily when he wrote his best book."[25] As late as 1936, Gandhi was reminding friends of Thoreau and his walks: "To appreciate all the advantages of walking you must read Thoreau."[26]

Second, Gandhi attached a religious symbolism to walking, as in pilgrimages or in the tours of itinerant religious preachers. For him, walking was a means of spiritual exercise too, of communicating and communing with people. His famous village tours to visit the poor and the oppressed were deliberately done on foot as a "spiritual act."[27] They had, he said, "the beauty and the necessity of pilgrimages." "People's hearts cannot be touched by a mad rush through space. They can be by quiet, personal, intimate contact with them."[28] By taking this view of walking, he was but following the example of kindred spirits "in all climes and ages" who had experienced "the joy and beauty of traveling on foot." "All the great reformers of the world who have from time to time effected religious revolutions have eschewed the use of vehicles and walked thousands of miles for delivering their mission. Yet, by the intensity of their faith and the strength of their realization, they were able to achieve what we, in our aeroplane age, with all the gee-gaws at our command, could hardly aspire to. Not mad rush, but unperturbed calmness brings wisdom."[29] It is interesting to note that Gandhi also listed Thomas F. Taylor's *Fallacy of Speed* (1909) in the appendix to *Hind Swaraj*. Taylor questioned the wisdom of the modern tendency to regard faster as better. Like Thoreau and Gandhi, he believed that modern speed militated against leisure in considerable sections of modern communities.[30]

## "Life without Principle"

Several critics have commented on the important place this essay occupies
in the Thoreau corpus. According to William Cain, it contains "a distilled
statement" of Thoreau's beliefs.[31] Richardson calls it "the tactical polemical
obverse of *Walden*": whereas the latter tells us what to live for, this essay
tells us what not to live for. It is "Thoreau's most puritanical piece," without
being Calvinistic; it is an attack against "both Protestant ethic and the spirit
of capitalism." Considered by many to be "Thoreau's best, most concentrated statement on his major message," it is the equivalent of Emerson's
"Self-Reliance."[32] Len Gougeon sees "Life without Principle" as an attack
on America's "restless materialism" and its impact on American culture.[33]

Gandhi's interest in this work arose from his broader interest in the
question of the impact of industrial capitalism on society in general and
India in particular. Of the twenty works in appendix I of *Hind Swaraj* recommended for further reading, more than half were on nineteenth-century
industrial capitalism; six were on the social impact of the Industrial Revolution on Great Britain, and two on the impact of colonial capitalism on
India.[34] "Life without Principle" belongs to this genre of books, and it was
the sole entry on the impact of nineteenth-century capitalism on the United
States. It was Gandhi's hope that Indians who were anxious to embark on
the path of economic development would learn from the experiences of
Great Britain and the United States.

"Life without Principle," Gandhi implied, contained a timely warning
for Indians. Nineteenth-century business capitalism in the United States
had a questionable impact on American culture, politics, and journalism.
It was promoting a philosophy of life that seemed to lack a transcendent
spiritual principle. "Let us consider the way in which we spend our lives,"
the essay begins. "This world is a place of business. What an infinite bustle!
. . . There is no Sabbath. . . . It is nothing but work, work, work." Nothing
is more opposed to poetry, philosophy, and life itself, moans Thoreau, than
this "incessant business."[35] It has made moneymaking the sole object of
labor, depriving it of any transcending moral end. And "the ways of making
money today almost without exception lead downwards." Even the intellectuals ("writers and lecturers") are no exception: they succumb to the lure
of fame and popularity.[36] The California gold rush is cited as symptomatic

of modern economic life. The greatest "disgrace on mankind," it has the support not only of merchants but also of "philosophers and prophets, so called." It turns making a living into something akin to gambling or living by luck. "And it is called enterprise!"[37]

Business culture is distorting the meaning of freedom itself, for it sees freedom merely in political terms—as freedom from colonial rule. America escaped colonial rule only to come under the rule of "an economical and moral tyrant"—business. To be "born free," warns Thoreau, is not the same as "living free." Political freedom, in its full sense, should mean "moral freedom," that is, "the freedom to be free."[38] Instead of leading to full freedom, political freedom has led to the new economic slavery to business.

At the root of the all-consuming devotion to trade, commerce, manufacture, and agriculture is the marginalization of the soul. The soul does not get its due share in the new culture. "There is a part of us which is not represented," Thoreau complains. "It is taxation without representation."[39] Because of this, life in the world of business culture lacks a solid foundation. Though we select granite stones for the foundations of our dwellings, "we do not ourselves rest on an underpinning of granitic truth."[40] We do not "worship truth, but the reflection of truth."[41] The outcome of all this is that there is no inwardness to life. As our inward life fails, our dependence on trivialities increases in the same proportion. Conversation degenerates into gossip. We have no time to listen ourselves.[42] We are industrious, yet we do not spend our time well.[43]

One of the worst effects of modern business culture has been on journalism. Newspapers reflect the values of the business world. Thoreau finds it "too much to read one newspaper per week." The news the papers print is not news but "the stalest repetition." The newspapers trivialize life issues. The stratum of human experience with which they are concerned is thinner than the paper on which the news is printed.[44] The "facts" they print appear to float in the atmosphere, "insignificant as the sporules of fungi," and impinge only on "the surface of our minds."[45] They threaten "the mind's chastity."[46]

The impact of modern business culture on politics is perhaps greatest. Politics lacks "a high and earnest purpose." It is interested more in potatoes than in culture. Though it ought to be a part of "the vital functions of human society," in a culture dominated by business, it produces a sort of social dyspepsia. It is, "as it were, the grizzard of society, full of grit and gravel, and the two political parties are its opposite halves. . . . Not only individuals, but states, have thus confirmed dyspepsia."[47]

Although the tone of "Life without Principle" is negative, its overall aim is positive—to appeal to the people to find a cure for the malaise spreading through American culture. The cure consists in restoring the balance between material interests and spiritual aspirations. This calls for an inner awareness of the nature of the malady, a psychological and spiritual self-mobilization. If we have "desecrated ourselves," it is time that we "re-consecrate ourselves." "Read not the Times, read the Eternities." We have to show that we are not all husk and shell but have "tender and living kernel to us."[48]

The question arises as to why Gandhi would recommend this essay to the readers of *Hind Swaraj*. The answer is that the issues it raises were of interest not only to Americans but also to Indians and to people everywhere who were concerned with the harmful consequences of the domination of modern life by business culture. Thoreau was correct in thinking that this dominance had upset the balance between the interests of the body and those of the soul, between the secular and the spiritual. These ideas resonated with Gandhi, for he too was trying to restore the right balance between *artha* (material interests of power and wealth) and *moksha* (a transcending spirituality) in India. In the past, India had ascribed undue importance to spirituality to the point of neglecting the economic well-being of the people. One of Gandhi's life missions was to restore the correct balance between the material and spiritual goals of life. He was afraid, however, that Indians were in danger of adopting uncritically the nineteenth-century American model. For those who were tempted, "Life without Principle" had a salutary warning. Gandhi's point was not that India should not embark on economic reconstruction. It was that India should do so without losing its balance. Economic development should not lead to a divorce between the secular and the spiritual.

In this respect, Gandhi's own 1916 lecture on the relationship of economic development to spiritual development may be profitably read as a companion piece to "Life without Principle." In that lecture, he raises the question of whether spiritual progress increases in the same proportion as economic progress.[49] The answer is that it does not. Economic progress and spiritual progress follow different sets of rules. That is why economic progress does not automatically produce spiritual progress. He makes his point by a masterly analysis of the parable of the rich young man in Mark 10:17–31. This young man, though very rich, is spiritually vacuous. An inner emptiness exists despite his wealth—wealth justly acquired, as the parable is careful to point out. Jesus' advice to the young man is that if he is serious about making spiritual progress, he has to make a serious adjustment in his life—which the young man is unwilling to do. Because he cannot make the required change, he goes away grieved. Gandhi's main point is that all societies that embark on economic development should integrate economic progress with the requirements of spiritual development.

There was no doubt in Gandhi's mind that India needed economic and political development. The question, however, was whether it could be achieved without sacrificing spiritual development. The examples of nineteenth-century Great Britain and the United States were not reassuring. As he states in *Hind Swaraj,* "It would [be] a folly to assume that an Indian Rockefeller would be better than the American Rockefeller."[50] One way to avoid such folly is to learn from essays such as "Life without Principle."

## "The Duty of Civil Disobedience"

This essay made a lasting impact on Gandhi. The paraphrase of 1907 and *Satyagraha Pamphlet No. 1* of 1919 help us determine what he found in it that was relevant to his purpose. What interested him most was its political theory, particularly the theory of the moral basis of the state. Although the paraphrase and the pamphlet make no mention of the Mexican War, those writings are fully appreciative of the context of the anti-slavery movement in the United States. "Historians say," the opening page of the paraphrase begins, "that the chief cause of the abolition of slavery in America was Thoreau's imprisonment and the publication by him of the above mentioned book after his release. Both his example and writings are at present exactly applicable to the Indians in the Transvaal."[51]

Four ideas from this essay greatly impressed Gandhi. The first concerned the moral basis of government and the state. To be strictly just, government must have the sanction of the governed. This idea found its way into the famous "Declaration of Independence" that Gandhi wrote in 1930 to launch the radical phase of the Indian nationalist movement. Indians had a right to choose their own government, and if any government deprived them of that right, they had the right "to alter or abolish it."[52]

The second idea concerned the relationship of the individual to the state. In some respects, the individual was subject to the power of the state, but in some other respects, he or she was independent of it. Gandhi agreed with Thoreau that there would never be a truly free and enlightened state until the state recognized the individual as a higher and independent power from which all its own power and authority were derived and treated him or her accordingly.[53] Possessing "a higher and independent power," the citizen has the right and the duty to resist the state when it acts unjustly.[54]

The role of conscience further strengthens the right to resist the unjust state. Conscience makes us "men" first and subjects afterward. Actions arising from principles of this sort change things and relations: they are equivalent to peaceful revolution. A decision based on one's conscience has priority over a decision based on the will of the majority. It is "a great error" to believe that justice prevails in a country in which "everything is decided by a majority vote." It is a "mere superstition" to believe that "what is done by the multitude is bound to be right." Conscience, not majorities, should decide what is right and wrong. "Those who obey their sense of justice while holding the reins of government are always found to be in conflict with the state."[55]

The term Gandhi often uses for conscience is *inner voice.* Inner voice, according to him, is the voice of truth. We have access to the voice of truth only through relative truth—truth as we see it and as conscience approves it. It is therefore necessary to train ourselves to discern what is true in relative truth, lest we fell into the error of moral subjectivism. The study of moral philosophy, the acquisition of self-discipline, and consultation with persons of moral probity and experience are necessary to acquire the habit of correct moral discernment. "Definite rules have been laid down to help us realize Truth, and we can know Truth only by following them. Hence, just as we cannot know geometry without studying it, so also it is not pos- sible for anybody to hear the inner voice without the necessary effort and training. Hence, according to my definition, a murderer cannot cite inner voice in defense of his act."[56]

The third idea concerned the need to limit government's power over the citizen. "That government is best which governs least" is the famous motto of Thoreau that Gandhi adopted as his own. The state is, of course, a necessary institution, but there are things that citizens, both individually and in small groups, can achieve without the interference of the state. The following is Gandhi's commentary on Thoreau's motto: "This means that when people come into possession of political power, the interference with the freedom of the people is reduced to a minimum. In other words, a nation that runs its affairs smoothly and effectively without much State interference is truly democratic. Where such a condition is absent, the form of government is democratic in name [only]."[57]

The fourth idea was that the duty to disobey an unjust law requires prompt, concrete action. It is true that a good constitutional state normally provides means of self-correction. Unfortunately, these means (such as voting) are slow and cumbersome. "When the majority shall at length vote for the abolition of slavery, it will be because there is but little slavery left to be abolished."[58] Mere profession of opposition to injustice is not enough; to be credible, it must be followed by action. "There are thousands who in opinion are opposed to slavery, but act contrary to their view." They sit down "with their hands in their pockets and say that they know not what to do, and do nothing. At the most they give lectures and send petitions. There are nine hundred and ninety nine persons who profess virtue to one virtuous man. Yet he who acts virtuously, though he be the only one, is of far greater worth than those who only profess it."[59] Given this, one should take immediate action and resist unjust laws even if the majority does not join, and even if the action costs dearly in terms of personal suffering, such as imprisonment and loss of income and property. "If there is only one man in Massachusetts who is opposed to slavery, he should effectually withdraw his support from the government, both in person and property, without waiting till there is majority on his side. For, he is not alone. God is ever on his side. Any man more right than his neighbors constitutes a majority of one already."[60] If only one person in Massachusetts refuses to pay taxes in order to oppose slavery and is locked up in jail for it, "it would be the abolition of slavery in America. What is once well done is done for ever." Thoreau's famous dictum that, under a government that imprisons any person unjustly, "the true place for a just man is also a prison"[61] went straight to Gandhi's heart. Suffering in vindication of the rights of conscience and for the sake of justice was thought to have special moral efficacy. Moreover, he linked the voluntary acceptance of his jail term with nonviolence and the ascetic ideal of self-suffering. "Thoreau in his immortal essay shows that civil disobedience, not violence is the true remedy. In civil disobedience, the resister suffers the consequences of disobedience. This was what Daniel did when he disobeyed the law of the Medes and Persians. That is what John Bunyan did and that is what the *raiyats* [peasants] have done in India from time immemorial. It is the law of our being. Violence is the law of the beast in us. Self-suffering, i.e., civil resistance, is the law of the man in us. It is rarely that the occasion for civil resistance arises in a well-ordered State."[62]

Gandhi readily endorsed the theory that the state's authority over the life, liberty, and property of its citizens is never absolute or unconditional. It is conditional on the state's behavior being just. And the state's behavior is never just when it imprisons a just citizen who justly disobeys specific laws. A corollary to this theory is that the practice of civil disobedience requires an attitude of detachment from the comforts associated with civic life, liberty, and property. A civil disobedient should be prepared to sacrifice these benefits for the sake of justice and to accept gladly the discomforts of prison and the loss of friends, income, and property.

Gandhi was an experienced practitioner of civil disobedience. Between 1908 and 1942 he was imprisoned ten times for a total of about five years and ten months. He found in Thoreau's dictum much solace and encouragement. By going to jail, he wrote, Thoreau had "sanctified" his essay. It was written "for all time," and its "incisive logic unanswerable."[63] Again, "As Thoreau has said, loss of liberty, wealth and intense suffering were the only course of honorable conduct under an unjust government."[64] "I think with Thoreau that the citizen who resists the evil government must ignore property rights."[65] "Thoreau told the truth when he said that possession of riches under an evil government was a sin and poverty was a virtue."[66] "Let them remember Thoreau's immortal words that possession is a vice and poverty a virtue in a tyrannical State."[67]

## The Extent of Thoreau's Impact

Although there is universal agreement on the fact of Thoreau's impact on Gandhi's political thought, there is some difference of opinion about its actual extent. Gandhi himself made three points on this matter. The first is that he started his movement in South Africa a year before he read Thoreau. Therefore, Thoreau did not contribute to its genesis. Second, there is a conceptual difference between civil disobedience and satyagraha. Third, Thoreau's actual role was to confirm and morally support what Gandhi had already started in South Africa.

Writing to a friend in 1935, Gandhi stated the following: "The statement that I had derived my idea of civil disobedience from the writings of Thoreau is wrong. The resistance to authority in South Africa was well advanced before I got the essay of Thoreau on civil disobedience. But the movement was then known as passive resistance. As it was incomplete I had coined the word *satyagraha* for the Gujarati readers. When I saw the title of Thoreau's great essay, I began the use of this phrase to explain our struggle to English readers. But I found that even civil disobedience failed to convey the full meaning of the struggle. I therefore adopted the phrase civil resistance. Non-violence was always an integral part of our struggle."[68]

As for the origin of the concept of satyagraha, the following is Gandhi's account. In 1906, when the resistance movement against racist legislation in South Africa began, he did not know what to call the movement. "None of us knew what name to give our movement. I then used the term 'passive resistance' in describing it. I did not quite understand the implications of 'passive resistance,' as I called it. I only knew that some new principle had come into being. As the struggle advanced, the phrase 'passive resistance' gave rise to confusion and it appeared shameful to permit this great struggle to be known only by an English name."[69] He therefore invited the readers of *Indian Opinion* to make suggestions. One suggestion was to call it the *sadagraha* movement. *Sad* in Gujarati means "a good cause," and *agraha*, "firmness." Thus, *sadagraha* means "firmness in a good cause." Gandhi was not fully satisfied with this new term either. He changed *sadagraha* to *satyagraha*. *Satya* in Gujarati means "truth," so *satyagraha* means "firmness in holding on to truth." From January 1908 onward, he called his movement *satyagraha* and gave up the phrase *passive resistance.*[70]

The focus of Gandhi's movement, then, was on truth. As he put it, "Civil disobedience is disobedience to untruth, and it becomes 'civil' if it is 'truthful' in its manner."[71] However, at different periods of its development, the Gandhian movement had used four different terms to describe itself—satyagraha, passive resistance, civil disobedience, and noncooperation. This caused confusion in the minds of many observers, so to remedy this, Gandhi wrote an article for *Young India* in 1921, which I reproduce here despite its length:

> Satyagraha . . . is literally holding on to Truth and it means, therefore, Truth-force. Truth is soul or spirit. It is, therefore, known as soul-force. It excludes the use of violence, because man is not capable of knowing the absolute truth and, therefore, is not competent to punish. The word was coined in South Africa to distinguish the non-violent resistance of the Indians of South Africa from the cotemporary "passive resistance" of the suffragettes and others. It is not conceived as a weapon of the weak.
>
> Passive resistance is used in the orthodox English sense and covers the suffragette movement as well as the resistance of the nonconformists. Passive resistance has been conceived and is regarded as a weapon of the weak. Whilst it avoids violence, being not open to the weak, it does not exclude its use if, in the opinion of a passive resister, the occasion demands it. However, it has always been distinguished from armed resistance and its application was at one time confined to Christian martyrs.
>
> Civil disobedience is civil breach of unmoral statutory enactments. The expression was, so far as I am aware, coined by Thoreau to signify his own resistance to the laws of a slave state. He has left a masterly treatise on the duty of civil disobedience. But Thoreau was not perhaps an out-and-out champion of non-violence. Probably, also, Thoreau limited his breach to statutory laws to the revenue law, i.e., payment of taxes,[72] whereas the term "civil disobedience" as practiced in 1919 covered a breach of any statutory and unmoral law. It signified the resister's outlawry in a civil, i.e., non-violent manner. He invoked sanctions of the law and cheerfully suffered imprisonment. It is a branch of *satyagraha.*
>
> Non-cooperation predominantly implies withdrawing of cooperation from the state that in the non-cooperator's view has become corrupt and excludes civil disobedience of the fierce type described above. By its very nature, non-cooperation is even open to children of understanding and can be safely practiced by the masses. Civil disobedience presupposes the habit of willing obedience to laws without fear of their sanctions. It can therefore be practiced only as a last resort and by a select few in the first instance at any rate. Non-cooperation, too, like civil disobedience is a branch of *satyagraha* which includes all non-violent resistance for the vindication of Truth.[73]

In a letter written in 1934, he made further comments on the subject: "Civil disobedience is not necessarily an accurate expression of the attitude indicated in 'civil resistance.' 'Civil disobedience' may also indicate an attitude of mind. The term 'civil disobedience' was first used by Thoreau. I didn't like it because it didn't suggest all that I had in mind. Looking for a new phrase, I fixed upon 'civil resistance.' The current phrase was 'passive resistance.' But my way of resistance or the force which I had in mind was not passive. It was active, but 'active' might also mean violent. The word 'civil' suggests nothing but non-violence. I therefore joined it with 'resistance.'"[74]

In 1942 Gandhi specified the exact nature of Thoreau's influence on him: "through his essay on the 'Duty of Civil Disobedience,'" Thoreau provided "scientific confirmation" of what Gandhi was doing in South Africa.[75]

In the light of the foregoing discussion, Richardson's interpretation of Thoreau's influence on Gandhi is untenable. It makes four claims. First, Thoreau domesticated "into an American context" the Hindu concept of *moksha*, or final liberation of the spirit. Second, he transcended the Hindu view that the quest for *moksha* requires acquiescence in outward tyranny. Third, he gave back to India its own tradition, "improved and made practicable." Finally, Gandhi's concept of *swaraj* as expressed in *Hind Swaraj* drew explicitly on Thoreau.[76]

Richardson, in my view, exaggerates the sophistication of Thoreau's knowledge of Hindu philosophy. Because of this, he misjudges the relevance of Thoreau for a helpful understanding of modern India in general and for Gandhi's *Hind Swaraj* in particular. It is true that Thoreau had read in translation (early translations, at that) such works as *The Laws of Manu*, parts of *Mahabharata*, *Vishnu Purana*, the *Samkhya Karika*, Kalidasa's *Sakuntala*, the *Harivansam*, the Sama Veda, and the Bhagavad Gita.[77] In "Walking" he appears to endorse the traditional view of *Vishnu Purana* that the pursuit of *artha* (politics and economics) is incompatible with the pursuit of spiritual liberation or *moksha*.[78] His praise of *The Laws of Manu*, a work that represents social hierarchy in its most oppressive form, is indicative of his limited understanding of the impact of its teachings on Indian society. One has only to contrast Thoreau's admiration for *The Laws of Manu* with its public burning in India in 1927 by the followers of A. R. Ambedkar, the Columbia University–educated jurist and political thinker, leader of the much despised Untouchables, and future chairman of the drafting committee of India's modern constitution (1950).

To cap it all, Gandhi took no note of Thoreau's comments on Hindu philosophy. His deep and enduring appreciation of Thoreau was based solely on his political essays. Thoreau had nothing to do with Gandhi's interpretation of the meaning of *swaraj* as it appears in *Hind Swaraj*.[79]

## Thoreau and Gandhi: A Comparison

Although there are many points in common between these two thinkers, there are also some interesting differences between them. This makes them apt subjects for comparative political thought. The conceptual differences between civil disobedience and satyagraha have already been noted. There are three other points on which Thoreau and Gandhi can be compared; they concern the relationship of civil disobedience or satyagraha to social reform, violence, and virtue.

As for the relationship of civil disobedience to social reform, Thoreau saw very clearly the need for the abolition of slavery. Some critics still debate the extent of Thoreau's commitment to reform, however. Even though there is a collection of his writings entitled *Reform Papers,* and even though the two essays Gandhi honored include the issue of reform, the debate continues.[80] There is no question that Thoreau was dissatisfied with slavery and that American society was in need of internal reform. And as noted in "Walking," the reform of the individual is the key to the reform of society. The individual has to experience true inner freedom, which can be found only in "wildness" and retreat from society and polity. At the same time, as Gougeon points out, Thoreau finally came to the conclusion that the reform of individuals through self-culture can occur only in a well-ordered polity that guarantees personal freedom.[81]

In Gandhi's mind, there was no doubt whatsoever about the necessary connection between civil disobedience and social reform, or what he called "constructive programme." In 1941 he published a thesis entitled "Constructive Programme: Its Meaning and Place."[82] In the Gandhi corpus, its importance is second only to that of *Hind Swaraj.* Its main argument is that social reform, carried out by voluntary organizations, has an indispensable role in a free society. Voluntary organizations are better equipped to bring about certain types of social reform than are the agencies of the state. The greater the number of voluntary agencies in a society, the less violent that society will be, and the less dependent on the state the citizens will be. Voluntary agencies hold the key to creating a government that governs the least.

Constructive programme, according to Gandhi, represents the positive side of politics, while satyagraha represents its negative side. Satyagraha is protest politics. But a society cannot live by protest alone. Its normal life has to be lived by constructive citizenship. That is to say, in Gandhi's philosophy, satyagraha is not the whole of politics; it is only part of the broader vision of politics. As he puts it, satyagraha is for rare occasions and for the few, while constructive programme is for always and to be carried out by everyone.[83] The metaphor of the paralyzed hand attempting to lift a spoon, which he uses toward the end of "Constructive Programme," says it all: "For my handling of civil disobedience without the constructive programme will be like a paralyzed hand attempting to lift a spoon."[84]

A second area of comparison is their respective stands on nonviolence. As Jack Turner has argued, Thoreau believes that liberators of society may resort to revolutionary violence on the basis of natural right. A "contingent willingness" to kill or be killed in resistance to political evil is consistent with Thoreau's philosophy. Thoreau does not stand in the way of morally concerned citizens who want to end the state's monopoly of legitimate violence.[85]

Gandhi's concept of nonviolence recognizes the right to use legitimate violence in self-defense both private and public. However, in the exercise of satyagraha, this right does not and may not come into play. His famous definition of *satyagraha* makes this clear enough. "Passive resistance [satyagraha] is a method of securing rights by personal suffering; it is the reverse of resistance by arms. When I refuse to do a thing repugnant to my conscience, I use soul-force."[86] Gandhi staked his reputation as an original political thinker on this specific issue. Hitherto, violence had been used in the name of political rights, such as in street riots, regicide, or armed revolutions. Gandhi believes there is a better way of securing political rights, that of nonviolence, and that this new way marks an advance in political ethics. With regard to the narrow issue of securing rights in open, free, democratic societies, he was absolutely opposed to the use of violence.

The third area of comparison between Thoreau and Gandhi concerns the role of virtue in resistance politics or satyagraha. Here again, a distinction is necessary as far as Gandhi is concerned. Those who wanted to practice satyagraha in the heroic sense were expected to practice four specific virtues—chastity, voluntary poverty, truthfulness, and fearlessness.[87] Others who practiced satyagraha for reasons of expediency were not bound by these virtues, even though the virtue of nonviolence was obligatory. Chastity and truthfulness are included in this list in deference to Indian moral philosophy. "Chastity," writes Gandhi, "is one of the greatest disciplines without which the mind cannot attain firmness."[88] As for voluntary poverty, "pecuniary ambition" and civil disobedience in the heroic sense do not go well together. No one is expected to throw money away, but a practitioner of satyagraha is expected "to be indifferent to it." Finally, the civil disobedient has to have the virtue of courage so that he or she may be free from the fear of losing friends, relatives, property, and even life itself.[89]

Thoreau does not write systematically on the need for virtue. However, it is clear—for example, in "Life without Principle"—that one of his criticisms of modern capitalist culture is its disregard for moral virtue. And who can forget the distinction he draws in "The Duty of Civil Disobedience" between "the nine hundred and ninety nine" patrons of virtue and "one virtuous man"? As noted earlier, one of the attributes of character that attracted Gandhi to Thoreau was his moral earnestness.

I conclude with an evaluation of the broader contributions these two thinkers have made to the field of comparative political thought. Thoreau made two contributions in this regard. The first is his lasting impact on Gandhi's political thought through the three essays discussed in this chapter. The second is his signal to future generations of American intellectuals that they should take a serious interest in Indian thought. Even though this interest did not influence Gandhi in any way—or modern Indian political thought, for that matter—it nevertheless sets a very good example for his compatriots. It reminds them that to be well educated in the contemporary world, it is no longer sufficient to be conversant with the political philosophy of one's own culture. To be politically literate in today's world, they need to cross their canonical boundaries and engage in serious comparative political thought. Thoreau was a pioneer in this regard. Accordingly, his contributions in this area should be evaluated not in terms of the depth of his knowledge of Indian thought (which he lacked) but in terms of his recognition of the need to learn from Indian thought.

Gandhi made a similar contribution to comparative political thought. He taught his Indian compatriots how to cross the canonical boundaries of their own culture and absorb new ideas from America and elsewhere, without losing their intellectual identity. The story of the transformation of civil disobedience or passive resistance into satyagraha is a story of how to practice comparative political thought in our times. Crossing canonical boundaries does not mean or require abandoning one's canon.[90] It means updating it and making it relevant to modern times. Gandhi was able to integrate what was universal in Thoreau's essays into the new Indian canon without undermining the latter's integrity. Here I must refer once again to appendix I of *Hind Swaraj,* a major text of the new Indian political canon. It invites Indians to integrate the thoughts of such Western authors as Plato, Tolstoy, Ruskin, Thoreau, and others within the framework of the new Indian canon. Gandhi's mode of comparative political thought has universal application.

# Notes

1. M. K. Gandhi to Premabehn Kantak, January 17, 1931, in *The Collected Works of Mahatma Gandhi,* 100 vols. (New Delhi: Publications Division, Government of India, 1958–1994), 45:95. The generous statement about Thoreau is followed immediately by the following sentence: "Perhaps I should drop Thoreau from this list." How are we to interpret this sudden change of mind? I do not think it should be interpreted as a put-down of Thoreau. Rather, I believe it means that Thoreau came fourth on the list.

2. Thoreau's essay is traditionally known as "On the Duty of Civil Disobedience" or "Civil Disobedience." Gandhi idiosyncratically referred to it as "The Duty of Civil Disobedience."

3. On October 12, 1929, Gandhi wrote to Henry S. Salt, Thoreau's biographer, the following: "My first introduction to Thoreau's writings was I think in 1907 or later when I was in the thick of passive resistance struggle. A friend sent me Thoreau's essay on civil disobedience. It left a deep impression upon me" (*Collected Works,* 41:553).

4. Ibid., 7:217–18, 228–30.

5. Ibid., 267.

6. Ibid., 9:159.

7. Ibid., 10:386.

8. Ibid., 7:510. The prize was ten guineas.

9. Ibid., 9:183.

10. M. K. Gandhi, *Hind Swaraj and Other Writings,* ed. Anthony J. Parel (Cambridge: Cambridge University Press, 1997), 6.

11. Gandhi, *Collected Works,* 10:446.

12. Ibid., 11:123.

13. Indulal Yagnik, *Gandhi as I Knew Him* (Delhi: Danish-Mahal, 1943), 16.

14. Gandhi, *Collected Works,* 15:497–502. There were twenty-one such leaflets in all, and this collection of extracts from Thoreau was given the singular honor of being the first in the series.

15. Robert D. Richardson Jr., *Henry Thoreau: A Life of the Mind* (Berkeley: University of California Press, 1986), 224.

16. Henry David Thoreau, "Walking," in *The Portable Thoreau,* rev. ed., ed. Carl Bode (New York: Penguin Books, 1982), 592.

17. Ibid., 594.

18. Ibid., 599.

19. Ibid., 611.

20. Ibid., 618.

21. Ibid., 623–24.

22. Gandhi, *Collected Works,* 12:24.

23. Ibid., 43:169.

24. Ibid., 12:24.

25. Ibid., 13:270.

26. Ibid., 63:94.

27. Ibid., 58:2.

28. Ibid., 213.

29. Ibid., 59:68–69.

30. See Gandhi, *Hind Swaraj,* xliii–xliv.

31. William Cain, ed., *A Historical Guide to Henry David Thoreau* (Oxford: Oxford University Press, 2000), 51.

32. Richardson, *Henry Thoreau,* 332–33.

33. Len Gougeon, "Thoreau and Reform," in *The Cambridge Companion to Henry David Thoreau,* ed. Joel Myerson (Cambridge: Cambridge University Press, 1995), 206.

34. The books critical of the social impact of nineteenth-century economic changes in Great Britain were *A New Crusade* (1903) by Godfrey Blount, *Civilization: Its Cause and Cure* (1897) by Edward Carpenter, *Unto This Last* (1860) and *"A Joy for Ever" and Its Prince in the Market* (1857, 1880) by John Ruskin, *The White Slaves of England* (1897) by Robert H. Sherard, and *The Fallacy of Speed* (1909) by Thomas F. Taylor. The books on Indian economics were *Poverty and Un-British Rule in India* (1901) by Dadabhai Naoroji and the two-volume *Economic History of India* (1904) by R. C. Dutt.

35. Henry David Thoreau, "Life without Principle," in *The Portable Thoreau,* 632.

36. Ibid., 634.

37. Ibid., 639.

38. Ibid., 650.

39. Ibid.

40. Ibid., 644.

41. Ibid., 650.

42. Ibid., 645.

43. Ibid., 636.

44. Ibid., 646.

45. Ibid.

46. Ibid., 647.

47. Ibid., 654.

48. Ibid., 649.

49. For the text of this lecture, see Gandhi, *Hind Swaraj,* 156–64.

50. Ibid., 108.

51. Gandhi, *Collected Works,* 7:217.

52. Ibid., 42:384. It is very likely that Gandhi's language here was influenced by the language of the American Declaration of Independence too.

53. *Satyagraha Pamphlet No. 1,* ibid., 15:501–2.

54. Ibid., 497.

55. Gandhi's paraphrase, ibid., 7:218.

56. Gandhi, *Collected Works,* 56:182.

57. Ibid., 62:92.

58. Ibid., 7:229.

59. Ibid.

60. Ibid.

61. Ibid., 230.

62. Gandhi, *Collected Works,* 16:51.

63. Ibid., 7:304–5.

64. Ibid., 18:169.

65. Ibid., 33:398.

66. Ibid., 36:105.

67. Ibid., 70:145.

68. Ibid., 61:401.

69. M. K. Gandhi, *Satyagraha in South Africa,* 2nd ed. (Ahmedabad: Navajivan, 1972), 102. The phrase *passive resistance* was used by British nonconformists against the Education Act of 1902 and by British suffragettes (ibid., 104).

70. Gandhi, *Collected Works,* 8:23.

71. Ibid., 131.

72. I am grateful to Jack Turner for pointing out that Gandhi was incorrect in saying that Thoreau limited his civil disobedience to revenue laws. He assisted many slaves to escape, thus disobeying the Fugitive Slave Law.

73. Gandhi, *Collected Works,* 19:466–67.

74. Ibid., 58:54.

75. Ibid., 76:358.

76. Richardson, *Henry Thoreau,* 316–17.

77. Ibid., 106–9, 204–9.

78. Thoreau, "Walking," 623–24.

79. Gandhi's meaning of *swaraj* in *Hind Swaraj* is based on his own original interpretation of how *artha* (the pursuit of politics and economics) can be harmonized with *moksha* (the pursuit of spiritual liberation). I have developed this point in Anthony J. Parel, ed., *Gandhi, Freedom and Self-Rule* (Lanham, MD: Lexington Books, 2000), 1–25; *Hind Swaraj and Other Writings;* and *Gandhi's Philosophy and the Quest for Harmony* (Cambridge: Cambridge University Press, 2006).

80. For a survey of the debate, see Gougeon, "Thoreau and Reform," 194–96.

81. Ibid., 196.

82. For the text, see Gandhi, *Collected Works,* 75:146–66; *Hind Swaraj,* 170–81.

83. Gandhi, *Collected Works,* 75:61.

84. Ibid., 166.

85. Jack Turner, "Performing Conscience: Thoreau, Political Action and the Plea for John Brown," in *Political Theory* 33 (August 2005): 459–62 (revised and reprinted as chapter 6 of this volume).

86. Gandhi, *Hind Swaraj,* 90.

87. See ibid., 96–99.

88. Ibid., 97.

89. Ibid., 98.

90. I have developed this point further in Anthony J. Parel, "Gandhi and the Emergence of the Modern Indian Political Canon," *Review of Politics* 70 (2008): 40–63.

# CHAPTER 15

# Thoreau, Adorno, and the Critical Potential of Particularity

*Shannon L. Mariotti*

DESPITE VAST DIFFERENCES of time, space, and context, Henry David Thoreau and Theodor W. Adorno similarly identify a critically valuable quality in particular things. As he shows especially in the aphorisms of *Minima Moralia*, Adorno thinks particular objects contain dissonant "nonidentical" qualities that can be drawn out to highlight the illusory harmonies of late modern society.[1] Adorno's aphorisms enact the practice of negative dialectics: he focuses on seemingly insignificant things (the taboo on "talking shop," hobbies, ideals of beauty) and shows how they, like monads, contain an image of the contradictions and antagonisms of modern society. Thoreau enacts a more corporealized version of Adorno's negative dialectics: for Thoreau, "little things" such as wild apples or the tiny huckleberry valuably encapsulate rupturing contradictions that can be drawn out toward a critique of the seemingly smooth machinations of a rapidly modernizing nineteenth-century society.

Adorno's understanding of the critical potential of particular objects helps us better understand the political significance of Thoreau's so-called nature writings. There are important sympathies between Adorno's notion of the "nonidentical" and Thoreau's quest in nature for the "wild" potential contained within particular objects. Both Thoreau and Adorno show us how confrontations with particular objects that resist (and illuminate) the domesticating, categorizing, containing logic of modernity can stimulate critical capacities that work against these conventional ways of thinking and perceiving, in democratically valuable ways.

There is something strikingly similar about the *ways* Thoreau and

Adorno see. Both, in contrast to the abstracting idealist gaze, employ what Adorno calls a "microscopic gaze."[2] Both Thoreau and Adorno often focus on apparently minor things as a pathway toward broader critiques of society at large.[3] Their eyes move from small, seemingly insignificant, particular things to broader, more general things, and not in the other direction. For both, "little things" encapsulate something of the universal but also contain a critique of it. Thoreau and Adorno are interested in the ways particular things depart from general trends and go against the grain of convention. In this way, paying attention to particularity can both inspire criticism of "what is" and contain the possibility of an alternative to convention and the status quo. They enact their politics in their engagement with particular things.

## Adorno's Critique of the Logic of Identity and Idealism

For Adorno, particular objects contain contradictory, rupturing possibilities we are blind to and dissonant speech we do not hear. If we would linger with these objects, they would help us see the illusory harmonies of the logics of modern capitalist society. Adorno dialectically engages the object in ways that avoid both projecting the self onto it and approaching it as a "fact," as "given" or self-explanatory: the thinker actively and creatively, but noninstrumentally and "without anxiety," engages the object to draw out an image of its rupturing, critical potential.[4] If we looked closely at technology, at the designs of our homes, at how people tell lies, how they chase after buses, at manners and notions of tact, small talk, sleepless nights, gift giving, customer service, love, marriage, or divorce, we could illuminate contradictions that highlight an unharmonious modern reality.[5] If approached the right way, these objects would allow us to see how the identifying and abstracting logics of modernity mask violence, damage life, and turn us into unthinking, conforming, alienated, machine-like creatures. In *Minima Moralia,* Adorno trains his truthful yet transformative "microscopic gaze" on these objects, highlighting aspects that refuse to be synthesized, unified, or reconciled. In this way, Adorno illuminates what he calls the "nonidentical."

Conventional ways of thinking, represented through the idealist dialectic and the logic of abstract exchange, act as an obstacle to this critical practice. In the interest of maintaining harmony, stability, and the status quo, they blind us to all that is unharmonious, rupturing, and negative.

When we are guided by these logics, when we see in abstract and identifying ways, we become conformists and tend to let the authority of the collective rule. Such a life can barely be called living, for Adorno: it is a dull, lifeless, monotonous, and formulaic mode of experience. This "damaged life" or "vanished life" is alienated life.[6] It describes the personal, psychological, and social effects of modernity characterized by the urge to "identify," to classify and categorize that which is other, particular, unique, different, and nonidentical.

Adorno's philosophical argument rests on a critique of idealist dialectics, of a logic that seeks to resolve all contradiction and reconcile all differences. Hegel exemplifies this positive version of the dialectic, where the universal and the particular find unity in the subject. Adorno critiques Hegel's notion of the absolute subject, but his primary objection is that Hegel's dialectics represents a "system," a "form of presenting a totality to which nothing remains extraneous" (*Negative Dialectics,* 24). This system consumes all: every difference and particularity is a contradiction to be overcome. As Adorno says, "The name of dialectics says no more, to begin with, than that objects do not go into their concepts without leaving a remainder" (*Negative Dialectics,* 4). But under an identifying dialectic, this remainder (the nonidentical) is seen as simply a contradiction to be reconciled. Its unique qualities are violated in the rush to systematize: "What we differentiate will appear divergent, dissonant, negative for just as long as the structure of our consciousness obliges it to strive for unity; as long as the demand for totality will be its measure for whatever is not identical with it" (*Negative Dialectics,* 5).

The appearance of the nonidentical is inevitable, as concepts never fully cover their objects. As J. M. Bernstein says, something inevitably "slips through the unifying net"; "contradictions testify to antagonisms in reality."[7] For Adorno, dialectics is driven by "the consistent sense of nonidentity," by the recognition that there is always something that escapes and eludes this unified way of thinking. Particular things indicate the presence of these remainders that resist the systematizing logic of modernity, but there are other logics at work in society that attempt to silence the dissonant call of particular things that disrupt, challenge, contradict, and antagonize more harmonious ways of thinking.

The traditional dialectic masks this inevitable nonidentity and, smoothing over the disjuncture, instead "serves the end of reconcilement" (*Nega-*

*tive Dialectics,* 6). The logic of identity is also reflected in the capitalist system of abstract exchange, whereby one thing can be replaced by another different and unique thing as long as they have equivalent monetary value; these two logics do similar violence to specific objects in the interest of promoting fungibility between disparate things (*Negative Dialectics,* 146). Adorno sees the exchange or barter principle (*Tauschprinzip*) as originally and foundationally related (*urverwandt*) to the principle of identification: it is an "ur" relationship.[8] The exchange principle reduces X and Y to an equal monetary value and holds them to be identical and interchangeable, even though they are actually very different. The exchange principle also turns subjects into objects, transforming the subject's labor into a calculation of hourly wages. The "obligation to become identical" that the principle of exchange "imposes on the whole world" involves a tendency to abstract away from particular objects, which lose their particularity and uniqueness (*Negative Dialectics,* 146). We simply see them as a means to the end of exchange and profit, or as a subset of a category or concept that is supposed to capture the object completely.

The object is treated instrumentally and only as a means to an end. Identity does violence to the object in abstracting away its difference and particularity. This logic also deadens experience by imposing sameness on the world.[9] It tries to silence the rupturing qualities of particular objects:

> Unquestionably, one who submits to the dialectical discipline has to pay dearly in the qualitative variety of experience. Still, in the administered world the impoverishment of experience by dialectics, which outrages healthy opinion, proves appropriate to the abstract monotony of that world. Its agony is the world's agony raised to a concept. (*Negative Dialectics,* 6)[10]

Adorno makes us first feel this loss and then models how to work against it. Negative dialectics is the practice he enacts against this alienated sensibility, teaching us to pay attention to particular objects, to hear their dissonance. To try to restore the object's ability to speak and to work against the deadening power of the logic of identity is to engage in the practice of negative dialectics. Adorno's negative dialectics is an "anti-system" that shines light on what has hitherto been neglected by traditional philosophy and idealist dialectics, what was dismissed by Hegel and Plato alike as "transitory and insignificant": the nonidentical and the particular, that which eludes general concepts, that which cannot be subsumed (*Negative Dialectics,* 8).

## Negative Dialectics and Adorno's Microscopic Gaze

The logics of identity and exchange both fail to recognize "the preponderance of the object" (*Negative Dialectics,* 183). Adorno says we must learn to see with our eye on the object, not on its category. We need to let our eye linger on the object and employ a "microscopic gaze." As Susan Buck-Morss shows, the microscopic gaze Adorno adopted was deeply influenced by Walter Benjamin's way of seeing (in fact, this was the phrase Adorno used to describe Benjamin's gaze).[11] Adorno is interested in the kinds of particular phenomena that Hegel dismissed as "foul existence."[12] Adorno focuses on seemingly minor phenomena that, at first glance, seem unlikely to yield any larger critique of bourgeois society: gift giving, astrology, running in the streets, children's fairy tales. But he uses these particular phenomena as ways to illuminate the dominating and alienating tendencies of modern society. As Buck-Morss says: "What distinguished Adorno's approach was not only his Hegelian assertion of the dialectical relationship between the particular and the general but the fact that, unlike Hegel, he found the general within the very surface characteristics of the particular, and indeed, within those that were seemingly insignificant, atypical or extreme."[13] For Adorno, the particular is not a part of the whole or something that can be subsumed. The particular is like a monad that contains an image of the whole that can be interpreted to yield a critique of bourgeois society.[14] Particular objects contain a truth, to be released through the interpretation of the thinker.

But the particular also contains "truth" in another sense: these phenomena, in their resistance to the whole, in their nonidentity, in their contradictions, testify to an alternative possibility to the bourgeois "false" life. As Buck-Morss says, there is "a utopian dimension" to the particular: "The transitoriness of particulars was the promise of a different future, while their small size, their elusiveness to categorization implied a defiance of the very social structure they expressed."[15]

This microscopic gaze disrupts the logic of identity that works in the interest of bourgeois powers. The principle of identity is conservative: it smoothes over the chasms between disparate things that characterize capitalist society. The logics of identity and exchange would have us believe that the subject's labor and the wage he is paid are truly fungible and equivalent, giving the appearance that the whole system is stable, unified, and harmonious. To give another example, it is also in the interest of power to try to smooth over any potential conflict between the individual's own life ambitions and society's need to manipulate individuals into certain modes of living:

> Experience forbids the resolution in the unity of consciousness of whatever appears contradictory. For instance, a contradiction like the one between the definition which an individual knows as his own and his "role," the definition forced upon him by society when he would make his living—such a contradiction cannot be brought under any unity without manipulation, without the insertion of some wretched cover concepts that will make the crucial differences vanish. (*Negative Dialectics*, 152)

To engage in the practice of negative dialectics is to highlight these experiential differences, to widen the contradiction, to work against the false manipulation of the identity principle. Negative dialectics describes this continual process of upsetting "what is," highlighting its contingency and instability. As Seyla Benhabib puts it, for Adorno, "The task of the critic is to illuminate those cracks in the totality, those fissures in the social net, those moments of disharmony and discrepancy, through which the untruth of the whole is revealed and glimmers of another life become visible."[16] But we can get to this critical point only by paying attention to the difference, particularity, and uniqueness of objects. This is why the "preponderance of the object" is so important as a limit to power for Adorno.

As we will see, while walking and in his writings on "Wild Apples" and "Huckleberries," Thoreau employs a similar gaze. He draws out the "wild" qualities of "little things" like huckleberries or apples toward a critique of the domesticating and taming tendencies of modern society. Thoreau, like Adorno, focuses on seemingly insignificant things to disrupt the abstract logics of modernity. In his nature writings, Thoreau enacts a dissonant critique of modern society that is deeply sympathetic to Adorno's practice of negative dialectics.

## Thoreau and Modernization: Man as Machine

What features of his own nascent modernity does Thoreau criticize? What is the topography of his nineteenth-century context? Thoreau was born in 1817 and died in 1862. His life span corresponds to the era historians recognize as an especially intense period of urbanization and industrialization in Massachusetts and in the United States generally. The first half of the nineteenth century saw many changes: on the broadest level, the population increased throughout the state, and there was a general shift from rural ways of life to more urban lifestyles. As historians Richard Brown and Jack Tager note: "After 1780 and especially in the decades after 1820, the population grew swiftly, at rates comparable to the most dynamic periods of colonial settlement. . . . The population density had risen from 33 persons per square mile in 1780 to 153 persons per square mile in 1860. Massachusetts became the most thickly settled state in the union, save only for tiny Rhode Island."[17]

As the population increased and as transportation became less arduous, there were incentives for farmers to grow surplus to supply the nearby markets of Boston. The railroads were a major factor in opening up new markets for farmers, thus prompting a shift away from family-based subsistence farming toward market-oriented farming.[18] Yet while new markets opened up for profit-oriented farmers, agriculture declined overall, and more people moved toward manufacturing. The years from 1790 to 1860 saw a shift from household or workshop production of consumer goods to factory-based production.[19] During this process of urbanization, "the more people turned to market production, even on this small scale, the more thoroughly they became enmeshed in the world of commerce."[20] This was the era of the textile boom. The mill city in Lowell, Massachusetts (about fifteen miles from Concord), was created in 1826, and although this was an extreme form of urbanization, the model was repeated to a lesser degree throughout the state: "What was happening in Lowell, urbanization based on industry, was far more rapid and intense than in other towns. Yet the direction was the same almost everywhere in Massachusetts during the first half of the nineteenth century."[21] As Brown and Tager note, "Between 1820 and the Civil War, Massachusetts turned toward industry and away from agriculture. From a labor force where 60% of workers were in agriculture, by 1865 only 13% were on farms. . . . Now workers were largely employees, no longer owning property or small businesses. The demand for skilled artisans declined and self-employment became unusual. Workers had become dependent on others for employment."[22]

Accompanying these changes were more general shifts in values, ideals, and lifestyles. A more bourgeois class of people began to develop in Massachusetts. People became more concerned with fashion and the goings-on of "society." By looking at which consumer items became popular, we can see the shift in people's material desires and aspirations to greater refinement and "gentility": "The production of consumer goods—items like clothing, home furnishings, musical instruments and books—reflected the radical changes in American ways of life between 1800 and 1860. These were the years when semi-subsistence farming all but disappeared and the ideals of bourgeois comfort and amenities characteristic of the Victorian age supplanted the rustic simplicity that religious beliefs and economic realities had forced on the majority of people from Winthrop's day to John Hancock's."[23]

Modernization during Thoreau's lifetime entailed greater organization, greater coordination of activities, and systematizing of behaviors. Instead of individuals self-sufficiently producing most of their own goods, they coordinated their needs and desires with the market. The number of people working for themselves declined, and more people became employees, with more rigid codes of conduct governing their behavior. The population increased; people began living in closer proximity to others and were able to compare and model their own lifestyles on the lifestyles of others, following popular styles and fashions. As transportation technologies advanced, routines emerged.

With the railroads came the possibility of selling surplus agricultural produce; those who continued farming cultivated larger swaths of land, no longer farming for only their own families. The activities of weeks and months took on greater regularity and predictability, following the railroad timetables, the demands for goods in Boston, and the schedules of employers. The introduction of the railroad in Concord was, for Thoreau, a major factor in the increasingly routine and formulaic ordering of the day. In the "Sounds" chapter of *Walden*, Thoreau describes how the regular whistles of the trains going to and from Boston became a marker of time and a dictator of action:

> I watch the passage of the morning cars with the same feeling that I do the rising of the sun, which is hardly more regular. . . . If the enterprise were as innocent as it is early! . . . If the enterprise were as heroic and commanding as it is protracted and unwearied! . . . The startings and arrivals of the cars are now the epochs in the village day. They come and go with such regularity and precision, and their whistle can be heard so far, that the farmers set their

clocks by them, and thus one well-conducted institution regulates a whole country.[24]

People moved in time to the railroads, which moved in time with the market. The farmers in the country sent raw materials to Boston: cotton and wool. The factories and the "restless city merchants" sent back finished products: woven cloth and silk.

> Here come your groceries, country: your rations, countrymen! Nor is there any man so independent on his farm that he can say them nay. And here's your pay for them! screams the countryman's whistle. . . . Up comes the cotton, down goes the woven cloth; up comes the silk, down goes the woolen; up come the books, but down goes the wit that writes them. (*Walden,* 115)

Activity was coordinated on increasingly large scales: the railroads indeed "regulate[d] a whole country," and people timed their days by the whistle of the train. The railroad coordinated activity to make certain artificial patterns of action look natural, like fate, as regular and inevitable as the rising and setting of the sun.

The face of the land reflected these social changes. In his essay "The Forests and Fields of Concord: An Ecological History, 1750–1850," Brian Donahue describes a Concord being rapidly depleted of timber and of good farmland.[25] Because of the great need for firewood, the forests of Concord were reduced to about half the town's surface by the end of the colonial era. By 1850, only 11 percent of Concord remained wooded.[26] Donahue says, "The most important thing about the forest in this period is that it was being wiped out. In Concord, 'woodland' dropped from roughly a quarter to about a tenth of the land surface of the town. The drop was particularly sharp after 1820."[27] By 1860, "virtually all of the forest in Concord was either managed woodlot or 'new woods' that had occupied abandoned farmland. There was no 'virgin' forest left; and most of the mature second growth timber had been cut as well."[28]

With all these changes, something was lost. Experience, like nature, became tamed and domesticated. People were cultivated, just as nature was increasingly becoming the material for consumption and industry. Activities conformed to expected patterns. People's lives took on predictable shapes. Thoreau identifies a corresponding watering down of experience; he is constantly urging himself and his readers to bite more deeply into life, to experience in unconventional ways, and to move past expected and formulaic ways of thinking and acting. For Thoreau, lifestyle expectations, habits, manners, and codes of conduct eviscerate real life and real experience, which are defined by that which negates regularizing. Life, for Thoreau, is a unique and unexpected surplus that exceeds common expectations. As he says in the chapter "Where I Lived and What I Lived For," "I went to the woods because I wished to live deliberately, to front only the essential facts of life, and see if I could not learn what it had to teach, and not, when I came to die, discover that I had not lived. I did not wish to live what was not life . . . I wanted to live deep and suck out all the marrow of life" (*Walden,* 90). Thoreau is trying to address a problem of modern life. Lives are not lived because the individual does not experiment for himself or herself: "Here is life, an experiment to a great extent untried by me; but it does not avail me that they have tried it" (*Walden,* 9). Thoreau contrasts *living* with modern ways of simply *getting a living,* where we conform to the market and to conventional ways of making money. As he says in "Life without Principle," "There is no more fatal blunderer than he who consumes the greater part of his life getting his living."[29] He begins that essay by saying, "Let us consider the way in which we spend our lives," punning that we literally buy our way out of real life ("Life," 156). As he often does, Thoreau opposes the market with life and living.

Thoreau often uses the term *common sense* to describe this alienated sensibility. For example, in the conclusion to *Walden,* he calls our "dullest perception" common sense and says, "the commonest sense is the sense of men asleep, which they express by snoring" (325). Common sense evokes images of the self-evident, the obvious, ideas that are immediately available to understanding. If something is common sense, it is accessible to an everyday, mainstream sensibility. But for Thoreau, these ways of thinking problematically follow conventional patterns. Thoreau's notion of common sense corresponds to Adorno's notion of "damaged life." For Thoreau, to be alienated is to think what we are expected to think, to say what we are expected to say. Like Adorno, Thoreau places the greatest value on the part of us that can negate, say no, and think against the grain of common thought. But this is the capacity that is eviscerated when we use a common and everyday sensibility. Thoreau wants to "transcend" this common sensibility by awakening an ability to negate familiar modes of perception for something more wild, unexpected, unpredictable, and idiosyncratic.

Thoreau thinks we are seductively alienated by routine, habit, patterns of conduct, formulas for how we should behave: all this tames and domesticates the self so that we can scarcely negate convention at all. Thoreau explicitly ties these tendencies to the processes of modernization taking place around him. In the opening passages of *Walden,* he says, "I have traveled a good deal in Concord; and everywhere, in shops and offices, and fields, the inhabitants have appeared to me to be doing penance in a thousand remarkable ways" (4). Their "penance" is to inherit farms that give them no choice in how to order their lives, but rather map out their destinies for them.[30] It is not the activity of farming itself that Thoreau objects to, but the lack of choice involved in most people's livelihood: their lives follow a pattern they have not themselves created.

Consequently, in losing the ability to negate, to choose, to experiment outside of convention, "the better part of the man is soon plowed into the soil for compost" (*Walden,* 5). The laboring man "has no time to be anything but a machine" (*Walden,* 6). Thoreau argues that we are slaves to majority sentiment, to conventions that have settled within us, to public opinions we have privatized. We have, so to speak, internalized external authority so that we do not even recognize that we have not chosen how to order our lives: we *think* we have freely chosen. Thoreau says, "it is hard to have a Southern overseer; it is worse to have a Northern one; but worst of all when you are the slave driver of yourself. . . . Public opinion is a weak tyrant compared with our own private opinion" (*Walden,* 7). Men are not aware of their lack of choice: "It appears as if men had deliberately chosen the common mode of living because they preferred it to any other. Yet they honestly think there is no choice left" (*Walden,* 8).

We are not content with this state of affairs: "The mass of men lead lives of quiet desperation" (*Walden,* 8). Thoreau notices that "the incessant anxiety and strain of some is a well-nigh incurable form of disease" (*Walden,* 11). Yet we deny that change is possible: "So thoroughly and sincerely are we compelled to live, reverencing our life and denying the possibility of change. This is the only way, we say; but there are as many ways as there can be drawn radii from one center" (*Walden,* 11). In his essay "Walking," Thoreau again draws our attention to the dire effects of the ways our lives have become routinized by modernization: "When sometimes I am reminded that the mechanics and shopkeepers stay in their shops not only all the forenoon, but all the afternoon too, sitting with crossed legs . . . I think that they deserve some credit for not having all committed suicide long ago."[31] These men are not "living" in the way Thoreau understands the term, because they conform to the patterns of the market and stay in their shops all day. They are nearly dead already, because they are being buried by sedimented social conventions. For Thoreau, as for Adorno, "life does not live" when our thoughts and actions conform to the expected, conventional patterns of modernity.

## Thoreau and Huckleberrying

Huckleberrying exemplifies the kind of practice that counteracts these modern forces of alienation by allowing us to withdraw from society for a time, but huckleberrying is a practice that also enacts and prompts the change in perception that Thoreau sees as necessary if we are really to *live* rather than sleepwalk through life as unthinking, uncritical machines.[32] Like a more bodily, physical, and corporealized practice of negative dialectics, the primary changes that come from huckleberrying are changes in perception. Huckleberrying teaches us to think outside of traditional norms and ways of seeing the world, to escape conventions instead of just accepting them. Huckleberrying teaches us to form our own opinions by paying attention to detail, to the little things. This practice fosters our ability to notice particularity and uniqueness. After reading the essay, we learn that the abstract category of "huckleberries" actually tells us nothing about these wild fruits. Through modeling attention to detail and critical perception, Thoreau tells us a much richer story about huckleberries, history, convention, perception, and practices that can makes us real citizens.

Thoreau begins his essay "Huckleberries" with two themes: "little things" and "education." He tells us that he is going against conventional wisdom about what is important: he is going to speak about "little things" that are often deemed insignificant. He says, "Many public speakers are accustomed, as I think foolishly, to talk about what they call *little things* in a patronising way sometimes."[33] He says that "what is thought to be covered by the word *education*—whether reading, writing or 'rithmetic—is a great thing, but almost all that constitutes education is a little thing in the estimation of such speakers as I refer to" ("Huckleberries," 468). Here Thoreau contrasts "what is thought to be covered by the word *education*" with his own definition of education: he is going to show us how education is really about "little things."

After this brief introduction, Thoreau seems to forget his self-professed topic of education and presents a rather straightforward natural history of huckleberries. (This kind of seeming digression is typical of Thoreau's excursionary style of writing: he walks around a topic, looking at it from unexpected angles, and rarely addresses his subject matter head-on.) Thoreau tells us when these berries ripen. He tells us what different types of huckleberries exist and describes each variety. He tells us where they grow and what they taste like. He gives us the etymology of their names.

About midway through the essay, Thoreau begins to attach huckleberries explicitly to a certain kind of lifestyle when he recounts testimonies of Native American uses of these wild fruits. (As I will show, however, even his natural history descriptions of these fruits constitute an "education" in an alternative way of thinking, seeing, and perceiving.) He emphasizes how Native Americans taught whites about huckleberries, not the other way around, and argues for the restoration of the berries' aboriginal names. Thoreau describes how Native Americans used the berries and lauds them for living simply on natural resources instead of supporting themselves by growing tobacco, with all its concomitant evils, such as slavery ("Huckleberries," 487).

But the object is clearly not just to live simply and subsist on huckleberries. The primary value of huckleberries, for Thoreau, consists in the act of gathering them: "For my part, I would not exchange fruits with them—for the object is not merely to get a ship-load of something which you can eat or sell, but the pleasure of gathering it is to be taken into the account" ("Huckleberries," 486). Thoreau counts himself lucky to be his family's appointed huckleberry collector: "They at home got nothing but the pudding, a comparatively heavy affair—but I got the afternoon out of doors. . . . They got only the plums that were in the pudding, but I got the far sweeter plums that never go into it" ("Huckleberries," 491). Thoreau says he learned more in the huckleberry field than he ever learned in school:

> I well remember with what a sense of freedom and spirit of adventure I used to take my way across the fields with my pail . . . and I would not now exchange such an expansion of all my being for all the learning in the world. Liberation and enlargement—such is the fruit which all culture aims to secure. I suddenly knew more about my books than if I had never ceased studying them.

I found myself in a schoolroom where I could not fail to see and hear things worth seeing and hearing—where I could not help getting my lesson—for my lesson came to me. ("Huckleberries," 492)

In fact, huckleberrying is such an important activity for Thoreau that he speaks of it as a career: "I served my apprenticeship and have since done considerable journeywork in the huckleberry field. Though I never paid for my schooling and clothing in that way, it was some of the best schooling that I got, and paid for itself" ("Huckleberries," 491).

Thoreau still has not spelled out exactly *what* he has learned from huckleberrying. Nevertheless, he goes on to argue for the preservation of public spaces of natural beauty. He argues for the creation of parks and wants primitive natural spaces preserved as common space. This is all linked to the ways nature educates us. As he says, "we boast of our system of education, but why stop at schoolmasters and schoolhouses? We are all schoolmasters and our schoolhouse is the universe. To attend chiefly to the desk or schoolhouse, while we neglect the scenery in which it is placed, is absurd" ("Huckleberries," 500). He wants the heads of states and towns to see the preservation of nature as politically important and as an investment in the polity ("Huckleberries," 496). But why are public spaces in nature politically important? How is huckleberrying a politically important education, as Thoreau understands the terms *political* and *education*? This appears to be the topic of his essay, yet these are the questions seemingly left unanswered. Thoreau has told us that huckleberrying is important. But he has not told us *how* it is important. Thoreau's answer, in part, is in the following passage:

As in old times they who dwelt on the heath, remote from towns, being backward to adopt the doctrines which prevailed in towns, were called heathen in a bad sense, so I trust that we dwellers in the huckleberry pastures, which are our heathlands, shall be slow to adopt the notions of large towns and cities, though perchance we may be nicknamed huckleberry people. ("Huckleberries," 491)

If alienation for Thoreau seems to be about a loss of critical faculties, a loss of the ability to negate, to think for ourselves, then the practice of huckleberrying teaches us how to begin to recover some of these lost parts of the self. Huckleberrying shows us how to be heathens with respect to the mainstream ways of life that Thoreau sees as alienated. Huckleberrying is action oriented toward social change, but the target of that change is the individual. In calling for the preservation of natural spaces like huckleberry pastures, Thoreau signals that alienation is a political problem: He thinks that "citizens" act like machines, and he wants to teach them how to act like critical, independent individuals. The huckleberry fields are a space where this political education can take place, where we can work against the tendency to act like conformist and unthinking subjects and work on being "heathens" who hesitate to accept prevailing doctrines and ways of life.

In broad terms, then, Thoreau recommends huckleberrying as a countervailing practice against the modern loss of critical capacities of negation. But in fact, he models this practice himself in the essay in specific ways. I would like to look beyond what he says to what Thoreau *does* in the essay itself. He begins with a seeming digression from the topic of "little things" and "education" into a minute natural history of the berries themselves. But as I noted earlier, this is not a digression at all. Thoreau is modeling how we might see the world if we could learn to be "huckleberry people," if we could learn to be less alienated. Thoreau models this mode of perception: he pays such close attention to these small berries that he is able to describe them in the most minute detail. He is able to tell us, "if you look closely at a huckleberry you will see that it is dotted, as if sprinkled over with a yellow dust or meal, which looks as if it could be rubbed off" ("Huckleberries," 471). He observes the changes the huckleberry has gone through from the nineteenth of June to early August ("Huckleberries," 470). There are many pages with precise descriptions of Thoreau's observations of these small berries. But none of this is a digression from the topic of education; rather, Thoreau is enacting the outcome of this education in the huckleberry pastures. Huckleberrying is a practice that can teach us to see for ourselves, to think for ourselves. Thoreau models the importance of noticing particularity. Huckleberries are by no means a universal category. Rather, each variety of huckleberry gets individual consideration and is differentiated from other types in several ways. There is the late whortleberry, the hairy huckleberry, the deerberry or squaw huckleberry, among others. And in Thoreau's eyes, each is unique and cannot be completely subsumed by the category "huckleberry." Each type of huckleberry is different at different times of year and in different localities. Thoreau thinks it is important and vital to perceive these particularities: only then can we truly understand huckleberries.

As a heathen huckleberryer, Thoreau is also skeptical about widely accepted historical stories. He consults authoritative texts to show how the white man did not "discover" huckleberries. He describes a counterhistory of Native American use of huckleberries that begins in 1615 and goes all the way to his present day of the mid-1800s: "Hence you see that the Indians from time immemorial, down to the present day, all over the northern part of America—have made far more extensive use of the whortleberry [huckleberry]—at all seasons and in various ways—than we—and that they were far more important to them than us" ("Huckleberries," 484). In presenting this history, Thoreau thinks against commonly accepted opinion and the conventional wisdom of society. This is the kind of critical thinking that such practices can teach us.

Thoreau associates huckleberrying with paying attention to particularity in a way that works against the logic of abstract exchange. Huckleberrying gives "preponderance to the object," to borrow Adorno's term: we get to know the berries in all their uniqueness instead of just seeing them as objects to be exchanged for objects of "equal" value. Under the logic of abstract exchange, we abstract away from the particular features of the object and think only of its fungibility with other objects. Thoreau describes the transformation that even huckleberries undergo under the logic of abstract exchange:

> The fruits do not yield their true flavor to the purchaser of them, not to him who raises them for the market. There is but one way to obtain it, yet few take that way. If you would know the true flavor of huckleberries, ask the cow-boy or the partridge. It is a vulgar error to suppose that you had tasted huckleberries who never plucked them. A huckleberry never reaches Boston; they have not been known there since they grew on her three hills. The ambrosial and essential part of the fruit is lost with the bloom which is rubbed off in the market-cart, and they become mere provender. As long as Eternal Justice remains, not one innocent huckleberry can be transported thither from the country hills. (*Walden,* 164)

Thoreau notes that those who purchase huckleberries in the market miss their "true flavor," which derives from the experience of plucking them in the fields: "It is a vulgar error to suppose that you had tasted huckleberries who never plucked them." When abstract exchange makes disparate things fungible, we do not experience things for themselves; we think of objects as means to other ends. Here, huckleberries become a means to profit and are reduced to "mere provender," mere food to eat or to sell as nourishment. In choosing to discuss the commodification of huckleberries, a notoriously market-resistant fruit, he signals the increasing pervasiveness of the market and the drive toward commodification. Huckleberries are wild fruits that resist being domesticated (think of Mark Twain's Huckleberry Finn, the boy who could not be "sivilized"; Twain and Thoreau both draw on the same untamable qualities of this fruit.)[34] The bushes most often die if they are transplanted and thrive only in specific kinds of terrain. The berries themselves do not ship well. Despite this, attempts are made to ship them to Boston markets. Here, Thoreau signals the increasing reach of the logic of exchange.

In "The Bean-Field" chapter of *Walden*, Thoreau describes another instance when his ability to know the object might have been threatened by the profit motive and the logic of exchange. At Walden Pond, Thoreau has a bean field, but he makes it clear that his aim is not profit but rather a true knowledge of beans. He is "determined to know beans" and, through this experience, to know himself and be more "attached" to the earth: "What shall I learn of beans or beans of me?" (*Walden*, 155). Thoreau implies that if profit had been his motive, he would never have gotten to know either beans or himself: the experience of planting, hoeing, weeding, threshing, and picking over would not have been rich if his only concern had been the goods he could buy with his bean money: "It was a singular experience that long acquaintance which I cultivated with beans" (*Walden*, 161). Instead of just seeing the beans as a means to profit, Thoreau speaks of "knowing," "cherishing," and "cultivating" a relationship with them. He eventually sold the beans, though not for a profit, and this part "was the hardest of all" because of his intimacy with them (*Walden*, 161).

Huckleberrying, like hoeing beans, is a practice that changes the way we perceive in politically important ways. Thoreau wants to let these objects speak, and he recognizes how the market drowns out their voices. These practices teach us to see carefully, to pay attention to particularity; for Thoreau, seeing for ourselves is related to thinking for ourselves, to avoiding unthinking conformity to conventions. It seems especially important for Thoreau that practices that work against alienation, such as walking or huckleberrying, be bodily and physical. For Thoreau, we cannot work against alienation by sitting in a chair and trying very hard to think for ourselves. This is an important difference from Adorno's less corporeal and more cognitive practice of negative dialectics. Although both work toward sharpening our capacities for critical negation, for Thoreau, the changes in how we think and perceive seem to come from how we move our bodies, how we shift our spatial arrangements. As Thoreau says in *Walden*, "My head is hands and feet" (98). To some extent, we change what the head does by changing what the hands and feet do. The dissonant critique that Thoreau draws from particular things is strongly connected to his body's movement.

## Thoreau's "Wild Apples"

In his essay "Wild Apples," Thoreau describes a similarly violent process of abstract exchange. He claims that the most important qualities of wild apples are lost when they are "vulgarized" by being bought and sold. The objects that end up in the market are not apples at all:

> There is thus about all natural products a certain volatile and ethereal qual-
> ity which represents their highest value, and which cannot be vulgarized, or
> bought or sold. . . . When I see a particularly mean man carrying a load of fair
> and fragrant early apples to market, I seem to see a contest going on between
> him and his horse, on the one side, and the apples on the other and, to my
> mind, the apples always gain it. . . . Our driver begins to lose his load the
> moment he tries to transport them to where they do not belong. . . . Though
> he gets out from time to time, and feels of them, and thinks they are all there,
> I see the stream of their evanescent and celestial qualities going to heaven
> from his cart, while the pulp and skin and core only are going to market. They
> are not apples but pomace.[35]

Pomace is the pulpy material that remains after the juice has been extracted from a fruit. Thoreau is saying that, in the market, no apple is sold; there, one finds only the remains after the fruit's vital, "volatile" quality has been removed.

The evanescence of the important qualities of objects is an effect of the market. Thoreau describes watching a farmer during apple harvest time, "between the fifth and twentieth of October":

> [He is] selecting some choice barrels to fulfil an order. He turns a specked
> one over many times before he leaves it out. If I were to tell what is passing

> in my mind, I should say that every one was specked which he had handled; for he rubs off all the bloom, and those fugacious ethereal qualities leave it. ("Wild Apples," 449)

The quality Thoreau values in the apple is that which cannot be captured; it is unstable, prone to flying away, fleeting. It is ethereal and intangible. This defining quality of the wild apple resists the market, resists commodification, so that if apples are sold, they are not apples at all, but only the pulp that remains after the fruit's essential qualities have been drained. To sell an apple is to commit violence against their highest quality: their wildness, their nonidentity, to use Adorno's term.

In the essay "Wild Apples," Thoreau implies that the attempt to cultivate, domesticate, and commodify wild apples reflects a broader trend in society. He begins the essay by saying, "It is remarkable how closely the history of the Apple-tree is connected with that of man" ("Wild Apples," 444). He goes on to say that there are several varieties of indigenous wild apples in North America, but the cultivated apple, the rosy, milder-tasting orchard apple, was brought to America by the British, who got it from the Romans:

> We have also two or three varieties of indigenous apples in North America. The cultivated apple-tree was first introduced into this country by the earliest settlers, and it is thought to do as well or better here than anywhere else. Probably some of the varieties which are now cultivated were first introduced into Britain by the Romans. ("Wild Apples," 445)

Having already told us that the history of humans and the history of the apple reflect each other, Thoreau now draws a parallel between imperialism and the cultivated apple. In one sentence he names two empires, the Roman and the British. The Romans passed on varieties of cultivated apples to the British, after conquering them to extend the Roman Empire. Interestingly, Thoreau says these apples have thrived in America as in few other places. He draws a connection between the cultivation of apples and acts of conquest and empire: this makes sense, as both seek to homogenize, control, domesticate. Just as he critiques the ways modernity tames humans, Thoreau denigrates cultivated apples: they may be sweet smelling and uniformly pretty, but they have been drained of their "spirited flavor," are "mild," and "commonly turn out to be very tame" ("Wild Apples," 458).

We get a clear picture of the wild apples Thoreau values when he extols one particular apple tree, growing on the side of a cliff, that he has seen in his walks. This is the most truly wild apple. It grows in a forbidden, rocky terrain and was never planted at all. Thoreau says that apple trees are often found in terrain that is too rocky or too distant for the farmer to bother with them. Such trees are wholly uncultivated: "There are, or were recently, extensive orchards there standing without order. Nay, they spring up wild and bear well there in the midst of pine, birches, maples and oaks" ("Wild Apples," 451). The wild apple tree on the cliff is the exemplar of this species. It is in such an inhospitable place that its owner is not even aware that he owns this tree. The fruits of the tree cannot be sold, and they cannot even be eaten, since the tree grows in such an inaccessible place.

> It was a rank wild growth, with many green leaves on it still, and made an impression of thorniness. . . . The owner knows nothing of it. . . . When I go by this shrub thus late and hardy, and see its dangling fruit, I respect the tree, and I am grateful for Nature's bounty, even though I cannot eat it. Here on this rugged and woody hill-side has grown an apple-tree, not planted by man, no relic of the former orchard, but a natural growth, like the pines and oak. Most fruits which we prize and use depend entirely on our care. Corn and grain, potatoes, peaches, melons, etc., depend on our plantings; but the apple emulates man's independence and enterprise. . . . Even the sourest and crabbedest apple, growing in the most unfavorable position, suggests such thoughts as these, it is so noble a fruit. ("Wild Apples," 451)

This tree's resistance to cultivation ennobles it. Its untamed quality embodies the independence Thoreau wants to encourage in humans.

Thoreau extols the sourness and unfavorable nature of both apple and tree. Everything about this "rank" and "wild" growth is unharmonious and uneasy, even the word Thoreau chooses to describe it: *crabbedest*. Something is "crabbed" when it is unpleasing, rough, "perverse," or "cross-grained."[36] If *euphony* is defined by a pleasant, smooth sound, often marked by long vowel sounds and liquid consonants such as *L* and *R*, then *crabbedest* seems to be the opposite of euphony: cacophony or dissonance.[37] With an ear for the relationship between style and content, Thoreau invokes an awkward word to describe this singularly incommodious tree. It grows on a precipice. Never having been touched by human hands, it likely yields the most mottled, speckled, wormy apples. Their taste would not be mild or sweet but would have the real sourness, "zest," "*tang*," or "*smack*" that

Thoreau relishes ("Wild Apples," 458; emphasis in original). These apples, even in their flavor, wake us up, startle and unsettle us.

Such fruits work against the domestication of all that is different and nonidentical, a tendency that, like the cultivated apple, has thrived in America. The need to seek out wild experiences and taste wild apples, so to speak, is politically important to Thoreau because the imperialist tendency to drive out "volatile" and "ethereal" qualities, to do violence against what is nonidentical, is getting stronger.

> The era of the Wild Apple will soon be past. It is a fruit which will probably become extinct in New England. You may still wander through old orchards of native fruit of great extent, which for the most part went to the cider mill, now all gone to decay. . . . Ah, poor man, there are many pleasures which he will not know! . . . I see nobody planting trees today in such out-of-the-way places, along the lonely roads and lanes, and at the bottom of the dells in the woods. Now that they have grafted trees, and pay a price for them, they collect them into a plat by their houses, and fence them in,—and the end of it all will be that we shall be compelled to look for our apples in a barrel. ("Wild Apples," 467)

Thoreau foresees a future where there will be no wild apples left, where all trees are grafted and fenced in as property. Every owner will account for his trees. And the only apples we will get will be the apples we can buy. This is the future Thoreau tries to work against through huckleberrying, walking, and courting the wild.

## The Political Value of Particular Things

For Thoreau and Adorno, there is a political value in how particular things change the ways we think and perceive. Both articulate their unconventional politics through their engagement with the particular: through the practice of negative dialectics for Adorno, and through excursions into wild nature for Thoreau. Both also associate these practices with more democratic possibilities. But what connection do their dissonant ways of thinking have to the participatory, intersubjective politics we typically associate with the idea of democracy? Thoreau and Adorno are notoriously dismissive of the conventional, mainstream political activities of their day. But does this mean they see all forms of "street-level" politics as inherently, necessarily useless and corrupt? I would argue against this interpretation. Instead, both Thoreau and Adorno see the cultivation of critical thinking practices as consonant with, and essential to, a more truly democratic politics.

Before we can form self-governing bodies, we must become self-governing individuals. This suggests that democracy is not just a structure of political institutions but an individual practice, a way of being in the world. The possibility of democracy depends on changing the ways we think and perceive. Adorno and Thoreau are suspicious of conventional politics, not because they reject politics *as such* but because it is so often conducted in uncritical, alienated, unthinking ways. They urge us to engage particular things to activate and cultivate our critical capacities, to work against the mainstream social forces that threaten our ability to negate and think against convention and the status quo. Thoreau and Adorno engage particular things in ways that disrupt, fracture, break apart, and negate the systematizing monotonies, conventional abstract logics, and illusory harmonies of modern mainstream society.[38] But these unconventional microlevel practices are conducted toward the end of cultivating more truly democratic citizens. Meaningful participatory, intersubjective, street-level politics is a possibility that can occur only when it is populated with individuals who are capable of critical, negative, independent thought. Negative dialectics, for Adorno, and confronting the wild, for Thoreau, are not valuable simply as prepolitical practices that prepare us for "real" politics: they are themselves politically valuable. In this way, Thoreau and Adorno push us to expand our conceptions of what counts as political and democratic, to widen the parameters of democratic political practice.

For Adorno, the loss of critical capacities is a fundamental problem for democracies, which promise that people will think and decide for themselves. In an essay titled "Critique," Adorno describes the democratic value of this critical practice: "Critique is essential to all democracy. Not only does democracy require the freedom to criticize and need critical impulses. Democracy is nothing less than defined by critique."[39] He is concerned with people's willingness to follow the lead of others, to conform to conventional opinion, to bend to the will of seemingly immutable historical forces. He argues that for a state to be truly democratic, it must have politically mature, autonomous, critical, thinking citizens.[40] Without such constituents, it is a democracy in name only. Adorno argues that "democracy, according to its very idea, promises people that they themselves would make decisions

about their world."[41] Negative dialectics, by enacting the critical consciousness that is rooted in the realization that things might be otherwise, that
existing conditions are not necessary, that we might think against the status
quo, becomes a valuable democratic political practice.

The connections Adorno makes between cultivating our critical capacities and the possibility of democracy help us better understand how
huckleberrying enacts Thoreau's politics. Thoreau is not a political theorist
in a conventional sense; he does not provide us with a fully fleshed out,
normative vision of the political state he wants to bring about. He does not
address the question of what mass-based social changes might result from
huckleberrying or picking wild apples or other practices in which we confront
the "wild." But he does reach toward a more truly democratic polity, and
he sees these critical practices as opening up more democratic possibilities.
His excursions into nature are part and parcel of that democratic vision. But
because of their unconventional form, Thoreau's democratic practices have
been characterized as a waste of time, politically speaking.

In his funeral eulogy, Emerson criticized Thoreau for not living up
to his full potential; Emerson thought Thoreau was born for greater positions and more important commands than huckleberry "captain." But in
criticizing Thoreau for leading a huckleberry party instead of an empire, for
failing to become a social engineer, Emerson misunderstands his project.
Emerson's eulogy helped solidify the dominant interpretation of Thoreau as
inadequately concerned with society and politics.[42] As Emerson says:

> Had his genius been only contemplative, he had been fitted to his life, but
> with his energy and practical ability he seemed born for great enterprise and
> for command; and I so much regret the loss of his rare powers of action, that
> I cannot help counting it a fault in him that he had no ambition. Wanting this,
> instead of engineering for all America, he was the captain of a huckleberry
> party. Pounding beans is good to the end of pounding empires one of these
> days; but if, at the end of years, it is still only beans![43]

Here, Emerson's notions of political and social leadership are constrained
by the conventional understanding of politics as plans for wide-scale social
change (though, in other texts, Emerson too is critical of mass reform). Emerson fails to appreciate that these kinds of actions are highly problematic
for Thoreau. Being a social engineer and "pounding empires" is antithetical
to Thoreau's theoretical position. He is critical of the urge to empire, to

dominate, control, and "pound" things into shape. But Thoreau is also less optimistic about the value of the "great enterprises" and mass movements that Emerson wanted him to lead. Thoreau has more faith in political action conducted in a different register: a more microcosmic, particular level that changes patterns of individual thought. Ultimately, Emerson misrepresents Thoreau's choice: he presents Thoreau as having chosen contemplation over action, mindlessly leading huckleberry parties instead of helping to create political change. But for Thoreau, huckleberrying *is itself* a political practice: it cultivates the critical capacities he sees as necessary if we are to be truly democratic citizens instead of "machines."

While walking, Thoreau looks closely at wild apples and huckleberries: these particular things prompt him to question the practices of domestication, cultivation, taming, abstract exchange, and conventional notions of politics that characterize a modern society where men act as machines. Thoreau directs his gaze toward the seemingly insignificant objects that "philosophically-schooled authors" (to borrow Adorno's phrase) would disregard. But for Thoreau, these "little things" contain qualities that stimulate critical negation. While walking in the fields and woods and confronting "the wild," he thinks dissonant thoughts about Main Street and all it represents: for example, conventional practices of buying a house, etiquette, abstract exchange, labor, furniture, railroads. These practices are political for Thoreau because they recuperate the critical capacities that define the truly democratic citizen as opposed to the wooden citizen-as-machine. Thoreau famously writes:

> The mass of men serve the State thus, not as men mainly but as machines, with their bodies. . . . In most cases, there is no free exercise whatever of the judgment or of the moral sense; but they put themselves on a level with wood and earth and stones, and wooden men can perhaps be manufactured that will serve the purpose as well.[44]

He asks, "Is a democracy, such as we know it, the last improvement possible in government? Is it not possible to take a step further toward recognizing and organizing the rights of man?" ("Resistance," 89). Thoreau seems to push us toward realizing a more truly democratic government in which we act less like machines. Paying attention to the dissonant qualities contained in particular things helps us work against becoming these kinds of automatons who move through preset patterns and think in terms of established conventions. This, in itself, is part of the practice of democracy.

Interestingly, both Thoreau and Adorno also portray paying attention to particular things, and drawing out their rupturing possibilities, as throwing a wrench into the machinery of modern society to open up more democratic possibilities. Adorno says that collective delusions "are rational in the sense that they rely on societal tendencies and that anyone who so reacts knows he is in accord with the spirit of the times. . . . Whoever doesn't entertain any idle thoughts doesn't throw any wrenches into the machinery."[45] Anyone who acts as an automaton, unthinkingly, idly, upholds the "smooth logic" of "what is" instead of thinking against reified modern social norms. Voicing a similar concern, Thoreau tells us that the "mass of men" serve the state as "machines" but advises us to be critical of the state and of injustice: "Let your life be a counter friction to stop the machine" ("Resistance," 73–74). When the machinery of politics runs smoothly, men do not think for themselves. This is the state of affairs that Thoreau thinks characterizes conventional, everyday politics. This is the condition he wants to disrupt: "I am not responsible for the successful working of the machinery of society. I am not the son of the engineer" ("Resistance," 81). Thoreau enacts his democratic politics on a different register; in this way, he valuably expands our notions of "the political."

Democratic politics, for both Thoreau and Adorno, depends on modest, small-scale, daily, seemingly insignificant practices. Whether we are talking about walking, huckleberrying, or negative dialectics, we are ultimately talking about practices that draw out the critical potential of particular things, incite us to appreciate what is unique despite the force of sameness, and inspire us think for ourselves against the power of convention. Adorno breaks apart the "abstract monotony" and "smooth logic" of a modern society under the sway of an idealist dialectic that violently reconciles and synthesizes everything unique and different. Negative dialectics engages particular objects to force recognition of, and widen, these cracks in the system, to highlight the "damaged life" of modern society. Thoreau's thought is similarly opposed to illusory harmonies. We see him praise "thorny" wild apple trees and fruits that taste "acidic," "crabbed," "sour," and "sharp." On a different level, in analyzing huckleberries and wild apples, he is prompted to critique the logics of abstract exchange, imperialism, and the instrumentalization of nature.

These are inglorious, inconspicuous, individual acts that change our perception, that sharpen our ability to think. But for Thoreau and Adorno, these practices have a critical potential that exceeds their humble appearance. They awaken us to what is violated and lost through the abstract ways of thinking that increasingly characterize modern society. By seeking out particularity, they both try to rupture, fracture, and negate these smoothing, taming, and domesticating logics. The alienating logics of modern society violate our ability to hear the dissonant call of the "nonidentical" or the "wild," but for Thoreau and Adorno, paying attention to particularity bears valuable fruit for democracy. The critical capacities we recuperate through these excursions are vital for meaningful democratic citizenship.

## Notes

I would like to acknowledge the people who have helped with my larger project on Thoreau and Adorno, of which this chapter is one piece. In particular, I thank Susan Buck-Morss, Anna Marie Smith, Jason Frank, and Isaac Kramnick for their insight and encouragement. I also thank Samuel Frederick for his constant and invaluable help in translating Adorno's words from the original German. Jack Turner, Tom Dumm, and Ed Royce provided valuable editorial advice, substantive criticism, and useful suggestions. Finally, I would like to thank my partner David Rando for his love and support.

1. Theodor Adorno, *Minima Moralia: Reflections from Damaged Life,* trans. E. F. N. Jephcott (London: Verso, 1974).

2. As Susan Buck-Morss notes, Adorno used this term in reference to Walter Benjamin's work. But Adorno, influenced by Benjamin, also adopted this "microscopic gaze." Susan Buck-Morss, *The Origin of Negative Dialectics* (New York: Free Press, 1977), 74.

3. In my book *Thoreau's Democratic Withdrawal: Alienation, Participation, and Modernity* (Madison: University of Wisconsin Press, forthcoming), I identify marked differences between Emerson's more abstracting gaze (which, using his own term, I call "focal distancing") and the way Thoreau sees. The sympathies between Thoreau and Adorno help name the differences between Emerson and Thoreau and show how Thoreau's thought resists the "transcendentalist" label.

4. Theodor Adorno, *Negative Dialectics,* trans. E. B. Ashton (New York: Continuum, 1973), 27; hereafter cited in text.

5. These are all particular things that Adorno explores in the aphorisms of *Minima Moralia.*

6. Adorno, *Minima Moralia*, 59. Adorno refers to "damaged life" in the subtitle of the book (*Reflections from Damaged Life*) and to "vanished life" in his aphorisms.

7. J. M. Bernstein, "Negative Dialectics as Fate," in *The Cambridge Companion to Adorno*, ed. Tom Huhn (New York: Cambridge University Press, 2004), 36.

8. Theodor Adorno, *Negative Dialektik, Gesammelte Schriften Band 6* (Darmstadt: Wissenchaftliche Buchgesellschaft, 1998), 149.

9. As Martin Jay says, this general decay of experience is a primary indicator of the modern crisis: "There is, in short, an implied loss of something that once existed and has been seriously damaged, if not entirely destroyed, in the present. Variously attributed to the traumas of world war, modern technologies of information, and the 'atemporal, technified process of the production of material goods,' which seems another way to say capitalist industrialization, the decay of something called experience is for Adorno an index of the general crisis of modern life." Martin Jay, "Is Experience Still in Crisis? Reflections on a Frankfurt School Lament," in *Cambridge Companion to Adorno*, 131.

10. In the original German, the phrase translated here as "has to pay dearly" is put much more strongly as "has to pay with a bitter sacrifice": "*hat fraglos mit bitterem Opfer an der qualitativen Mannigfaltigkeit der Erfahrung zu zahlen.*" Adorno, *Negative Dialektik*, 18.

11. Buck-Morss, *Origin of Negative Dialectics*, 74.

12. Ibid., 73.

13. Ibid., 74.

14. Ibid., 76.

15. Ibid.

16. Seyla Benhabib, *Critique, Norm, and Utopia* (New York: Columbia University Press, 1986), 181.

17. Richard D. Brown and Jack Tager, *Massachusetts: A Concise History* (Amherst: University of Massachusetts Press, 2000), 116–17.

18. Ibid., 115.

19. Ibid., 115–16.

20. Ibid., 119.

21. Ibid., 125.

22. Ibid., 165.

23. Ibid., 164.

24. Henry David Thoreau, *Walden*, ed. J. Lyndon Shanley (Princeton, NJ: Princeton University Press, [1854] 2004), 116; hereafter cited in text.

25. Brian Donahue, "The Forests and Fields of Concord: An Ecological History, 1750–1850," in *Concord: The Social History of a New England Town 1750–1850*, ed. David Hackett Fischer (Waltham, MA: Brandeis University Press, 1984).

26. Ibid., 32.

27. Ibid., 57.

28. Ibid., 60.

29. Henry David Thoreau, "Life without Principle," in *The Higher Law: Thoreau on Civil Disobedience and Reform*, ed. Wendell Glick (Princeton, NJ: Princeton University Press, 2004), 160; hereafter cited in text as "Life."

30. Interestingly, in "Self-Reliance," Emerson uses the term "penance" in a similar way. As he says, "men do what is called a good action, as some piece of courage or charity, much as they would pay a fine in expiation of daily non-appearance on parade. Their works are done as an apology or extenuation of their being in the world,—as invalids and the insane pay a high board. Their virtues are penances. I do not wish to expiate, but to live." Ralph Waldo Emerson, "Self-Reliance," in *Essays: First Series*, vol. 2, ed. Joseph Slater, *The Collected Works of Ralph Waldo Emerson* (Cambridge, MA: Belknap Press of Harvard University Press, 1979), 31. For both Thoreau and Emerson, doing this "penance" is contrasted with really "living."

31. Henry David Thoreau, "Walking," in *Collected Essays and Poems*, ed. Elizabeth Hall Witherell (New York: Library of America, 2001), 227; hereafter cited in the text.

32. In his essay "Thoreau's Later Natural History Writings," Ronald Wesley Hoag also notes the democratic tendencies of Thoreau's "Huckleberries." As Hoag says, "Even Thoreau's tone in this essay is unusually democratic, as when he assures his readers that 'It is my own way of living that I complain of as well as yours' or speaks companionably of 'we dwellers in the huckleberry pastures.' His friendliness is tactical, for in this essay the target of reform is entire communities rather than individuals." However, Hoag focuses only on the democratic tone of the piece and the democratic imperative to preserve more natural spaces to be held in common, as public spaces. He does not explore how, for Thoreau, the practice of huckleberrying itself educates us about being more critical and independent democratic citizens. Furthermore, Hoag does not describe the huckleberry fields themselves as a political space for the formation of a new type of citizen; in his reading, Thoreau is simply saying that a democracy needs to maintain and preserve wild spaces, but these spaces themselves are not a new ground for politics but more of a space of retreat. Ronald Wesley Hoag, "Thoreau's Later Natural History Writings," in *The Cambridge Companion to Henry David Thoreau*, ed. Joel Myerson (New York: Cambridge University Press, 1995), 162.

33. Henry David Thoreau, "Huckleberries," in *Collected Essays and Poems*, 468; hereafter cited in text.

34. In his article titled "Huckleberries and Humans: On the Naming of Huckleberry Finn," James L. Colwell explores the origins of that classic rascal's

name. He notes Thoreau's passages on the wildness of the berry from *Walden*. Although Colwell finds no evidence that Twain was influenced by Thoreau's writings in naming his hero, he concludes that Twain, like Thoreau, capitalized on the huckleberry's resistance to civilization. Apparently, Twain also considered naming his hero Mulberry. As Colwell says, "Precisely how and when Twain hit upon 'Huckleberry' remains a mystery, but it was apparent from the start that he made an excellent choice" (70). Colwell notes the sympathy between the boy who resists polite society and the berry that resists domestication: "Twain chose well— probably better than he knew—when he named Huck, for there is a characteristic of that small berry that makes it a superb symbol for the boy and his life. Through all of the history of American civilization, the huckleberry has resisted attempts at its domestication" (74). Like the berry itself, Colwell concludes that "Twain's Huckleberry, too, never reaches the city. He, in his way, was a determined social innocent, preferring to flee the American society rather than submit to its domestication. Wealth and most other human possessions were as burdensome to him as to any Thoreauvian: he wanted no part of 'sivilization.' Thus the botanic huckleberry's preference for the wilder reaches of the American woods nicely parallels that same inclination on the part of the literary Huckleberry. At the end of his *Adventures*, he is preparing to 'light out for the territory ahead of the rest' rather than suffer any further efforts at taming him. Huckleberry Finn was indeed well named" (74). James L. Colwell, "Huckleberries and Humans: On the Naming of Huckleberry Finn," *PMLA* 86, no. 1 (1971): 70–76.

35. Henry David Thoreau, "Wild Apples," in *Collected Essays and Poems*, 448; hereafter cited in text.

36. See the entry for "crabbed" in *Oxford English Reference Dictionary*, rev. 2nd ed., ed. Judy Pearsall and Bill Trumble (New York: Oxford University Press, 2002).

37. See "euphony," ibid.

38. My book *Thoreau's Democratic Withdrawal* explores the paradoxical yet necessary "politics of withdrawal" of both Thoreau and Adorno. I also analyze these themes in "Critique from the Margins: Adorno and the Politics of Withdrawal," *Political Theory* 36, no. 3 (2008): 456–65.

39. Theodor Adorno, "Critique," in *Critical Models: Interventions and Catchwords* (New York: Columbia University Press, 1998), 281.

40. In a 1959 lecture that was later a radio address and then an essay, Adorno describes the ways of thinking that characterized the Nazi era, shows how they continued to characterize the post-Nazi era despite the advent of German parliamentary democracy, and discusses what might be done to create a more truly democratic Germany. Adorno argues that for Nazism to be consigned to the past, people must become citizens capable of thinking for themselves, instead of au-

thoritarian subjects with weak egos who seek the safety of the collective. Changes in the economic order must be made if such citizens are to be created: a democracy based on self-determination cannot exist in an economic structure that makes people feel powerless and dependent. But Adorno spends most of his time discussing the conformist ways of thinking that characterize life under an authoritarian regime and showing how they persist under German parliamentary democracy. His major point is that a democracy is not created only by instituting a new form of political rule. Democracy depends, initially, on creating citizens who are capable of engaging in the practice of critique. The first published version of the essay even included a formal discussion between Adorno and his students, who pressed him to clarify parts of his lecture even more explicitly. Theodor Adorno, "The Meaning of Working through the Past," in *Critical Models,* 92. See also Theodor Adorno, "Appendix 1: Discussion of Professor Adorno's Lecture 'The Meaning of Working through the Past,'" ibid.

41. Adorno, "Appendix 1," 296.

42. As Robert Sattelmeyer and other scholars have noted, Emerson seemed to use his now famous eulogy for Thoreau as a chance to settle some scores and remind everyone that he thought Thoreau had wasted his life by not being more of a traditional social or political leader. As Sattelmeyer notes, "Emerson's eulogy seems particularly designed to present Thoreau's life as one of renunciation and withdrawal. . . . Emerson's account of Thoreau makes him a renouncer, an iconoclast . . . and a hermit and ascetic." Robert Sattelmeyer, "Thoreau and Emerson," in *Cambridge Companion to Thoreau,* 37.

43. Ralph Waldo Emerson, introduction to *Walden and Other Writings* (New York: Modern Library, 2000), xxviii.

44. Henry David Thoreau, "Resistance to Civil Government," in *Higher Law,* 66; hereafter cited in text as "Resistance."

45. Adorno, "The Meaning of Working through the Past," 92.

# CHAPTER 16

# Thoreau, Cavell, and the Foundations of True Political Expression

*Andrew Norris*

I desire to speak somewhere *without* bounds; like a man in a waking moment, to men in their waking moments; for I am convinced that I cannot exaggerate enough even to lay the foundation of a true expression.
—Thoreau, *Walden*

THE PUBLICATION OF Stanley Cavell's *The Senses of Walden* in 1972 was an extraordinary event in Thoreau scholarship. Thoreau's reputation had waxed and waned, but by the early 1970s the obscurity to which he had seemed fated at his death was well past. The author and hero of "Civil Disobedience" had achieved lasting fame and considerable status as a political thinker via his influence on Tolstoy, Gandhi, Martin Luther King Jr., and the Dutch anti-Nazi resistance in the Second World War, and *Walden* was widely acknowledged to be his masterpiece. Although this acknowledgment was reflected in significant work in fields as diverse as literary criticism, natural history, and American studies, *Walden* had yet to be recognized as making a significant contribution to *philosophy;* indeed, it is rare even today, more than thirty years later, to hear one claim any distinctively philosophical interest in this most praised of Thoreau's books. In Cavell's study, moreover, Thoreau's magnum opus was taken up by a philosopher who worked outside the tradition of American pragmatism, the philosophical tradition that comes closest to grudgingly granting a place if not to Thoreau then to his mentor Emerson. Perhaps most importantly, in *The Senses of Walden*, *Walden* was read by a mind as unorthodox and fiercely independent as its author's own. Given the kind of book Cavell set out to write, this was of necessity the case. *The Senses of Walden* is not simply a reading of *Walden* but, as its title suggests, a reading of it that takes the form of a rewriting of it, a reiteration of its senses or meanings, and hence its perceptions and senses of the world.

The first line of Cavell's preface asks, "What hope is there in a book about a book?"[1] Cavell goes on to make clear that this is not meant to distinguish the plight of his book about *Walden* from Thoreau's book about Walden, for in writing about Walden, Thoreau describes and plumbs not only the pond, Walden, but also his own experience of that pond, what he did at and with it. And the first thing Thoreau chooses to tell us of what he did there is to write *Walden*.[2] As Cavell puts it, "*Walden* is itself about a book, about its own writing and reading."[3] Since this is exactly what Cavell's book is about—the writing and reading of *Walden*—Cavell is doing Thoreau's work over, reinscribing and repeating it, as one might repeat the words of another.[4] The titles of the chapters of Cavell's book underline the importance of this for his understanding of Thoreau's work. *Walden* is divided into eighteen chapters, only the third ("Reading") and possibly the fourth ("Sounds") and eleventh ("Higher Laws") of which refer even indirectly to linguistic matters; *The Senses of Walden* is divided into three chapters ("Words," "Sentences," and "Portions") that, taken together, do just this. Whereas Thoreau's titles, for the most part, name things in the world ("The Bean-Field," "The Village," "Winter Animals") or ways of being in the world or events in the world ("Solitude," "House-Warming"), Cavell's titles name three forms in which our utterances might be meaningful, or make sense: as independent words, as sentences, and as paragraphs, verses, quatrains, or other portions of text.[5] If these are the senses of *Walden*, however, this distinction must be one of approach or emphasis rather than topic. And the fact that Cavell writes of the *senses* rather than the *meanings* of *Walden* announces plainly enough that these are to be understood as ways of perceiving and experiencing the world, like hearing, smelling, touching, tasting, and seeing. If Thoreau knows the world so well that he can show it to us as something we have not yet seen, this is not because he experienced it more directly in his hut than did others back in Concord; rather, it is because, in writing of it, he comes closer to the language with which we give shape and heft to the real in what Cavell describes as our "wording of the world."[6] Though written in prose, *Walden* is poetry of the kind Shelley describes in his "Defense of Poetry" when he argues that the poet is "the unacknowledged legislator of the world" who alone can keep language from dying over time; in losing the ability to represent the world in its complexity as opposed to mere "classes of thoughts," one loses the ability to give voice to "the nobler purposes of human interaction."[7] Poets "in the most universal sense of the word" can thus reinvigorate a dying language because of their ability, first, to "behold intensely the present as it is [and] the future in the present," and second, to "express the influence of society or nature upon their own minds" in "vitally metaphorical" language that "communicates [the pleasure of that expression] to others, and gathers a sort of reduplication from that community."[8] In romantic poetry such as Thoreau's, we are meant to find the ability to sense the world and the society lost in the senses of our degenerate language.

This is true even in those texts in which Thoreau seems to set his face against society much more decisively than he does in *Walden*. In "Walking," for instance, Thoreau writes of coming to see that the Mississippi is "a Rhine stream of a different kind; that the foundations of castles were yet to be laid, and the famous bridges were yet to be thrown over the river. And I felt that *this was the heroic age itself*, though we know it not, for the hero is commonly the simplest and obscurest of men."[9] Although this is no doubt a reiteration of Thoreau's repeated claim to find the strange within the familiar, and the world within Concord, one should not overlook the words Thoreau italicizes, words that announce this discovery as one with the writing of the epic announcing it. The heroic age of the Rhine's castles and bridges is a *literary* age, one made real in song and verse. In the absence of sagas celebrating them, who would know one's heroes? It is no surprise, then, that Thoreau goes on in "Walking" to ask, "Where is the literature which gives expression to Nature?"[10] If "the simplest and obscurest of men" are to be revealed as the heroes they are—which is to say, are to become the heroes they are—this will require not a new heroic world but a poetry adequate to a heroic world.

If we as readers fail to note Thoreau's demand for a literature adequate to the world, we will continue to read *Walden* as first and foremost an account of "Life in the Woods," forgetting that Thoreau himself thought the subtitle announcing the book as such misleading enough that he instructed his publishers to remove it eight years after the book's initial 1854 publication.[11] Indeed, Thoreau takes care to emphasize early on in *Walden* the limitations of such a woodsman's life as a solution to the miserable fact that "the mass of men live lives of quiet desperation." "From the desperate city," he writes, "you go into the desperate country, and have to console yourself with the bravery of minks and muskrats. . . . But it is a characteristic of wisdom not to do desperate things."[12] It is not simply in removing himself to Walden that Thoreau puts himself in a position to address our condition; he does so by writing *Walden*.[13] Our failure to appreciate this receives unfortunate encouragement in Emerson's distorted but influential portrait of Thoreau in his memoir, according to which Thoreau is a *character* first and a writer only by way of reporting on that character.[14] But there is also a difficulty peculiar to the romantic project of writing poetry that will be adequate to a world and a mode of life that is not yet that of its readers.[15] As Thoreau puts it in "Reading," a chapter title that instructs us to expect some guide to the approach to *Walden*, "The heroic books . . . will always be written in a language dead to degenerate times, and we must laboriously seek the meaning of each word and line, conjecturing a larger sense than common use permits of what wisdom and valor and generosity we have."[16] In the case of *Walden*, this involves learning how to read the book's basic "vital metaphors," those that concern the relation between life at Walden as Thoreau depicts it and the writing of *Walden*. As Cavell puts it, if "it is hard to keep in mind that the hero of this book is its writer," this is "because we seem to be shown this hero doing everything under the sun but, except very infrequently, writing. It takes a while to recognize that each of his actions is the act of a writer."[17] Writing as Thoreau does is a way of being in the world, for oneself and one's readers, that is adequate to that world. It is, as Cavell puts it, redemptive.

Thoreau indicates some of the difficulties and apparent paradoxes of such writing in the second paragraph of *Walden*, in his sly discussion of the questions posed by his townsmen that provoked the apparent self-absorption of *Walden*:

> I should not obtrude my affairs so much on the notice of my readers if very particular inquiries had not been made by my townsmen concerning my mode of life, which some would call impertinent, though they do not appear to me impertinent, but, considering the circumstances, very natural and pertinent. Some have asked what I got to eat; if I did not feel lonesome; if I was not afraid; and the like. Others have been curious to learn what portion of my income I devoted to charitable purposes; and some, who have large

families, how many poor children I maintained. I will therefore ask those of my readers who feel no particular interest in me if I undertake to answer some of these questions in this book. In most books, the *I*, or first person, is omitted; in this it will be retained; that, in respect to egotism, is the main difference. We commonly do not remember that it is, after all, always the first person that is speaking.[18]

Since it is impossible to imagine a *Walden* in which Thoreau does not figure as prominently as he does, this is a characteristically roundabout way of saying that it is because of his townsmen's questions that he writes the book at all.[19] To put the point differently, Thoreau announces here that the questioning of his townsmen reveals them to require the lessons Thoreau can teach regarding the *I*, the use of the first person, and its role in Thoreau's "mode of life." The townsmen ask Thoreau about his mode of life but do not expect him to use the first person in answering them. They think, then, that Thoreau can sensibly give an account of himself without speaking for himself. This reveals that they do not know how to speak for themselves, how to represent themselves—a disastrous lack in "our democratic New England towns," which pride themselves on being governed by the will of the people.[20] Further, if we read Thoreau's words in light of Cavell's observation that they often require "an emphasis other than, or in addition to, the one their surface grammar suggests," we can see that Thoreau worries here that in the common omission of the *I*, his townsmen have literally omitted *themselves* from their lives.[21] Having forgotten themselves and removed themselves from the world, they are dead to it, as Thoreau more or less announces when he writes with bitter irony that in *Walden* he "would fain say something, not so much concerning the Chinese and Sandwich Islanders, as you who read these pages, who are said to live in New England; something about your condition, especially your outward condition or circumstances in this world, what it is, whether it is necessary that it be as bad as it is, whether it cannot be improved as well as not."[22]

Thoreau's townsmen "are said to live in New England" by others because they do not announce this themselves in their own speech, an omission that has everything to do with Thoreau's ironic suggestion that they do not, in fact, *live* there, do not live *there*. The answer to the question with which Cavell begins his "reduplication" of *Walden*, "What hope is there in a book about a book?" is thus the hope that we might find ourselves where we are, that we might awake to our lives.[23] "Moral reform is," Thoreau says, "the effort to throw off sleep"—a sleep we falsely attribute to the dead and that better characterizes our own inability and refusal to live where we are now.[24] But a book that attempts such reform will of necessity strike those of us in the circumstances of Thoreau's townsmen—the people for whom the book is written, whose dead lives call for it—as "impertinent" and "unnatural" in its suggestion that we are not yet there, that we still slumber, that in our thoughtlessness we are beside ourselves in an insane way.[25] Thoreau's own attempt to answer his townsmen is one that will, of necessity, provoke their, and our, distrust and suspicion. Thoreau's announcement of this in the opening pages of his book is the first of his efforts to awaken us.

The fact that our heroes are, as Thoreau says, obscure as well as simple is, then, not so much a matter of how they are spoken of but a matter of how they speak, of how they leave themselves out. The true hero, whose heroism is realized in the sense of both being made conscious and being made real, is he who awakens to his life here, where he is, his everyday "simple" life, and to his voicing of it; a hero is he who awakens to the common and, in so doing, fulfills and transforms it. It is crucial for Cavell's reading of Thoreau that the existential and the semantic or linguistic thus line up. Immediately before writing *The Senses of Walden* in 1970–1971, Cavell published a collection of essays, *Must We Mean What We Say?* in which, among other things, he defends a mode of ordinary language philosophy that, though derived from the work of J. L. Austin, is far more explicitly "existentially" oriented than Austin's—as well as far more openly aligned with the project of romantic poetry sketched by Shelley. Whereas Austin focused on using the analysis of ordinary language as a way of revealing the philosophical errors of positivists such as A. J. Ayer, Cavell presents it as a way of returning us to an everyday or ordinary life we had failed to make our own, and thus as a mode of access to an "eventual everyday" in which our meanings and our lives would come together, as they currently do not. If, as Wittgenstein claims, we need to "lead words back from their metaphysical to their everyday use," this is because the everyday as we live it is the uncanny site of our self-estrangement.[26] Ordinary language philosophy as Cavell practices it combats what he describes as "a version of what Socrates calls the unexamined life" in its engagement with our failure to attend to what we are saying and how we are saying it, our failure to really mean what we are saying, and our failure to really *do* all the things we attempt to do with our speech, as individuals and as members of political communities.[27]

The title of Cavell's collection is intended to be a provocation. According to Cavell, as strange as it may sound, we must not always mean what we say, not simply because we sometimes say things we do not mean (such as when we tell fibs and lies) but because we sometimes try to *mean* things we cannot actually mean by certain words and in certain circumstances; in so doing, we refuse to mean what we *are* saying. As an example, Cavell imagines someone asking, in quite ordinary circumstances, "Would you like to use my scooter?" and insisting that, in so asking, he is not suggesting that the person asked may use the scooter if she wishes. In ordinary circumstances, Cavell points out, this question *has* to be an offer, not an inquiry into the other's state of mind: "The 'pragmatic implications' of our utterances are (or, if we are feeling perverse, or tempted to speak carelessly, or chafing under an effort of honesty, let us say *must be*) *meant;* . . . they are an essential part of what we mean when we say something, of what it is to mean something."[28] Of someone who insists, in the face of the disappointment and irritation of others, that in asking "Would you like to use my scooter?" he "just wants to know what's on your mind," Cavell concludes, he has "tuned out, become incomprehensible."[29] Unable to foist a meaning on his words that they, in this context, will not bear, and unwilling to make the meaning that they do bear his own, the speaker succeeds in meaning nothing, exactly—a predicament that should recall Nietzsche's diagnosis of the nihilist as one who chooses "to will the nothing."[30]

Although this is a trivial example, the lesson is a central one for Cavell's understanding of philosophy in general and of skepticism in particular, an attitude toward the world and toward "other minds" that Cavell finds to be of far greater significance and extent than is usually supposed. In numerous aspects of our lives, but particularly when we reflect on freedom, knowledge, and the question of the real *überhaupt,* we fall, Cavell argues, into similar senseless expressions and positions. We try to say that we do quite ordinary things *voluntarily*—such as running family errands in unexceptional circumstances—and lead ourselves to believe that everything we do that is not a response to actual coercion is voluntary and hence open to moral appraisal—as if an entire way of life could be open to moral appraisal at any time, by anyone. This is to lose sight of the fact that we say an act is *voluntary* only if there is something unusual or out of the ordinary about it; in so doing, we lose sight of the very particular sort of thing it is to evaluate an act's moral worth.[31] We say, "I know there are material objects" or "I am not now dreaming" and try to *mean* such statements as applying to reality *as such,* in the absence of a particular context in which things are seen to be fishy, material, or dreamt, and thus in the absence of any desire to make a particular claim to knowledge of a particular thing.[32] In so doing, we pride ourselves on achieving a kind of objectivity in which we set ourselves aside and yet still say something about the world, as if language were a matter of statements and facts aligning themselves with one another, with human beings such as ourselves acting as only an unreliable medium of exchange.[33]

Language, in short, is something we see at times as wholly pliable and responsive to our whims, and at other times as rigid and unyielding, of an impersonal significance far beyond any meaning humble beings such as ourselves might give it. For Cavell, each of these alternatives expresses an unhealthy fantasy symptomatic of a more general failure to accept the mode of our existence in the world, the ways our language games and corresponding forms of life are responsive to as well as expressive of our needs and desires in given situations, but in a manner in which individual assertion and communal commitment check and balance each other. Language is not primarily a matter of either unmediated self-assertion or the impersonal recording of facts, but of individual speakers and writers expressing themselves to one another. "There must," Cavell argues, "in grammar, be reasons for what you say, or be point in your saying of something, if what you say is to be comprehensible. We can understand what the *words* mean apart from understanding why you say them; but apart from understanding the point of your saying them we cannot understand what *you* mean."[34] In the model of "objectivity" sketched above, this is set aside in a fantasy of self-effacement: "In philosophizing we come to be dissatisfied with answers which depend upon *our* meaning something by an expression, as though what *we* meant by it were more or less arbitrary. . . . It is as though we try to get the world to provide answers in a way which is independent of our *claiming* something to be so."[35] Although my utterances need to express my sense of what is worth saying in the specific circumstances in which I speak, the fact that that sense is *mine* does not leave it subject to my arbitrary decision, any more than my sense of what is beautiful or just or rude is subject to such decision. That we live together in a common language requires and demonstrates a shared sense of what follows from what, a sense of what saying X in these circumstances means and implies. It is a central aspect of that sense that I cannot say—in the sense of meaningfully uttering words—just anything at any time in any context, and I cannot willfully impose meanings on my words that magically transcend the conditions of common interaction, expression, and understanding. This is a matter of the community's practice, of the practice of individuals who are, as Cavell puts it, "in attunement with one another."[36] It is we, in our practice, in our interactions with one another and with the world at large, who decide how we will speak. And in trying to say things we cannot quite mean, we reveal ourselves to be in conflict not with some extraordinary set of linguistic rules composed by either God or nature but with ourselves.

In presenting himself as capable of giving and receiving instruction here, the ordinary language philosopher speaks for his fellows and sees himself spoken for by them in their reflections of our life in language. It is because Cavell is a member of the same "form of life" as the scooter owner that he can remind him of what it is possible to mean, here and now, by his words. Ordinary language philosophy is thus an extraordinary medium of deliberation in which our discussions are not so much "intersubjective" as they are reflective of (and upon) a commonality as basic to our identity as our status as discrete "subjects." Cavell compares it to Kant's characterization, in the third *Critique,* of our common considerations of what is and is not beautiful. Kant argues there that our aesthetic, reflective judgments are universal but nonetheless subjective.[37] In saying that something is beautiful, I do not simply announce that I find it so but that others should find it so as well, that *we* find it beautiful. My judgment is thus *publicke,* as opposed to the merely "private judgments" of the "taste of sense," the pleasures we feel in the warmth of the sun, steak, Pepsi, and, in Kant's famous if rather obscure example, canary wine.[38] As Kant puts it, in making such judgments, we express ourselves in the "universal voice" or *allgemeine Stimme.*[39] The common sense this voice articulates is, however, a matter of what we (as subjects) *feel,* not what we can *prove.* When we announce that we find something to be beautiful we are, Kant says, "suitors for agreement from everyone else," but we are in no position to *demand* their assent to our judgment, there being no rules to which we might appeal for authority.[40] Instead, we present our subjective judgment as *exemplary* and ask others to share it.[41]

Thoreau, who turns his face to the woods because his fellow citizens "were not likely to find me any room in the court house," is just such an exemplary judge and speaker; he is one who confronts much the same

set of metaphysical fantasies, confusions, and internal conflicts as does
the ordinary language philosopher: "Thoreau is doing with our ordinary
assertions what Wittgenstein does with our more patently philosophical
assertions—bringing them back to a context in which they are alive. It is
the appeal from ordinary language to itself; a rebuke of our lives by what
we may know of them, if we will."[42] Thoreau's townsmen resemble Cavell's
skeptical philosopher in their expectation that Thoreau can, as it were, let
his words speak for him and give an account of his mode of life without
expressing himself and making his words his own. His townsmen expect the
same of themselves and hence succeed, like the "curious" scooter owner, in
meaning nothing and, in so doing, leading lives that are robbed of meaning
they would otherwise have. Their culture is, as Cavell puts it, characterized by an "esotericism" in which they attempt to deny or transcend the
public meanings of their terms as well as their personal engagement with
those public meanings and the community in which they are forged.[43] The
exoteric, however, cannot be set aside in favor of the esoteric; rather, the
disjunction between the two is one that splits the speaker's words and sets
the speaker against him- or herself. In combating his culture's esotericism
through his example, Thoreau struggles to bring his townsmen back to their
words and thus to themselves; it is, as Cavell puts it, "his subject that the
word and the reader can only be awakened together."[44]

Thoreau's appeal and example are presented in *Walden:* it is as a writer
that Thoreau instructs his townsmen how to begin to live, which involves
speaking and writing and, in so doing, accepting the terms of public discourse and the public life in which they live. Thoreau notes that he builds
his house one mile from the nearest neighbor; Cavell rightly notes that
this is just far enough to be seen, as an example must be.[45] If the writer of
Walden wants to be seen, it is in large part as the writer of *Walden*. The
"reduplications" from the community that the romantic poet evokes involve
its members in making their language their own, as Thoreau does his in
*Walden;* this means, first, making *Thoreau's* language their own, which is
to say, learning how to read his book.[46] The difficulty of this is constantly
stressed by Cavell, and he rightly alerts us to the fact that Thoreau himself
is quite explicit about the challenges this involves.[47] As we have already
seen, Thoreau maintains that "the heroic books . . . will always be written
in a language dead to degenerate times, and we must laboriously seek the
meaning of each word and line, conjecturing a larger sense than common

use permits of what wisdom and valor and generosity we have."[48] Cavell identifies heroic writing with what Thoreau elsewhere describes as the "Scriptures of nations," texts that are often unnoticed for what they are and bear the task of giving a nation its language. This entails not giving German to Germans or English to Americans, as our more xenophobic fellow citizens might hope, but giving language as it is to people who as yet have failed to make themselves present in their language and to see its working in their lives and see themselves in it.[49]

> Writing—heroic writing, the writing of a nation's scripture—must assume the conditions of language as such; re-experience, as it were, the fact that there is such a thing as language at all and assume responsibility for it—find a way to acknowledge it—until the nation is capable of serious speech again. Writing must assume responsibility, in particular, for three of the features it lives upon: (1) that every mark of a language means something in the language, one thing rather than another; that a language is totally, systematically meaningful; (2) that words and their orderings are meant by human beings, that they contain (or conceal) their beliefs, express (or deny) their convictions; and (3) that the saying of something when and as it is said is as significant as the meaning and ordering of the words said.[50]

These three aspects of language that make possible writing such as Thoreau's are clearly three faces of the teaching of ordinary language philosophy as Cavell understands it. Language is systematically meaningful in ways that we ordinarily fail to notice. Most if not all of Austin's readers are, for instance, surprised to learn that, if they are native English speakers, they say "How do you know?" and "Why do you believe?" but not "Why do you know?" and "How do you believe?"[51] The systematic nature of our own linguistic practice is something that a nation's scripture needs to reveal to us. But this systematic practice is one that rests on the ability of individual speakers to express *themselves* in their words. Linguistic expressions have meaning insofar as they are *our* expressions; their meaning is our own. And our expressions, of necessity, reveal the concrete details of the situation in which we speak and write. A question such as "Is our government our enemy?" means something very different if our government spies on us and manipulates our elections than if no such unpleasant revelations are made.

To show all this is not to show anything new but to reveal what has been there all along, to help us *realize* what our ordinary practice entails and thus return us to it. As Thoreau emphasizes again and again, such revelations, to self and other, require a *deliberate* practice. Thoreau famously says he went to Walden because he wished "to live deliberately," and he associates such a deliberate life with the writing of *Walden*.[52] "Books," he writes,

> must be read as deliberately and reservedly as they were written. It is not enough even to be able to speak the language of that nation by which they are written, for there is a memorable interval between the spoken and the written language, the language heard and the language read. The one is commonly transitory, a tongue, a dialect merely, almost brutish, and we learn it unconsciously, like the brutes, of our mothers. The other is the maturity and experience of that; if that is our mother tongue, this is our father tongue, a reserved and select expression, too significant to be heard by the ear, which we must be born again in order to speak.[53]

Cavell emphasizes in his reading of this passage that the "'father tongue' is not a new lexicon or syntax at our disposal, but precisely a rededication to the inescapable and utterly specific syllables upon which we are already disposed."[54] It is, in effect, the "tongue" of the eventual everyday that Cavell seeks in ordinary language philosophy. In each case, we are *reborn*—a fact that explains Thoreau's preference here for the father tongue over the mother tongue. As Cavell explains: "A son of man is born of woman; but rebirth, according to our Bible, is the business of the father."[55] The rebirth of Walden involves baptism in the waters of Walden Pond and, by extension, *Walden,* the book Thoreau endeavors to write in the father tongue. For *Walden* to be read as deliberately and reservedly as it was written requires that its readers master the tongue in which it is written and thus allow themselves and their language to be reborn.

Thoreau introduces the concept of the mother tongue in "The Service," one of his earliest pieces, written in 1840 but published posthumously. Here our mother tongue is said to be music, the "voice" of both "the brave man" and of God.[56] But at that point, he does not see the need or perhaps the possibility of a father tongue; one speaks the mother tongue of music, or one speaks with words. In introducing the idea of the father tongue, he introduces the idea that we might be redeemed in ways that require our going *forward* rather than back, in ways that require us to *pass through* the alienation and confusion that characterize our current state.[57] For Cavell, this is a crucial feature of *Walden*. Thoreau begins his book by implying that his readers are as good as dead, are haunting their lives, because he wants to wake them up. "I do not," Thoreau writes, "propose to write an ode to dejection, but to brag as lustily as chanticleer in the morning, standing on his roost, if only to wake my neighbors up."[58] But if waking up means becoming conscious, one must first become conscious of one's lack of consciousness. "We must learn," Thoreau says, "to reawaken and keep ourselves awake."[59] This sounds paradoxical only because we do not usually wake ourselves up, at least in this sense, and because we do not usually will ourselves to sleep—our sleep is not usually a grotesque form of "penance."[60] Thoreau's task in *Walden* is to teach us how to wake up, and to do that, he must first wake us up himself, show us that we have been sleeping, that the lives we lead are not yet our own and that the words we speak do not yet bear the meanings we give them—all tasks Thoreau begins in the unsettling opening pages of his book.

The first step in overcoming our estrangement from ourselves and from our language is acknowledging that estrangement. As Cavell puts it, Thoreau "has secrets which can only be told to strangers. The secrets are not his, and they are not the confidences of others. They are secrets because few are anxious to know them; all but one or two wish to remain foreign. Only those who recognize themselves as strangers can be told them, because those who think themselves familiars will think they have already heard what the writer is saying."[61] They will mistake the current everyday for the eventual everyday it might be. Thoreau, as we have seen, "would fain say something . . . about your condition, especially your outward condition or circumstances in this world, what it is, whether it is necessary that it be as bad as it is, whether it cannot be improved as well as not." Cavell asks of this famous passage, "Why does this watchman of the private sea insist especially upon his readers' outward condition or circumstances in this world?" and answers:

> Because the outward position or circumstance in this world is precisely the position of outwardness, outsideness to the world, distance from it, the position of stranger. The first step in attending to our education is to observe the strangeness of our lives, our estrangement from ourselves, the lack of necessity in what we profess to be necessary. The second step is to grasp the true necessity of human strangeness as such, the opportunity of outwardness.[62]

The opportunity of outwardness is the possibility of moving forward into our father tongue, actively inheriting our language as opposed to passively repeating it. That we are sleeping means that we might yet wake, a process in which Thoreau sees endless promise, as he announces in the closing words of *Walden:* "The light which puts out our eyes is darkness to us. Only that day dawns to which we are awake. There is more day to dawn. The sun is but a morning star."[63]

If waking to our lives is to write and read the father tongue, to be, in effect, born again, it is a *conversion process,* one in which we turn and face ourselves as we are.[64] This concern may seem to be of only indirect political significance. Thoreau indicates that he thinks otherwise in his sole reference in *Walden* to the events celebrated in his "Civil Disobedience." Although Thoreau was arrested and put in jail while living out at Walden Pond, he had not paid his poll taxes for years. His resistance to the U.S. government's support of slavery and its prosecution of the imperialist and unjust war against Mexico—a war that threatened to expand the extent of the slaveholding territories—was evidently not undertaken on the basis of Thoreau's life at Walden. But Thoreau, strikingly, suggests that something like this was in fact the case. Immediately before describing his arrest, Thoreau recounts walking at night in the woods near the pond, a recounting that leads him to consider the modes of conversion made possible at Walden:

> Not till we are completely lost, or turned round,—for a man needs only to be turned round once with his eyes shut in this world to be lost,—do we appreciate the vastness and strangeness of Nature. Every man has to learn the points of compass again as often as he awakes, whether from sleep or any abstraction. Not till we are lost, in other words, do we begin to find ourselves, and realize where we are and the infinite extent of our relations.

It is precisely *here* that Thoreau refers to "Civil Disobedience":

> One afternoon, near the end of the first summer, when I went to the village to get a shoe from the cobbler's, I was seized and put into jail, because, as I have elsewhere related, I did not pay a tax to, or recognize the authority of, the state which buys and sells men, women, and children, like cattle at the door of its senate-house.[65]

Thoreau could not be clearer that sleep as he understands it is a form of abstraction from reality; that waking to it is a conversion experience open only to the lost; and that the reality to which that conversion brings us round is characterized by infinite relations between people and things that carry with them significant moral and political obligations.

The turn back here is one that moves in opposition to the drift of much of our current political and religious talk, which Thoreau condemns as degrading patriotism on the one hand and a parochial obsession with "our church" on the other.[66] "The task of literature," as Cavell puts it, "is to rescue the word from both politics and religion."[67] Cavell expands on this elsewhere: "That our meaning a word is our return to it and its return to us—our occurring to one another—is expressed by the word's literality, its being just these letters, just here, rather than any others. In religion and politics, literality is defeated because we allow our choices to be made for us."[68] As we have seen, the choices that are up to us involve our words, what we say, not what we mean with those words: "We have a choice over our words, but not their meaning. Their meaning is in their language; and our possession of the language is the way we live it."[69] If we allow others to make the choices that are open to us (for instance, by limiting reasonable religious and political speech to that which respects the compromises of the church and the Constitution), we attempt to compensate for this by choosing the meaning of what is said. (One might say that the fantasy that such things are "subjective" and thus "voluntarily" or "freely" chosen is the correlate of our failure to accept the burden of the freedom we really do or could have.) The attempt to impose a meaning on those words that is not their own (to insist that all our actions might be done voluntarily or involuntarily, that any question we might ask is really just a way of asking, "What is on your mind?") reflects not our choices but our abdication of them, or, more properly, our abdication of the work of being present enough in our lives and our language to intelligibly choose anything.

The example Cavell gives from politics is denser and harder to understand than it at first appears: "In politics we allow ourselves to say, e.g., that a man is a fugitive who is merely running from enslavement. That is an attempted choice of meaning, not an autonomous choice of words. Beyond the bondage to institutions, we have put nature in bondage, bound it to our uses and to our hurried capacities for sensing, rather than learning of its autonomy."[70] It is plain enough that Cavell means to indicate that a fugitive flees from more than "merely" enslavement. But beyond that it gets trickier. What we "allow ourselves to say" appears to be—and is—a statement about *fugitives*. That Cavell has something else in mind as well is indicated by his awkward construction: "a man is a fugitive who is merely running from enslavement." This is a definition not just of a fugitive, a kind of man, but of *man* as such: a *man* is a fugitive who is merely running from enslavement. This is what we allow ourselves to say, and in doing so, we attempt to choose the meaning of our terms in ways that our terms will not allow. But if this is not what the terms mean, what *do* they mean? First, that a man is a fugitive who flees more than merely enslavement—that he, or rather we, also flee justice and nature. Locke's depiction of us as creatures who in health seek freedom and fair trade and face opposition only from without, from tyrants and other "Beasts of Prey" who choose to live by a rule other than that of reason and common equity, needs amending.[71] Second, that a man is a fugitive who flees freedom as well as enslavement and who finds his "escape from freedom" in flight. Third, and following from this, that a man as such is not a fugitive, and that living as if one were a fugitive is a betrayal of nature, of one's own nature. A fugitive is one who seeks freedom in flight, but our freedom is to be achieved not in flight but in standing still.

In "Visitors," Thoreau mocks the "runaway slaves with plantation manners" who visited him and "listened from time to time, like that fox in the fable, as if they heard the hounds a-baying on their track, and looked at me beseechingly, as much to say,—'O Christian, will you send me back?'" In immediately going on to speak of a "real runaway slave" he had helped, Thoreau makes it plain that he is not denying the fact of chattel slavery and the need of flight from it, but only the latter's adequacy. That a slave in Maryland must flee to the North to find freedom does not mean that a person in Massachusetts must or can find his or her freedom in flight. Our commitment to flight, our sense that freedom is found in flight, expresses our *hurried* capacities for sensing, our reluctance to speak and live, as Thoreau puts it, deliberately: "It appears," Thoreau writes, "as if men had deliberately chosen the common mode of living because they preferred it to any other. Yet they honestly think there is no choice left."[72] What appears to be an exercise of freedom is a denial of it, of its possibility. Denying ourselves the freedom to choose the lives we desire, we live like slaves. Finding ourselves incapable of stepping back from ourselves and our lives, we submit to our lives, submit to ourselves. "I sometimes wonder," Thoreau (the author of "A Plea for Captain John Brown") writes,

> that we can be so frivolous, I may almost say, as to attend to the gross but somewhat foreign form of servitude called Negro Slavery, there are so many keen and subtle masters that enslave both north and south. It is hard to have

a southern overseer; it is worse to have a northern one; but worst of all when you are slave-driver of yourself.[73]

Trapped in the quiet desperation of lives that are not our own, lives that represent our submission rather than our fulfillment, we naturally identify freedom with flight, with escape: when there is no choice left, the only choice is to flee. But doing so leaves us unable to do any of the things Thoreau's neighbors, in their initial questioning of him, rightfully take to be essential parts of a "mode of life" worth living: getting something to eat, avoiding being lonesome and afraid, being charitable, helping to raise children. Hence we spend our days shifting unhappily back and forth between fantasies of inevitability and fantasies of whimsy. As Cavell puts it in regard to the questions *Walden* was written to answer, Thoreau's "problem—at once philosophical, religious, literary, and, I will argue, political—is to get us to ask the questions, and then show us that we do not know what we are asking, and then to show us that we have the answer."[74] Only in this way is autonomy and democracy, or people power (*demos kratos*), possible.[75] Thoreau announces twice in *Walden* that he moved to Walden Pond on July 4, during a period he describes in characteristically elliptical fashion as one of personal crisis.[76] This, as is widely recognized, is Thoreau's way of declaring his independence, a declaration that throws into question the sufficiency of Jefferson's and the nation's. As Cavell puts it, "America's revolution never happened. The colonists fought a war against England all right, and they won it. But it was not a war of independence that was won, because we are not free; nor was even secession the outcome, because we have not departed from the conditions England lives under, either in our literature or in our political and economic lives."[77] Cavell goes on to ask, as others have not, why Thoreau emphasizes that he went to Walden Pond on the Fourth of July "by accident."[78] Cavell suggests, quite rightly, that the answer has to do with the superficiality of our understanding of what independence and hence freedom consist of. Although Thoreau acknowledges fortuitous accidents in his life and in nature, he suggests that we reserve our respect for "only what is inevitable and has a right to be."[79] Our freedom does not pass this test. We are free from the interference of others, perhaps, but we are not yet free in ourselves; our freedom does not flow from within, as it would if it were necessary, if it had a right to be.

To be a fugitive, as we say a man is, is to move *quickly*. To be free or autonomous requires standing still and accepting the limits of that freedom in nature, in language, and in others. (As Austin suggests, the fact that we cannot do everything voluntarily does not mean that we do it involuntarily, and the fact that we cannot choose whether to say we do everything voluntarily does not mean that we are constrained.) Cavell notes, "The most characteristic of [Thoreau's] reflexive descriptions is that of finding himself in some attitude or locale."[80] A free life as an individual and a citizen requires self-knowledge; this, in turn, requires knowing where one is. "For the most part," Thoreau writes, "we are not where we are, but in a false position."[81] He calls it a *position*, not just a situation, as this false position is our own stance toward the world, our aversion to it, our lack of interest in the reality of our own lives.[82] And this position is *ours*, not just mine and not just yours. "Practically," Thoreau writes, "the old have no very important advice to give the young, their own experience has been so partial, and their lives have been such miserable failures, for private reasons, as they must believe."[83] But the reasons are *public* ones. Thoreau himself finds no *private* relief at Walden from our shared condition, which he as much as announces in 1854's "Slavery in Massachusetts." Here, as in *Walden*, Thoreau condemns the servitude of his fellow citizens, their inability to accept that the solution to a problem they wish to locate in Nebraska and the South begins in Massachusetts, in their own homes. "I walk toward one of our ponds, but what signifies the beauty of nature when men are base? We walk to lakes to see our serenity reflected in them; when we are not serene, we go not to them. Who can be serene in a country where both the rulers and the ruled are without principle?"[84] If Thoreau finds some relief at "one of our ponds," it is a relief not in flight but in achieving a position from which he might address his fellow citizens. Thoreau may have lived alone at Walden Pond, but he wrote *Walden* for us.

## Notes

I am grateful to Jack Turner for his helpful comments on an earlier version of this chapter and to Adam Thurshwell for urging upon me, some years ago, the importance and complexity of the task of understanding what makes it possible to wake up and act politically.

1. Stanley Cavell, *The Senses of Walden*, exp. ed. (San Francisco: North Point Press, 1981), xiii.

2. Writing is indeed the first thing Thoreau describes himself doing in the open-

ing sentence of the book: "When I wrote the following pages, or rather the bulk of them, I lived alone, in the woods, a mile from any neighbor." Henry David Thoreau, *Walden and Civil Disobedience* (New York: Penguin, 1983), 45. That Thoreau does not see fit to mention that he was finishing *A Week on the Concord and Merrimack Rivers* when he moved to Walden Pond in 1845 seems to support Cavell's effort to superimpose life at Walden and the writing of *Walden* on each other.

3. Cavell, *Senses of Walden*, xiii.

4. As Cavell notes, to repeat the words of another is to make them your own, to give them your own interpretation. Conversely, repeating the words of another sometimes entails letting them alone, accepting that you cannot master them but must be led by them, as when one is led by verses of another's poetry that one has committed to memory. Cavell signals this when he opens his book by writing of *Walden* as one of "the very greatest masterpieces," of which one "knows, without stint, how unspeakably better they are than anything that can be said about them." Cavell, *Senses of Walden*, 3; for the previous point, see 35.

5. Cavell indicates why there is no chapter on the text in its entirety in "The Philosopher in American Life (Toward Thoreau and Emerson)," in *In Quest of the Ordinary* (Chicago: University of Chicago Press, 1988), 18: "While philosophizing is a product of reading, the reading is not especially that of books, especially not of what we think of as books of philosophy. The reading is of whatever is before you. Where this happens to be a verbal matter, what you read are words and sentences, at most pages. Whole books are not read, any more than they are written, at a sitting; not exactly or simply because they are too long but because they would dictate the length of a session of reading, whereas meditation is either to be broken off or to bring itself to an end."

6. Cavell, *Senses of Walden*, 44: "A fact has two surfaces because a fact is not merely an event in the world but the assertion of an event, the wording of the world." Facts are not reported in language; they *are* in language.

7. The "language" of poets "marks the before unapprehended relations of things, and perpetuates their apprehension, until the words which represent them become through time signs for portions and classes of thoughts, instead of pictures of integral thoughts; and then, if no new poets should arise to create afresh the associations which have been thus disorganized, language will be dead to all the nobler purposes of human intercourse." Percy Bysshe Shelley, "A Defense of Poetry," in *Critical Theory since Plato*, ed. Hazard Adams (New York: Harcourt, Brace Jovanovich, 1971), 500. Cavell refers only in passing to Shelley, but he notes that transcendentalism as established in the writing of Emerson and Thoreau "is what became of romanticism in America." Cavell, *Senses of Walden*, 33; Cavell, "Philosopher in American Life," 6.

8. Shelley, "Defense of Poetry," 500–501. Poets are not just "the institutors of

laws" but "the authors of language" as such. Shelley is himself adamant that "the distinction between poets and prose-writers is a vulgar error."

9. Henry David Thoreau, "Walking," in *Henry David Thoreau: Collected Essays and Poems*, ed. Elizabeth Hall Witherell (New York: Library of America, 2001), 239. The heroic is an abiding concern in *Walden*, most pointedly in Thoreau's characterization of the kind of book he set out to write.

10. Thoreau, "Walking," 244. As Hans Sluga reminded me, the twelfth- and thirteenth-century robber barons who built the castles along the Rhine became "heroic" only in the early nineteenth century, when the romantic poets rediscovered the ruins of those castles.

11. Walter Harding, *The Days of Henry Thoreau: A Biography* (Princeton, NJ: Princeton University Press, 1992), 458.

12. Thoreau, *Walden*, 50.

13. Cavell, *Senses of Walden*, 70.

14. As Robert Sattelmeyer notes, "What Thoreau was *not* in Emerson's version is a writer. Remarkably, Emerson refers to Thoreau's writing only in passing, makes no mention of his career, and offers no description of his books and principal essays. The only selections of Thoreau's prose that Emerson quotes are snippets from his then-unpublished Journal, a decision that reinforces that essay's subtext that Thoreau was chiefly a 'character' who chose not to participate in the life of his times, someone who perversely produced his best writing for no audience but himself." Robert Sattelmeyer, "Thoreau and Emerson," in *The Cambridge Companion to Henry David Thoreau*, ed. Joel Myerson (Cambridge: Cambridge University Press, 1995), 37. Cavell suggests that he might not quite share this appraisal in *Senses of Walden*, 12.

15. The extent of these difficulties depends on the degree to which the audience is "naturally" inclined to an adequate relation to the world and to their words; Shelley, for instance, seems much more optimistic on this account than does Thoreau, who pictures the natural as a hard-won achievement.

16. Thoreau, *Walden*, 145.

17. Cavell, *Senses of Walden*, 5.

18. Thoreau, *Walden*, 45.

19. An initial draft of part of *Walden* was entitled "A History of Myself." See the editor's "Chronology" in *Collected Essays and Poems*, 650.

20. Thoreau, *Walden*, 65. Thoreau is clearly hearkening back here to Emerson's "Self-Reliance," where Emerson observes: "Man is timid and apologetic; he is no longer upright; he dares not say 'I think,' 'I am,' but quotes some saint or sage." Ralph Waldo Emerson, "Self-Reliance," in *Emerson: Essays and Lectures*, ed. Joel Porte (New York: Library of America, 1983), 270. This is a connection

that becomes more important to Cavell over time, as Emerson comes to eclipse Thoreau in his thought.

21. Cavell, *Senses of Walden,* 66.

22. Thoreau, *Walden,* 46.

23. It should be clear that the failure to do so, the fact that what is most common is lost in obscurity or, better, obscures itself, is not the result of any special failing particular to the community of New England. It is no *accident* that they or we might have avoided; it is something more like a sin with which humans are born, an unhappiness that, as Cavell puts it, "is natural to us but at the same time unnatural" ("Philosopher in American Life," 9). Thoreau does not say he would fain say something that does not concern people in distant lands, but this is not his primary focus ("not so much" his focus); his object is his audience ("you who read these pages") and, more particularly, his fellow citizens. The relation between these two is raised quietly by Thoreau's distinction between his readers and his townsmen.

24. Thoreau, *Walden,* 128, 365. The theme of the living dead runs throughout *Walden;* see, for example, 135, 179, 199.

25. "With thinking we may be beside ourselves in a sane sense" (Thoreau, *Walden,* 180).

26. Ludwig Wittgenstein, *Philosophical Investigations,* trans. G. E. M. Anscombe (New York: Macmillan, 1958), I, §116. Cavell gives a wonderfully succinct account of his reading of this turn in Wittgenstein in "The Wittgensteinian Event," in *Philosophy the Day after Tomorrow* (Cambridge, MA: Belknap, 2005). I discuss the distinctively political aspects of this in Andrew Norris, "Das Politische als das Metaphysische und das Alltägliche," in *Wittgenstein: Philosophie als „Arbeit an Einem selbst"* (München: Wilhelm Fink Verlag, forthcoming).

27. Cavell, "Wittgensteinian Event," 123; compare the earlier references to Socrates in Stanley Cavell, "Must We Mean What We Say?" in *Must We Mean What We Say?* (Cambridge: Cambridge University Press, 1969), 40, 43.

28. Cavell, "Must We Mean What We Say?" 32. The scooter example is found in Stanley Cavell, "Ending the Waiting Game: A Reading of Beckett's *Endgame,*" in the same collection.

29. Cavell, "Ending the Waiting Game," 123–24. It is essential to attend to the details here. What is incomprehensible is the appeal to *mere curiosity* in *ordinary* circumstances. We can imagine circumstances in which I am not making an offer by asking this question. But these are not circumstances in which I ask simply to find out your desires. Imagine, for example, that many people at a party want to use my scooter, and I am trying to determine how long each one can ride it and still allow others to try it out, or whether there is time to allow everyone who wants

to ride to do so. Here I might ask, "Would you like to use my scooter?" without offering it or (in the second case) without being sure that I would eventually offer it. But even here, I do not ask just to find out what is on your mind.

30. Friedrich Nietzsche, *Zur Genealogie der Moral,* in *Jenseits von Gut und Böse, Zur Genealogie der Moral,* ed. Girogio Colli and Mazzino Montinari (München: Walter de Gruyter, 1999), 339. I retain the definite article so as not to lose Nietzsche's contrast between this and simply not willing.

31. The claim concerning the voluntary is Austin's, from his classic essay "A Plea for Excuses." Cavell defends it and expands on it in "Must We Mean What We Say?" On "normal action" and the sphere of moral evaluation, see in particular 7n5. On the question of when and how moral evaluation takes place, see Stanley Cavell, *The Claim of Reason: Wittgenstein, Skepticism, Morality, and Tragedy* (New York: Oxford University Press, 1979), pt. 3.

32. These latter claims are central to Cavell's magnum opus, *The Claim of Reason,* which Cavell was finishing as he wrote *The Senses of Walden.* A full defense and explanation of them are beyond the scope of this chapter. I discuss them at more length in the introduction to *The Claim to Community: Stanley Cavell and Political Philosophy,* ed. Andrew Norris (Stanford, CA: Stanford University Press, 2006), and in the second chapter of my manuscript "Publicity and Partiality: Ordinary Language and Political Reflection in the Work of Stanley Cavell." See also Stephen Affeldt, "The Ground of Mutuality: Criteria, Judgment, and Intelligibility in Stephen Muhall and Stanley Cavell," *European Journal of Philosophy* 6, no. 1 (1998), and Edward Witherspoon, "Houses, Flowers, and Frameworks: Cavell and Mulhall on the Moral of Skepticism," *European Journal of Philosophy* 10, no. 2 (2002).

33. For many, following the initial positivist reception of Wittgenstein's early work, this would serve as a good description of the *Tractatus Logico-Philosophicus.*

34. Cavell, *Claim of Reason,* 206.

35. Ibid., 215–16.

36. Ibid., 32.

37. Stanley Cavell, "Aesthetic Problems in Modern Philosophy," in *Must We Mean What We Say?* 74.

38. Immanuel Kant, *The Critique of Judgment,* trans. J. C. Meredith (Oxford: Clarendon, 1989), 54; Immanuel Kant, *Kritik der Urteilskraft* (Hamburg: Felix Meiner Verlag, 1990), 52.

39. Kant, *Critique of Judgment,* 56; Kant, *Kritik der Urteilskraft,* 54.

40. Kant, *Critique of Judgment,* 82. Kant distinguishes there the common sense he has in mind—the *sensus communis aestheticus*—from "common understanding [*gemeinen Verstande*], which is also sometimes called common sense (*sensus communis logicus*): for the judgment of the latter is not one by feeling, but

always one by concepts, though usually only in the shape of obscurely represented principles."

41. Ibid., 84.

42. Thoreau, *Walden,* 62; Cavell, *Senses of Walden,* 92.

43. Cavell, *Senses of Walden,* xv; compare 81, where Cavell describes the habit of Thoreau's neighbors to take everything in a "literary" rather than a practical sense.

44. Ibid., 59.

45. Ibid., 11.

46. Cavell argues convincingly that an important part of Thoreau's claim to be writing philosophy rests on his invention of a new vocabulary of assessment, one that takes up familiar terms such as *account, settle, redemption, living, interest,* and *terms* and gives these terms new meanings. See Cavell, "Philosopher in American Life," 19.

47. See, for example, Cavell, *The Senses of Walden,* 35.

48. Thoreau, *Walden,* 145.

49. Ibid., 152; Cavell, *Senses of Walden,* 14, 6.

50. Cavell, *Senses of Walden,* 33–34.

51. J. L. Austin, "Other Minds," in *Philosophical Papers,* ed. J. O. Urmson and G. J. Warnock (New York: Oxford University Press, 1961), 46.

52. Thoreau, *Walden,* 135.

53. Ibid., 146.

54. Cavell, *Senses of Walden,* 16.

55. Ibid.

56. Henry David Thoreau, "The Service," in *Collected Essays and Poems,* 12, 13.

57. It is, I think, no coincidence that Nietzsche argues that the proper response to the passive nihilism of our lives as we now live them requires passing *through* nihilism, *affirming* it.

58. Thoreau, *Walden,* 128. Cavell indicates the centrality of these lines (which were originally the epigraph to *Walden*) to his reading and rewriting of *Walden* in *Senses of Walden,* 36. On our "dead-and-alive" status, compare Thoreau, *Walden,* 199.

59. Thoreau, *Walden,* 134.

60. Ibid., 46.

61. Cavell, *Senses of Walden,* 92.

62. Ibid., 55.

63. Thoreau, *Walden,* 382. This connects back to Thoreau's desire for the heroic: "Morning brings back the heroic ages" (*Walden,* 133). Cavell embraces this sense of life's endless possibility: "The fate of having a self—of being human—is

one in which the self is *always* to be found, fated to be sought, or not; recognized, or not" (*Senses of Walden*, 53; emphasis added).

64. Conversion is a major theme in Cavell's work. I discuss this in Andrew Norris, "Political Revisions: Stanley Cavell and Political Philosophy," *Political Theory* 30, no. 6 (December 2002), reprinted in *Claim to Community*.

65. Thoreau, *Walden*, 217.

66. See, respectively, ibid., 68, 369, 153.

67. Cavell, *Senses of Walden*, 31.

68. Ibid., 63. As I read him, Cavell's reference to literality is meant to develop a line of thought suggested in Thoreau's striking and beautiful question, "Why do precisely these objects which we behold make a world?" (*Walden*, 272).

69. Cavell, *Senses of Walden*, 63.

70. Ibid., 64.

71. John Locke, *Two Treatises of Government*, ed. Peter Laslett (Cambridge: Cambridge University, 1963), II, secs. 11, 16, 19.

72. Thoreau, *Walden*, 50.

73. Ibid., 49.

74. Cavell, *Senses of Walden*, 47.

75. People debate the extent and nature of Thoreau's commitment to democracy. But even in "Civil Disobedience," where he says he imagines possible improvements to "democracy, such as we know it," he remains committed to the idea that our lives should express our power, not our subordination. The question of majority rule is something quite different. Thoreau, *Walden*, 413.

76. Thoreau, *Walden*, 88, 128, 66. See Cavell's discussion of the latter passage in *Senses of Walden*, 43.

77. Cavell, *Senses of Walden*, 7.

78. Thoreau, *Walden*, 128.

79. Ibid., 140.

80. Cavell, *Senses of Walden*, 53.

81. Thoreau, *Walden*, 376.

82. "It would be a fair summary of the book's motive to say that it invites us to take an interest in our lives, and teaches us how" (Cavell, *Senses of Walden*, 67).

83. Thoreau, *Walden*, 51.

84. Thoreau, "Slavery in Massachusetts," in *Collected Essays and Poems*, 346.

# Selected Bibliography

## Works by Thoreau

Thoreau, Henry David. *Cape Cod,* ed. Joseph J. Moldenhauer. Princeton, NJ: Princeton University Press, 1988.

———. *The Correspondence of Henry David Thoreau,* ed. Carl Bode and Walter Harding. New York: New York University Press, 1958.

———. *Early Essays and Miscellanies,* ed. Joseph J. Moldenhauer and Edwin Moser, with Alexander C. Kern. Princeton, NJ: Princeton University Press, 1975.

———. *Excursions,* ed. Joseph J. Moldenhauer. Princeton, NJ: Princeton University Press, 2007.

———. *Faith in a Seed: The Dispersion of Seeds and Other Late Natural History Writings,* ed. Bradley P. Dean. Washington, DC: Island Press/Shearwater Books, 1993.

———. *Henry David Thoreau: Collected Essays and Poems,* ed. Elizabeth Hall Witherell. New York: Library of America, 2001.

———. *Huckleberries,* ed. Leo Stoller. New York and Iowa City: New York Public Library and Windhover Press, 1970.

———. *Journal (1837–1854),* ed. Elizabeth Hall Witherell et al. 8 vols. Princeton, NJ: Princeton University Press, 1981–2009.

———. *The Journal of Henry David Thoreau,* ed. Bradford Torrey and Francis Allen. 14 vols. Boston: Houghton Mifflin, 1906.

———. *The Maine Woods,* ed. Joseph J. Moldenhauer. Princeton, NJ: Princeton University Press, 1972.

———. *Reform Papers,* ed. Wendell Glick. Princeton, NJ: Princeton University Press, 1973.

———. *Translations,* ed. K. P. Van Anglen. Princeton, NJ: Princeton University Press, 1986.

———. *Walden,* ed. J. Lyndon Shanley. Princeton, NJ: Princeton University Press, 1971.

———. *A Week on the Concord and Merrimack Rivers,* ed. Carl F. Hovde, William L. Howarth, and Elizabeth Hall Witherell. Princeton, NJ: Princeton University Press, 1980.

———. *Wild Fruits: Thoreau's Rediscovered Last Manuscript,* ed. Bradley P. Dean. New York: W. W. Norton, 2000.

## Biographies of Thoreau

Harding, Walter. *The Days of Henry Thoreau: A Biography.* Rev. ed. Princeton, NJ: Princeton University Press, 1992.

Richardson, Robert D. *Henry Thoreau: A Life of the Mind.* Berkeley: University of California Press, 1992.

## Works on Thoreau's Ethics and Politics

Abbott, Philip. "Henry David Thoreau, the State of Nature, and the Redemption of Liberalism." *Journal of Politics* 47, no. 1 (1985): 182–208.

Allen, Thomas. "Clockwork Nation: Modern Time, Moral Perfectionism, and American Identity in Catharine Beecher and Henry Thoreau." *Journal of American Studies* 39, no. 1 (2005): 65–86.

Becker, Christian. "Thoreau's Economic Philosophy." *European Journal of the History of Economic Thought* 15, no. 2 (2008): 211–46.

Bellis, Peter J. *Writing Revolution: Aesthetics and Politics in Hawthorne, Whitman, and Thoreau.* Athens: University of Georgia Press, 2003.

Bennett, Jane. *Thoreau's Nature: Ethics, Politics, and the Wild.* New ed. Lanham, MD: Rowman and Littlefield, 2002.

Buell, Lawrence. *The Environmental Imagination: Thoreau, Nature Writing, and the Formation of American Culture.* Cambridge, MA: Harvard University Press, 1995.

Buranelli, Vincent. "The Case against Thoreau." *Ethics* 67, no. 4 (1957): 257–68.

———. "The Verdict on Thoreau." *Ethics* 70, no. 1 (1959): 64–65.

Cafaro, Philip. "Thoreau, Leopold, and Carson: Toward an Environmental Virtue Ethics." *Environmental Ethics* 23, no. 1 (2001): 3–17.

———. *Thoreau's Living Ethics: Walden and the Pursuit of Virtue.* Athens: University of Georgia Press, 2006.

Cavell, Stanley. "Night and Day: Heidegger and Thoreau." In *Appropriating Heidegger,* ed. James E. Faulconer and Mark A. Wrathall, 30–49. Cambridge: Cambridge University Press, 2000.

———. "The Philosopher in American Life (toward Thoreau and Emerson)." Chap. 3 in *Emerson's Transcendental Etudes*, ed. David Justin Hodge. Stanford, CA: Stanford University Press, 2003.

———. *The Senses of Walden.* Exp. ed. Chicago: University of Chicago Press, 1992.

Diggins, John Patrick. "Thoreau, Marx, and the 'Riddle' of Alienation." *Social Research* 39, no. 4 (1972): 571–98.

Duban, James. "Conscience and Consciousness: The Liberal Christian Context of Thoreau's Political Ethics." *New England Quarterly* 60, no. 2 (1987): 208–22.

Dumm, Thomas L. *A Politics of the Ordinary.* New York: New York University Press, 1999.

Eulau, Heinz. "Wayside Challenger: Some Remarks on the Politics of Henry David Thoreau." *Antioch Review* 9, no. 4 (1949): 509–22.

Fergenson, Laraine. "Thoreau, Daniel Berrigan, and the Problem of Transcendental Politics." *Soundings* 65 (1982): 103–22.

Francis, Richard. *Transcendental Utopias: Individual and Community at Brook Farm, Fruitlands, and Walden.* Ithaca, NY: Cornell University Press, 1997.

Furtak, Rick Anthony. "Skepticism and Perceptual Faith: Henry David Thoreau and Stanley Cavell on Seeing and Believing." *Transactions of the Charles S. Peirce Society* 43, no. 3 (2007): 542–61.

———. "Thoreau's Emotional Stoicism." *Journal of Speculative Philosophy* 17, no. 2 (2003): 122–32.

Garber, Frederick. *Thoreau's Redemptive Imagination.* New York: New York University Press, 1977.

Gougeon, Len. "Thoreau and Reform." In *The Cambridge Companion to Henry David Thoreau,* ed. Joel Myerson, 194–214. Cambridge: Cambridge University Press, 1995.

Hanley, Ryan Patrick. "Thoreau among His Heroes." *Philosophy and Literature* 25, no. 1 (2001): 59–74.

Hodder, Alan D. *Thoreau's Ecstatic Witness.* New Haven, CT: Yale University Press, 2001.

Howarth, William L. *The Book of Concord: Thoreau's Life as a Writer.* New York: Viking, 1982.

Hyde, Lewis. "Henry Thoreau, John Brown, and the Problem of Prophetic Action." *Raritan* 22, no. 2 (2002): 125–44.

Kaplan, Morris B. "Queer Citizenship: Thoreau's 'Civil Disobedience' and the Ethics of Self-Making." Chap. 6 in *Sexual Justice: Democratic Citizenship and the Politics of Desire.* New York: Routledge, 1997.

Kateb, George. "Democratic Individuality and the Meaning of Rights." In *Liberalism and the Moral Life,* ed. Nancy L. Rosenblum, 183–206. Cambridge, MA: Harvard University Press, 1989.

————. *The Inner Ocean: Individualism and Democratic Culture.* Ithaca, NY: Cornell University Press, 1992.

————. "Wildness and Conscience: Thoreau and Emerson." Chap. 11 in *Patriotism and Other Mistakes.* New Haven, CT: Yale University Press, 2006.

Ketcham, Ralph L. "Some Thoughts on Buranelli's Case against Thoreau." *Ethics* 69, no. 3 (1959): 206–8.

Kritzberg, Barry. "Thoreau, Slavery, and Resistance to Civil Government." *Massachusetts Review* 30, no. 4 (1989): 535–65.

Lane, Ruth. "Standing 'Aloof' from the State: Thoreau on Self-Government." *Review of Politics* 67, no. 2 (2005): 283–310.

Madden, Marian C., and Edward H. Madden. "Buffs and Rebuffs: Emerson, Parker, and Thoreau." *Transactions of the Charles S. Peirce Society* 30, no. 1 (1994): 1–32.

Mariotti, Shannon L. *Thoreau's Democratic Withdrawal: Alienation, Participation, and Modernity.* Madison: University of Wisconsin Press, 2010.

Marshall, Mason. "Freedom through Critique: Thoreau's Service to Others." *Transactions of the Charles S. Peirce Society* 41, no. 2 (2005): 395–427.

McWilliams, Wilson Carey. "Emerson and Thoreau: The All and the One." Chap. 11 in *The Idea of Fraternity in America.* Berkeley: University of California Press, 1973.

Meyer, Michael. *Several More Lives to Live: Thoreau's Political Reputation in America.* Westport, CT: Greenwood Press, 1977.

————. "Thoreau and Black Emigration." *American Literature* 53, no. 3 (1981): 380–96.

Nabers, Deak. "Thoreau's Natural Constitution." *American Literary History* 19, no. 4 (2007): 824–48.

Nelson, Dana D. "Thoreau, Manhood, and Race: Quiet Desperation versus Representative Isolation." In *A Historical Guide to Henry David Thoreau,* ed. William E. Cain, 61–93. Oxford: Oxford University Press, 2000.

Neufeldt, Leonard N. *The Economist: Henry Thoreau and Enterprise.* New York: Oxford University Press, 1989.

Newman, Lance. *Our Common Dwelling: Henry Thoreau, Transcendentalism, and the Class Politics of Nature.* New York: Palgrave Macmillan, 2005.

Parrington, Vernon Louis. "Henry Thoreau: Transcendental Economist." In *Main Currents in American Thought: An Interpretation of American Literature from the Beginnings to 1920.* Vol. 2, *1800–1860: The Romantic Revolution in America,* 400–413. New York: Harcourt, Brace, 1930.

Robinson, David M. *Natural Life: Thoreau's Worldly Transcendentalism.* Ithaca, NY: Cornell University Press, 2004.

Rosenblum, Nancy L. "Heroic Individualism and the Spectacle of Diversity." Chap.

5 in *Another Liberalism: Romanticism and the Reconstruction of Liberal Thought*. Cambridge, MA: Harvard University Press, 1987.

———. Introduction to *Thoreau: Political Writings*, ed. Nancy L. Rosenblum, vii–xxxi. Cambridge: Cambridge University Press, 1996.

———. "Thoreau's Militant Conscience." *Political Theory* 9, no. 1 (1981): 81–110.

Rosenwald, Lawrence A. "The Theory, Practice, and Influence of Thoreau's Civil Disobedience." In *A Historical Guide to Henry David Thoreau*, ed. William E. Cain, 153–79. Oxford: Oxford University Press, 2000.

Saito, Naoko. "Citizenship without Inclusion: Religious Democracy after Dewey, Emerson, and Thoreau." *Journal of Speculative Philosophy* 18, no. 3 (2004): 203–15.

———. "Perfectionism and the Love of Humanity: Democracy as a Way of Life after Dewey, Thoreau, and Cavell." *Journal of Speculative Philosophy* 20, no. 2 (2006): 93–105.

———. "Truth Is Translated: Cavell's Thoreau and the Transcendence of America." *Journal of Speculative Philosophy* 21, no. 2 (2007): 124–32.

Sayre, Robert F. *Thoreau and the American Indians*. Princeton, NJ: Princeton University Press, 1977.

Shulman, George. "Thoreau, the Reluctant Prophet: Moral Witness and Poetic Vision in Politics." Chap. 2 in *American Prophecy: Race and Redemption in American Political Culture*. Minneapolis: University of Minnesota Press, 2008.

Simon, Myron. "Thoreau and Anarchism." *Michigan Quarterly Review* 23, no. 3 (1984): 360–84.

Tauber, Alfred I. *Henry David Thoreau and the Moral Agency of Knowing*. Berkeley: University of California Press, 2001.

Taylor, Bob Pepperman. *America's Bachelor Uncle: Thoreau and the American Polity*. Lawrence: University Press of Kansas, 1996.

Teichgraeber, Richard F. *Sublime Thoughts/Penny Wisdom: Situating Emerson and Thoreau in the American Market*. Baltimore, MD: Johns Hopkins University Press, 1995.

Walker, Brian. "Thoreau on Democratic Cultivation." *Political Theory* 29, no. 2 (2001): 155–89.

Worley, Sam McGuire. *Emerson, Thoreau, and the Role of the Cultural Critic*. Albany: State University of New York Press, 2001.

# Contributors

**Jane Bennett** is professor of political science at Johns Hopkins University. She is the author of *Thoreau's Nature: Ethics, Politics, and the Wild* and *The Enchantment of Modern Life: Attachments, Crossings, and Ethics.* Her new book, *Vibrant Matter: A Political Ecology of Things,* is forthcoming.

**William Chaloupka** is professor of political science at Colorado State University. He is the author of *Everybody Knows: Cynicism in America* and the coeditor, with Jane Bennett, of *In the Nature of Things: Language, Politics, and the Environment.*

**Thomas L. Dumm** is professor of political science at Amherst College. He is the author of *Democracy and Punishment, united states, Michel Foucault and the Politics of Freedom, A Politics of the Ordinary,* and *Loneliness as a Way of Life.*

**Christopher A. Dustin** is associate professor of philosophy at College of the Holy Cross. He is the coauthor, with Joanna E. Ziegler, of *Practicing Mortality: Art, Philosophy, and Contemplative Seeing.*

**Harry V. Jaffa** is professor emeritus of government at Claremont McKenna College and the Claremont Graduate School. He is the author of *Crisis of the House Divided: An Interpretation of the Issues in the Lincoln-Douglas Debates* and *A New Birth of Freedom: Abraham Lincoln and the Coming of the Civil War.*

**Leigh Kathryn Jenco** is assistant professor of political science at the National University of Singapore. Her articles have appeared in *American Political Science Review, Political Theory,* and *Review of Politics.* She is currently completing a book entitled *Making the Political: Founding and Action in the Political Theory of Zhang Shizhao.*

**Melissa Lane** taught for fifteen years at the University of Cambridge before becoming professor of politics at Princeton University in 2009. Her books include *Method and Politics in Plato's Statesman* and *Plato's Progeny: How Plato and Socrates Still Captivate the Modern Mind.* She also wrote the new introduction for the Penguin Classics edition of Plato's *Republic.*

**Shannon L. Mariotti** is assistant professor of political science at Southwestern University. She is the author of *Thoreau's Democratic Withdrawal: Alienation, Participation, and Modernity.* Her work has also appeared in *Political Theory.*

**Susan McWilliams** is assistant professor of politics at Pomona College. Her work has appeared in *Perspectives on Political Science, Commonweal,* and *Boston Review.* She is currently working on a book about the history of travel literature in Western political thought.

**Andrew Norris** is associate professor of political science at the University of California–Santa Barbara. He is the editor of *Politics, Metaphysics, and Death: Essays on Giorgio Agamben's Homo Sacer* and *The Claim to Community: Essays on Stanley Cavell and Political Philosophy.* He is currently completing a book entitled *Publicity and Partiality: Political Reflection in the Work of Stanley Cavell.*

**Anthony J. Parel** is professor emeritus of political science at the University of Calgary. He is the author of *The Machiavellian Cosmos* and *Gandhi's Philosophy and the Quest for Harmony* and the editor of *Gandhi: "Hind Swaraj" and Other Writings* and *Gandhi, Freedom, and Self-Rule.* He is also the coeditor, with Judith Brown, of the forthcoming *Cambridge Companion to Gandhi.*

**Nancy L. Rosenblum** is Senator Joseph S. Clark Professor of Ethics in

Politics and Government at Harvard University. She is the author of *Another Liberalism: Romanticism and the Reconstruction of Liberal Thought, Membership and Morals: The Personal Uses of Pluralism in America,* and *On the Side of the Angels: An Appreciation of Parties and Partisanship.* She is also the editor of *Thoreau: Political Writings* and is currently working on a book-length study of Thoreau, entitled *The Quality of Life.*

**George Shulman** is a professor at the Gallatin School of Individualized Study at New York University, where he teaches political theory and American studies. He is most recently the author of *American Prophecy: Race and Redemption in American Political Culture.*

**Bob Pepperman Taylor** is professor of political science at the University of Vermont. His books include *America's Bachelor Uncle: Thoreau and the American Polity* and *Citizenship and Democratic Doubt: The Legacy of Progressive Thought.*

**Jack Turner** is assistant professor of political science at the University of Washington. His articles have appeared in *Political Theory, Raritan,* and *Polity.* He is currently completing a book exploring the relationship among American individualism, racial injustice, and democratic citizenship.

**Brian Walker** is associate professor of political science at the University of California–Los Angeles. His articles have appeared in *American Political Science Review, Political Theory,* and *Canadian Journal of Political Science.* He is currently completing a book examining cultivation thinking in Thoreau's Confucian notebook and comparing Confucian and American ways of thinking about individuality, culture, and public service.

# Index